Selling Price $3.95

NUMBERS GUIDE
FOR
REAL ESTATE

W9-CUW-005

Publication No. 176
Delphi Order No. 176PB
ISBN 0-930306-01-5

Computed and Published by:
Delphi Information Sciences Corporation
1414 Sixth Street
Santa Monica, California 90401

Copyright © 1976 All Rights Reserved
Delphi Information Sciences Corporation

Other Products from Delphi Available thru Bookstores and Stationery Stores

* Payment Tables for Monthly Mortgage Loans

These pocket-size, stitch-bound books provide the monthly payment necessary to amortize a loan.

Publication No. 475 — $2.50 each
Covering interest rates from:
7% thru 12% by ¼% & 1/10% jumps

Publication No. 674 — $3.95 each
Covering interest rates from:
8% thru 14% by ¼% jumps

* Mortgage Yield Tables

These tables are designed to rapidly determine yields on discounted mortgages. It is also used to find Annual Percentage Rates (APR) and to calculate the complete disclosure for a Truth-in-Lending statement where a Brokerage fee has been charged.

It covers interest rates from 6% thru 12%, and 10 maturities (1 year to 10 years); plus a No Due Date section for loans where the due date is unknown.

$25.00 each

If ordering directly from the publisher, add 55¢ for shipping and handling. All orders must be prepaid. California residents add 6% for sales tax. Send all orders to the attention of:

Thomas D. Kinsey
Delphi Information Sciences Corporation
1414 Sixth Street
Santa Monica, California 90401

"How to Use These Tables"
Instructions Starting on Page 182

• TABLE OF CONTENTS •

LOAN TO APPRAISED VALUE
CONVENTIONAL LOANS

APPRAISED VALUE	R A T I O S					
	50%	60%	65%	70%	75%	80%
10000	5000	6000	6500	7000	7500	8000
11000	5500	6600	7150	7700	8250	8800
12000	6000	7200	7800	8400	9000	9600
13000	6500	7800	8450	9100	9750	10400
14000	7000	8400	9100	9800	10500	11200
15000	7500	9000	9750	10500	11250	12000
16000	8000	9600	10400	11200	12000	12800
17000	8500	10200	11050	11900	12750	13600
18000	9000	10800	11700	12600	13500	14400
19000	9500	11400	12350	13300	14250	15200
20000	10000	12000	13000	14000	15000	16000
21000	10500	12600	13650	14700	15750	16800
22000	11000	13200	14300	15400	16500	17600
23000	11500	13800	14950	16100	17250	18400
24000	12000	14400	15600	16800	18000	19200
25000	12500	15000	16250	17500	18750	20000
26000	13000	15600	16900	18200	19500	20800
27000	13500	16200	17550	18900	20250	21600
28000	14000	16800	18200	19600	21000	22400
29000	14500	17400	18850	20300	21750	23200
30000	15000	18000	19500	21000	22500	24000
31000	15500	18600	20150	21700	23250	24800
32000	16000	19200	20800	22400	24000	25600
33000	16500	19800	21450	23100	24750	26400
34000	17000	20400	22100	23800	25500	27200
35000	17500	21000	22750	24500	26250	28000
36000	18000	21600	23400	25200	27000	28800
37000	18500	22200	24050	25900	27750	29600
38000	19000	22800	24700	26600	28500	30400
39000	19500	23400	25350	27300	29250	31200
40000	20000	24000	26000	28000	30000	32000
41000	20500	24600	26650	28700	30750	32800
42000	21000	25200	27300	29400	31500	33600
43000	21500	25800	27950	30100	32250	34400
44000	22000	26400	28600	30800	33000	35200
45000	22500	27000	29250	31500	33750	36000
46000	23000	27600	29900	32200	34500	36800
47000	23500	28200	30550	32900	35250	37600
48000	24000	28800	31200	33600	36000	38400
49000	24500	29400	31850	34300	36750	39200
50000	25000	30000	32500	35000	37500	40000
51000	25500	30600	33150	35700	38250	40800
52000	26000	31200	33800	36400	39000	41600
53000	26500	31800	34450	37100	39750	42400
54000	27000	32400	35100	37800	40500	43200
55000	27500	33000	35750	38500	41250	44000
56000	28000	33600	36400	39200	42000	44800
57000	28500	34200	37050	39900	42750	45600
58000	29000	34800	37700	40600	43500	46400
59000	29500	35400	38350	41300	44250	47200
60000	30000	36000	39000	42000	45000	48000
61000	30500	36600	39650	42700	45750	48800
62000	31000	37200	40300	43400	46500	49600
63000	31500	37800	40950	44100	47250	50400
64000	32000	38400	41600	44800	48000	51200
65000	32500	39000	42250	45500	48750	52000
66000	33000	39600	42900	46200	49500	52800
67000	33500	40200	43550	46900	50250	53600
68000	34000	40800	44200	47600	51000	54400
69000	34500	41400	44850	48300	51750	55200

LOAN TO APPRAISED VALUE
CONVENTIONAL LOANS

APPRAISED VALUE	R A T I O S					
	50%	60%	65%	70%	75%	80%
70000	35000	42000	45500	49000	52500	56000
71000	35500	42600	46150	49700	53250	56800
72000	36000	43200	46800	50400	54000	57600
73000	36500	43800	47450	51100	54750	58400
74000	37000	44400	48100	51800	55500	59200
75000	37500	45000	48750	52500	56250	60000
76000	38000	45600	49400	53200	57000	60800
77000	38500	46200	50050	53900	57750	61600
78000	39000	46800	50700	54600	58500	62400
79000	39500	47400	51350	55300	59250	63200
80000	40000	48000	52000	56000	60000	64000
81000	40500	48600	52650	56700	60750	64800
82000	41000	49200	53300	57400	61500	65600
83000	41500	49800	53950	58100	62250	66400
84000	42000	50400	54600	58800	63000	67200
85000	42500	51000	55250	59500	63750	68000
86000	43000	51600	55900	60200	64500	68800
87000	43500	52200	56550	60900	65250	69600
88000	44000	52800	57200	61600	66000	70400
89000	44500	53400	57850	62300	66750	71200
90000	45000	54000	58500	63000	67500	72000
91000	45500	54600	59150	63700	68250	72800
92000	46000	55200	59800	64400	69000	73600
93000	46500	55800	60450	65100	69750	74400
94000	47000	56400	61100	65800	70500	75200
95000	47500	57000	61750	66500	71250	76000
96000	48000	57600	62400	67200	72000	76800
97000	48500	58200	63050	67900	72750	77600
98000	49000	58800	63700	68600	73500	78400
99000	49500	59400	64350	69300	74250	79200
100000	50000	60000	65000	70000	75000	80000
101000	50500	60600	65650	70700	75750	80800
102000	51000	61200	66300	71400	76500	81600
103000	51500	61800	66950	72100	77250	82400
104000	52000	62400	67600	72800	78000	83200
105000	52500	63000	68250	73500	78750	84000
106000	53000	63600	68900	74200	79500	84800
107000	53500	64200	69550	74900	80250	85600
108000	54000	64800	70200	75600	81000	86400
109000	54500	65400	70850	76300	81750	87200
110000	55000	66000	71500	77000	82500	88000
111000	55500	66600	72150	77700	83250	88800
112000	56000	67200	72800	78400	84000	89600
113000	56500	67800	73450	79100	84750	90400
114000	57000	68400	74100	79800	85500	91200
115000	57500	69000	74750	80500	86250	92000
116000	58000	69600	75400	81200	87000	92800
117000	58500	70200	76050	81900	87750	93600
118000	59000	70800	76700	82600	88500	94400
119000	59500	71400	77350	83300	89250	95200
120000	60000	72000	78000	84000	90000	96000
121000	60500	72600	78650	84700	90750	96800
122000	61000	73200	79300	85400	91500	97600
123000	61500	73800	79950	86100	92250	98400
124000	62000	74400	80600	86800	93000	99200
125000	62500	75000	81250	87500	93750	100000
126000	63000	75600	81900	88200	94500	100800
127000	63500	76200	82550	88900	95250	101600
128000	64000	76800	83200	89600	96000	102400
129000	64500	77400	83850	90300	96750	103200

7%

MONTHLY AMORTIZING PAYMENTS

AMOUNT OF LOAN	NUMBER OF YEARS IN TERM							
	3	5	10	15	20	25	30	35
10	.31	.20	.12	.09	.08	.08	.07	.07
20	.62	.40	.24	.18	.16	.15	.14	.13
25	.78	.50	.30	.23	.20	.18	.17	.16
30	.93	.60	.35	.27	.24	.22	.20	.20
40	1.24	.80	.47	.36	.32	.29	.27	.26
50	1.55	1.00	.59	.45	.39	.36	.34	.32
60	1.86	1.19	.70	.54	.47	.43	.40	.39
70	2.17	1.39	.82	.63	.55	.50	.47	.45
75	2.32	1.49	.88	.68	.59	.54	.50	.48
80	2.48	1.59	.93	.72	.63	.57	.54	.52
90	2.78	1.79	1.05	.81	.70	.64	.60	.58
100	3.09	1.99	1.17	.90	.78	.71	.67	.64
200	6.18	3.97	2.33	1.80	1.56	1.42	1.34	1.28
300	9.27	5.95	3.49	2.70	2.33	2.13	2.00	1.92
400	12.36	7.93	4.65	3.60	3.11	2.83	2.67	2.56
500	15.44	9.91	5.81	4.50	3.88	3.54	3.33	3.20
600	18.53	11.89	6.97	5.40	4.66	4.25	4.00	3.84
700	21.62	13.87	8.13	6.30	5.43	4.95	4.66	4.48
800	24.71	15.85	9.29	7.20	6.21	5.66	5.33	5.12
900	27.79	17.83	10.45	8.09	6.98	6.37	5.99	5.75
1000	30.88	19.81	11.62	8.99	7.76	7.07	6.66	6.39
2000	61.76	39.61	23.23	17.98	15.51	14.14	13.31	12.78
3000	92.64	59.41	34.84	26.97	23.26	21.21	19.96	19.17
4000	123.51	79.21	46.45	35.96	31.02	28.28	26.62	25.56
5000	154.39	99.01	58.06	44.95	38.77	35.34	33.27	31.95
6000	185.27	118.81	69.67	53.93	46.52	42.41	39.92	38.34
7000	216.14	138.61	81.28	62.92	54.28	49.48	46.58	44.72
8000	247.02	158.41	92.89	71.91	62.03	56.55	53.23	51.11
9000	277.90	178.22	104.50	80.90	69.78	63.62	59.88	57.50
10000	308.78	198.02	116.11	89.89	77.53	70.68	66.54	63.89
11000	339.65	217.82	127.72	98.88	85.29	77.75	73.19	70.28
12000	370.53	237.62	139.34	107.86	93.04	84.82	79.84	76.67
13000	401.41	257.42	150.95	116.85	100.79	91.89	86.49	83.06
14000	432.28	277.22	162.56	125.84	108.55	98.95	93.15	89.44
15000	463.16	297.03	174.17	134.83	116.30	106.02	99.80	95.83
16000	494.04	316.82	185.78	143.82	124.05	113.09	106.45	102.22
17000	524.92	336.63	197.39	152.81	131.81	120.16	113.11	108.61
18000	555.79	356.43	209.00	161.79	139.56	127.23	119.76	115.00
19000	586.67	376.23	220.61	170.78	147.31	134.29	126.41	121.39
20000	617.55	396.03	232.22	179.77	155.06	141.36	133.07	127.78
21000	648.42	415.84	243.83	188.76	162.82	148.43	139.72	134.16
22000	679.30	435.63	255.44	197.75	170.57	155.50	146.37	140.55
23000	710.18	455.43	267.05	206.74	178.32	162.56	153.02	146.94
24000	741.06	475.23	278.67	215.72	186.08	169.63	159.68	153.33
25000	771.93	495.03	290.28	224.71	193.83	176.70	166.33	159.72
26000	802.81	514.84	301.89	233.70	201.58	183.77	172.98	166.11
27000	833.69	534.64	313.50	242.69	209.34	190.84	179.64	172.50
28000	864.56	554.44	325.11	251.68	217.09	197.90	186.29	178.88
29000	895.44	574.24	336.72	260.67	224.84	204.97	192.94	185.27
30000	926.32	594.04	348.33	269.65	232.59	212.04	199.60	191.66
31000	957.20	613.84	359.94	278.64	240.35	219.11	206.25	198.05
32000	988.07	633.64	371.55	287.63	248.10	226.17	212.90	204.44
33000	1018.95	653.44	383.16	296.62	255.85	233.24	219.55	210.83
34000	1049.83	673.25	394.77	305.61	263.61	240.31	226.21	217.22
35000	1080.70	693.05	406.38	314.59	271.36	247.38	232.86	223.60
36000	1111.58	712.85	418.00	323.58	279.11	254.45	239.51	229.99
37000	1142.46	732.65	429.61	332.57	286.87	261.51	246.17	236.38
38000	1173.33	752.45	441.22	341.56	294.62	268.58	252.82	242.77
39000	1204.21	772.25	452.83	350.55	302.37	275.65	259.47	249.16
40000	1235.09	792.05	464.44	359.54	310.12	282.72	266.13	255.55

MONTHLY AMORTIZING PAYMENTS

AMOUNT OF LOAN	NUMBER OF YEARS IN TERM						
	10	15	20	25	30	35	40
41000	476.05	368.52	317.88	289.78	272.78	261.94	254.79
42000	487.66	377.51	325.63	296.85	279.43	268.32	261.01
43000	499.27	386.50	333.38	303.92	286.09	274.71	267.22
44000	510.88	395.49	341.14	310.99	292.74	281.10	273.43
45000	522.49	404.48	348.89	318.06	299.39	287.49	279.65
46000	534.10	413.47	356.64	325.12	306.04	293.88	285.86
47000	545.71	422.45	364.40	332.19	312.70	300.27	292.08
48000	557.33	431.44	372.15	339.26	319.35	306.66	298.29
49000	568.94	440.43	379.90	346.33	326.00	313.04	304.51
50000	580.55	449.42	387.65	353.39	332.66	319.43	310.72
51000	592.16	458.41	395.41	360.46	339.31	325.82	316.93
52000	603.77	467.40	403.16	367.53	345.96	332.21	323.15
53000	615.38	476.38	410.91	374.60	352.62	338.60	329.36
54000	626.99	485.37	418.67	381.67	359.27	344.99	335.58
55000	638.60	494.36	426.42	388.73	365.92	351.38	341.79
56000	650.21	503.35	434.17	395.80	372.57	357.76	348.01
57000	661.82	512.34	441.93	402.87	379.23	364.15	354.22
58000	673.43	521.33	449.68	409.94	385.88	370.54	360.44
59000	685.05	530.31	457.43	417.00	392.53	376.93	366.65
60000	696.66	539.30	465.18	424.07	399.19	383.32	372.86
61000	708.27	548.29	472.94	431.14	405.84	389.71	379.08
62000	719.88	557.28	480.69	438.21	412.49	396.10	385.29
63000	731.49	566.27	488.44	445.28	419.15	402.48	391.51
64000	743.10	575.26	496.20	452.34	425.80	408.87	397.72
65000	754.71	584.24	503.95	459.41	432.45	415.26	403.94
66000	766.32	593.23	511.70	466.48	439.10	421.65	410.15
67000	777.93	602.22	519.46	473.55	445.76	428.04	416.36
68000	789.54	611.21	527.21	480.61	452.41	434.43	422.58
69000	801.15	620.20	534.96	487.68	459.06	440.82	428.79
70000	812.76	629.18	542.71	494.75	465.72	447.20	435.01
71000	824.38	638.17	550.47	501.82	472.37	453.59	441.22
72000	835.99	647.16	558.22	508.89	479.02	459.98	447.44
73000	847.60	656.15	565.97	515.95	485.68	466.37	453.65
74000	859.21	665.14	573.73	523.02	492.33	472.76	459.86
75000	870.82	674.13	581.48	530.09	498.98	479.15	466.08
76000	882.43	683.11	589.23	537.16	505.63	485.54	472.29
77000	894.04	692.10	596.99	544.22	512.29	491.92	478.51
78000	905.65	701.09	604.74	551.29	518.94	498.31	484.72
79000	917.26	710.08	612.49	558.36	525.59	504.70	490.94
80000	928.87	719.07	620.24	565.43	532.25	511.09	497.15
81000	940.48	728.06	628.00	572.50	538.90	517.48	503.36
82000	952.09	737.04	635.75	579.56	545.55	523.87	509.58
83000	963.71	746.03	643.50	586.63	552.21	530.26	515.79
84000	975.32	755.02	651.26	593.70	558.86	536.64	522.01
85000	986.93	764.01	659.01	600.77	565.51	543.03	528.22
86000	998.54	773.00	666.76	607.84	572.17	549.42	534.44
87000	1010.15	781.99	674.52	614.90	578.82	555.81	540.65
88000	1021.76	790.97	682.27	621.97	585.47	562.20	546.86
89000	1033.37	799.96	690.02	629.04	592.12	568.59	553.08
90000	1044.98	808.95	697.77	636.11	598.78	574.98	559.29
91000	1056.59	817.94	705.53	643.17	605.43	581.36	565.51
92000	1068.20	826.93	713.28	650.24	612.08	587.75	571.72
93000	1079.81	835.92	721.03	657.31	618.74	594.14	577.94
94000	1091.42	844.90	728.79	664.38	625.39	600.53	584.15
95000	1103.04	853.89	736.54	671.45	632.04	606.92	590.36
96000	1114.65	862.88	744.29	678.51	638.70	613.31	596.58
97000	1126.26	871.87	752.04	685.58	645.35	619.70	602.79
98000	1137.87	880.86	759.80	692.65	652.00	626.08	609.01
99000	1149.48	889.84	767.55	699.72	658.65	632.47	615.22
100000	1161.09	898.83	775.30	706.78	665.31	638.86	621.44

7¼%

MONTHLY AMORTIZING PAYMENTS

AMOUNT OF LOAN	NUMBER OF YEARS IN TERM							
	3	5	10	15	20	25	30	35
10	.31	.20	.12	.10	.08	.08	.07	.07
20	.62	.40	.24	.19	.16	.15	.14	.14
25	.78	.50	.30	.23	.20	.19	.18	.17
30	.93	.60	.36	.28	.24	.22	.21	.20
40	1.24	.80	.47	.37	.32	.29	.28	.27
50	1.55	1.00	.59	.46	.40	.37	.35	.33
60	1.86	1.20	.71	.55	.48	.44	.41	.40
70	2.17	1.40	.83	.64	.56	.51	.48	.46
75	2.33	1.50	.89	.69	.60	.55	.52	.50
80	2.48	1.60	.94	.74	.64	.58	.55	.53
90	2.79	1.80	1.06	.83	.72	.66	.62	.60
100	3.10	2.00	1.18	.92	.80	.73	.69	.66
200	6.20	3.99	2.35	1.83	1.59	1.45	1.37	1.32
300	9.30	5.98	3.53	2.74	2.38	2.17	2.05	1.97
400	12.40	7.97	4.70	3.66	3.17	2.90	2.73	2.63
500	15.50	9.96	5.88	4.57	3.96	3.62	3.42	3.29
600	18.60	11.96	7.05	5.48	4.75	4.34	4.10	3.94
700	21.70	13.95	8.22	6.40	5.54	5.06	4.78	4.60
800	24.80	15.94	9.40	7.31	6.33	5.79	5.46	5.26
900	27.90	17.93	10.57	8.22	7.12	6.51	6.14	5.91
1000	31.00	19.92	11.75	9.13	7.91	7.23	6.83	6.57
2000	61.99	39.84	23.49	18.26	15.81	14.46	13.65	13.13
3000	92.98	59.76	35.23	27.39	23.72	21.69	20.47	19.70
4000	123.97	79.68	46.97	36.52	31.62	28.92	27.29	26.26
5000	154.96	99.60	58.71	45.65	39.52	36.15	34.11	32.83
6000	185.95	119.52	70.45	54.78	47.43	43.37	40.94	39.39
7000	216.95	139.44	82.19	63.91	55.33	50.60	47.76	45.96
8000	247.94	159.36	93.93	73.03	63.24	57.83	54.58	52.52
9000	278.93	179.28	105.67	82.16	71.14	65.06	61.40	59.09
10000	309.92	199.20	117.41	91.29	79.04	72.29	68.22	65.65
11000	340.91	219.12	129.15	100.42	86.95	79.51	75.04	72.22
12000	371.90	239.04	140.89	109.55	94.85	86.74	81.87	78.78
13000	402.89	258.96	152.63	118.68	102.75	93.97	88.69	85.35
14000	433.89	278.88	164.37	127.81	110.66	101.20	95.51	91.91
15000	464.88	298.80	176.11	136.93	118.56	108.43	102.33	98.48
16000	495.87	318.71	187.85	146.06	126.47	115.65	109.15	105.04
17000	526.86	338.63	199.59	155.19	134.37	122.88	115.97	111.60
18000	557.85	358.55	211.33	164.32	142.27	130.11	122.80	118.17
19000	588.84	378.47	223.07	173.45	150.18	137.34	129.62	124.73
20000	619.84	398.39	234.81	182.58	158.08	144.57	136.44	131.30
21000	650.83	418.31	246.55	191.71	165.98	151.79	143.26	137.86
22000	681.82	438.23	258.29	200.83	173.89	159.02	150.08	144.43
23000	712.81	458.15	270.03	209.96	181.79	166.25	156.91	150.99
24000	743.80	478.07	281.77	219.09	189.70	173.48	163.73	157.56
25000	774.79	497.99	293.51	228.22	197.60	180.71	170.55	164.12
26000	805.78	517.91	305.25	237.35	205.50	187.93	177.37	170.69
27000	836.78	537.83	316.99	246.48	213.41	195.16	184.19	177.25
28000	867.77	557.75	328.73	255.61	221.31	202.39	191.01	183.82
29000	898.76	577.67	340.47	264.74	229.21	209.62	197.84	190.38
30000	929.75	597.59	352.21	273.86	237.12	216.85	204.66	196.95
31000	960.74	617.51	363.95	282.99	245.02	224.08	211.48	203.51
32000	991.73	637.42	375.69	292.12	252.93	231.30	218.30	210.07
33000	1022.73	657.34	387.43	301.25	260.83	238.53	225.12	216.64
34000	1053.72	677.26	399.17	310.38	268.73	245.76	231.94	223.20
35000	1084.71	697.18	410.91	319.51	276.64	252.99	238.77	229.77
36000	1115.70	717.10	422.65	328.64	284.54	260.22	245.59	236.33
37000	1146.69	737.02	434.39	337.76	292.44	267.44	252.41	242.90
38000	1177.68	756.94	446.13	346.89	300.35	274.67	259.23	249.46
39000	1208.67	776.86	457.87	356.02	308.25	281.90	266.05	256.03
40000	1239.67	796.78	469.61	365.15	316.16	289.13	272.88	262.59

8

MONTHLY AMORTIZING PAYMENTS

AMOUNT OF LOAN	NUMBER OF YEARS IN TERM						
	10	15	20	25	30	35	40
41000	481.35	374.28	324.06	296.36	279.70	269.16	262.27
42000	493.09	383.41	331.96	303.58	286.52	275.72	268.67
43000	504.83	392.54	339.87	310.81	293.34	282.29	275.06
44000	516.57	401.66	347.77	318.04	300.16	288.85	281.46
45000	528.31	410.79	355.67	325.27	306.98	295.42	287.86
46000	540.05	419.92	363.58	332.50	313.81	301.98	294.25
47000	551.79	429.05	371.48	339.72	320.63	308.54	300.65
48000	563.53	438.18	379.39	346.95	327.45	315.11	307.05
49000	575.27	447.31	387.29	354.18	334.27	321.67	313.44
50000	587.01	456.44	395.19	361.41	341.09	328.24	319.84
51000	598.75	465.57	403.10	368.64	347.91	334.80	326.24
52000	610.49	474.69	411.00	375.86	354.74	341.37	332.63
53000	622.23	483.82	418.90	383.09	361.56	347.93	339.03
54000	633.97	492.95	426.81	390.32	368.38	354.50	345.43
55000	645.71	502.08	434.71	397.55	375.20	361.06	351.82
56000	657.45	511.21	442.62	404.78	382.02	367.63	358.22
57000	669.19	520.34	450.52	412.00	388.85	374.19	364.62
58000	680.93	529.47	458.42	419.23	395.67	380.76	371.01
59000	692.67	538.59	466.33	426.46	402.49	387.32	377.41
60000	704.41	547.72	474.23	433.69	409.31	393.89	383.81
61000	716.15	556.85	482.13	440.92	416.13	400.45	390.20
62000	727.89	565.98	490.04	448.15	422.95	407.01	396.60
63000	739.63	575.11	497.94	455.37	429.78	413.58	403.00
64000	751.37	584.24	505.85	462.60	436.60	420.14	409.40
65000	763.11	593.37	513.75	469.83	443.42	426.71	415.79
66000	774.85	602.49	521.65	477.06	450.24	433.27	422.19
67000	786.59	611.62	529.56	484.29	457.06	439.84	428.59
68000	798.33	620.75	537.46	491.51	463.88	446.40	434.98
69000	810.07	629.88	545.36	498.74	470.71	452.97	441.38
70000	821.81	639.01	553.27	505.97	477.53	459.53	447.78
71000	833.55	648.14	561.17	513.20	484.35	466.10	454.17
72000	845.29	657.27	569.08	520.43	491.17	472.66	460.57
73000	857.03	666.39	576.98	527.65	497.99	479.23	466.97
74000	868.77	675.52	584.88	534.88	504.82	485.79	473.36
75000	880.51	684.65	592.79	542.11	511.64	492.36	479.76
76000	892.25	693.78	600.69	549.34	518.46	498.92	486.16
77000	903.99	702.91	608.59	556.57	525.28	505.48	492.55
78000	915.73	712.04	616.50	563.79	532.10	512.05	498.95
79000	927.47	721.17	624.40	571.02	538.92	518.61	505.35
80000	939.21	730.30	632.31	578.25	545.75	525.18	511.74
81000	950.95	739.42	640.21	585.48	552.57	531.74	518.14
82000	962.69	748.55	648.11	592.71	559.39	538.31	524.54
83000	974.43	757.68	656.02	599.93	566.21	544.87	530.93
84000	986.17	766.81	663.92	607.16	573.03	551.44	537.33
85000	997.91	775.94	671.82	614.39	579.85	558.00	543.73
86000	1009.65	785.07	679.73	621.62	586.68	564.57	550.12
87000	1021.39	794.20	687.63	628.85	593.50	571.13	556.52
88000	1033.13	803.32	695.54	636.08	600.32	577.70	562.92
89000	1044.87	812.45	703.44	643.30	607.14	584.26	569.31
90000	1056.61	821.58	711.34	650.53	613.96	590.83	575.71
91000	1068.35	830.71	719.25	657.76	620.79	597.39	582.11
92000	1080.09	839.84	727.15	664.99	627.61	603.95	588.50
93000	1091.83	848.97	735.05	672.22	634.43	610.52	594.90
94000	1103.57	858.10	742.96	679.44	641.25	617.08	601.30
95000	1115.31	867.23	750.86	686.67	648.07	623.65	607.69
96000	1127.05	876.35	758.77	693.90	654.89	630.21	614.09
97000	1138.80	885.48	766.67	701.13	661.72	636.78	620.49
98000	1150.54	894.61	774.57	708.36	668.54	643.34	626.88
99000	1162.28	903.74	782.48	715.58	675.36	649.91	633.28
100000	1174.02	912.87	790.38	722.81	682.18	656.47	639.68

7½%

MONTHLY AMORTIZING PAYMENTS

AMOUNT OF LOAN	NUMBER OF YEARS IN TERM							
	3	5	10	15	20	25	30	35
10	.32	.21	.12	.10	.09	.08	.07	.07
20	.63	.41	.24	.19	.17	.15	.14	.14
25	.78	.51	.30	.24	.21	.19	.18	.17
30	.94	.61	.36	.28	.25	.23	.21	.21
40	1.25	.81	.48	.38	.33	.30	.28	.27
50	1.56	1.01	.60	.47	.41	.37	.35	.34
60	1.87	1.21	.72	.56	.49	.45	.42	.41
70	2.18	1.41	.84	.65	.57	.52	.49	.48
75	2.34	1.51	.90	.70	.61	.56	.53	.51
80	2.49	1.61	.95	.75	.65	.60	.56	.54
90	2.80	1.81	1.07	.84	.73	.67	.63	.61
100	3.12	2.01	1.19	.93	.81	.74	.70	.68
200	6.23	4.01	2.38	1.86	1.62	1.48	1.40	1.35
300	9.34	6.02	3.57	2.79	2.42	2.22	2.10	2.03
400	12.45	8.02	4.75	3.71	3.23	2.96	2.80	2.70
500	15.56	10.02	5.94	4.64	4.03	3.70	3.50	3.38
600	18.67	12.03	7.13	5.57	4.84	4.44	4.20	4.05
700	21.78	14.03	8.31	6.49	5.64	5.18	4.90	4.72
800	24.89	16.04	9.50	7.42	6.45	5.92	5.60	5.40
900	28.00	18.04	10.69	8.35	7.26	6.66	6.30	6.07
1000	31.11	20.04	11.88	9.28	8.06	7.39	7.00	6.75
2000	62.22	40.08	23.75	18.55	16.12	14.78	13.99	13.49
3000	93.32	60.12	35.62	27.82	24.17	22.17	20.98	20.23
4000	124.43	80.16	47.49	37.09	32.23	29.56	27.97	26.97
5000	155.54	100.19	59.36	46.36	40.28	36.95	34.97	33.72
6000	186.64	120.23	71.23	55.63	48.34	44.34	41.96	40.46
7000	217.75	140.27	83.10	64.90	56.40	51.73	48.95	47.20
8000	248.85	160.31	94.97	74.17	64.45	59.12	55.94	53.94
9000	279.96	180.35	106.84	83.44	72.51	66.51	62.93	60.69
10000	311.07	200.38	118.71	92.71	80.56	73.90	69.93	67.43
11000	342.17	220.42	130.58	101.98	88.62	81.29	76.92	74.17
12000	373.28	240.46	142.45	111.25	96.68	88.68	83.91	80.91
13000	404.39	260.50	154.32	120.52	104.73	96.07	90.90	87.66
14000	435.49	280.54	166.19	129.79	112.79	103.46	97.90	94.40
15000	466.60	300.57	178.06	139.06	120.84	110.85	104.89	101.14
16000	497.70	320.61	189.93	148.33	128.90	118.24	111.88	107.88
17000	528.81	340.65	201.80	157.60	136.96	125.63	118.87	114.63
18000	559.92	360.69	213.67	166.87	145.01	133.02	125.86	121.37
19000	591.02	380.73	225.54	176.14	153.07	140.41	132.86	128.11
20000	622.13	400.76	237.41	185.41	161.12	147.80	139.85	134.85
21000	653.24	420.80	249.28	194.68	169.18	155.19	146.84	141.60
22000	684.34	440.84	261.15	203.95	177.24	162.58	153.83	148.34
23000	715.45	460.88	273.02	213.22	185.29	169.97	160.82	155.08
24000	746.55	480.92	284.89	222.49	193.35	177.36	167.82	161.82
25000	777.66	500.95	296.76	231.76	201.40	184.75	174.81	168.57
26000	808.77	520.99	308.63	241.03	209.46	192.14	181.80	175.31
27000	839.87	541.03	320.50	250.30	217.52	199.53	188.79	182.05
28000	870.98	561.07	332.37	259.57	225.57	206.92	195.79	188.79
29000	902.09	581.11	344.24	268.84	233.63	214.31	202.78	195.54
30000	933.19	601.14	356.11	278.11	241.68	221.70	209.77	202.28
31000	964.30	621.18	367.98	287.38	249.74	229.09	216.76	209.02
32000	995.40	641.22	379.85	296.65	257.79	236.48	223.75	215.76
33000	1026.51	661.26	391.72	305.92	265.85	243.87	230.75	222.51
34000	1057.62	681.30	403.59	315.19	273.91	251.26	237.74	229.25
35000	1088.72	701.33	415.46	324.46	281.96	258.65	244.73	235.99
36000	1119.83	721.37	427.33	333.73	290.02	266.04	251.72	242.73
37000	1150.94	741.41	439.20	343.00	298.07	273.43	258.71	249.47
38000	1182.04	761.45	451.07	352.27	306.13	280.82	265.71	256.22
39000	1213.15	781.48	462.94	361.54	314.19	288.21	272.70	262.96
40000	1244.25	801.52	474.81	370.81	322.24	295.60	279.69	269.70

10

MONTHLY AMORTIZING PAYMENTS

AMOUNT OF LOAN	NUMBER OF YEARS IN TERM						
	10	15	20	25	30	35	40
41000	486.68	380.08	330.30	302.99	286.68	276.44	269.81
42000	498.55	389.35	338.35	310.38	293.68	283.19	276.39
43000	510.42	398.62	346.41	317.77	300.67	289.93	282.98
44000	522.29	407.89	354.47	325.16	307.66	296.67	289.56
45000	534.16	417.16	362.52	332.55	314.65	303.41	296.14
46000	546.03	426.43	370.58	339.94	321.64	310.16	302.72
47000	557.90	435.70	378.63	347.33	328.64	316.90	309.30
48000	569.77	444.97	386.69	354.72	335.63	323.64	315.88
49000	581.64	454.24	394.75	362.11	342.62	330.38	322.46
50000	593.51	463.51	402.80	369.50	349.61	337.13	329.04
51000	605.38	472.78	410.86	376.89	356.60	343.87	335.62
52000	617.25	482.05	418.91	384.28	363.60	350.61	342.20
53000	629.12	491.32	426.97	391.67	370.59	357.35	348.78
54000	640.99	500.59	435.03	399.06	377.58	364.10	355.36
55000	652.86	509.86	443.08	406.45	384.57	370.84	361.94
56000	664.73	519.13	451.14	413.84	391.57	377.58	368.52
57000	676.61	528.40	459.19	421.23	398.56	384.32	375.11
58000	688.48	537.67	467.25	428.62	405.55	391.07	381.69
59000	700.35	546.94	475.30	436.01	412.54	397.81	388.27
60000	712.22	556.21	483.36	443.40	419.53	404.55	394.85
61000	724.09	565.48	491.42	450.79	426.53	411.29	401.43
62000	735.96	574.75	499.47	458.18	433.52	418.04	408.01
63000	747.83	584.02	507.53	465.57	440.51	424.78	414.59
64000	759.70	593.29	515.58	472.96	447.50	431.52	421.17
65000	771.57	602.56	523.64	480.35	454.49	438.26	427.75
66000	783.44	611.83	531.70	487.74	461.49	445.01	434.33
67000	795.31	621.10	539.75	495.13	468.48	451.75	440.91
68000	807.18	630.37	547.81	502.52	475.47	458.49	447.49
69000	819.05	639.64	555.86	509.91	482.46	465.23	454.07
70000	830.92	648.91	563.92	517.30	489.46	471.97	460.65
71000	842.79	658.18	571.98	524.69	496.45	478.72	467.24
72000	854.66	667.45	580.03	532.08	503.44	485.46	473.82
73000	866.53	676.72	588.09	539.47	510.43	492.20	480.40
74000	878.40	685.99	596.14	546.86	517.42	498.94	486.98
75000	890.27	695.26	604.20	554.25	524.42	505.69	493.56
76000	902.14	704.53	612.26	561.64	531.41	512.43	500.14
77000	914.01	713.80	620.31	569.03	538.40	519.17	506.72
78000	925.88	723.07	628.37	576.42	545.39	525.91	513.30
79000	937.75	732.34	636.42	583.81	552.38	532.66	519.88
80000	949.62	741.61	644.48	591.20	559.38	539.40	526.46
81000	961.49	750.89	652.54	598.59	566.37	546.14	533.04
82000	973.36	760.16	660.59	605.98	573.36	552.88	539.62
83000	985.23	769.43	668.65	613.37	580.35	559.63	546.20
84000	997.10	778.70	676.70	620.76	587.35	566.37	552.78
85000	1008.97	787.97	684.76	628.15	594.34	573.11	559.37
86000	1020.84	797.24	692.82	635.54	601.33	579.85	565.95
87000	1032.71	806.51	700.87	642.93	608.32	586.60	572.53
88000	1044.58	815.78	708.93	650.32	615.31	593.34	579.11
89000	1056.45	825.05	716.98	657.71	622.31	600.08	585.69
90000	1068.32	834.32	725.04	665.10	629.30	606.82	592.27
91000	1080.19	843.59	733.09	672.49	636.29	613.57	598.85
92000	1092.06	852.86	741.15	679.88	643.28	620.31	605.43
93000	1103.93	862.13	749.21	687.27	650.27	627.05	612.01
94000	1115.80	871.40	757.26	694.66	657.27	633.79	618.59
95000	1127.67	880.67	765.32	702.05	664.26	640.54	625.17
96000	1139.54	889.94	773.37	709.44	671.25	647.28	631.75
97000	1151.41	899.21	781.43	716.83	678.24	654.02	638.33
98000	1163.28	908.48	789.49	724.22	685.24	660.76	644.91
99000	1175.15	917.75	797.54	731.61	692.23	667.51	651.50
100000	1187.02	927.02	805.60	739.00	699.22	674.25	658.08

7¾%

MONTHLY AMORTIZING PAYMENTS

AMOUNT OF LOAN	NUMBER OF YEARS IN TERM							
	3	5	10	15	20	25	30	35
10	.32	.21	.13	.10	.09	.08	.08	.07
20	.63	.41	.25	.19	.17	.16	.15	.14
25	.79	.51	.31	.24	.21	.19	.18	.18
30	.94	.61	.37	.29	.25	.23	.22	.21
40	1.25	.81	.49	.38	.33	.31	.29	.28
50	1.57	1.01	.61	.48	.42	.38	.36	.35
60	1.88	1.21	.73	.57	.50	.46	.43	.42
70	2.19	1.42	.85	.66	.58	.53	.51	.49
75	2.35	1.52	.91	.71	.62	.57	.54	.52
80	2.50	1.62	.97	.76	.66	.61	.58	.56
90	2.81	1.82	1.09	.85	.74	.68	.65	.63
100	3.13	2.02	1.21	.95	.83	.76	.72	.70
200	6.25	4.04	2.41	1.89	1.65	1.52	1.44	1.39
300	9.37	6.05	3.61	2.83	2.47	2.27	2.15	2.08
400	12.49	8.07	4.81	3.77	3.29	3.03	2.87	2.77
500	15.62	10.08	6.01	4.71	4.11	3.78	3.59	3.47
600	18.74	12.10	7.21	5.65	4.93	4.54	4.30	4.16
700	21.86	14.11	8.41	6.59	5.75	5.29	5.02	4.85
800	24.98	16.13	9.61	7.54	6.57	6.05	5.74	5.54
900	28.10	18.15	10.81	8.48	7.39	6.80	6.45	6.23
1000	31.23	20.16	12.01	9.42	8.21	7.56	7.17	6.93
2000	62.45	40.32	24.01	18.83	16.42	15.11	14.33	13.85
3000	93.67	60.48	36.01	28.24	24.63	22.66	21.50	20.77
4000	124.89	80.63	48.01	37.66	32.84	30.22	28.66	27.69
5000	156.11	100.79	60.01	47.07	41.05	37.77	35.83	34.61
6000	187.33	120.95	72.01	56.48	49.26	45.32	42.99	41.54
7000	218.55	141.10	84.01	65.89	57.47	52.88	50.15	48.46
8000	249.77	161.26	96.01	75.31	65.68	60.43	57.32	55.38
9000	281.00	181.42	108.01	84.72	73.89	67.98	64.48	62.30
10000	312.22	201.57	120.02	94.13	82.10	75.54	71.65	69.22
11000	343.44	221.73	132.02	103.55	90.31	83.09	78.81	76.14
12000	374.66	241.89	144.02	112.96	98.52	90.64	85.97	83.07
13000	405.88	262.05	156.02	122.37	106.73	98.20	93.14	89.99
14000	437.10	282.20	168.02	131.78	114.94	105.75	100.30	96.91
15000	468.32	302.36	180.02	141.20	123.15	113.30	107.47	103.83
16000	499.54	322.52	192.02	150.61	131.36	120.86	114.63	110.75
17000	530.76	342.67	204.02	160.02	139.57	128.41	121.80	117.67
18000	561.99	362.83	216.02	169.43	147.78	135.96	128.96	124.60
19000	593.21	382.99	228.03	178.85	155.99	143.52	136.12	131.52
20000	624.43	403.14	240.03	188.26	164.19	151.07	143.29	138.44
21000	655.65	423.30	252.03	197.67	172.40	158.62	150.45	145.36
22000	686.87	443.46	264.03	207.09	180.61	166.18	157.62	152.28
23000	718.09	463.62	276.03	216.50	188.82	173.73	164.78	159.21
24000	749.31	483.77	288.03	225.91	197.03	181.28	171.94	166.13
25000	780.53	503.93	300.03	235.32	205.24	188.84	179.11	173.05
26000	811.76	524.09	312.03	244.74	213.45	196.39	186.27	179.97
27000	842.98	544.24	324.03	254.15	221.66	203.94	193.44	186.89
28000	874.20	564.40	336.03	263.56	229.87	211.50	200.60	193.81
29000	905.42	584.56	348.04	272.97	238.08	219.05	207.76	200.74
30000	936.64	604.71	360.04	282.39	246.29	226.60	214.93	207.66
31000	967.86	624.87	372.04	291.80	254.50	234.16	222.09	214.58
32000	999.08	645.03	384.04	301.21	262.71	241.71	229.26	221.50
33000	1030.30	665.18	396.04	310.63	270.92	249.26	236.42	228.42
34000	1061.52	685.34	408.04	320.04	279.13	256.82	243.59	235.34
35000	1092.75	705.50	420.04	329.45	287.34	264.37	250.75	242.27
36000	1123.97	725.66	432.04	338.86	295.55	271.92	257.91	249.19
37000	1155.19	745.81	444.04	348.28	303.76	279.48	265.08	256.11
38000	1186.41	765.97	456.05	357.69	311.97	287.03	272.24	263.03
39000	1217.63	786.13	468.05	367.10	320.17	294.58	279.41	269.95
40000	1248.85	806.28	480.05	376.52	328.38	302.14	286.57	276.88

MONTHLY AMORTIZING PAYMENTS

AMOUNT OF LOAN	NUMBER OF YEARS IN TERM						
	10	15	20	25	30	35	40
41000	492.05	385.93	336.59	309.69	293.73	283.80	277.42
42000	504.05	395.34	344.80	317.24	300.90	290.72	284.19
43000	516.05	404.75	353.01	324.80	308.06	297.64	290.95
44000	528.05	414.17	361.22	332.35	315.23	304.56	297.72
45000	540.05	423.58	369.43	339.90	322.39	311.48	304.48
46000	552.05	432.99	377.64	347.46	329.55	318.41	311.25
47000	564.05	442.40	385.85	355.01	336.72	325.33	318.02
48000	576.06	451.82	394.06	362.56	343.88	332.25	324.78
49000	588.06	461.23	402.27	370.12	351.05	339.17	331.55
50000	600.06	470.64	410.48	377.67	358.21	346.09	338.31
51000	612.06	480.06	418.69	385.22	365.38	353.01	345.08
52000	624.06	489.47	426.90	392.78	372.54	359.94	351.85
53000	636.06	498.88	435.11	400.33	379.70	366.86	358.61
54000	648.06	508.29	443.32	407.88	386.87	373.78	365.38
55000	660.06	517.71	451.53	415.44	394.03	380.70	372.15
56000	672.06	527.12	459.74	422.99	401.20	387.62	378.91
57000	684.06	536.53	467.95	430.54	408.36	394.55	385.68
58000	696.07	545.94	476.16	438.10	415.52	401.47	392.44
59000	708.07	555.36	484.36	445.65	422.69	408.39	399.21
60000	720.07	564.77	492.57	453.20	429.85	415.31	405.98
61000	732.07	574.18	500.78	460.76	437.02	422.23	412.74
62000	744.07	583.60	508.99	468.31	444.18	429.15	419.51
63000	756.07	593.01	517.20	475.86	451.34	436.08	426.28
64000	768.07	602.42	525.41	483.42	458.51	443.00	433.04
65000	780.07	611.83	533.62	490.97	465.67	449.92	439.81
66000	792.08	621.25	541.83	498.52	472.84	456.84	446.57
67000	804.08	630.66	550.04	506.08	480.00	463.76	453.34
68000	816.08	640.07	558.25	513.63	487.17	470.68	460.11
69000	828.08	649.49	566.46	521.18	494.33	477.61	466.87
70000	840.08	658.90	574.67	528.74	501.49	484.53	473.64
71000	852.08	668.31	582.88	536.29	508.66	491.45	480.41
72000	864.08	677.72	591.09	543.84	515.82	498.37	487.17
73000	876.08	687.14	599.30	551.39	522.99	505.29	493.94
74000	888.08	696.55	607.51	558.95	530.15	512.22	500.70
75000	900.08	705.96	615.72	566.50	537.31	519.14	507.47
76000	912.09	715.37	623.93	574.05	544.48	526.06	514.24
77000	924.09	724.79	632.14	581.61	551.64	532.98	521.00
78000	936.09	734.20	640.34	589.16	558.81	539.90	527.77
79000	948.09	743.61	648.55	596.71	565.97	546.82	534.53
80000	960.09	753.03	656.76	604.27	573.13	553.75	541.30
81000	972.09	762.44	664.97	611.82	580.30	560.67	548.07
82000	984.09	771.85	673.18	619.37	587.46	567.59	554.83
83000	996.09	781.26	681.39	626.93	594.63	574.51	561.60
84000	1008.09	790.68	689.60	634.48	601.79	581.43	568.37
85000	1020.10	800.09	697.81	642.03	608.96	588.35	575.13
86000	1032.10	809.50	706.02	649.59	616.12	595.28	581.90
87000	1044.10	818.91	714.23	657.14	623.28	602.20	588.66
88000	1056.10	828.33	722.44	664.69	630.45	609.12	595.43
89000	1068.10	837.74	730.65	672.25	637.61	616.04	602.20
90000	1080.10	847.15	738.86	679.80	644.78	622.96	608.96
91000	1092.10	856.57	747.07	687.35	651.94	629.89	615.73
92000	1104.10	865.98	755.28	694.91	659.10	636.81	622.50
93000	1116.10	875.39	763.49	702.46	666.27	643.73	629.26
94000	1128.10	884.80	771.70	710.01	673.43	650.65	636.03
95000	1140.11	894.22	779.91	717.57	680.60	657.57	642.79
96000	1152.11	903.63	788.12	725.12	687.76	664.49	649.56
97000	1164.11	913.04	796.33	732.67	694.92	671.42	656.33
98000	1176.11	922.46	804.53	740.23	702.09	678.34	663.09
99000	1188.11	931.87	812.74	747.78	709.25	685.26	669.86
100000	1200.11	941.28	820.95	755.33	716.42	692.18	676.62

MONTHLY AMORTIZING PAYMENTS

AMOUNT OF LOAN	NUMBER OF YEARS IN TERM							
	3	5	10	15	20	25	30	35
10	.32	.21	.13	.10	.09	.08	.08	.08
20	.63	.41	.25	.20	.17	.16	.15	.15
25	.79	.51	.31	.24	.21	.20	.19	.18
30	.95	.61	.37	.29	.26	.24	.23	.22
40	1.26	.82	.49	.39	.34	.31	.30	.29
50	1.57	1.02	.61	.48	.42	.39	.37	.36
60	1.89	1.22	.73	.58	.51	.47	.45	.43
70	2.20	1.42	.85	.67	.59	.55	.52	.50
75	2.36	1.53	.91	.72	.63	.58	.56	.54
80	2.51	1.63	.98	.77	.67	.62	.59	.57
90	2.83	1.83	1.10	.87	.76	.70	.67	.64
100	3.14	2.03	1.22	.96	.84	.78	.74	.72
200	6.27	4.06	2.43	1.92	1.68	1.55	1.47	1.43
300	9.41	6.09	3.64	2.87	2.51	2.32	2.21	2.14
400	12.54	8.12	4.86	3.83	3.35	3.09	2.94	2.85
500	15.67	10.14	6.07	4.78	4.19	3.86	3.67	3.56
600	18.81	12.17	7.28	5.74	5.02	4.64	4.41	4.27
700	21.94	14.20	8.50	6.69	5.86	5.41	5.14	4.98
800	25.07	16.23	9.71	7.65	6.70	6.18	5.88	5.69
900	28.21	18.25	10.92	8.61	7.53	6.95	6.61	6.40
1000	31.34	20.28	12.14	9.56	8.37	7.72	7.34	7.11
2000	62.68	40.56	24.27	19.12	16.73	15.44	14.68	14.21
3000	94.01	60.83	36.40	28.67	25.10	23.16	22.02	21.31
4000	125.35	81.11	48.54	38.23	33.46	30.88	29.36	28.42
5000	156.69	101.39	60.67	47.79	41.83	38.60	36.69	35.52
6000	188.02	121.66	72.80	57.34	50.19	46.31	44.03	42.62
7000	219.36	141.94	84.93	66.90	58.56	54.03	51.37	49.72
8000	250.70	162.22	97.07	76.46	66.92	61.75	58.71	56.83
9000	282.03	182.49	109.20	86.01	75.28	69.47	66.04	63.93
10000	313.37	202.77	121.33	95.57	83.65	77.19	73.38	71.03
11000	344.71	223.05	133.47	105.13	92.01	84.90	80.72	78.13
12000	376.04	243.32	145.60	114.68	100.38	92.62	88.06	85.24
13000	407.38	263.60	157.73	124.24	108.74	100.34	95.39	92.34
14000	438.71	283.87	169.86	133.80	117.11	108.06	102.73	99.44
15000	470.05	304.15	182.00	143.35	125.47	115.78	110.07	106.54
16000	501.39	324.43	194.13	152.91	133.84	123.50	117.41	113.65
17000	532.72	344.70	206.26	162.47	142.20	131.21	124.74	120.75
18000	564.06	364.98	218.39	172.02	150.56	138.93	132.08	127.85
19000	595.40	385.26	230.53	181.58	158.93	146.65	139.42	134.95
20000	626.73	405.53	242.66	191.14	167.29	154.37	146.76	142.06
21000	658.07	425.81	254.79	200.69	175.66	162.09	154.10	149.16
22000	689.41	446.09	266.93	210.25	184.02	169.80	161.43	156.26
23000	720.74	466.36	279.06	219.80	192.39	177.52	168.77	163.37
24000	752.08	486.64	291.19	229.36	200.75	185.24	176.11	170.47
25000	783.41	506.91	303.32	238.92	209.12	192.96	183.45	177.57
26000	814.75	527.19	315.46	248.47	217.48	200.68	190.78	184.67
27000	846.09	547.47	327.59	258.03	225.84	208.40	198.12	191.78
28000	877.42	567.74	339.72	267.59	234.21	216.11	205.46	198.88
29000	908.76	588.02	351.86	277.14	242.57	223.83	212.80	205.98
30000	940.10	608.30	363.99	286.70	250.94	231.55	220.13	213.08
31000	971.43	628.57	376.12	296.26	259.30	239.27	227.47	220.19
32000	1002.77	648.85	388.25	305.81	267.67	246.99	234.81	227.29
33000	1034.11	669.13	400.39	315.37	276.03	254.70	242.15	234.39
34000	1065.44	689.40	412.52	324.93	284.39	262.42	249.48	241.49
35000	1096.78	709.68	424.65	334.48	292.76	270.14	256.82	248.60
36000	1128.11	729.96	436.78	344.04	301.12	277.86	264.16	255.70
37000	1159.45	750.23	448.92	353.60	309.49	285.58	271.50	262.80
38000	1190.79	770.51	461.05	363.15	317.85	293.30	278.84	269.90
39000	1222.12	790.78	473.18	372.71	326.22	301.01	286.17	277.01
40000	1253.46	811.06	485.32	382.27	334.58	308.73	293.51	284.11

14

MONTHLY AMORTIZING PAYMENTS

AMOUNT OF LOAN	NUMBER OF YEARS IN TERM						
	10	15	20	25	30	35	40
41000	497.45	391.82	342.95	316.45	300.85	291.21	285.08
42000	509.58	401.38	351.31	324.17	308.19	298.31	292.04
43000	521.71	410.94	359.67	331.89	315.52	305.42	298.99
44000	533.85	420.49	368.04	339.60	322.86	312.52	305.94
45000	545.98	430.05	376.40	347.32	330.20	319.62	312.90
46000	558.11	439.60	384.77	355.04	337.54	326.73	319.85
47000	570.24	449.16	393.13	362.76	344.87	333.83	326.80
48000	582.38	458.72	401.50	370.48	352.21	340.93	333.75
49000	594.51	468.27	409.86	378.19	359.55	348.03	340.71
50000	606.64	477.83	418.23	385.91	366.89	355.14	347.66
51000	618.78	487.39	426.59	393.63	374.22	362.24	354.61
52000	630.91	496.94	434.95	401.35	381.56	369.34	361.57
53000	643.04	506.50	443.32	409.07	388.90	376.44	368.52
54000	655.17	516.06	451.68	416.79	396.24	383.55	375.47
55000	667.31	525.61	460.05	424.50	403.58	390.65	382.43
56000	679.44	535.17	468.41	432.22	410.91	397.75	389.38
57000	691.57	544.73	476.78	439.94	418.25	404.85	396.33
58000	703.71	554.28	485.14	447.66	425.59	411.96	403.29
59000	715.84	563.84	493.50	455.38	432.93	419.06	410.24
60000	727.97	573.40	501.87	463.09	440.26	426.16	417.19
61000	740.10	582.95	510.23	470.81	447.60	433.26	424.15
62000	752.24	592.51	518.60	478.53	454.94	440.37	431.10
63000	764.37	602.07	526.96	486.25	462.28	447.47	438.05
64000	776.50	611.62	535.33	493.97	469.61	454.57	445.00
65000	788.63	621.18	543.69	501.69	476.95	461.67	451.96
66000	800.77	630.74	552.06	509.40	484.29	468.78	458.91
67000	812.90	640.29	560.42	517.12	491.63	475.88	465.86
68000	825.03	649.85	568.78	524.84	498.96	482.98	472.82
69000	837.17	659.40	577.15	532.56	506.30	490.09	479.77
70000	849.30	668.96	585.51	540.28	513.64	497.19	486.72
71000	861.43	678.52	593.88	547.99	520.98	504.29	493.68
72000	873.56	688.07	602.24	555.71	528.32	511.39	500.63
73000	885.70	697.63	610.61	563.43	535.65	518.50	507.58
74000	897.83	707.19	618.97	571.15	542.99	525.60	514.54
75000	909.96	716.74	627.34	578.87	550.33	532.70	521.49
76000	922.09	726.30	635.70	586.59	557.67	539.80	528.44
77000	934.23	735.86	644.06	594.30	565.00	546.91	535.40
78000	946.36	745.41	652.43	602.02	572.34	554.01	542.35
79000	958.49	754.97	660.79	609.74	579.68	561.11	549.30
80000	970.63	764.53	669.16	617.46	587.02	568.21	556.25
81000	982.76	774.08	677.52	625.18	594.35	575.32	563.21
82000	994.89	783.64	685.89	632.89	601.69	582.42	570.16
83000	1007.02	793.20	694.25	640.61	609.03	589.52	577.11
84000	1019.16	802.75	702.61	648.33	616.37	596.62	584.07
85000	1031.29	812.31	710.98	656.05	623.70	603.73	591.02
86000	1043.42	821.87	719.34	663.77	631.04	610.83	597.97
87000	1055.56	831.42	727.71	671.49	638.38	617.93	604.93
88000	1067.69	840.98	736.07	679.20	645.72	625.03	611.88
89000	1079.82	850.54	744.44	686.92	653.06	632.14	618.83
90000	1091.95	860.09	752.80	694.64	660.39	639.24	625.79
91000	1104.09	869.65	761.17	702.36	667.73	646.34	632.74
92000	1116.22	879.20	769.53	710.08	675.07	653.45	639.69
93000	1128.35	888.76	777.89	717.79	682.41	660.55	646.64
94000	1140.48	898.32	786.26	725.51	689.74	667.65	653.60
95000	1152.62	907.87	794.62	733.23	697.08	674.75	660.55
96000	1164.75	917.43	802.99	740.95	704.42	681.86	667.50
97000	1176.88	926.99	811.35	748.67	711.76	688.96	674.46
98000	1189.02	936.54	819.72	756.38	719.09	696.06	681.41
99000	1201.15	946.10	828.08	764.10	726.43	703.16	688.36
100000	1213.28	955.66	836.45	771.82	733.77	710.27	695.32

8¼%

MONTHLY AMORTIZING PAYMENTS

AMOUNT OF LOAN	NUMBER OF YEARS IN TERM							
	3	5	10	15	20	25	30	35
10	.32	.21	.13	.10	.09	.08	.08	.08
20	.63	.41	.25	.20	.18	.16	.16	.15
25	.79	.51	.31	.25	.22	.20	.19	.19
30	.95	.62	.37	.30	.26	.24	.23	.22
40	1.26	.82	.50	.39	.35	.32	.31	.30
50	1.58	1.02	.62	.49	.43	.40	.38	.37
60	1.89	1.23	.74	.59	.52	.48	.46	.44
70	2.21	1.43	.86	.68	.60	.56	.53	.51
75	2.36	1.53	.92	.73	.64	.60	.57	.55
80	2.52	1.64	.99	.78	.69	.64	.61	.59
90	2.84	1.84	1.11	.88	.77	.71	.68	.66
100	3.15	2.04	1.23	.98	.86	.79	.76	.73
200	6.30	4.08	2.46	1.95	1.71	1.58	1.51	1.46
300	9.44	6.12	3.68	2.92	2.56	2.37	2.26	2.19
400	12.59	8.16	4.91	3.89	3.41	3.16	3.01	2.92
500	15.73	10.20	6.14	4.86	4.27	3.95	3.76	3.65
600	18.88	12.24	7.36	5.83	5.12	4.74	4.51	4.38
700	22.02	14.28	8.59	6.80	5.97	5.52	5.26	5.10
800	25.17	16.32	9.82	7.77	6.82	6.31	6.02	5.83
900	28.31	18.36	11.04	8.74	7.67	7.10	6.77	6.56
1000	31.46	20.40	12.27	9.71	8.53	7.89	7.52	7.29
2000	62.91	40.80	24.54	19.41	17.05	15.77	15.03	14.57
3000	94.36	61.19	36.80	29.11	25.57	23.66	22.54	21.86
4000	125.81	81.59	49.07	38.81	34.09	31.54	30.06	29.14
5000	157.26	101.99	61.33	48.51	42.61	39.43	37.57	36.43
6000	188.72	122.38	73.60	58.21	51.13	47.31	45.08	43.71
7000	220.17	142.78	85.86	67.91	59.65	55.20	52.59	51.00
8000	251.62	163.18	98.13	77.62	68.17	63.08	60.11	58.28
9000	283.07	183.57	110.39	87.32	76.69	70.97	67.62	65.57
10000	314.52	203.97	122.66	97.02	85.21	78.85	75.13	72.85
11000	345.98	224.36	134.92	106.72	93.73	86.73	82.64	80.14
12000	377.43	244.76	147.19	116.42	102.25	94.62	90.16	87.42
13000	408.88	265.16	159.45	126.12	110.77	102.50	97.67	94.71
14000	440.33	285.55	171.72	135.82	119.29	110.39	105.18	101.99
15000	471.78	305.95	183.98	145.53	127.81	118.27	112.69	109.28
16000	503.23	326.35	196.25	155.23	136.34	126.16	120.21	116.56
17000	534.69	346.74	208.51	164.93	144.86	134.04	127.72	123.85
18000	566.14	367.14	220.78	174.63	153.38	141.93	135.23	131.13
19000	597.59	387.53	233.04	184.33	161.90	149.81	142.75	138.42
20000	629.04	407.93	245.31	194.03	170.42	157.70	150.26	145.70
21000	660.49	428.33	257.58	203.73	178.94	165.58	157.77	152.99
22000	691.95	448.72	269.84	213.44	187.46	173.46	165.28	160.27
23000	723.40	469.12	282.11	223.14	195.98	181.35	172.80	167.56
24000	754.85	489.52	294.37	232.84	204.50	189.23	180.31	174.84
25000	786.30	509.91	306.64	242.54	213.02	197.12	187.82	182.13
26000	817.75	530.31	318.90	252.24	221.54	205.00	195.33	189.41
27000	849.20	550.70	331.17	261.94	230.06	212.89	202.85	196.70
28000	880.66	571.10	343.43	271.64	238.58	220.77	210.36	203.98
29000	912.11	591.50	355.70	281.35	247.10	228.66	217.87	211.27
30000	943.56	611.89	367.96	291.05	255.62	236.54	225.38	218.55
31000	975.01	632.29	380.23	300.75	264.15	244.42	232.90	225.84
32000	1006.46	652.69	392.49	310.45	272.67	252.31	240.41	233.12
33000	1037.92	673.08	404.76	320.15	281.19	260.19	247.92	240.41
34000	1069.37	693.48	417.02	329.85	289.71	268.08	255.44	247.69
35000	1100.82	713.87	429.29	339.55	298.23	275.96	262.95	254.98
36000	1132.27	734.27	441.55	349.26	306.75	283.85	270.46	262.26
37000	1163.72	754.67	453.82	358.96	315.27	291.73	277.98	269.55
38000	1195.17	775.06	466.08	368.66	323.79	299.62	285.49	276.83
39000	1226.63	795.46	478.35	378.36	332.31	307.50	293.00	284.12
40000	1258.08	815.86	490.62	388.06	340.83	315.39	300.51	291.40

MONTHLY AMORTIZING PAYMENTS

AMOUNT OF LOAN	NUMBER OF YEARS IN TERM						
	10	15	20	25	30	35	40
41000	502.88	397.76	349.35	323.27	308.02	298.69	292.80
42000	515.15	407.46	357.87	331.15	315.54	305.97	299.94
43000	527.41	417.17	366.39	339.04	323.05	313.26	307.08
44000	539.68	426.87	374.91	346.92	330.56	320.54	314.23
45000	551.94	436.57	383.43	354.81	338.07	327.83	321.37
46000	564.21	446.27	391.96	362.69	345.59	335.11	328.51
47000	576.47	455.97	400.48	370.58	353.10	342.40	335.65
48000	588.74	465.67	409.00	378.46	360.61	349.68	342.79
49000	601.00	475.37	417.52	386.35	368.13	356.97	349.93
50000	613.27	485.08	426.04	394.23	375.64	364.25	357.07
51000	625.53	494.78	434.56	402.11	383.15	371.54	364.22
52000	637.80	504.48	443.08	410.00	390.66	378.82	371.36
53000	650.06	514.18	451.60	417.88	398.18	386.11	378.50
54000	662.33	523.88	460.12	425.77	405.69	393.39	385.64
55000	674.59	533.58	468.64	433.65	413.20	400.68	392.78
56000	686.86	543.28	477.16	441.54	420.71	407.96	399.92
57000	699.12	552.99	485.68	449.42	428.23	415.24	407.06
58000	711.39	562.69	494.20	457.31	435.74	422.53	414.21
59000	723.66	572.39	502.72	465.19	443.25	429.81	421.35
60000	735.92	582.09	511.24	473.08	450.76	437.10	428.49
61000	748.19	591.79	519.77	480.96	458.28	444.38	435.63
62000	760.45	601.49	528.29	488.84	465.79	451.67	442.77
63000	772.72	611.19	536.81	496.73	473.30	458.95	449.91
64000	784.98	620.89	545.33	504.61	480.82	466.24	457.05
65000	797.25	630.60	553.85	512.50	488.33	473.52	464.20
66000	809.51	640.30	562.37	520.38	495.84	480.81	471.34
67000	821.78	650.00	570.89	528.27	503.35	488.09	478.48
68000	834.04	659.70	579.41	536.15	510.87	495.38	485.62
69000	846.31	669.40	587.93	544.04	518.38	502.66	492.76
70000	858.57	679.10	596.45	551.92	525.89	509.95	499.90
71000	870.84	688.80	604.97	559.80	533.40	517.23	507.04
72000	883.10	698.51	613.49	567.69	540.92	524.52	514.18
73000	895.37	708.21	622.01	575.57	548.43	531.80	521.33
74000	907.63	717.91	630.53	583.46	555.94	539.09	528.47
75000	919.90	727.61	639.05	591.34	563.45	546.37	535.61
76000	932.16	737.31	647.57	599.23	570.97	553.66	542.75
77000	944.43	747.01	656.10	607.11	578.48	560.94	549.89
78000	956.70	756.71	664.62	615.00	585.99	568.23	557.03
79000	968.96	766.42	673.14	622.88	593.51	575.51	564.17
80000	981.23	776.12	681.66	630.77	601.02	582.80	571.32
81000	993.49	785.82	690.18	638.65	608.53	590.08	578.46
82000	1005.76	795.52	698.70	646.53	616.04	597.37	585.60
83000	1018.02	805.22	707.22	654.42	623.56	604.65	592.74
84000	1030.29	814.92	715.74	662.30	631.07	611.94	599.88
85000	1042.55	824.62	724.26	670.19	638.58	619.22	607.02
86000	1054.82	834.33	732.78	678.07	646.09	626.51	614.16
87000	1067.08	844.03	741.30	685.96	653.61	633.79	621.31
88000	1079.35	853.73	749.82	693.84	661.12	641.08	628.45
89000	1091.61	863.43	758.34	701.73	668.63	648.36	635.59
90000	1103.88	873.13	766.86	709.61	676.14	655.65	642.73
91000	1116.14	882.83	775.38	717.49	683.66	662.93	649.87
92000	1128.41	892.53	783.91	725.38	691.17	670.22	657.01
93000	1140.67	902.24	792.43	733.26	698.68	677.50	664.15
94000	1152.94	911.94	800.95	741.15	706.20	684.79	671.30
95000	1165.20	921.64	809.47	749.03	713.71	692.07	678.44
96000	1177.47	931.34	817.99	756.92	721.22	699.36	685.58
97000	1189.74	941.04	826.51	764.80	728.73	706.64	692.72
98000	1202.00	950.74	835.03	772.69	736.25	713.93	699.86
99000	1214.27	960.44	843.55	780.57	743.76	721.21	707.00
100000	1226.53	970.15	852.07	788.46	751.27	728.50	714.14

8½%

MONTHLY AMORTIZING PAYMENTS

AMOUNT OF LOAN	NUMBER OF YEARS IN TERM							
	3	5	10	15	20	25	30	35
10	.32	.21	.13	.10	.09	.09	.08	.08
20	.64	.42	.25	.20	.18	.17	.16	.15
25	.79	.52	.31	.25	.22	.21	.20	.19
30	.95	.62	.38	.30	.27	.25	.24	.23
40	1.27	.83	.50	.40	.35	.33	.31	.30
50	1.58	1.03	.62	.50	.44	.41	.39	.38
60	1.90	1.24	.75	.60	.53	.49	.47	.45
70	2.21	1.44	.87	.69	.61	.57	.54	.53
75	2.37	1.54	.93	.74	.66	.61	.58	.57
80	2.53	1.65	1.00	.79	.70	.65	.62	.60
90	2.85	1.85	1.12	.89	.79	.73	.70	.68
100	3.16	2.06	1.24	.99	.87	.81	.77	.75
200	6.32	4.11	2.48	1.97	1.74	1.62	1.54	1.50
300	9.48	6.16	3.72	2.96	2.61	2.42	2.31	2.25
400	12.63	8.21	4.96	3.94	3.48	3.23	3.08	2.99
500	15.79	10.26	6.20	4.93	4.34	4.03	3.85	3.74
600	18.95	12.31	7.44	5.91	5.21	4.84	4.62	4.49
700	22.10	14.37	8.68	6.90	6.08	5.64	5.39	5.23
800	25.26	16.42	9.92	7.88	6.95	6.45	6.16	5.98
900	28.42	18.47	11.16	8.87	7.82	7.25	6.93	6.73
1000	31.57	20.52	12.40	9.85	8.68	8.06	7.69	7.47
2000	63.14	41.04	24.80	19.70	17.36	16.11	15.38	14.94
3000	94.71	61.55	37.20	29.55	26.04	24.16	23.07	22.41
4000	126.28	82.07	49.60	39.39	34.72	32.21	30.76	29.88
5000	157.84	102.59	62.00	49.24	43.40	40.27	38.45	37.35
6000	189.41	123.10	74.40	59.09	52.07	48.32	46.14	44.82
7000	220.98	143.62	86.79	68.94	60.75	56.37	53.83	52.29
8000	252.55	164.14	99.19	78.78	69.43	64.42	61.52	59.75
9000	284.11	184.65	111.59	88.63	78.11	72.48	69.21	67.22
10000	315.68	205.17	123.99	98.48	86.79	80.53	76.90	74.69
11000	347.25	225.69	136.39	108.33	95.47	88.58	84.59	82.16
12000	378.82	246.20	148.79	118.17	104.14	96.63	92.27	89.63
13000	410.38	266.72	161.19	128.02	112.82	104.68	99.96	97.10
14000	441.95	287.24	173.58	137.87	121.50	112.74	107.65	104.57
15000	473.52	307.75	185.98	147.72	130.18	120.79	115.34	112.03
16000	505.09	328.27	198.38	157.56	138.86	128.84	123.03	119.50
17000	536.65	348.79	210.78	167.41	147.53	136.89	130.72	126.97
18000	568.22	369.30	223.18	177.26	156.21	144.95	138.41	134.44
19000	599.79	389.82	235.58	187.11	164.89	153.00	146.10	141.91
20000	631.36	410.34	247.98	196.95	173.57	161.05	153.79	149.38
21000	662.92	430.85	260.37	206.80	182.25	169.10	161.48	156.85
22000	694.49	451.37	272.77	216.65	190.93	177.15	169.17	164.31
23000	726.06	471.89	285.17	226.50	199.60	185.21	176.86	171.78
24000	757.63	492.40	297.57	236.34	208.28	193.26	184.54	179.25
25000	789.19	512.92	309.97	246.19	216.96	201.31	192.23	186.72
26000	820.76	533.43	322.37	256.04	225.64	209.36	199.92	194.19
27000	852.33	553.95	334.77	265.88	234.32	217.42	207.61	201.66
28000	883.90	574.47	347.16	275.73	243.00	225.47	215.30	209.13
29000	915.46	594.98	359.56	285.58	251.67	233.52	222.99	216.59
30000	947.03	615.50	371.96	295.43	260.35	241.57	230.68	224.06
31000	978.60	636.02	384.36	305.27	269.03	249.63	238.37	231.53
32000	1010.17	656.53	396.76	315.12	277.71	257.68	246.06	239.00
33000	1041.73	677.05	409.16	324.97	286.39	265.73	253.75	246.47
34000	1073.30	697.57	421.56	334.82	295.06	273.78	261.44	253.94
35000	1104.87	718.08	433.95	344.66	303.74	281.83	269.12	261.41
36000	1136.44	738.60	446.35	354.51	312.42	289.89	276.81	268.87
37000	1168.00	759.12	458.75	364.36	321.10	297.94	284.50	276.34
38000	1199.57	779.63	471.15	374.21	329.78	305.99	292.19	283.81
39000	1231.14	800.15	483.55	384.05	338.46	314.04	299.88	291.28
40000	1262.71	820.67	495.95	393.90	347.13	322.10	307.57	298.75

MONTHLY AMORTIZING PAYMENTS

AMOUNT OF LOAN	NUMBER OF YEARS IN TERM						
	10	15	20	25	30	35	40
41000	508.35	403.75	355.81	330.15	315.26	306.22	300.57
42000	520.74	413.60	364.49	338.20	322.95	313.69	307.90
43000	533.14	423.44	373.17	346.25	330.64	321.16	315.24
44000	545.54	433.29	381.85	354.30	338.33	328.62	322.57
45000	557.94	443.14	390.53	362.36	346.02	336.09	329.90
46000	570.34	452.99	399.20	370.41	353.71	343.56	337.23
47000	582.74	462.83	407.88	378.46	361.39	351.03	344.56
48000	595.14	472.68	416.56	386.51	369.08	358.50	351.89
49000	607.53	482.53	425.24	394.57	376.77	365.97	359.22
50000	619.93	492.37	433.92	402.62	384.46	373.44	366.55
51000	632.33	502.22	442.59	410.67	392.15	380.90	373.88
52000	644.73	512.07	451.27	418.72	399.84	388.37	381.21
53000	657.13	521.92	459.95	426.78	407.53	395.84	388.54
54000	669.53	531.76	468.63	434.83	415.22	403.31	395.88
55000	681.93	541.61	477.31	442.88	422.91	410.78	403.21
56000	694.32	551.46	485.99	450.93	430.60	418.25	410.54
57000	706.72	561.31	494.66	458.98	438.29	425.72	417.87
58000	719.12	571.15	503.34	467.04	445.97	433.18	425.20
59000	731.52	581.00	512.02	475.09	453.66	440.65	432.53
60000	743.92	590.85	520.70	483.14	461.35	448.12	439.86
61000	756.32	600.70	529.38	491.19	469.04	455.59	447.19
62000	768.72	610.54	538.06	499.25	476.73	463.06	454.52
63000	781.11	620.39	546.73	507.30	484.42	470.53	461.85
64000	793.51	630.24	555.41	515.35	492.11	478.00	469.19
65000	805.91	640.09	564.09	523.40	499.80	485.46	476.52
66000	818.31	649.93	572.77	531.45	507.49	492.93	483.85
67000	830.71	659.78	581.45	539.51	515.18	500.40	491.18
68000	843.11	669.63	590.12	547.56	522.87	507.87	498.51
69000	855.51	679.48	598.80	555.61	530.56	515.34	505.84
70000	867.90	689.32	607.48	563.66	538.24	522.81	513.17
71000	880.30	699.17	616.16	571.71	545.93	530.28	520.50
72000	892.70	709.02	624.84	579.77	553.62	537.74	527.83
73000	905.10	718.86	633.52	587.82	561.31	545.21	535.16
74000	917.50	728.71	642.19	595.87	569.00	552.68	542.49
75000	929.90	738.56	650.87	603.93	576.69	560.15	549.83
76000	942.30	748.41	659.55	611.98	584.38	567.62	557.16
77000	954.69	758.25	668.23	620.03	592.07	575.09	564.49
78000	967.09	768.10	676.91	628.08	599.76	582.56	571.82
79000	979.49	777.95	685.59	636.13	607.45	590.02	579.15
80000	991.89	787.80	694.26	644.19	615.14	597.49	586.48
81000	1004.29	797.64	702.94	652.24	622.82	604.96	593.81
82000	1016.69	807.49	711.62	660.29	630.51	612.43	601.14
83000	1029.09	817.34	720.30	668.34	638.20	619.90	608.47
84000	1041.48	827.19	728.98	676.40	645.89	627.37	615.80
85000	1053.88	837.03	737.65	684.45	653.58	634.84	623.13
86000	1066.28	846.88	746.33	692.50	661.27	642.31	630.47
87000	1078.68	856.73	755.01	700.55	668.96	649.77	637.80
88000	1091.08	866.58	763.69	708.60	676.65	657.24	645.13
89000	1103.48	876.42	772.37	716.66	684.34	664.71	652.46
90000	1115.88	886.27	781.05	724.71	692.03	672.18	659.79
91000	1128.27	896.12	789.72	732.76	699.72	679.65	667.12
92000	1140.67	905.97	798.40	740.81	707.41	687.12	674.45
93000	1153.07	915.81	807.08	748.87	715.09	694.59	681.78
94000	1165.47	925.66	815.76	756.92	722.78	702.05	689.11
95000	1177.87	935.51	824.44	764.97	730.47	709.52	696.44
96000	1190.27	945.35	833.12	773.02	738.16	716.99	703.78
97000	1202.67	955.20	841.79	781.08	745.85	724.46	711.11
98000	1215.06	965.05	850.47	789.13	753.54	731.93	718.44
99000	1227.46	974.90	859.15	797.18	761.23	739.40	725.77
100000	1239.86	984.74	867.83	805.23	768.92	746.87	733.10

8¾%

MONTHLY AMORTIZING PAYMENTS

AMOUNT OF LOAN	NUMBER OF YEARS IN TERM							
	3	5	10	15	20	25	30	35
10	.32	.21	.13	.10	.09	.09	.08	.08
20	.64	.42	.26	.20	.18	.17	.16	.16
25	.80	.52	.32	.25	.23	.21	.20	.20
30	.96	.62	.38	.30	.27	.25	.24	.23
40	1.27	.83	.51	.40	.36	.33	.32	.31
50	1.59	1.04	.63	.50	.45	.42	.40	.39
60	1.91	1.24	.76	.60	.54	.50	.48	.46
70	2.22	1.45	.88	.70	.62	.58	.56	.54
75	2.38	1.55	.94	.75	.67	.62	.60	.58
80	2.54	1.66	1.01	.80	.71	.66	.63	.62
90	2.86	1.86	1.13	.90	.80	.74	.71	.69
100	3.17	2.07	1.26	1.00	.89	.83	.79	.77
200	6.34	4.13	2.51	2.00	1.77	1.65	1.58	1.54
300	9.51	6.20	3.76	3.00	2.66	2.47	2.37	2.30
400	12.68	8.26	5.02	4.00	3.54	3.29	3.15	3.07
500	15.85	10.32	6.27	5.00	4.42	4.12	3.94	3.83
600	19.02	12.39	7.52	6.00	5.31	4.94	4.73	4.60
700	22.18	14.45	8.78	7.00	6.19	5.76	5.51	5.36
800	25.35	16.51	10.03	8.00	7.07	6.58	6.30	6.13
900	28.52	18.58	11.28	9.00	7.96	7.40	7.09	6.89
1000	31.69	20.64	12.54	10.00	8.84	8.23	7.87	7.66
2000	63.37	41.28	25.07	19.99	17.68	16.45	15.74	15.31
3000	95.06	61.92	37.60	29.99	26.52	24.67	23.61	22.97
4000	126.74	82.55	50.14	39.98	35.35	32.89	31.47	30.62
5000	158.42	103.19	62.67	49.98	44.19	41.11	39.34	38.27
6000	190.11	123.83	75.20	59.97	53.03	49.33	47.21	45.93
7000	221.79	144.47	87.73	69.97	61.86	57.56	55.07	53.58
8000	253.47	165.10	100.27	79.96	70.70	65.78	62.94	61.23
9000	285.16	185.74	112.80	89.96	79.54	74.00	70.81	68.89
10000	316.84	206.38	125.33	99.95	88.38	82.22	78.68	76.54
11000	348.52	227.01	137.86	109.94	97.21	90.44	86.54	84.19
12000	380.21	247.65	150.40	119.94	106.05	98.66	94.41	91.85
13000	411.89	268.29	162.93	129.93	114.89	106.88	102.28	99.50
14000	443.57	288.93	175.46	139.93	123.72	115.11	110.14	107.16
15000	475.26	309.56	188.00	149.92	132.56	123.33	118.01	114.81
16000	506.94	330.20	200.53	159.92	141.40	131.55	125.88	122.46
17000	538.62	350.84	213.06	169.91	150.24	139.77	133.74	130.12
18000	570.31	371.48	225.59	179.91	159.07	147.99	141.61	137.77
19000	601.99	392.11	238.13	189.90	167.91	156.21	149.48	145.42
20000	633.68	412.75	250.66	199.89	176.75	164.43	157.35	153.08
21000	665.36	433.39	263.19	209.89	185.58	172.66	165.21	160.73
22000	697.04	454.02	275.72	219.88	194.42	180.88	173.08	168.38
23000	728.73	474.66	288.26	229.88	203.26	189.10	180.95	176.04
24000	760.41	495.30	300.79	239.87	212.10	197.32	188.81	183.69
25000	792.09	515.94	313.32	249.87	220.93	205.54	196.68	191.35
26000	823.78	536.57	325.85	259.86	229.77	213.76	204.55	199.00
27000	855.46	557.21	338.39	269.86	238.61	221.98	212.41	206.65
28000	887.14	577.85	350.92	279.85	247.44	230.21	220.28	214.31
29000	918.83	598.48	363.45	289.85	256.28	238.43	228.15	221.96
30000	950.51	619.12	375.99	299.84	265.12	246.65	236.02	229.61
31000	982.19	639.76	388.52	309.83	273.96	254.87	243.88	237.27
32000	1013.88	660.40	401.05	319.83	282.79	263.09	251.75	244.92
33000	1045.56	681.03	413.58	329.82	291.63	271.31	259.62	252.57
34000	1077.24	701.67	426.12	339.82	300.47	279.53	267.48	260.23
35000	1108.93	722.31	438.65	349.81	309.30	287.76	275.35	267.88
36000	1140.61	742.95	451.18	359.81	318.14	295.98	283.22	275.54
37000	1172.29	763.58	463.71	369.80	326.98	304.20	291.08	283.19
38000	1203.98	784.22	476.25	379.80	335.82	312.42	298.95	290.84
39000	1235.66	804.86	488.78	389.79	344.65	320.64	306.82	298.50
40000	1267.35	825.49	501.31	399.78	353.49	328.86	314.69	306.15

MONTHLY AMORTIZING PAYMENTS

AMOUNT OF LOAN	NUMBER OF YEARS IN TERM						
	10	15	20	25	30	35	40
41000	513.84	409.78	362.33	337.08	322.55	313.80	308.39
42000	526.38	419.77	371.16	345.31	330.42	321.46	315.92
43000	538.91	429.77	380.00	353.53	338.29	329.11	323.44
44000	551.44	439.76	388.84	361.75	346.15	336.76	330.96
45000	563.98	449.76	397.67	369.97	354.02	344.42	338.48
46000	576.51	459.75	406.51	378.19	361.89	352.07	346.00
47000	589.04	469.75	415.35	386.41	369.75	359.73	353.53
48000	601.57	479.74	424.19	394.63	377.62	367.38	361.05
49000	614.11	489.73	433.02	402.86	385.49	375.03	368.57
50000	626.64	499.73	441.86	411.08	393.36	382.69	376.09
51000	639.17	509.72	450.70	419.30	401.22	390.34	383.61
52000	651.70	519.72	459.53	427.52	409.09	397.99	391.13
53000	664.24	529.71	468.37	435.74	416.96	405.65	398.66
54000	676.77	539.71	477.21	443.96	424.82	413.30	406.18
55000	689.30	549.70	486.05	452.18	432.69	420.95	413.70
56000	701.83	559.70	494.88	460.41	440.56	428.61	421.22
57000	714.37	569.69	503.72	468.63	448.42	436.26	428.74
58000	726.90	579.69	512.56	476.85	456.29	443.92	436.26
59000	739.43	589.68	521.39	485.07	464.16	451.57	443.79
60000	751.97	599.67	530.23	493.29	472.03	459.22	451.31
61000	764.50	609.67	539.07	501.51	479.89	466.88	458.83
62000	777.03	619.66	547.91	509.73	487.76	474.53	466.35
63000	789.56	629.66	556.74	517.96	495.63	482.18	473.87
64000	802.10	639.65	565.58	526.18	503.49	489.84	481.39
65000	814.63	649.65	574.42	534.40	511.36	497.49	488.92
66000	827.16	659.64	583.25	542.62	519.23	505.14	496.44
67000	839.69	669.64	592.09	550.84	527.09	512.80	503.96
68000	852.23	679.63	600.93	559.06	534.96	520.45	511.48
69000	864.76	689.62	609.77	567.28	542.83	528.11	519.00
70000	877.29	699.62	618.60	575.51	550.70	535.76	526.52
71000	889.82	709.61	627.44	583.73	558.56	543.41	534.05
72000	902.36	719.61	636.28	591.95	566.43	551.07	541.57
73000	914.89	729.60	645.11	600.17	574.30	558.72	549.09
74000	927.42	739.60	653.95	608.39	582.16	566.37	556.61
75000	939.96	749.59	662.79	616.61	590.03	574.03	564.13
76000	952.49	759.59	671.63	624.83	597.90	581.68	571.65
77000	965.02	769.58	680.46	633.06	605.76	589.33	579.18
78000	977.55	779.57	689.30	641.28	613.63	596.99	586.70
79000	990.09	789.57	698.14	649.50	621.50	604.64	594.22
80000	1002.62	799.56	706.97	657.72	629.37	612.30	601.74
81000	1015.15	809.56	715.81	665.94	637.23	619.95	609.26
82000	1027.68	819.55	724.65	674.16	645.10	627.60	616.78
83000	1040.22	829.55	733.48	682.38	652.97	635.26	624.31
84000	1052.75	839.54	742.32	690.61	660.83	642.91	631.83
85000	1065.28	849.54	751.16	698.83	668.70	650.56	639.35
86000	1077.82	859.53	760.00	707.05	676.57	658.22	646.87
87000	1090.35	869.53	768.83	715.27	684.43	665.87	654.39
88000	1102.88	879.52	777.67	723.49	692.30	673.52	661.92
89000	1115.41	889.51	786.51	731.71	700.17	681.18	669.44
90000	1127.95	899.51	795.34	739.93	708.04	688.83	676.96
91000	1140.48	909.50	804.18	748.16	715.90	696.49	684.48
92000	1153.01	919.50	813.02	756.38	723.77	704.14	692.00
93000	1165.54	929.49	821.86	764.60	731.64	711.79	699.52
94000	1178.08	939.49	830.69	772.82	739.50	719.45	707.05
95000	1190.61	949.48	839.53	781.04	747.37	727.10	714.57
96000	1203.14	959.48	848.37	789.26	755.24	734.75	722.09
97000	1215.67	969.47	857.20	797.48	763.10	742.41	729.61
98000	1228.21	979.46	866.04	805.71	770.97	750.06	737.13
99000	1240.74	989.46	874.88	813.93	778.84	757.71	744.65
100000	1253.27	999.45	883.72	822.15	786.71	765.37	752.18

9%

MONTHLY AMORTIZING PAYMENTS

AMOUNT OF LOAN	NUMBER OF YEARS IN TERM							
	3	5	10	15	20	25	30	35
10	.32	.21	.13	.11	.09	.09	.09	.08
20	.64	.42	.26	.21	.18	.17	.17	.16
25	.80	.52	.32	.26	.23	.21	.21	.20
30	.96	.63	.39	.31	.27	.26	.25	.24
40	1.28	.84	.51	.41	.36	.34	.33	.32
50	1.59	1.04	.64	.51	.45	.42	.41	.40
60	1.91	1.25	.77	.61	.54	.51	.49	.48
70	2.23	1.46	.89	.71	.63	.59	.57	.55
75	2.39	1.56	.96	.77	.68	.63	.61	.59
80	2.55	1.67	1.02	.82	.72	.68	.65	.63
90	2.87	1.87	1.15	.92	.81	.76	.73	.71
100	3.18	2.08	1.27	1.02	.90	.84	.81	.79
200	6.36	4.16	2.54	2.03	1.80	1.68	1.61	1.57
300	9.54	6.23	3.81	3.05	2.70	2.52	2.42	2.36
400	12.72	8.31	5.07	4.06	3.60	3.36	3.22	3.14
500	15.90	10.38	6.34	5.08	4.50	4.20	4.03	3.92
600	19.08	12.46	7.61	6.09	5.40	5.04	4.83	4.71
700	22.26	14.54	8.87	7.10	6.30	5.88	5.64	5.49
800	25.44	16.61	10.14	8.12	7.20	6.72	6.44	6.28
900	28.62	18.69	11.41	9.13	8.10	7.56	7.25	7.06
1000	31.80	20.76	12.67	10.15	9.00	8.40	8.05	7.84
2000	63.60	41.52	25.34	20.29	18.00	16.79	16.10	15.68
3000	95.40	62.28	38.01	30.43	27.00	25.18	24.14	23.52
4000	127.20	83.04	50.68	40.58	35.99	33.57	32.19	31.36
5000	159.00	103.80	63.34	50.72	44.99	41.96	40.24	39.20
6000	190.80	124.56	76.01	60.86	53.99	50.36	48.28	47.04
7000	222.60	145.31	88.68	71.00	62.99	58.75	56.33	54.88
8000	254.40	166.07	101.35	81.15	71.98	67.14	64.37	62.72
9000	286.20	186.83	114.01	91.29	80.98	75.53	72.42	70.56
10000	318.00	207.59	126.68	101.43	89.98	83.92	80.47	78.40
11000	349.80	228.35	139.35	111.57	98.97	92.32	88.51	86.24
12000	381.60	249.11	152.02	121.72	107.97	100.71	96.56	94.08
13000	413.40	269.86	164.68	131.86	116.97	109.10	104.61	101.92
14000	445.20	290.62	177.35	142.00	125.97	117.49	112.65	109.76
15000	477.00	311.38	190.02	152.14	134.96	125.88	120.70	117.60
16000	508.80	332.14	202.69	162.29	143.96	134.28	128.74	125.44
17000	540.60	352.90	215.35	172.43	152.96	142.67	136.79	133.28
18000	572.40	373.66	228.02	182.57	161.96	151.06	144.84	141.12
19000	604.20	394.41	240.69	192.72	170.95	159.45	152.88	148.96
20000	636.00	415.17	253.36	202.86	179.95	167.84	160.93	156.80
21000	667.80	435.93	266.02	213.00	188.95	176.24	168.98	164.64
22000	699.60	456.69	278.69	223.14	197.94	184.63	177.02	172.48
23000	731.40	477.45	291.36	233.29	206.94	193.02	185.07	180.32
24000	763.20	498.21	304.03	243.43	215.94	201.41	193.11	188.16
25000	795.00	518.96	316.69	253.57	224.94	209.80	201.16	196.00
26000	826.80	539.72	329.36	263.71	233.93	218.20	209.21	203.84
27000	858.60	560.48	342.03	273.86	242.93	226.59	217.25	211.68
28000	890.40	581.24	354.70	284.00	251.93	234.98	225.30	219.52
29000	922.20	602.00	367.36	294.14	260.93	243.37	233.35	227.36
30000	954.00	622.76	380.03	304.28	269.92	251.76	241.39	235.20
31000	985.80	643.51	392.70	314.43	278.92	260.16	249.44	243.04
32000	1017.60	664.27	405.37	324.57	287.92	268.55	257.48	250.88
33000	1049.40	685.03	418.04	334.71	296.91	276.94	265.53	258.72
34000	1081.20	705.79	430.70	344.86	305.91	285.33	273.58	266.56
35000	1113.00	726.55	443.37	355.00	314.91	293.72	281.62	274.40
36000	1144.80	747.31	456.04	365.14	323.91	302.12	289.67	282.24
37000	1176.60	768.06	468.71	375.28	332.90	310.51	297.72	290.08
38000	1208.39	788.82	481.37	385.43	341.90	318.90	305.76	297.92
39000	1240.19	809.58	494.04	395.57	350.90	327.29	313.81	305.76
40000	1271.99	830.34	506.71	405.71	359.90	335.68	321.85	313.60

22

MONTHLY AMORTIZING PAYMENTS

AMOUNT OF LOAN	NUMBER OF YEARS IN TERM						
	10	15	20	25	30	35	40
41000	519.38	415.85	368.89	344.08	329.90	321.44	316.26
42000	532.04	426.00	377.89	352.47	337.95	329.28	323.98
43000	544.71	436.14	386.89	360.86	345.99	337.12	331.69
44000	557.38	446.28	395.88	369.25	354.04	344.96	339.40
45000	570.05	456.42	404.88	377.64	362.09	352.80	347.12
46000	582.71	466.57	413.88	386.04	370.13	360.64	354.83
47000	595.38	476.71	422.88	394.43	378.18	368.48	362.54
48000	608.05	486.85	431.87	402.82	386.22	376.32	370.26
49000	620.72	497.00	440.87	411.21	394.27	384.16	377.97
50000	633.38	507.14	449.87	419.60	402.32	392.00	385.69
51000	646.05	517.28	458.87	428.00	410.36	399.84	393.40
52000	658.72	527.42	467.86	436.39	418.41	407.68	401.11
53000	671.39	537.57	476.86	444.78	426.45	415.52	408.83
54000	684.05	547.71	485.86	453.17	434.50	423.36	416.54
55000	696.72	557.85	494.85	461.56	442.55	431.20	424.25
56000	709.39	567.99	503.85	469.95	450.59	439.04	431.97
57000	722.06	578.14	512.85	478.35	458.64	446.88	439.68
58000	734.72	588.28	521.85	486.74	466.69	454.72	447.39
59000	747.39	598.42	530.84	495.13	474.73	462.56	455.11
60000	760.06	608.56	539.84	503.52	482.78	470.40	462.82
61000	772.73	618.71	548.84	511.91	490.82	478.24	470.54
62000	785.39	628.85	557.84	520.31	498.87	486.08	478.25
63000	798.06	638.99	566.83	528.70	506.92	493.92	485.96
64000	810.73	649.14	575.83	537.09	514.96	501.76	493.68
65000	823.40	659.28	584.83	545.48	523.01	509.60	501.39
66000	836.07	669.42	593.82	553.87	531.06	517.44	509.10
67000	848.73	679.56	602.82	562.27	539.10	525.28	516.82
68000	861.40	689.71	611.82	570.66	547.15	533.12	524.53
69000	874.07	699.85	620.82	579.05	555.19	540.96	532.24
70000	886.74	709.99	629.81	587.44	563.24	548.80	539.96
71000	899.40	720.13	638.81	595.83	571.29	556.64	547.67
72000	912.07	730.28	647.81	604.23	579.33	564.48	555.39
73000	924.74	740.42	656.80	612.62	587.38	572.32	563.10
74000	937.41	750.56	665.80	621.01	595.43	580.16	570.81
75000	950.07	760.70	674.80	629.40	603.47	588.00	578.53
76000	962.74	770.85	683.80	637.79	611.52	595.84	586.24
77000	975.41	780.99	692.79	646.19	619.56	603.68	593.95
78000	988.08	791.13	701.79	654.58	627.61	611.52	601.67
79000	1000.74	801.28	710.79	662.97	635.66	619.36	609.38
80000	1013.41	811.42	719.79	671.36	643.70	627.20	617.09
81000	1026.08	821.56	728.78	679.75	651.75	635.04	624.81
82000	1038.75	831.70	737.78	688.15	659.80	642.88	632.52
83000	1051.41	841.85	746.78	696.54	667.84	650.72	640.24
84000	1064.08	851.99	755.77	704.93	675.89	658.56	647.95
85000	1076.75	862.13	764.77	713.32	683.93	666.40	655.66
86000	1089.42	872.27	773.77	721.71	691.98	674.24	663.38
87000	1102.08	882.42	782.77	730.11	700.03	682.08	671.09
88000	1114.75	892.56	791.76	738.50	708.07	689.92	678.80
89000	1127.42	902.70	800.76	746.89	716.12	697.76	686.52
90000	1140.09	912.84	809.76	755.28	724.17	705.60	694.23
91000	1152.75	922.99	818.76	763.67	732.21	713.44	701.94
92000	1165.42	933.13	827.75	772.07	740.26	721.28	709.66
93000	1178.09	943.27	836.75	780.46	748.30	729.12	717.37
94000	1190.76	953.42	845.75	788.85	756.35	736.96	725.08
95000	1203.42	963.56	854.74	797.24	764.40	744.80	732.80
96000	1216.09	973.70	863.74	805.63	772.44	752.64	740.51
97000	1228.76	983.84	872.74	814.03	780.49	760.48	748.23
98000	1241.43	993.99	881.74	822.42	788.54	768.32	755.94
99000	1254.10	1004.13	890.73	830.81	796.58	776.16	763.65
100000	1266.76	1014.27	899.73	839.20	804.63	784.00	771.37

9¼%

MONTHLY AMORTIZING PAYMENTS

AMOUNT OF LOAN	NUMBER OF YEARS IN TERM							
	3	5	10	15	20	25	30	35
10	.32	.21	.13	.11	.10	.09	.09	.09
20	.64	.42	.26	.21	.19	.18	.17	.17
25	.80	.53	.33	.26	.23	.22	.21	.21
30	.96	.63	.39	.31	.28	.26	.25	.25
40	1.28	.84	.52	.42	.37	.35	.33	.33
50	1.60	1.05	.65	.52	.46	.43	.42	.41
60	1.92	1.26	.77	.62	.55	.52	.50	.49
70	2.24	1.47	.90	.73	.65	.60	.58	.57
75	2.40	1.57	.97	.78	.69	.65	.62	.61
80	2.56	1.68	1.03	.83	.74	.69	.66	.65
90	2.88	1.88	1.16	.93	.83	.78	.75	.73
100	3.20	2.09	1.29	1.03	.92	.86	.83	.81
200	6.39	4.18	2.57	2.06	1.84	1.72	1.65	1.61
300	9.58	6.27	3.85	3.09	2.75	2.57	2.47	2.41
400	12.77	8.36	5.13	4.12	3.67	3.43	3.30	3.22
500	15.96	10.44	6.41	5.15	4.58	4.29	4.12	4.02
600	19.15	12.53	7.69	6.18	5.50	5.14	4.94	4.82
700	22.35	14.62	8.97	7.21	6.42	6.00	5.76	5.62
800	25.54	16.71	10.25	8.24	7.33	6.86	6.59	6.43
900	28.73	18.80	11.53	9.27	8.25	7.71	7.41	7.23
1000	31.92	20.88	12.81	10.30	9.16	8.57	8.23	8.03
2000	63.84	41.76	25.61	20.59	18.32	17.13	16.46	16.06
3000	95.75	62.64	38.41	30.88	27.48	25.70	24.69	24.09
4000	127.67	83.52	51.22	41.17	36.64	34.26	32.91	32.11
5000	159.59	104.40	64.02	51.46	45.80	42.82	41.14	40.14
6000	191.50	125.28	76.82	61.76	54.96	51.39	49.37	48.17
7000	223.42	146.16	89.63	72.05	64.12	59.95	57.59	56.20
8000	255.33	167.04	102.43	82.34	73.27	68.52	65.82	64.22
9000	287.25	187.92	115.23	92.63	82.43	77.08	74.05	72.25
10000	319.17	208.80	128.04	102.92	91.59	85.64	82.27	80.28
11000	351.08	229.68	140.84	113.22	100.75	94.21	90.50	88.31
12000	383.00	250.56	153.64	123.51	109.91	102.77	98.73	96.33
13000	414.92	271.44	166.45	133.80	119.07	111.33	106.95	104.36
14000	446.83	292.32	179.25	144.09	128.23	119.90	115.18	112.39
15000	478.75	313.20	192.05	154.38	137.39	128.46	123.41	120.42
16000	510.66	334.08	204.86	164.68	146.54	137.03	131.63	128.44
17000	542.58	354.96	217.66	174.97	155.70	145.59	139.86	136.47
18000	574.50	375.84	230.46	185.26	164.86	154.15	148.09	144.50
19000	606.41	396.72	243.27	195.55	174.02	162.72	156.31	152.53
20000	638.33	417.60	256.07	205.84	183.18	171.28	164.54	160.55
21000	670.25	438.48	268.87	216.14	192.34	179.85	172.77	168.58
22000	702.16	459.36	281.68	226.43	201.50	188.41	180.99	176.61
23000	734.08	480.24	294.48	236.72	210.65	196.97	189.22	184.64
24000	765.99	501.12	307.28	247.01	219.81	205.54	197.45	192.66
25000	797.91	522.00	320.09	257.30	228.97	214.10	205.67	200.69
26000	829.83	542.88	332.89	267.59	238.13	222.66	213.90	208.72
27000	861.74	563.76	345.69	277.89	247.29	231.23	222.13	216.75
28000	893.66	584.64	358.50	288.18	256.45	239.79	230.35	224.77
29000	925.58	605.52	371.30	298.47	265.61	248.36	238.58	232.80
30000	957.49	626.40	384.10	308.76	274.77	256.92	246.81	240.83
31000	989.41	647.28	396.91	319.05	283.92	265.48	255.03	248.86
32000	1021.32	668.16	409.71	329.35	293.08	274.05	263.26	256.88
33000	1053.24	689.04	422.51	339.64	302.24	282.61	271.49	264.91
34000	1085.16	709.92	435.32	349.93	311.40	291.17	279.71	272.94
35000	1117.07	730.80	448.12	360.22	320.56	299.74	287.94	280.97
36000	1148.99	751.68	460.92	370.51	329.72	308.30	296.17	288.99
37000	1180.90	772.56	473.73	380.81	338.88	316.87	304.39	297.02
38000	1212.82	793.44	486.53	391.10	348.03	325.43	312.62	305.05
39000	1244.74	814.32	499.33	401.39	357.19	333.99	320.85	313.08
40000	1276.65	835.20	512.14	411.68	366.35	342.56	329.08	321.10

24

MONTHLY AMORTIZING PAYMENTS

AMOUNT OF LOAN	NUMBER OF YEARS IN TERM						
	10	15	20	25	30	35	40
41000	524.94	421.97	375.51	351.12	337.30	329.13	324.18
42000	537.74	432.27	384.67	359.69	345.53	337.16	332.08
43000	550.55	442.56	393.83	368.25	353.76	345.19	339.99
44000	563.35	452.85	402.99	376.81	361.98	353.21	347.90
45000	576.15	463.14	412.15	385.38	370.21	361.24	355.80
46000	588.96	473.43	421.30	393.94	378.44	369.27	363.71
47000	601.76	483.73	430.46	402.50	386.66	377.29	371.62
48000	614.56	494.02	439.62	411.07	394.89	385.32	379.52
49000	627.37	504.31	448.78	419.63	403.12	393.35	387.43
50000	640.17	514.60	457.94	428.20	411.34	401.38	395.34
51000	652.97	524.89	467.10	436.76	419.57	409.40	403.24
52000	665.78	535.18	476.26	445.32	427.80	417.43	411.15
53000	678.58	545.48	485.41	453.89	436.02	425.46	419.06
54000	691.38	555.77	494.57	462.45	444.25	433.49	426.96
55000	704.18	566.06	503.73	471.02	452.48	441.51	434.87
56000	716.99	576.35	512.89	479.58	460.70	449.54	442.77
57000	729.79	586.64	522.05	488.14	468.93	457.57	450.68
58000	742.59	596.94	531.21	496.71	477.16	465.60	458.59
59000	755.40	607.23	540.37	505.27	485.38	473.62	466.49
60000	768.20	617.52	549.53	513.83	493.61	481.65	474.40
61000	781.00	627.81	558.68	522.40	501.84	489.68	482.31
62000	793.81	638.10	567.84	530.96	510.06	497.71	490.21
63000	806.61	648.40	577.00	539.53	518.29	505.73	498.12
64000	819.41	658.69	586.16	548.09	526.52	513.76	506.03
65000	832.22	668.98	595.32	556.65	534.74	521.79	513.93
66000	845.02	679.27	604.48	565.22	542.97	529.82	521.84
67000	857.82	689.56	613.64	573.78	551.20	537.84	529.75
68000	870.63	699.86	622.79	582.34	559.42	545.87	537.65
69000	883.43	710.15	631.95	590.91	567.65	553.90	545.56
70000	896.23	720.44	641.11	599.47	575.88	561.93	553.47
71000	909.04	730.73	650.27	608.04	584.10	569.95	561.37
72000	921.84	741.02	659.43	616.60	592.33	577.98	569.28
73000	934.64	751.32	668.59	625.16	600.56	586.01	577.19
74000	947.45	761.61	677.75	633.73	608.78	594.04	585.09
75000	960.25	771.90	686.91	642.29	617.01	602.06	593.00
76000	973.05	782.19	696.06	650.86	625.24	610.09	600.91
77000	985.86	792.48	705.22	659.42	633.47	618.12	608.81
78000	998.66	802.77	714.38	667.98	641.69	626.15	616.72
79000	1011.46	813.07	723.54	676.55	649.92	634.17	624.63
80000	1024.27	823.36	732.70	685.11	658.15	642.20	632.53
81000	1037.07	833.65	741.86	693.67	666.37	650.23	640.44
82000	1049.87	843.94	751.02	702.24	674.60	658.26	648.35
83000	1062.68	854.23	760.17	710.80	682.83	666.28	656.25
84000	1075.48	864.53	769.33	719.37	691.05	674.31	664.16
85000	1088.28	874.82	778.49	727.93	699.28	682.34	672.07
86000	1101.09	885.11	787.65	736.49	707.51	690.37	679.97
87000	1113.89	895.40	796.81	745.06	715.73	698.39	687.88
88000	1126.69	905.69	805.97	753.62	723.96	706.42	695.79
89000	1139.50	915.99	815.13	762.18	732.19	714.45	703.69
90000	1152.30	926.28	824.29	770.75	740.41	722.47	711.60
91000	1165.10	936.57	833.44	779.31	748.64	730.50	719.51
92000	1177.91	946.86	842.60	787.88	756.87	738.53	727.41
93000	1190.71	957.15	851.76	796.44	765.09	746.56	735.32
94000	1203.51	967.45	860.92	805.00	773.32	754.58	743.23
95000	1216.32	977.74	870.08	813.57	781.55	762.61	751.13
96000	1229.12	988.03	879.24	822.13	789.77	770.64	759.04
97000	1241.92	998.32	888.40	830.70	798.00	778.67	766.95
98000	1254.73	1008.61	897.55	839.26	806.23	786.69	774.85
99000	1267.53	1018.91	906.71	847.82	814.45	794.72	782.76
100000	1280.33	1029.20	915.87	856.39	822.68	802.75	790.67

9½%

MONTHLY AMORTIZING PAYMENTS

AMOUNT OF LOAN	NUMBER OF YEARS IN TERM							
	3	5	10	15	20	25	30	35
10	.33	.22	.13	.11	.10	.09	.09	.09
20	.65	.43	.26	.21	.19	.18	.17	.17
25	.81	.53	.33	.27	.24	.22	.22	.21
30	.97	.64	.39	.32	.28	.27	.26	.25
40	1.29	.85	.52	.42	.38	.35	.34	.33
50	1.61	1.06	.65	.53	.47	.44	.43	.42
60	1.93	1.27	.78	.63	.56	.53	.51	.50
70	2.25	1.48	.91	.74	.66	.62	.59	.58
75	2.41	1.58	.98	.79	.70	.66	.64	.62
80	2.57	1.69	1.04	.84	.75	.70	.68	.66
90	2.89	1.90	1.17	.94	.84	.79	.76	.74
100	3.21	2.11	1.30	1.05	.94	.88	.85	.83
200	6.41	4.21	2.59	2.09	1.87	1.75	1.69	1.65
300	9.61	6.31	3.89	3.14	2.80	2.63	2.53	2.47
400	12.82	8.41	5.18	4.18	3.73	3.50	3.37	3.29
500	16.02	10.51	6.47	5.23	4.67	4.37	4.21	4.11
600	19.22	12.61	7.77	6.27	5.60	5.25	5.05	4.93
700	22.43	14.71	9.06	7.31	6.53	6.12	5.89	5.76
800	25.63	16.81	10.36	8.36	7.46	6.99	6.73	6.58
900	28.83	18.91	11.65	9.40	8.39	7.87	7.57	7.40
1000	32.04	21.01	12.94	10.45	9.33	8.74	8.41	8.22
2000	64.07	42.01	25.88	20.89	18.65	17.48	16.82	16.44
3000	96.10	63.01	38.82	31.33	27.97	26.22	25.23	24.65
4000	128.14	84.01	51.76	41.77	37.29	34.95	33.64	32.87
5000	160.17	105.01	64.70	52.22	46.61	43.69	42.05	41.09
6000	192.20	126.02	77.64	62.66	55.93	52.43	50.46	49.30
7000	224.24	147.02	90.58	73.10	65.25	61.16	58.86	57.52
8000	256.27	168.02	103.52	83.54	74.58	69.90	67.27	65.73
9000	288.30	189.02	116.46	93.99	83.90	78.64	75.68	73.95
10000	320.33	210.02	129.40	104.43	93.22	87.37	84.09	82.17
11000	352.37	231.03	142.34	114.87	102.54	96.11	92.50	90.38
12000	384.40	252.03	155.28	125.31	111.86	104.85	100.91	98.60
13000	416.43	273.03	168.22	135.75	121.18	113.59	109.32	106.81
14000	448.47	294.03	181.16	146.20	130.50	122.32	117.72	115.03
15000	480.50	315.03	194.10	156.64	139.82	131.06	126.13	123.25
16000	512.53	336.03	207.04	167.08	149.15	139.80	134.54	131.46
17000	544.57	357.04	219.98	177.52	158.47	148.53	142.95	139.68
18000	576.60	378.04	232.92	187.97	167.79	157.27	151.36	147.90
19000	608.63	399.04	245.86	198.41	177.11	166.01	159.77	156.11
20000	640.66	420.04	258.80	208.85	186.43	174.74	168.18	164.33
21000	672.70	441.04	271.74	219.29	195.75	183.48	176.58	172.54
22000	704.73	462.05	284.68	229.73	205.07	192.22	184.99	180.76
23000	736.76	483.05	297.62	240.18	214.40	200.96	193.40	188.98
24000	768.80	504.05	310.56	250.62	223.72	209.69	201.81	197.19
25000	800.83	525.05	323.50	261.06	233.04	218.43	210.22	205.41
26000	832.86	546.05	336.44	271.50	242.36	227.17	218.63	213.62
27000	864.89	567.06	349.38	281.95	251.68	235.90	227.04	221.84
28000	896.93	588.06	362.32	292.39	261.00	244.64	235.44	230.06
29000	928.96	609.06	375.26	302.83	270.32	253.38	243.85	238.27
30000	960.99	630.06	388.20	313.27	279.64	262.11	252.26	246.49
31000	993.03	651.06	401.14	323.71	288.97	270.85	260.67	254.70
32000	1025.06	672.06	414.08	334.16	298.29	279.59	269.08	262.92
33000	1057.09	693.07	427.02	344.60	307.61	288.32	277.49	271.14
34000	1089.13	714.07	439.96	355.04	316.93	297.06	285.90	279.35
35000	1121.16	735.07	452.90	365.48	326.25	305.80	294.30	287.57
36000	1153.19	756.07	465.84	375.93	335.57	314.54	302.71	295.79
37000	1185.22	777.07	478.78	386.37	344.89	323.27	311.12	304.00
38000	1217.26	798.08	491.72	396.81	354.21	332.01	319.53	312.22
39000	1249.29	819.08	504.66	407.25	363.54	340.75	327.94	320.43
40000	1281.32	840.08	517.60	417.69	372.86	349.48	336.35	328.65

MONTHLY AMORTIZING PAYMENTS

AMOUNT OF LOAN	NUMBER OF YEARS IN TERM						
	10	15	20	25	30	35	40
41000	530.53	428.14	382.18	358.22	344.76	336.87	332.13
42000	543.47	438.58	391.50	366.96	353.16	345.08	340.23
43000	556.41	449.02	400.82	375.69	361.57	353.30	348.33
44000	569.35	459.46	410.14	384.43	369.98	361.51	356.43
45000	582.29	469.91	419.46	393.17	378.39	369.73	364.53
46000	595.23	480.35	428.79	401.91	386.80	377.95	372.63
47000	608.17	490.79	438.11	410.64	395.21	386.16	380.73
48000	621.11	501.23	447.43	419.38	403.62	394.38	388.83
49000	634.05	511.68	456.75	428.12	412.02	402.59	396.94
50000	646.99	522.12	466.07	436.85	420.43	410.81	405.04
51000	659.93	532.56	475.39	445.59	428.84	419.03	413.14
52000	672.87	543.00	484.71	454.33	437.25	427.24	421.24
53000	685.81	553.44	494.03	463.06	445.66	435.46	429.34
54000	698.75	563.89	503.36	471.80	454.07	443.68	437.44
55000	711.69	574.33	512.68	480.54	462.47	451.89	445.54
56000	724.63	584.77	522.00	489.28	470.88	460.11	453.64
57000	737.57	595.21	531.32	498.01	479.29	468.32	461.74
58000	750.51	605.66	540.64	506.75	487.70	476.54	469.84
59000	763.45	616.10	549.96	515.49	496.11	484.76	477.94
60000	776.39	626.54	559.28	524.22	504.52	492.97	486.04
61000	789.33	636.98	568.61	532.96	512.93	501.19	494.14
62000	802.27	647.42	577.93	541.70	521.33	509.40	502.24
63000	815.21	657.87	587.25	550.43	529.74	517.62	510.34
64000	828.15	668.31	596.57	559.17	538.15	525.84	518.44
65000	841.09	678.75	605.89	567.91	546.56	534.05	526.55
66000	854.03	689.19	615.21	576.64	554.97	542.27	534.65
67000	866.97	699.64	624.53	585.38	563.38	550.48	542.75
68000	879.91	710.08	633.85	594.12	571.79	558.70	550.85
69000	892.85	720.52	643.18	602.86	580.19	566.92	558.95
70000	905.79	730.96	652.50	611.59	588.60	575.13	567.05
71000	918.73	741.40	661.82	620.33	597.01	583.35	575.15
72000	931.67	751.85	671.14	629.07	605.42	591.57	583.25
73000	944.61	762.29	680.46	637.80	613.83	599.78	591.35
74000	957.55	772.73	689.78	646.54	622.24	608.00	599.45
75000	970.49	783.17	699.10	655.28	630.65	616.21	607.55
76000	983.43	793.62	708.42	664.01	639.05	624.43	615.65
77000	996.37	804.06	717.75	672.75	647.46	632.65	623.75
78000	1009.31	814.50	727.07	681.49	655.87	640.86	631.85
79000	1022.25	824.94	736.39	690.23	664.28	649.08	639.95
80000	1035.19	835.38	745.71	698.96	672.69	657.29	648.05
81000	1048.13	845.83	755.03	707.70	681.10	665.51	656.15
82000	1061.06	856.27	764.35	716.44	689.51	673.73	664.26
83000	1074.00	866.71	773.67	725.17	697.91	681.94	672.36
84000	1086.94	877.15	783.00	733.91	706.32	690.16	680.46
85000	1099.88	887.60	792.32	742.65	714.73	698.37	688.56
86000	1112.82	898.04	801.64	751.38	723.14	706.59	696.66
87000	1125.76	908.48	810.96	760.12	731.55	714.81	704.76
88000	1138.70	918.92	820.28	768.86	739.96	723.02	712.86
89000	1151.64	929.36	829.60	777.60	748.37	731.24	720.96
90000	1164.58	939.81	838.92	786.33	756.77	739.46	729.06
91000	1177.52	950.25	848.24	795.07	765.18	747.67	737.16
92000	1190.46	960.69	857.57	803.81	773.59	755.89	745.26
93000	1203.40	971.13	866.89	812.54	782.00	764.10	753.36
94000	1216.34	981.58	876.21	821.28	790.41	772.32	761.46
95000	1229.28	992.02	885.53	830.02	798.82	780.54	769.56
96000	1242.22	1002.46	894.85	838.75	807.23	788.75	777.66
97000	1255.16	1012.90	904.17	847.49	815.63	796.97	785.76
98000	1268.10	1023.35	913.49	856.23	824.04	805.18	793.87
99000	1281.04	1033.79	922.81	864.96	832.45	813.40	801.97
100000	1293.98	1044.23	932.14	873.70	840.86	821.62	810.07

MONTHLY AMORTIZING PAYMENTS

AMOUNT OF LOAN	NUMBER OF YEARS IN TERM							
	3	5	10	15	20	25	30	35
10	.33	.22	.14	.11	.10	.09	.09	.09
20	.65	.43	.27	.22	.19	.18	.18	.17
25	.81	.53	.33	.27	.24	.23	.22	.22
30	.97	.64	.40	.32	.29	.27	.26	.26
40	1.29	.85	.53	.43	.38	.36	.35	.34
50	1.61	1.06	.66	.53	.48	.45	.43	.43
60	1.93	1.27	.79	.64	.57	.54	.52	.51
70	2.26	1.48	.92	.75	.67	.63	.61	.59
75	2.42	1.59	.99	.80	.72	.67	.65	.64
80	2.58	1.69	1.05	.85	.76	.72	.69	.68
90	2.90	1.91	1.18	.96	.86	.81	.78	.76
100	3.22	2.12	1.31	1.06	.95	.90	.86	.85
200	6.43	4.23	2.62	2.12	1.90	1.79	1.72	1.69
300	9.65	6.34	3.93	3.18	2.85	2.68	2.58	2.53
400	12.86	8.45	5.24	4.24	3.80	3.57	3.44	3.37
500	16.08	10.57	6.54	5.30	4.75	4.46	4.30	4.21
600	19.29	12.68	7.85	6.36	5.70	5.35	5.16	5.05
700	22.51	14.79	9.16	7.42	6.64	6.24	6.02	5.89
800	25.72	16.90	10.47	8.48	7.59	7.13	6.88	6.73
900	28.94	19.02	11.77	9.54	8.54	8.03	7.74	7.57
1000	32.15	21.13	13.08	10.60	9.49	8.92	8.60	8.41
2000	64.30	42.25	26.16	21.19	18.98	17.83	17.19	16.82
3000	96.45	63.38	39.24	31.79	28.46	26.74	25.78	25.22
4000	128.60	84.50	52.31	42.38	37.95	35.65	34.37	33.63
5000	160.75	105.63	65.39	52.97	47.43	44.56	42.96	42.03
6000	192.90	126.75	78.47	63.57	56.92	53.47	51.55	50.44
7000	225.05	147.87	91.54	74.16	66.40	62.38	60.15	58.85
8000	257.20	169.00	104.62	84.75	75.89	71.30	68.74	67.25
9000	289.35	190.12	117.70	95.35	85.37	80.21	77.33	75.66
10000	321.50	211.25	130.78	105.94	94.86	89.12	85.92	84.06
11000	353.65	232.37	143.85	116.53	104.34	98.03	94.51	92.47
12000	385.80	253.50	156.93	127.13	113.83	106.94	103.10	100.88
13000	417.95	274.62	170.01	137.72	123.31	115.85	111.70	109.28
14000	450.10	295.74	183.08	148.32	132.80	124.76	120.29	117.69
15000	482.25	316.87	196.16	158.91	142.28	133.68	128.88	126.09
16000	514.40	337.99	209.24	169.50	151.77	142.59	137.47	134.50
17000	546.55	359.12	222.31	180.10	161.25	151.50	146.06	142.91
18000	578.70	380.24	235.39	190.69	170.74	160.41	154.65	151.31
19000	610.85	401.37	248.47	201.28	180.22	169.32	163.24	159.72
20000	643.00	422.49	261.55	211.88	189.71	178.23	171.84	168.12
21000	675.15	443.61	274.62	222.47	199.19	187.14	180.43	176.53
22000	707.30	464.74	287.70	233.06	208.68	196.06	189.02	184.93
23000	739.45	485.86	300.78	243.66	218.16	204.97	197.61	193.34
24000	771.60	506.99	313.85	254.25	227.65	213.88	206.20	201.75
25000	803.75	528.11	326.93	264.85	237.13	222.79	214.79	210.15
26000	835.90	549.24	340.01	275.44	246.62	231.70	223.39	218.56
27000	868.05	570.36	353.08	286.03	256.10	240.61	231.98	226.96
28000	900.20	591.48	366.16	296.63	265.59	249.52	240.57	235.37
29000	932.35	612.61	379.24	307.22	275.07	258.43	249.16	243.78
30000	964.50	633.73	392.32	317.81	284.56	267.35	257.75	252.18
31000	996.65	654.86	405.39	328.41	294.05	276.26	266.34	260.59
32000	1028.80	675.98	418.47	339.00	303.53	285.17	274.93	268.99
33000	1060.95	697.11	431.55	349.59	313.02	294.08	283.53	277.40
34000	1093.10	718.23	444.62	360.19	322.50	302.99	292.12	285.81
35000	1125.25	739.35	457.70	370.78	331.99	311.90	300.71	294.21
36000	1157.40	760.48	470.78	381.38	341.47	320.81	309.30	302.62
37000	1189.55	781.60	483.85	391.97	350.96	329.73	317.89	311.02
38000	1221.70	802.73	496.93	402.56	360.44	338.64	326.48	319.43
39000	1253.85	823.85	510.01	413.16	369.93	347.55	335.08	327.83
40000	1286.00	844.97	523.09	423.75	379.41	356.46	343.67	336.24

MONTHLY AMORTIZING PAYMENTS

AMOUNT OF LOAN	NUMBER OF YEARS IN TERM						
	10	15	20	25	30	35	40
41000	536.16	434.34	388.90	365.37	352.26	344.65	340.12
42000	549.24	444.94	398.38	374.28	360.85	353.05	348.42
43000	562.32	455.53	407.87	383.19	369.44	361.46	356.72
44000	575.39	466.12	417.35	392.11	378.03	369.86	365.01
45000	588.47	476.72	426.84	401.02	386.62	378.27	373.31
46000	601.55	487.31	436.32	409.93	395.22	386.68	381.60
47000	614.63	497.91	445.81	418.84	403.81	395.08	389.90
48000	627.70	508.50	455.29	427.75	412.40	403.49	398.19
49000	640.78	519.09	464.78	436.66	420.99	411.89	406.49
50000	653.86	529.69	474.26	445.57	429.58	420.30	414.78
51000	666.93	540.28	483.75	454.49	438.17	428.71	423.08
52000	680.01	550.87	493.23	463.40	446.77	437.11	431.38
53000	693.09	561.47	502.72	472.31	455.36	445.52	439.67
54000	706.16	572.06	512.20	481.22	463.95	453.92	447.97
55000	719.24	582.65	521.69	490.13	472.54	462.33	456.26
56000	732.32	593.25	531.17	499.04	481.13	470.74	464.56
57000	745.40	603.84	540.66	507.95	489.72	479.14	472.85
58000	758.47	614.44	550.14	516.86	498.31	487.55	481.15
59000	771.55	625.03	559.63	525.78	506.91	495.95	489.44
60000	784.63	635.62	569.12	534.69	515.50	504.36	497.74
61000	797.70	646.22	578.60	543.60	524.09	512.76	506.04
62000	810.78	656.81	588.09	552.51	532.68	521.17	514.33
63000	823.86	667.40	597.57	561.42	541.27	529.58	522.63
64000	836.93	678.00	607.06	570.33	549.86	537.98	530.92
65000	850.01	688.59	616.54	579.24	558.46	546.39	539.22
66000	863.09	699.18	626.03	588.16	567.05	554.79	547.51
67000	876.17	709.78	635.51	597.07	575.64	563.20	555.81
68000	889.24	720.37	645.00	605.98	584.23	571.61	564.10
69000	902.32	730.97	654.48	614.89	592.82	580.01	572.40
70000	915.40	741.56	663.97	623.80	601.41	588.42	580.70
71000	928.47	752.15	673.45	632.71	610.00	596.82	588.99
72000	941.55	762.75	682.94	641.62	618.60	605.23	597.29
73000	954.63	773.34	692.42	650.54	627.19	613.64	605.58
74000	967.70	783.93	701.91	659.45	635.78	622.04	613.88
75000	980.78	794.53	711.39	668.36	644.37	630.45	622.17
76000	993.86	805.12	720.88	677.27	652.96	638.85	630.47
77000	1006.94	815.71	730.36	686.18	661.55	647.26	638.77
78000	1020.01	826.31	739.85	695.09	670.15	655.66	647.06
79000	1033.09	836.90	749.33	704.00	678.74	664.07	655.36
80000	1046.17	847.50	758.82	712.91	687.33	672.48	663.65
81000	1059.24	858.09	768.30	721.83	695.92	680.88	671.95
82000	1072.32	868.68	777.79	730.74	704.51	689.29	680.24
83000	1085.40	879.28	787.27	739.65	713.10	697.69	688.54
84000	1098.48	889.87	796.76	748.56	721.69	706.10	696.83
85000	1111.55	900.46	806.24	757.47	730.29	714.51	705.13
86000	1124.63	911.06	815.73	766.38	738.88	722.91	713.43
87000	1137.71	921.65	825.21	775.29	747.47	731.32	721.72
88000	1150.78	932.24	834.70	784.21	756.06	739.72	730.02
89000	1163.86	942.84	844.18	793.12	764.65	748.13	738.31
90000	1176.94	953.43	853.67	802.03	773.24	756.54	746.61
91000	1190.01	964.03	863.16	810.94	781.84	764.94	754.90
92000	1203.09	974.62	872.64	819.85	790.43	773.35	763.20
93000	1216.17	985.21	882.13	828.76	799.02	781.75	771.49
94000	1229.25	995.81	891.61	837.67	807.61	790.16	779.79
95000	1242.32	1006.40	901.10	846.59	816.20	798.56	788.09
96000	1255.40	1016.99	910.58	855.50	824.79	806.97	796.38
97000	1268.48	1027.59	920.07	864.41	833.38	815.38	804.68
98000	1281.55	1038.18	929.55	873.32	841.98	823.78	812.97
99000	1294.63	1048.77	939.04	882.23	850.57	832.19	821.27
100000	1307.71	1059.37	948.52	891.14	859.16	840.59	829.56

10%

MONTHLY AMORTIZING PAYMENTS

AMOUNT OF LOAN	NUMBER OF YEARS IN TERM							
	3	5	10	15	20	25	30	35
10	.33	.22	.14	.11	.10	.10	.09	.09
20	.65	.43	.27	.22	.20	.19	.18	.18
25	.81	.54	.34	.27	.25	.23	.22	.22
30	.97	.64	.40	.33	.29	.28	.27	.26
40	1.30	.85	.53	.43	.39	.37	.36	.35
50	1.62	1.07	.67	.54	.49	.46	.44	.43
60	1.94	1.28	.80	.65	.58	.55	.53	.52
70	2.26	1.49	.93	.76	.68	.64	.62	.61
75	2.43	1.60	1.00	.81	.73	.69	.66	.65
80	2.59	1.70	1.06	.86	.78	.73	.71	.69
90	2.91	1.92	1.19	.97	.87	.82	.79	.78
100	3.23	2.13	1.33	1.08	.97	.91	.88	.86
200	6.46	4.25	2.65	2.15	1.94	1.82	1.76	1.72
300	9.69	6.38	3.97	3.23	2.90	2.73	2.64	2.58
400	12.91	8.50	5.29	4.30	3.87	3.64	3.52	3.44
500	16.14	10.63	6.61	5.38	4.83	4.55	4.39	4.30
600	19.37	12.75	7.93	6.45	5.80	5.46	5.27	5.16
700	22.59	14.88	9.26	7.53	6.76	6.37	6.15	6.02
800	25.82	17.00	10.58	8.60	7.73	7.27	7.03	6.88
900	29.05	19.13	11.90	9.68	8.69	8.18	7.90	7.74
1000	32.27	21.25	13.22	10.75	9.66	9.09	8.78	8.60
2000	64.54	42.50	26.44	21.50	19.31	18.18	17.56	17.20
3000	96.81	63.75	39.65	32.24	28.96	27.27	26.33	25.80
4000	129.07	84.99	52.87	42.99	38.61	36.35	35.11	34.39
5000	161.34	106.24	66.08	53.74	48.26	45.44	43.88	42.99
6000	193.61	127.49	79.30	64.48	57.91	54.53	52.66	51.59
7000	225.88	148.73	92.51	75.23	67.56	63.61	61.44	60.18
8000	258.14	169.98	105.73	85.97	77.21	72.70	70.21	68.78
9000	290.41	191.23	118.94	96.72	86.86	81.79	78.99	77.38
10000	322.68	212.48	132.16	107.47	96.51	90.88	87.76	85.97
11000	354.94	233.72	145.37	118.21	106.16	99.96	96.54	94.57
12000	387.21	254.97	158.59	128.96	115.81	109.05	105.31	103.17
13000	419.48	276.22	171.80	139.70	125.46	118.14	114.09	111.76
14000	451.75	297.46	185.02	150.45	135.11	127.22	122.87	120.36
15000	484.01	318.71	198.23	161.20	144.76	136.31	131.64	128.96
16000	516.28	339.96	211.45	171.94	154.41	145.40	140.42	137.55
17000	548.55	361.20	224.66	182.69	164.06	154.48	149.19	146.15
18000	580.81	382.45	237.88	193.43	173.71	163.57	157.97	154.75
19000	613.08	403.70	251.09	204.18	183.36	172.66	166.74	163.34
20000	645.35	424.95	264.31	214.93	193.01	181.75	175.52	171.94
21000	677.62	446.19	277.52	225.67	202.66	190.83	184.30	180.54
22000	709.88	467.44	290.74	236.42	212.31	199.92	193.07	189.13
23000	742.15	488.69	303.95	247.16	221.96	209.01	201.85	197.73
24000	774.42	509.93	317.17	257.91	231.61	218.09	210.62	206.33
25000	806.68	531.18	330.38	268.66	241.26	227.18	219.40	214.92
26000	838.95	552.43	343.60	279.40	250.91	236.27	228.17	223.52
27000	871.22	573.68	356.81	290.15	260.56	245.35	236.95	232.12
28000	903.49	594.92	370.03	300.89	270.21	254.44	245.73	240.71
29000	935.75	616.17	383.24	311.64	279.86	263.53	254.50	249.31
30000	968.02	637.42	396.46	322.39	289.51	272.62	263.28	257.91
31000	1000.29	658.66	409.67	333.13	299.16	281.70	272.05	266.50
32000	1032.55	679.91	422.89	343.88	308.81	290.79	280.83	275.10
33000	1064.82	701.16	436.10	354.62	318.46	299.88	289.60	283.70
34000	1097.09	722.40	449.32	365.37	328.11	308.96	298.38	292.29
35000	1129.36	743.65	462.53	376.12	337.76	318.05	307.16	300.89
36000	1161.62	764.90	475.75	386.86	347.41	327.14	315.93	309.49
37000	1193.89	786.15	488.96	397.61	357.06	336.22	324.71	318.08
38000	1226.16	807.39	502.18	408.35	366.71	345.31	333.48	326.68
39000	1258.43	828.64	515.39	419.10	376.36	354.40	342.26	335.28
40000	1290.69	849.89	528.61	429.85	386.01	363.49	351.03	343.87

MONTHLY AMORTIZING PAYMENTS

AMOUNT OF LOAN	NUMBER OF YEARS IN TERM						
	10	15	20	25	30	35	40
41000	541.82	440.59	395.66	372.57	359.81	352.47	348.15
42000	555.04	451.34	405.31	381.66	368.59	361.07	356.65
43000	568.25	462.09	414.96	390.75	377.36	369.66	365.14
44000	581.47	472.83	424.61	399.83	386.14	378.26	373.63
45000	594.68	483.58	434.26	408.92	394.91	386.86	382.12
46000	607.90	494.32	443.91	418.01	403.69	395.45	390.61
47000	621.11	505.07	453.57	427.09	412.46	404.05	399.10
48000	634.33	515.82	463.22	436.18	421.24	412.65	407.60
49000	647.54	526.56	472.87	445.27	430.02	421.24	416.09
50000	660.76	537.31	482.52	454.36	438.79	429.84	424.58
51000	673.97	548.05	492.17	463.44	447.57	438.44	433.07
52000	687.19	558.80	501.82	472.53	456.34	447.03	441.56
53000	700.40	569.55	511.47	481.62	465.12	455.63	450.05
54000	713.62	580.29	521.12	490.70	473.89	464.23	458.54
55000	726.83	591.04	530.77	499.79	482.67	472.82	467.04
56000	740.05	601.78	540.42	508.88	491.45	481.42	475.53
57000	753.26	612.53	550.07	517.96	500.22	490.02	484.02
58000	766.48	623.28	559.72	527.05	509.00	498.62	492.51
59000	779.69	634.02	569.37	536.14	517.77	507.21	501.00
60000	792.91	644.77	579.02	545.23	526.55	515.81	509.49
61000	806.12	655.51	588.67	554.31	535.32	524.41	517.98
62000	819.34	666.26	598.32	563.40	544.10	533.00	526.48
63000	832.55	677.01	607.97	572.49	552.88	541.60	534.97
64000	845.77	687.75	617.62	581.57	561.65	550.20	543.46
65000	858.98	698.50	627.27	590.66	570.43	558.79	551.95
66000	872.20	709.24	636.92	599.75	579.20	567.39	560.44
67000	885.41	719.99	646.57	608.83	587.98	575.99	568.93
68000	898.63	730.74	656.22	617.92	596.75	584.58	577.42
69000	911.85	741.48	665.87	627.01	605.53	593.18	585.92
70000	925.06	752.23	675.52	636.10	614.31	601.78	594.41
71000	938.28	762.97	685.17	645.18	623.08	610.37	602.90
72000	951.49	773.72	694.82	654.27	631.86	618.97	611.39
73000	964.71	784.47	704.47	663.36	640.63	627.57	619.88
74000	977.92	795.21	714.12	672.44	649.41	636.16	628.37
75000	991.14	805.96	723.77	681.53	658.18	644.76	636.86
76000	1004.35	816.70	733.42	690.62	666.96	653.36	645.36
77000	1017.57	827.45	743.07	699.70	675.74	661.95	653.85
78000	1030.78	838.20	752.72	708.79	684.51	670.55	662.34
79000	1044.00	848.94	762.37	717.88	693.29	679.15	670.83
80000	1057.21	859.69	772.02	726.97	702.06	687.74	679.32
81000	1070.43	870.44	781.67	736.05	710.84	696.34	687.81
82000	1083.64	881.18	791.32	745.14	719.61	704.94	696.30
83000	1096.86	891.93	800.97	754.23	728.39	713.53	704.80
84000	1110.07	902.67	810.62	763.31	737.17	722.13	713.29
85000	1123.29	913.42	820.27	772.40	745.94	730.73	721.78
86000	1136.50	924.17	829.92	781.49	754.72	739.32	730.27
87000	1149.72	934.91	839.57	790.57	763.49	747.92	738.76
88000	1162.93	945.66	849.22	799.66	772.27	756.52	747.25
89000	1176.15	956.40	858.87	808.75	781.04	765.11	755.74
90000	1189.36	967.15	868.52	817.84	789.82	773.71	764.24
91000	1202.58	977.90	878.17	826.92	798.60	782.31	772.73
92000	1215.79	988.64	887.82	836.01	807.37	790.90	781.22
93000	1229.01	999.39	897.48	845.10	816.15	799.50	789.71
94000	1242.22	1010.13	907.13	854.18	824.92	808.10	798.20
95000	1255.44	1020.88	916.78	863.27	833.70	816.69	806.69
96000	1268.65	1031.63	926.43	872.36	842.47	825.29	815.19
97000	1281.87	1042.37	936.08	881.44	851.25	833.89	823.68
98000	1295.08	1053.12	945.73	890.53	860.03	842.48	832.17
99000	1308.30	1063.86	955.38	899.62	868.80	851.08	840.66
100000	1321.51	1074.61	965.03	908.71	877.58	859.68	849.15

10¼%

MONTHLY AMORTIZING PAYMENTS

AMOUNT OF LOAN	NUMBER OF YEARS IN TERM							
	3	5	10	15	20	25	30	35
10	.33	.22	.14	.11	.10	.10	.09	.09
20	.65	.43	.27	.22	.20	.19	.18	.18
25	.81	.54	.34	.28	.25	.24	.23	.22
30	.98	.65	.41	.33	.30	.28	.27	.27
40	1.30	.86	.54	.44	.40	.38	.36	.36
50	1.62	1.07	.67	.55	.50	.47	.45	.44
60	1.95	1.29	.81	.66	.59	.56	.54	.53
70	2.27	1.50	.94	.77	.69	.65	.63	.62
75	2.43	1.61	1.01	.82	.74	.70	.68	.66
80	2.60	1.71	1.07	.88	.79	.75	.72	.71
90	2.92	1.93	1.21	.99	.89	.84	.81	.80
100	3.24	2.14	1.34	1.09	.99	.93	.90	.88
200	6.48	4.28	2.68	2.18	1.97	1.86	1.80	1.76
300	9.72	6.42	4.01	3.27	2.95	2.78	2.69	2.64
400	12.96	8.55	5.35	4.36	3.93	3.71	3.59	3.52
500	16.20	10.69	6.68	5.45	4.91	4.64	4.49	4.40
600	19.44	12.83	8.02	6.54	5.89	5.56	5.38	5.28
700	22.67	14.96	9.35	7.63	6.88	6.49	6.28	6.16
800	25.91	17.10	10.69	8.72	7.86	7.42	7.17	7.04
900	29.15	19.24	12.02	9.81	8.84	8.34	8.07	7.91
1000	32.39	21.38	13.36	10.90	9.82	9.27	8.97	8.79
2000	64.77	42.75	26.71	21.80	19.64	18.53	17.93	17.58
3000	97.16	64.12	40.07	32.70	29.45	27.80	26.89	26.37
4000	129.54	85.49	53.42	43.60	39.27	37.06	35.85	35.16
5000	161.93	106.86	66.77	54.50	49.09	46.32	44.81	43.95
6000	194.31	128.23	80.13	65.40	58.90	55.59	53.77	52.74
7000	226.70	149.60	93.48	76.30	68.72	64.85	62.73	61.52
8000	259.08	170.97	106.84	87.20	78.54	74.12	71.69	70.31
9000	291.47	192.34	120.19	98.10	88.35	83.38	80.65	79.10
10000	323.85	213.71	133.54	109.00	98.17	92.64	89.62	87.89
11000	356.24	235.08	146.90	119.90	107.99	101.91	98.58	96.68
12000	388.62	256.45	160.25	130.80	117.80	111.17	107.54	105.47
13000	421.01	277.82	173.61	141.70	127.62	120.43	116.50	114.26
14000	453.39	299.19	186.96	152.60	137.44	129.70	125.46	123.04
15000	485.78	320.56	200.31	163.50	147.25	138.96	134.42	131.83
16000	518.16	341.93	213.67	174.40	157.07	148.23	143.38	140.62
17000	550.54	363.30	227.02	185.30	166.88	157.49	152.34	149.41
18000	582.93	384.67	240.38	196.20	176.70	166.75	161.30	158.20
19000	615.31	406.04	253.73	207.10	186.52	176.02	170.26	166.99
20000	647.70	427.41	267.08	218.00	196.33	185.28	179.23	175.78
21000	680.08	448.78	280.44	228.89	206.15	194.55	188.19	184.56
22000	712.47	470.15	293.79	239.79	215.97	203.81	197.15	193.35
23000	744.85	491.52	307.14	250.69	225.78	213.07	206.11	202.14
24000	777.24	512.89	320.50	261.59	235.60	222.34	215.07	210.93
25000	809.62	534.26	333.85	272.49	245.42	231.60	224.03	219.72
26000	842.01	555.63	347.21	283.39	255.23	240.86	232.99	228.51
27000	874.39	577.00	360.56	294.29	265.05	250.13	241.95	237.30
28000	906.78	598.37	373.91	305.19	274.87	259.39	250.91	246.08
29000	939.16	619.74	387.27	316.09	284.68	268.66	259.87	254.87
30000	971.55	641.11	400.62	326.99	294.50	277.92	268.84	263.66
31000	1003.93	662.48	413.98	337.89	304.31	287.18	277.80	272.45
32000	1036.32	683.85	427.33	348.79	314.13	296.45	286.76	281.24
33000	1068.70	705.22	440.68	359.69	323.95	305.71	295.72	290.03
34000	1101.08	726.59	454.04	370.59	333.76	314.98	304.68	298.82
35000	1133.47	747.96	467.39	381.49	343.58	324.24	313.64	307.60
36000	1165.85	769.33	480.75	392.39	353.40	333.50	322.60	316.39
37000	1198.24	790.70	494.10	403.29	363.21	342.77	331.56	325.18
38000	1230.62	812.08	507.45	414.19	373.03	352.03	340.52	333.97
39000	1263.01	833.45	520.81	425.09	382.85	361.29	349.48	342.76
40000	1295.39	854.82	534.16	435.99	392.66	370.56	358.45	351.55

32

MONTHLY AMORTIZING PAYMENTS

AMOUNT OF LOAN	NUMBER OF YEARS IN TERM						
	10	15	20	25	30	35	40
41000	547.51	446.88	402.48	379.82	367.41	360.34	356.22
42000	560.87	457.78	412.30	389.09	376.37	369.12	364.91
43000	574.22	468.68	422.11	398.35	385.33	377.91	373.60
44000	587.58	479.58	431.93	407.61	394.29	386.70	382.29
45000	600.93	490.48	441.74	416.88	403.25	395.49	390.97
46000	614.28	501.38	451.56	426.14	412.21	404.28	399.66
47000	627.64	512.28	461.38	435.41	421.17	413.07	408.35
48000	640.99	523.18	471.19	444.67	430.13	421.86	417.04
49000	654.35	534.08	481.01	453.93	439.09	430.64	425.73
50000	667.70	544.98	490.83	463.20	448.06	439.43	434.41
51000	681.05	555.88	500.64	472.46	457.02	448.22	443.10
52000	694.41	566.78	510.46	481.72	465.98	457.01	451.79
53000	707.76	577.68	520.28	490.99	474.94	465.80	460.48
54000	721.12	588.58	530.09	500.25	483.90	474.59	469.17
55000	734.47	599.48	539.91	509.52	492.86	483.38	477.86
56000	747.82	610.38	549.73	518.78	501.82	492.16	486.54
57000	761.18	621.28	559.54	528.04	510.78	500.95	495.23
58000	774.53	632.18	569.36	537.31	519.74	509.74	503.92
59000	787.89	643.08	579.17	546.57	528.70	518.53	512.61
60000	801.24	653.98	588.99	555.83	537.67	527.32	521.30
61000	814.59	664.88	598.81	565.10	546.63	536.11	529.98
62000	827.95	675.77	608.62	574.36	555.59	544.90	538.67
63000	841.30	686.67	618.44	583.63	564.55	553.68	547.36
64000	854.65	697.57	628.26	592.89	573.51	562.47	556.05
65000	868.01	708.47	638.07	602.15	582.47	571.26	564.74
66000	881.36	719.37	647.89	611.42	591.43	580.05	573.43
67000	894.72	730.27	657.71	620.68	600.39	588.84	582.11
68000	908.07	741.17	667.52	629.95	609.35	597.63	590.80
69000	921.42	752.07	677.34	639.21	618.31	606.42	599.49
70000	934.78	762.97	687.16	648.47	627.28	615.20	608.18
71000	948.13	773.87	696.97	657.74	636.24	623.99	616.87
72000	961.49	784.77	706.79	667.00	645.20	632.78	625.55
73000	974.84	795.67	716.60	676.26	654.16	641.57	634.24
74000	988.19	806.57	726.42	685.53	663.12	650.36	642.93
75000	1001.55	817.47	736.24	694.79	672.08	659.15	651.62
76000	1014.90	828.37	746.05	704.06	681.04	667.94	660.31
77000	1028.26	839.27	755.87	713.32	690.00	676.72	669.00
78000	1041.61	850.17	765.69	722.58	698.96	685.51	677.68
79000	1054.96	861.07	775.50	731.85	707.93	694.30	686.37
80000	1068.32	871.97	785.32	741.11	716.89	703.09	695.06
81000	1081.67	882.87	795.14	750.38	725.85	711.88	703.75
82000	1095.02	893.76	804.95	759.64	734.81	720.67	712.44
83000	1108.38	904.66	814.77	768.90	743.77	729.46	721.12
84000	1121.73	915.56	824.59	778.17	752.73	738.24	729.81
85000	1135.09	926.46	834.40	787.43	761.69	747.03	738.50
86000	1148.44	937.36	844.22	796.69	770.65	755.82	747.19
87000	1161.79	948.26	854.03	805.96	779.61	764.61	755.88
88000	1175.15	959.16	863.85	815.22	788.57	773.40	764.57
89000	1188.50	970.06	873.67	824.49	797.54	782.19	773.25
90000	1201.86	980.96	883.48	833.75	806.50	790.98	781.94
91000	1215.21	991.86	893.30	843.01	815.46	799.76	790.63
92000	1228.56	1002.76	903.12	852.28	824.42	808.55	799.32
93000	1241.92	1013.66	912.93	861.54	833.38	817.34	808.01
94000	1255.27	1024.56	922.75	870.81	842.34	826.13	816.69
95000	1268.63	1035.46	932.57	880.07	851.30	834.92	825.38
96000	1281.98	1046.36	942.38	889.33	860.26	843.71	834.07
97000	1295.33	1057.26	952.20	898.60	869.22	852.49	842.76
98000	1308.69	1068.16	962.02	907.86	878.18	861.28	851.45
99000	1322.04	1079.06	971.83	917.12	887.15	870.07	860.14
100000	1335.40	1089.96	981.65	926.39	896.11	878.86	868.82

10½%

MONTHLY AMORTIZING PAYMENTS

AMOUNT OF LOAN	NUMBER OF YEARS IN TERM							
	3	5	10	15	20	25	30	35
10	.33	.22	.14	.12	.10	.10	.10	.09
20	.66	.43	.27	.23	.20	.19	.19	.18
25	.82	.54	.34	.28	.25	.24	.23	.23
30	.98	.65	.41	.34	.30	.29	.28	.27
40	1.31	.86	.54	.45	.40	.38	.37	.36
50	1.63	1.08	.68	.56	.50	.48	.46	.45
60	1.96	1.29	.81	.67	.60	.57	.55	.54
70	2.28	1.51	.95	.78	.70	.67	.65	.63
75	2.44	1.62	1.02	.83	.75	.71	.69	.68
80	2.61	1.72	1.08	.89	.80	.76	.74	.72
90	2.93	1.94	1.22	1.00	.90	.85	.83	.81
100	3.26	2.15	1.35	1.11	1.00	.95	.92	.90
200	6.51	4.30	2.70	2.22	2.00	1.89	1.83	1.80
300	9.76	6.45	4.05	3.32	3.00	2.84	2.75	2.70
400	13.01	8.60	5.40	4.43	4.00	3.78	3.66	3.60
500	16.26	10.75	6.75	5.53	5.00	4.73	4.58	4.50
600	19.51	12.90	8.10	6.64	6.00	5.67	5.49	5.39
700	22.76	15.05	9.45	7.74	6.99	6.61	6.41	6.29
800	26.01	17.20	10.80	8.85	7.99	7.56	7.32	7.19
900	29.26	19.35	12.15	9.95	8.99	8.50	8.24	8.09
1000	32.51	21.50	13.50	11.06	9.99	9.45	9.15	8.99
2000	65.01	42.99	26.99	22.11	19.97	18.89	18.30	17.97
3000	97.51	64.49	40.49	33.17	29.96	28.33	27.45	26.95
4000	130.01	85.98	53.98	44.22	39.94	37.77	36.59	35.93
5000	162.52	107.47	67.47	55.27	49.92	47.21	45.74	44.91
6000	195.02	128.97	80.97	66.33	59.91	56.66	54.89	53.89
7000	227.52	150.46	94.46	77.38	69.89	66.10	64.04	62.87
8000	260.02	171.96	107.95	88.44	79.88	75.54	73.18	71.86
9000	292.53	193.45	121.45	99.49	89.86	84.98	82.33	80.84
10000	325.03	214.94	134.94	110.54	99.84	94.42	91.48	89.82
11000	357.53	236.44	148.43	121.60	109.83	103.86	100.63	98.80
12000	390.03	257.93	161.93	132.65	119.81	113.31	109.77	107.78
13000	422.54	279.43	175.42	143.71	129.79	122.75	118.92	116.76
14000	455.04	300.92	188.91	154.76	139.78	132.19	128.07	125.74
15000	487.54	322.41	202.41	165.81	149.76	141.63	137.22	134.73
16000	520.04	343.91	215.90	176.87	159.75	151.07	146.36	143.71
17000	552.55	365.40	229.39	187.92	169.73	160.52	155.51	152.69
18000	585.05	386.90	242.89	198.98	179.71	169.96	164.66	161.67
19000	617.55	408.39	256.38	210.03	189.70	179.40	173.81	170.65
20000	650.05	429.88	269.87	221.08	199.68	188.84	182.95	179.63
21000	682.56	451.38	283.37	232.14	209.66	198.28	192.10	188.61
22000	715.06	472.87	296.86	243.19	219.65	207.72	201.25	197.59
23000	747.56	494.36	310.36	254.25	229.63	217.17	210.40	206.58
24000	780.06	515.86	323.85	265.30	239.62	226.61	219.54	215.56
25000	812.57	537.35	337.34	276.35	249.60	236.05	228.69	224.54
26000	845.07	558.85	350.84	287.41	259.58	245.49	237.84	233.52
27000	877.57	580.34	364.33	298.46	269.57	254.93	246.98	242.50
28000	910.07	601.83	377.82	309.52	279.55	264.38	256.13	251.48
29000	942.58	623.33	391.32	320.57	289.54	273.82	265.28	260.46
30000	975.08	644.82	404.81	331.62	299.52	283.26	274.43	269.45
31000	1007.58	666.32	418.30	342.68	309.50	292.70	283.57	278.43
32000	1040.08	687.81	431.80	353.73	319.49	302.14	292.72	287.41
33000	1072.59	709.30	445.29	364.79	329.47	311.58	301.87	296.39
34000	1105.09	730.80	458.78	375.84	339.45	321.03	311.02	305.37
35000	1137.59	752.29	472.28	386.89	349.44	330.47	320.16	314.35
36000	1170.09	773.79	485.77	397.95	359.42	339.91	329.31	323.33
37000	1202.60	795.28	499.26	409.00	369.41	349.35	338.46	332.31
38000	1235.10	816.77	512.76	420.06	379.39	358.79	347.61	341.30
39000	1267.60	838.27	526.25	431.11	389.37	368.24	356.75	350.28
40000	1300.10	859.76	539.74	442.16	399.36	377.68	365.90	359.26

MONTHLY AMORTIZING PAYMENTS

AMOUNT OF LOAN	NUMBER OF YEARS IN TERM						
	10	15	20	25	30	35	40
41000	553.24	453.22	409.34	387.12	375.05	368.24	364.32
42000	566.73	464.27	419.32	396.56	384.20	377.22	373.20
43000	580.23	475.33	429.31	406.00	393.34	386.20	382.09
44000	593.72	486.38	439.29	415.44	402.49	395.18	390.98
45000	607.21	497.43	449.28	424.89	411.64	404.17	399.86
46000	620.71	508.49	459.26	434.33	420.79	413.15	408.75
47000	634.20	519.54	469.24	443.77	429.93	422.13	417.63
48000	647.69	530.60	479.23	453.21	439.08	431.11	426.52
49000	661.19	541.65	489.21	462.65	448.23	440.09	435.40
50000	674.68	552.70	499.19	472.10	457.37	449.07	444.29
51000	688.17	563.76	509.18	481.54	466.52	458.05	453.18
52000	701.67	574.81	519.16	490.98	475.67	467.03	462.06
53000	715.16	585.87	529.15	500.42	484.82	476.02	470.95
54000	728.65	596.92	539.13	509.86	493.96	485.00	479.83
55000	742.15	607.97	549.11	519.30	503.11	493.98	488.72
56000	755.64	619.03	559.10	528.75	512.26	502.96	497.60
57000	769.13	630.08	569.08	538.19	521.41	511.94	506.49
58000	782.63	641.14	579.07	547.63	530.55	520.92	515.38
59000	796.12	652.19	589.05	557.07	539.70	529.90	524.26
60000	809.61	663.24	599.03	566.51	548.85	538.89	533.15
61000	823.11	674.30	609.02	575.96	558.00	547.87	542.03
62000	836.60	685.35	619.00	585.40	567.14	556.85	550.92
63000	850.10	696.41	628.98	594.84	576.29	565.83	559.80
64000	863.59	707.46	638.97	604.28	585.44	574.81	568.69
65000	877.08	718.51	648.95	613.72	594.59	583.79	577.58
66000	890.58	729.57	658.94	623.16	603.73	592.77	586.46
67000	904.07	740.62	668.92	632.61	612.88	601.75	595.35
68000	917.56	751.68	678.90	642.05	622.03	610.74	604.23
69000	931.06	762.73	688.89	651.49	631.18	619.72	613.12
70000	944.55	773.78	698.87	660.93	640.32	628.70	622.00
71000	958.04	784.84	708.85	670.37	649.47	637.68	630.89
72000	971.54	795.89	718.84	679.82	658.62	646.66	639.78
73000	985.03	806.95	728.82	689.26	667.76	655.64	648.66
74000	998.52	818.00	738.81	698.70	676.91	664.62	657.55
75000	1012.02	829.05	748.79	708.14	686.06	673.61	666.43
76000	1025.51	840.11	758.77	717.58	695.21	682.59	675.32
77000	1039.00	851.16	768.76	727.02	704.35	691.57	684.20
78000	1052.50	862.22	778.74	736.47	713.50	700.55	693.09
79000	1065.99	873.27	788.73	745.91	722.65	709.53	701.98
80000	1079.48	884.32	798.71	755.35	731.80	718.51	710.86
81000	1092.98	895.38	808.69	764.79	740.94	727.49	719.75
82000	1106.47	906.43	818.68	774.23	750.09	736.47	728.63
83000	1119.97	917.49	828.66	783.68	759.24	745.46	737.52
84000	1133.46	928.54	838.64	793.12	768.39	754.44	746.40
85000	1146.95	939.59	848.63	802.56	777.53	763.42	755.29
86000	1160.45	950.65	858.61	812.00	786.68	772.40	764.18
87000	1173.94	961.70	868.60	821.44	795.83	781.38	773.06
88000	1187.43	972.76	878.58	830.88	804.98	790.36	781.95
89000	1200.93	983.81	888.56	840.33	814.12	799.34	790.83
90000	1214.42	994.86	898.55	849.77	823.27	808.33	799.72
91000	1227.91	1005.92	908.53	859.21	832.42	817.31	808.60
92000	1241.41	1016.97	918.51	868.65	841.57	826.29	817.49
93000	1254.90	1028.03	928.50	878.09	850.71	835.27	826.38
94000	1268.39	1039.08	938.48	887.54	859.86	844.25	835.26
95000	1281.89	1050.13	948.47	896.98	869.01	853.23	844.15
96000	1295.38	1061.19	958.45	906.42	878.15	862.21	853.03
97000	1308.87	1072.24	968.43	915.86	887.30	871.19	861.92
98000	1322.37	1083.30	978.42	925.30	896.45	880.18	870.80
99000	1335.86	1094.35	988.40	934.74	905.60	889.16	879.69
100000	1349.35	1105.40	998.38	944.19	914.74	898.14	888.58

10¾%

MONTHLY AMORTIZING PAYMENTS

AMOUNT OF LOAN	NUMBER OF YEARS IN TERM							
	3	5	10	15	20	25	30	35
10	.33	.22	.14	.12	.11	.10	.10	.10
20	.66	.44	.28	.23	.21	.20	.19	.19
25	.82	.55	.35	.29	.26	.25	.24	.23
30	.98	.65	.41	.34	.31	.29	.29	.28
40	1.31	.87	.55	.45	.41	.39	.38	.37
50	1.64	1.09	.69	.57	.51	.49	.47	.46
60	1.96	1.30	.82	.68	.61	.58	.57	.56
70	2.29	1.52	.96	.79	.72	.68	.66	.65
75	2.45	1.63	1.03	.85	.77	.73	.71	.69
80	2.61	1.73	1.10	.90	.82	.77	.75	.74
90	2.94	1.95	1.23	1.01	.92	.87	.85	.83
100	3.27	2.17	1.37	1.13	1.02	.97	.94	.92
200	6.53	4.33	2.73	2.25	2.04	1.93	1.87	1.84
300	9.79	6.49	4.10	3.37	3.05	2.89	2.81	2.76
400	13.05	8.65	5.46	4.49	4.07	3.85	3.74	3.68
500	16.32	10.81	6.82	5.61	5.08	4.82	4.67	4.59
600	19.58	12.98	8.19	6.73	6.10	5.78	5.61	5.51
700	22.84	15.14	9.55	7.85	7.11	6.74	6.54	6.43
800	26.10	17.30	10.91	8.97	8.13	7.70	7.47	7.35
900	29.36	19.46	12.28	10.09	9.14	8.66	8.41	8.26
1000	32.63	21.62	13.64	11.21	10.16	9.63	9.34	9.18
2000	65.25	43.24	27.27	22.42	20.31	19.25	18.67	18.36
3000	97.87	64.86	40.91	33.63	30.46	28.87	28.01	27.53
4000	130.49	86.48	54.54	44.84	40.61	38.49	37.34	36.71
5000	163.11	108.09	68.17	56.05	50.77	48.11	46.68	45.88
6000	195.73	129.71	81.81	67.26	60.92	57.73	56.01	55.06
7000	228.35	151.33	95.44	78.47	71.07	67.35	65.35	64.23
8000	260.97	172.95	109.08	89.68	81.22	76.97	74.68	73.41
9000	293.59	194.57	122.71	100.89	91.38	86.59	84.02	82.58
10000	326.21	216.18	136.34	112.10	101.53	96.21	93.35	91.76
11000	358.83	237.80	149.98	123.31	111.68	105.84	102.69	100.93
12000	391.45	259.42	163.61	134.52	121.83	115.46	112.02	110.11
13000	424.07	281.04	177.25	145.73	131.98	125.08	121.36	119.28
14000	456.69	302.66	190.88	156.94	142.14	134.70	130.69	128.46
15000	489.31	324.27	204.51	168.15	152.29	144.32	140.03	137.63
16000	521.93	345.89	218.15	179.36	162.44	153.94	149.36	146.81
17000	554.55	367.51	231.78	190.57	172.59	163.56	158.70	155.98
18000	587.17	389.13	245.41	201.78	182.75	173.18	168.03	165.16
19000	619.79	410.75	259.05	212.99	192.90	182.80	177.37	174.33
20000	652.41	432.36	272.68	224.19	203.05	192.42	186.70	183.51
21000	685.03	453.98	286.32	235.40	213.20	202.04	196.04	192.68
22000	717.65	475.60	299.95	246.61	223.36	211.67	205.37	201.86
23000	750.28	497.22	313.58	257.82	233.51	221.29	214.71	211.03
24000	782.90	518.84	327.22	269.03	243.66	230.91	224.04	220.21
25000	815.52	540.45	340.85	280.24	253.81	240.53	233.38	229.38
26000	848.14	562.07	354.49	291.45	263.96	250.15	242.71	238.56
27000	880.76	583.69	368.12	302.66	274.12	259.77	252.04	247.73
28000	913.38	605.31	381.75	313.87	284.27	269.39	261.38	256.91
29000	946.00	626.93	395.39	325.08	294.42	279.01	270.71	266.08
30000	978.62	648.54	409.02	336.29	304.57	288.63	280.05	275.26
31000	1011.24	670.16	422.65	347.50	314.73	298.25	289.38	284.43
32000	1043.86	691.78	436.29	358.71	324.88	307.87	298.72	293.61
33000	1076.48	713.40	449.92	369.92	335.03	317.50	308.05	302.78
34000	1109.10	735.02	463.56	381.13	345.18	327.12	317.39	311.96
35000	1141.72	756.63	477.19	392.34	355.34	336.74	326.72	321.13
36000	1174.34	778.25	490.82	403.55	365.49	346.36	336.06	330.31
37000	1206.96	799.87	504.46	414.76	375.64	355.98	345.39	339.48
38000	1239.58	821.49	518.09	425.97	385.79	365.60	354.73	348.66
39000	1272.20	843.11	531.73	437.17	395.94	375.22	364.06	357.83
40000	1304.82	864.72	545.36	448.38	406.10	384.84	373.40	367.01

AMOUNT OF LOAN	NUMBER OF YEARS IN TERM						
	10	15	20	25	30	35	40
41000	558.99	459.59	416.25	394.46	382.73	376.18	372.45
42000	572.63	470.80	426.40	404.08	392.07	385.36	381.53
43000	586.26	482.01	436.55	413.70	401.40	394.53	390.62
44000	599.90	493.22	446.71	423.33	410.74	403.71	399.70
45000	613.53	504.43	456.86	432.95	420.07	412.88	408.78
46000	627.16	515.64	467.01	442.57	429.41	422.06	417.87
47000	640.80	526.85	477.16	452.19	438.74	431.23	426.95
48000	654.43	538.06	487.31	461.81	448.08	440.41	436.04
49000	668.06	549.27	497.47	471.43	457.41	449.58	445.12
50000	681.70	560.48	507.62	481.05	466.75	458.76	454.20
51000	695.33	571.69	517.77	490.67	476.08	467.93	463.29
52000	708.97	582.90	527.92	500.29	485.42	477.11	472.37
53000	722.60	594.11	538.08	509.91	494.75	486.28	481.46
54000	736.23	605.32	548.23	519.54	504.08	495.46	490.54
55000	749.87	616.53	558.38	529.16	513.42	504.63	499.62
56000	763.50	627.74	568.53	538.78	522.75	513.81	508.71
57000	777.14	638.95	578.69	548.40	532.09	522.98	517.79
58000	790.77	650.15	588.84	558.02	541.42	532.16	526.88
59000	804.40	661.36	598.99	567.64	550.76	541.33	535.96
60000	818.04	672.57	609.14	577.26	560.09	550.51	545.04
61000	831.67	683.78	619.29	586.88	569.43	559.68	554.13
62000	845.30	694.99	629.45	596.50	578.76	568.86	563.21
63000	858.94	706.20	639.60	606.12	588.10	578.03	572.30
64000	872.57	717.41	649.75	615.74	597.43	587.21	581.38
65000	886.21	728.62	659.90	625.37	606.77	596.38	590.46
66000	899.84	739.83	670.06	634.99	616.10	605.56	599.55
67000	913.47	751.04	680.21	644.61	625.44	614.73	608.63
68000	927.11	762.25	690.36	654.23	634.77	623.91	617.72
69000	940.74	773.46	700.51	663.85	644.11	633.08	626.80
70000	954.38	784.67	710.67	673.47	653.44	642.26	635.88
71000	968.01	795.88	720.82	683.09	662.78	651.43	644.97
72000	981.64	807.09	730.97	692.71	672.11	660.61	654.05
73000	995.28	818.30	741.12	702.33	681.45	669.78	663.13
74000	1008.91	829.51	751.27	711.95	690.78	678.96	672.22
75000	1022.55	840.72	761.43	721.57	700.12	688.13	681.30
76000	1036.18	851.93	771.58	731.20	709.45	697.31	690.39
77000	1049.81	863.13	781.73	740.82	718.79	706.48	699.47
78000	1063.45	874.34	791.88	750.44	728.12	715.66	708.55
79000	1077.08	885.55	802.04	760.06	737.46	724.83	717.64
80000	1090.71	896.76	812.19	769.68	746.79	734.01	726.72
81000	1104.35	907.97	822.34	779.30	756.12	743.18	735.81
82000	1117.98	919.18	832.49	788.92	765.46	752.36	744.89
83000	1131.62	930.39	842.65	798.54	774.79	761.53	753.97
84000	1145.25	941.60	852.80	808.16	784.13	770.71	763.06
85000	1158.88	952.81	862.95	817.78	793.46	779.88	772.14
86000	1172.52	964.02	873.10	827.40	802.80	789.06	781.23
87000	1186.15	975.23	883.25	837.03	812.13	798.23	790.31
88000	1199.79	986.44	893.41	846.65	821.47	807.41	799.39
89000	1213.42	997.65	903.56	856.27	830.80	816.58	808.48
90000	1227.05	1008.86	913.71	865.89	840.14	825.76	817.56
91000	1240.69	1020.07	923.86	875.51	849.47	834.93	826.65
92000	1254.32	1031.28	934.02	885.13	858.81	844.11	835.73
93000	1267.95	1042.49	944.17	894.75	868.14	853.28	844.81
94000	1281.59	1053.70	954.32	904.37	877.48	862.46	853.90
95000	1295.22	1064.91	964.47	913.99	886.81	871.63	862.98
96000	1308.86	1076.12	974.62	923.61	896.15	880.81	872.07
97000	1322.49	1087.32	984.78	933.23	905.48	889.98	881.15
98000	1336.12	1098.53	994.93	942.86	914.82	899.16	890.23
99000	1349.76	1109.74	1005.08	952.48	924.15	908.33	899.32
100000	1363.39	1120.95	1015.23	962.10	933.49	917.51	908.40

11%

MONTHLY AMORTIZING PAYMENTS

AMOUNT OF LOAN	NUMBER OF YEARS IN TERM							
	3	5	10	15	20	25	30	35
10	.33	.22	.14	.12	.11	.10	.10	.10
20	.66	.44	.28	.23	.21	.20	.20	.19
25	.82	.55	.35	.29	.26	.25	.24	.24
30	.99	.66	.42	.35	.31	.30	.29	.29
40	1.31	.87	.56	.46	.42	.40	.39	.38
50	1.64	1.09	.69	.57	.52	.50	.48	.47
60	1.97	1.31	.83	.69	.62	.59	.58	.57
70	2.30	1.53	.97	.80	.73	.69	.67	.66
75	2.46	1.64	1.04	.86	.78	.74	.72	.71
80	2.62	1.74	1.11	.91	.83	.79	.77	.75
90	2.95	1.96	1.24	1.03	.93	.89	.86	.85
100	3.28	2.18	1.38	1.14	1.04	.99	.96	.94
200	6.55	4.35	2.76	2.28	2.07	1.97	1.91	1.88
300	9.83	6.53	4.14	3.41	3.10	2.95	2.86	2.82
400	13.10	8.70	5.51	4.55	4.13	3.93	3.81	3.75
500	16.37	10.88	6.89	5.69	5.17	4.91	4.77	4.69
600	19.65	13.05	8.27	6.82	6.20	5.89	5.72	5.63
700	22.92	15.22	9.65	7.96	7.23	6.87	6.67	6.56
800	26.20	17.40	11.02	9.10	8.26	7.85	7.62	7.50
900	29.47	19.57	12.40	10.23	9.29	8.83	8.58	8.44
1000	32.74	21.75	13.78	11.37	10.33	9.81	9.53	9.37
2000	65.48	43.49	27.56	22.74	20.65	19.61	19.05	18.74
3000	98.22	65.23	41.33	34.10	30.97	29.41	28.57	28.11
4000	130.96	86.97	55.11	45.47	41.29	39.21	38.10	37.48
5000	163.70	108.72	68.88	56.83	51.61	49.01	47.62	46.85
6000	196.44	130.46	82.66	68.20	61.94	58.81	57.14	56.22
7000	229.18	152.20	96.43	79.57	72.26	68.61	66.67	65.59
8000	261.91	173.94	110.21	90.93	82.58	78.41	76.19	74.96
9000	294.65	195.69	123.98	102.30	92.90	88.22	85.71	84.33
10000	327.39	217.43	137.76	113.66	103.22	98.02	95.24	93.70
11000	360.13	239.17	151.53	125.03	113.55	107.82	104.76	103.07
12000	392.87	260.91	165.31	136.40	123.87	117.62	114.28	112.44
13000	425.61	282.66	179.08	147.76	134.19	127.42	123.81	121.81
14000	458.35	304.40	192.86	159.13	144.51	137.22	133.33	131.18
15000	491.09	326.14	206.63	170.49	154.83	147.02	142.85	140.55
16000	523.82	347.88	220.41	181.86	165.16	156.82	152.38	149.92
17000	556.56	369.63	234.18	193.23	175.48	166.62	161.90	159.29
18000	589.30	391.37	247.96	204.59	185.80	176.43	171.42	168.66
19000	622.04	413.11	261.73	215.96	196.12	186.23	180.95	178.03
20000	654.78	434.85	275.51	227.32	206.44	196.03	190.47	187.40
21000	687.52	456.60	289.28	238.69	216.76	205.83	199.99	196.77
22000	720.26	478.34	303.06	250.06	227.09	215.63	209.52	206.14
23000	753.00	500.08	316.83	261.42	237.41	225.43	219.04	215.51
24000	785.73	521.82	330.61	272.79	247.73	235.23	228.56	224.87
25000	818.47	543.57	344.38	284.15	258.05	245.03	238.09	234.24
26000	851.21	565.31	358.16	295.52	268.37	254.83	247.61	243.61
27000	883.95	587.05	371.93	306.89	278.70	264.64	257.13	252.98
28000	916.69	608.79	385.71	318.25	289.02	274.44	266.66	262.35
29000	949.43	630.54	399.48	329.62	299.34	284.24	276.18	271.72
30000	982.17	652.28	413.26	340.98	309.66	294.04	285.70	281.09
31000	1014.91	674.02	427.03	352.35	319.98	303.84	295.23	290.46
32000	1047.64	695.76	440.81	363.72	330.31	313.64	304.75	299.83
33000	1080.38	717.50	454.58	375.08	340.63	323.44	314.27	309.20
34000	1113.12	739.25	468.36	386.45	350.95	333.24	323.79	318.57
35000	1145.86	760.99	482.13	397.81	361.27	343.04	333.32	327.94
36000	1178.60	782.73	495.91	409.18	371.59	352.85	342.84	337.31
37000	1211.34	804.47	509.68	420.55	381.91	362.65	352.36	346.68
38000	1244.08	826.22	523.46	431.91	392.24	372.45	361.89	356.05
39000	1276.81	847.96	537.23	443.28	402.56	382.25	371.41	365.42
40000	1309.55	869.70	551.01	454.64	412.88	392.05	380.93	374.79

MONTHLY AMORTIZING PAYMENTS

AMOUNT OF LOAN	NUMBER OF YEARS IN TERM						
	10	15	20	25	30	35	40
41000	564.78	466.01	423.20	401.85	390.46	384.16	380.61
42000	578.56	477.38	433.52	411.65	399.98	393.53	389.89
43000	592.33	488.74	443.85	421.45	409.50	402.90	399.17
44000	606.11	500.11	454.17	431.25	419.03	412.27	408.45
45000	619.88	511.47	464.49	441.06	428.55	421.64	417.74
46000	633.66	522.84	474.81	450.86	438.07	431.01	427.02
47000	647.43	534.21	485.13	460.66	447.60	440.38	436.30
48000	661.21	545.57	495.46	470.46	457.12	449.74	445.59
49000	674.98	556.94	505.78	480.26	466.64	459.11	454.87
50000	688.76	568.30	516.10	490.06	476.17	468.48	464.15
51000	702.53	579.67	526.42	499.86	485.69	477.85	473.44
52000	716.31	591.04	536.74	509.66	495.21	487.22	482.72
53000	730.08	602.40	547.06	519.46	504.74	496.59	492.00
54000	743.86	613.77	557.39	529.27	514.26	505.96	501.28
55000	757.63	625.13	567.71	539.07	523.78	515.33	510.57
56000	771.41	636.50	578.03	548.87	533.31	524.70	519.85
57000	785.18	647.87	588.35	558.67	542.83	534.07	529.13
58000	798.96	659.23	598.67	568.47	552.35	543.44	538.42
59000	812.73	670.60	609.00	578.27	561.88	552.81	547.70
60000	826.51	681.96	619.32	588.07	571.40	562.18	556.98
61000	840.28	693.33	629.64	597.87	580.92	571.55	566.26
62000	854.06	704.70	639.96	607.68	590.45	580.92	575.55
63000	867.83	716.06	650.28	617.48	599.97	590.29	584.83
64000	881.61	727.43	660.61	627.28	609.49	599.66	594.11
65000	895.38	738.79	670.93	637.08	619.02	609.03	603.40
66000	909.16	750.16	681.25	646.88	628.54	618.40	612.68
67000	922.93	761.52	691.57	656.68	638.06	627.77	621.96
68000	936.71	772.89	701.89	666.48	647.58	637.14	631.25
69000	950.48	784.26	712.21	676.28	657.11	646.51	640.53
70000	964.26	795.62	722.54	686.08	666.63	655.88	649.81
71000	978.03	806.99	732.86	695.89	676.15	665.24	659.09
72000	991.81	818.35	743.18	705.69	685.68	674.61	668.38
73000	1005.58	829.72	753.50	715.49	695.20	683.98	677.66
74000	1019.36	841.09	763.82	725.29	704.72	693.35	686.94
75000	1033.13	852.45	774.15	735.09	714.25	702.72	696.23
76000	1046.91	863.82	784.47	744.89	723.77	712.09	705.51
77000	1060.68	875.18	794.79	754.69	733.29	721.46	714.79
78000	1074.46	886.55	805.11	764.49	742.82	730.83	724.07
79000	1088.23	897.92	815.43	774.29	752.34	740.20	733.36
80000	1102.01	909.28	825.76	784.10	761.86	749.57	742.64
81000	1115.78	920.65	836.08	793.90	771.39	758.94	751.92
82000	1129.56	932.01	846.40	803.70	780.91	768.31	761.21
83000	1143.33	943.38	856.72	813.50	790.43	777.68	770.49
84000	1157.11	954.75	867.04	823.30	799.96	787.05	779.77
85000	1170.88	966.11	877.37	833.10	809.48	796.42	789.06
86000	1184.66	977.48	887.69	842.90	819.00	805.79	798.34
87000	1198.43	988.84	898.01	852.70	828.53	815.16	807.62
88000	1212.21	1000.21	908.33	862.50	838.05	824.53	816.90
89000	1225.98	1011.58	918.65	872.31	847.57	833.90	826.19
90000	1239.76	1022.94	928.97	882.11	857.10	843.27	835.47
91000	1253.53	1034.31	939.30	891.91	866.62	852.64	844.75
92000	1267.31	1045.67	949.62	901.71	876.14	862.01	854.04
93000	1281.08	1057.04	959.94	911.51	885.67	871.38	863.32
94000	1294.86	1068.41	970.26	921.31	895.19	880.75	872.60
95000	1308.63	1079.77	980.58	931.11	904.71	890.11	881.88
96000	1322.41	1091.14	990.91	940.91	914.24	899.48	891.17
97000	1336.18	1102.50	1001.23	950.71	923.76	908.85	900.45
98000	1349.96	1113.87	1011.55	960.52	933.28	918.22	909.73
99000	1363.73	1125.24	1021.87	970.32	942.81	927.59	919.02
100000	1377.51	1136.60	1032.19	980.12	952.33	936.96	928.30

11¼%

MONTHLY AMORTIZING PAYMENTS

AMOUNT OF LOAN	NUMBER OF YEARS IN TERM							
	3	5	10	15	20	25	30	35
10	.33	.22	.14	.12	.11	.10	.10	.10
20	.66	.44	.28	.24	.21	.20	.20	.20
25	.83	.55	.35	.29	.27	.25	.25	.24
30	.99	.66	.42	.35	.32	.30	.30	.29
40	1.32	.88	.56	.47	.42	.40	.39	.39
50	1.65	1.10	.70	.58	.53	.50	.49	.48
60	1.98	1.32	.84	.70	.63	.60	.59	.58
70	2.31	1.54	.98	.81	.74	.70	.68	.67
75	2.47	1.65	1.05	.87	.79	.75	.73	.72
80	2.63	1.75	1.12	.93	.84	.80	.78	.77
90	2.96	1.97	1.26	1.04	.95	.90	.88	.87
100	3.29	2.19	1.40	1.16	1.05	1.00	.98	.96
200	6.58	4.38	2.79	2.31	2.10	2.00	1.95	1.92
300	9.86	6.57	4.18	3.46	3.15	3.00	2.92	2.87
400	13.15	8.75	5.57	4.61	4.20	4.00	3.89	3.83
500	16.43	10.94	6.96	5.77	5.25	5.00	4.86	4.79
600	19.72	13.13	8.36	6.92	6.30	5.99	5.83	5.74
700	23.01	15.31	9.75	8.07	7.35	6.99	6.80	6.70
800	26.29	17.50	11.14	9.22	8.40	7.99	7.78	7.66
900	29.58	19.69	12.53	10.38	9.45	8.99	8.75	8.61
1000	32.86	21.87	13.92	11.53	10.50	9.99	9.72	9.57
2000	65.72	43.74	27.84	23.05	20.99	19.97	19.43	19.13
3000	98.58	65.61	41.76	34.58	31.48	29.95	29.14	28.70
4000	131.43	87.47	55.67	46.10	41.98	39.93	38.86	38.26
5000	164.29	109.34	69.59	57.62	52.47	49.92	48.57	47.83
6000	197.15	131.21	83.51	69.15	62.96	59.90	58.28	57.39
7000	230.01	153.08	97.42	80.67	73.45	69.88	67.99	66.96
8000	262.86	174.94	111.34	92.19	83.95	79.86	77.71	76.52
9000	295.72	196.81	125.26	103.72	94.44	89.85	87.42	86.09
10000	328.58	218.68	139.17	115.24	104.93	99.83	97.13	95.65
11000	361.43	240.55	153.09	126.76	115.42	109.81	106.84	105.22
12000	394.29	262.41	167.01	138.29	125.92	119.79	116.56	114.78
13000	427.15	284.28	180.92	149.81	136.41	129.78	126.27	124.35
14000	460.01	306.15	194.84	161.33	146.90	139.76	135.98	133.91
15000	492.86	328.01	208.76	172.86	157.39	149.74	145.69	143.48
16000	525.72	349.88	222.68	184.38	167.89	159.72	155.41	153.04
17000	558.58	371.75	236.59	195.90	178.38	169.71	165.12	162.61
18000	591.44	393.62	250.51	207.43	188.87	179.69	174.83	172.17
19000	624.29	415.48	264.43	218.95	199.36	189.67	184.54	181.74
20000	657.15	437.35	278.34	230.47	209.86	199.65	194.26	191.30
21000	690.01	459.22	292.26	242.00	220.35	209.64	203.97	200.87
22000	722.86	481.09	306.18	253.52	230.84	219.62	213.68	210.43
23000	755.72	502.95	320.09	265.04	241.33	229.60	223.40	220.00
24000	788.58	524.82	334.01	276.57	251.83	239.58	233.11	229.56
25000	821.44	546.69	347.93	288.09	262.32	249.56	242.82	239.13
26000	854.29	568.56	361.84	299.61	272.81	259.55	252.53	248.69
27000	887.15	590.42	375.76	311.14	283.30	269.53	262.25	258.26
28000	920.01	612.29	389.68	322.66	293.80	279.51	271.96	267.82
29000	952.86	634.16	403.59	334.18	304.29	289.49	281.67	277.39
30000	985.72	656.02	417.51	345.71	314.78	299.48	291.38	286.95
31000	1018.58	677.89	431.43	357.23	325.27	309.46	301.10	296.52
32000	1051.44	699.76	445.35	368.76	335.77	319.44	310.81	306.08
33000	1084.29	721.63	459.26	380.28	346.26	329.42	320.52	315.65
34000	1117.15	743.49	473.18	391.80	356.75	339.41	330.23	325.21
35000	1150.01	765.36	487.10	403.33	367.24	349.39	339.95	334.78
36000	1182.87	787.23	501.01	414.85	377.74	359.37	349.66	344.34
37000	1215.72	809.10	514.93	426.37	388.23	369.35	359.37	353.91
38000	1248.58	830.96	528.85	437.90	398.72	379.34	369.08	363.47
39000	1281.44	852.83	542.76	449.42	409.21	389.32	378.80	373.04
40000	1314.29	874.70	556.68	460.94	419.71	399.30	388.51	382.60

AMOUNT OF LOAN	NUMBER OF YEARS IN TERM						
	10	15	20	25	30	35	40
41000	570.60	472.47	430.20	409.28	398.22	392.17	388.79
42000	584.51	483.99	440.69	419.27	407.93	401.73	398.27
43000	598.43	495.51	451.19	429.25	417.65	411.30	407.76
44000	612.35	507.04	461.68	439.23	427.36	420.86	417.24
45000	626.27	518.56	472.17	449.21	437.07	430.43	426.72
46000	640.18	530.08	482.66	459.20	446.79	439.99	436.20
47000	654.10	541.61	493.16	469.18	456.50	449.56	445.69
48000	668.02	553.13	503.65	479.16	466.21	459.12	455.17
49000	681.93	564.65	514.14	489.14	475.92	468.69	464.65
50000	695.85	576.18	524.63	499.12	485.64	478.25	474.13
51000	709.77	587.70	535.13	509.11	495.35	487.82	483.62
52000	723.68	599.22	545.62	519.09	505.06	497.38	493.10
53000	737.60	610.75	556.11	529.07	514.77	506.95	502.58
54000	751.52	622.27	566.60	539.05	524.49	516.51	512.06
55000	765.43	633.79	577.10	549.04	534.20	526.08	521.55
56000	779.35	645.32	587.59	559.02	543.91	535.64	531.03
57000	793.27	656.84	598.08	569.00	553.62	545.21	540.51
58000	807.18	668.36	608.57	578.98	563.34	554.77	549.99
59000	821.10	679.89	619.07	588.97	573.05	564.34	559.48
60000	835.02	691.41	629.56	598.95	582.76	573.90	568.96
61000	848.94	702.94	640.05	608.93	592.47	583.47	578.44
62000	862.85	714.46	650.54	618.91	602.19	593.03	587.92
63000	876.77	725.98	661.04	628.90	611.90	602.60	597.41
64000	890.69	737.51	671.53	638.88	621.61	612.16	606.89
65000	904.60	749.03	682.02	648.86	631.32	621.73	616.37
66000	918.52	760.55	692.51	658.84	641.04	631.29	625.85
67000	932.44	772.08	703.01	668.83	650.75	640.86	635.34
68000	946.35	783.60	713.50	678.81	660.46	650.42	644.82
69000	960.27	795.12	723.99	688.79	670.18	659.99	654.30
70000	974.19	806.65	734.48	698.77	679.89	669.55	663.79
71000	988.10	818.17	744.98	708.76	689.60	679.12	673.27
72000	1002.02	829.69	755.47	718.74	699.31	688.68	682.75
73000	1015.94	841.22	765.96	728.72	709.03	698.25	692.23
74000	1029.86	852.74	776.45	738.70	718.74	707.81	701.72
75000	1043.77	864.26	786.95	748.68	728.45	717.38	711.20
76000	1057.69	875.79	797.44	758.67	738.16	726.94	720.68
77000	1071.61	887.31	807.93	768.65	747.88	736.51	730.16
78000	1085.52	898.83	818.42	778.63	757.59	746.07	739.65
79000	1099.44	910.36	828.92	788.61	767.30	755.64	749.13
80000	1113.36	921.88	839.41	798.60	777.01	765.20	758.61
81000	1127.27	933.40	849.90	808.58	786.73	774.77	768.09
82000	1141.19	944.93	860.39	818.56	796.44	784.33	777.58
83000	1155.11	956.45	870.89	828.54	806.15	793.89	787.06
84000	1169.02	967.97	881.38	838.53	815.86	803.46	796.54
85000	1182.94	979.50	891.87	848.51	825.58	813.02	806.02
86000	1196.86	991.02	902.37	858.49	835.29	822.59	815.51
87000	1210.77	1002.54	912.86	868.47	845.00	832.15	824.99
88000	1224.69	1014.07	923.35	878.46	854.72	841.72	834.47
89000	1238.61	1025.59	933.84	888.44	864.43	851.28	843.95
90000	1252.53	1037.12	944.34	898.42	874.14	860.85	853.44
91000	1266.44	1048.64	954.83	908.40	883.85	870.41	862.92
92000	1280.36	1060.16	965.32	918.39	893.57	879.98	872.40
93000	1294.28	1071.69	975.81	928.37	903.28	889.54	881.88
94000	1308.19	1083.21	986.31	938.35	912.99	899.11	891.37
95000	1322.11	1094.73	996.80	948.33	922.70	908.67	900.85
96000	1336.03	1106.26	1007.29	958.31	932.42	918.24	910.33
97000	1349.94	1117.78	1017.78	968.30	942.13	927.80	919.81
98000	1363.86	1129.30	1028.28	978.28	951.84	937.37	929.30
99000	1377.78	1140.83	1038.77	988.26	961.55	946.93	938.78
100000	1391.69	1152.35	1049.26	998.24	971.27	956.50	948.26

11½%

MONTHLY AMORTIZING PAYMENTS

AMOUNT OF LOAN	NUMBER OF YEARS IN TERM							
	3	5	10	15	20	25	30	35
10	.33	.22	.15	.12	.11	.11	.10	.10
20	.66	.44	.29	.24	.22	.21	.20	.20
25	.83	.55	.36	.30	.27	.26	.25	.25
30	.99	.66	.43	.36	.32	.31	.30	.30
40	1.32	.88	.57	.47	.43	.41	.40	.40
50	1.65	1.10	.71	.59	.54	.51	.50	.49
60	1.98	1.32	.85	.71	.64	.61	.60	.59
70	2.31	1.54	.99	.82	.75	.72	.70	.69
75	2.48	1.65	1.06	.88	.80	.77	.75	.74
80	2.64	1.76	1.13	.94	.86	.82	.80	.79
90	2.97	1.98	1.27	1.06	.96	.92	.90	.88
100	3.30	2.20	1.41	1.17	1.07	1.02	1.00	.98
200	6.60	4.40	2.82	2.34	2.14	2.04	1.99	1.96
300	9.90	6.60	4.22	3.51	3.20	3.05	2.98	2.93
400	13.20	8.80	5.63	4.68	4.27	4.07	3.97	3.91
500	16.49	11.00	7.03	5.85	5.34	5.09	4.96	4.89
600	19.79	13.20	8.44	7.01	6.40	6.10	5.95	5.86
700	23.09	15.40	9.85	8.18	7.47	7.12	6.94	6.84
800	26.39	17.60	11.25	9.35	8.54	8.14	7.93	7.81
900	29.68	19.80	12.66	10.52	9.60	9.15	8.92	8.79
1000	32.98	22.00	14.06	11.69	10.67	10.17	9.91	9.77
2000	65.96	43.99	28.12	23.37	21.33	20.33	19.81	19.53
3000	98.93	65.98	42.18	35.05	32.00	30.50	29.71	29.29
4000	131.91	87.98	56.24	46.73	42.66	40.66	39.62	39.05
5000	164.89	109.97	70.30	58.41	53.33	50.83	49.52	48.81
6000	197.86	131.96	84.36	70.10	63.99	60.99	59.42	58.57
7000	230.84	153.95	98.42	81.78	74.66	71.16	69.33	68.33
8000	263.81	175.95	112.48	93.46	85.32	81.32	79.23	78.09
9000	296.79	197.94	126.54	105.14	95.98	91.49	89.13	87.85
10000	329.77	219.93	140.60	116.82	106.65	101.65	99.03	97.62
11000	362.74	241.92	154.66	128.51	117.31	111.82	108.94	107.38
12000	395.72	263.92	168.72	140.19	127.98	121.98	118.84	117.14
13000	428.69	285.91	182.78	151.87	138.64	132.15	128.74	126.90
14000	461.67	307.90	196.84	163.55	149.31	142.31	138.65	136.66
15000	494.65	329.89	210.90	175.23	159.97	152.48	148.55	146.42
16000	527.62	351.89	224.96	186.92	170.63	162.64	158.45	156.18
17000	560.60	373.88	239.02	198.60	181.30	172.80	168.35	165.94
18000	593.57	395.87	253.08	210.28	191.96	182.97	178.26	175.70
19000	626.55	417.86	267.14	221.96	202.63	193.13	188.16	185.47
20000	659.53	439.86	281.20	233.64	213.29	203.30	198.06	195.23
21000	692.50	461.85	295.26	245.32	223.96	213.46	207.97	204.99
22000	725.48	483.84	309.31	257.01	234.62	223.63	217.87	214.75
23000	758.45	505.83	323.37	268.69	245.28	233.79	227.77	224.51
24000	791.43	527.83	337.43	280.37	255.95	243.96	237.67	234.27
25000	824.41	549.82	351.49	292.05	266.61	254.12	247.58	244.03
26000	857.38	571.81	365.55	303.73	277.28	264.29	257.48	253.79
27000	890.36	593.81	379.61	315.42	287.94	274.45	267.38	263.55
28000	923.33	615.80	393.67	327.10	298.61	284.62	277.29	273.32
29000	956.31	637.79	407.73	338.78	309.27	294.78	287.19	283.08
30000	989.29	659.78	421.79	350.46	319.93	304.95	297.09	292.84
31000	1022.26	681.78	435.85	362.14	330.60	315.11	307.00	302.60
32000	1055.24	703.77	449.91	373.83	341.26	325.28	316.90	312.36
33000	1088.21	725.76	463.97	385.51	351.93	335.44	326.80	322.12
34000	1121.19	747.75	478.03	397.19	362.59	345.60	336.70	331.88
35000	1154.17	769.75	492.09	408.87	373.26	355.77	346.61	341.64
36000	1187.14	791.74	506.15	420.55	383.92	365.93	356.51	351.40
37000	1220.12	813.73	520.21	432.24	394.58	376.10	366.41	361.16
38000	1253.09	835.72	534.27	443.92	405.25	386.26	376.32	370.93
39000	1286.07	857.72	548.33	455.60	415.91	396.43	386.22	380.69
40000	1319.05	879.71	562.39	467.28	426.58	406.59	396.12	390.45

AMOUNT OF LOAN	NUMBER OF YEARS IN TERM						
	10	15	20	25	30	35	40
41000	576.45	478.96	437.24	416.76	406.02	400.21	397.00
42000	590.51	490.64	447.91	426.92	415.93	409.97	406.68
43000	604.57	502.33	458.57	437.09	425.83	419.73	416.37
44000	618.62	514.01	469.23	447.25	435.73	429.49	426.05
45000	632.68	525.69	479.90	457.42	445.64	439.25	435.73
46000	646.74	537.37	490.56	467.58	455.54	449.01	445.41
47000	660.80	549.05	501.23	477.75	465.44	458.78	455.10
48000	674.86	560.74	511.89	487.91	475.34	468.54	464.78
49000	688.92	572.42	522.56	498.07	485.25	478.30	474.46
50000	702.98	584.10	533.22	508.24	495.15	488.06	484.15
51000	717.04	595.78	543.88	518.40	505.05	497.82	493.83
52000	731.10	607.46	554.55	528.57	514.96	507.58	503.51
53000	745.16	619.15	565.21	538.73	524.86	517.34	513.19
54000	759.22	630.83	575.88	548.90	534.76	527.10	522.88
55000	773.28	642.51	586.54	559.06	544.67	536.86	532.56
56000	787.34	654.19	597.21	569.23	554.57	546.63	542.24
57000	801.40	665.87	607.87	579.39	564.47	556.39	551.93
58000	815.46	677.56	618.53	589.56	574.37	566.15	561.61
59000	829.52	689.24	629.20	599.72	584.28	575.91	571.29
60000	843.58	700.92	639.86	609.89	594.18	585.67	580.97
61000	857.64	712.60	650.53	620.05	604.08	595.43	590.66
62000	871.70	724.28	661.19	630.22	613.99	605.19	600.34
63000	885.76	735.96	671.86	640.38	623.89	614.95	610.02
64000	899.82	747.65	682.52	650.55	633.79	624.71	619.71
65000	913.88	759.33	693.18	660.71	643.69	634.47	629.39
66000	927.93	771.01	703.85	670.87	653.60	644.24	639.07
67000	941.99	782.69	714.51	681.04	663.50	654.00	648.75
68000	956.05	794.37	725.18	691.20	673.40	663.76	658.44
69000	970.11	806.06	735.84	701.37	683.31	673.52	668.12
70000	984.17	817.74	746.51	711.53	693.21	683.28	677.80
71000	998.23	829.42	757.17	721.70	703.11	693.04	687.49
72000	1012.29	841.10	767.83	731.86	713.01	702.80	697.17
73000	1026.35	852.78	778.50	742.03	722.92	712.56	706.85
74000	1040.41	864.47	789.16	752.19	732.82	722.32	716.53
75000	1054.47	876.15	799.83	762.36	742.72	732.09	726.22
76000	1068.53	887.83	810.49	772.52	752.63	741.85	735.90
77000	1082.59	899.51	821.16	782.69	762.53	751.61	745.58
78000	1096.65	911.19	831.82	792.85	772.43	761.37	755.26
79000	1110.71	922.87	842.48	803.02	782.34	771.13	764.95
80000	1124.77	934.56	853.15	813.18	792.24	780.89	774.63
81000	1138.83	946.24	863.81	823.34	802.14	790.65	784.31
82000	1152.89	957.92	874.48	833.51	812.04	800.41	794.00
83000	1166.95	969.60	885.14	843.67	821.95	810.17	803.68
84000	1181.01	981.28	895.81	853.84	831.85	819.94	813.36
85000	1195.07	992.97	906.47	864.00	841.75	829.70	823.04
86000	1209.13	1004.65	917.13	874.17	851.66	839.46	832.73
87000	1223.19	1016.33	927.80	884.33	861.56	849.22	842.41
88000	1237.24	1028.01	938.46	894.50	871.46	858.98	852.09
89000	1251.30	1039.69	949.13	904.66	881.36	868.74	861.78
90000	1265.36	1051.38	959.79	914.83	891.27	878.50	871.46
91000	1279.42	1063.06	970.46	924.99	901.17	888.26	881.14
92000	1293.48	1074.74	981.12	935.16	911.07	898.02	890.82
93000	1307.54	1086.42	991.78	945.32	920.98	907.78	900.51
94000	1321.60	1098.10	1002.45	955.49	930.88	917.55	910.19
95000	1335.66	1109.79	1013.11	965.65	940.78	927.31	919.87
96000	1349.72	1121.47	1023.78	975.82	950.68	937.07	929.56
97000	1363.78	1133.15	1034.44	985.98	960.59	946.83	939.24
98000	1377.84	1144.83	1045.11	996.14	970.49	956.59	948.92
99000	1391.90	1156.51	1055.77	1006.31	980.39	966.35	958.60
100000	1405.96	1168.19	1066.43	1016.47	990.30	976.11	968.29

11¾%

MONTHLY AMORTIZING PAYMENTS

AMOUNT OF LOAN	NUMBER OF YEARS IN TERM							
	3	5	10	15	20	25	30	35
10	.34	.23	.15	.12	.11	.11	.11	.10
20	.67	.45	.29	.24	.22	.21	.21	.20
25	.83	.56	.36	.30	.28	.26	.26	.25
30	1.00	.67	.43	.36	.33	.32	.31	.30
40	1.33	.89	.57	.48	.44	.42	.41	.40
50	1.66	1.11	.72	.60	.55	.52	.51	.50
60	1.99	1.33	.86	.72	.66	.63	.61	.60
70	2.32	1.55	1.00	.83	.76	.73	.71	.70
75	2.49	1.66	1.07	.89	.82	.78	.76	.75
80	2.65	1.77	1.14	.95	.87	.83	.81	.80
90	2.98	2.00	1.28	1.07	.98	.94	.91	.90
100	3.31	2.22	1.43	1.19	1.09	1.04	1.01	1.00
200	6.62	4.43	2.85	2.37	2.17	2.07	2.02	2.00
300	9.93	6.64	4.27	3.56	3.26	3.11	3.03	2.99
400	13.24	8.85	5.69	4.74	4.34	4.14	4.04	3.99
500	16.55	11.06	7.11	5.93	5.42	5.18	5.05	4.98
600	19.86	13.28	8.53	7.11	6.51	6.21	6.06	5.98
700	23.17	15.49	9.95	8.29	7.59	7.25	7.07	6.98
800	26.48	17.70	11.37	9.48	8.67	8.28	8.08	7.97
900	29.79	19.91	12.79	10.66	9.76	9.32	9.09	8.97
1000	33.10	22.12	14.21	11.85	10.84	10.35	10.10	9.96
2000	66.20	44.24	28.41	23.69	21.68	20.70	20.19	19.92
3000	99.29	66.36	42.61	35.53	32.52	31.05	30.29	29.88
4000	132.39	88.48	56.82	47.37	43.35	41.40	40.38	39.84
5000	165.48	110.60	71.02	59.21	54.19	51.74	50.48	49.79
6000	198.58	132.71	85.22	71.05	65.03	62.09	60.57	59.75
7000	231.67	154.83	99.43	82.89	75.86	72.44	70.66	69.71
8000	264.77	176.95	113.63	94.74	86.70	82.79	80.76	79.67
9000	297.86	199.07	127.83	106.58	97.54	93.14	90.85	89.63
10000	330.96	221.19	142.03	118.42	108.38	103.48	100.95	99.58
11000	364.05	243.31	156.24	130.26	119.21	113.83	111.04	109.54
12000	397.15	265.42	170.44	142.10	130.05	124.18	121.13	119.50
13000	430.24	287.54	184.64	153.94	140.89	134.53	131.23	129.46
14000	463.34	309.66	198.85	165.78	151.72	144.88	141.32	139.42
15000	496.43	331.78	213.05	177.62	162.56	155.22	151.42	149.37
16000	529.53	353.90	227.25	189.47	173.40	165.57	161.51	159.33
17000	562.62	376.02	241.46	201.31	184.24	175.92	171.60	169.29
18000	595.72	398.13	255.66	213.15	195.07	186.27	181.70	179.25
19000	628.81	420.25	269.86	224.99	205.91	196.62	191.79	189.21
20000	661.91	442.37	284.06	236.83	216.75	206.96	201.89	199.16
21000	695.00	464.49	298.27	248.67	227.58	217.31	211.98	209.12
22000	728.10	486.61	312.47	260.51	238.42	227.66	222.08	219.08
23000	761.19	508.73	326.67	272.36	249.26	238.01	232.17	229.04
24000	794.29	530.84	340.88	284.20	260.09	248.36	242.26	239.00
25000	827.38	552.96	355.08	296.04	270.93	258.70	252.36	248.95
26000	860.48	575.08	369.28	307.88	281.77	269.05	262.45	258.91
27000	893.57	597.20	383.48	319.72	292.61	279.40	272.55	268.87
28000	926.67	619.32	397.69	331.56	303.44	289.75	282.64	278.83
29000	959.76	641.44	411.89	343.40	314.28	300.10	292.73	288.79
30000	992.86	663.55	426.09	355.24	325.12	310.44	302.83	298.74
31000	1025.95	685.67	440.30	367.09	335.95	320.79	312.92	308.70
32000	1059.05	707.79	454.50	378.93	346.79	331.14	323.02	318.66
33000	1092.14	729.91	468.70	390.77	357.63	341.49	333.11	328.62
34000	1125.24	752.03	482.91	402.61	368.47	351.84	343.20	338.57
35000	1158.33	774.15	497.11	414.45	379.30	362.18	353.30	348.53
36000	1191.43	796.26	511.31	426.29	390.14	372.53	363.39	358.49
37000	1224.52	818.38	525.51	438.13	400.98	382.88	373.49	368.45
38000	1257.62	840.50	539.72	449.97	411.81	393.23	383.58	378.41
39000	1290.71	862.62	553.92	461.82	422.65	403.58	393.67	388.36
40000	1323.81	884.74	568.12	473.66	433.49	413.92	403.77	398.32

MONTHLY AMORTIZING PAYMENTS

AMOUNT OF LOAN	NUMBER OF YEARS IN TERM						
	10	15	20	25	30	35	40
41000	582.33	485.50	444.32	424.27	413.86	408.28	405.23
42000	596.53	497.34	455.16	434.62	423.96	418.24	415.12
43000	610.73	509.18	466.00	444.97	434.05	428.20	425.00
44000	624.93	521.02	476.84	455.32	444.15	438.15	434.89
45000	639.14	532.86	487.67	465.66	454.24	448.11	444.77
46000	653.34	544.71	498.51	476.01	464.33	458.07	454.65
47000	667.54	556.55	509.35	486.36	474.43	468.03	464.54
48000	681.75	568.39	520.18	496.71	484.52	477.99	474.42
49000	695.95	580.23	531.02	507.06	494.62	487.94	484.30
50000	710.15	592.07	541.86	517.40	504.71	497.90	494.19
51000	724.36	603.91	552.70	527.75	514.80	507.86	504.07
52000	738.56	615.75	563.53	538.10	524.90	517.82	513.95
53000	752.76	627.59	574.37	548.45	534.99	527.78	523.84
54000	766.96	639.44	585.21	558.80	545.09	537.73	533.72
55000	781.17	651.28	596.04	569.14	555.18	547.69	543.61
56000	795.37	663.12	606.88	579.49	565.27	557.65	553.49
57000	809.57	674.96	617.72	589.84	575.37	567.61	563.37
58000	823.78	686.80	628.56	600.19	585.46	577.57	573.26
59000	837.98	698.64	639.39	610.54	595.56	587.52	583.14
60000	852.18	710.48	650.23	620.88	605.65	597.48	593.02
61000	866.38	722.33	661.07	631.23	615.74	607.44	602.91
62000	880.59	734.17	671.90	641.58	625.84	617.40	612.79
63000	894.79	746.01	682.74	651.93	635.93	627.36	622.67
64000	908.99	757.85	693.58	662.28	646.03	637.31	632.56
65000	923.20	769.69	704.41	672.62	656.12	647.27	642.44
66000	937.40	781.53	715.25	682.97	666.22	657.23	652.33
67000	951.60	793.37	726.09	693.32	676.31	667.19	662.21
68000	965.81	805.21	736.93	703.67	686.40	677.14	672.09
69000	980.01	817.06	747.76	714.02	696.50	687.10	681.98
70000	994.21	828.90	758.60	724.36	706.59	697.06	691.86
71000	1008.41	840.74	769.44	734.71	716.69	707.02	701.74
72000	1022.62	852.58	780.27	745.06	726.78	716.98	711.63
73000	1036.82	864.42	791.11	755.41	736.87	726.93	721.51
74000	1051.02	876.26	801.95	765.76	746.97	736.89	731.39
75000	1065.23	888.10	812.79	776.10	757.06	746.85	741.28
76000	1079.43	899.94	823.62	786.45	767.16	756.81	751.16
77000	1093.63	911.79	834.46	796.80	777.25	766.77	761.05
78000	1107.83	923.63	845.30	807.15	787.34	776.72	770.93
79000	1122.04	935.47	856.13	817.50	797.44	786.68	780.81
80000	1136.24	947.31	866.97	827.84	807.53	796.64	790.70
81000	1150.44	959.15	877.81	838.19	817.63	806.60	800.58
82000	1164.65	970.99	888.64	848.54	827.72	816.56	810.46
83000	1178.85	982.83	899.48	858.89	837.82	826.51	820.35
84000	1193.05	994.68	910.32	869.24	847.91	836.47	830.23
85000	1207.26	1006.52	921.16	879.58	858.00	846.43	840.11
86000	1221.46	1018.36	931.99	889.93	868.10	856.39	850.00
87000	1235.66	1030.20	942.83	900.28	878.19	866.35	859.88
88000	1249.86	1042.04	953.67	910.63	888.29	876.30	869.77
89000	1264.07	1053.88	964.50	920.98	898.38	886.26	879.65
90000	1278.27	1065.72	975.34	931.32	908.47	896.22	889.53
91000	1292.47	1077.56	986.18	941.67	918.57	906.18	899.42
92000	1306.68	1089.41	997.02	952.02	928.66	916.14	909.30
93000	1320.88	1101.25	1007.85	962.37	938.76	926.09	919.18
94000	1335.08	1113.09	1018.69	972.72	948.85	936.05	929.07
95000	1349.28	1124.93	1029.53	983.06	958.94	946.01	938.95
96000	1363.49	1136.77	1040.36	993.41	969.04	955.97	948.83
97000	1377.69	1148.61	1051.20	1003.76	979.13	965.93	958.72
98000	1391.89	1160.45	1062.04	1014.11	989.23	975.88	968.60
99000	1406.10	1172.30	1072.87	1024.46	999.32	985.84	978.49
100000	1420.30	1184.14	1083.71	1034.80	1009.41	995.80	988.37

12%

MONTHLY AMORTIZING PAYMENTS

AMOUNT OF LOAN	NUMBER OF YEARS IN TERM							
	3	5	10	15	20	25	30	35
10	.34	.23	.15	.13	.12	.11	.11	.11
20	.67	.45	.29	.25	.23	.22	.21	.21
25	.84	.56	.36	.31	.28	.27	.26	.26
30	1.00	.67	.44	.37	.34	.32	.31	.31
40	1.33	.89	.58	.49	.45	.43	.42	.41
50	1.67	1.12	.72	.61	.56	.53	.52	.51
60	2.00	1.34	.87	.73	.67	.64	.62	.61
70	2.33	1.56	1.01	.85	.78	.74	.73	.72
75	2.50	1.67	1.08	.91	.83	.79	.78	.77
80	2.66	1.78	1.15	.97	.89	.85	.83	.82
90	2.99	2.01	1.30	1.09	1.00	.95	.93	.92
100	3.33	2.23	1.44	1.21	1.11	1.06	1.03	1.02
200	6.65	4.45	2.87	2.41	2.21	2.11	2.06	2.04
300	9.97	6.68	4.31	3.61	3.31	3.16	3.09	3.05
400	13.29	8.90	5.74	4.81	4.41	4.22	4.12	4.07
500	16.61	11.13	7.18	6.01	5.51	5.27	5.15	5.08
600	19.93	13.35	8.61	7.21	6.61	6.32	6.18	6.10
700	23.26	15.58	10.05	8.41	7.71	7.38	7.21	7.11
800	26.58	17.80	11.48	9.61	8.81	8.43	8.23	8.13
900	29.90	20.03	12.92	10.81	9.91	9.48	9.26	9.14
1000	33.22	22.25	14.35	12.01	11.02	10.54	10.29	10.16
2000	66.43	44.49	28.70	24.01	22.03	21.07	20.58	20.32
3000	99.65	66.74	43.05	36.01	33.04	31.60	30.86	30.47
4000	132.86	88.98	57.39	48.01	44.05	42.13	41.15	40.63
5000	166.08	111.23	71.74	60.01	55.06	52.67	51.44	50.78
6000	199.29	133.47	86.09	72.02	66.07	63.20	61.72	60.94
7000	232.51	155.72	100.43	84.02	77.08	73.73	72.01	71.09
8000	265.72	177.96	114.78	96.02	88.09	84.26	82.29	81.25
9000	298.93	200.21	129.13	108.02	99.10	94.80	92.58	91.40
10000	332.15	222.45	143.48	120.02	110.11	105.33	102.87	101.56
11000	365.36	244.69	157.82	132.02	121.12	115.86	113.15	111.72
12000	398.58	266.94	172.17	144.03	132.14	126.39	123.44	121.87
13000	431.79	289.18	186.52	156.03	143.15	136.92	133.72	132.03
14000	465.01	311.43	200.86	168.03	154.16	147.46	144.01	142.18
15000	498.22	333.67	215.21	180.03	165.17	157.99	154.30	152.34
16000	531.43	355.92	229.56	192.03	176.18	168.52	164.58	162.49
17000	564.65	378.16	243.91	204.03	187.19	179.05	174.87	172.65
18000	597.86	400.41	258.25	216.04	198.20	189.59	185.16	182.80
19000	631.08	422.65	272.60	228.04	209.21	200.12	195.44	192.96
20000	664.29	444.89	286.95	240.04	220.22	210.65	205.73	203.11
21000	697.51	467.14	301.29	252.04	231.23	221.18	216.01	213.27
22000	730.72	489.38	315.64	264.04	242.24	231.71	226.30	223.43
23000	763.93	511.63	329.99	276.04	253.25	242.25	236.59	233.58
24000	797.15	533.87	344.34	288.05	264.27	252.78	246.87	243.74
25000	830.36	556.12	358.68	300.05	275.28	263.31	257.16	253.89
26000	863.58	578.36	373.03	312.05	286.29	273.84	267.44	264.05
27000	896.79	600.61	387.38	324.05	297.30	284.38	277.73	274.20
28000	930.01	622.85	401.72	336.05	308.31	294.91	288.02	284.36
29000	963.22	645.09	416.07	348.05	319.32	305.44	298.30	294.51
30000	996.43	667.34	430.42	360.06	330.33	315.97	308.59	304.67
31000	1029.65	689.58	444.76	372.06	341.34	326.50	318.87	314.83
32000	1062.86	711.83	459.11	384.06	352.35	337.04	329.16	324.98
33000	1096.08	734.07	473.46	396.06	363.36	347.57	339.45	335.14
34000	1129.29	756.32	487.81	408.06	374.37	358.10	349.73	345.29
35000	1162.51	778.56	502.15	420.06	385.39	368.63	360.02	355.45
36000	1195.72	800.81	516.50	432.07	396.40	379.17	370.31	365.60
37000	1228.93	823.05	530.85	444.07	407.41	389.70	380.59	375.76
38000	1262.15	845.29	545.19	456.07	418.42	400.23	390.88	385.91
39000	1295.36	867.54	559.54	468.07	429.43	410.76	401.16	396.07
40000	1328.58	889.78	573.89	480.07	440.44	421.29	411.45	406.22

AMOUNT OF LOAN	NUMBER OF YEARS IN TERM						
	10	15	20	25	30	35	40
41000	588.24	492.07	451.45	431.83	421.74	416.38	413.49
42000	602.58	504.08	462.46	442.36	432.02	426.54	423.57
43000	616.93	516.08	473.47	452.89	442.31	436.69	433.66
44000	631.28	528.08	484.48	463.42	452.59	446.85	443.74
45000	645.62	540.08	495.49	473.96	462.88	457.00	453.83
46000	659.97	552.08	506.50	484.49	473.17	467.16	463.91
47000	674.32	564.08	517.52	495.02	483.45	477.31	474.00
48000	688.67	576.09	528.53	505.55	493.74	487.47	484.08
49000	703.01	588.09	539.54	516.08	504.03	497.62	494.17
50000	717.36	600.09	550.55	526.62	514.31	507.78	504.25
51000	731.71	612.09	561.56	537.15	524.60	517.94	514.34
52000	746.05	624.09	572.57	547.68	534.88	528.09	524.42
53000	760.40	636.09	583.58	558.21	545.17	538.25	534.51
54000	774.75	648.10	594.59	568.75	555.46	548.40	544.59
55000	789.10	660.10	605.60	579.28	565.74	558.56	554.68
56000	803.44	672.10	616.61	589.81	576.03	568.71	564.76
57000	817.79	684.10	627.62	600.34	586.31	578.87	574.85
58000	832.14	696.10	638.63	610.88	596.60	589.02	584.93
59000	846.48	708.10	649.65	621.41	606.89	599.18	595.02
60000	860.83	720.11	660.66	631.94	617.17	609.33	605.10
61000	875.18	732.11	671.67	642.47	627.46	619.49	615.19
62000	889.52	744.11	682.68	653.00	637.74	629.65	625.27
63000	903.87	756.11	693.69	663.54	648.03	639.80	635.36
64000	918.22	768.11	704.70	674.07	658.32	649.96	645.44
65000	932.57	780.11	715.71	684.60	668.60	660.11	655.53
66000	946.91	792.12	726.72	695.13	678.89	670.27	665.61
67000	961.26	804.12	737.73	705.67	689.18	680.42	675.70
68000	975.61	816.12	748.74	716.20	699.46	690.58	685.78
69000	989.95	828.12	759.75	726.73	709.75	700.73	695.87
70000	1004.30	840.12	770.77	737.26	720.03	710.89	705.95
71000	1018.65	852.12	781.78	747.79	730.32	721.05	716.04
72000	1033.00	864.13	792.79	758.33	740.61	731.20	726.12
73000	1047.34	876.13	803.80	768.86	750.89	741.36	736.21
74000	1061.69	888.13	814.81	779.39	761.18	751.51	746.29
75000	1076.04	900.13	825.82	789.92	771.46	761.67	756.38
76000	1090.38	912.13	836.83	800.46	781.75	771.82	766.46
77000	1104.73	924.13	847.84	810.99	792.04	781.98	776.55
78000	1119.08	936.14	858.85	821.52	802.32	792.13	786.63
79000	1133.43	948.14	869.86	832.05	812.61	802.29	796.72
80000	1147.77	960.14	880.87	842.58	822.90	812.44	806.80
81000	1162.12	972.14	891.88	853.12	833.18	822.60	816.89
82000	1176.47	984.14	902.90	863.65	843.47	832.76	826.97
83000	1190.81	996.14	913.91	874.18	853.75	842.91	837.06
84000	1205.16	1008.15	924.92	884.71	864.04	853.07	847.14
85000	1219.51	1020.15	935.93	895.25	874.33	863.22	857.23
86000	1233.86	1032.15	946.94	905.78	884.61	873.38	867.31
87000	1248.20	1044.15	957.95	916.31	894.90	883.53	877.40
88000	1262.55	1056.15	968.96	926.84	905.18	893.69	887.48
89000	1276.90	1068.15	979.97	937.37	915.47	903.84	897.57
90000	1291.24	1080.16	990.98	947.91	925.76	914.00	907.65
91000	1305.59	1092.16	1001.99	958.44	936.04	924.16	917.74
92000	1319.94	1104.16	1013.00	968.97	946.33	934.31	927.82
93000	1334.28	1116.16	1024.02	979.50	956.61	944.47	937.91
94000	1348.63	1128.16	1035.03	990.04	966.90	954.62	947.99
95000	1362.98	1140.16	1046.04	1000.57	977.19	964.78	958.08
96000	1377.33	1152.17	1057.05	1011.10	987.47	974.93	968.16
97000	1391.67	1164.17	1068.06	1021.63	997.76	985.09	978.25
98000	1406.02	1176.17	1079.07	1032.16	1008.05	995.24	988.33
99000	1420.37	1188.17	1090.08	1042.70	1018.33	1005.40	998.42
100000	1434.71	1200.17	1101.09	1053.23	1028.62	1015.55	1008.50

CONSTANT ANNUAL PERCENT

The Annual Debt Service needed to Amortize a Loan Amount

YEARS	6.00%	6.25%	6.50%	6.60%	6.75%	7.00%	7.20%	7.25%
1	103.28	103.42	103.56	103.61	103.69	103.83	103.94	103.97
2	53.18	53.32	53.46	53.51	53.59	53.73	53.84	53.86
3	36.51	36.64	36.78	36.83	36.92	37.05	37.16	37.19
4	28.18	28.32	28.46	28.51	28.60	28.74	28.85	28.87
5	23.20	23.34	23.48	23.54	23.62	23.76	23.87	23.90
6	19.89	20.03	20.17	20.23	20.32	20.46	20.57	20.60
7	17.53	17.67	17.82	17.88	17.96	18.11	18.23	18.26
8	15.77	15.92	16.06	16.12	16.21	16.36	16.48	16.51
9	14.41	14.56	14.71	14.77	14.86	15.01	15.13	15.16
10	13.32	13.47	13.63	13.69	13.78	13.93	14.06	14.09
11	12.44	12.59	12.75	12.81	12.90	13.06	13.19	13.22
12	11.71	11.87	12.02	12.09	12.18	12.34	12.47	12.50
13	11.10	11.25	11.41	11.48	11.57	11.74	11.87	11.90
14	10.57	10.74	10.90	10.96	11.06	11.22	11.36	11.39
15	10.13	10.29	10.45	10.52	10.62	10.79	10.92	10.95
16	9.74	9.90	10.07	10.14	10.24	10.41	10.54	10.58
17	9.40	9.56	9.73	9.80	9.90	10.08	10.21	10.25
18	9.10	9.27	9.44	9.51	9.61	9.79	9.93	9.96
19	8.83	9.00	9.18	9.25	9.35	9.53	9.67	9.71
20	8.60	8.77	8.95	9.02	9.12	9.30	9.45	9.48
21	8.39	8.56	8.74	8.81	8.92	9.10	9.25	9.28
22	8.20	8.38	8.56	8.63	8.74	8.92	9.07	9.11
23	8.03	8.21	8.39	8.46	8.57	8.76	8.91	8.95
24	7.87	8.05	8.24	8.31	8.42	8.61	8.77	8.80
25	7.73	7.92	8.10	8.18	8.29	8.48	8.64	8.67
26	7.60	7.79	7.98	8.05	8.17	8.36	8.52	8.56
28	7.38	7.57	7.76	7.84	7.96	8.16	8.31	8.35
30	7.19	7.39	7.58	7.66	7.78	7.98	8.15	8.19
35	6.84	7.04	7.25	7.33	7.46	7.67	7.84	7.88
40	6.60	6.81	7.03	7.11	7.24	7.46	7.63	7.68

YEARS	7.50%	7.75%	7.80%	8.00%	8.25%	8.40%	8.50%	8.75%
1	104.11	104.25	104.28	104.39	104.52	104.61	104.66	104.80
2	54.00	54.14	54.16	54.27	54.41	54.49	54.55	54.68
3	37.33	37.47	37.49	37.60	37.74	37.83	37.88	38.02
4	29.01	29.15	29.18	29.30	29.44	29.52	29.58	29.72
5	24.05	24.19	24.22	24.33	24.48	24.56	24.62	24.76
6	20.75	20.89	20.92	21.04	21.19	21.28	21.33	21.48
7	18.41	18.55	18.58	18.70	18.85	18.94	19.00	19.15
8	16.66	16.81	16.84	16.96	17.12	17.21	17.27	17.43
9	15.31	15.47	15.50	15.62	15.78	15.87	15.94	16.09
10	14.24	14.40	14.43	14.56	14.72	14.81	14.88	15.04
11	13.38	13.54	13.57	13.70	13.86	13.96	14.02	14.19
12	12.66	12.83	12.86	12.99	13.15	13.25	13.32	13.49
13	12.06	12.23	12.26	12.40	12.56	12.67	12.73	12.90
14	11.56	11.73	11.76	11.90	12.07	12.17	12.24	12.41
15	11.12	11.30	11.33	11.47	11.64	11.75	11.82	11.99
16	10.75	10.92	10.96	11.10	11.28	11.38	11.45	11.63
17	10.42	10.60	10.64	10.78	10.96	11.07	11.14	11.32
18	10.14	10.32	10.35	10.50	10.68	10.79	10.87	11.05
19	9.89	10.07	10.11	10.25	10.44	10.55	10.63	10.81
20	9.67	9.85	9.89	10.04	10.22	10.34	10.41	10.60
21	9.47	9.66	9.69	9.85	10.04	10.15	10.23	10.42
22	9.29	9.48	9.52	9.67	9.87	9.98	10.06	10.26
23	9.14	9.33	9.37	9.52	9.72	9.83	9.91	10.11
24	9.00	9.19	9.23	9.38	9.58	9.70	9.78	9.98
25	8.87	9.06	9.10	9.26	9.46	9.58	9.66	9.87
26	8.75	8.95	8.99	9.15	9.35	9.47	9.56	9.76
28	8.55	8.76	8.80	8.96	9.17	9.29	9.37	9.58
30	8.39	8.60	8.64	8.81	9.02	9.14	9.23	9.44
35	8.09	8.31	8.35	8.52	8.74	8.87	8.96	9.18
40	7.90	8.12	8.16	8.34	8.57	8.71	8.80	9.03

CONSTANT ANNUAL PERCENT

The Annual Debt Service needed to Amortize
a Loan Amount

YEARS	RATE							
	9.00%	9.25%	9.50%	9.60%	9.75%	10.00%	10.20%	10.25%
1	104.94	105.08	105.22	105.28	105.36	105.50	105.61	105.64
2	54.82	54.96	55.10	55.15	55.24	55.37	55.48	55.51
3	38.16	38.30	38.44	38.50	38.58	38.72	38.83	38.86
4	29.86	30.00	30.15	30.21	30.29	30.44	30.55	30.58
5	24.91	25.06	25.20	25.26	25.35	25.50	25.61	25.64
6	21.63	21.78	21.93	21.99	22.08	22.23	22.35	22.38
7	19.31	19.46	19.61	19.67	19.77	19.92	20.05	20.08
8	17.58	17.74	17.89	17.96	18.05	18.21	18.34	18.37
9	16.25	16.41	16.57	16.64	16.73	16.89	17.02	17.06
10	15.20	15.36	15.53	15.59	15.69	15.86	15.99	16.02
11	14.35	14.52	14.69	14.75	14.85	15.02	15.16	15.19
12	13.66	13.83	14.00	14.07	14.17	14.34	14.48	14.51
13	13.08	13.25	13.42	13.49	13.60	13.77	13.92	13.95
14	12.59	12.76	12.94	13.01	13.12	13.30	13.44	13.48
15	12.17	12.35	12.53	12.60	12.71	12.90	13.04	13.08
16	11.81	12.00	12.18	12.25	12.36	12.55	12.70	12.74
17	11.51	11.69	11.88	11.95	12.07	12.25	12.41	12.45
18	11.24	11.43	11.61	11.69	11.81	12.00	12.15	12.19
19	11.00	11.19	11.39	11.46	11.58	11.78	11.93	11.97
20	10.80	10.99	11.19	11.26	11.38	11.58	11.74	11.78
21	10.61	10.81	11.01	11.09	11.21	11.41	11.57	11.61
22	10.45	10.65	10.85	10.93	11.06	11.26	11.42	11.46
23	10.31	10.51	10.72	10.80	10.92	11.13	11.29	11.33
24	10.18	10.39	10.59	10.68	10.80	11.01	11.18	11.22
25	10.07	10.28	10.48	10.57	10.69	10.90	11.07	11.12
26	9.97	10.18	10.39	10.47	10.60	10.81	10.98	11.03
28	9.80	10.01	10.22	10.31	10.44	10.66	10.83	10.87
30	9.66	9.87	10.09	10.18	10.31	10.53	10.71	10.75
35	9.41	9.63	9.86	9.95	10.09	10.32	10.50	10.55
40	9.26	9.49	9.72	9.81	9.95	10.19	10.38	10.43

YEARS	RATE							
	10.50%	10.75%	10.80%	11.00%	11.25%	11.50%	11.75%	12.00%
1	105.78	105.92	105.95	106.06	106.20	106.34	106.48	106.62
2	55.65	55.79	55.82	55.93	56.07	56.21	56.35	56.49
3	39.00	39.14	39.17	39.29	39.43	39.57	39.71	39.86
4	30.72	30.87	30.90	31.01	31.16	31.31	31.45	31.60
5	25.79	25.94	25.97	26.09	26.24	26.39	26.54	26.69
6	22.53	22.69	22.72	22.84	22.99	23.15	23.30	23.46
7	20.23	20.39	20.42	20.55	20.71	20.86	21.02	21.18
8	18.53	18.69	18.72	18.85	19.01	19.18	19.34	19.50
9	17.22	17.39	17.42	17.55	17.72	17.88	18.05	18.22
10	16.19	16.36	16.39	16.53	16.70	16.87	17.04	17.22
11	15.37	15.54	15.57	15.71	15.89	16.06	16.24	16.41
12	14.69	14.87	14.90	15.04	15.22	15.40	15.58	15.76
13	14.13	14.31	14.35	14.49	14.67	14.86	15.04	15.22
14	13.66	13.84	13.88	14.03	14.21	14.40	14.59	14.78
15	13.26	13.45	13.49	13.64	13.83	14.02	14.21	14.40
16	12.93	13.12	13.15	13.31	13.50	13.69	13.89	14.08
17	12.64	12.83	12.87	13.02	13.22	13.42	13.62	13.81
18	12.39	12.58	12.62	12.78	12.98	13.18	13.38	13.58
19	12.17	12.37	12.41	12.57	12.77	12.97	13.18	13.38
20	11.98	12.18	12.22	12.39	12.59	12.80	13.00	13.21
21	11.82	12.02	12.06	12.23	12.43	12.64	12.85	13.06
22	11.67	11.88	11.92	12.09	12.30	12.51	12.72	12.94
23	11.54	11.75	11.79	11.96	12.18	12.39	12.61	12.82
24	11.43	11.64	11.69	11.86	12.07	12.29	12.51	12.72
25	11.33	11.55	11.59	11.76	11.98	12.20	12.42	12.64
26	11.24	11.46	11.50	11.68	11.90	12.12	12.34	12.56
28	11.09	11.32	11.36	11.54	11.76	11.99	12.21	12.44
30	10.98	11.20	11.25	11.43	11.66	11.88	12.11	12.34
35	10.78	11.01	11.06	11.24	11.48	11.71	11.95	12.19
40	10.66	10.90	10.95	11.14	11.38	11.62	11.86	12.10

MONTHLY PAYMENT NEEDED TO AMORTIZE A $1000 LOAN

YEARS	4.00%	4.25%	4.50%	4.75%	5.00%	5.25%	5.50%	5.75%
1	85.15	85.27	85.38	85.50	85.61	85.73	85.84	85.96
2	43.43	43.54	43.65	43.76	43.88	43.99	44.10	44.21
3	29.53	29.64	29.75	29.86	29.98	30.09	30.20	30.31
4	22.58	22.70	22.81	22.92	23.03	23.15	23.26	23.38
5	18.42	18.53	18.65	18.76	18.88	18.99	19.11	19.22
6	15.65	15.76	15.88	15.99	16.11	16.23	16.34	16.46
7	13.67	13.79	13.91	14.02	14.14	14.26	14.38	14.49
8	12.19	12.31	12.43	12.55	12.66	12.78	12.90	13.03
9	11.05	11.16	11.28	11.40	11.52	11.64	11.76	11.89
10	10.13	10.25	10.37	10.49	10.61	10.73	10.86	10.98
11	9.38	9.50	9.62	9.75	9.87	9.99	10.12	10.25
12	8.76	8.88	9.01	9.13	9.25	9.38	9.51	9.63
13	8.24	8.36	8.48	8.61	8.74	8.86	8.99	9.12
14	7.79	7.91	8.04	8.17	8.29	8.42	8.55	8.68
15	7.40	7.53	7.65	7.78	7.91	8.04	8.18	8.31
16	7.06	7.19	7.32	7.45	7.58	7.71	7.85	7.98
17	6.77	6.90	7.03	7.16	7.29	7.43	7.56	7.70
18	6.51	6.64	6.77	6.90	7.04	7.17	7.31	7.45
19	6.27	6.40	6.54	6.67	6.81	6.95	7.08	7.22
20	6.06	6.20	6.33	6.47	6.60	6.74	6.88	7.03
21	5.88	6.01	6.15	6.28	6.42	6.56	6.70	6.85
22	5.71	5.84	5.98	6.12	6.26	6.40	6.54	6.69
23	5.55	5.69	5.83	5.97	6.11	6.25	6.40	6.54
24	5.41	5.55	5.69	5.83	5.97	6.12	6.27	6.41
25	5.28	5.42	5.56	5.71	5.85	6.00	6.15	6.30
26	5.17	5.31	5.45	5.59	5.74	5.89	6.04	6.19
28	4.96	5.10	5.24	5.39	5.54	5.69	5.84	6.00
30	4.78	4.92	5.07	5.22	5.37	5.53	5.68	5.84
35	4.43	4.58	4.74	4.89	5.05	5.21	5.38	5.54
40	4.18	4.34	4.50	4.66	4.83	4.99	5.16	5.33

YEARS	6.00%	6.10%	6.20%	6.25%	6.30%	6.40%	6.50%	6.60%
1	86.07	86.12	86.16	86.19	86.21	86.26	86.30	86.35
2	44.33	44.37	44.42	44.44	44.46	44.51	44.55	44.60
3	30.43	30.47	30.52	30.54	30.56	30.61	30.65	30.70
4	23.49	23.54	23.58	23.60	23.63	23.67	23.72	23.77
5	19.34	19.38	19.43	19.45	19.48	19.52	19.57	19.62
6	16.58	16.63	16.67	16.70	16.72	16.77	16.81	16.86
7	14.61	14.66	14.71	14.73	14.76	14.81	14.85	14.90
8	13.15	13.20	13.24	13.27	13.29	13.34	13.39	13.44
9	12.01	12.06	12.11	12.13	12.16	12.21	12.26	12.31
10	11.11	11.16	11.21	11.23	11.26	11.31	11.36	11.41
11	10.37	10.42	10.47	10.50	10.53	10.58	10.63	10.68
12	9.76	9.82	9.87	9.89	9.92	9.97	10.02	10.08
13	9.25	9.30	9.36	9.38	9.41	9.46	9.52	9.57
14	8.82	8.87	8.92	8.95	8.98	9.03	9.09	9.14
15	8.44	8.50	8.55	8.58	8.61	8.66	8.72	8.77
16	8.12	8.17	8.23	8.26	8.28	8.34	8.40	8.45
17	7.84	7.89	7.95	7.98	8.00	8.06	8.12	8.17
18	7.59	7.64	7.70	7.73	7.76	7.81	7.87	7.93
19	7.37	7.42	7.48	7.51	7.54	7.60	7.65	7.71
20	7.17	7.23	7.29	7.31	7.34	7.40	7.46	7.52
21	6.99	7.05	7.11	7.14	7.17	7.23	7.29	7.35
22	6.84	6.89	6.95	6.98	7.01	7.07	7.13	7.19
23	6.69	6.75	6.81	6.84	6.87	6.93	7.00	7.06
24	6.56	6.63	6.69	6.72	6.75	6.81	6.87	6.93
25	6.45	6.51	6.57	6.60	6.63	6.69	6.76	6.82
26	6.34	6.40	6.47	6.50	6.53	6.59	6.65	6.72
28	6.16	6.22	6.28	6.31	6.35	6.41	6.48	6.54
30	6.00	6.06	6.13	6.16	6.19	6.26	6.33	6.39
35	5.71	5.77	5.84	5.88	5.91	5.98	6.05	6.12
40	5.51	5.58	5.65	5.68	5.72	5.79	5.86	5.93

MONTHLY PAYMENT NEEDED TO AMORTIZE A $1000 LOAN

YEARS	RATE							
	6.70%	6.75%	6.80%	6.90%	7.00%	7.10%	7.20%	7.25%
1	86.39	86.42	86.44	86.49	86.53	86.58	86.62	86.65
2	44.64	44.66	44.69	44.73	44.78	44.82	44.87	44.89
3	30.75	30.77	30.79	30.84	30.88	30.93	30.97	31.00
4	23.81	23.84	23.86	23.90	23.95	24.00	24.04	24.07
5	19.66	19.69	19.71	19.76	19.81	19.85	19.90	19.92
6	16.91	16.93	16.96	17.01	17.05	17.10	17.15	17.17
7	14.95	14.98	15.00	15.05	15.10	15.15	15.20	15.22
8	13.49	13.51	13.54	13.59	13.64	13.69	13.74	13.76
9	12.36	12.39	12.41	12.46	12.51	12.56	12.61	12.64
10	11.46	11.49	11.51	11.56	11.62	11.67	11.72	11.75
11	10.73	10.76	10.78	10.84	10.89	10.94	10.99	11.02
12	10.13	10.16	10.18	10.24	10.29	10.34	10.40	10.42
13	9.62	9.65	9.68	9.73	9.79	9.84	9.89	9.92
14	9.19	9.22	9.25	9.30	9.36	9.41	9.47	9.50
15	8.83	8.85	8.88	8.94	8.99	9.05	9.11	9.13
16	8.51	8.54	8.56	8.62	8.68	8.73	8.79	8.82
17	8.23	8.26	8.29	8.34	8.40	8.46	8.52	8.55
18	7.99	8.01	8.04	8.10	8.16	8.22	8.28	8.31
19	7.77	7.80	7.83	7.89	7.95	8.01	8.07	8.10
20	7.58	7.61	7.64	7.70	7.76	7.82	7.88	7.91
21	7.41	7.44	7.47	7.53	7.59	7.65	7.71	7.74
22	7.26	7.29	7.32	7.38	7.44	7.50	7.56	7.59
23	7.12	7.15	7.18	7.24	7.30	7.37	7.43	7.46
24	6.99	7.03	7.06	7.12	7.18	7.25	7.31	7.34
25	6.88	6.91	6.95	7.01	7.07	7.14	7.20	7.23
26	6.78	6.81	6.84	6.91	6.97	7.04	7.10	7.14
28	6.60	6.64	6.67	6.74	6.80	6.87	6.93	6.97
30	6.46	6.49	6.52	6.59	6.66	6.73	6.79	6.83
35	6.18	6.22	6.25	6.32	6.39	6.46	6.53	6.57
40	6.00	6.04	6.07	6.15	6.22	6.29	6.37	6.40

YEARS	RATE							
	7.30%	7.40%	7.50%	7.60%	7.70%	7.75%	7.80%	7.90%
1	86.67	86.72	86.76	86.81	86.85	86.88	86.90	86.95
2	44.91	44.96	45.00	45.05	45.10	45.12	45.14	45.19
3	31.02	31.07	31.11	31.16	31.20	31.23	31.25	31.30
4	24.09	24.14	24.18	24.23	24.28	24.30	24.32	24.37
5	19.95	20.00	20.04	20.09	20.14	20.16	20.19	20.23
6	17.20	17.25	17.30	17.34	17.39	17.42	17.44	17.49
7	15.24	15.29	15.34	15.39	15.44	15.47	15.49	15.54
8	13.79	13.84	13.89	13.94	13.99	14.01	14.04	14.09
9	12.66	12.71	12.77	12.82	12.87	12.89	12.92	12.97
10	11.77	11.82	11.88	11.93	11.98	12.01	12.03	12.08
11	11.05	11.10	11.15	11.21	11.26	11.29	11.31	11.37
12	10.45	10.50	10.56	10.61	10.67	10.69	10.72	10.77
13	9.95	10.00	10.06	10.11	10.17	10.20	10.22	10.28
14	9.52	9.58	9.64	9.69	9.75	9.78	9.80	9.86
15	9.16	9.22	9.28	9.33	9.39	9.42	9.45	9.50
16	8.85	8.91	8.96	9.02	9.08	9.11	9.14	9.20
17	8.58	8.63	8.69	8.75	8.81	8.84	8.87	8.93
18	8.34	8.40	8.45	8.51	8.57	8.60	8.63	8.69
19	8.13	8.19	8.25	8.31	8.37	8.40	8.43	8.49
20	7.94	8.00	8.06	8.12	8.18	8.21	8.25	8.31
21	7.77	7.83	7.90	7.96	8.02	8.05	8.08	8.15
22	7.63	7.69	7.75	7.81	7.88	7.91	7.94	8.00
23	7.49	7.56	7.62	7.68	7.75	7.78	7.81	7.87
24	7.37	7.44	7.50	7.57	7.63	7.66	7.70	7.76
25	7.27	7.33	7.39	7.46	7.53	7.56	7.59	7.66
26	7.17	7.23	7.30	7.36	7.43	7.46	7.50	7.56
28	7.00	7.07	7.13	7.20	7.27	7.30	7.34	7.40
30	6.86	6.93	7.00	7.07	7.13	7.17	7.20	7.27
35	6.61	6.68	6.75	6.82	6.89	6.93	6.96	7.04
40	6.44	6.51	6.59	6.66	6.73	6.77	6.81	6.88

MONTHLY PAYMENT NEEDED TO
AMORTIZE A $1000 LOAN

YEARS	RATE							
	8.00%	8.10%	8.20%	8.25%	8.30%	8.40%	8.50%	8.60%
1	86.99	87.04	87.09	87.11	87.13	87.18	87.22	87.27
2	45.23	45.28	45.32	45.35	45.37	45.41	45.46	45.51
3	31.34	31.39	31.43	31.46	31.48	31.53	31.57	31.62
4	24.42	24.46	24.51	24.54	24.56	24.61	24.65	24.70
5	20.28	20.33	20.38	20.40	20.43	20.47	20.52	20.57
6	17.54	17.59	17.64	17.66	17.69	17.73	17.78	17.83
7	15.59	15.64	15.69	15.72	15.74	15.79	15.84	15.89
8	14.14	14.19	14.24	14.27	14.29	14.35	14.40	14.45
9	13.02	13.08	13.13	13.15	13.18	13.23	13.28	13.34
10	12.14	12.19	12.24	12.27	12.30	12.35	12.40	12.46
11	11.42	11.47	11.53	11.56	11.58	11.64	11.69	11.75
12	10.83	10.88	10.94	10.97	10.99	11.05	11.11	11.16
13	10.34	10.39	10.45	10.48	10.50	10.56	10.62	10.67
14	9.92	9.98	10.03	10.06	10.09	10.15	10.20	10.26
15	9.56	9.62	9.68	9.71	9.74	9.79	9.85	9.91
16	9.25	9.31	9.37	9.40	9.43	9.49	9.55	9.61
17	8.99	9.05	9.11	9.14	9.17	9.23	9.29	9.35
18	8.75	8.82	8.88	8.91	8.94	9.00	9.06	9.12
19	8.55	8.61	8.67	8.70	8.74	8.80	8.86	8.92
20	8.37	8.43	8.49	8.53	8.56	8.62	8.68	8.75
21	8.21	8.27	8.34	8.37	8.40	8.46	8.53	8.59
22	8.07	8.13	8.20	8.23	8.26	8.32	8.39	8.45
23	7.94	8.00	8.07	8.10	8.13	8.20	8.27	8.33
24	7.83	7.89	7.96	7.99	8.02	8.09	8.16	8.22
25	7.72	7.79	7.86	7.89	7.92	7.99	8.06	8.12
26	7.63	7.70	7.77	7.80	7.83	7.90	7.97	8.04
28	7.47	7.54	7.61	7.64	7.68	7.75	7.82	7.89
30	7.34	7.41	7.48	7.52	7.55	7.62	7.69	7.77
35	7.11	7.18	7.25	7.29	7.33	7.40	7.47	7.55
40	6.96	7.03	7.11	7.15	7.18	7.26	7.34	7.41

YEARS	RATE							
	8.70%	8.75%	8.80%	8.90%	9.00%	9.10%	9.20%	9.25%
1	87.32	87.34	87.36	87.41	87.46	87.50	87.55	87.57
2	45.55	45.58	45.60	45.64	45.69	45.74	45.78	45.80
3	31.67	31.69	31.71	31.76	31.80	31.85	31.90	31.92
4	24.75	24.77	24.80	24.84	24.89	24.94	24.99	25.01
5	20.62	20.64	20.67	20.71	20.76	20.81	20.86	20.88
6	17.88	17.91	17.93	17.97	18.03	18.08	18.13	18.15
7	15.94	15.97	15.99	16.04	16.09	16.14	16.20	16.22
8	14.50	14.53	14.55	14.60	14.66	14.71	14.76	14.79
9	13.39	13.42	13.44	13.49	13.55	13.60	13.65	13.68
10	12.51	12.54	12.56	12.62	12.67	12.73	12.78	12.81
11	11.80	11.83	11.86	11.91	11.97	12.02	12.08	12.10
12	11.22	11.24	11.27	11.33	11.39	11.44	11.50	11.53
13	10.73	10.76	10.79	10.84	10.90	10.96	11.02	11.05
14	10.32	10.35	10.38	10.44	10.49	10.55	10.61	10.64
15	9.97	10.00	10.03	10.09	10.15	10.21	10.27	10.30
16	9.67	9.70	9.73	9.79	9.85	9.91	9.97	10.00
17	9.41	9.44	9.47	9.53	9.59	9.65	9.72	9.75
18	9.18	9.21	9.24	9.31	9.37	9.43	9.49	9.53
19	8.98	9.02	9.05	9.11	9.17	9.24	9.30	9.33
20	8.81	8.84	8.87	8.94	9.00	9.07	9.13	9.16
21	8.66	8.69	8.72	8.79	8.85	8.92	8.98	9.01
22	8.52	8.55	8.59	8.65	8.72	8.78	8.85	8.88
23	8.40	8.43	8.46	8.53	8.60	8.66	8.73	8.77
24	8.29	8.32	8.36	8.42	8.49	8.56	8.63	8.66
25	8.19	8.23	8.26	8.33	8.40	8.47	8.53	8.57
26	8.11	8.14	8.17	8.24	8.31	8.38	8.45	8.49
28	7.96	7.99	8.03	8.10	8.17	8.24	8.31	8.35
30	7.84	7.87	7.91	7.98	8.05	8.12	8.20	8.23
35	7.62	7.66	7.70	7.77	7.84	7.92	7.99	8.03
40	7.49	7.53	7.56	7.64	7.72	7.80	7.87	7.91

MONTHLY PAYMENT NEEDED TO AMORTIZE A $1000 LOAN

YEARS	9.30%	9.40%	9.50%	9.60%	9.70%	9.75%	9.80%	9.90%
1	87.60	87.64	87.69	87.73	87.78	87.80	87.83	87.87
2	45.83	45.87	45.92	45.97	46.01	46.03	46.06	46.10
3	31.94	31.99	32.04	32.08	32.13	32.15	32.18	32.23
4	25.03	25.08	25.13	25.18	25.22	25.25	25.27	25.32
5	20.91	20.96	21.01	21.06	21.10	21.13	21.15	21.20
6	18.18	18.23	18.28	18.33	18.38	18.41	18.43	18.48
7	16.25	16.30	16.35	16.40	16.45	16.48	16.50	16.55
8	14.81	14.86	14.92	14.97	15.02	15.05	15.07	15.13
9	13.71	13.76	13.81	13.87	13.92	13.95	13.98	14.03
10	12.84	12.89	12.94	13.00	13.05	13.08	13.11	13.16
11	12.13	12.19	12.24	12.30	12.36	12.38	12.41	12.47
12	11.55	11.61	11.67	11.73	11.78	11.81	11.84	11.90
13	11.07	11.13	11.19	11.25	11.31	11.34	11.37	11.42
14	10.67	10.73	10.79	10.85	10.91	10.94	10.97	11.03
15	10.33	10.39	10.45	10.51	10.57	10.60	10.63	10.69
16	10.03	10.09	10.15	10.22	10.28	10.31	10.34	10.40
17	9.78	9.84	9.90	9.97	10.03	10.06	10.09	10.15
18	9.56	9.62	9.68	9.75	9.81	9.84	9.88	9.94
19	9.37	9.43	9.49	9.56	9.62	9.65	9.69	9.75
20	9.20	9.26	9.33	9.39	9.46	9.49	9.52	9.59
21	9.05	9.11	9.18	9.25	9.31	9.35	9.38	9.45
22	8.92	8.98	9.05	9.12	9.18	9.22	9.25	9.32
23	8.80	8.87	8.93	9.00	9.07	9.11	9.14	9.21
24	8.70	8.76	8.83	8.90	8.97	9.01	9.04	9.11
25	8.60	8.67	8.74	8.81	8.88	8.92	8.95	9.02
26	8.52	8.59	8.66	8.73	8.80	8.84	8.87	8.94
28	8.38	8.45	8.52	8.60	8.67	8.70	8.74	8.81
30	8.27	8.34	8.41	8.49	8.56	8.60	8.63	8.71
35	8.07	8.15	8.22	8.30	8.37	8.41	8.45	8.53
40	7.95	8.03	8.11	8.18	8.26	8.30	8.34	8.42

YEARS	10.00%	10.25%	10.50%	10.75%	11.00%	11.25%	11.50%	12.00%
1	87.92	88.04	88.15	88.27	88.39	88.50	88.62	88.85
2	46.15	46.27	46.38	46.50	46.61	46.73	46.85	47.08
3	32.27	32.39	32.51	32.63	32.74	32.86	32.98	33.22
4	25.37	25.49	25.61	25.73	25.85	25.97	26.09	26.34
5	21.25	21.38	21.50	21.62	21.75	21.87	22.00	22.25
6	18.53	18.66	18.78	18.91	19.04	19.17	19.30	19.56
7	16.61	16.74	16.87	17.00	17.13	17.26	17.39	17.66
8	15.18	15.31	15.45	15.58	15.71	15.85	15.98	16.26
9	14.08	14.22	14.36	14.49	14.63	14.77	14.91	15.19
10	13.22	13.36	13.50	13.64	13.78	13.92	14.06	14.35
11	12.52	12.67	12.81	12.95	13.10	13.24	13.39	13.68
12	11.96	12.10	12.25	12.39	12.54	12.69	12.84	13.14
13	11.48	11.63	11.78	11.93	12.08	12.23	12.38	12.69
14	11.09	11.24	11.39	11.54	11.70	11.85	12.01	12.32
15	10.75	10.90	11.06	11.21	11.37	11.53	11.69	12.01
16	10.46	10.62	10.78	10.94	11.10	11.26	11.42	11.74
17	10.22	10.38	10.54	10.70	10.86	11.02	11.19	11.52
18	10.00	10.16	10.33	10.49	10.66	10.82	10.99	11.32
19	9.82	9.98	10.15	10.31	10.48	10.65	10.82	11.16
20	9.66	9.82	9.99	10.16	10.33	10.50	10.67	11.02
21	9.51	9.68	9.85	10.02	10.19	10.37	10.54	10.89
22	9.39	9.56	9.73	9.90	10.08	10.25	10.43	10.78
23	9.28	9.45	9.62	9.80	9.98	10.15	10.33	10.69
24	9.18	9.35	9.53	9.71	9.89	10.06	10.25	10.61
25	9.09	9.27	9.45	9.63	9.81	9.99	10.17	10.54
26	9.01	9.19	9.37	9.55	9.74	9.92	10.10	10.47
28	8.88	9.07	9.25	9.43	9.62	9.81	9.99	10.37
30	8.78	8.97	9.15	9.34	9.53	9.72	9.91	10.29
35	8.60	8.79	8.99	9.18	9.37	9.57	9.77	10.16
40	8.50	8.69	8.89	9.09	9.29	9.49	9.69	10.09

QUARTERLY PAYMENT NEEDED TO AMORTIZE A $1000 LOAN

YEARS	RATE							
	4.00%	4.25%	4.50%	4.75%	5.00%	5.25%	5.50%	5.75%
1	256.29	256.68	257.08	257.47	257.87	258.26	258.66	259.05
2	130.70	131.06	131.42	131.78	132.14	132.50	132.86	133.23
3	88.85	89.21	89.56	89.91	90.26	90.62	90.97	91.33
4	67.95	68.30	68.65	69.00	69.35	69.70	70.06	70.41
5	55.42	55.77	56.12	56.47	56.83	57.18	57.54	57.89
6	47.00	47.43	47.78	48.14	48.49	48.85	49.21	49.57
7	41.13	41.48	41.84	42.19	42.55	42.91	43.28	43.64
8	36.68	37.03	37.39	37.75	38.11	38.48	38.84	39.21
9	33.22	33.58	33.94	34.30	34.67	35.04	35.41	35.78
10	30.46	30.82	31.19	31.56	31.93	32.30	32.67	33.05
11	28.21	28.58	28.94	29.32	29.69	30.07	30.45	30.83
12	26.34	26.71	27.08	27.46	27.84	28.22	28.60	28.99
13	24.76	25.13	25.51	25.89	26.27	26.66	27.05	27.44
14	23.41	23.79	24.17	24.55	24.94	25.33	25.73	26.13
15	22.25	22.63	23.01	23.40	23.79	24.19	24.59	24.99
16	21.24	21.62	22.01	22.40	22.80	23.20	23.60	24.01
17	20.34	20.73	21.12	21.52	21.92	22.33	22.74	23.15
18	19.56	19.95	20.34	20.74	21.15	21.56	21.97	22.39
19	18.85	19.25	19.65	20.05	20.46	20.88	21.30	21.72
20	18.22	18.62	19.03	19.44	19.85	20.27	20.69	21.12
21	17.66	18.06	18.47	18.88	19.30	19.72	20.15	20.59
22	17.15	17.55	17.97	18.38	18.81	19.23	19.67	20.10
23	16.68	17.09	17.51	17.93	18.36	18.79	19.23	19.67
24	16.26	16.67	17.09	17.52	17.95	18.39	18.83	19.28
25	15.87	16.29	16.71	17.14	17.58	18.02	18.47	18.92
26	15.52	15.94	16.37	16.80	17.24	17.69	18.14	18.59
28	14.89	15.32	15.75	16.20	16.64	17.10	17.56	18.02
30	14.35	14.79	15.23	15.68	16.14	16.60	17.07	17.54
35	13.31	13.76	14.22	14.69	15.17	15.65	16.14	16.63
40	12.56	13.03	13.51	14.00	14.49	14.99	15.50	16.01

YEARS	RATE							
	6.00%	6.25%	6.50%	6.75%	7.00%	7.25%	7.50%	7.75%
1	259.45	259.85	260.24	260.64	261.04	261.43	261.83	262.23
2	133.59	133.95	134.32	134.68	135.05	135.41	135.78	136.15
3	91.68	92.04	92.40	92.76	93.12	93.48	93.84	94.20
4	70.77	71.13	71.49	71.84	72.20	72.57	72.93	73.29
5	58.25	58.61	58.97	59.33	59.70	60.06	60.43	60.79
6	49.93	50.29	50.66	51.02	51.39	51.76	52.13	52.50
7	44.01	44.37	44.74	45.11	45.49	45.86	46.24	46.62
8	39.58	39.95	40.33	40.70	41.08	41.46	41.85	42.23
9	36.16	36.53	36.91	37.30	37.68	38.07	38.45	38.85
10	33.43	33.81	34.20	34.59	34.98	35.37	35.76	36.16
11	31.22	31.60	31.99	32.39	32.78	33.18	33.58	33.99
12	29.38	29.77	30.17	30.57	30.97	31.38	31.78	32.19
13	27.84	28.24	28.64	29.04	29.45	29.86	30.28	30.69
14	26.53	26.93	27.34	27.75	28.16	28.58	29.00	29.42
15	25.40	25.81	26.22	26.64	27.06	27.48	27.91	28.34
16	24.42	24.84	25.25	25.68	26.10	26.53	26.97	27.40
17	23.57	23.99	24.41	24.84	25.27	25.71	26.15	26.59
18	22.81	23.24	23.67	24.10	24.54	24.98	25.43	25.88
19	22.15	22.58	23.01	23.45	23.90	24.34	24.80	25.25
20	21.55	21.99	22.43	22.88	23.33	23.78	24.24	24.70
21	21.02	21.46	21.91	22.36	22.82	23.28	23.74	24.21
22	20.55	20.99	21.45	21.90	22.36	22.83	23.30	23.77
23	20.12	20.57	21.03	21.49	21.95	22.42	22.90	23.38
24	19.73	20.19	20.65	21.11	21.59	22.06	22.54	23.03
25	19.38	19.84	20.30	20.78	21.25	21.74	22.22	22.71
26	19.05	19.52	19.99	20.47	20.95	21.44	21.93	22.43
28	18.49	18.97	19.45	19.94	20.43	20.93	21.43	21.94
30	18.02	18.51	19.00	19.50	20.00	20.50	21.02	21.53
35	17.14	17.64	18.16	18.67	19.20	19.72	20.26	20.80
40	16.53	17.06	17.59	18.13	18.67	19.21	19.77	20.32

QUARTERLY PAYMENT NEEDED TO AMORTIZE A $1000 LOAN

YEARS	8.00%	8.25%	8.50%	8.75%	9.00%	9.25%	9.50%	9.75%
1	262.63	263.03	263.43	263.82	264.22	264.62	265.02	265.42
2	136.51	136.88	137.25	137.62	137.99	138.36	138.73	139.10
3	94.56	94.93	95.29	95.66	96.02	96.39	96.76	97.12
4	73.66	74.02	74.39	74.75	75.12	75.49	75.86	76.23
5	61.16	61.53	61.90	62.27	62.65	63.02	63.40	63.77
6	52.88	53.25	53.63	54.01	54.39	54.77	55.15	55.53
7	46.99	47.38	47.76	48.14	48.53	48.92	49.31	49.70
8	42.62	43.00	43.39	43.79	44.18	44.57	44.97	45.37
9	39.24	39.63	40.03	40.43	40.83	41.23	41.64	42.05
10	36.56	36.96	37.37	37.77	38.18	38.59	39.01	39.42
11	34.39	34.80	35.21	35.63	36.04	36.46	36.88	37.31
12	32.61	33.02	33.44	33.86	34.29	34.71	35.14	35.58
13	31.11	31.54	31.96	32.39	32.82	33.26	33.70	34.14
14	29.85	30.28	30.71	31.15	31.59	32.03	32.48	32.93
15	28.77	29.21	29.65	30.09	30.54	30.99	31.44	31.90
16	27.84	28.29	28.73	29.19	29.64	30.10	30.56	31.02
17	27.04	27.49	27.94	28.40	28.86	29.32	29.79	30.26
18	26.33	26.79	27.25	27.71	28.18	28.65	29.13	29.61
19	25.71	26.18	26.64	27.11	27.59	28.07	28.55	29.04
20	25.17	25.64	26.11	26.59	27.07	27.55	28.04	28.54
21	24.68	25.16	25.64	26.12	26.61	27.10	27.60	28.10
22	24.25	24.73	25.22	25.71	26.20	26.70	27.20	27.71
23	23.86	24.35	24.84	25.34	25.84	26.34	26.85	27.36
24	23.52	24.01	24.51	25.01	25.52	26.03	26.54	27.06
25	23.21	23.71	24.21	24.72	25.23	25.75	26.27	26.79
26	22.93	23.43	23.94	24.46	24.97	25.49	26.02	26.55
28	22.45	22.96	23.48	24.01	24.53	25.07	25.60	26.14
30	22.05	22.58	23.11	23.64	24.18	24.72	25.27	25.81
35	21.34	21.89	22.44	22.99	23.55	24.11	24.68	25.25
40	20.88	21.45	22.02	22.59	23.16	23.74	24.32	24.91

YEARS	10.00%	10.25%	10.50%	10.75%	11.00%	11.25%	11.50%	12.00%
1	265.82	266.22	266.62	267.02	267.43	267.83	268.23	269.03
2	139.47	139.84	140.22	140.59	140.96	141.34	141.71	142.46
3	97.49	97.86	98.23	98.60	98.97	99.35	99.72	100.47
4	76.60	76.98	77.35	77.73	78.10	78.48	78.86	79.62
5	64.15	64.53	64.91	65.29	65.68	66.06	66.45	67.22
6	55.92	56.30	56.69	57.08	57.47	57.87	58.26	59.05
7	50.09	50.49	50.88	51.28	51.68	52.08	52.49	53.30
8	45.77	46.18	46.58	46.99	47.40	47.81	48.22	49.05
9	42.46	42.87	43.28	43.70	44.12	44.54	44.96	45.81
10	39.84	40.26	40.68	41.11	41.54	41.97	42.40	43.27
11	37.74	38.16	38.60	39.03	39.47	39.90	40.35	41.23
12	36.01	36.45	36.89	37.33	37.78	38.22	38.67	39.58
13	34.58	35.03	35.47	35.93	36.38	36.84	37.30	38.22
14	33.38	33.83	34.29	34.75	35.21	35.68	36.14	37.09
15	32.36	32.82	33.29	33.75	34.23	34.70	35.18	36.14
16	31.49	31.96	32.43	32.91	33.39	33.87	34.35	35.33
17	30.74	31.22	31.70	32.18	32.67	33.16	33.65	34.65
18	30.09	30.57	31.06	31.55	32.05	32.55	33.05	34.06
19	29.52	30.02	30.51	31.01	31.51	32.02	32.53	33.55
20	29.03	29.53	30.03	30.54	31.05	31.56	32.08	33.12
21	28.60	29.10	29.61	30.13	30.64	31.16	31.68	32.74
22	28.22	28.73	29.25	29.76	30.29	30.81	31.34	32.41
23	27.88	28.40	28.92	29.45	29.98	30.51	31.04	32.12
24	27.58	28.11	28.63	29.17	29.70	30.24	30.78	31.87
25	27.32	27.85	28.38	28.92	29.46	30.00	30.55	31.65
26	27.08	27.62	28.16	28.70	29.25	29.79	30.35	31.46
28	26.68	27.23	27.78	28.33	28.89	29.45	30.01	31.14
30	26.37	26.92	27.48	28.04	28.61	29.18	29.75	30.89
35	25.82	26.39	26.97	27.55	28.14	28.72	29.31	30.49
40	25.50	26.09	26.68	27.27	27.87	28.47	29.07	30.27

SEMI-ANNUAL PAYMENT NEEDED TO AMORTIZE A $1000 LOAN

YEARS	RATE 4.00%	4.25%	4.50%	4.75%	5.00%	5.25%	5.50%	5.75%
1	515.05	516.00	516.94	517.89	518.83	519.78	520.72	521.67
2	262.63	263.43	264.22	265.02	265.82	266.62	267.43	268.23
3	178.53	179.28	180.04	180.80	181.55	182.31	183.08	183.84
4	136.51	137.25	137.99	138.73	139.47	140.22	140.96	141.71
5	111.33	112.06	112.79	113.53	114.26	115.00	115.74	116.49
6	94.56	95.29	96.02	96.76	97.49	98.23	98.97	99.72
7	82.61	83.34	84.07	84.80	85.54	86.28	87.03	87.78
8	73.66	74.39	75.12	75.86	76.60	77.35	78.10	78.86
9	66.71	67.44	68.18	68.93	69.68	70.43	71.19	71.95
10	61.16	61.90	62.65	63.40	64.15	64.91	65.68	66.45
11	56.64	57.38	58.13	58.89	59.65	60.42	61.19	61.97
12	52.88	53.63	54.39	55.15	55.92	56.69	57.47	58.26
13	49.70	50.46	51.23	52.00	52.77	53.56	54.35	55.14
14	46.99	47.76	48.53	49.31	50.09	50.88	51.68	52.49
15	44.65	45.43	46.20	46.99	47.78	48.58	49.39	50.20
16	42.62	43.39	44.18	44.97	45.77	46.58	47.40	48.22
17	40.82	41.61	42.40	43.20	44.01	44.83	45.65	46.49
18	39.24	40.03	40.83	41.64	42.46	43.28	44.12	44.96
19	37.83	38.62	39.43	40.25	41.08	41.91	42.75	43.60
20	36.56	37.37	38.18	39.01	39.84	40.68	41.54	42.40
21	35.42	36.24	37.06	37.89	38.73	39.59	40.45	41.32
22	34.39	35.21	36.04	36.88	37.74	38.60	39.47	40.35
23	33.46	34.29	35.12	35.97	36.83	37.70	38.58	39.47
24	32.61	33.44	34.29	35.14	36.01	36.89	37.78	38.67
25	31.83	32.67	33.52	34.39	35.26	36.15	37.05	37.95
26	31.11	31.96	32.82	33.70	34.58	35.47	36.38	37.30
28	29.85	30.71	31.59	32.48	33.38	34.29	35.21	36.14
30	28.77	29.65	30.54	31.44	32.36	33.29	34.23	35.18
35	26.67	27.58	28.51	29.45	30.40	31.37	32.35	33.34
40	25.17	26.11	27.07	28.04	29.03	30.03	31.05	32.08

YEARS	RATE 6.00%	6.25%	6.50%	6.75%	7.00%	7.25%	7.50%	7.75%
1	522.62	523.56	524.51	525.46	526.41	527.35	528.30	529.25
2	269.03	269.84	270.64	271.45	272.26	273.06	273.87	274.68
3	184.60	185.37	186.13	186.90	187.67	188.44	189.22	189.99
4	142.46	143.21	143.97	144.72	145.48	146.24	147.00	147.77
5	117.24	117.98	118.74	119.49	120.25	121.01	121.77	122.53
6	100.47	101.22	101.97	102.73	103.49	104.25	105.02	105.79
7	88.53	89.29	90.05	90.81	91.58	92.35	93.12	93.89
8	79.62	80.38	81.15	81.92	82.69	83.47	84.25	85.04
9	72.71	73.48	74.26	75.04	75.82	76.61	77.40	78.20
10	67.22	68.00	68.78	69.57	70.37	71.16	71.97	72.77
11	62.75	63.54	64.33	65.13	65.94	66.75	67.56	68.38
12	59.05	59.85	60.65	61.46	62.28	63.10	63.92	64.76
13	55.94	56.75	57.56	58.38	59.21	60.04	60.88	61.72
14	53.30	54.12	54.94	55.77	56.61	57.45	58.30	59.16
15	51.02	51.85	52.69	53.53	54.38	55.23	56.09	56.96
16	49.05	49.89	50.73	51.59	52.45	53.31	54.19	55.07
17	47.33	48.18	49.03	49.89	50.76	51.64	52.53	53.42
18	45.81	46.67	47.53	48.41	49.29	50.18	51.08	51.98
19	44.46	45.33	46.21	47.09	47.99	48.89	49.80	50.71
20	43.27	44.15	45.03	45.93	46.83	47.74	48.66	49.59
21	42.20	43.09	43.98	44.89	45.80	46.73	47.66	48.60
22	41.23	42.13	43.04	43.96	44.88	45.82	46.76	47.71
23	40.37	41.28	42.19	43.12	44.06	45.00	45.95	46.92
24	39.58	40.50	41.43	42.37	43.31	44.27	45.23	46.20
25	38.87	39.80	40.74	41.68	42.64	43.60	44.58	45.56
26	38.22	39.16	40.11	41.06	42.03	43.01	43.99	44.98
28	37.09	38.04	39.01	39.99	40.97	41.97	42.97	43.99
30	36.14	37.11	38.09	39.09	40.09	41.11	42.13	43.16
35	34.34	35.36	36.38	37.42	38.47	39.52	40.59	41.67
40	33.12	34.17	35.23	36.31	37.39	38.48	39.59	40.70

SEMI-ANNUAL PAYMENT NEEDED TO AMORTIZE A $1000 LOAN

YEARS	RATE 8.00%	8.25%	8.50%	8.75%	9.00%	9.25%	9.50%	9.75%
1	530.20	531.15	532.10	533.05	534.00	534.95	535.91	536.86
2	275.50	276.31	277.12	277.93	278.73	279.56	280.38	281.20
3	190.77	191.54	192.32	193.10	193.88	194.67	195.45	196.24
4	148.53	149.30	150.07	150.84	151.61	152.39	153.17	153.95
5	123.30	124.06	124.84	125.61	126.38	127.16	127.94	128.72
6	106.56	107.33	108.11	108.89	109.67	110.46	111.25	112.04
7	94.67	95.46	96.24	97.03	97.83	98.62	99.42	100.22
8	85.82	86.62	87.42	88.22	89.02	89.83	90.64	91.46
9	79.00	79.80	80.61	81.42	82.24	83.06	83.89	84.72
10	73.59	74.40	75.22	76.05	76.88	77.72	78.56	79.40
11	69.20	70.03	70.87	71.71	72.55	73.40	74.25	75.11
12	65.59	66.43	67.28	68.13	68.99	69.86	70.72	71.60
13	62.57	63.43	64.29	65.15	66.03	66.90	67.79	68.68
14	60.02	60.89	61.76	62.64	63.53	64.42	65.32	66.22
15	57.84	58.72	59.60	60.50	61.40	62.30	63.21	64.13
16	55.95	56.85	57.75	58.65	59.57	60.49	61.41	62.35
17	54.32	55.23	56.14	57.06	57.99	58.92	59.86	60.81
18	52.89	53.81	54.74	55.67	56.61	57.56	58.51	59.47
19	51.64	52.57	53.51	54.45	55.41	56.37	57.33	58.31
20	50.53	51.47	52.42	53.38	54.35	55.32	56.30	57.29
21	49.55	50.50	51.46	52.44	53.41	54.40	55.39	56.39
22	48.67	49.64	50.61	51.60	52.59	53.58	54.59	55.60
23	47.89	48.87	49.85	50.85	51.85	52.86	53.88	54.90
24	47.19	48.18	49.17	50.18	51.19	52.22	53.24	54.28
25	46.56	47.56	48.57	49.58	50.61	51.64	52.68	53.73
26	45.99	47.00	48.02	49.05	50.08	51.13	52.18	53.23
28	45.01	46.04	47.08	48.13	49.19	50.25	51.32	52.40
30	44.21	45.26	46.32	47.38	48.46	49.54	50.63	51.73
35	42.75	43.84	44.94	46.05	47.17	48.29	49.42	50.56
40	41.82	42.95	44.08	45.23	46.38	47.53	48.69	49.86

YEARS	RATE 10.00%	10.25%	10.50%	10.75%	11.00%	11.25%	11.50%	12.00%
1	537.81	538.76	539.72	540.67	541.62	542.58	543.53	545.44
2	282.02	282.84	283.66	284.48	285.30	286.12	286.95	288.60
3	197.02	197.81	198.60	199.39	200.18	200.98	201.77	203.37
4	154.73	155.51	156.29	157.08	157.87	158.66	159.45	161.04
5	129.51	130.30	131.09	131.88	132.67	133.47	134.27	135.87
6	112.83	113.63	114.43	115.23	116.03	116.84	117.65	119.28
7	101.03	101.84	102.65	103.47	104.28	105.11	105.93	107.59
8	92.27	93.10	93.92	94.75	95.59	96.42	97.27	98.96
9	85.55	86.39	87.23	88.08	88.92	89.78	90.64	92.36
10	80.25	81.10	81.96	82.82	83.68	84.55	85.43	87.19
11	75.98	76.84	77.72	78.59	79.48	80.36	81.25	83.05
12	72.48	73.36	74.25	75.14	76.04	76.94	77.85	79.68
13	69.57	70.47	71.37	72.28	73.20	74.12	75.04	76.91
14	67.13	68.04	68.96	69.89	70.82	71.76	72.70	74.60
15	65.06	65.99	66.92	67.86	68.81	69.76	70.72	72.65
16	63.29	64.23	65.18	66.14	67.10	68.07	69.04	71.01
17	61.76	62.72	63.69	64.66	65.63	66.62	67.61	69.60
18	60.44	61.41	62.39	63.38	64.37	65.37	66.37	68.40
19	59.29	60.28	61.27	62.27	63.28	64.29	65.31	67.36
20	58.28	59.28	60.29	61.31	62.33	63.35	64.38	66.47
21	57.40	58.41	59.43	60.46	61.49	62.53	63.58	65.69
22	56.62	57.65	58.68	59.72	60.77	61.82	62.88	65.01
23	55.93	56.97	58.02	59.07	60.13	61.19	62.26	64.42
24	55.32	56.37	57.43	58.49	59.56	60.64	61.72	63.90
25	54.78	55.84	56.91	57.99	59.07	60.15	61.25	63.45
26	54.30	55.37	56.45	57.54	58.63	59.72	60.83	63.05
28	53.49	54.58	55.68	56.78	57.89	59.01	60.13	62.39
30	52.83	53.94	55.06	56.18	57.31	58.45	59.59	61.88
35	51.70	52.85	54.01	55.17	56.33	57.50	58.68	61.04
40	51.03	52.21	53.40	54.58	55.77	56.97	58.17	60.58

ANNUAL PAYMENT NEEDED TO AMORTIZE A $1000 LOAN

YEARS	RATE							
	4.00%	4.25%	4.50%	4.75%	5.00%	5.25%	5.50%	5.75%
2	530.20	532.10	534.00	535.91	537.81	539.72	541.62	543.53
3	360.35	362.06	363.78	365.49	367.21	368.94	370.66	372.39
4	275.50	277.12	278.75	280.38	282.02	283.66	285.30	286.95
5	224.63	226.21	227.80	229.39	230.98	232.58	234.18	235.79
6	190.77	192.32	193.88	195.45	197.02	198.60	200.18	201.77
7	166.61	168.16	169.71	171.26	172.82	174.39	175.97	177.55
8	148.53	150.07	151.61	153.17	154.73	156.29	157.87	159.45
9	134.50	136.03	137.58	139.13	140.70	142.27	143.84	145.43
10	123.30	124.84	126.38	127.94	129.51	131.09	132.67	134.27
11	114.15	115.70	117.25	118.82	120.39	121.98	123.58	125.18
12	106.56	108.11	109.67	111.25	112.83	114.43	116.03	117.65
13	100.15	101.71	103.28	104.86	106.46	108.07	109.69	111.32
14	94.67	96.24	97.83	99.42	101.03	102.65	104.28	105.93
15	89.95	91.53	93.12	94.73	96.35	97.98	99.63	101.29
16	85.82	87.42	89.02	90.64	92.27	93.92	95.59	97.27
17	82.20	83.81	85.42	87.06	88.70	90.37	92.05	93.74
18	79.00	80.61	82.24	83.89	85.55	87.23	88.92	90.64
19	76.14	77.77	79.41	81.07	82.75	84.44	86.16	87.88
20	73.59	75.22	76.88	78.56	80.25	81.96	83.68	85.43
21	71.29	72.94	74.61	76.29	78.00	79.73	81.47	83.23
22	69.20	70.87	72.55	74.25	75.98	77.72	79.48	81.25
23	67.31	68.99	70.69	72.40	74.14	75.90	77.67	79.47
24	65.59	67.28	68.99	70.72	72.48	74.25	76.04	77.85
25	64.02	65.72	67.44	69.19	70.96	72.75	74.55	76.38
26	62.57	64.29	66.03	67.79	69.57	71.37	73.20	75.04
27	61.24	62.97	64.72	66.50	68.30	70.12	71.96	73.82
28	60.02	61.76	63.53	65.32	67.13	68.96	70.82	72.70
30	57.84	59.60	61.40	63.21	65.06	66.92	68.81	70.72
35	53.58	55.41	57.28	59.16	61.08	63.02	64.98	66.97
40	50.53	52.42	54.35	56.30	58.28	60.29	62.33	64.38

YEARS	RATE							
	6.00%	6.25%	6.50%	6.75%	7.00%	7.25%	7.50%	7.75%
2	545.44	547.35	549.27	551.18	553.10	555.01	556.93	558.85
3	374.11	375.85	377.58	379.32	381.06	382.80	384.54	386.29
4	288.60	290.25	291.91	293.57	295.23	296.90	298.57	300.25
5	237.40	239.02	240.64	242.27	243.90	245.53	247.17	248.81
6	203.37	204.97	206.57	208.18	209.80	211.42	213.05	214.68
7	179.14	180.73	182.34	183.94	185.56	187.18	188.81	190.44
8	161.04	162.64	164.24	165.85	167.47	169.10	170.73	172.37
9	147.03	148.63	150.24	151.86	153.49	155.13	156.77	158.42
10	135.87	137.49	139.11	140.74	142.38	144.03	145.69	147.36
11	126.80	128.42	130.06	131.71	133.36	135.03	136.70	138.39
12	119.28	120.92	122.57	124.23	125.91	127.59	129.28	130.99
13	112.97	114.62	116.29	117.97	119.66	121.36	123.07	124.79
14	107.59	109.26	110.95	112.64	114.35	116.07	117.80	119.55
15	102.97	104.66	106.36	108.07	109.80	111.54	113.29	115.06
16	98.96	100.66	102.38	104.12	105.86	107.62	109.40	111.18
17	95.45	97.17	98.91	100.66	102.43	104.21	106.01	107.81
18	92.36	94.10	95.86	97.63	99.42	101.22	103.03	104.86
19	89.63	91.39	93.16	94.95	96.76	98.58	100.42	102.27
20	87.19	88.97	90.76	92.57	94.40	96.24	98.10	99.97
21	85.01	86.81	88.62	90.45	92.29	94.16	96.03	97.93
22	83.05	84.86	86.70	88.55	90.41	92.29	94.19	96.11
23	81.28	83.12	84.97	86.83	88.72	90.62	92.54	94.48
24	79.68	81.53	83.40	85.29	87.19	89.12	91.06	93.01
25	78.23	80.10	81.99	83.89	85.82	87.76	89.72	91.69
26	76.91	78.79	80.70	82.62	84.57	86.53	88.50	90.50
27	75.70	77.61	79.53	81.47	83.43	85.41	87.41	89.42
28	74.60	76.52	78.46	80.42	82.40	84.39	86.41	88.44
30	72.65	74.61	76.58	78.58	80.59	82.62	84.68	86.75
35	68.98	71.01	73.07	75.14	77.24	79.35	81.49	83.64
40	66.47	68.57	70.70	72.85	75.01	77.20	79.41	81.63

ANNUAL PAYMENT NEEDED TO AMORTIZE A $1000 LOAN

YEARS	RATE 8.00%	8.25%	8.50%	8.75%	9.00%	9.25%	9.50%	9.75%
2	560.77	562.70	564.62	566.55	568.47	570.40	572.33	574.26
3	388.04	389.79	391.54	393.30	395.06	396.82	398.58	400.35
4	301.93	303.61	305.29	306.98	308.67	310.37	312.07	313.77
5	250.46	252.11	253.77	255.43	257.10	258.77	260.44	262.12
6	216.32	217.96	219.61	221.27	222.92	224.59	226.26	227.93
7	192.08	193.72	195.37	197.03	198.70	200.37	202.04	203.72
8	174.02	175.67	177.34	179.00	180.68	182.36	184.05	185.75
9	160.08	161.75	163.43	165.11	166.80	168.50	170.21	171.92
10	149.03	150.72	152.41	154.11	155.83	157.54	159.27	161.01
11	140.08	141.78	143.50	145.22	146.95	148.69	150.44	152.20
12	132.70	134.42	136.16	137.90	139.66	141.42	143.19	144.98
13	126.53	128.27	130.03	131.79	133.57	135.36	137.16	138.97
14	121.33	123.07	124.85	126.64	128.44	130.25	132.07	133.91
15	116.83	118.62	120.43	122.24	124.06	125.90	127.75	129.61
16	112.98	114.79	116.62	118.46	120.30	122.17	124.04	125.92
17	109.63	111.47	113.32	115.18	117.05	118.94	120.84	122.75
18	106.71	108.56	110.44	112.32	114.22	116.13	118.05	119.99
19	104.13	106.01	107.91	109.81	111.74	113.67	115.62	117.58
20	101.86	103.76	105.68	107.61	109.55	111.51	113.48	115.47
21	99.84	101.76	103.70	105.65	107.62	109.60	111.60	113.61
22	98.04	99.98	101.94	103.92	105.91	107.91	109.93	111.96
23	96.43	98.39	100.38	102.37	104.39	106.41	108.45	110.51
24	94.98	96.97	98.97	100.99	103.03	105.08	107.14	109.21
25	93.68	95.69	97.72	99.76	101.81	103.88	105.96	108.06
26	92.51	94.54	96.59	98.65	100.72	102.81	104.91	107.03
27	91.45	93.50	95.57	97.64	99.74	101.85	103.97	106.11
28	90.49	92.56	94.64	96.74	98.86	100.99	103.13	105.29
30	88.83	90.94	93.06	95.19	97.34	99.51	101.69	103.88
35	85.81	87.99	90.19	92.41	94.64	96.89	99.14	101.41
40	83.87	86.12	88.39	90.67	92.96	95.27	97.59	99.92

YEARS	RATE 10.00%	10.25%	10.50%	10.75%	11.00%	11.25%	11.50%	12.00%
2	576.20	578.13	580.06	582.00	583.94	585.88	587.82	591.70
3	402.12	403.89	405.66	407.44	409.22	411.00	412.78	416.35
4	315.48	317.18	318.90	320.61	322.33	324.05	325.78	329.24
5	263.80	265.49	267.18	268.88	270.58	272.28	273.99	277.41
6	229.61	231.30	232.99	234.68	236.38	238.09	239.80	243.23
7	205.41	207.10	208.80	210.51	212.22	213.94	215.66	219.12
8	187.45	189.16	190.87	192.60	194.33	196.06	197.80	201.31
9	173.65	175.37	177.11	178.86	180.61	182.37	184.13	187.68
10	162.75	164.50	166.26	168.03	169.81	171.59	173.38	176.99
11	153.97	155.74	157.53	159.32	161.13	162.94	164.76	168.42
12	146.77	148.57	150.38	152.20	154.03	155.87	157.72	161.44
13	140.78	142.61	144.45	146.30	148.16	150.02	151.90	155.68
14	135.75	137.61	139.47	141.35	143.23	145.13	147.04	150.88
15	131.48	133.36	135.25	137.16	139.07	140.99	142.93	146.83
16	127.82	129.73	131.65	133.58	135.52	137.47	139.44	143.40
17	124.67	126.60	128.55	130.51	132.48	134.46	136.45	140.46
18	121.94	123.90	125.87	127.85	129.85	131.85	133.87	137.94
19	119.55	121.54	123.54	125.55	127.57	129.60	131.65	135.77
20	117.46	119.48	121.50	123.53	125.58	127.64	129.71	133.88
21	115.63	117.66	119.71	121.77	123.84	125.93	128.02	132.25
22	114.01	116.07	118.14	120.22	122.32	124.43	126.54	130.82
23	112.58	114.66	116.75	118.86	120.98	123.11	125.25	129.56
24	111.30	113.41	115.52	117.65	119.79	121.94	124.11	128.47
25	110.17	112.30	114.43	116.58	118.75	120.92	123.10	127.50
26	109.16	111.31	113.47	115.64	117.82	120.01	122.22	126.66
27	108.26	110.43	112.60	114.79	116.99	119.21	121.43	125.91
28	107.46	109.64	111.83	114.04	116.26	118.49	120.73	125.25
30	106.08	108.30	110.53	112.78	115.03	117.29	119.57	124.15
35	103.69	105.99	108.29	110.61	112.93	115.27	117.61	122.32
40	102.26	104.62	106.98	109.35	111.72	114.11	116.50	121.31

6%

LOAN PROGRESS CHART
Showing remaining balance on $1000 loan

AGE OF LOAN	2	3	5	6	8	10	12	14	15	16	17	18	19	AGE OF LOAN
					ORIGINAL TERM IN YEARS									
1	515	686	823	857	900	925	941	953	958	962	965	968	971	1
2		353	635	706	793	845	879	903	913	921	928	934	940	2
3			436	545	680	760	813	850	865	877	889	898	907	3
4			225	374	560	670	743	794	814	832	847	860	872	4
5				193	432	574	668	734	760	783	802	820	835	5
6					297	473	589	671	703	731	755	777	796	6
7					153	365	505	603	642	676	705	731	754	7
8						250	416	532	578	617	652	683	710	8
9						129	321	456	509	555	596	631	663	9
10							220	375	436	490	536	577	613	10
11							113	290	359	420	473	519	560	11
12								199	277	346	405	457	504	12
13								102	190	267	333	392	444	13
14									98	183	257	323	381	14
15										94	177	249	313	15
16											91	171	242	16
17												88	166	17
18													86	18

AGE OF LOAN	20	21	22	23	24	25	26	27	28	29	30	35	40	AGE OF LOAN
					ORIGINAL TERM IN YEARS									
1	973	975	977	979	981	982	984	985	986	987	988	991	994	1
2	945	949	953	957	960	963	966	968	971	973	975	982	987	2
3	915	922	928	934	939	943	947	951	955	958	961	972	980	3
4	883	892	901	909	916	922	928	933	938	942	946	962	973	4
5	849	861	872	882	891	899	907	913	920	925	931	951	965	5
6	813	828	842	854	865	875	884	893	901	908	914	939	957	6
7	775	793	809	824	838	850	861	871	880	889	896	927	948	7
8	734	756	775	793	808	823	836	848	859	869	878	914	938	8
9	691	716	739	759	777	794	809	823	836	847	858	900	928	9
10	645	674	700	723	744	764	781	797	811	825	837	885	918	10
11	597	629	659	685	709	731	751	769	785	801	815	869	906	11
12	545	582	615	645	672	697	719	739	758	775	791	852	894	12
13	490	532	569	602	633	660	685	708	729	748	766	835	882	13
14	432	478	520	557	591	621	649	675	698	719	739	816	868	14
15	371	422	468	509	546	580	613	641	665	689	710	796	854	15
16	305	361	412	458	499	537	571	602	630	656	680	775	839	16
17	235	298	353	404	449	490	528	562	593	622	648	752	823	17
18	162	230	291	346	396	441	482	520	554	586	614	728	805	18
19	83	158	225	285	339	389	434	475	512	547	578	703	787	19
20		81	154	220	279	333	382	427	468	506	540	676	768	20
21			79	151	216	274	328	377	421	462	499	647	747	21
22				78	148	212	270	323	371	416	456	617	726	22
23					76	145	208	266	318	366	410	586	703	23
24						75	143	205	262	314	362	550	678	24
25							74	141	202	258	310	514	652	25
26								73	139	200	255	475	624	26
27									71	137	197	434	595	27
28										71	135	390	564	28
29											70	344	531	29
30												295	496	30
31												243	458	31
32												187	419	32
33												129	377	33
34												66	332	34
35													285	35

LOAN PROGRESS CHART
Showing remaining balance on $1000 loan

AGE OF LOAN	2	3	5	6	8	10	12	14	15	16	17	18	19	AGE OF LOAN
1	517	690	827	861	903	928	945	956	961	965	968	971	974	1
2		357	641	712	800	852	886	910	919	927	934	940	946	2
3			442	552	689	769	822	859	874	887	898	907	916	3
4			229	381	569	681	754	806	826	843	858	872	884	4
5				197	442	586	681	748	774	797	816	834	849	5
6					305	485	603	686	719	747	771	793	812	6
7					158	376	519	620	659	693	723	749	772	7
8						259	429	549	596	636	671	702	730	8
9						134	333	472	527	575	616	652	684	9
10							230	391	454	509	556	598	635	10
11							119	303	375	438	492	540	583	11
12								209	291	362	424	478	526	12
13								108	201	281	351	412	466	13
14									104	194	272	341	401	14
15									100	188	264	332		15
16										97	182	257		16
17											94	177		17
18												92		18

AGE OF LOAN	20	21	22	23	24	25	26	27	28	29	30	35	40	AGE OF LOAN
1	976	978	980	982	983	985	986	987	988	989	990	993	995	1
2	951	955	959	962	965	968	971	973	975	977	979	986	990	2
3	923	930	936	941	946	951	955	958	962	965	967	978	985	3
4	894	903	912	919	926	932	937	942	947	951	955	969	979	4
5	863	875	885	895	904	912	919	925	931	936	941	960	973	5
6	829	844	857	869	880	890	899	907	914	921	927	950	966	6
7	793	811	827	842	855	867	877	887	896	904	911	940	959	7
8	754	775	795	812	828	842	854	866	877	886	895	929	951	8
9	712	738	760	780	799	815	830	843	856	867	877	917	943	9
10	668	697	723	746	767	786	804	819	833	846	858	904	934	10
11	620	653	683	710	734	756	775	793	809	824	838	890	925	11
12	569	606	640	671	698	723	745	765	784	800	816	875	914	12
13	514	556	594	629	659	687	712	735	756	775	792	859	903	13
14	455	503	545	584	618	649	678	703	727	748	767	842	892	14
15	392	445	493	535	574	609	640	669	695	719	740	824	879	15
16	324	383	436	484	526	565	600	632	661	687	711	804	866	16
17	251	317	375	428	476	518	557	592	624	654	680	783	851	17
18	173	246	310	369	421	468	511	550	585	620	647	761	836	18
19	90	169	241	305	362	415	462	504	543	579	611	737	819	19
20		88	166	236	300	357	409	456	498	537	573	711	802	20
21			86	163	232	295	352	403	450	493	532	683	782	21
22				84	160	229	291	347	399	445	488	653	762	22
23					83	158	226	287	343	394	441	621	740	23
24						82	156	223	284	339	390	587	717	24
25							81	154	220	281	336	550	691	25
26								79	152	218	278	511	664	26
27									79	150	215	469	635	27
28										78	149	423	604	28
29											77	375	571	29
30												323	535	30
31												267	497	31
32												207	456	32
33												143	412	33
34												74	364	34
35													314	35

7¼%

LOAN PROGRESS CHART
Showing remaining balance on $1000 loan

AGE OF LOAN	2	3	5	6	8	10	12	14	15	16	17	18	19	AGE OF LOAN
1	518	690	828	862	904	929	946	957	962	966	969	972	975	1
2		358	643	714	801	853	887	911	921	929	936	942	947	2
3			444	554	691	772	825	862	876	889	900	909	918	3
4			230	383	572	684	757	809	829	846	861	875	886	4
5				198	444	589	685	751	778	800	820	837	852	5
6					307	488	607	690	723	751	775	797	816	6
7					159	379	523	624	663	698	728	754	777	7
8						262	433	553	600	641	676	707	734	8
9						136	336	477	532	579	621	657	689	9
10							232	394	458	513	561	603	640	10
11							120	306	379	443	497	546	588	11
12								211	295	366	429	484	532	12
13								110	203	284	355	417	471	13
14									105	196	276	345	406	14
15									102	190	268	336		15
16										99	185	261		16
17											96	180		17
18												93		18

AGE OF LOAN	20	21	22	23	24	25	26	27	28	29	30	35	40	AGE OF LOAN
1	977	979	981	982	984	985	986	988	989	989	990	994	996	1
2	952	956	960	964	967	969	972	974	976	978	980	987	991	2
3	925	932	938	943	948	952	956	960	963	966	969	979	986	3
4	897	906	914	922	928	934	940	944	949	953	957	971	980	4
5	866	878	889	898	907	915	922	928	934	939	944	962	974	5
6	833	848	861	873	884	893	902	910	917	924	930	953	968	6
7	797	815	831	846	859	871	881	891	900	908	915	943	961	7
8	759	780	799	817	832	846	859	870	881	890	899	932	954	8
9	718	743	765	785	804	820	835	848	860	872	882	921	946	9
10	673	702	728	752	773	792	809	824	839	851	863	908	938	10
11	626	659	689	716	740	761	781	799	815	830	843	895	929	11
12	574	612	646	677	704	729	751	771	790	806	822	880	919	12
13	519	562	601	635	666	694	719	742	763	781	799	865	908	13
14	460	509	552	590	625	656	684	710	733	755	774	848	897	14
15	397	451	499	542	581	616	647	676	702	726	747	831	885	15
16	328	388	442	490	533	572	607	639	668	695	719	811	872	16
17	255	322	381	434	482	525	564	600	632	661	688	791	858	17
18	176	250	315	374	427	475	518	557	593	625	655	769	843	18
19	91	172	245	310	368	421	469	512	551	587	619	745	827	19
20		89	169	241	305	363	415	463	506	545	581	719	809	20
21			88	166	237	300	358	410	458	501	540	692	791	21
22				86	163	233	296	354	405	453	496	662	771	22
23					85	161	230	293	349	401	448	630	749	23
24						83	159	227	289	346	397	596	726	24
25							82	157	225	286	342	559	701	25
26								81	155	222	284	520	674	26
27									80	153	220	477	645	27
28										80	152	431	614	28
29											79	382	581	29
30												330	545	30
31												273	506	31
32												212	465	32
33												146	420	33
34												76	373	34
35													321	35

LOAN PROGRESS CHART
Showing remaining balance on $1000 loan

AGE OF LOAN	2	3	5	6	8	10	12	14	15	16	17	18	19	AGE OF LOAN
					ORIGINAL TERM IN YEARS									
1	519	691	829	863	905	930	947	958	962	966	970	973	975	1
2		359	644	715	803	855	889	913	922	930	937	943	949	2
3			445	556	693	774	827	864	878	891	902	912	920	3
4			231	384	574	687	760	811	832	849	864	877	889	4
5				199	446	592	688	755	781	804	823	840	856	5
6					309	491	610	694	726	755	779	801	820	6
7					160	382	527	628	668	702	732	758	781	7
8						264	436	557	604	645	681	712	739	8
9						137	339	481	536	584	626	662	694	9
10							234	398	463	518	566	609	646	10
11							122	310	383	447	502	551	594	11
12								214	298	370	434	489	537	12
13								111	206	288	359	422	477	13
14									107	199	279	349	411	14
15										103	193	272	341	15
16											100	188	265	16
17												97	183	17
18													95	18

AGE OF LOAN	20	21	22	23	24	25	26	27	28	29	30	35	40	AGE OF LOAN
					ORIGINAL TERM IN YEARS									
1	978	980	981	983	985	986	987	988	989	990	991	994	996	1
2	953	958	961	965	968	971	973	975	977	979	981	987	991	2
3	927	934	940	945	950	954	958	961	965	968	970	980	987	3
4	899	908	917	924	931	936	942	947	951	955	959	973	982	4
5	869	881	892	901	910	917	924	931	936	941	946	964	976	5
6	836	851	865	876	887	897	905	913	920	927	933	955	970	6
7	801	819	835	850	863	875	885	895	903	911	918	946	964	7
8	763	785	804	821	837	851	863	875	885	894	903	935	957	8
9	723	748	770	791	809	825	840	853	865	876	886	924	949	9
10	679	708	734	757	778	797	814	830	844	856	868	912	941	10
11	631	665	695	722	746	767	787	805	821	835	848	899	932	11
12	580	618	652	683	710	735	757	777	796	812	827	886	923	12
13	525	568	607	641	672	700	726	748	769	788	805	871	913	13
14	466	515	558	597	632	663	691	717	740	761	781	854	902	14
15	402	456	505	548	587	623	654	683	709	733	754	837	890	15
16	333	394	448	496	540	579	614	647	676	702	726	818	878	16
17	259	326	387	440	489	532	572	607	639	669	695	798	864	17
18	179	254	320	380	434	482	525	565	601	633	663	776	850	18
19	93	175	249	315	374	427	476	519	559	595	627	753	834	19
20		91	172	245	310	369	422	470	513	553	589	727	817	20
21			89	169	241	306	364	417	465	508	548	700	799	21
22				88	167	238	302	360	412	460	504	671	779	22
23					86	164	234	298	356	408	456	639	758	23
24						85	162	232	295	352	404	605	735	24
25							84	160	229	292	349	568	710	25
26								83	158	227	289	528	683	26
27									82	157	225	486	655	27
28										81	155	440	624	28
29											81	390	590	29
30												336	554	30
31												279	516	31
32												217	474	32
33												150	429	33
34												78	381	34
35													328	35

7¾%

LOAN PROGRESS CHART
Showing remaining balance on $1000 loan

AGE OF LOAN	2	3	5	6	8	10	12	14	15	16	17	18	19	AGE OF LOAN
				ORIGINAL TERM IN YEARS										
1	519	692	830	864	906	931	947	959	963	967	970	973	976	1
2		359	646	717	805	857	891	914	924	932	939	945	950	2
3			447	558	695	776	829	866	881	893	904	914	922	3
4			232	386	577	689	763	814	834	852	867	880	892	4
5				200	449	595	691	758	784	807	827	844	859	5
6					311	494	614	697	730	759	783	805	823	6
7					161	384	530	632	672	706	736	762	785	7
8						266	440	561	609	650	685	717	744	8
9						138	342	485	541	589	631	667	699	9
10							237	402	467	523	571	614	651	10
11							123	313	387	452	507	556	599	11
12								217	301	375	438	494	543	12
13								112	209	292	364	427	482	13
14									108	202	283	354	416	14
15									105	196	275	345		15
16											102	191	269	16
17												99	186	17
18													97	18

AGE OF LOAN	20	21	22	23	24	25	26	27	28	29	30	35	40	AGE OF LOAN
				ORIGINAL TERM IN YEARS										
1	978	980	982	984	985	986	988	989	990	990	991	994	996	1
2	955	962	963	966	969	972	974	976	978	980	982	988	992	2
3	929	936	942	947	952	956	960	963	966	969	971	981	988	3
4	902	911	919	926	933	939	944	949	953	957	960	974	983	4
5	872	884	895	904	912	920	927	933	939	944	948	966	978	5
6	840	855	868	880	891	900	909	916	923	930	936	958	972	6
7	806	824	840	854	867	878	889	898	907	915	922	949	966	7
8	768	790	809	826	841	855	867	879	889	898	907	939	959	8
9	728	753	775	796	814	830	844	858	870	880	890	928	952	9
10	684	713	739	763	784	802	819	835	849	861	873	916	944	10
11	637	671	701	727	751	773	792	810	826	841	854	904	936	11
12	586	624	659	689	716	741	763	783	802	818	833	890	927	12
13	531	574	613	648	679	707	732	755	775	794	811	876	918	13
14	472	520	564	603	638	670	698	724	747	768	787	860	907	14
15	407	462	511	555	594	629	661	690	716	740	761	843	896	15
16	338	399	454	503	547	586	622	654	683	709	733	825	884	16
17	263	331	392	446	495	539	579	614	647	676	703	805	870	17
18	182	258	325	386	440	489	532	572	608	641	670	784	856	18
19	95	178	253	320	380	434	482	526	566	602	635	760	841	19
20		93	175	249	315	375	428	477	521	561	597	735	824	20
21			91	172	245	311	370	424	472	516	556	708	803	21
22				89	170	242	307	366	419	467	511	679	787	22
23					88	167	239	304	362	415	463	648	766	23
24						87	165	236	300	359	411	614	743	24
25							86	163	234	297	355	577	719	25
26								85	162	231	295	537	692	26
27									84	160	229	494	664	27
28										83	159	446	633	28
29											82	398	600	29
30												343	564	30
31												285	525	31
32												222	483	32
33												153	433	33
34												80	389	34
35													336	35

LOAN PROGRESS CHART
Showing remaining balance on $1000 loan

AGE OF LOAN	2	3	5	6	8	10	12	14	15	16	17	18	19	AGE OF LOAN
					ORIGINAL TERM IN YEARS									
1	520	693	831	865	907	932	948	960	964	968	971	974	977	1
2		360	647	718	806	858	892	916	925	933	940	946	951	2
3			448	560	697	778	831	868	883	895	906	916	924	3
4			233	388	579	692	766	817	837	854	869	883	894	4
5				202	451	598	694	761	788	810	830	847	862	5
6					313	497	617	701	734	762	787	808	827	6
7					163	387	534	636	676	710	740	766	789	7
8						268	443	565	613	654	690	721	749	8
9						139	345	489	545	593	635	672	704	9
10							239	406	471	528	576	619	656	10
11							124	316	391	456	512	561	600	11
12								219	305	379	443	499	548	12
13								114	211	295	368	432	487	13
14									110	205	287	358	421	14
15										106	199	279	350	15
16											103	193	273	16
17												101	189	17
18													98	18

AGE OF LOAN	20	21	22	23	24	25	26	27	28	29	30	35	40	AGE OF LOAN
					ORIGINAL TERM IN YEARS									
1	979	981	983	984	986	987	988	989	990	991	992	995	996	1
2	956	960	964	967	970	973	975	977	979	981	983	989	993	2
3	931	938	943	949	953	957	961	964	968	970	973	982	988	3
4	904	913	921	929	935	941	946	951	955	959	962	975	984	4
5	875	887	897	907	915	923	930	936	941	946	951	968	979	5
6	844	859	872	883	894	903	912	919	926	933	938	960	974	6
7	810	828	844	858	871	882	892	902	910	918	925	951	968	7
8	773	794	813	830	846	859	872	883	893	902	910	942	962	8
9	733	758	780	800	818	834	849	862	874	885	894	931	955	9
10	689	719	745	768	789	808	824	840	853	866	877	920	948	10
11	642	676	706	733	757	779	798	816	831	846	859	908	940	11
12	592	630	664	695	722	747	769	789	807	824	839	895	931	12
13	537	580	619	654	685	713	738	761	781	800	817	881	922	13
14	477	526	570	609	645	676	705	730	753	774	793	866	912	14
15	413	468	517	561	601	636	668	697	723	746	768	849	901	15
16	343	405	460	509	553	593	629	661	690	716	740	831	889	16
17	267	336	398	453	502	546	586	622	654	684	710	812	876	17
18	185	262	330	391	446	495	539	579	615	648	678	791	862	18
19	96	181	257	325	386	440	489	534	574	610	643	768	847	19
20		94	178	253	320	381	435	484	528		605	743	831	20
21			93	175	250	316	376	430	479	523	564	716	814	21
22				91	173	246	312	372	426	475	519	688	795	22
23					90	171	243	309	368	422	471	656	774	23
24						89	169	241	306	365	418	622	752	24
25							88	167	238	303	362	585	728	25
26								87	165	236	301	546	701	26
27									86	164	234	502	673	27
28										85	162	456	642	28
29											84	405	609	29
30												350	573	30
31												291	534	31
32												227	492	32
33												157	446	33
34												82	397	34
35													343	35

8¼%

LOAN PROGRESS CHART
Showing remaining balance on $1000 loan

AGE OF LOAN	ORIGINAL TERM IN YEARS													AGE OF LOAN
	2	3	5	6	8	10	12	14	15	16	17	18	19	
1	521	694	831	866	908	933	949	960	965	969	972	975	977	1
2		361	648	720	808	860	894	917	927	934	941	947	953	2
3			450	561	699	781	834	871	885	897	908	918	926	3
4			234	389	581	695	769	820	840	857	872	885	897	4
5				203	454	601	698	765	791	814	833	850	865	5
6					315	500	621	705	738	766	791	812	831	6
7					164	390	537	640	680	715	745	771	794	7
8						271	447	570	617	659	695	726	753	8
9						141	349	493	549	598	640	677	709	9
10							242	410	476	532	581	624	662	10
11							126	320	395	461	517	567	610	11
12								222	308	383	448	504	554	12
13								115	214	299	372	436	493	13
14									111	207	290	363	427	14
15									108	201	283	355		15
16										105	196	277		16
17											102	192		17
18												100		18

AGE OF LOAN	ORIGINAL TERM IN YEARS													AGE OF LOAN
	20	21	22	23	24	25	26	27	28	29	30	35	40	
1	979	981	983	985	986	987	989	990	990	991	992	995	997	1
2	957	961	965	968	971	974	976	978	980	982	983	989	993	2
3	933	939	945	950	955	959	963	966	969	972	974	983	989	3
4	907	916	924	931	937	943	948	953	957	960	964	977	985	4
5	878	890	900	910	918	925	932	938	943	948	953	970	980	5
6	847	862	875	887	897	906	915	922	929	935	941	962	975	6
7	814	832	848	862	874	886	896	905	914	921	928	954	970	7
8	777	799	818	835	850	863	876	887	897	906	914	945	964	8
9	738	763	785	805	823	839	853	866	878	889	898	935	958	9
10	695	724	750	773	794	813	829	845	858	871	882	924	951	10
11	648	682	712	739	763	784	803	821	837	851	864	912	943	11
12	597	636	670	701	728	753	775	795	813	829	844	900	935	12
13	542	586	625	660	691	719	744	767	787	806	823	886	926	13
14	483	532	576	616	651	683	711	737	760	781	800	871	916	14
15	418	474	523	568	607	643	675	704	730	753	774	855	906	15
16	347	410	466	515	560	600	635	668	697	723	747	837	894	16
17	271	341	403	459	508	553	593	629	661	691	717	818	882	17
18	188	266	335	397	452	502	546	587	623	656	685	798	869	18
19	98	184	261	330	391	447	496	541	581	617	650	775	854	19
20		96	181	257	326	387	441	491	536	576	613	751	838	20
21			94	179	254	321	382	437	486	531	571	724	821	21
22				93	176	251	318	378	433	482	527	696	802	22
23					92	174	248	314	375	429	478	665	782	23
24						91	172	245	311	371	426	631	760	24
25							89	170	243	309	368	594	736	25
26								89	168	241	306	554	710	26
27									88	167	239	511	682	27
28										87	166	464	651	28
29											86	413	618	29
30												357	582	30
31												297	543	31
32												232	501	32
33												161	455	33
34												84	404	34
35													350	35

LOAN PROGRESS CHART
Showing remaining balance on $1000 loan

AGE OF LOAN	2	3	5	6	8	10	12	14	15	16	17	18	19	AGE OF LOAN
1	521	694	832	867	909	934	950	961	966	969	973	975	978	1
2		362	650	721	810	861	895	919	928	936	943	949	954	2
3			451	563	701	783	836	873	887	899	910	919	928	3
4			235	391	584	697	771	823	843	860	875	888	899	4
5				204	456	604	701	768	794	817	836	853	868	5
6					317	503	624	709	742	770	794	816	834	6
7					165	393	541	644	684	719	749	775	798	7
8						273	450	574	622	663	699	730	758	8
9						142	352	497	554	603	645	682	714	9
10							244	414	480	537	586	629	667	10
11							127	323	400	465	522	572	615	11
12								224	312	387	452	509	559	12
13								117	217	302	377	441	498	13
14									113	210	294	367	432	14
15										109	204	287	359	15
16											106	199	280	16
17												104	195	17
18													102	18

AGE OF LOAN	20	21	22	23	24	25	26	27	28	29	30	35	40	AGE OF LOAN
1	980	982	984	985	987	988	989	990	991	992	992	995	997	1
2	958	962	966	969	972	975	977	979	981	983	984	990	994	2
3	935	941	947	952	956	960	964	967	970	973	975	984	990	3
4	909	918	926	933	939	945	950	954	958	962	966	978	986	4
5	881	893	903	912	921	928	934	940	946	951	955	971	982	5
6	851	865	878	890	900	909	918	925	932	938	943	964	977	6
7	818	836	851	865	878	889	899	909	917	924	931	956	972	7
8	782	803	822	839	854	867	880	890	900	909	917	947	966	8
9	743	768	790	810	828	844	858	871	882	893	902	938	960	9
10	700	729	755	778	799	818	834	849	863	875	886	928	953	10
11	654	687	717	744	768	790	809	826	842	856	868	916	946	11
12	603	642	676	707	734	759	781	801	818	835	849	904	938	12
13	548	592	631	666	697	725	750	773	793	812	828	891	930	13
14	488	538	583	622	657	689	717	743	766	787	806	876	921	14
15	423	479	529	574	614	649	681	710	736	760	781	861	910	15
16	352	415	472	522	566	606	642	675	704	730	754	843	899	16
17	275	346	409	465	515	559	600	636	669	698	725	825	887	17
18	191	270	340	403	458	508	553	594	630	663	693	805	874	18
19	99	187	266	335	397	453	503	548	588	625	658	782	860	19
20		98	184	262	331	392	448	498	543	583	620	758	845	20
21			96	182	258	327	388	443	493	538	579	732	828	21
22				95	179	255	323	384	439	489	534	704	810	22
23					93	177	252	320	381	436	486	673	790	23
24						92	175	250	317	378	432	639	768	24
25							91	173	247	314	375	602	744	25
26								90	172	245	312	562	719	26
27									90	170	244	519	691	27
28										89	169	472	660	28
29											88	420	627	29
30												364	591	30
31												303	552	31
32												237	509	32
33												164	463	33
34												86	412	34
35													357	35

8¾%

LOAN PROGRESS CHART
Showing remaining balance on $1000 loan

AGE OF LOAN	2	3	5	6	8	10	12	14	15	16	17	18	19	AGE OF LOAN
1	522	695	833	867	910	935	951	962	966	970	973	976	979	1
2		363	651	723	811	863	897	920	929	937	944	950	955	2
3			453	565	704	785	838	875	889	901	912	921	930	3
4			236	393	586	700	774	825	845	862	877	890	902	4
5				205	458	607	704	771	797	820	839	853	871	5
6					319	506	628	712	745	774	798	819	838	6
7					166	396	545	648	688	723	753	779	802	7
8						275	454	578	626	668	704	735	762	8
9						144	355	501	558	607	650	687	719	9
10							247	418	484	542	591	634	672	10
11							129	326	404	470	527	577	621	11
12								227	315	391	457	514	565	12
13								118	219	306	381	446	503	13
14									114	213	298	372	437	14
15									111	207	291	364		15
16										108	202	284		16
17										105	198			17
18											103			18

AGE OF LOAN	20	21	22	23	24	25	26	27	28	29	30	35	40	AGE OF LOAN
1	981	983	984	986	987	988	989	990	991	992	993	995	997	1
2	960	964	967	970	973	976	978	980	982	983	985	991	994	2
3	937	943	949	953	958	962	965	969	971	974	976	985	991	3
4	912	920	928	935	941	947	952	956	960	964	967	979	987	4
5	884	896	906	915	923	930	937	943	948	953	957	973	983	5
6	854	869	882	893	903	912	921	928	934	940	946	966	978	6
7	822	839	855	869	882	893	903	912	920	927	934	958	973	7
8	786	807	826	843	858	871	883	894	904	913	920	950	968	8
9	747	773	795	815	832	848	862	875	886	897	906	941	962	9
10	705	734	760	784	804	823	839	854	867	879	890	930	956	10
11	659	693	723	750	773	795	814	831	847	860	873	920	949	11
12	609	647	682	713	740	765	786	806	824	840	854	908	942	12
13	554	598	637	672	704	731	756	779	799	817	834	895	934	13
14	494	544	589	628	664	695	724	749	772	793	811	881	925	14
15	428	485	535	580	620	656	688	717	743	766	787	866	915	15
16	357	421	477	528	573	613	649	681	711	737	761	849	904	16
17	279	351	414	471	521	566	607	643	676	705	732	831	893	17
18	194	274	345	408	465	515	560	601	637	670	700	811	880	18
19	101	191	270	340	403	459	510	555	596	632	665	789	866	19
20		99	188	266	336	398	454	505	550	591	628	766	851	20
21			98	185	263	332	394	450	500	546	587	740	835	21
22				96	183	259	328	390	446	496	542	712	817	22
23					95	180	257	325	387	443	493	681	797	23
24						94	179	254	322	384	439	647	776	24
25							93	177	252	320	381	611	753	25
26								92	175	250	318	571	727	26
27									91	174	248	527	699	27
28										91	173	479	669	28
29											90	428	636	29
30												371	600	30
31												309	561	31
32												242	518	32
33												168	471	33
34												88	420	34
35													364	35

LOAN PROGRESS CHART
Showing remaining balance on $1000 loan

AGE OF LOAN	2	3	5	6	8	10	12	14	15	16	17	18	19	AGE OF LOAN
							ORIGINAL TERM IN YEARS							
1	522	696	834	868	911	935	951	963	967	971	974	977	979	1
2		364	653	724	813	865	898	922	931	939	945	951	956	2
3			454	567	706	787	840	877	891	903	914	923	931	3
4			237	395	589	703	777	828	848	865	880	893	904	4
5			206	461	610	707	775	801	823	843	859	874		5
6				321	509	631	716	749	777	802	823	841		6
7				168	398	548	652	692	727	757	783	806		7
8					277	457	582	630	672	708	739	767		8
9					145	358	505	563	612	654	691	724		9
10						249	422	489	546	596	639	677		10
11						130	330	408	474	532	582	626		11
12							230	319	396	462	520	570		12
13							120	222	310	385	451	509		13
14								116	216	302	376	442		14
15									113	210	294	368		15
16										110	205	288		16
17											107	201		17
18												105		18

AGE OF LOAN	20	21	22	23	24	25	26	27	28	29	30	35	40	AGE OF LOAN
					ORIGINAL TERM IN YEARS									
1	981	983	985	986	988	989	990	991	992	992	993	996	997	1
2	961	965	968	971	974	977	979	981	983	984	986	991	994	2
3	938	945	950	955	959	962	967	970	973	975	978	986	991	3
4	914	923	930	937	943	949	954	958	962	965	969	980	988	4
5	887	898	909	918	926	933	939	945	950	955	959	974	984	5
6	858	872	885	896	906	915	923	931	937	943	948	968	980	6
7	826	843	859	873	885	896	906	915	923	930	936	960	975	7
8	791	812	831	847	862	875	887	898	907	916	924	952	970	8
9	752	777	799	819	837	852	866	879	890	900	910	944	965	9
10	710	740	766	789	809	827	844	858	872	884	894	934	959	10
11	664	698	728	755	779	800	819	836	851	865	878	924	952	11
12	614	653	688	718	746	770	792	812	829	845	859	912	945	12
13	559	604	643	678	710	737	762	785	805	823	839	900	937	13
14	499	550	595	634	670	702	730	755	778	799	817	886	929	14
15	433	491	541	587	627	662	695	723	749	772	793	871	919	15
16	362	426	483	534	579	620	656	688	717	743	767	855	909	16
17	283	355	420	477	527	573	613	650	682	712	738	837	898	17
18	197	278	350	414	471	522	567	608	644	677	707	818	885	18
19	103	194	274	345	409	466	516	562	603	640	673	796	872	19
20		101	191	270	341	404	461	512	557	598	635	773	857	20
21			100	188	267	337	400	457	507	553	594	747	841	21
22				98	186	264	334	397	453	504	549	719	824	22
23					97	184	261	331	393	449	500	689	805	23
24						96	182	259	328	390	446	655	783	24
25							95	180	257	326	388	619	761	25
26								94	179	255	323	579	735	26
27									93	177	253	535	708	27
28										93	176	487	678	28
29											92	435	645	29
30												378	609	30
31												315	570	31
32												247	527	32
33												172	479	33
34												90	428	34
35													372	35

9¼%

LOAN PROGRESS CHART
Showing remaining balance on $1000 loan

AGE OF LOAN	2	3	5	6	8	10	12	14	15	16	17	18	19	AGE OF LOAN
1	523	697	835	869	911	936	952	963	968	971	975	977	980	1
2		364	654	726	814	866	900	923	932	940	947	952	957	2
3			456	569	708	790	842	879	893	905	916	925	933	3
4			238	396	591	705	780	831	851	868	882	895	906	4
5				207	463	613	710	778	804	826	846	862	877	5
6					323	512	635	720	753	781	805	826	845	6
7					169	401	552	656	696	731	761	787	810	7
8						280	461	586	635	676	712	744	771	8
9						146	361	509	567	616	659	696	729	9
10							252	425	493	551	601	644	682	10
11							132	333	412	479	537	587	631	11
12								232	322	400	467	525	575	12
13								121	225	313	390	456	514	13
14									118	218	305	381	447	14
15									114	213	298	373		15
16										111	208	292		16
17											109	204		17
18												107		18

AGE OF LOAN	20	21	22	23	24	25	26	27	28	29	30	35	40	AGE OF LOAN
1	982	984	985	987	988	989	990	991	992	993	994	996	998	1
2	962	966	969	972	975	978	980	982	983	985	986	992	995	2
3	940	946	952	957	961	965	968	971	974	976	979	987	992	3
4	916	925	932	939	945	951	955	960	963	967	970	982	989	4
5	890	901	911	920	928	935	941	947	952	957	961	976	985	5
6	861	875	888	899	909	918	926	933	939	945	950	969	981	6
7	830	847	863	876	889	899	909	918	926	933	939	962	977	7
8	795	816	835	851	866	879	891	901	911	919	927	955	972	8
9	757	782	804	824	841	857	871	883	895	904	913	947	967	9
10	715	745	771	793	814	832	848	863	876	888	898	937	961	10
11	670	704	734	760	784	805	824	841	856	870	882	927	955	11
12	620	659	693	724	751	776	797	817	834	850	864	916	948	12
13	565	610	649	684	715	743	768	790	810	828	844	904	941	13
14	505	556	601	641	676	708	736	761	784	805	823	891	932	14
15	439	496	547	593	633	669	701	730	755	779	799	876	923	15
16	366	431	489	540	586	626	662	695	724	750	773	861	913	16
17	287	360	425	483	534	579	620	657	689	719	745	843	903	17
18	200	282	355	420	477	528	574	615	651	684	714	823	891	18
19	105	197	278	350	415	472	523	569	610	647	680	803	878	19
20		103	194	274	346	410	467	518	564	605	643	780	863	20
21			101	191	271	342	406	463	514	560	602	755	848	21
22				100	189	268	339	403	460	511	557	727	830	22
23					99	187	266	336	399	456	507	697	812	23
24						98	185	263	334	397	453	663	791	24
25							97	184	261	331	394	627	768	25
26								96	182	259	329	587	743	26
27									95	181	258	543	716	27
28										95	180	495	686	28
29											94	442	653	29
30												384	618	30
31												321	578	31
32												252	535	32
33												175	488	33
34												92	436	34
35													379	35

LOAN PROGRESS CHART
Showing remaining balance on $1000 loan

AGE OF LOAN	|	2	3	5	6	8	10	12	14	15	16	17	18	19
						ORIGINAL TERM IN YEARS								
1		524	698	836	870	912	937	953	964	968	972	975	978	980
2			365	656	727	816	868	901	925	934	941	948	954	959
3				457	570	710	792	845	881	895	907	918	927	935
4				240	398	594	708	782	833	853	870	885	898	909
5					208	465	616	714	781	807	829	849	865	880
6						325	515	638	723	756	784	809	830	848
7						170	404	555	660	700	735	765	791	813
8							282	464	590	639	681	717	748	775
9							148	364	513	571	621	664	701	733
10								254	429	497	555	606	649	687
11								133	337	416	483	542	592	636
12									235	326	404	471	530	581
13									123	227	317	394	461	519
14										119	221	309	385	452
15											116	216	302	378
16												113	211	296
17													110	207
18														108

AGE OF LOAN	|	20	21	22	23	24	25	26	27	28	29	30	35	40
						ORIGINAL TERM IN YEARS								
1		982	984	986	987	989	990	991	992	992	993	994	996	998
2		963	967	970	973	976	978	981	982	984	986	987	992	995
3		942	948	953	958	962	966	969	972	975	977	980	988	992
4		918	927	934	941	947	952	957	961	965	968	971	983	989
5		893	904	914	923	930	937	943	949	954	958	962	977	986
6		864	879	891	902	912	921	929	936	942	947	951	971	982
7		833	851	866	880	892	903	912	921	929	935	942	964	978
8		799	820	839	855	870	883	894	905	914	922	930	957	974
9		762	787	809	828	845	861	875	887	898	908	917	949	969
10		720	750	775	798	819	837	853	867	880	892	902	940	963
11		675	709	739	766	789	810	829	846	861	874	886	931	957
12		625	664	699	730	757	781	803	822	839	855	869	920	951
13		570	615	655	699	721	749	774	796	816	834	850	908	944
14		510	561	607	647	682	714	742	767	790	810	828	896	936
15		444	502	553	599	639	675	707	736	762	785	805	881	927
16		371	437	495	546	592	633	669	701	730	756	780	866	918
17		291	365	431	489	540	586	627	663	696	725	752	849	907
18		203	286	360	425	483	535	581	622	658	691	721	830	896
19		106	200	282	355	420	478	530	576	617	654	687	809	883
20			105	197	279	351	416	474	525	571	613	650	787	869
21				103	194	276	348	412	470	521	567	609	762	854
22					102	192	273	345	409	466	518	564	735	837
23						101	190	270	342	406	463	514	704	818
24							100	189	268	339	403	460	671	798
25								99	187	266	337	400	635	776
26									98	186	264	335	595	751
27										97	184	262	551	724
28											96	183	503	695
29												96	450	662
30													391	626
31													327	587
32													256	543
33													179	496
34													94	443
35														386

9¾%

LOAN PROGRESS CHART
Showing remaining balance on $1000 loan

AGE OF LOAN	ORIGINAL TERM IN YEARS													AGE OF LOAN
	2	3	5	6	8	10	12	14	15	16	17	18	19	
1	524	698	837	871	913	938	954	965	969	973	976	978	981	1
2	366	657	729	818	869	903	926	935	943	949	955	960		2
3		459	572	712	794	847	883	897	909	920	929	937		3
4		241	400	596	711	785	836	856	873	887	900	911		4
5			210	468	619	717	784	810	832	852	868	883		5
6				327	518	642	727	760	788	812	833	852		6
7				171	407	559	664	704	739	769	795	817		7
8					284	448	594	643	685	721	752	780		8
9					149	367	518	576	626	668	706	738		9
10						257	433	501	560	610	654	692		10
11							134	340	420	488	546	597	642	11
12								238	330	408	476	535	586	12
13								125	230	320	398	466	524	13
14									121	224	313	390	457	14
15									117	218	306	382		15
16										115	214	300		16
17											112	210		17
18												110		18

AGE OF LOAN	ORIGINAL TERM IN YEARS													AGE OF LOAN
	20	21	22	23	24	25	26	27	28	29	30	35	40	
1	983	985	986	988	989	990	991	992	993	994	994	996	998	1
2	964	968	971	974	977	979	981	983	985	986	988	993	995	2
3	943	949	955	959	964	967	971	973	976	978	981	989	993	3
4	921	929	936	943	949	954	959	963	966	970	973	984	990	4
5	895	906	916	925	933	940	946	951	956	960	964	978	987	5
6	868	882	894	905	915	923	931	938	944	950	955	973	983	6
7	837	854	870	883	895	906	915	924	931	938	944	966	980	7
8	803	824	843	859	873	886	898	908	917	925	933	959	975	8
9	766	791	813	832	850	865	878	891	901	911	920	952	971	9
10	725	755	780	803	823	841	857	871	884	896	906	944	966	10
11	680	714	744	771	794	815	834	850	865	878	890	934	960	11
12	631	670	705	735	762	786	808	827	844	860	873	924	954	12
13	576	621	661	696	727	755	779	801	821	839	855	912	947	13
14	515	567	612	653	688	720	748	773	796	816	834	900	939	14
15	449	508	559	605	645	681	713	742	768	791	811	886	931	15
16	376	442	501	552	598	639	675	708	737	763	786	871	922	16
17	295	370	436	495	546	592	633	670	703	732	758	854	912	17
18	206	291	365	431	489	541	587	628	665	698	728	836	900	18
19	108	203	287	361	426	484	536	582	624	661	694	816	888	19
20		106	200	283	357	422	480	532	578	620	657	793	875	20
21			105	198	280	353	418	476	528	575	616	769	860	21
22				104	196	277	350	415	473	525	571	742	843	22
23					103	194	275	347	412	470	522	712	825	23
24						101	192	273	345	409	467	679	805	24
25							101	190	271	342	407	643	783	25
26								100	189	269	340	603	759	26
27									99	188	267	559	732	27
28										98	187	510	703	28
29											98	457	670	29
30												398	634	30
31												333	595	31
32												261	551	32
33												183	504	33
34												96	451	34
35													393	35

LOAN PROGRESS CHART
Showing remaining balance on $1000 loan

ORIGINAL TERM IN YEARS

AGE OF LOAN	2	3	5	6	8	10	12	14	15	16	17	18	19	AGE OF LOAN
1	525	699	838	872	914	939	955	965	970	973	976	979	981	1
2		367	658	730	819	871	904	927	936	944	950	956	961	2
3			460	574	714	796	849	885	899	911	922	930	938	3
4			242	401	598	713	788	839	858	875	890	902	913	4
5				211	470	622	720	787	813	835	855	871	885	5
6					329	521	645	730	763	791	816	837	855	6
7					173	410	562	668	708	743	773	799	821	7
8						286	471	598	647	689	725	757	784	8
9						150	370	522	580	630	673	710	743	9
10							259	437	506	565	615	659	697	10
11							136	343	424	492	551	602	647	11
12								240	333	412	481	540	591	12
13								126	233	324	403	471	530	13
14									122	227	316	394	462	14
15										119	221	310	387	15
16											116	217	304	16
17												114	213	17
18													112	18

ORIGINAL TERM IN YEARS

AGE OF LOAN	20	21	22	23	24	25	26	27	28	29	30	35	40	AGE OF LOAN
1	983	985	987	988	989	991	992	992	993	994	994	997	998	1
2	965	969	972	975	978	980	982	984	986	987	988	993	996	2
3	945	951	956	961	965	969	972	975	977	979	982	989	993	3
4	923	931	938	945	951	956	960	964	968	971	974	985	991	4
5	898	909	919	927	935	942	948	953	958	962	966	980	988	5
6	871	885	897	908	918	926	934	940	946	952	957	974	984	6
7	841	858	873	886	898	909	918	927	934	941	946	968	981	7
8	807	828	847	863	877	890	901	911	920	928	935	961	977	8
9	771	796	817	837	854	869	882	894	905	914	923	954	972	9
10	730	759	785	808	828	846	861	876	888	899	909	946	968	10
11	685	719	749	776	799	820	838	855	870	883	894	937	962	11
12	636	675	710	741	768	792	813	832	849	864	878	927	956	12
13	581	627	666	702	733	760	785	807	826	844	859	916	950	13
14	521	573	618	659	694	726	754	779	801	821	839	904	942	14
15	454	513	565	611	652	688	720	748	774	796	817	891	934	15
16	380	447	506	559	605	645	682	714	743	769	792	876	926	16
17	299	375	442	500	553	599	640	677	709	738	765	860	916	17
18	209	295	370	436	495	547	594	635	672	705	734	842	905	18
19	110	206	291	366	432	491	543	589	631	668	701	822	893	19
20		108	203	287	362	428	486	539	585	627	664	800	880	20
21			107	201	284	358	424	483	535	582	623	776	865	21
22				105	199	282	355	421	479	532	578	749	849	22
23					104	197	279	353	418	476	529	719	832	23
24						103	195	277	350	415	474	687	812	24
25							102	194	275	348	413	651	790	25
26								102	192	273	346	611	766	26
27									101	191	272	567	740	27
28										100	190	518	711	28
29											100	464	678	29
30												405	643	30
31												339	603	31
32												266	560	32
33												186	511	33
34												98	458	34
35													400	35

LOAN PROGRESS CHART
Showing remaining balance on $1000 loan

AGE OF LOAN	2	3	5	6	8	10	12	14	15	16	17	18	19	AGE OF LOAN
					ORIGINAL TERM IN YEARS									
1	525	700	839	873	915	939	955	966	970	974	977	980	982	1
2		368	660	732	821	872	906	929	937	945	952	957	962	2
3			462	576	716	798	851	887	901	913	923	932	940	3
4			243	403	601	716	790	841	861	878	892	904	915	4
5				212	473	625	723	790	816	838	857	874	888	5
6					331	524	648	734	767	795	819	840	858	6
7					174	412	566	671	712	747	777	802	825	7
8						289	475	602	651	693	730	761	788	8
9						152	373	526	584	634	678	715	747	9
10						261	441	510	569	620	664	702	10	
11							137	347	428	497	556	607	652	11
12							243	337	417	485	545	596	12	
13							128	236	328	407	475	535	13	
14								124	229	320	399	467	14	
15								121	224	314	391	15		
16									118	220	308	16		
17										115	216	17		
18											113	18		

AGE OF LOAN	20	21	22	23	24	25	26	27	28	29	30	35	40	AGE OF LOAN
					ORIGINAL TERM IN YEARS									
1	984	986	987	989	990	991	992	993	993	994	995	997	998	1
2	966	970	973	976	979	981	983	985	986	988	989	993	996	2
3	947	952	958	962	966	970	973	976	978	980	982	990	994	3
4	925	933	940	947	952	957	962	966	969	972	975	985	991	4
5	901	912	921	930	937	944	950	955	959	964	967	981	989	5
6	874	888	900	911	920	929	936	943	949	954	959	976	986	6
7	844	861	876	890	901	912	921	929	936	943	949	970	982	7
8	812	832	850	867	881	893	904	914	923	931	938	964	978	8
9	775	800	822	841	858	873	886	898	908	918	926	956	974	9
10	735	764	790	812	832	850	866	880	892	903	913	949	970	10
11	691	725	754	781	804	825	843	859	874	887	898	940	964	11
12	641	681	715	746	773	797	818	837	854	869	882	931	959	12
13	587	632	672	707	738	766	790	812	831	849	864	920	953	13
14	526	578	624	664	700	732	760	785	807	827	844	908	946	14
15	459	519	571	617	658	694	726	754	779	802	822	895	938	15
16	385	453	512	565	611	652	688	720	749	775	798	881	929	16
17	303	380	447	506	559	605	646	683	716	745	771	865	920	17
18	212	299	375	442	501	554	600	642	679	711	741	847	909	18
19	112	209	295	371	437	497	549	596	638	675	708	828	898	19
20		110	207	292	367	433	493	545	592	634	671	806	885	20
21			109	204	289	364	430	489	542	589	630	782	871	21
22				107	202	286	361	427	486	538	585	756	855	22
23					106	200	284	358	424	483	536	727	838	23
24						105	199	282	356	422	480	694	818	24
25							104	197	280	354	419	658	797	25
26								104	196	278	352	618	773	26
27									103	195	277	574	747	27
28										102	194	525	718	28
29											102	471	686	29
30												411	651	30
31												345	611	31
32												271	568	32
33												190	519	33
34												100	466	34
35													407	35

LOAN PROGRESS CHART
Showing remaining balance on $1000 loan

AGE OF LOAN	\(ORIGINAL TERM IN YEARS\) 2	3	5	6	8	10	12	14	15	16	17	18	19	AGE OF LOAN
1	526	701	839	874	916	940	956	967	971	975	978	980	982	1
2		369	661	733	822	874	907	930	939	946	953	958	963	2
3			463	578	718	800	853	889	903	915	925	934	941	3
4			244	405	603	719	793	844	863	880	894	907	917	4
5				213	475	628	726	793	819	841	860	877	891	5
6					333	527	652	737	770	798	822	843	861	6
7					175	415	570	675	716	751	780	806	828	7
8						291	478	606	656	698	734	765	792	8
9						153	377	530	589	639	682	719	752	9
10							264	445	514	574	625	661	707	10
11							139	350	432	501	561	612	657	11
12								245	340	421	490	550	601	12
13								129	238	331	411	480	540	13
14									125	232	324	403	472	14
15									122	227	318	396		15
16										119	223	312		16
17											117	219		17
18												115		18

AGE OF LOAN	\(ORIGINAL TERM IN YEARS\) 20	21	22	23	24	25	26	27	28	29	30	35	40	AGE OF LOAN
1	984	986	988	989	990	991	992	993	994	994	995	997	998	1
2	967	971	974	977	979	982	984	985	987	988	989	994	996	2
3	948	954	959	963	967	971	974	977	979	981	983	990	994	3
4	927	935	942	948	954	959	963	967	971	974	976	986	992	4
5	903	914	923	932	939	946	951	957	961	965	969	982	989	5
6	877	891	903	913	923	931	938	945	951	956	960	977	986	6
7	848	865	880	893	904	915	924	932	939	945	951	971	983	7
8	816	836	854	870	884	897	908	917	926	934	941	965	980	8
9	780	804	826	845	862	876	890	901	912	921	929	959	976	9
10	740	769	794	817	837	854	870	883	896	907	916	951	971	10
11	696	730	760	786	809	829	848	864	878	891	902	943	967	11
12	647	686	721	751	778	802	823	842	858	873	886	934	962	12
13	592	638	678	713	744	771	796	817	836	853	869	924	955	13
14	532	584	630	670	706	737	765	790	812	832	849	912	948	14
15	464	524	577	623	664	700	732	760	785	808	828	900	941	15
16	390	458	518	570	617	658	694	727	755	781	804	886	933	16
17	307	385	452	512	565	612	653	689	722	751	777	870	924	17
18	215	303	380	448	507	560	607	648	685	718	747	853	914	18
19	113	212	299	376	443	503	556	603	644	681	714	834	902	19
20		112	210	296	372	439	499	552	599	641	678	812	890	20
21			110	207	293	369	436	495	548	595	637	789	876	21
22				109	205	290	366	433	492	545	592	763	861	22
23					108	204	288	363	430	490	543	734	844	23
24						107	202	286	361	428	487	701	825	24
25							106	201	284	359	426	666	804	25
26								106	199	283	357	626	781	26
27									105	198	281	582	755	27
28										104	197	533	726	28
29											104		694	29
30												418	659	30
31												351	619	31
32												276	575	32
33												194	527	33
34												102	473	34
35													413	35

10¾%

LOAN PROGRESS CHART
Showing remaining balance on $1000 loan

AGE OF LOAN	ORIGINAL TERM IN YEARS													AGE OF LOAN
	2	3	5	6	8	10	12	14	15	16	17	18	19	
1	527	702	840	875	917	941	957	967	972	975	978	981	983	1
2		370	663	735	824	875	909	931	940	947	954	959	964	2
3			465	580	720	802	855	891	905	917	927	935	943	3
4			245	407	605	721	795	846	866	882	897	909	920	4
5				214	477	631	729	796	822	844	863	879	893	5
6					335	530	655	741	774	802	826	846	864	6
7					176	418	573	679	720	754	784	810	832	7
8						293	482	610	660	702	738	769	796	8
9						154	380	534	593	643	687	724	756	9
10							266	448	519	578	629	673	711	10
11							140	354	436	506	566	617	662	11
12								248	344	425	495	555	607	12
13								131	241	335	416	485	545	13
14									127	235	328	408	477	14
15									124	230	321	401		15
16										121	226	316		16
17											119	222		17
18												117		18

AGE OF LOAN	ORIGINAL TERM IN YEARS													AGE OF LOAN
	20	21	22	23	24	25	26	27	28	29	30	35	40	
1	985	987	988	989	991	992	993	993	994	995	996	997	998	1
2	968	972	975	978	980	982	984	986	987	989	990	994	997	2
3	950	955	960	965	969	972	975	978	980	982	984	991	995	3
4	929	937	944	950	956	960	965	969	972	975	978	987	993	4
5	906	916	926	934	941	948	953	958	963	967	970	983	990	5
6	880	894	906	916	925	933	941	947	953	958	962	978	987	6
7	851	868	883	896	907	918	926	934	941	948	953	973	984	7
8	820	840	858	874	888	900	911	920	929	936	943	967	981	8
9	784	809	830	849	866	880	893	905	915	924	932	961	977	9
10	745	774	799	821	841	858	874	887	899	910	919	954	973	10
11	701	735	764	791	814	834	852	868	882	894	906	946	969	11
12	652	691	726	756	783	807	828	846	863	877	890	937	963	12
13	598	643	683	718	749	777	801	822	841	858	873	927	958	13
14	537	590	636	676	712	743	771	795	817	837	854	916	951	14
15	470	530	583	629	670	706	738	766	791	813	833	904	944	15
16	395	463	524	576	623	664	700	733	761	787	809	890	936	16
17	311	389	458	518	571	618	659	696	728	757	783	875	928	17
18	218	307	385	453	513	566	613	655	692	724	754	858	918	18
19	115	215	303	381	449	509	562	609	651	688	721	839	907	19
20		113	213	300	377	445	505	558	605	647	685	819	895	20
21			112	211	297	374	442	502	555	602	644	795	881	21
22				111	209	295	371	439	499	552	599	769	866	22
23					110	207	293	369	436	496	549	741	850	23
24						109	205	291	367	434	494	709	831	24
25							108	204	289	365	432	673	810	25
26								107	203	288	363	633	787	26
27									107	202	286	589	762	27
28										106	201	540	733	28
29											106	485	702	29
30												424	666	30
31												357	627	31
32												281	583	32
33												197	535	33
34												104	480	34
35													420	35

LOAN PROGRESS CHART
Showing remaining balance on $1000 loan

AGE OF LOAN	2	3	5	6	8	10	12	14	15	16	17	18	19	AGE OF LOAN
					ORIGINAL TERM IN YEARS									
1	527	702	841	875	917	942	957	968	972	976	979	981	983	1
2		370	664	736	825	877	910	933	941	949	956	960	965	2
3			466	581	722	805	857	893	907	918	928	937	945	3
4			246	408	608	724	798	849	868	885	899	911	922	4
5				215	480	634	732	799	825	847	866	882	896	5
6					337	533	659	744	777	805	829	850	867	6
7					178	421	577	683	724	758	788	813	836	7
8						296	485	614	664	706	742	773	800	8
9						156	383	538	597	648	691	726	760	9
10							269	452	523	583	634	678	716	10
11							142	357	440	510	570	622	667	11
12								251	347	429	499	560	612	12
13								132	244	339	420	490	550	13
14									129	238	332	412	482	14
15										125	233	325	405	15
16											123	229	320	16
17												121	225	17
18													119	18

AGE OF LOAN	20	21	22	23	24	25	26	27	28	29	30	35	40	AGE OF LOAN
					ORIGINAL TERM IN YEARS									
1	985	987	989	990	991	992	993	994	994	995	995	997	999	1
2	969	973	976	979	981	983	985	987	988	989	990	995	997	2
3	951	957	962	966	970	973	976	979	981	983	985	991	997	3
4	931	939	946	952	957	962	966	970	973	976	979	988	993	4
5	908	919	928	936	943	950	955	960	964	968	972	984	991	5
6	883	896	908	919	928	936	943	949	955	960	964	979	988	6
7	855	872	886	899	910	920	929	937	944	950	955	974	985	7
8	823	844	862	877	891	903	914	923	931	939	945	969	982	8
9	788	813	834	853	869	884	897	908	918	927	935	963	979	9
10	749	778	803	826	845	862	877	891	903	913	923	956	975	10
11	706	740	769	795	818	838	856	872	886	898	909	948	970	11
12	657	697	731	762	788	812	832	851	867	881	894	940	965	12
13	603	649	689	724	755	782	806	827	846	863	877	930	960	13
14	542	595	641	682	717	749	776	801	822	842	859	920	954	14
15	475	535	588	635	676	712	743	771	796	818	838	908	947	15
16	399	469	529	582	629	670	706	739	767	792	815	895	940	16
17	315	394	463	524	577	624	665	702	734	763	789	880	931	17
18	221	311	390	459	519	572	619	661	698	731	760	863	922	18
19	117	219	308	386	454	515	568	616	657	694	727	845	911	19
20		115	216	305	382	451	511	565	612	654	691	824	899	20
21			114	214	302	379	448	508	562	609	651	801	886	21
22			113	212	299	377	445	505	559	606		776	872	22
23				112	210	297	374	442	503	556		747	855	23
24				111	209	295	372	440	500			716	837	24
25					110	207	294	370	438			680	817	25
26					109	206	292	368				641	794	26
27						109	205	291				596	769	27
28						108	204					547	741	28
29							108					492	709	29
30												431	674	30
31												363	635	31
32												286	591	32
33												201	542	33
34												106	488	34
35													427	35

11¼%

LOAN PROGRESS CHART
Showing remaining balance on $1000 loan

AGE OF LOAN	ORIGINAL TERM IN YEARS 2	3	5	6	8	10	12	14	15	16	17	18	19	AGE OF LOAN
1	528	703	842	876	918	943	958	969	973	976	979	982	984	1
2		371	666	738	827	878	911	934	942	950	956	961	966	2
3			468	583	725	807	859	895	909	920	930	939	946	3
4			247	410	610	726	801	851	871	887	901	913	924	4
5				217	482	636	735	802	828	850	869	885	899	5
6					339	536	662	748	780	808	832	853	870	6
7					179	424	580	687	727	762	792	817	839	7
8						298	488	618	668	710	746	777	804	8
9						157	386	542	601	652	695	733	765	9
10							271	456	527	587	639	683	721	10
11							143	361	444	514	575	627	672	11
12								254	351	433	504	564	617	12
13								134	247	342	424	495	555	13
14									130	241	335	417	487	14
15									127	236	329	410		15
16										124	231	324		16
17											122	228		17
18												120		18

AGE OF LOAN	ORIGINAL TERM IN YEARS 20	21	22	23	24	25	26	27	28	29	30	35	40	AGE OF LOAN
1	986	988	989	990	991	992	993	994	995	995	996	998	999	1
2	970	974	977	979	982	984	986	987	989	990	991	995	997	2
3	952	958	963	967	971	974	977	980	982	984	986	992	995	3
4	933	941	947	953	959	963	967	971	974	977	980	989	994	4
5	911	921	930	938	945	951	957	962	966	970	973	985	991	5
6	886	899	911	921	930	938	945	951	956	961	966	981	989	6
7	858	875	889	902	913	923	932	939	946	952	957	976	986	7
8	827	847	865	881	894	906	917	926	934	941	948	971	983	8
9	793	817	838	857	873	887	900	911	921	930	937	965	980	9
10	754	783	808	830	849	866	881	894	906	917	926	958	976	10
11	711	745	774	800	823	843	860	876	890	902	913	950	972	11
12	662	702	736	767	793	816	837	855	871	885	898	943	967	12
13	608	654	694	729	760	787	811	832	851	867	882	933	962	13
14	548	601	647	687	723	754	782	806	827	846	863	923	956	14
15	480	541	594	640	681	717	749	777	802	823	841	912	950	15
16	404	474	535	588	635	676	712	744	773	798	820	899	943	16
17	319	399	469	530	583	630	672	708	740	769	794	884	934	17
18	225	315	395	464	525	579	626	667	704	737	766	868	925	18
19	119	222	312	391	460	521	575	622	664	701	734	850	915	19
20		117	219	309	387	456	517	571	619	661	698	830	904	20
21			116	217	306	384	453	514	568	616	658	808	891	21
22				115	215	304	382	451	511	565	613	782	877	22
23					114	214	302	379	448	509	563	754	861	23
24						113	212	300	377	446	507	723	843	24
25							112	211	298	376	444	687	823	25
26								111	210	297	374	648	801	26
27									111	209	296	604	776	27
28										110	208	554	748	28
29											110	499	716	29
30												437	681	30
31												368	642	31
32												291	599	32
33												205	550	33
34												108	495	34
35													434	35

11½%

LOAN PROGRESS CHART

Showing remaining balance on $1000 loan

AGE OF LOAN	ORIGINAL TERM IN YEARS 2	3	5	6	8	10	12	14	15	16	17	18	19	AGE OF LOAN
1	529	704	843	877	919	943	959	969	973	977	980	982	984	1
2		372	667	739	828	880	913	935	944	951	957	962	967	2
3			470	585	727	809	861	897	910	922	932	940	947	3
4			248	412	612	729	803	854	873	889	903	915	926	4
5				218	485	639	738	805	831	853	871	887	901	5
6					341	539	665	751	784	812	835	856	873	6
7					180	426	584	690	731	766	795	821	843	7
8						300	492	622	672	714	750	781	808	8
9						159	389	546	606	656	700	737	769	9
10							274	460	531	592	643	687	725	10
11							145	364	448	519	580	632	677	11
12								256	354	437	508	569	622	12
13								135	249	346	429	499	560	13
14									132	244	339	421	492	14
15										129	239	333	414	15
16											126	234	328	16
17												124	231	17
18													122	18

AGE OF LOAN	ORIGINAL TERM IN YEARS 20	21	22	23	24	25	26	27	28	29	30	35	40	AGE OF LOAN
1	986	988	989	991	992	993	993	994	995	995	996	998	999	1
2	971	974	977	980	982	984	986	988	989	990	991	995	997	2
3	954	959	964	968	972	975	978	980	983	985	986	992	996	3
4	935	942	949	955	960	965	969	972	975	978	981	989	994	4
5	913	923	932	940	947	953	958	963	967	971	974	986	992	5
6	889	902	913	924	932	940	947	953	958	963	967	982	990	6
7	861	878	892	905	916	925	934	941	948	954	959	977	987	7
8	831	851	869	884	897	909	919	929	937	944	950	972	984	8
9	797	821	842	860	877	891	903	914	924	932	940	967	981	9
10	759	787	812	834	853	870	885	898	909	920	929	960	978	10
11	716	749	779	805	827	847	864	880	893	905	916	953	974	11
12	667	707	741	772	798	821	841	859	875	889	902	945	969	12
13	613	659	699	734	765	792	816	837	855	871	886	936	964	13
14	553	606	652	693	728	759	787	811	832	851	868	926	959	14
15	485	546	600	646	687	723	755	782	807	829	848	915	953	15
16	409	479	540	594	641	682	718	750	778	803	825	903	946	16
17	323	404	474	535	589	636	678	714	746	775	800	889	938	17
18	228	319	400	470	531	585	632	674	710	743	772	873	929	18
19	120	225	316	396	466	527	581	628	670	707	740	855	919	19
20		119	223	313	393	462	523	577	625	667	704	836	908	20
21			118	220	311	390	459	520	575	622	664	813	896	21
22				117	219	308	387	457	518	572	620	789	882	22
23					116	217	306	385	454	515	570	761	866	23
24						115	216	304	383	452	513	729	849	24
25							114	214	303	381	450	694	829	25
26								113	213	302	380	655	807	26
27									113	212	300	611	782	27
28										112	211	561	755	28
29											112	506	723	29
30												444	689	30
31												374	650	31
32												296	606	32
33												208	557	33
34												110	502	34
35													440	35

11¾%

LOAN PROGRESS CHART
Showing remaining balance on $1000 loan

AGE OF LOAN	2	3	5	6	8	10	12	14	15	16	17	18	19	AGE OF LOAN
						ORIGINAL TERM IN YEARS								
1	529	705	844	878	920	944	960	970	974	977	980	983	985	1
2		373	668	741	830	881	914	936	945	952	958	963	968	2
3			471	587	729	811	863	898	912	924	933	942	949	3
4			249	414	615	731	806	856	875	891	905	917	927	4
5				219	487	642	741	808	834	855	874	890	903	5
6					343	542	669	754	787	815	839	859	876	6
7					182	429	587	694	735	769	799	824	846	7
8						302	495	626	676	718	754	785	812	8
9						160	392	550	610	661	704	741	773	9
10							276	464	535	596	648	692	730	10
11							146	367	452	523	584	636	681	11
12								259	358	442	513	574	627	12
13								137	252	350	433	504	566	13
14									133	246	343	425	497	14
15										130	242	337	419	15
16											128	237	332	16
17												126	234	17
18													124	18

AGE OF LOAN	20	21	22	23	24	25	26	27	28	29	30	35	40	AGE OF LOAN
					ORIGINAL TERM IN YEARS									
1	987	988	990	991	992	993	994	994	995	996	996	998	999	1
2	972	975	978	981	983	985	987	988	990	991	992	996	998	2
3	955	961	965	969	973	976	979	981	983	985	987	993	996	3
4	936	944	951	957	962	966	970	973	977	979	982	990	994	4
5	915	925	934	942	949	955	960	965	969	972	975	987	993	5
6	891	905	916	926	935	942	949	955	960	965	969	983	990	6
7	865	881	895	908	919	928	936	944	950	956	961	978	988	7
8	835	855	872	887	900	912	922	931	939	946	952	974	985	8
9	801	825	846	864	880	894	906	917	927	935	942	968	982	9
10	763	792	817	838	857	874	889	901	913	923	931	962	979	10
11	720	754	784	809	832	851	868	884	897	909	919	956	975	11
12	672	712	746	776	803	826	846	864	879	893	906	948	971	12
13	619	665	705	740	770	797	821	841	859	875	890	939	966	13
14	558	611	658	698	734	765	792	816	837	856	872	930	961	14
15	490	552	605	652	693	729	760	788	812	834	852	919	955	15
16	413	484	546	600	647	688	724	756	784	809	830	907	948	16
17	327	409	479	541	595	642	684	720	752	780	805	893	941	17
18	231	324	404	475	537	591	638	680	717	749	777	878	932	18
19	122	228	324	401	471	533	587	635	676	713	746	860	923	19
20		121	224	317	398	468	530	584	631	674	711	841	912	20
21			119	224	315	395	465	527	581	629	671	819	900	21
22				118	222	313	392	462	524	578	626	795	886	22
23					117	220	311	390	460	522	576	767	871	23
24						117	219	309	388	458	520	736	854	24
25							116	218	308	387	456	701	835	25
26								115	217	306	385	662	813	26
27									115	216	305	618	789	27
28										114	215	568	761	28
29											114	513	730	29
30												450	696	30
31												380	657	31
32												301	613	32
33												212	564	33
34												112	509	34
35													447	35

LOAN PROGRESS CHART
Showing remaining balance on $1000 loan

AGE OF LOAN	2	3	5	6	8	10	12	14	15	16	17	18	19	AGE OF LOAN
					ORIGINAL	TERM	IN	YEARS						
1	530	706	845	879	921	945	960	971	975	978	981	983	985	1
2		374	670	742	831	883	915	938	946	953	959	964	969	2
3			473	589	731	813	865	900	914	925	935	943	950	3
4			250	415	617	734	808	858	877	894	907	919	929	4
5				220	489	645	744	811	837	858	877	892	902	5
6					345	545	672	758	790	818	842	862	879	6
7					183	432	590	698	738	773	802	828	849	7
8						305	499	630	680	722	758	789	815	8
9						161	395	554	614	665	708	745	777	9
10							279	468	540	600	652	696	735	10
11							148	371	456	528	589	641	686	11
12								262	361	446	518	579	632	12
13								139	255	353	437	509	571	13
14									135	249	347	430	501	14
15										132	245	341	424	15
16											130	240	336	16
17												127	237	17
18													126	18

AGE OF LOAN	20	21	22	23	24	25	26	27	28	29	30	35	40	AGE OF LOAN
				ORIGINAL	TERM	IN	YEARS							
1	987	989	990	991	992	993	994	995	995	996	996	998	999	1
2	973	976	979	982	984	986	987	989	990	991	992	996	998	2
3	956	962	966	970	974	977	980	982	984	986	988	993	996	3
4	938	946	952	958	963	967	971	975	978	980	982	990	995	4
5	917	928	936	944	951	957	962	966	970	974	977	987	993	5
6	894	907	918	928	937	944	951	957	962	966	970	984	991	6
7	868	884	898	910	921	930	939	946	952	958	963	980	989	7
8	838	858	875	890	903	915	925	934	941	948	954	975	986	8
9	805	829	850	868	884	897	909	920	929	938	945	970	984	9
10	767	796	821	842	861	878	892	905	916	926	934	964	980	10
11	725	759	788	814	836	855	872	887	900	912	922	958	977	11
12	677	717	751	781	807	830	850	868	883	897	909	950	973	12
13	624	670	710	745	775	802	825	846	864	880	894	942	968	13
14	563	617	663	704	739	770	797	821	842	860	876	933	963	14
15	495	557	611	657	698	734	765	793	817	838	857	922	958	15
16	418	489	551	605	652	694	730	761	789	814	835	910	951	16
17	332	413	485	547	601	648	689	726	758	786	811	897	944	17
18	234	328	409	480	542	597	644	686	723	755	783	882	936	18
19	124	231	325	406	477	539	593	641	683	720	752	865	926	19
20		123	229	322	403	473	536	590	638	680	717	846	916	20
21			121	227	319	400	471	533	587	635	677	825	904	21
22				120	225	317	398	468	530	585	633	800	891	22
23					119	224	315	395	466	528	583	773	876	23
24						119	222	314	394	464	526	742	859	24
25							118	221	312	392	462	708	840	25
26								117	220	311	391	669	819	26
27									117	219	310	625	795	27
28										116	219	575	768	28
29											116	519	737	29
30												457	703	30
31												386	664	31
32												306	621	32
33												216	571	33
34												114	516	34
35													453	35

REMAINING BALANCE TABLE

Showing remaining balance on $1000 loan

INTEREST RATE	DUE DATE YEARS	MONTHLY PAYBACK RATE (%)									
		.70	.80	.90	1.00	1.10	1.20	1.25	1.50	1.75	2.00
6%	1	975	963	951	938	926	914	907	877	846	815
	2	949	924	898	873	847	822	809	746	682	619
	3	921	882	843	803	764	725	705	607	508	410
	4	892	838	784	730	675	621	594	459	324	189
	5	860	791	721	651	581	512	477	302	128	
	6	827	741	654	568	482	395	352	136		
	7	792	688	584	480	376	271	219			
	8	754	632	509	386	263	140	79			
	9	715	572	429	286	144	1				
	10	672	508	344	181	17					
6½%	1	980	968	956	943	931	919	912	882	851	820
	2	960	934	908	883	857	832	819	755	691	627
	3	937	898	858	818	779	739	719	620	521	422
	4	913	859	804	750	695	640	613	476	340	203
	5	888	817	747	676	605	535	499	323	146	
	6	861	773	685	598	510	422	378	159		
	7	832	726	620	514	408	302	249			
	8	801	676	550	425	299	174	111			
	9	768	622	476	330	183	37				
	10	733	565	397	228	60					
6¾%	1	983	971	958	946	933	921	915	884	853	822
	2	965	939	914	888	862	837	824	760	696	632
	3	945	906	866	826	786	746	727	627	528	428
	4	924	870	815	760	705	650	622	485	348	210
	5	902	831	760	689	618	547	511	333	155	
	6	878	790	701	613	525	436	392	171		
	7	853	746	639	532	425	318	264			
	8	826	699	572	445	318	191	128			
	9	796	648	500	352	204	56				
	10	765	595	424	253	82					
7%	1	986	973	961	948	936	924	917	886	855	824
	2	970	944	919	893	867	842	829	765	700	636
	3	953	913	874	834	794	754	734	634	534	434
	4	936	880	825	770	715	660	632	494	356	218
	5	916	845	773	702	630	559	523	344	165	
	6	896	807	718	628	539	450	406	183		
	7	874	766	658	550	442	334	280	10		
	8	850	722	594	466	338	209	145			
	9	825	675	525	376	226	76	1			
	10	798	625	452	279	106					
7¼%	1	988	976	963	951	938	926	920	889	858	827
	2	975	950	924	898	872	847	834	769	705	641
	3	962	922	881	841	801	761	741	641	541	441
	4	947	891	836	780	725	669	642	503	364	225
	5	931	859	787	715	643	571	535	354	174	
	6	914	824	734	644	554	465	430	195		
	7	896	787	678	569	459	350	296	23		
	8	876	746	617	487	357	228	163			
	9	855	703	551	399	248	96	20			
	10	832	656	481	305	130					
7½%	1	991	978	966	953	941	929	922	891	860	829
	2	981	955	929	903	877	852	839	774	710	645
	3	970	930	889	849	809	769	749	648	547	447
	4	958	902	847	791	735	679	651	512	373	233
	5	946	873	801	728	655	583	547	365	184	3
	6	932	841	751	660	570	479	434	207		
	7	917	807	697	587	477	367	312	37		
	8	902	771	640	509	378	247	181			
	9	885	731	578	424	270	117	40			
	10	867	689	511	333	155					

REMAINING BALANCE TABLE

Showing remaining balance on $1000 loan

INTEREST RATE	DUE DATE YEARS	MONTHLY PAYBACK RATE (%)									
		.75	.80	.90	1.00	1.10	1.20	1.25	1.50	1.75	2.00
7¾%	1	987	981	968	956	944	931	925	894	863	832
	2	973	960	934	908	883	857	844	779	714	650
	3	958	938	897	857	817	776	756	655	554	453
	4	942	914	858	801	745	689	661	521	381	241
	5	924	887	814	741	668	595	559	376	194	11
	6	905	859	768	677	585	494	448	220		
	7	884	829	718	607	496	385	329	51		
	8	862	796	663	531	399	266	200			
	9	838	760	605	449	294	138	61			
	10	812	722	541	361	181					
8%	1	990	983	971	959	946	934	927	896	865	834
	2	978	965	939	914	888	862	849	784	719	654
	3	966	946	905	865	824	784	764	662	561	460
	4	953	925	869	812	756	699	671	530	390	249
	5	939	902	829	755	682	608	571	388	204	20
	6	923	877	785	693	601	509	463	233	3	
	7	907	851	738	626	514	402	346	66		
	8	888	822	688	554	420	286	219			
	9	869	790	633	475	318	160	82			
	10	848	756	573	390	207	24				
8¼%	1	992	986	974	961	949	936	930	899	868	836
	2	984	971	945	919	893	867	854	789	724	659
	3	975	954	914	873	832	791	771	669	568	466
	4	965	936	880	823	766	710	681	540	398	257
	5	954	917	843	769	695	621	584	399	214	29
	6	942	896	803	710	617	525	478	246	14	
	7	929	873	760	646	533	420	363	80		
	8	915	848	712	577	442	306	239			
	9	900	821	661	502	342	183	103			
	10	884	791	606	420	235	49				
8½%	1	995	989	976	964	951	939	932	901	870	839
	2	989	976	950	924	898	872	859	794	729	663
	3	983	963	922	881	840	799	779	677	575	472
	4	976	948	891	834	777	720	692	549	407	265
	5	969	932	857	783	708	634	597	411	225	38
	6	961	914	821	727	634	540	494	260	26	
	7	952	895	781	667	553	438	381	96		
	8	943	875	738	601	464	327	259			
	9	933	852	691	529	368	206	126			
	10	922	828	639	451	263	75				
8¾%	1	997	991	979	966	954	941	935	904	872	841
	2	995	981	955	929	903	877	864	799	733	668
	3	991	971	930	889	848	807	786	684	581	479
	4	988	959	902	845	788	731	702	559	416	273
	5	984	947	872	797	722	647	610	422	235	48
	6	980	933	839	745	650	556	509	273	38	
	7	976	918	803	688	572	457	399	111		
	8	971	902	764	625	487	349	280			
	9	966	884	721	557	394	231	149			
	10	960	865	674	483	292	102	6			
9%	1	1000	994	981	969	956	944	937	906	875	844
	2	1000	987	961	935	908	882	869	804	738	673
	3	1000	979	938	897	856	815	794	691	588	486
	4	1000	971	914	856	799	741	712	569	425	281
	5	1000	962	887	811	736	661	623	434	246	57
	6	1000	952	857	762	667	572	525	287	50	
	7	1000	942	825	709	593	476	418	127		
	8	1000	930	790	650	511	371	301			
	9	1000	917	752	586	421	255	173			
	10	1000	903	710	516	323	129	32			

REMAINING BALANCE TABLE

Showing remaining balance on $1000 loan

INTEREST RATE	DUE DATE YEARS	MONTHLY PAYBACK RATE (%)									
		.90	1.00	1.10	1.20	1.25	1.30	1.40	1.50	1.75	2.00
9¼%	1	984	971	959	946	940	934	921	909	877	846
	2	966	940	914	887	874	861	835	809	743	677
	3	947	905	864	823	802	781	740	699	596	492
	4	925	868	810	752	723	694	636	578	434	289
	5	902	826	750	674	636	598	522	446	257	67
	6	876	781	685	589	541	493	397	302	62	
	7	848	731	613	496	437	378	260	143		
	8	817	676	535	393	322	252	110			
	9	784	616	448	281	197	113				
	10	746	550	354	158	60					
9½%	1	986	974	961	949	943	936	924	911	880	849
	2	971	945	919	893	879	866	840	814	748	682
	3	955	914	872	831	810	789	748	706	603	499
	4	937	879	821	763	734	705	646	588	443	298
	5	917	841	764	688	650	612	535	459	268	77
	6	895	799	702	606	558	509	413	316	75	
	7	871	753	638	515	456	397	278	159		
	8	845	702	559	416	345	273	130			
	9	816	646	477	307	222	137				
	10	784	585	386	187	88					
9¾%	1	989	976	964	951	945	939	926	914	882	851
	2	977	951	924	898	885	871	845	819	753	687
	3	964	922	880	839	818	797	755	714	610	506
	4	949	890	832	774	744	715	657	598	452	306
	5	933	856	779	702	663	625	548	471	279	86
	6	915	818	720	623	574	526	428	331	88	
	7	895	775	656	536	476	416	296	176		
	8	874	729	584	440	368	295	151	6		
	9	850	678	506	334	248	162				
	10	823	621	419	217	117	16				
10%	1	992	979	966	954	948	941	929	916	885	853
	2	982	956	929	903	890	877	850	824	758	691
	3	972	930	889	847	826	805	763	721	617	513
	4	961	902	843	785	755	726	667	609	462	315
	5	948	871	794	716	677	639	561	484	290	97
	6	935	836	738	640	591	542	444	346	101	
	7	919	798	677	557	496	436	315	194		
	8	903	756	610	464	391	318	172	25		
	9	884	710	536	362	275	188	14			
	10	863	659	454	249	146	44				
10¼%	1	994	982	969	956	950	944	931	919	887	856
	2	988	961	935	908	895	882	855	829	762	696
	3	981	939	897	855	834	813	771	729	624	519
	4	973	914	855	796	766	737	678	619	471	324
	5	964	886	808	730	691	652	575	497	302	107
	6	955	856	757	658	608	559	460	361	114	
	7	944	822	700	578	517	456	333	211		
	8	932	784	637	489	415	341	193	45		
	9	919	743	567	390	302	214	38			
	10	905	697	489	281	177	74				
10½%	1	997	984	972	959	953	946	934	921	890	858
	2	993	967	940	914	900	887	860	834	767	701
	3	989	947	905	863	842	821	779	737	632	526
	4	985	926	866	807	777	748	688	629	481	332
	5	980	902	823	745	706	667	588	510	313	117
	6	975	875	776	676	626	576	477	377	128	
	7	969	846	723	599	538	476	353	229		
	8	963	813	664	514	439	365	215	66		
	9	955	777	598	420	330	241	63			
	10	947	736	526	315	209	104				

REMAINING BALANCE TABLE

Showing remaining balance on $1000 loan

INTEREST RATE	DUE DATE YEARS	MONTHLY PAYBACK RATE (%)									
		1.00	1.10	1.20	1.25	1.30	1.40	1.50	1.60	1.75	2.00
10¾%	1	987	974	962	955	949	936	924	911	892	861
	2	972	946	919	906	892	866	839	812	772	706
	3	956	914	871	850	829	787	745	702	639	533
	4	938	878	819	789	759	699	640	580	491	341
	5	918	839	760	720	681	602	523	444	325	128
	6	895	795	694	644	594	493	393	292	141	
	7	870	746	621	559	497	372	248	123		
	8	843	691	540	465	389	238	87			
	9	812	631	450	360	269	88				
	10	777	563	349	243	136					
11%	1	989	977	964	958	952	939	926	914	895	863
	2	978	951	924	911	898	871	844	817	777	711
	3	965	922	880	859	837	795	753	710	646	540
	4	950	890	830	800	770	710	650	590	500	350
	5	934	854	775	735	695	616	536	457	337	139
	6	916	814	713	662	612	510	409	307	155	
	7	895	770	644	581	518	392	267	141		
	8	873	720	567	490	414	261	108			
	9	847	664	481	389	298	115				
	10	819	602	385	277	168					
11¼%	1	992	979	967	961	954	942	929	916	897	866
	2	983	956	930	916	903	876	849	823	782	716
	3	973	931	888	867	846	803	760	718	654	548
	4	962	902	842	812	782	721	661	601	510	360
	5	950	870	790	750	710	630	550	470	350	149
	6	936	834	732	681	630	527	425	323	170	
	7	921	794	667	603	540	413	286	159		
	8	903	749	594	517	440	285	130			
	9	884	698	513	420	327	142				
	10	862	642	422	312	202					
11½%	1	995	982	969	963	957	944	931	919	900	868
	2	989	962	935	922	908	881	855	828	788	720
	3	982	939	897	875	854	811	768	726	662	555
	4	975	914	854	823	793	732	672	611	520	369
	5	966	886	805	765	725	644	563	483	362	161
	6	957	854	751	700	648	545	442	339	185	
	7	947	818	690	626	562	434	306	178		
	8	935	779	622	544	466	309	153			
	9	922	734	546	452	358	170				
	10	907	684	460	348	237	13				
11¾%	1	997	985	972	966	959	947	934	921	902	871
	2	994	967	941	927	914	887	860	833	793	725
	3	991	948	905	884	862	819	776	734	669	562
	4	987	926	866	835	805	744	683	622	531	378
	5	983	902	821	780	740	659	577	496	375	172
	6	978	875	771	719	667	563	459	355	199	
	7	973	844	714	650	585	455	326	197	2	
	8	967	809	651	572	493	335	176	18		
	9	960	770	580	484	389	199	8			
	10	953	726	499	386	273	46				
12%	1	1000	987	975	968	962	949	937	924	905	873
	2	1000	973	946	933	919	892	865	838	798	730
	3	1000	957	914	892	871	828	785	742	677	569
	4	1000	939	878	847	816	755	694	633	541	388
	5	1000	918	837	796	755	673	592	510	387	183
	6	1000	895	791	738	686	581	476	372	215	
	7	1000	869	739	673	608	477	347	216	20	
	8	1000	840	680	600	520	360	200	40		
	9	1000	807	614	518	421	228	36			
	10	1000	770	540	425	310	80				

MORTGAGE YIELD TABLES

SHOWING DISCOUNT (%) AT VARIOUS YIELDS,
MONTHLY PAYMENT RATES AND DUE DATES

DUE DATE	PAYT RATE	YIELD								
		7%	8%	9%	10%	11%	12%	13%	14%	15%
1 YR	.50	.96	1.92	2.86	3.79	4.71	5.63	6.53	7.42	8.31
	.75	.95	1.89	2.82	3.74	4.65	5.55	6.44	7.32	8.20
	1.00	.94	1.86	2.78	3.69	4.59	5.47	6.35	7.22	8.08
	1.25	.92	1.84	2.74	3.64	4.52	5.40	6.26	7.12	7.97
	1.50	.91	1.81	2.70	3.58	4.46	5.32	6.17	7.02	7.86
	1.75	.90	1.78	2.66	3.53	4.39	5.24	6.09	6.92	7.74
	2.00	.88	1.76	2.62	3.48	4.33	5.17	6.00	6.82	7.63
	8.61	.53	1.06	1.58	2.10	2.62	3.13	3.64	4.14	4.64
2 YRS	.50	1.86	3.69	5.47	7.22	8.94	10.62	12.27	13.89	15.47
	.75	1.81	3.58	5.31	7.02	8.68	10.32	11.92	13.49	15.03
	1.00	1.75	3.47	5.16	6.81	8.43	10.01	11.57	13.10	14.59
	1.25	1.70	3.36	5.00	6.60	8.17	9.71	11.22	12.70	14.16
	1.50	1.64	3.26	4.84	6.39	7.91	9.41	10.87	12.31	13.72
	1.75	1.59	3.15	4.68	6.18	7.66	9.10	10.52	11.92	13.28
	2.00	1.54	3.04	4.52	5.98	7.40	8.80	10.17	11.52	12.85
	4.43	1.01	2.00	2.99	3.95	4.91	5.85	6.78	7.69	8.59
3 YRS	.50	2.70	5.32	7.86	10.33	12.73	15.05	17.31	19.51	21.64
	.75	2.58	5.08	7.51	9.88	12.17	14.40	16.57	18.67	20.71
	1.00	2.46	4.85	7.17	9.42	11.62	13.75	15.82	17.83	19.79
	1.25	2.34	4.61	6.82	8.97	11.06	13.09	15.07	16.99	18.86
	1.50	2.22	4.37	6.47	8.52	10.50	12.44	14.32	16.16	17.94
	1.75	2.10	4.14	6.13	8.06	9.95	11.79	13.57	15.32	17.02
	2.00	1.98	3.90	5.78	7.61	9.39	11.13	12.83	14.48	16.09
	3.04	1.47	2.92	4.33	5.72	7.08	8.41	9.71	10.99	12.24
4 YRS	.50	3.48	6.83	10.05	13.14	16.12	18.99	21.74	24.40	26.95
	.75	3.27	6.42	9.45	12.37	15.18	17.88	20.49	23.00	25.42
	1.00	3.06	6.01	8.85	11.59	14.23	16.78	19.23	21.60	23.88
	1.25	2.85	5.60	8.25	10.81	13.29	15.67	17.98	20.20	22.35
	1.50	2.64	5.19	7.65	10.04	12.34	14.57	16.72	18.80	20.82
	1.75	2.43	4.78	7.06	9.26	11.40	13.46	15.47	17.41	19.28
	2.35	1.93	3.80	5.63	7.40	9.13	10.82	12.46	14.06	15.61
5 YRS	.50	4.21	8.22	12.04	15.69	19.16	22.48	25.64	28.65	31.53
	.75	3.89	7.60	11.14	14.52	17.75	20.84	23.79	26.60	29.29
	1.00	3.57	6.98	10.24	13.36	16.34	19.20	21.94	24.56	27.06
	1.25	3.24	6.35	9.33	12.19	14.94	17.56	20.09	22.51	24.83
	1.50	2.92	5.73	8.43	11.03	13.53	15.93	18.24	20.46	22.60
	1.93	2.37	4.65	6.87	9.01	11.08	13.09	15.03	16.91	18.74
6 YRS	.50	4.89	9.51	13.87	17.99	21.89	25.58	29.06	32.35	35.47
	.75	4.44	8.64	12.61	16.38	19.95	23.34	26.55	29.59	32.48
	1.00	3.98	7.77	11.36	14.77	18.02	21.11	24.04	26.83	29.49
	1.25	3.53	6.90	10.10	13.16	16.08	18.87	21.53	24.07	26.50
	1.66	2.79	5.48	8.06	10.54	12.93	15.23	17.44	19.57	21.62
7 YRS	.50	5.52	10.69	15.54	20.08	24.33	28.32	32.07	35.57	38.87
	.75	4.92	9.54	13.89	17.98	21.82	25.44	28.85	32.05	35.08
	1.00	4.32	8.39	12.24	15.88	19.31	22.56	25.63	28.53	31.28
	1.46	3.21	6.27	9.20	12.00	14.68	17.24	19.70	22.05	24.30
8 YRS	.50	6.11	11.79	17.06	21.97	26.53	30.76	34.71	38.38	41.79
	.75	5.34	10.33	14.99	19.34	23.40	27.20	30.75	34.07	37.18
	1.00	4.58	8.87	12.91	16.70	20.27	23.63	26.79	29.76	32.57
	1.31	3.61	7.04	10.30	13.40	16.34	19.14	21.81	24.35	26.77
9 YRS	.50	6.66	12.80	18.46	23.68	28.49	32.93	37.03	40.82	44.31
	1.20	4.00	7.78	11.35	14.72	17.91	20.93	23.79	26.50	29.06
10 YRS	.50	7.18	13.74	19.74	25.22	30.25	34.85	39.07	42.94	46.49
	1.11	4.38	8.50	12.36	15.99	19.40	22.62	25.64	28.50	31.19
UNTIL PAID	.75	7.13	13.53	19.28	24.47	29.15	33.38	37.22	40.71	43.89
	1.00	4.96	9.57	13.87	17.87	21.60	25.09	28.34	31.38	34.23
	1.25	3.82	7.44	10.87	14.11	17.19	20.11	22.89	25.52	28.02
	1.50	3.12	6.10	8.95	11.68	14.30	16.80	19.21	21.50	23.71
	1.75	2.63	5.17	7.61	9.97	12.24	14.44	16.55	18.59	20.56
	2.00	2.28	4.49	6.63	8.71	10.71	12.66	14.55	16.38	18.15

MORTGAGE YIELD TABLES 6%

SHOWING DISCOUNT (%) AT VARIOUS YIELDS,
MONTHLY PAYMENT RATES AND DUE DATES

16%	17%	18%	19%	YIELD 20%	21%	22%	23%	24%	BAL REMAIN
9.18	10.05	10.91	11.76	12.59	13.42	14.25	15.06	15.86	100.00
9.06	9.91	10.76	11.60	12.42	13.24	14.05	14.86	15.65	96.92
8.94	9.78	10.61	11.44	12.25	13.06	13.86	14.66	15.44	93.83
8.81	9.64	10.46	11.28	12.09	12.88	13.67	14.45	15.23	90.75
8.69	9.51	10.32	11.12	11.92	12.70	13.48	14.25	15.01	87.66
8.56	9.37	10.17	10.96	11.75	12.52	13.29	14.05	14.80	84.58
8.44	9.23	10.02	10.80	11.58	12.34	13.10	13.85	14.59	81.50
5.14	5.63	6.12	6.61	7.09	7.57	8.04	8.51	8.98	.00
17.02	18.54	20.03	21.49	22.92	24.33	25.70	27.05	28.37	100.00
16.54	18.02	19.47	20.89	22.29	23.65	24.99	26.31	27.60	93.64
16.06	17.50	18.91	20.29	21.65	22.98	24.29	25.56	26.82	87.28
15.58	16.98	18.35	19.70	21.01	22.31	23.58	24.82	26.04	80.93
15.10	16.46	17.79	19.10	20.38	21.64	22.87	24.08	25.27	74.57
14.62	15.94	17.23	18.50	19.74	20.96	22.16	23.34	24.49	68.21
14.14	15.42	16.67	17.90	19.11	20.29	21.45	22.60	23.72	61.85
9.48	10.36	11.22	12.08	12.92	13.75	14.57	15.38	16.17	.00
23.70	25.71	27.66	29.55	31.39	33.18	34.91	36.60	38.23	100.00
22.70	24.63	26.50	28.32	30.09	31.81	33.48	35.10	36.68	90.17
21.69	23.54	25.34	27.09	28.79	30.44	32.05	33.61	35.13	80.33
20.68	22.45	24.18	25.85	27.48	29.07	30.61	32.12	33.58	70.50
19.68	21.37	23.02	24.62	26.18	27.69	29.18	30.62	32.03	60.66
18.67	20.28	21.85	23.38	24.88	26.33	27.75	29.13	30.48	50.83
17.66	19.20	20.69	22.15	23.57	24.96	26.32	27.64	28.93	41.00
13.47	14.67	15.85	17.01	18.14	19.25	20.34	21.41	22.46	.00
29.40	31.77	34.04	36.23	38.34	40.37	42.32	44.20	46.01	100.00
27.74	29.99	32.15	34.23	36.24	38.18	40.04	41.84	43.57	86.48
26.08	28.21	30.26	32.23	34.14	35.98	37.76	39.47	41.13	72.95
24.43	26.43	28.37	30.24	32.04	33.79	35.48	37.11	38.69	59.43
22.77	24.65	26.47	28.24	29.95	31.60	33.20	34.75	36.25	45.90
21.11	22.87	24.58	26.24	27.85	29.41	30.92	32.38	33.81	32.38
17.13	18.61	20.05	21.46	22.82	24.16	25.46	26.73	27.96	.00
34.27	36.88	39.38	41.76	44.04	46.20	48.28	50.25	52.14	100.00
31.87	34.32	36.67	38.92	41.07	43.12	45.09	46.97	48.77	82.56
29.47	31.77	33.97	36.08	38.10	40.04	41.90	43.68	45.39	65.11
27.06	29.21	31.26	33.24	35.14	36.96	38.71	40.40	42.02	47.67
24.66	26.65	28.56	30.40	32.17	33.88	35.53	37.11	38.65	30.23
20.50	22.21	23.87	25.47	27.03	28.54	30.00	31.42	32.80	.00
38.42	41.21	43.84	46.34	48.71	50.95	53.07	55.07	56.98	100.00
35.22	37.81	40.28	42.62	44.84	46.95	48.96	50.86	52.67	78.40
32.01	34.42	36.71	38.90	40.97	42.96	44.85	46.65	48.37	56.80
28.81	31.03	33.15	35.17	37.11	38.96	40.74	42.44	44.06	35.19
23.60	25.50	27.34	29.11	30.81	32.45	34.04	35.57	37.05	.00
41.96	44.86	47.58	50.14	52.54	54.80	56.92	58.91	60.79	100.00
37.92	40.60	43.13	45.52	47.77	49.90	51.90	53.80	55.59	73.98
33.89	36.35	38.69	40.90	43.00	44.99	46.89	48.68	50.39	47.96
26.45	28.51	30.49	32.39	34.21	35.96	37.64	39.25	40.80	.00
44.98	47.94	50.70	53.28	55.68	57.92	60.01	61.97	63.79	100.00
40.09	42.82	45.38	47.78	50.03	52.14	54.13	56.00	57.75	69.29
35.21	37.70	40.06	42.28	44.38	46.37	48.24	50.02	51.71	38.59
29.08	31.27	33.37	35.37	37.28	39.11	40.85	42.52	44.11	.00
47.55	50.54	53.31	55.88	58.26	60.46	62.50	64.40	66.16	100.00
31.49	33.80	35.99	38.07	40.05	41.93	43.72	45.42	47.04	.00
49.75	52.74	55.50	58.03	60.37	62.52	64.51	66.34	68.03	100.00
33.72	36.12	38.39	40.53	42.55	44.47	46.29	48.01	49.65	.00

16%	17%	18%	19%	20%	21%	22%	23%	24%	MONTHS
46.79	49.45	51.88	54.12	56.18	58.08	59.84	61.47	62.98	220.27
36.90	39.40	41.75	43.96	46.03	47.98	49.82	51.55	53.19	138.98
30.39	32.65	34.80	36.85	38.80	40.66	42.43	44.11	45.72	102.42
25.83	27.86	29.81	31.68	33.48	35.21	36.86	38.46	39.99	81.30
22.46	24.29	26.06	27.78	29.43	31.03	32.57	34.06	35.51	67.46
19.87	21.54	23.16	24.73	26.25	27.73	29.17	30.56	31.91	57.68

SHOWING DISCOUNT (%) AT VARIOUS YIELDS,
MONTHLY PAYMENT RATES AND DUE DATES

DUE DATE	PAYT RATE	YIELD								
		7%	8%	9%	10%	11%	12%	13%	14%	15%
1 YR	.54	.48	1.44	2.38	3.32	4.24	5.16	6.06	6.96	7.85
	.75	.48	1.42	2.35	3.28	4.19	5.10	6.00	6.88	7.76
	1.00	.47	1.40	2.32	3.23	4.14	5.03	5.91	6.79	7.65
	1.25	.46	1.38	2.29	3.19	4.08	4.96	5.83	6.69	7.54
	1.50	.46	1.36	2.26	3.14	4.02	4.89	5.75	6.60	7.44
	1.75	.45	1.34	2.22	3.10	3.96	4.82	5.66	6.50	7.33
	2.00	.44	1.32	2.19	3.05	3.90	4.75	5.58	6.41	7.22
	8.63	.27	.80	1.32	1.84	2.36	2.87	3.38	3.89	4.39
2 YRS	.54	.93	2.76	4.56	6.32	8.05	9.74	11.39	13.02	14.61
	.75	.91	2.70	4.45	6.17	7.85	9.50	11.12	12.71	14.26
	1.00	.88	2.62	4.32	5.99	7.62	9.22	10.80	12.34	13.85
	1.25	.85	2.54	4.19	5.80	7.39	8.95	10.47	11.97	13.44
	1.50	.83	2.46	4.05	5.62	7.16	8.67	10.15	11.60	13.02
	1.75	.80	2.38	3.92	5.44	6.93	8.39	9.82	11.23	12.61
	2.00	.77	2.29	3.79	5.26	6.70	8.11	9.50	10.86	12.19
	4.45	.51	1.51	2.49	3.46	4.42	5.37	6.30	7.22	8.13
3 YRS	.54	1.35	3.99	6.55	9.04	11.45	13.80	16.08	18.29	20.43
	.75	1.30	3.84	6.31	8.71	11.04	13.30	15.49	17.63	19.70
	1.00	1.24	3.66	6.02	8.31	10.53	12.70	14.80	16.84	18.83
	1.25	1.18	3.48	5.73	7.91	10.03	12.09	14.10	16.05	17.95
	1.50	1.12	3.31	5.44	7.51	9.53	11.49	13.40	15.26	17.07
	1.75	1.06	3.13	5.15	7.11	9.03	10.89	12.71	14.47	16.20
	2.00	1.00	2.95	4.86	6.71	8.52	10.29	12.01	13.68	15.32
	3.06	.74	2.19	3.62	5.01	6.38	7.72	9.04	10.32	11.59
4 YRS	.54	1.74	5.12	8.37	11.50	14.51	17.40	20.19	22.87	25.45
	.75	1.65	4.86	7.95	10.93	13.80	16.56	19.21	21.77	24.24
	1.00	1.54	4.55	7.45	10.25	12.94	15.54	18.04	20.45	22.78
	1.25	1.44	4.24	6.95	9.56	12.08	14.52	16.87	19.13	21.32
	1.50	1.33	3.94	6.45	8.88	11.23	13.50	15.69	17.81	19.87
	1.75	1.23	3.63	5.95	8.20	10.37	12.48	14.52	16.50	18.41
	2.37	.97	2.86	4.70	6.50	8.24	9.94	11.60	13.22	14.79
5 YRS	.54	2.10	6.16	10.04	13.73	17.25	20.60	23.81	26.86	29.77
	.75	1.97	5.77	9.40	12.87	16.18	19.34	22.36	25.25	28.00
	1.00	1.81	5.30	8.65	11.84	14.90	17.83	20.63	23.31	25.88
	1.25	1.65	4.83	7.89	10.82	13.62	16.32	18.90	21.38	23.76
	1.50	1.48	4.36	7.13	9.79	12.35	14.80	17.17	19.44	21.63
	1.96	1.19	3.50	5.74	7.91	10.01	12.04	14.01	15.91	17.75
6 YRS	.54	2.44	7.13	11.56	15.74	19.70	23.44	26.98	30.33	33.50
	.75	2.25	6.58	10.68	14.56	18.24	21.72	25.02	28.15	31.12
	1.00	2.02	5.92	9.62	13.14	16.48	19.65	22.67	25.54	28.27
	1.25	1.80	5.26	8.56	11.71	14.72	17.58	20.32	22.93	25.42
	1.68	1.40	4.13	6.74	9.26	11.69	14.02	16.26	18.42	20.50
7 YRS	.54	2.76	8.02	12.95	17.57	21.90	25.96	29.78	33.35	36.71
	.75	2.51	7.29	11.79	16.02	20.00	23.74	27.26	30.57	33.69
	1.00	2.20	6.42	10.40	14.18	17.71	21.06	24.24	27.23	30.07
	1.48	1.61	4.73	7.70	10.55	13.27	15.88	18.37	20.76	23.05
8 YRS	.54	3.06	8.84	14.22	19.22	23.87	28.20	32.23	35.98	39.47
	.75	2.73	7.92	12.76	17.28	21.50	25.44	29.12	32.57	35.79
	1.00	2.34	6.81	11.00	14.94	18.65	22.13	25.40	28.48	31.38
	1.34	1.82	5.31	8.63	11.78	14.78	17.64	20.35	22.94	25.41
9 YRS	.54	3.33	9.60	15.38	20.72	25.64	30.18	34.38	38.26	41.85
	1.23	2.01	5.87	9.51	12.96	16.21	19.29	22.21	24.97	27.59
10 YRS	.54	3.59	10.30	16.45	22.07	27.22	31.95	36.28	40.25	43.90
	1.14	2.21	6.41	10.36	14.08	17.57	20.86	23.95	26.87	29.62
UNTIL PAID	.75	3.80	10.78	17.00	22.58	27.58	32.09	36.15	39.82	43.15
	1.00	2.58	7.46	11.99	16.20	20.12	23.76	27.16	30.34	33.30
	1.25	1.97	5.74	9.31	12.68	15.88	18.91	21.78	24.50	27.09
	1.50	1.59	4.67	7.62	10.44	13.14	15.72	18.19	20.56	22.83
	1.75	1.34	3.95	6.46	8.88	11.21	13.46	15.63	17.72	19.74
	2.00	1.16	3.42	5.61	7.73	9.79	11.78	13.71	15.58	17.39

SHOWING DISCOUNT (%) AT VARIOUS YIELDS,
MONTHLY PAYMENT RATES AND DUE DATES

16%	17%	18%	19%	YIELD 20%	21%	22%	23%	24%	BAL REMAIN
8.73	9.59	10.45	11.30	12.14	12.98	13.80	14.62	15.42	100.00
8.63	9.49	10.34	11.18	12.01	12.83	13.65	14.45	15.25	97.42
8.51	9.36	10.19	11.02	11.84	12.66	13.46	14.26	15.04	94.33
8.39	9.22	10.05	10.87	11.68	12.48	13.27	14.06	14.84	91.24
8.27	9.09	9.91	10.72	11.52	12.31	13.09	13.86	14.63	88.15
8.15	8.96	9.77	10.56	11.35	12.13	12.90	13.67	14.42	85.06
8.03	8.83	9.63	10.41	11.19	11.96	12.72	13.47	14.22	81.97
4.89	5.38	5.87	6.36	6.84	7.32	7.80	8.27	8.74	.00
16.17	17.70	19.20	20.66	22.10	23.51	24.90	26.25	27.58	100.00
15.79	17.28	18.75	20.18	21.59	22.97	24.32	25.65	26.95	94.68
15.33	16.78	18.21	19.61	20.98	22.32	23.64	24.93	26.20	88.29
14.87	16.29	17.67	19.03	20.36	21.67	22.95	24.21	25.44	81.90
14.42	15.79	17.13	18.45	19.75	21.02	22.26	23.48	24.68	75.51
13.96	15.29	16.59	17.87	19.13	20.36	21.57	22.76	23.93	69.12
13.50	14.79	16.06	17.30	18.52	19.71	20.89	22.04	23.17	62.73
9.02	9.90	10.77	11.63	12.48	13.31	14.13	14.94	15.75	.00
22.52	24.54	26.51	28.42	30.27	32.07	33.82	35.52	37.17	100.00
21.72	23.67	25.58	27.42	29.22	30.96	32.66	34.31	35.91	91.74
20.76	22.63	24.46	26.23	27.96	29.63	31.27	32.85	34.39	81.84
19.80	21.59	23.34	25.04	26.69	28.30	29.87	31.39	32.88	71.93
18.84	20.55	22.22	23.85	25.43	26.97	28.48	29.94	31.36	62.02
17.88	19.51	21.10	22.66	24.17	25.64	27.08	28.48	29.85	52.11
16.91	18.47	19.99	21.46	22.91	24.31	25.69	27.03	28.33	42.20
12.82	14.03	15.22	16.39	17.53	18.65	19.75	20.82	21.88	.00
27.93	30.32	32.62	34.84	36.97	39.02	41.00	42.90	44.73	100.00
26.61	28.90	31.10	33.23	35.27	37.24	39.15	40.98	42.74	88.61
25.03	27.19	29.28	31.29	33.24	35.11	36.92	38.67	40.36	74.95
23.44	25.48	27.45	29.36	31.20	32.98	34.70	36.36	37.97	61.29
21.85	23.77	25.63	27.43	29.17	30.85	32.48	34.05	35.58	47.63
20.27	22.06	23.80	25.49	27.13	28.72	30.25	31.75	33.20	33.96
16.32	17.81	19.27	20.69	22.07	23.42	24.73	26.01	27.26	.00
32.55	35.21	37.74	40.16	42.46	44.66	46.77	48.78	50.69	100.00
30.64	33.16	35.56	37.86	40.06	42.16	44.17	46.10	47.94	85.28
28.34	30.69	32.95	35.11	37.18	39.16	41.06	42.89	44.63	67.61
26.04	28.23	30.33	32.36	34.30	36.16	37.95	39.67	41.33	49.94
23.74	25.77	27.72	29.60	31.41	33.16	34.84	36.46	38.02	32.27
19.54	21.27	22.95	24.57	26.15	27.68	29.16	30.59	31.99	.00
36.50	39.33	42.02	44.56	46.97	49.25	51.41	53.45	55.39	100.00
33.94	36.61	39.14	41.55	43.83	46.00	48.06	50.02	51.87	81.71
30.87	33.34	35.69	37.93	40.07	42.10	44.04	45.89	47.65	59.77
27.80	30.07	32.24	34.32	36.31	38.21	40.02	41.76	43.43	37.83
22.51	24.44	26.30	28.09	29.82	31.49	33.10	34.65	36.15	.00
39.86	42.82	45.60	48.21	50.66	52.97	55.14	57.18	59.10	100.00
36.63	39.40	42.01	44.47	46.79	48.98	51.05	53.00	54.84	77.91
32.75	35.29	37.70	39.98	42.14	44.19	46.14	47.98	49.73	51.41
25.24	27.34	29.35	31.28	33.13	34.91	36.61	38.25	39.82	.00
42.73	45.76	48.59	51.23	53.69	55.99	58.14	60.15	62.02	100.00
38.81	41.64	44.29	46.77	49.10	51.28	53.33	55.26	57.07	73.86
34.12	36.69	39.12	41.42	43.58	45.63	47.56	49.39	51.12	42.49
27.75	29.99	32.13	34.17	36.11	37.97	39.75	41.45	43.07	.00
45.17	48.25	51.09	53.73	56.18	58.44	60.55	62.51	64.33	100.00
30.08	32.43	34.67	36.79	38.81	40.73	42.55	44.29	45.95	.00
47.26	50.35	53.19	55.80	58.21	60.44	62.49	64.39	66.14	100.00
32.22	34.67	36.98	39.17	41.24	43.21	45.07	46.83	48.50	.00
									MONTHS
46.18	48.94	51.46	53.77	55.89	57.84	59.64	61.30	62.84	237.12
36.07	38.67	41.10	43.38	45.51	47.52	49.41	51.19	52.86	144.42
29.54	31.87	34.08	36.19	38.19	40.10	41.91	43.64	45.29	105.14
25.00	27.09	29.09	31.01	32.85	34.62	36.32	37.95	39.51	82.94
21.68	23.56	25.37	27.12	28.81	30.44	32.02	33.54	35.01	68.56
19.15	20.85	22.50	24.10	25.65	27.16	28.62	30.04	31.42	58.47

MORTGAGE YIELD TABLES

SHOWING DISCOUNT (%) AT VARIOUS YIELDS,
MONTHLY PAYMENT RATES AND DUE DATES

DUE DATE	PAYT RATE	7%	8%	9%	10%	11%	12%	13%	14%	15%
1 YR	.56	.24	1.20	2.14	3.08	4.01	4.92	5.83	6.73	7.62
	.75	.24	1.19	2.12	3.05	3.97	4.87	5.77	6.66	7.54
	1.00	.23	1.17	2.09	3.01	3.91	4.81	5.69	6.57	7.44
	1.25	.23	1.15	2.06	2.96	3.86	4.74	5.61	6.48	7.33
	1.50	.23	1.14	2.03	2.92	3.80	4.67	5.53	6.38	7.23
	1.75	.22	1.12	2.00	2.88	3.75	4.60	5.45	6.29	7.12
	2.00	.22	1.10	1.97	2.84	3.69	4.54	5.37	6.20	7.02
	8.64	.13	.66	1.19	1.71	2.23	2.74	3.25	3.76	4.26
2 YRS	.56	.47	2.30	4.10	5.87	7.60	9.29	10.96	12.58	14.18
	.75	.46	2.25	4.01	5.74	7.43	9.09	10.72	12.31	13.88
	1.00	.44	2.19	3.90	5.57	7.22	8.83	10.41	11.96	13.47
	1.25	.43	2.12	3.78	5.40	7.00	8.56	10.09	11.60	13.07
	1.50	.41	2.05	3.66	5.23	6.78	8.29	9.78	11.24	12.67
	1.75	.40	1.98	3.54	5.06	6.56	8.03	9.47	10.88	12.27
	2.00	.39	1.92	3.42	4.89	6.34	7.76	9.15	10.52	11.86
	4.47	.25	1.26	2.24	3.22	4.18	5.13	6.06	6.98	7.89
3 YRS	.56	.67	3.32	5.90	8.39	10.82	13.17	15.46	17.68	19.83
	.75	.65	3.21	5.70	8.12	10.46	12.74	14.95	17.10	19.19
	1.00	.62	3.06	5.44	7.74	9.99	12.16	14.28	16.34	18.34
	1.25	.59	2.92	5.18	7.37	9.51	11.59	13.61	15.58	17.49
	1.50	.56	2.77	4.91	7.00	9.03	11.01	12.94	14.81	16.63
	1.75	.53	2.62	4.65	6.63	8.56	10.44	12.26	14.05	15.78
	2.00	.50	2.47	4.39	6.26	8.08	9.86	11.59	13.28	14.93
	3.08	.37	1.83	3.26	4.66	6.04	7.38	8.70	9.99	11.26
4 YRS	.56	.87	4.27	7.53	10.68	13.70	16.61	19.41	22.11	24.70
	.75	.83	4.07	7.20	10.20	13.09	15.88	18.57	21.15	23.64
	1.00	.78	3.81	6.74	9.56	12.28	14.91	17.43	19.87	22.22
	1.25	.72	3.56	6.29	8.93	11.47	13.93	16.30	18.59	20.80
	1.50	.67	3.30	5.84	8.29	10.66	12.95	15.17	17.31	19.38
	1.75	.62	3.04	5.38	7.65	9.85	11.98	14.04	16.03	17.97
	2.38	.48	2.39	4.24	6.04	7.80	9.51	11.17	12.79	14.37
5 YRS	.56	1.05	5.14	9.03	12.75	16.29	19.67	22.89	25.97	28.90
	.75	.99	4.84	8.52	12.03	15.38	18.58	21.64	24.56	27.35
	1.00	.91	4.45	7.83	11.07	14.17	17.13	19.97	22.68	25.28
	1.25	.83	4.06	7.15	10.11	12.95	15.68	18.29	20.80	23.21
	1.50	.75	3.66	6.46	9.15	11.74	14.23	16.62	18.92	21.14
	1.97	.59	2.92	5.18	7.36	9.47	11.51	13.49	15.41	17.26
6 YRS	.56	1.22	5.94	10.40	14.62	18.61	22.38	25.95	29.32	32.51
	.75	1.14	5.53	9.69	13.62	17.35	20.89	24.24	27.42	30.43
	1.00	1.02	4.98	8.73	12.30	15.69	18.91	21.97	24.88	27.65
	1.25	.91	4.42	7.77	10.97	14.02	16.92	19.69	22.34	24.87
	1.69	.70	3.45	6.08	8.62	11.06	13.41	15.67	17.84	19.94
7 YRS	.56	1.38	6.68	11.65	16.31	20.68	24.78	28.63	32.24	35.63
	.75	1.27	6.13	10.71	15.01	19.06	22.86	26.44	29.81	32.98
	1.00	1.11	5.40	9.45	13.27	16.88	20.29	23.52	26.56	29.44
	1.50	.81	3.95	6.95	9.82	12.57	15.19	17.71	20.11	22.42
8 YRS	.56	1.53	7.37	12.80	17.85	22.55	26.92	30.99	34.78	38.31
	.75	1.38	6.67	11.61	16.21	20.51	24.53	28.29	31.80	35.08
	1.00	1.19	5.74	10.02	14.03	17.80	21.35	24.68	27.82	30.77
	1.35	.91	4.44	7.79	10.97	14.00	16.88	19.62	22.23	24.72
9 YRS	.56	1.67	8.00	13.84	19.24	24.22	28.81	33.06	36.99	40.62
	1.24	.91	4.91	8.59	12.07	15.36	18.47	21.41	24.21	26.85
10 YRS	.56	1.79	8.59	14.80	20.49	25.71	30.49	34.88	38.91	42.61
	1.15	1.11	5.36	9.36	13.11	16.64	19.97	23.10	26.05	28.83
UNTIL PAID	.75	1.97	9.28	15.78	21.57	26.76	31.41	35.60	39.37	42.78
	1.00	1.32	6.34	11.00	15.32	19.34	23.07	26.55	29.80	32.82
	1.25	1.00	4.85	8.49	11.94	15.20	18.28	21.21	23.98	26.61
	1.50	.81	3.94	6.94	9.80	12.54	15.16	17.67	20.08	22.38
	1.75	.68	3.32	5.87	8.32	10.69	12.96	15.16	17.28	19.32
	2.00	.58	2.87	5.09	7.24	9.32	11.33	13.28	15.17	17.00

SHOWING DISCOUNT (%) AT VARIOUS YIELDS,
MONTHLY PAYMENT RATES AND DUE DATES

16%	17%	18%	19%	YIELD 20%	21%	22%	23%	24%	BAL REMAIN
8.50	9.37	10.23	11.08	11.92	12.75	13.58	14.39	15.20	100.00
8.41	9.27	10.12	10.96	11.80	12.62	13.44	14.25	15.05	97.68
8.29	9.14	9.98	10.81	11.64	12.45	13.26	14.06	14.85	94.58
8.18	9.02	9.84	10.67	11.48	12.28	13.08	13.86	14.64	91.49
8.06	8.89	9.71	10.52	11.32	12.11	12.89	13.67	14.44	88.40
7.95	8.76	9.57	10.37	11.15	11.94	12.71	13.48	14.23	85.30
7.83	8.63	9.43	10.22	10.99	11.76	12.53	13.28	14.03	82.21
4.76	5.26	5.75	6.23	6.72	7.20	7.67	8.15	8.62	.00
15.74	17.28	18.78	20.25	21.69	23.11	24.50	25.86	27.19	100.00
15.41	16.91	18.38	19.83	21.24	22.63	23.99	25.32	26.63	95.20
14.96	16.42	17.86	19.26	20.64	21.99	23.31	24.61	25.88	88.79
14.52	15.94	17.33	18.69	20.03	21.34	22.63	23.90	25.14	82.39
14.07	15.45	16.80	18.13	19.43	20.70	21.96	23.18	24.39	75.98
13.63	14.96	16.27	17.56	18.82	20.06	21.28	22.47	23.64	69.58
13.18	14.48	15.75	16.99	18.22	19.42	20.60	21.76	22.90	63.17
8.79	9.67	10.55	11.41	12.25	13.09	13.91	14.73	15.53	.00
21.93	23.96	25.93	27.85	29.71	31.52	33.28	34.98	36.64	100.00
21.22	23.19	25.11	26.97	28.78	30.54	32.24	33.90	35.52	92.54
20.28	22.18	24.01	25.80	27.54	29.23	30.87	32.47	34.02	82.60
19.35	21.16	22.92	24.63	26.30	27.92	29.49	31.03	32.52	72.65
18.41	20.14	21.82	23.46	25.05	26.61	28.12	29.59	31.03	62.71
17.47	19.12	20.72	22.29	23.81	25.30	26.74	28.15	29.53	52.76
16.53	18.10	19.63	21.12	22.57	23.99	25.37	26.72	28.03	42.82
12.50	13.72	14.91	16.08	17.22	18.35	19.45	20.53	21.59	.00
27.20	29.60	31.91	34.14	36.29	38.35	40.34	42.25	44.09	100.00
26.04	28.35	30.57	32.72	34.78	36.77	38.69	40.54	42.32	89.70
24.49	26.67	28.78	30.82	32.78	34.67	36.50	38.26	39.96	75.97
22.94	25.00	26.99	28.91	30.77	32.57	34.30	35.98	37.60	62.24
21.39	23.33	25.20	27.01	28.77	30.47	32.11	33.70	35.24	48.50
19.84	21.65	23.41	25.11	26.76	28.36	29.92	31.42	32.88	34.77
15.91	17.41	18.88	20.30	21.69	23.04	24.36	25.65	26.90	.00
31.70	34.37	36.92	39.35	41.68	43.89	46.01	48.04	49.97	100.00
30.01	32.56	34.99	37.32	39.55	41.67	43.71	45.65	47.52	86.66
27.76	30.15	32.43	34.61	36.71	38.71	40.64	42.48	44.25	68.88
25.52	27.73	29.86	31.90	33.87	35.75	37.56	39.30	40.98	51.10
23.27	25.32	27.29	29.20	31.03	32.79	34.49	36.13	37.71	33.31
19.06	20.80	22.49	24.12	25.71	27.24	28.73	30.18	31.58	.00
35.54	38.40	41.10	43.67	46.10	48.40	50.58	52.64	54.60	100.00
33.28	35.99	38.56	41.00	43.32	45.51	47.60	49.58	51.47	83.41
30.28	32.79	35.17	37.44	39.61	41.67	43.63	45.50	47.28	61.30
27.28	29.58	31.78	33.88	35.90	37.82	39.66	41.42	43.10	39.18
21.96	23.90	25.77	27.58	29.32	31.00	32.62	34.19	35.70	.00
38.81	41.80	44.60	47.24	49.72	52.06	54.25	56.31	58.26	100.00
35.96	38.74	41.43	43.93	46.28	48.51	50.61	52.59	54.46	79.94
32.17	34.75	37.19	39.51	41.70	43.78	45.75	47.62	49.40	53.19
24.63	26.74	28.77	30.72	32.58	34.37	36.09	37.74	39.33	.00
41.60	44.67	47.53	50.20	52.70	55.03	57.20	59.23	61.14	100.00
38.15	41.03	43.72	46.25	48.61	50.83	52.92	54.88	56.71	76.22
33.55	36.17	38.64	40.97	43.17	45.25	47.21	49.06	50.82	44.51
27.09	29.35	31.50	33.56	35.52	37.40	39.19	40.91	42.54	.00
43.98	47.10	49.98	52.66	55.14	57.44	59.57	61.56	63.41	100.00
29.36	31.74	34.00	36.14	38.18	40.12	41.96	43.72	45.39	.00
46.02	49.15	52.03	54.69	57.14	59.40	61.48	63.41	65.20	100.00
31.45	33.93	36.27	38.49	40.58	42.57	44.45	46.23	47.92	.00

16%	17%	18%	19%	20%	21%	22%	23%	24%	MONTHS
45.88	48.70	51.26	53.61	55.76	57.73	59.55	61.23	62.78	247.15
35.65	38.29	40.76	43.08	45.25	47.29	49.20	51.01	52.70	147.38
29.10	31.47	33.71	35.85	37.88	39.81	41.65	43.40	45.07	106.58
24.58	26.70	28.72	30.66	32.53	34.32	36.04	37.69	39.27	83.79
21.28	23.18	25.02	26.78	28.49	30.14	31.73	33.27	34.76	69.13
18.77	20.49	22.16	23.78	25.35	26.87	28.34	29.78	31.17	58.87

MORTGAGE YIELD TABLES

SHOWING DISCOUNT (%) AT VARIOUS YIELDS,
MONTHLY PAYMENT RATES AND DUE DATES

DUE DATE	PAYT RATE	YIELD								
		8%	9%	10%	11%	12%	13%	14%	15%	16%
1 YR	.58	.96	1.91	2.84	3.77	4.69	5.60	6.50	7.39	8.27
	.75	.95	1.89	2.82	3.74	4.65	5.55	6.44	7.32	8.19
	1.00	.94	1.86	2.78	3.69	4.58	5.47	6.35	7.22	8.08
	1.25	.92	1.84	2.74	3.63	4.52	5.39	6.26	7.12	7.97
	1.50	.91	1.81	2.70	3.58	4.45	5.32	6.17	7.02	7.85
	1.75	.90	1.78	2.66	3.53	4.39	5.24	6.08	6.92	7.74
	2.00	.88	1.76	2.62	3.48	4.33	5.16	5.99	6.82	7.63
	8.65	.53	1.06	1.58	2.10	2.61	3.12	3.63	4.13	4.65
2 YRS	.58	1.84	3.65	5.42	7.15	8.85	10.52	12.15	13.75	15.32
	.75	1.81	3.58	5.31	7.01	8.68	10.32	11.92	13.49	15.03
	1.00	1.75	3.47	5.16	6.81	8.43	10.01	11.57	13.10	14.59
	1.25	1.70	3.37	5.00	6.60	8.17	9.71	11.22	12.71	14.16
	1.50	1.65	3.26	4.84	6.40	7.92	9.41	10.88	12.32	13.73
	1.75	1.59	3.15	4.69	6.19	7.66	9.11	10.53	11.93	13.29
	2.00	1.54	3.05	4.53	5.98	7.41	8.81	10.18	11.53	12.86
	4.48	1.01	2.00	2.97	3.94	4.89	5.82	6.75	7.66	8.56
3 YRS	.58	2.66	5.24	7.75	10.18	12.54	14.84	17.07	19.23	21.33
	.75	2.58	5.09	7.52	9.88	12.18	14.41	16.57	18.68	20.72
	1.00	2.46	4.85	7.18	9.43	11.63	13.76	15.83	17.85	19.81
	1.25	2.34	4.62	6.83	8.98	11.08	13.11	15.09	17.02	18.89
	1.50	2.22	4.38	6.49	8.54	10.53	12.47	14.36	16.19	17.98
	1.75	2.10	4.15	6.15	8.09	9.98	11.82	13.62	15.36	17.07
	2.00	1.98	3.92	5.80	7.64	9.43	11.17	12.88	14.53	16.15
	3.09	1.47	2.90	4.31	5.69	7.04	8.36	9.66	10.93	12.17
4 YRS	.58	3.41	6.70	9.86	12.90	15.82	18.64	21.35	23.95	26.46
	.75	3.28	6.43	9.46	12.39	15.20	17.91	20.52	23.03	25.46
	1.00	3.07	6.02	8.87	11.62	14.27	16.82	19.28	21.65	23.94
	1.25	2.86	5.62	8.28	10.85	13.34	15.73	18.04	20.27	22.43
	1.50	2.65	5.22	7.69	10.09	12.40	14.64	16.80	18.90	20.92
	1.75	2.45	4.81	7.10	9.32	11.47	13.55	15.56	17.52	19.40
	2.39	1.91	3.77	5.58	7.35	9.07	10.74	12.37	13.96	15.50
5 YRS	.58	4.11	8.03	11.77	15.33	18.73	21.98	25.07	28.02	30.84
	.75	3.90	7.62	11.17	14.57	17.81	20.90	23.86	26.68	29.38
	1.00	3.58	7.01	10.29	13.42	16.42	19.29	22.04	24.67	27.18
	1.25	3.27	6.40	9.40	12.28	15.03	17.68	20.22	22.65	24.99
	1.50	2.95	5.79	8.51	11.13	13.65	16.07	18.40	20.64	22.79
	1.98	2.34	4.61	6.80	8.93	10.98	12.97	14.90	16.77	18.57
6 YRS	.58	4.75	9.25	13.49	17.51	21.31	24.91	28.31	31.53	34.58
	.75	4.46	8.68	12.67	16.46	20.05	23.45	26.67	29.72	32.62
	1.00	4.01	7.82	11.44	14.88	18.15	21.25	24.20	27.01	29.68
	1.25	3.57	6.97	10.21	13.30	16.25	19.06	21.74	24.30	26.75
	1.70	2.76	5.42	7.97	10.43	12.79	15.07	17.26	19.37	21.40
7 YRS	.58	5.35	10.36	15.06	19.47	23.60	27.48	31.13	34.55	37.76
	.75	4.95	9.61	13.98	18.10	21.97	25.60	29.03	32.25	35.29
	1.00	4.37	8.48	12.37	16.04	19.51	22.78	25.88	28.81	31.57
	1.51	3.17	6.19	9.09	11.85	14.50	17.04	19.46	21.79	24.01
8 YRS	.58	5.89	11.38	16.48	21.22	25.64	29.75	33.58	37.15	40.48
	.75	5.40	10.43	15.12	19.51	23.60	27.43	31.00	34.35	37.47
	1.00	4.65	9.01	13.10	16.94	20.55	23.94	27.14	30.14	32.97
	1.36	3.56	6.94	10.15	13.21	16.11	18.88	21.52	24.03	26.42
9 YRS	.58	6.40	12.31	17.76	22.79	27.44	31.74	35.71	39.39	42.80
	1.25	3.94	7.65	11.17	14.49	17.64	20.61	23.43	26.10	28.64
10 YRS	.58	6.87	13.16	18.92	24.20	29.04	33.49	37.57	41.32	44.77
	1.16	4.30	8.34	12.14	15.71	19.07	22.24	25.22	28.03	30.69
UNTIL PAID	.75	7.68	14.48	20.53	25.91	30.72	35.04	38.92	42.42	45.58
	1.00	5.18	9.97	14.41	18.53	22.36	25.93	29.24	32.33	35.22
	1.25	3.94	7.66	11.18	14.50	17.65	20.62	23.44	26.12	28.65
	1.50	3.19	6.24	9.15	11.93	14.60	17.14	19.58	21.92	24.15
	1.75	2.68	5.27	7.75	10.15	12.46	14.68	16.82	18.89	20.88
	2.00	2.32	4.56	6.73	8.84	10.87	12.85	14.76	16.61	18.40

17%	18%	19%	20%	YIELD 21%	22%	23%	24%	25%	BAL REMAIN
9.14	10.00	10.85	11.69	12.53	13.36	14.17	14.98	15.78	100.00
9.05	9.91	10.75	11.59	12.42	13.24	14.05	14.85	15.64	97.93
8.93	9.77	10.61	11.43	12.25	13.06	13.86	14.65	15.43	94.84
8.81	9.64	10.46	11.27	12.08	12.88	13.66	14.45	15.22	91.74
8.68	9.50	10.31	11.12	11.91	12.70	13.47	14.24	15.01	88.64
8.56	9.37	10.17	10.96	11.74	12.52	13.28	14.04	14.80	85.54
8.43	9.23	10.02	10.80	11.57	12.34	13.09	13.84	14.58	82.44
5.13	5.62	6.11	6.59	7.07	7.55	8.02	8.50	8.96	.00
16.85	18.36	19.84	21.29	22.70	24.09	25.46	26.79	28.10	100.00
16.54	18.02	19.47	20.89	22.28	23.65	24.99	26.30	27.59	95.72
16.06	17.50	18.91	20.30	21.65	22.98	24.29	25.57	26.82	89.30
15.59	16.98	18.36	19.70	21.02	22.31	23.58	24.83	26.05	82.88
15.11	16.47	17.80	19.11	20.39	21.65	22.88	24.09	25.28	76.46
14.63	15.95	17.24	18.51	19.76	20.98	22.18	23.36	24.51	70.04
14.16	15.44	16.69	17.92	19.13	20.31	21.48	22.62	23.74	63.62
9.44	10.32	11.18	12.03	12.87	13.70	14.51	15.32	16.11	.00
23.37	25.36	27.28	29.15	30.97	32.73	34.44	36.11	37.73	100.00
22.71	24.64	26.51	28.34	30.11	31.83	33.50	35.12	36.70	93.34
21.71	23.56	25.36	27.11	28.82	30.47	32.08	33.64	35.17	83.36
20.72	22.49	24.22	25.89	27.53	29.12	30.66	32.17	33.63	73.38
19.72	21.42	23.07	24.67	26.24	27.76	29.24	30.69	32.10	63.40
18.73	20.34	21.92	23.45	24.95	26.40	27.82	29.21	30.56	53.41
17.73	19.27	20.77	22.23	23.66	25.05	26.41	27.73	29.02	43.43
13.39	14.59	15.77	16.92	18.04	19.15	20.23	21.30	22.34	.00
28.88	31.21	33.44	35.60	37.68	39.67	41.60	43.45	45.24	100.00
27.79	30.03	32.20	34.29	36.30	38.23	40.10	41.90	43.63	90.80
26.15	28.28	30.33	32.31	34.22	36.07	37.85	39.56	41.22	77.00
24.51	26.52	28.46	30.34	32.15	33.90	35.60	37.23	38.81	63.19
22.87	24.77	26.60	28.37	30.08	31.74	33.34	34.90	36.40	49.39
21.24	23.01	24.73	26.39	28.01	29.58	31.09	32.57	33.99	35.59
17.01	18.48	19.91	21.31	22.67	23.99	25.29	26.55	27.78	.00
33.53	36.10	38.55	40.89	43.12	45.26	47.30	49.24	51.11	100.00
31.96	34.46	36.77	39.03	41.18	43.24	45.20	47.09	48.89	88.07
29.59	31.90	34.11	36.23	38.26	40.20	42.07	43.85	45.57	70.17
27.23	29.38	31.45	33.43	35.34	37.17	38.93	40.62	42.24	52.27
24.86	26.86	28.78	30.63	32.42	34.13	35.79	37.38	38.92	34.37
20.33	22.02	23.67	25.26	26.81	28.31	29.76	31.17	32.54	.00
37.46	40.19	42.78	45.23	47.55	49.75	51.83	53.81	55.69	100.00
35.36	37.97	40.44	42.79	45.02	47.13	49.14	51.05	52.87	85.14
32.22	34.64	36.94	39.13	41.22	43.21	45.11	46.91	48.64	62.85
29.08	31.31	33.44	35.48	37.42	39.29	41.07	42.77	44.41	40.56
23.36	25.25	27.07	28.82	30.51	32.15	33.72	35.24	36.71	.00
40.78	43.61	46.28	48.79	51.14	53.36	55.45	57.41	59.26	100.00
38.14	40.84	43.38	45.77	48.03	50.16	52.17	54.07	55.86	82.00
34.19	36.67	39.02	41.25	43.36	45.36	47.25	49.05	50.76	55.00
26.15	28.19	30.15	32.03	33.84	35.57	37.24	38.85	40.37	.00
43.58	46.48	49.18	51.70	54.06	56.26	58.32	60.25	62.05	100.00
40.40	43.14	45.71	48.12	50.38	52.50	54.49	56.35	58.11	78.63
35.63	38.14	40.51	42.74	44.85	46.85	48.73	50.51	52.20	46.58
28.70	30.87	32.95	34.93	36.83	38.63	40.36	42.02	43.60	.00
45.95	48.87	51.58	54.09	56.43	58.60	60.61	62.49	64.23	100.00
31.04	33.32	35.49	37.55	39.51	41.37	43.15	44.84	46.44	.00
47.95	50.87	53.57	56.06	58.35	60.48	62.44	64.25	65.94	100.00
33.19	35.56	37.80	39.92	41.93	43.83	45.63	47.34	48.96	.00

17%	18%	19%	20%	21%	22%	23%	24%	25%	MONTHS
48.45	51.06	53.45	55.63	57.63	59.46	61.16	62.72	64.17	258.59
37.91	40.42	42.78	44.98	47.05	49.00	50.82	52.54	54.15	150.52
31.06	33.34	35.51	37.57	39.53	41.39	43.16	44.85	46.46	108.08
26.29	28.35	30.32	32.20	34.02	35.75	37.42	39.02	40.56	84.67
22.80	24.66	26.43	28.17	29.84	31.45	33.00	34.50	35.95	69.71
20.14	21.82	23.46	25.04	26.57	28.06	29.51	30.91	32.27	59.29

MORTGAGE YIELD TABLES

SHOWING DISCOUNT (%) AT VARIOUS YIELDS,
MONTHLY PAYMENT RATES AND DUE DATES

DUE DATE	PAYT RATE	YIELD								
		8%	9%	10%	11%	12%	13%	14%	15%	16%
1 YR	.60	.72	1.67	2.61	3.54	4.46	5.36	6.26	7.16	8.04
	.75	.71	1.65	2.59	3.51	4.42	5.32	6.21	7.10	7.97
	1.00	.70	1.63	2.55	3.46	4.36	5.25	6.13	7.00	7.86
	1.25	.69	1.61	2.51	3.41	4.30	5.17	6.04	6.90	7.75
	1.50	.68	1.59	2.48	3.36	4.24	5.10	5.96	6.81	7.64
	1.75	.67	1.56	2.44	3.31	4.17	5.03	5.87	6.71	7.53
	2.00	.66	1.54	2.41	3.26	4.11	4.95	5.79	6.61	7.43
	8.66	.40	.93	1.45	1.97	2.48	3.00	3.50	4.01	4.51
2 YRS	.60	1.38	3.19	4.97	6.70	8.41	10.08	11.72	13.32	14.89
	.75	1.36	3.14	4.88	6.59	8.27	9.91	11.52	13.10	14.65
	1.00	1.32	3.05	4.74	6.40	8.03	9.62	11.19	12.72	14.22
	1.25	1.28	2.95	4.59	6.20	7.78	9.33	10.85	12.34	13.80
	1.50	1.24	2.86	4.45	6.01	7.54	9.04	10.52	11.96	13.38
	1.75	1.20	2.77	4.31	5.82	7.30	8.75	10.18	11.58	12.96
	2.00	1.16	2.67	4.16	5.62	7.06	8.46	9.85	11.20	12.53
	4.49	.75	1.75	2.73	3.69	4.65	5.59	6.51	7.43	8.33
3 YRS	.60	1.99	4.59	7.10	9.55	11.92	14.22	16.46	18.63	20.74
	.75	1.94	4.47	6.92	9.30	11.61	13.86	16.04	18.16	20.22
	1.00	1.85	4.26	6.60	8.88	11.09	13.24	15.33	17.36	19.33
	1.25	1.76	4.06	6.29	8.46	10.56	12.62	14.61	16.55	18.44
	1.50	1.67	3.85	5.97	8.03	10.04	11.99	13.90	15.75	17.55
	1.75	1.58	3.65	5.66	7.61	9.52	11.37	13.18	14.94	16.66
	2.00	1.49	3.44	5.34	7.19	8.99	10.75	12.47	14.14	15.77
	3.10	1.10	2.54	3.95	5.34	6.69	8.02	9.32	10.60	11.85
4 YRS	.60	2.56	5.86	9.04	12.09	15.03	17.86	20.58	23.21	25.75
	.75	2.47	5.65	8.72	11.67	14.51	17.25	19.89	22.42	24.87
	1.00	2.31	5.30	8.18	10.95	13.62	16.20	18.69	21.08	23.39
	1.25	2.16	4.94	7.63	10.23	12.74	15.15	17.49	19.74	21.92
	1.50	2.00	4.59	7.09	9.51	11.85	14.11	16.29	18.40	20.44
	1.75	1.85	4.24	6.55	8.79	10.96	13.06	15.09	17.06	18.97
	2.41	1.44	3.31	5.13	6.90	8.63	10.31	11.94	13.54	15.09
5 YRS	.60	3.08	7.03	10.79	14.37	17.79	21.06	24.17	27.15	29.98
	.75	2.94	6.71	10.31	13.74	17.02	20.16	23.15	26.00	28.73
	1.00	2.71	6.17	9.49	12.66	15.70	18.60	21.38	24.04	26.59
	1.25	2.47	5.64	8.67	11.59	14.38	17.05	19.62	22.09	24.45
	1.50	2.23	5.10	7.86	10.51	13.06	15.50	17.86	20.13	22.31
	1.99	1.76	4.04	6.25	8.38	10.45	12.45	14.39	16.27	18.09
6 YRS	.60	3.56	8.09	12.37	16.42	20.25	23.87	27.30	30.54	33.61
	.75	3.37	7.65	11.71	15.55	19.19	22.64	25.91	29.00	31.94
	1.00	3.03	6.90	10.57	14.06	17.38	20.53	23.52	26.37	29.07
	1.25	2.70	6.15	9.44	12.58	15.56	18.41	21.13	23.73	26.21
	1.72	2.08	4.75	7.32	9.80	12.18	14.47	16.68	18.80	20.85
7 YRS	.60	4.01	9.06	13.80	18.25	22.42	26.34	30.02	33.47	36.71
	.75	3.75	8.49	12.94	17.12	21.05	24.75	28.23	31.51	34.59
	1.00	3.31	7.50	11.45	15.18	18.71	22.03	25.18	28.15	30.97
	1.52	2.38	5.43	8.35	11.14	13.81	16.36	18.81	21.15	23.40
8 YRS	.60	4.42	9.95	15.10	19.89	24.35	28.51	32.38	35.99	39.35
	.75	4.09	9.22	14.01	18.48	22.65	26.55	30.19	33.60	36.78
	1.00	3.53	7.97	12.14	16.06	19.73	23.19	26.44	29.50	32.37
	1.38	2.68	6.09	9.33	12.41	15.35	18.14	20.80	23.33	25.75
9 YRS	.60	4.80	10.77	16.28	21.37	26.07	30.42	34.44	38.16	41.61
	1.26	2.96	6.72	10.27	13.62	16.80	19.81	22.66	25.35	27.91
10 YRS	.60	5.15	11.51	17.34	22.69	27.59	32.09	36.23	40.03	43.53
	1.17	3.24	7.32	11.16	14.77	18.17	21.37	24.39	27.23	29.92
UNTIL PAID	.75	5.98	13.11	19.43	25.03	30.01	34.47	38.46	42.05	45.29
	1.00	3.96	8.90	13.47	17.70	21.63	25.28	28.67	31.83	34.77
	1.25	3.00	6.80	10.39	13.78	16.99	20.03	22.90	25.62	28.20
	1.50	2.42	5.52	8.48	11.31	14.02	16.60	19.08	21.45	23.72
	1.75	2.03	4.65	7.17	9.60	11.94	14.19	16.36	18.46	20.47
	2.00	1.75	4.02	6.22	8.35	10.41	12.40	14.34	16.21	18.02

MORTGAGE YIELD TABLES 7¼%

SHOWING DISCOUNT (%) AT VARIOUS YIELDS,
MONTHLY PAYMENT RATES AND DUE DATES

17%	18%	19%	20%	YIELD 21%	22%	23%	24%	25%	BAL REMAIN
8.91	9.77	10.63	11.47	12.31	13.13	13.95	14.76	15.56	100.00
8.84	9.69	10.54	11.38	12.21	13.03	13.84	14.65	15.44	98.19
8.72	9.56	10.40	11.22	12.04	12.85	13.65	14.45	15.23	95.09
8.60	9.43	10.25	11.07	11.88	12.68	13.47	14.25	15.02	91.99
8.47	9.30	10.11	10.91	11.71	12.50	13.28	14.05	14.82	88.89
8.35	9.16	9.97	10.76	11.54	12.32	13.09	13.85	14.61	85.78
8.23	9.03	9.82	10.60	11.38	12.14	12.90	13.66	14.40	82.68
5.00	5.50	5.98	6.47	6.95	7.43	7.90	8.37	8.84	.00
16.43	17.94	19.42	20.88	22.30	23.69	25.06	26.40	27.71	100.00
16.16	17.65	19.11	20.54	21.94	23.31	24.66	25.98	27.27	96.25
15.70	17.14	18.56	19.95	21.32	22.65	23.96	25.25	26.51	89.81
15.23	16.64	18.02	19.37	20.69	21.99	23.27	24.52	25.75	83.37
14.77	16.13	17.47	18.78	20.07	21.34	22.58	23.80	24.99	76.94
14.30	15.63	16.93	18.20	19.45	20.68	21.89	23.07	24.23	70.50
13.84	15.12	16.38	17.62	18.83	20.02	21.19	22.34	23.47	64.07
9.22	10.09	10.96	11.81	12.65	13.48	14.30	15.10	15.90	.00
22.79	24.78	26.71	28.59	30.41	32.19	33.91	35.58	37.20	100.00
22.22	24.17	26.05	27.89	29.67	31.41	33.09	34.73	36.32	94.15
21.25	23.11	24.93	26.69	28.40	30.07	31.69	33.27	34.80	84.13
20.27	22.06	23.80	25.49	27.13	28.73	30.29	31.81	33.28	74.11
19.30	21.01	22.67	24.29	25.86	27.40	28.89	30.35	31.76	64.09
18.33	19.96	21.54	23.09	24.59	26.06	27.49	28.89	30.25	54.07
17.35	18.90	20.41	21.89	23.32	24.72	26.09	27.43	28.73	44.05
13.07	14.28	15.45	16.61	17.74	18.85	19.94	21.01	22.05	.00
28.16	30.50	32.75	34.92	37.00	39.01	40.95	42.81	44.61	100.00
27.22	29.49	31.68	33.78	35.81	37.77	39.65	41.47	43.22	91.91
25.62	27.77	29.84	31.84	33.77	35.63	37.43	39.16	40.84	78.03
24.02	26.05	28.01	29.90	31.73	33.50	35.21	36.86	38.45	64.16
22.42	24.33	26.17	27.96	29.69	31.36	32.98	34.55	36.07	50.29
20.81	22.61	24.34	26.02	27.65	29.23	30.76	32.25	33.69	36.42
16.61	18.09	19.52	20.93	22.29	23.63	24.93	26.19	27.43	.00
32.69	35.28	37.75	40.10	42.35	44.50	46.56	48.52	50.40	100.00
31.34	33.84	36.22	38.50	40.67	42.76	44.75	46.65	48.48	89.49
29.03	31.36	33.60	35.74	37.80	39.76	41.65	43.45	45.19	71.48
26.72	28.89	30.98	32.99	34.92	36.77	38.55	40.25	41.90	53.46
24.40	26.42	28.36	30.23	32.04	33.77	35.44	37.05	38.61	35.45
19.85	21.56	23.21	24.82	26.37	27.88	29.34	30.76	32.13	.00
36.52	39.28	41.89	44.36	46.70	48.92	51.02	53.02	54.91	100.00
34.73	37.37	39.88	42.26	44.51	46.66	48.70	50.63	52.47	86.89
31.65	34.10	36.43	38.65	40.77	42.78	44.70	46.53	48.28	64.43
28.57	30.83	32.99	35.05	37.02	38.91	40.71	42.44	44.09	41.96
22.82	24.72	26.55	28.32	30.02	31.67	33.25	34.78	36.26	.00
39.76	42.62	45.31	47.85	50.23	52.47	54.58	56.57	58.44	100.00
37.50	40.24	42.81	45.25	47.54	49.70	51.74	53.67	55.49	84.10
33.63	36.14	38.53	40.79	42.93	44.95	46.88	48.70	50.43	56.85
25.55	27.61	29.59	31.48	33.30	35.05	36.73	38.34	39.89	.00
42.49	45.42	48.15	50.71	53.09	55.33	57.41	59.36	61.19	100.00
39.76	42.55	45.17	47.61	49.91	52.06	54.09	55.99	57.77	81.10
35.08	37.63	40.04	42.31	44.45	46.48	48.39	50.19	51.90	48.70
28.05	30.24	32.34	34.34	36.25	38.07	39.82	41.49	43.08	.00
44.80	47.76	50.51	53.05	55.42	57.62	59.67	61.57	63.34	100.00
30.34	32.65	34.84	36.92	38.90	40.78	42.57	44.28	45.90	.00
46.75	49.72	52.45	54.98	57.31	59.47	61.46	63.31	65.02	100.00
32.45	34.84	37.11	39.25	41.28	43.20	45.02	46.75	48.39	.00
									MONTHS
48.21	50.87	53.29	55.50	57.53	59.38	61.09	62.67	64.13	271.87
37.52	40.08	42.48	44.72	46.82	48.79	50.64	52.38	54.01	153.86
30.64	32.96	35.16	37.25	39.23	41.12	42.92	44.63	46.26	109.63
25.89	27.97	29.96	31.87	33.71	35.47	37.15	38.78	40.33	85.58
22.42	24.29	26.10	27.85	29.53	31.16	32.73	34.25	35.71	70.31
19.78	21.48	23.13	24.73	26.28	27.78	29.24	30.66	32.03	59.71

7½%   MORTGAGE YIELD TABLES

SHOWING DISCOUNT (%) AT VARIOUS YIELDS,
MONTHLY PAYMENT RATES AND DUE DATES

DUE DATE	PAYT RATE	YIELD								
		8%	9%	10%	11%	12%	13%	14%	15%	16%
1 YR	.62	.48	1.43	2.37	3.30	4.22	5.13	6.03	6.92	7.81
	.75	.48	1.42	2.35	3.28	4.19	5.10	5.99	6.88	7.75
	1.00	.47	1.40	2.32	3.23	4.13	5.03	5.91	6.78	7.65
	1.25	.46	1.38	2.29	3.19	4.08	4.96	5.83	6.69	7.54
	1.50	.46	1.36	2.26	3.14	4.02	4.89	5.74	6.59	7.43
	1.75	.45	1.34	2.22	3.10	3.96	4.81	5.66	6.50	7.33
	2.00	.44	1.32	2.19	3.05	3.90	4.74	5.58	6.40	7.22
	8.68	.27	.79	1.32	1.84	2.35	2.87	3.37	3.88	4.38
2 YRS	.62	.92	2.76	4.51	6.26	7.97	9.64	11.28	12.89	14.47
	.75	.91	2.70	4.45	6.17	7.85	9.50	11.12	12.71	14.26
	1.00	.88	2.62	4.32	5.99	7.62	9.23	10.80	12.34	13.85
	1.25	.85	2.54	4.19	5.81	7.39	8.95	10.47	11.97	13.44
	1.50	.83	2.46	4.06	5.62	7.16	8.67	10.15	11.60	13.03
	1.75	.80	2.38	3.92	5.44	6.93	8.39	9.83	11.24	12.62
	2.00	.77	2.30	3.79	5.26	6.70	8.12	9.51	10.87	12.21
	4.50	.50	1.50	2.48	3.45	4.41	5.35	6.28	7.19	8.09
3 YRS	.62	1.33	3.93	6.46	8.91	11.29	13.60	15.85	18.03	20.15
	.75	1.30	3.84	6.31	8.71	11.04	13.30	15.50	17.64	19.71
	1.00	1.24	3.67	6.03	8.32	10.54	12.71	14.81	16.86	18.85
	1.25	1.18	3.49	5.74	7.92	10.05	12.11	14.12	16.08	17.98
	1.50	1.12	3.31	5.45	7.53	9.55	11.52	13.43	15.30	17.11
	1.75	1.06	3.14	5.16	7.13	9.05	10.92	12.74	14.52	16.24
	2.00	1.00	2.96	4.88	6.74	8.56	10.33	12.05	13.74	15.38
	3.11	.73	2.18	3.60	4.99	6.35	7.68	8.99	10.27	11.52
4 YRS	.62	1.71	5.02	8.21	11.28	14.24	17.08	19.82	22.46	24.99
	.75	1.65	4.87	7.97	10.95	13.82	16.58	19.24	21.81	24.28
	1.00	1.55	4.57	7.47	10.27	12.97	15.58	18.09	20.50	22.84
	1.25	1.45	4.26	6.98	9.60	12.13	14.57	16.93	19.20	21.40
	1.50	1.34	3.96	6.48	8.92	11.28	13.56	15.77	17.90	19.96
	1.75	1.24	3.65	5.99	8.25	10.44	12.56	14.61	16.60	18.53
	2.42	.96	2.84	4.67	6.45	8.18	9.87	11.52	13.12	14.68
5 YRS	.62	2.05	6.02	9.81	13.41	16.86	20.14	23.28	26.27	29.13
	.75	1.98	5.79	9.43	12.91	16.23	19.40	22.43	25.32	28.08
	1.00	1.82	5.33	8.69	11.90	14.97	17.91	20.72	23.42	25.99
	1.25	1.66	4.87	7.94	10.89	13.71	16.42	19.02	21.51	23.90
	1.50	1.50	4.40	7.19	9.88	12.45	14.93	17.32	19.61	21.81
	2.00	1.18	3.47	5.69	7.84	9.92	11.93	13.88	15.77	17.60
6 YRS	.62	2.38	6.93	11.25	15.32	19.18	22.83	26.29	29.56	32.65
	.75	2.26	6.61	10.73	14.63	18.32	21.82	25.13	28.28	31.25
	1.00	2.04	5.96	9.69	13.23	16.59	19.79	22.82	25.71	28.46
	1.25	1.82	5.32	8.66	11.84	14.87	17.76	20.51	23.15	25.66
	1.73	1.39	4.08	6.67	9.16	11.56	13.87	16.09	18.23	20.29
7 YRS	.62	2.67	7.77	12.55	17.03	21.24	25.19	28.90	32.39	35.66
	.75	2.52	7.34	11.87	16.12	20.12	23.89	27.43	30.76	33.89
	1.00	2.23	6.49	10.51	14.31	17.89	21.27	24.47	27.49	30.35
	1.53	1.59	4.67	7.61	10.42	13.11	15.69	18.15	20.51	22.78
8 YRS	.62	2.95	8.53	13.73	18.57	23.07	27.27	31.18	34.83	38.23
	.75	2.76	7.99	12.87	17.43	21.68	25.65	29.36	32.83	36.07
	1.00	2.38	6.91	11.16	15.15	18.90	22.42	25.73	28.84	31.76
	1.39	1.79	5.23	8.50	11.62	14.58	17.39	20.08	22.63	25.07
9 YRS	.62	3.20	9.23	14.80	19.94	24.70	29.09	33.16	36.93	40.42
	1.28	1.98	5.79	9.37	12.75	15.96	19.00	21.87	24.60	27.18
10 YRS	.62	3.43	9.87	15.76	21.17	26.14	30.70	34.89	38.74	42.29
	1.19	2.16	6.29	10.18	13.83	17.26	20.50	23.55	26.43	29.14
UNTIL PAID	.75	4.15	11.66	18.28	24.11	29.29	33.89	38.00	41.69	45.00
	1.00	2.70	7.79	12.49	16.85	20.88	24.62	28.09	31.32	34.32
	1.25	2.03	5.92	9.58	13.05	16.32	19.41	22.34	25.11	27.73
	1.50	1.63	4.77	7.80	10.68	13.42	16.05	18.57	20.97	23.27
	1.75	1.37	4.03	6.58	9.05	11.42	13.70	15.90	18.02	20.06
	2.00	1.18	3.48	5.70	7.86	9.94	11.96	13.91	15.80	17.63

SHOWING DISCOUNT (%) AT VARIOUS YIELDS,
MONTHLY PAYMENT RATES AND DUE DATES

| | | | | YIELD | | | | | BAL |
17%	18%	19%	20%	21%	22%	23%	24%	25%	REMAIN
8.68	9.54	10.40	11.24	12.08	12.91	13.73	14.54	15.34	100.00
8.62	9.48	10.33	11.17	12.00	12.82	13.64	14.44	15.24	98.45
8.50	9.35	10.19	11.02	11.84	12.65	13.45	14.25	15.04	95.34
8.38	9.22	10.05	10.86	11.67	12.48	13.27	14.05	14.83	92.24
8.27	9.09	9.91	10.71	11.51	12.30	13.08	13.86	14.62	89.13
8.15	8.96	9.76	10.56	11.35	12.13	12.90	13.66	14.42	86.03
8.03	8.83	9.62	10.41	11.18	11.95	12.71	13.47	14.21	82.92
4.88	5.37	5.86	6.34	6.83	7.30	7.78	8.25	8.72	.00
16.01	17.53	19.01	20.47	21.89	23.29	24.66	26.01	27.32	100.00
15.79	17.28	18.74	20.18	21.59	22.97	24.32	25.65	26.95	96.77
15.33	16.79	18.21	19.61	20.98	22.32	23.64	24.93	26.20	90.32
14.88	16.29	17.68	19.03	20.37	21.67	22.96	24.21	25.45	83.87
14.43	15.80	17.14	18.46	19.76	21.03	22.27	23.50	24.70	77.42
13.97	15.30	16.61	17.89	19.15	20.38	21.59	22.78	23.95	70.97
13.52	14.81	16.07	17.32	18.53	19.73	20.91	22.06	23.19	64.52
8.99	9.86	10.73	11.58	12.43	13.26	14.08	14.89	15.69	.00
22.20	24.20	26.14	28.03	29.86	31.64	33.37	35.05	36.68	100.00
21.73	23.69	25.59	27.44	29.24	30.98	32.68	34.33	35.93	94.97
20.78	22.66	24.48	26.26	27.99	29.66	31.30	32.88	34.43	84.91
19.83	21.63	23.38	25.08	26.74	28.35	29.92	31.44	32.93	74.86
18.88	20.60	22.27	23.90	25.49	27.03	28.54	30.00	31.43	64.80
17.93	19.57	21.16	22.72	24.24	25.72	27.16	28.56	29.93	54.74
16.98	18.54	20.06	21.54	22.99	24.40	25.78	27.12	28.43	44.68
12.75	13.96	15.14	16.30	17.43	18.55	19.64	20.71	21.76	.00
27.44	29.79	32.05	34.23	36.33	38.35	40.30	42.18	43.98	100.00
26.65	28.94	31.15	33.28	35.33	37.30	39.20	41.04	42.80	93.03
25.09	27.26	29.35	31.37	33.32	35.19	37.01	38.76	40.45	79.08
23.52	25.57	27.55	29.46	31.31	33.09	34.81	36.48	38.09	65.14
21.96	23.88	25.75	27.55	29.30	30.98	32.62	34.20	35.73	51.20
20.39	22.20	23.95	25.64	27.29	28.88	30.42	31.92	33.38	37.25
16.21	17.69	19.13	20.54	21.92	23.26	24.56	25.84	27.08	.00
31.85	34.46	36.94	39.32	41.58	43.75	45.82	47.80	49.69	100.00
30.72	33.25	35.66	37.96	40.17	42.27	44.29	46.21	48.06	90.93
28.46	30.82	33.08	35.25	37.33	39.32	41.22	43.05	44.80	72.80
26.20	28.40	30.51	32.54	34.49	36.36	38.16	39.89	41.55	54.67
23.93	25.97	27.94	29.83	31.65	33.40	35.09	36.72	38.29	36.54
19.37	21.09	22.75	24.37	25.93	27.45	28.92	30.35	31.73	.00
35.59	38.36	41.00	43.49	45.85	48.09	50.21	52.23	54.14	100.00
34.08	36.76	39.30	41.71	44.00	46.18	48.24	50.21	52.06	88.68
31.07	33.55	35.91	38.16	40.31	42.35	44.29	46.15	47.91	66.03
28.05	30.34	32.53	34.62	36.61	38.52	40.35	42.09	43.76	43.39
22.28	24.19	26.04	27.82	29.53	31.19	32.78	34.33	35.81	.00
38.74	41.63	44.35	46.91	49.32	51.58	53.71	55.72	57.62	100.00
36.84	39.62	42.24	44.71	47.04	49.24	51.31	53.26	55.11	86.25
33.05	35.60	38.02	40.31	42.49	44.54	46.49	48.34	50.10	58.74
24.94	27.02	29.02	30.93	32.76	34.52	36.22	37.84	39.40	.00
41.40	44.36	47.13	49.71	52.13	54.39	56.50	58.48	60.33	100.00
39.11	41.95	44.61	47.10	49.43	51.62	53.68	55.61	57.42	83.63
34.52	37.11	39.56	41.87	44.04	46.10	48.04	49.87	51.60	50.88
27.39	29.61	31.72	33.74	35.67	37.51	39.27	40.95	42.56	.00
43.65	46.65	49.43	52.01	54.41	56.64	58.72	60.65	62.45	100.00
29.64	31.97	34.18	36.28	38.28	40.18	41.99	43.71	45.35	.00
45.55	48.56	51.34	53.90	56.27	58.46	60.49	62.36	64.10	100.00
31.70	34.12	36.41	38.58	40.63	42.57	44.41	46.16	47.82	.00
									MONTHS
47.99	50.69	53.15	55.39	57.43	59.31	61.04	62.63	64.10	287.58
37.12	39.73	42.17	44.45	46.58	48.58	50.45	52.21	53.87	157.42
30.21	32.57	34.80	36.92	38.94	40.85	42.67	44.40	46.05	111.25
25.47	27.58	29.60	31.54	33.40	35.18	36.88	38.52	40.10	86.51
22.03	23.92	25.75	27.52	29.22	30.87	32.45	33.99	35.47	70.91
19.41	21.13	22.79	24.41	25.98	27.49	28.97	30.40	31.78	60.14

7¾% MORTGAGE YIELD TABLES

SHOWING DISCOUNT (%) AT VARIOUS YIELDS, MONTHLY PAYMENT RATES AND DUE DATES

DUE DATE	PAYT RATE	YIELD								
		8%	9%	10%	11%	12%	13%	14%	15%	16%
1 YR	.65	.24	1.19	2.13	3.06	3.99	4.90	5.80	6.69	7.58
	.75	.24	1.18	2.12	3.05	3.96	4.87	5.77	6.66	7.53
	1.00	.23	1.17	2.09	3.00	3.91	4.80	5.69	6.56	7.43
	1.25	.23	1.15	2.06	2.96	3.85	4.74	5.61	6.47	7.33
	1.50	.23	1.13	2.03	2.92	3.80	4.67	5.53	6.38	7.22
	1.75	.22	1.12	2.00	2.88	3.74	4.60	5.45	6.29	7.12
	2.00	.22	1.10	1.97	2.84	3.69	4.53	5.37	6.20	7.02
	8.69	.13	.66	1.19	1.71	2.22	2.74	3.25	3.75	4.25
2 YRS	.65	.46	2.28	4.06	5.81	7.52	9.20	10.85	12.46	14.04
	.75	.46	2.25	4.01	5.74	7.43	9.09	10.72	12.31	13.87
	1.00	.44	2.19	3.90	5.57	7.22	8.83	10.41	11.96	13.48
	1.25	.43	2.12	3.78	5.40	7.00	8.56	10.10	11.60	13.08
	1.50	.41	2.05	3.66	5.24	6.78	8.30	9.79	11.24	12.68
	1.75	.40	1.99	3.54	5.07	6.56	8.03	9.47	10.89	12.28
	2.00	.39	1.92	3.42	4.90	6.35	7.77	9.16	10.53	11.88
	4.51	.25	1.25	2.24	3.21	4.16	5.11	6.04	6.96	7.86
3 YRS	.65	.66	3.28	5.81	8.27	10.66	12.98	15.24	17.43	19.56
	.75	.65	3.21	5.70	8.12	10.47	12.75	14.96	17.11	19.20
	1.00	.62	3.07	5.44	7.75	10.00	12.18	14.30	16.36	18.36
	1.25	.59	2.92	5.18	7.39	9.53	11.61	13.63	15.60	17.52
	1.50	.56	2.77	4.92	7.02	9.05	11.04	12.97	14.84	16.67
	1.75	.53	2.63	4.67	6.65	8.58	10.47	12.30	14.09	15.83
	2.00	.50	2.48	4.41	6.28	8.11	9.90	11.64	13.33	14.98
	3.12	.37	1.82	3.24	4.64	6.00	7.34	8.65	9.94	11.20
4 YRS	.65	.85	4.19	7.39	10.48	13.45	16.31	19.06	21.71	24.26
	.75	.83	4.08	7.21	10.22	13.12	15.91	18.59	21.18	23.68
	1.00	.78	3.82	6.76	9.59	12.32	14.94	17.48	19.92	22.28
	1.25	.73	3.57	6.31	8.96	11.52	13.98	16.36	18.66	20.88
	1.50	.67	3.32	5.87	8.33	10.71	13.02	15.24	17.40	19.48
	1.75	.62	3.06	5.42	7.70	9.91	12.05	14.13	16.13	18.08
	2.43	.48	2.37	4.21	6.00	7.74	9.44	11.09	12.70	14.27
5 YRS	.65	1.03	5.02	8.82	12.46	15.92	19.23	22.38	25.40	28.27
	.75	.99	4.86	8.54	12.06	15.42	18.63	21.70	24.63	27.42
	1.00	.91	4.47	7.87	11.12	14.23	17.21	20.05	22.78	25.39
	1.25	.83	4.08	7.20	10.18	13.04	15.78	18.41	20.93	23.35
	1.50	.75	3.70	6.52	9.24	11.85	14.35	16.76	19.08	21.31
	2.02	.59	2.90	5.13	7.29	9.38	11.41	13.37	15.27	17.11
6 YRS	.65	1.19	5.78	10.12	14.23	18.12	21.79	25.28	28.57	31.69
	.75	1.14	5.55	9.73	13.69	17.43	20.98	24.35	27.53	30.56
	1.00	1.03	5.01	8.79	12.38	15.80	19.04	22.12	25.04	27.83
	1.25	.92	4.47	7.86	11.08	14.16	17.09	19.88	22.55	25.10
	1.74	.69	3.41	6.02	8.52	10.94	13.26	15.50	17.66	19.73
7 YRS	.65	1.34	6.47	11.29	15.82	20.06	24.05	27.79	31.31	34.61
	.75	1.27	6.18	10.78	15.11	19.13	23.00	26.60	29.99	33.17
	1.00	1.12	5.46	9.55	13.41	17.05	20.49	23.74	26.81	29.71
	1.55	.80	3.90	6.86	9.70	12.41	15.01	17.49	19.87	22.15
8 YRS	.65	1.47	7.11	12.36	17.24	21.79	26.03	29.98	33.67	37.10
	.75	1.39	6.73	11.71	16.35	20.69	24.74	28.52	32.05	35.35
	1.00	1.20	5.83	10.16	14.23	18.04	21.63	25.00	28.16	31.14
	1.40	.90	4.37	7.67	10.81	13.80	16.64	19.35	21.93	24.39
9 YRS	.65	1.60	7.69	13.32	18.52	23.32	27.77	31.89	35.70	39.23
	1.29	.99	4.82	8.45	11.87	15.11	18.18	21.09	23.84	26.45
10 YRS	.65	1.72	8.22	14.19	19.66	24.69	29.30	33.54	37.45	41.04
	1.20	1.09	5.26	9.19	12.88	16.35	19.62	22.71	25.61	28.36
UNTIL PAID	.75	2.16	10.11	17.06	23.17	28.55	33.31	37.55	41.33	44.72
	1.00	1.38	6.63	11.48	15.96	20.10	23.94	27.49	30.79	33.86
	1.25	1.03	5.01	8.76	12.29	15.63	18.79	21.77	24.59	27.25
	1.50	.83	4.04	7.10	10.03	12.82	15.49	18.04	20.48	22.82
	1.75	.69	3.39	5.98	8.48	10.88	13.20	15.42	17.57	19.64
	2.00	.59	2.92	5.17	7.35	9.46	11.50	13.48	15.39	17.24

SHOWING DISCOUNT (%) AT VARIOUS YIELDS,
MONTHLY PAYMENT RATES AND DUE DATES

17%	18%	19%	20%	YIELD 21%	22%	23%	24%	25%	BAL REMAIN
8.45	9.32	10.17	11.02	11.86	12.69	13.51	14.32	15.12	100.00
8.40	9.26	10.12	10.96	11.79	12.62	13.43	14.24	15.04	98.70
8.29	9.14	9.98	10.81	11.63	12.45	13.25	14.05	14.84	95.60
8.17	9.01	9.84	10.66	11.47	12.27	13.07	13.86	14.63	92.49
8.06	8.88	9.70	10.51	11.31	12.10	12.89	13.66	14.43	89.38
7.94	8.76	9.56	10.36	11.15	11.93	12.71	13.47	14.23	86.27
7.83	8.63	9.43	10.21	10.99	11.76	12.52	13.28	14.03	83.16
4.75	5.24	5.73	6.22	6.70	7.18	7.66	8.13	8.60	.00
15.59	17.11	18.60	20.06	21.49	22.89	24.26	25.61	26.93	100.00
15.41	16.91	18.38	19.82	21.24	22.62	23.98	25.32	26.62	97.31
14.96	16.42	17.86	19.26	20.64	21.99	23.31	24.61	25.88	90.85
14.52	15.94	17.33	18.70	20.04	21.35	22.64	23.90	25.14	84.37
14.08	15.46	16.81	18.14	19.44	20.71	21.97	23.20	24.40	77.90
13.64	14.97	16.29	17.57	18.84	20.08	21.29	22.49	23.66	71.44
13.20	14.49	15.76	17.01	18.24	19.44	20.62	21.78	22.92	64.97
8.76	9.64	10.50	11.36	12.21	13.04	13.86	14.67	15.47	.00
21.62	23.63	25.58	27.47	29.31	31.09	32.83	34.52	36.15	100.00
21.23	23.21	25.12	26.99	28.80	30.55	32.26	33.92	35.54	95.79
20.31	22.20	24.04	25.83	27.57	29.26	30.90	32.50	34.06	85.70
19.38	21.19	22.95	24.67	26.34	27.96	29.54	31.08	32.57	75.60
18.45	20.18	21.87	23.51	25.11	26.66	28.18	29.65	31.09	65.51
17.52	19.17	20.78	22.35	23.88	25.37	26.82	28.23	29.61	55.41
16.59	18.17	19.70	21.19	22.65	24.07	25.46	26.81	28.13	45.31
12.43	13.64	14.83	15.99	17.13	18.25	19.35	20.42	21.48	.00
26.71	29.08	31.35	33.55	35.66	37.69	39.65	41.54	43.35	100.00
26.08	28.39	30.62	32.76	34.83	36.83	38.75	40.60	42.38	94.16
24.55	26.74	28.85	30.89	32.85	34.75	36.58	38.35	40.05	80.14
23.02	25.09	27.08	29.01	30.88	32.68	34.42	36.10	37.72	66.13
21.49	23.43	25.32	27.14	28.90	30.60	32.25	33.85	35.39	52.11
19.96	21.78	23.55	25.26	26.92	28.53	30.08	31.60	33.06	38.10
15.80	17.29	18.74	20.16	21.54	22.89	24.20	25.48	26.73	.00
31.02	33.64	36.14	38.53	40.81	43.00	45.08	47.07	48.98	100.00
30.09	32.65	35.09	37.42	39.65	41.78	43.82	45.77	47.63	92.40
27.88	30.27	32.56	34.75	36.85	38.86	40.79	42.64	44.41	74.15
25.67	27.90	30.03	32.09	34.06	35.95	37.77	39.51	41.19	55.90
23.46	25.52	27.51	29.42	31.26	33.03	34.74	36.38	37.97	37.65
18.89	20.62	22.30	23.92	25.49	27.02	28.50	29.93	31.33	.00
34.65	37.45	40.10	42.62	45.00	47.26	49.40	51.44	53.36	100.00
33.42	36.14	38.72	41.16	43.48	45.69	47.78	49.77	51.65	90.49
30.47	32.99	35.39	37.67	39.84	41.91	43.88	45.75	47.54	67.67
27.53	29.84	32.06	34.17	36.20	38.13	39.98	41.74	43.44	44.84
21.73	23.66	25.52	27.31	29.04	30.70	32.31	33.86	35.36	.00
37.72	40.64	43.39	45.97	48.40	50.69	52.85	54.88	56.79	100.00
36.17	39.00	41.66	44.17	46.53	48.76	50.86	52.85	54.72	88.43
32.46	35.05	37.51	39.83	42.04	44.12	46.10	47.98	49.76	60.66
24.34	26.43	28.44	30.37	32.22	34.00	35.70	37.34	38.91	.00
40.31	43.31	46.11	48.72	51.16	53.45	55.59	57.59	59.47	100.00
38.44	41.33	44.04	46.57	48.95	51.17	53.26	55.22	57.06	86.21
33.94	36.58	39.07	41.41	43.62	45.71	47.68	49.54	51.30	53.10
26.73	28.97	31.10	33.14	35.08	36.94	38.72	40.42	42.04	.00
42.50	45.54	48.36	50.97	53.41	55.67	57.77	59.73	61.56	100.00
28.93	31.28	33.52	35.64	37.66	39.58	41.40	43.15	44.80	.00
44.35	47.40	50.22	52.82	55.23	57.45	59.51	61.42	63.19	100.00
30.95	33.40	35.71	37.90	39.97	41.94	43.80	45.57	47.25	.00

									MONTHS
47.77	50.52	53.01	55.28	57.35	59.25	60.99	62.59	64.06	306.65
36.72	39.38	41.86	44.18	46.34	48.37	50.27	52.05	53.73	161.24
29.78	32.17	34.44	36.60	38.64	40.58	42.42	44.18	45.85	112.94
25.05	27.19	29.24	31.20	33.08	34.88	36.61	38.27	39.86	87.47
21.63	23.55	25.40	27.19	28.91	30.57	32.17	33.72	35.22	71.54
19.04	20.77	22.46	24.09	25.67	27.21	28.69	30.13	31.53	60.58

MORTGAGE YIELD TABLES

SHOWING DISCOUNT (%) AT VARIOUS YIELDS,
MONTHLY PAYMENT RATES AND DUE DATES

DUE DATE	PAYT RATE	9%	10%	11%	12%	13%	14%	15%	16%	17%
						YIELD				
1 YR	.67	.95	1.90	2.83	3.75	4.67	5.57	6.46	7.35	8.22
	.75	.95	1.89	2.82	3.73	4.64	5.54	6.43	7.31	8.19
	1.00	.94	1.86	2.78	3.68	4.58	5.47	6.35	7.21	8.07
	1.25	.92	1.83	2.74	3.63	4.52	5.39	6.26	7.11	7.96
	1.50	.91	1.81	2.70	3.58	4.45	5.31	6.17	7.01	7.85
	1.75	.90	1.78	2.66	3.53	4.39	5.24	6.08	6.91	7.74
	2.00	.88	1.76	2.62	3.48	4.32	5.16	5.99	6.81	7.63
	8.70	.53	1.05	1.58	2.09	2.61	3.12	3.62	4.12	4.62
2 YRS	.67	1.82	3.61	5.36	7.08	8.76	10.41	12.03	13.62	15.17
	.75	1.81	3.58	5.31	7.01	8.68	10.31	11.92	13.49	15.03
	1.00	1.75	3.47	5.16	6.81	8.43	10.02	11.57	13.10	14.59
	1.25	1.70	3.37	5.00	6.60	8.17	9.72	11.23	12.71	14.16
	1.50	1.65	3.26	4.84	6.40	7.92	9.42	10.88	12.32	13.73
	1.75	1.59	3.16	4.69	6.19	7.67	9.12	10.54	11.93	13.30
	2.00	1.54	3.05	4.53	5.99	7.42	8.82	10.20	11.55	12.87
	4.52	1.00	1.99	2.96	3.92	4.87	5.80	6.72	7.63	8.53
3 YRS	.67	2.62	5.17	7.64	10.04	12.37	14.63	16.83	18.96	21.04
	.75	2.58	5.09	7.52	9.89	12.18	14.42	16.58	18.69	20.73
	1.00	2.46	4.86	7.18	9.44	11.64	13.78	15.85	17.87	19.83
	1.25	2.35	4.63	6.84	9.00	11.10	13.14	15.12	17.05	18.92
	1.50	2.23	4.39	6.50	8.56	10.55	12.50	14.39	16.23	18.02
	1.75	2.11	4.16	6.16	8.11	10.01	11.86	13.66	15.41	17.11
	2.00	1.99	3.93	5.82	7.67	9.46	11.22	12.92	14.59	16.21
	3.13	1.46	2.88	4.28	5.65	7.00	8.31	9.60	10.87	12.11
4 YRS	.67	3.35	6.57	9.67	12.66	15.53	18.30	20.96	23.52	25.99
	.75	3.28	6.44	9.48	12.41	15.22	17.94	20.55	23.07	25.49
	1.00	3.08	6.04	8.90	11.65	14.30	16.86	19.33	21.71	24.00
	1.25	2.87	5.64	8.32	10.89	13.38	15.79	18.11	20.35	22.51
	1.50	2.67	5.24	7.73	10.14	12.46	14.71	16.88	18.98	21.02
	1.75	2.46	4.85	7.15	9.38	11.54	13.64	15.66	17.62	19.52
	2.44	1.90	3.74	5.54	7.29	9.00	10.66	12.28	13.86	15.39
5 YRS	.67	4.01	7.84	11.50	14.99	18.31	21.49	24.52	27.41	30.18
	.75	3.91	7.64	11.21	14.61	17.86	20.96	23.92	26.75	29.46
	1.00	3.60	7.04	10.33	13.48	16.49	19.37	22.13	24.77	27.30
	1.25	3.29	6.44	9.46	12.35	15.13	17.79	20.34	22.79	25.14
	1.50	2.98	5.84	8.59	11.23	13.76	16.20	18.55	20.80	22.97
	2.03	2.32	4.57	6.74	8.85	10.89	12.86	14.77	16.62	18.41
6 YRS	.67	4.62	9.00	13.13	17.05	20.76	24.27	27.59	30.73	33.71
	.75	4.48	8.72	12.73	16.53	20.14	23.55	26.78	29.85	32.75
	1.00	4.04	7.88	11.52	14.98	18.27	21.40	24.36	27.19	29.87
	1.25	3.61	7.04	10.32	13.44	16.41	19.24	21.95	24.53	26.99
	1.75	2.73	5.36	7.89	10.32	12.66	14.91	17.08	19.17	21.19
7 YRS	.67	5.18	10.04	14.60	18.88	22.90	26.68	30.23	33.56	36.70
	.75	4.99	9.67	14.07	18.21	22.10	25.76	29.20	32.44	35.49
	1.00	4.41	8.57	12.50	16.20	19.70	23.00	26.12	29.07	31.85
	1.56	3.13	6.11	8.97	11.71	14.32	16.83	19.23	21.53	23.73
8 YRS	.67	5.69	10.98	15.92	20.51	24.79	28.78	32.51	35.98	39.22
	.75	5.44	10.52	15.26	19.67	23.80	27.65	31.25	34.61	37.76
	1.00	4.71	9.13	13.28	17.17	20.82	24.25	27.47	30.50	33.35
	1.41	3.51	6.84	10.01	13.02	15.89	18.62	21.22	23.70	26.07
9 YRS	.67	6.15	11.84	17.09	21.95	26.45	30.61	34.47	38.04	41.35
	1.30	3.87	7.53	10.99	14.26	17.36	20.30	23.08	25.71	28.22
10 YRS	.67	6.58	12.61	18.15	23.23	27.91	32.20	36.16	39.80	43.15
	1.21	4.22	8.19	11.92	15.43	18.74	21.86	24.80	27.57	30.19
UNTIL PAID	.75	8.45	15.79	22.18	27.79	32.73	37.10	40.99	44.45	47.56
	1.00	5.43	10.43	15.04	19.30	23.23	26.88	30.26	33.39	36.31
	1.25	4.07	7.90	11.52	14.92	18.14	21.18	24.05	26.77	29.34
	1.50	3.27	6.39	9.36	12.20	14.92	17.51	19.99	22.36	24.62
	1.75	2.74	5.37	7.90	10.34	12.68	14.94	17.11	19.21	21.22
	2.00	2.36	4.64	6.84	8.98	11.04	13.04	14.97	16.85	18.66

MORTGAGE YIELD TABLES

8%

SHOWING DISCOUNT (%) AT VARIOUS YIELDS,
MONTHLY PAYMENT RATES AND DUE DATES

18%	19%	20%	21%	YIELD 22%	23%	24%	25%	26%	BAL REMAIN
9.09	9.95	10.80	11.63	12.47	13.29	14.10	14.91	15.70	100.00
9.05	9.90	10.75	11.58	12.41	13.23	14.04	14.84	15.63	98.96
8.92	9.77	10.60	11.42	12.24	13.05	13.85	14.64	15.42	95.85
8.80	9.63	10.45	11.27	12.07	12.87	13.66	14.44	15.21	92.74
8.68	9.50	10.31	11.11	11.90	12.69	13.47	14.24	15.00	89.63
8.55	9.36	10.16	10.95	11.74	12.51	13.28	14.04	14.79	86.51
8.43	9.23	10.01	10.80	11.57	12.33	13.09	13.84	14.58	83.40
5.12	5.61	6.10	6.58	7.06	7.53	8.01	8.48	8.94	.00
16.69	18.18	19.65	21.08	22.49	23.87	25.22	26.54	27.84	100.00
16.53	18.01	19.46	20.89	22.28	23.65	24.99	26.30	27.59	97.84
16.06	17.50	18.91	20.30	21.65	22.98	24.29	25.57	26.82	91.36
15.59	16.99	18.36	19.71	21.03	22.32	23.59	24.84	26.06	84.87
15.12	16.48	17.81	19.12	20.40	21.66	22.89	24.10	25.29	78.39
14.65	15.96	17.26	18.53	19.77	21.00	22.20	23.37	24.53	71.91
14.17	15.45	16.71	17.94	19.15	20.33	21.50	22.64	23.77	65.42
9.41	10.28	11.14	11.98	12.82	13.64	14.46	15.26	16.05	.00
23.05	25.01	26.91	28.75	30.55	32.29	33.99	35.63	37.23	100.00
22.72	24.65	26.53	28.35	30.12	31.84	33.52	35.14	36.72	96.62
21.74	23.59	25.39	27.14	28.85	30.50	32.11	33.68	35.20	86.49
20.75	22.53	24.25	25.93	27.57	29.16	30.71	32.22	33.68	76.35
19.76	21.46	23.12	24.72	26.29	27.82	29.30	30.75	32.16	66.22
18.78	20.40	21.98	23.52	25.01	26.48	27.90	29.29	30.64	56.09
17.79	19.34	20.84	22.31	23.74	25.13	26.50	27.82	29.12	45.95
13.32	14.51	15.68	16.82	17.95	19.05	20.13	21.19	22.22	.00
28.37	30.66	32.86	34.98	37.03	39.00	40.90	42.73	44.49	100.00
27.83	30.08	32.25	34.34	36.35	38.29	40.16	41.96	43.69	95.30
26.21	28.35	30.40	32.39	34.30	36.15	37.93	39.65	41.31	81.22
24.60	26.61	28.56	30.44	32.26	34.01	35.71	37.35	38.93	67.13
22.98	24.88	26.72	28.49	30.21	31.88	33.49	35.05	36.56	53.04
21.36	23.15	24.87	26.55	28.17	29.74	31.26	32.74	34.18	38.95
16.89	18.35	19.77	21.16	22.51	23.83	25.12	26.37	27.60	.00
32.82	35.34	37.74	40.04	42.24	44.34	46.35	48.27	50.10	100.00
32.04	34.51	36.87	39.13	41.28	43.35	45.32	47.20	49.01	93.88
29.71	32.03	34.25	36.37	38.41	40.36	42.23	44.02	45.73	75.51
27.39	29.55	31.63	33.62	35.53	37.37	39.13	40.83	42.46	57.14
25.06	27.07	29.00	30.86	32.66	34.38	36.04	37.64	39.19	38.77
20.15	21.84	23.47	25.05	26.59	28.07	29.52	30.92	32.28	.00
36.54	39.21	41.75	44.15	46.43	48.59	50.65	52.59	54.44	100.00
35.51	38.12	40.60	42.96	45.19	47.31	49.32	51.24	53.05	92.33
32.42	34.85	37.16	39.36	41.46	43.45	45.36	47.17	48.90	69.32
29.34	31.58	33.72	35.77	37.73	39.60	41.39	43.10	44.74	46.32
23.13	25.00	26.80	28.54	30.22	31.84	33.40	34.91	36.37	.00
39.65	42.42	45.03	47.49	49.80	51.98	54.03	55.97	57.79	100.00
38.36	41.06	43.61	46.01	48.28	50.41	52.43	54.33	56.13	90.66
34.49	36.98	39.34	41.58	43.70	45.70	47.61	49.41	51.12	62.63
25.84	27.87	29.81	31.68	33.47	35.18	36.84	38.42	39.95	.00
42.25	45.08	47.73	50.20	52.51	54.68	56.71	58.61	60.39	100.00
40.70	43.45	46.03	48.45	50.71	52.84	54.83	56.70	58.46	88.84
36.04	38.56	40.95	43.19	45.31	47.31	49.20	50.98	52.67	55.38
28.32	30.48	32.53	34.49	36.37	38.16	39.88	41.52	43.09	.00
44.43	47.28	49.93	52.40	54.69	56.83	58.81	60.67	62.39	100.00
30.59	32.85	34.99	37.03	38.97	40.82	42.58	44.25	45.85	.00
46.25	49.11	51.74	54.19	56.44	58.53	60.47	62.27	63.94	100.00
32.67	35.01	37.22	39.32	41.30	43.18	44.97	46.67	48.28	.00

18%	19%	20%	21%	22%	23%	24%	25%	26%	MONTHS
50.36	52.89	55.19	57.28	59.19	60.94	62.55	64.04	65.41	330.68
39.02	41.55	43.90	46.10	48.16	50.09	51.89	53.59	55.18	165.34
31.77	34.08	36.26	38.34	40.30	42.17	43.95	45.64	47.24	114.70
26.79	28.87	30.86	32.76	34.58	36.33	38.01	39.62	41.16	88.46
23.17	25.04	26.85	28.59	30.27	31.89	33.46	34.97	36.42	72.18
20.42	22.12	23.77	25.36	26.91	28.41	29.87	31.28	32.65	61.02

MORTGAGE YIELD TABLES

SHOWING DISCOUNT (%) AT VARIOUS YIELDS,
MONTHLY PAYMENT RATES AND DUE DATES

DUE DATE	PAYT RATE	9%	10%	11%	12%	13%	14%	15%	16%	17%
	.69	.71	1.66	2.59	3.52	4.43	5.34	6.23	7.12	7.99
	.75	.71	1.65	2.58	3.51	4.42	5.32	6.21	7.09	7.97
	1.00	.70	1.63	2.55	3.46	4.36	5.25	6.13	7.00	7.86
1 YR	1.25	.69	1.61	2.51	3.41	4.29	5.17	6.04	6.90	7.75
	1.50	.68	1.58	2.48	3.36	4.23	5.10	5.95	6.80	7.64
	1.75	.67	1.56	2.44	3.31	4.17	5.03	5.87	6.70	7.53
	2.00	.66	1.54	2.41	3.26	4.11	4.95	5.78	6.61	7.42
	8.71	.40	.92	1.45	1.96	2.48	2.99	3.49	4.00	4.50
	.69	1.37	3.16	4.92	6.64	8.33	9.98	11.60	13.19	14.75
	.75	1.36	3.14	4.88	6.59	8.27	9.91	11.52	13.10	14.64
	1.00	1.32	3.05	4.74	6.40	8.03	9.62	11.19	12.72	14.22
2 YRS	1.25	1.28	2.95	4.60	6.21	7.79	9.33	10.85	12.34	13.80
	1.50	1.24	2.86	4.45	6.01	7.54	9.05	10.52	11.97	13.38
	1.75	1.20	2.77	4.31	5.82	7.30	8.76	10.19	11.59	12.97
	2.00	1.16	2.68	4.17	5.63	7.06	8.47	9.86	11.21	12.55
	4.53	.75	1.74	2.72	3.68	4.63	5.56	6.49	7.40	8.29
	.69	1.97	4.52	7.00	9.41	11.75	14.02	16.23	18.37	20.45
	.75	1.94	4.47	6.92	9.30	11.62	13.87	16.05	18.17	20.23
	1.00	1.85	4.27	6.61	8.89	11.10	13.25	15.34	17.37	19.35
3 YRS	1.25	1.77	4.06	6.30	8.47	10.58	12.64	14.63	16.58	18.47
	1.50	1.68	3.86	5.99	8.05	10.06	12.02	13.93	15.78	17.59
	1.75	1.59	3.66	5.67	7.64	9.55	11.41	13.22	14.98	16.70
	2.00	1.50	3.46	5.36	7.22	9.03	10.79	12.51	14.19	15.82
	3.15	1.09	2.53	3.93	5.31	6.65	7.98	9.27	10.54	11.78
	.69	2.51	5.75	8.87	11.87	14.75	17.53	20.21	22.79	25.27
	.75	2.47	5.66	8.73	11.69	14.54	17.28	19.92	22.46	24.91
	1.00	2.32	5.31	8.20	10.98	13.66	16.24	18.73	21.13	23.45
4 YRS	1.25	2.17	4.96	7.66	10.27	12.78	15.21	17.55	19.81	21.99
	1.50	2.01	4.61	7.13	9.56	11.91	14.17	16.37	18.49	20.54
	1.75	1.86	4.26	6.59	8.85	11.03	13.14	15.18	17.16	19.08
	2.45	1.42	3.28	5.09	6.85	8.56	10.23	11.86	13.44	14.99
	.69	3.01	6.86	10.54	14.05	17.40	20.59	23.64	26.56	29.34
	.75	2.95	6.73	10.34	13.78	17.07	20.21	23.21	26.08	28.81
	1.00	2.72	6.20	9.54	12.72	15.77	18.69	21.48	24.15	26.70
5 YRS	1.25	2.48	5.67	8.73	11.66	14.47	17.16	19.74	22.22	24.59
	1.50	2.25	5.15	7.93	10.60	13.17	15.64	18.01	20.29	22.48
	2.04	1.74	4.00	6.19	8.31	10.36	12.34	14.27	16.13	17.93
	.69	3.47	7.87	12.04	15.98	19.72	23.25	26.60	29.77	32.78
	.75	3.39	7.69	11.76	15.62	19.27	22.74	26.02	29.13	32.07
6 YRS	1.00	3.06	6.95	10.65	14.16	17.50	20.66	23.67	26.54	29.26
	1.25	2.73	6.22	9.54	12.70	15.72	18.59	21.33	23.95	26.44
	1.77	2.05	4.70	7.24	9.69	12.05	14.32	16.50	18.61	20.64
	.69	3.88	8.78	13.38	17.70	21.76	25.57	29.15	32.52	35.68
	.75	3.78	8.54	13.02	17.23	21.18	24.90	28.40	31.69	34.79
7 YRS	1.00	3.34	7.57	11.57	15.33	18.89	22.24	25.41	28.41	31.24
	1.57	2.35	5.36	8.24	11.00	13.64	16.16	18.58	20.90	23.12
	.69	4.27	9.61	14.59	19.23	23.55	27.58	31.35	34.86	38.13
	.75	4.13	9.31	14.13	18.64	22.84	26.76	30.43	33.85	37.06
8 YRS	1.00	3.58	8.08	12.31	16.27	19.99	23.48	26.76	29.85	32.75
	1.43	2.64	6.00	9.19	12.24	15.13	17.89	20.51	23.02	25.40
9 YRS	.69	4.61	10.36	15.67	20.58	25.13	29.34	33.24	36.85	40.21
	1.31	2.91	6.61	10.10	13.41	16.54	19.50	22.31	24.97	27.50
10 YRS	.69	4.93	11.04	16.64	21.78	26.51	30.86	34.87	38.55	41.95
	1.23	3.18	7.19	10.96	14.51	17.85	21.01	23.98	26.78	29.43
	.75	6.65	14.44	21.17	27.03	32.16	36.67	40.66	44.21	47.38
	1.00	4.17	9.33	14.08	18.47	22.51	26.25	29.71	32.92	35.89
UNTIL PAID	1.25	3.10	7.02	10.72	14.20	17.48	20.58	23.51	26.27	28.89
	1.50	2.48	5.66	8.68	11.57	14.33	16.97	19.48	21.89	24.19
	1.75	2.07	4.74	7.31	9.78	12.16	14.45	16.65	18.77	20.81
	2.00	1.78	4.09	6.32	8.48	10.57	12.59	14.55	16.44	18.28

MORTGAGE YIELD TABLES 8¼%

SHOWING DISCOUNT (%) AT VARIOUS YIELDS, MONTHLY PAYMENT RATES AND DUE DATES

18%	19%	20%	21%	YIELD 22%	23%	24%	25%	26%	BAL REMAIN
8.86	9.72	10.57	11.41	12.24	13.07	13.88	14.69	15.48	100.00
8.83	9.69	10.53	11.37	12.20	13.02	13.83	14.64	15.43	99.22
8.71	9.56	10.39	11.22	12.04	12.85	13.65	14.44	15.22	96.10
8.59	9.42	10.25	11.06	11.87	12.67	13.46	14.24	15.02	92.99
8.47	9.29	10.10	10.91	11.70	12.49	13.27	14.04	14.81	89.87
8.35	9.16	9.96	10.75	11.54	12.32	13.09	13.85	14.60	86.76
8.23	9.03	9.82	10.60	11.37	12.14	12.90	13.65	14.39	83.64
4.99	5.48	5.97	6.45	6.93	7.41	7.88	8.35	8.82	.00
16.27	17.77	19.24	20.68	22.09	23.47	24.82	26.15	27.46	100.00
16.16	17.65	19.10	20.53	21.93	23.31	24.65	25.97	27.27	98.38
15.70	17.14	18.56	19.95	21.32	22.65	23.96	25.25	26.51	91.88
15.24	16.64	18.02	19.37	20.70	22.00	23.28	24.53	25.76	85.38
14.78	16.14	17.48	18.79	20.08	21.35	22.59	23.81	25.00	78.88
14.31	15.64	16.94	18.21	19.47	20.70	21.90	23.09	24.25	72.38
13.85	15.14	16.40	17.64	18.85	20.04	21.21	22.36	23.49	65.88
9.18	10.05	10.91	11.76	12.60	13.43	14.24	15.05	15.84	.00
22.47	24.44	26.35	28.20	30.00	31.75	33.45	35.11	36.71	100.00
22.23	24.18	26.07	27.90	29.69	31.42	33.11	34.75	36.34	97.46
21.27	23.14	24.95	26.72	28.43	30.10	31.72	33.30	34.83	87.28
20.31	22.09	23.83	25.53	27.17	28.78	30.34	31.85	33.33	77.11
19.34	21.05	22.72	24.34	25.92	27.45	28.95	30.41	31.83	66.94
18.38	20.01	21.60	23.15	24.66	26.13	27.57	28.96	30.33	56.77
17.42	18.97	20.48	21.96	23.40	24.81	26.18	27.52	28.82	46.60
13.00	14.20	15.37	16.52	17.64	18.75	19.83	20.90	21.94	.00
27.66	29.96	32.18	34.31	36.37	38.35	40.26	42.10	43.87	100.00
27.26	29.54	31.72	33.83	35.86	37.82	39.71	41.53	43.28	96.46
25.68	27.84	29.91	31.92	33.85	35.72	37.51	39.25	40.93	82.30
24.10	26.14	28.10	30.00	31.84	33.61	35.32	36.97	38.57	68.14
22.52	24.44	26.29	28.09	29.82	31.50	33.12	34.70	36.22	53.98
20.94	22.74	24.48	26.17	27.81	29.39	30.93	32.42	33.87	39.82
16.49	17.96	19.39	20.78	22.14	23.47	24.76	26.02	27.25	.00
32.00	34.53	36.96	39.27	41.49	43.60	45.62	47.56	49.40	100.00
31.43	33.93	36.31	38.60	40.78	42.86	44.86	46.77	48.59	95.38
29.15	31.49	33.74	35.88	37.94	39.92	41.80	43.62	45.35	76.89
26.87	29.06	31.16	33.17	35.11	36.97	38.75	40.46	42.11	58.40
24.59	26.63	28.58	30.46	32.27	34.02	35.69	37.31	38.87	39.91
19.68	21.37	23.02	24.61	26.15	27.65	29.10	30.51	31.88	.00
35.62	38.32	40.88	43.30	45.60	47.78	49.85	51.82	53.68	100.00
34.87	37.52	40.03	42.42	44.68	46.83	48.87	50.81	52.65	94.20
31.85	34.31	36.65	38.88	41.00	43.02	44.95	46.79	48.53	71.01
28.82	31.10	33.27	35.34	37.32	39.22	41.03	42.76	44.42	47.82
22.59	24.47	26.29	28.04	29.73	31.36	32.94	34.46	35.92	.00
38.66	41.46	44.09	46.58	48.91	51.11	53.19	55.15	56.99	100.00
37.71	40.46	43.04	45.48	47.78	49.95	52.00	53.93	55.75	92.93
33.92	36.45	38.84	41.11	43.26	45.30	47.23	49.06	50.79	64.63
25.25	27.29	29.25	31.13	32.93	34.67	36.33	37.93	39.47	.00
41.20	44.06	46.73	49.23	51.57	53.77	55.82	57.74	59.55	100.00
40.05	42.85	45.48	47.94	50.24	52.40	54.43	56.33	58.11	91.54
35.48	38.05	40.47	42.75	44.90	46.93	48.85	50.66	52.37	57.71
27.68	29.85	31.92	33.90	35.80	37.61	39.34	40.99	42.58	.00
43.32	46.21	48.89	51.39	53.71	55.88	57.89	59.77	61.53	100.00
29.90	32.18	34.34	36.40	38.36	40.23	42.00	43.69	45.31	.00
45.09	47.99	50.67	53.14	55.44	57.56	59.53	61.36	63.06	100.00
31.93	34.30	36.53	38.65	40.66	42.56	44.37	46.09	47.71	.00
									MONTHS
50.23	52.79	55.11	57.22	59.15	60.91	62.53	64.02	65.40	362.68
38.66	41.23	43.63	45.86	47.95	49.90	51.73	53.45	55.06	169.77
31.36	33.71	35.93	38.03	40.02	41.92	43.72	45.43	47.05	116.55
26.39	28.49	30.51	32.43	34.28	36.05	37.75	39.38	40.94	89.49
22.78	24.68	26.51	28.27	29.97	31.60	33.19	34.71	36.18	72.83
20.05	21.77	23.44	25.05	26.62	28.13	29.60	31.02	32.41	61.48

MORTGAGE YIELD TABLES

SHOWING DISCOUNT (%) AT VARIOUS YIELDS,
MONTHLY PAYMENT RATES AND DUE DATES

DUE DATE	PAYT RATE	9%	10%	11%	12%	13%	14%	15%	16%	17%
1 YR	.71	.48	1.42	2.36	3.28	4.20	5.10	6.00	6.89	7.77
	1.00	.47	1.40	2.32	3.23	4.13	5.02	5.91	6.78	7.64
	1.25	.46	1.38	2.29	3.18	4.07	4.95	5.82	6.68	7.54
	1.50	.46	1.36	2.25	3.14	4.02	4.88	5.74	6.59	7.43
	1.75	.45	1.34	2.22	3.09	3.96	4.81	5.66	6.50	7.32
	2.00	.44	1.32	2.19	3.05	3.90	4.74	5.58	6.40	7.22
	2.25	.44	1.30	2.16	3.00	3.84	4.67	5.49	6.31	7.11
	8.72	.26	.79	1.31	1.83	2.35	2.86	3.37	3.87	4.37
2 YRS	.71	.91	2.71	4.47	6.20	7.89	9.55	11.17	12.76	14.33
	1.00	.88	2.62	4.32	5.99	7.62	9.23	10.80	12.34	13.85
	1.25	.85	2.54	4.19	5.81	7.39	8.95	10.48	11.97	13.44
	1.50	.83	2.46	4.06	5.63	7.17	8.68	10.16	11.61	13.03
	1.75	.80	2.38	3.93	5.45	6.94	8.40	9.84	11.24	12.63
	2.00	.77	2.30	3.80	5.27	6.71	8.13	9.52	10.88	12.22
	2.25	.75	2.22	3.67	5.09	6.48	7.85	9.19	10.51	11.81
	4.55	.50	1.49	2.47	3.44	4.39	5.33	6.25	7.16	8.06
3 YRS	.71	1.31	3.87	6.36	8.78	11.13	13.41	15.63	17.78	19.87
	1.00	1.24	3.67	6.03	8.33	10.56	12.72	14.83	16.88	18.87
	1.25	1.18	3.50	5.75	7.94	10.06	12.13	14.15	16.10	18.01
	1.50	1.12	3.32	5.46	7.55	9.57	11.54	13.46	15.33	17.15
	1.75	1.06	3.15	5.18	7.15	9.08	10.95	12.78	14.56	16.29
	2.00	1.00	2.97	4.89	6.76	8.59	10.36	12.10	13.79	15.43
	2.25	.95	2.80	4.61	6.37	8.10	9.78	11.41	13.01	14.57
	3.16	.73	2.17	3.58	4.96	6.31	7.64	8.94	10.21	11.46
4 YRS	.71	1.67	4.93	8.06	11.08	13.98	16.77	19.46	22.05	24.55
	1.00	1.55	4.58	7.49	10.30	13.01	15.61	18.13	20.55	22.89
	1.25	1.45	4.28	7.00	9.63	12.17	14.62	16.99	19.27	21.47
	1.50	1.35	3.98	6.52	8.97	11.34	13.63	15.84	17.99	20.05
	1.75	1.25	3.68	6.03	8.30	10.51	12.64	14.70	16.70	18.64
	2.00	1.14	3.38	5.54	7.64	9.67	11.65	13.56	15.42	17.22
	2.46	.95	2.82	4.63	6.40	8.12	9.80	11.43	13.03	14.58
5 YRS	.71	2.01	5.88	9.58	13.19	16.48	19.70	22.77	25.70	28.50
	1.00	1.82	5.35	8.73	11.95	15.04	17.99	20.81	23.51	26.10
	1.25	1.67	4.90	7.99	10.96	13.80	16.52	19.14	21.64	24.04
	1.50	1.51	4.44	7.26	9.96	12.56	15.06	17.46	19.77	21.99
	1.75	1.35	3.99	6.52	8.97	11.32	13.59	15.78	17.89	19.93
	2.05	1.16	3.44	5.64	7.77	9.83	11.83	13.76	15.63	17.45
6 YRS	.71	2.31	6.75	10.95	14.92	18.68	22.24	25.62	28.81	31.84
	1.00	2.06	6.01	9.76	13.32	16.71	19.92	22.97	25.88	28.63
	1.25	1.84	5.37	8.74	11.95	15.01	17.93	20.71	23.36	25.89
	1.50	1.62	4.74	7.73	10.58	13.32	15.94	18.44	20.84	23.14
	1.78	1.37	4.03	6.60	9.06	11.44	13.72	15.92	18.04	20.08
7 YRS	.71	2.59	7.53	12.17	16.52	20.61	24.46	28.07	31.47	34.66
	1.00	2.25	6.56	10.62	14.45	18.06	21.47	24.69	27.74	30.61
	1.25	1.96	5.72	9.29	12.66	15.87	18.91	21.80	24.54	27.14
	1.58	1.57	4.61	7.51	10.29	12.95	15.49	17.93	20.27	22.51
8 YRS	.71	2.84	8.24	13.26	17.95	22.31	26.38	30.18	33.73	37.04
	1.00	2.41	7.01	11.31	15.35	19.14	22.70	26.04	29.18	32.13
	1.25	2.04	5.95	9.64	13.13	16.43	19.54	22.49	25.28	27.92
	1.44	1.76	5.15	8.38	11.45	14.37	17.15	19.80	22.33	24.73
9 YRS	.71	3.08	8.88	14.24	19.21	23.80	28.06	32.01	35.66	39.06
	1.33	1.95	5.68	9.21	12.55	15.71	18.70	21.54	24.23	26.78
10 YRS	.71	3.29	9.46	15.12	20.33	25.12	29.52	33.57	37.31	40.76
	1.24	2.12	6.18	9.99	13.58	16.96	20.15	23.15	25.98	28.66
UNTIL PAID	1.00	2.85	8.19	13.09	17.61	21.76	25.60	29.15	32.43	35.47
	1.25	2.10	6.12	9.89	13.45	16.81	19.97	22.95	25.77	28.43
	1.50	1.68	4.91	7.99	10.93	13.73	16.41	18.97	21.41	23.74
	1.75	1.40	4.11	6.71	9.22	11.63	13.95	16.18	18.33	20.40
	2.00	1.20	3.54	5.80	7.98	10.10	12.14	14.12	16.04	17.89
	2.25	1.05	3.11	5.10	7.04	8.93	10.76	12.53	14.26	15.94

SHOWING DISCOUNT (%) AT VARIOUS YIELDS,
MONTHLY PAYMENT RATES AND DUE DATES

18%	19%	20%	21%	YIELD 22%	23%	24%	25%	26%	BAL REMAIN
8.64	9.49	10.35	11.19	12.02	12.84	13.66	14.47	15.27	100.00
8.50	9.34	10.18	11.01	11.83	12.64	13.45	14.24	15.03	96.36
8.38	9.22	10.04	10.86	11.67	12.47	13.26	14.05	14.82	93.24
8.26	9.09	9.90	10.71	11.51	12.30	13.08	13.85	14.62	90.12
8.15	8.96	9.76	10.56	11.34	12.12	12.89	13.66	14.41	87.00
8.03	8.83	9.62	10.40	11.18	11.95	12.71	13.46	14.21	83.88
7.91	8.70	9.48	10.25	11.02	11.78	12.53	13.27	14.00	80.76
4.86	5.36	5.85	6.33	6.81	7.29	7.76	8.23	8.70	.00
15.86	17.36	18.83	20.27	21.69	23.07	24.43	25.76	27.07	100.00
15.33	16.79	18.21	19.61	20.98	22.32	23.64	24.93	26.20	92.40
14.88	16.29	17.68	19.04	20.37	21.68	22.96	24.22	25.45	85.88
14.43	15.80	17.15	18.47	19.77	21.04	22.28	23.51	24.71	79.37
13.98	15.31	16.62	17.90	19.16	20.39	21.61	22.80	23.96	72.85
13.53	14.82	16.09	17.33	18.55	19.75	20.93	22.08	23.22	66.34
13.08	14.33	15.56	16.76	17.95	19.11	20.25	21.37	22.47	59.82
8.95	9.83	10.69	11.54	12.38	13.21	14.03	14.83	15.63	.00
21.90	23.87	25.79	27.65	29.46	31.22	32.92	34.58	36.20	100.00
20.80	22.68	24.51	26.29	28.01	29.69	31.33	32.92	34.46	88.09
19.86	21.66	23.41	25.12	26.78	28.39	29.96	31.49	32.98	77.88
18.92	20.64	22.32	23.95	25.54	27.09	28.60	30.06	31.49	67.67
17.98	19.62	21.22	22.78	24.30	25.78	27.23	28.64	30.01	57.46
17.04	18.60	20.13	21.61	23.07	24.48	25.86	27.21	28.52	47.24
16.10	17.58	19.03	20.45	21.83	23.18	24.50	25.78	27.04	37.03
12.68	13.88	15.06	16.21	17.34	18.45	19.54	20.60	21.65	.00
26.95	29.26	31.49	33.64	35.71	37.70	39.62	41.47	43.25	100.00
25.15	27.32	29.42	31.44	33.39	35.28	37.09	38.84	40.54	83.39
23.60	25.66	27.64	29.56	31.41	33.20	34.92	36.59	38.21	69.16
22.06	23.99	25.86	27.67	29.42	31.12	32.76	34.34	35.88	54.93
20.51	22.33	24.08	25.79	27.44	29.04	30.59	32.10	33.55	40.70
18.96	20.66	22.31	23.90	25.46	26.96	28.42	29.85	31.23	26.46
16.09	17.56	19.00	20.40	21.77	23.10	24.40	25.66	26.90	.00
31.18	33.73	36.17	38.50	40.73	42.86	44.90	46.85	48.71	100.00
28.58	30.95	33.22	35.39	37.47	39.47	41.38	43.21	44.97	78.29
26.35	28.56	30.68	32.72	34.68	36.56	38.36	40.09	41.76	59.68
24.12	26.17	28.15	30.05	31.88	33.65	35.34	36.98	38.55	41.07
21.89	23.79	25.62	27.38	29.09	30.73	32.32	33.86	35.35	22.46
19.21	20.91	22.56	24.16	25.72	27.22	28.68	30.10	31.48	.00
34.71	37.43	40.01	42.45	44.77	46.97	49.06	51.04	52.93	100.00
31.26	33.75	36.13	38.39	40.54	42.59	44.54	46.40	48.17	72.73
28.30	30.60	32.80	34.90	36.91	38.83	40.66	42.41	44.09	49.35
25.34	27.45	29.47	31.42	33.28	35.07	36.78	38.43	40.01	25.98
22.05	23.95	25.78	27.54	29.24	30.89	32.47	34.00	35.48	.00
37.67	40.49	43.16	45.66	48.02	50.25	52.35	54.32	56.19	100.00
33.33	35.90	38.33	40.64	42.82	44.88	46.84	48.70	50.46	66.68
29.61	31.96	34.20	36.33	38.35	40.28	42.12	43.87	45.54	38.12
24.65	26.71	28.68	30.58	32.40	34.14	35.82	37.43	38.98	.00
40.14	43.03	45.74	48.27	50.64	52.86	54.93	56.88	58.71	100.00
34.91	37.52	39.98	42.30	44.48	46.55	48.49	50.33	52.07	60.09
30.42	32.80	35.05	37.18	39.21	41.14	42.97	44.71	46.37	25.89
27.03	29.22	31.31	33.31	35.22	37.05	38.79	40.46	42.06	.00
42.21	45.13	47.85	50.38	52.74	54.93	56.97	58.88	60.66	100.00
29.20	31.50	33.69	35.77	37.75	39.63	41.43	43.13	44.76	.00
43.94	46.87	49.59	52.10	54.43	56.58	58.58	60.44	62.17	100.00
31.19	33.58	35.84	37.99	40.02	41.94	43.77	45.50	47.15	.00
									MONTHS
38.29	40.91	43.35	45.62	47.74	49.72	51.58	53.31	54.94	174.57
30.95	33.33	35.58	37.72	39.74	41.66	43.48	45.21	46.86	118.48
25.98	28.11	30.15	32.10	33.98	35.77	37.49	39.13	40.71	90.54
22.39	24.31	26.16	27.94	29.66	31.31	32.91	34.45	35.94	73.50
19.68	21.42	23.10	24.73	26.31	27.84	29.33	30.77	32.16	61.94
17.57	19.16	20.70	22.20	23.65	25.07	26.45	27.79	29.10	53.56

MORTGAGE YIELD TABLES

SHOWING DISCOUNT (%) AT VARIOUS YIELDS,
MONTHLY PAYMENT RATES AND DUE DATES

DUE DATE	PAYT RATE	YIELD 9%	10%	11%	12%	13%	14%	15%	16%	17%
1 YR	.73	.24	1.18	2.12	3.05	3.97	4.87	5.77	6.66	7.54
	1.00	.23	1.17	2.09	3.00	3.91	4.80	5.68	6.56	7.43
	1.25	.23	1.15	2.06	2.96	3.85	4.73	5.61	6.47	7.32
	1.50	.23	1.13	2.03	2.92	3.80	4.67	5.53	6.38	7.22
	1.75	.22	1.12	2.00	2.88	3.74	4.60	5.45	6.29	7.12
	2.00	.22	1.10	1.97	2.83	3.69	4.53	5.37	6.20	7.01
	2.25	.22	1.09	1.94	2.79	3.63	4.47	5.29	6.10	6.91
	8.73	.13	.66	1.18	1.70	2.22	2.73	3.24	3.74	4.24
2 YRS	.73	.46	2.26	4.02	5.75	7.45	9.11	10.74	12.34	13.91
	1.00	.44	2.19	3.90	5.57	7.22	8.83	10.41	11.96	13.48
	1.25	.43	2.12	3.78	5.41	7.00	8.56	10.10	11.60	13.08
	1.50	.41	2.05	3.66	5.24	6.78	8.30	9.79	11.25	12.68
	1.75	.40	1.99	3.54	5.07	6.57	8.04	9.48	10.90	12.29
	2.00	.39	1.92	3.43	4.90	6.35	7.78	9.17	10.54	11.89
	2.25	.37	1.86	3.31	4.74	6.14	7.51	8.86	10.19	11.49
	4.56	.25	1.25	2.23	3.19	4.15	5.09	6.02	6.93	7.83
3 YRS	.73	.66	3.23	5.73	8.15	10.51	12.80	15.02	17.18	19.28
	1.00	.62	3.07	5.45	7.76	10.01	12.19	14.31	16.37	18.38
	1.25	.59	2.93	5.19	7.40	9.54	11.63	13.65	15.63	17.54
	1.50	.56	2.78	4.94	7.03	9.08	11.06	12.99	14.88	16.71
	1.75	.53	2.63	4.68	6.67	8.61	10.50	12.34	14.13	15.87
	2.00	.50	2.49	4.42	6.31	8.14	9.93	11.68	13.38	15.04
	2.25	.47	2.34	4.17	5.94	7.68	9.37	11.02	12.63	14.20
	3.17	.37	1.81	3.22	4.61	5.97	7.30	8.60	9.88	11.13
4 YRS	.73	.84	4.11	7.25	10.28	13.20	16.01	18.71	21.32	23.83
	1.00	.78	3.83	6.78	9.61	12.35	14.98	17.52	19.97	22.33
	1.25	.73	3.58	6.34	8.99	11.56	14.03	16.42	18.72	20.95
	1.50	.68	3.33	5.90	8.37	10.77	13.08	15.32	17.48	19.57
	1.75	.63	3.08	5.46	7.75	9.98	12.13	14.21	16.23	18.18
	2.00	.57	2.83	5.01	7.13	9.19	11.18	13.11	14.99	16.80
	2.48	.48	2.35	4.17	5.95	7.68	9.37	11.01	12.61	14.17
5 YRS	.73	1.00	4.90	8.62	12.18	15.57	18.80	21.89	24.84	27.66
	1.00	.92	4.49	7.91	11.17	14.29	17.28	20.14	22.87	25.49
	1.25	.84	4.11	7.24	10.24	13.12	15.88	18.52	21.06	23.49
	1.50	.76	3.73	6.58	9.32	11.95	14.47	16.90	19.24	21.48
	1.75	.68	3.35	5.92	8.39	10.77	13.07	15.28	17.42	19.48
	2.06	.58	2.87	5.08	7.23	9.30	11.31	13.25	15.14	16.96
6 YRS	.73	1.16	5.62	9.85	13.85	17.64	21.23	24.63	27.85	30.90
	1.00	1.04	5.05	8.85	12.47	15.90	19.16	22.26	25.20	28.00
	1.25	.93	4.52	7.94	11.19	14.29	17.25	20.07	22.76	25.32
	1.50	.82	3.99	7.02	9.91	12.69	15.34	17.88	20.31	22.64
	1.79	.69	3.37	5.95	8.43	10.82	13.12	15.34	17.47	19.53
7 YRS	.73	1.29	6.27	10.95	15.34	19.47	23.35	26.99	30.42	33.64
	1.00	1.14	5.52	9.65	13.54	17.22	20.68	23.96	27.05	29.97
	1.25	.99	4.82	8.44	11.88	15.14	18.23	21.16	23.94	26.58
	1.60	.79	3.85	6.77	9.57	12.26	14.82	17.28	19.63	21.89
8 YRS	.73	1.42	6.86	11.94	16.66	21.07	25.18	29.02	32.61	35.95
	1.00	1.22	5.91	10.30	14.41	18.27	21.90	25.30	28.49	31.50
	1.25	1.03	5.02	8.78	12.34	15.69	18.86	21.86	24.70	27.38
	1.45	.88	4.31	7.56	10.66	13.60	16.41	19.08	21.63	24.06
9 YRS	.73	1.54	7.40	12.82	17.84	22.48	26.79	30.77	34.47	37.91
	1.34	.98	4.74	8.31	11.68	14.87	17.90	20.76	23.48	26.06
10 YRS	.73	1.64	7.88	13.61	18.88	23.72	28.18	32.28	36.07	39.56
	1.25	1.06	5.16	9.02	12.65	16.06	19.28	22.32	25.18	27.89
UNTIL PAID	1.00	1.46	6.99	12.06	16.71	20.99	24.94	28.57	31.93	35.04
	1.25	1.07	5.18	9.05	12.69	16.11	19.34	22.38	25.25	27.96
	1.50	.85	4.14	7.28	10.27	13.12	15.84	18.44	20.92	23.29
	1.75	.71	3.46	6.10	8.65	11.09	13.44	15.70	17.88	19.97
	2.00	.60	2.97	5.26	7.47	9.61	11.68	13.69	15.62	17.50
	2.25	.53	2.61	4.63	6.59	8.49	10.34	12.13	13.88	15.57

MORTGAGE YIELD TABLES   8¾%

SHOWING DISCOUNT (%) AT VARIOUS YIELDS,
MONTHLY PAYMENT RATES AND DUE DATES

| | | | | YIELD | | | | | BAL |
18%	19%	20%	21%	22%	23%	24%	25%	26%	REMAIN
8.41	9.27	10.12	10.96	11.80	12.62	13.44	14.25	15.05	100.00
8.28	9.13	9.97	10.80	11.62	12.44	13.24	14.04	14.83	96.62
8.17	9.01	9.83	10.65	11.46	12.27	13.06	13.85	14.63	93.49
8.05	8.88	9.70	10.51	11.31	12.10	12.88	13.66	14.42	90.37
7.94	8.75	9.56	10.36	11.15	11.93	12.70	13.47	14.22	87.25
7.83	8.63	9.42	10.21	10.99	11.76	12.52	13.27	14.02	84.12
7.71	8.50	9.28	10.06	10.83	11.59	12.34	13.08	13.82	81.00
4.74	5.23	5.72	6.21	6.69	7.17	7.64	8.11	8.58	.00
15.44	16.94	18.42	19.87	21.28	22.67	24.04	25.37	26.68	100.00
14.96	16.43	17.86	19.26	20.64	21.99	23.31	24.61	25.89	92.92
14.53	15.95	17.34	18.70	20.04	21.36	22.64	23.91	25.15	86.39
14.09	15.47	16.82	18.14	19.45	20.72	21.98	23.21	24.41	79.86
13.65	14.99	16.30	17.59	18.85	20.09	21.31	22.50	23.68	73.33
13.21	14.51	15.78	17.03	18.25	19.46	20.64	21.80	22.94	66.80
12.77	14.03	15.26	16.47	17.66	18.83	19.97	21.10	22.21	60.27
8.72	9.60	10.46	11.32	12.16	12.99	13.81	14.62	15.41	.00
21.32	23.30	25.23	27.10	28.91	30.68	32.39	34.06	35.68	100.00
20.33	22.22	24.06	25.85	27.59	29.29	30.93	32.53	34.09	88.90
19.41	21.22	22.99	24.71	26.38	28.00	29.58	31.12	32.62	78.65
18.49	20.23	21.91	23.56	25.16	26.72	28.24	29.71	31.15	68.40
17.57	19.23	20.84	22.41	23.94	25.43	26.89	28.31	29.69	58.15
16.65	18.23	19.77	21.26	22.73	24.15	25.54	26.90	28.22	47.90
15.73	17.23	18.69	20.12	21.51	22.87	24.19	25.49	26.75	37.65
12.36	13.57	14.75	15.90	17.04	18.15	19.24	20.31	21.36	.00
26.24	28.57	30.81	32.97	35.05	37.05	38.98	40.84	42.63	100.00
24.61	26.80	28.92	30.96	32.93	34.83	36.66	38.43	40.14	84.50
23.10	25.17	27.17	29.11	30.98	32.78	34.53	36.21	37.84	70.20
21.59	23.54	25.43	27.26	29.02	30.73	32.39	33.99	35.54	55.89
20.08	21.91	23.68	25.40	27.07	28.68	30.25	31.77	33.24	41.58
18.57	20.28	21.94	23.55	25.12	26.64	28.11	29.54	30.93	27.28
15.69	17.17	18.61	20.02	21.39	22.73	24.03	25.31	26.55	.00
30.36	32.93	35.39	37.73	39.98	42.12	44.18	46.14	48.01	100.00
28.00	30.33	32.69	34.89	37.00	39.01	40.95	42.80	44.57	79.71
25.82	28.06	30.20	32.26	34.24	36.14	37.97	39.72	41.40	60.97
23.64	25.72	27.72	29.64	31.49	33.27	34.98	36.64	38.23	42.24
21.46	23.38	25.23	27.01	28.73	30.40	32.00	33.56	35.05	23.51
18.73	20.44	22.11	23.72	25.28	26.79	28.26	29.69	31.07	.00
33.80	36.54	39.14	41.61	43.94	46.16	48.27	50.27	52.17	100.00
30.66	33.19	35.60	37.89	40.07	42.14	44.12	46.00	47.80	74.47
27.77	30.10	32.33	34.46	36.49	38.43	40.28	42.04	43.73	50.91
24.87	27.01	29.06	31.02	32.91	34.72	36.45	38.12	39.72	27.35
21.51	23.42	25.26	27.04	28.75	30.41	32.00	33.54	35.03	.00
36.68	39.53	42.22	44.75	47.13	49.38	51.50	53.50	55.39	100.00
32.73	35.34	37.81	40.15	42.36	44.46	46.44	48.33	50.11	68.76
29.09	31.48	33.75	35.91	37.96	39.91	41.78	43.55	45.24	39.93
24.05	26.13	28.12	30.03	31.86	33.62	35.31	36.94	38.50	.00
39.08	42.01	44.74	47.30	49.70	51.94	54.05	56.02	57.87	100.00
34.32	36.98	39.48	41.84	44.06	46.15	48.13	49.99	51.75	62.54
29.93	32.34	34.62	36.79	38.85	40.80	42.66	44.43	46.11	27.95
26.38	28.59	30.70	32.71	34.64	36.48	38.24	39.93	41.54	.00
41.10	44.06	46.81	49.38	51.76	53.98	56.06	57.99	59.79	100.00
28.50	30.83	33.03	35.13	37.13	39.03	40.85	42.57	44.22	.00
42.78	45.76	48.51	51.06	53.42	55.61	57.64	59.53	61.28	100.00
30.45	32.86	35.15	37.32	39.37	41.31	43.16	44.91	46.57	.00
									MONTHS
37.92	40.59	43.07	45.38	47.54	49.54	51.42	53.18	54.84	179.80
30.52	32.94	35.23	37.40	39.46	41.40	43.25	45.00	46.67	120.50
25.56	27.72	29.79	31.77	33.67	35.48	37.22	38.88	40.48	91.64
21.99	23.93	25.81	27.61	29.35	31.02	32.64	34.19	35.70	74.19
19.31	21.07	22.77	24.42	26.01	27.56	29.05	30.51	31.91	62.42
17.22	18.82	20.38	21.89	23.36	24.79	26.18	27.54	28.85	53.91

9% MORTGAGE YIELD TABLES

SHOWING DISCOUNT (%) AT VARIOUS YIELDS,
MONTHLY PAYMENT RATES AND DUE DATES

DUE DATE	PAYT RATE	YIELD								
		10%	11%	12%	13%	14%	15%	16%	17%	18%
1 YR	.75	.95	1.89	2.81	3.73	4.64	5.54	6.43	7.31	8.18
	1.00	.93	1.86	2.77	3.68	4.58	5.46	6.34	7.21	8.07
	1.25	.92	1.83	2.74	3.63	4.51	5.39	6.25	7.11	7.96
	1.50	.91	1.81	2.70	3.58	4.45	5.31	6.17	7.01	7.85
	1.75	.90	1.78	2.66	3.53	4.39	5.24	6.08	6.91	7.73
	2.00	.88	1.76	2.62	3.48	4.32	5.16	5.99	6.81	7.62
	2.25	.87	1.73	2.58	3.42	4.26	5.08	5.90	6.71	7.51
	8.75	.53	1.05	1.57	2.09	2.60	3.11	3.61	4.12	4.61
2 YRS	.75	1.81	3.58	5.31	7.01	8.68	10.31	11.91	13.48	15.02
	1.00	1.75	3.47	5.16	6.81	8.43	10.02	11.57	13.10	14.60
	1.25	1.70	3.37	5.00	6.60	8.18	9.72	11.23	12.71	14.17
	1.50	1.65	3.26	4.85	6.40	7.93	9.42	10.89	12.33	13.74
	1.75	1.59	3.16	4.69	6.20	7.68	9.12	10.55	11.94	13.31
	2.00	1.54	3.05	4.54	5.99	7.42	8.83	10.21	11.56	12.88
	2.25	1.49	2.95	4.38	5.79	7.17	8.53	9.86	11.17	12.46
	4.57	1.00	1.98	2.95	3.91	4.85	5.78	6.70	7.60	8.49
3 YRS	.75	2.58	5.09	7.53	9.89	12.19	14.42	16.59	18.70	20.75
	1.00	2.47	4.86	7.19	9.45	11.65	13.79	15.87	17.89	19.85
	1.25	2.35	4.63	6.85	9.01	11.11	13.16	15.14	17.08	18.95
	1.50	2.23	4.40	6.52	8.57	10.58	12.52	14.42	16.26	18.06
	1.75	2.12	4.18	6.18	8.14	10.04	11.89	13.69	15.45	17.16
	2.00	2.00	3.95	5.85	7.70	9.50	11.26	12.97	14.64	16.27
	2.25	1.88	3.72	5.51	7.26	8.96	10.62	12.24	13.83	15.37
	3.18	1.45	2.87	4.26	5.62	6.96	8.27	9.55	10.81	12.04
4 YRS	.75	3.29	6.45	9.49	12.43	15.25	17.97	20.58	23.10	25.53
	1.00	3.08	6.06	8.92	11.68	14.34	16.90	19.38	21.76	24.06
	1.25	2.88	5.66	8.35	10.93	13.43	15.84	18.17	20.42	22.58
	1.50	2.68	5.27	7.77	10.19	12.52	14.78	16.96	19.07	21.11
	1.75	2.48	4.88	7.20	9.44	11.62	13.72	15.76	17.73	19.64
	2.00	2.28	4.48	6.62	8.70	10.71	12.66	14.55	16.38	18.16
	2.49	1.88	3.72	5.50	7.24	8.93	10.58	12.19	13.76	15.28
5 YRS	.75	3.92	7.67	11.24	14.65	17.91	21.02	23.99	26.82	29.54
	1.00	3.62	7.07	10.38	13.54	16.56	19.46	22.22	24.87	27.41
	1.25	3.31	6.48	9.52	12.43	15.22	17.90	20.46	22.92	25.28
	1.50	3.00	5.89	8.66	11.32	13.88	16.34	18.70	20.97	23.15
	1.75	2.70	5.30	7.80	10.21	12.54	14.78	16.94	19.02	21.03
	2.08	2.30	4.53	6.68	8.77	10.79	12.74	14.64	16.47	18.25
6 YRS	.75	4.50	8.76	12.79	16.61	20.22	23.65	26.89	29.97	32.88
	1.00	4.07	7.93	11.60	15.09	18.39	21.53	24.52	27.36	30.05
	1.25	3.64	7.11	10.42	13.56	16.56	19.42	22.15	24.74	27.22
	1.50	3.22	6.29	9.23	12.04	14.73	17.31	19.77	22.13	24.39
	1.80	2.70	5.30	7.80	10.21	12.52	14.75	16.90	18.97	20.97
7 YRS	.75	5.02	9.73	14.16	18.32	22.23	25.91	29.37	32.62	35.68
	1.00	4.46	8.66	12.62	16.35	19.88	23.21	26.35	29.32	32.12
	1.25	3.89	7.58	11.07	14.39	17.53	20.50	23.33	26.01	28.56
	1.61	3.08	6.04	8.86	11.56	14.15	16.62	19.00	21.27	23.45
8 YRS	.75	5.49	10.61	15.38	19.83	23.99	27.86	31.48	34.86	38.03
	1.00	4.78	9.26	13.45	17.39	21.08	24.54	27.79	30.85	33.72
	1.25	4.07	7.90	11.52	14.94	18.17	21.22	24.11	26.84	29.42
	1.47	3.45	6.74	9.86	12.83	15.67	18.36	20.93	23.38	25.72
9 YRS	.75	5.92	11.40	16.46	21.16	25.51	29.54	33.29	36.76	39.99
	1.35	4.81	7.40	10.81	14.03	17.09	19.98	22.72	25.33	27.80
10 YRS	.75	6.31	12.10	17.43	22.32	26.84	30.99	34.82	38.36	41.62
	1.27	4.14	8.04	11.71	15.16	18.41	21.48	24.38	27.11	29.70
UNTIL PAID	1.00	5.73	10.98	15.79	20.20	24.25	27.98	31.42	34.60	37.54
	1.25	4.21	8.17	11.90	15.40	18.69	21.80	24.72	27.49	30.09
	1.50	3.36	6.55	9.60	12.50	15.27	17.91	20.43	22.83	25.14
	1.75	2.79	5.48	8.06	10.54	12.92	15.22	17.42	19.54	21.59
	2.00	2.40	4.72	6.96	9.12	11.22	13.24	15.20	17.10	18.93
	2.25	2.10	4.14	6.13	8.05	9.92	11.73	13.49	15.20	16.87

MORTGAGE YIELD TABLES 9%

SHOWING DISCOUNT (%) AT VARIOUS YIELDS,
MONTHLY PAYMENT RATES AND DUE DATES

19%	20%	21%	22%	YIELD 23%	24%	25%	26%	27%	BAL REMAIN
9.04	9.90	10.74	11.57	12.40	13.22	14.03	14.83	15.62	100.00
8.92	9.76	10.59	11.42	12.23	13.04	13.84	14.63	15.41	96.87
8.80	9.63	10.45	11.26	12.07	12.86	13.65	14.43	15.20	93.75
8.67	9.49	10.30	11.10	11.90	12.68	13.46	14.23	14.99	90.62
8.55	9.36	10.16	10.95	11.73	12.51	13.27	14.03	14.78	87.49
8.43	9.22	10.01	10.79	11.56	12.33	13.08	13.83	14.57	84.37
8.30	9.09	9.87	10.63	11.40	12.15	12.90	13.63	14.36	81.24
5.11	5.60	6.08	6.56	7.04	7.52	7.99	8.46	8.92	.00
16.53	18.01	19.46	20.88	22.28	23.64	24.98	26.30	27.58	100.00
16.06	17.50	18.91	20.30	21.65	22.98	24.29	25.57	26.82	93.45
15.59	16.99	18.37	19.71	21.03	22.33	23.60	24.84	26.07	86.91
15.13	16.48	17.82	19.13	20.41	21.67	22.90	24.12	25.31	80.36
14.66	15.98	17.27	18.54	19.79	21.01	22.21	23.39	24.55	73.81
14.19	15.47	16.72	17.95	19.16	20.35	21.52	22.66	23.79	67.26
13.72	14.96	16.18	17.37	18.54	19.69	20.83	21.94	23.03	60.72
9.37	10.24	11.09	11.94	12.77	13.59	14.40	15.20	15.99	.00
22.73	24.67	26.54	28.37	30.14	31.86	33.53	35.16	36.74	100.00
21.76	23.61	25.42	27.17	28.87	30.53	32.14	33.71	35.24	89.71
20.78	22.56	24.29	25.97	27.61	29.20	30.75	32.26	33.73	79.42
19.81	21.51	23.16	24.78	26.35	27.87	29.36	30.81	32.23	69.14
18.83	20.45	22.04	23.58	25.08	26.55	27.97	29.36	30.72	58.85
17.85	19.40	20.91	22.38	23.82	25.22	26.58	27.91	29.21	48.56
16.88	18.35	19.78	21.19	22.55	23.89	25.19	26.47	27.71	38.27
13.25	14.43	15.59	16.73	17.85	18.95	20.02	21.07	22.11	.00
27.87	30.12	32.29	34.38	36.40	38.34	40.21	42.02	43.75	100.00
26.27	28.41	30.47	32.46	34.38	36.23	38.02	39.74	41.40	85.62
24.68	26.70	28.65	30.54	32.36	34.12	35.82	37.47	39.05	71.24
23.08	24.99	26.83	28.62	30.34	32.01	33.63	35.19	36.70	56.86
21.49	23.28	25.01	26.69	28.32	29.90	31.43	32.92	34.35	42.48
19.89	21.57	23.19	24.77	26.30	27.79	29.24	30.64	32.00	28.10
16.77	18.22	19.64	21.02	22.36	23.67	24.95	26.20	27.41	.00
32.12	34.60	36.96	39.22	41.39	43.45	45.43	47.32	49.12	100.00
29.83	32.16	34.38	36.51	38.55	40.51	42.38	44.18	45.90	81.14
27.54	29.72	31.80	33.80	35.72	37.56	39.34	41.04	42.67	62.29
25.27	27.29	29.22	31.09	32.89	34.62	36.29	37.90	39.45	43.43
22.96	24.83	26.63	28.38	30.06	31.68	33.25	34.76	36.22	24.58
19.98	21.65	23.21	24.84	26.36	27.84	29.20	30.67	32.02	.00
35.65	38.27	40.76	43.12	45.35	47.48	49.50	51.41	53.23	100.00
32.85	35.06	37.38	39.59	41.69	43.69	45.60	47.42	49.15	76.25
29.59	31.85	34.00	36.06	38.02	39.90	41.70	43.42	45.06	52.50
26.56	28.63	30.62	32.53	34.36	36.12	37.80	39.42	40.97	28.74
22.89	24.75	26.53	28.26	29.92	31.53	33.08	34.58	36.03	.00
38.57	41.28	43.84	46.25	48.52	50.66	52.68	54.58	56.38	100.00
34.77	37.28	39.66	41.90	44.03	46.04	47.95	49.76	51.48	70.89
30.98	33.29	35.47	37.56	39.54	41.42	43.22	44.94	46.57	41.79
25.54	27.55	29.47	31.32	33.09	34.80	36.44	38.01	39.52	.00
40.98	43.75	46.34	48.76	51.03	53.16	55.16	57.03	58.79	100.00
36.43	38.97	41.36	43.62	45.75	47.75	49.65	51.43	53.12	65.04
31.87	34.19	36.39	38.48	40.46	42.35	44.13	45.84	47.45	30.07
27.95	30.08	32.12	34.06	35.92	37.69	39.39	41.02	42.58	.00
42.98	45.77	48.37	50.78	53.04	55.14	57.10	58.93	60.64	100.00
30.14	32.38	34.50	36.51	38.43	40.26	42.01	43.67	45.25	.00
44.64	47.43	50.02	52.41	54.63	56.69	58.61	60.39	62.05	100.00
32.14	34.45	36.64	38.71	40.68	42.55	44.32	46.00	47.60	.00
									MONTHS
40.27	42.79	45.14	47.33	49.37	51.27	53.05	54.71	56.27	185.53
32.55	34.88	37.08	39.17	41.14	43.01	44.79	46.47	48.07	122.63
27.32	29.42	31.43	33.35	35.19	36.95	38.63	40.25	41.80	92.77
23.55	25.45	27.27	29.03	30.72	32.36	33.93	35.45	36.92	74.90
20.71	22.43	24.09	25.70	27.26	28.78	30.24	31.66	33.04	62.90
18.48	20.06	21.58	23.07	24.51	25.91	27.28	28.61	29.90	54.27

MORTGAGE YIELD TABLES

SHOWING DISCOUNT (%) AT VARIOUS YIELDS,
MONTHLY PAYMENT RATES AND DUE DATES

DUE DATE	PAYT RATE	YIELD								
		10%	11%	12%	13%	14%	15%	16%	17%	18%
1 YR	.77	.71	1.65	2.58	3.50	4.41	5.31	6.20	7.08	7.95
	1.00	.70	1.63	2.55	3.45	4.35	5.24	6.12	6.99	7.85
	1.25	.69	1.61	2.51	3.41	4.29	5.17	6.04	6.90	7.75
	1.50	.68	1.58	2.48	3.36	4.23	5.10	5.95	6.80	7.64
	1.75	.67	1.56	2.44	3.31	4.17	5.02	5.87	6.70	7.53
	2.00	.66	1.54	2.40	3.26	4.11	4.95	5.78	6.61	7.42
	2.25	.65	1.52	2.37	3.21	4.05	4.88	5.70	6.51	7.31
	8.76	.40	.92	1.44	1.96	2.47	2.98	3.49	3.99	4.49
2 YRS	.77	1.35	3.13	4.87	6.57	8.24	9.88	11.49	13.06	14.61
	1.00	1.32	3.05	4.74	6.40	8.03	9.62	11.19	12.72	14.22
	1.25	1.28	2.95	4.60	6.21	7.79	9.34	10.86	12.35	13.81
	1.50	1.24	2.86	4.45	6.02	7.55	9.05	10.53	11.97	13.39
	1.75	1.20	2.77	4.31	5.83	7.31	8.77	10.20	11.60	12.97
	2.00	1.16	2.68	4.17	5.63	7.07	8.48	9.87	11.22	12.56
	2.25	1.12	2.59	4.03	5.44	6.83	8.20	9.54	10.85	12.14
	4.58	.75	1.73	2.71	3.66	4.61	5.54	6.46	7.37	8.26
3 YRS	.77	1.94	4.45	6.90	9.27	11.58	13.82	16.00	18.11	20.17
	1.00	1.86	4.27	6.62	8.90	11.11	13.26	15.36	17.39	19.37
	1.25	1.77	4.07	6.31	8.48	10.60	12.66	14.66	16.60	18.50
	1.50	1.68	3.87	6.00	8.07	10.09	12.05	13.96	15.82	17.62
	1.75	1.59	3.67	5.69	7.66	9.57	11.44	13.26	15.03	16.75
	2.00	1.51	3.47	5.38	7.24	9.06	10.83	12.56	14.24	15.88
	2.25	1.42	3.27	5.07	6.83	8.55	10.22	11.86	13.45	15.01
	3.19	1.09	2.51	3.91	5.28	6.62	7.93	9.22	10.48	11.72
4 YRS	.77	2.46	5.64	8.70	11.65	14.49	17.22	19.85	22.38	24.82
	1.00	2.33	5.33	8.22	11.01	13.69	16.28	18.78	21.18	23.51
	1.25	2.17	4.98	7.69	10.30	12.83	15.26	17.61	19.88	22.07
	1.50	2.02	4.64	7.16	9.60	11.96	14.24	16.44	18.57	20.63
	1.75	1.87	4.29	6.63	8.90	11.10	13.22	15.28	17.27	19.19
	2.00	1.72	3.95	6.11	8.20	10.23	12.20	14.11	15.96	17.76
	2.50	1.41	3.26	5.05	6.80	8.50	10.16	11.77	13.35	14.88
5 YRS	.77	2.94	6.71	10.30	13.73	17.01	20.14	23.13	25.99	28.71
	1.00	2.73	6.23	9.58	12.78	15.84	18.77	21.57	24.25	26.81
	1.25	2.50	5.71	8.79	11.73	14.56	17.26	19.86	22.35	24.73
	1.50	2.27	5.19	7.99	10.69	13.28	15.76	18.15	20.45	22.66
	1.75	2.04	4.67	7.20	9.64	12.00	14.26	16.45	18.55	20.58
	2.09	1.73	3.97	6.13	8.23	10.26	12.23	14.14	15.98	17.77
6 YRS	.77	3.37	7.66	11.72	15.57	19.21	22.66	25.93	29.03	31.97
	1.00	3.08	7.00	10.72	14.25	17.61	20.80	23.82	26.70	29.44
	1.25	2.76	6.28	9.63	12.82	15.86	18.76	21.52	24.16	26.67
	1.50	2.43	5.56	8.54	11.39	14.12	16.73	19.23	21.62	23.91
	1.81	2.03	4.65	7.16	9.59	11.92	14.16	16.33	18.41	20.42
7 YRS	.77	3.76	8.52	12.98	17.18	21.12	24.83	28.32	31.60	34.69
	1.00	3.38	7.65	11.68	15.48	19.06	22.44	25.64	28.65	31.50
	1.25	2.95	6.70	10.25	13.62	16.81	19.84	22.71	25.43	28.02
	1.62	2.32	5.29	8.14	10.86	13.47	15.96	18.36	20.65	22.85
8 YRS	.77	4.12	9.28	14.10	18.59	22.79	26.70	30.36	33.78	36.97
	1.00	3.63	8.19	12.47	16.48	20.24	23.76	27.08	30.19	33.11
	1.25	3.09	7.00	10.69	14.17	17.45	20.56	23.50	26.27	28.90
	1.48	2.60	5.91	9.06	12.06	14.92	17.64	20.23	22.70	25.06
9 YRS	.77	4.44	9.97	15.09	19.84	24.23	28.31	32.10	35.61	38.87
	1.37	2.86	6.50	9.93	13.19	16.27	19.19	21.97	24.59	27.09
10 YRS	.77	4.73	10.59	15.97	20.93	25.49	29.70	33.58	37.16	40.47
	1.28	3.12	7.05	10.76	14.25	17.54	20.64	23.57	26.33	28.94
UNTIL PAID	1.00	4.42	9.85	14.82	19.37	23.54	27.38	30.91	34.16	37.16
	1.25	3.22	7.27	11.08	14.66	18.03	21.20	24.18	27.00	29.65
	1.50	2.55	5.81	8.91	11.86	14.67	17.36	19.92	22.36	24.69
	1.75	2.12	4.84	7.46	9.98	12.40	14.72	16.96	19.11	21.18
	2.00	1.81	4.16	6.43	8.62	10.74	12.79	14.78	16.69	18.55
	2.25	1.59	3.65	5.66	7.60	9.49	11.32	13.10	14.83	16.51

MORTGAGE YIELD TABLES 9¼%

SHOWING DISCOUNT (%) AT VARIOUS YIELDS,
MONTHLY PAYMENT RATES AND DUE DATES

19%	20%	21%	22%	YIELD 23%	24%	25%	26%	27%	BAL REMAIN
8.82	9.67	10.52	11.35	12.18	13.00	13.81	14.61	15.41	100.00
8.71	9.55	10.38	11.21	12.03	12.84	13.64	14.43	15.22	97.13
8.59	9.42	10.24	11.06	11.86	12.66	13.45	14.23	15.01	94.00
8.47	9.29	10.10	10.90	11.70	12.49	13.27	14.04	14.80	90.87
8.35	9.16	9.96	10.75	11.53	12.31	13.08	13.84	14.60	87.74
8.23	9.02	9.81	10.60	11.37	12.14	12.89	13.65	14.39	84.61
8.11	8.89	9.67	10.44	11.21	11.96	12.71	13.45	14.18	81.48
4.98	5.47	5.96	6.44	6.92	7.39	7.87	8.34	8.80	.00
16.12	17.60	19.06	20.48	21.88	23.25	24.59	25.91	27.20	100.00
15.70	17.14	18.56	19.95	21.32	22.65	23.97	25.25	26.51	93.98
15.24	16.65	18.03	19.38	20.70	22.01	23.28	24.54	25.76	87.42
14.78	16.15	17.49	18.80	20.09	21.36	22.60	23.82	25.01	80.86
14.33	15.65	16.95	18.23	19.48	20.71	21.92	23.10	24.26	74.29
13.87	15.16	16.41	17.65	18.87	20.06	21.23	22.39	23.51	67.73
13.41	14.65	15.88	17.08	18.26	19.41	20.55	21.67	22.77	61.17
9.14	10.01	10.87	11.72	12.55	13.38	14.19	14.99	15.78	.00
22.17	24.11	25.99	27.82	29.60	31.33	33.01	34.64	36.23	100.00
21.29	23.16	24.98	26.74	28.46	30.13	31.75	33.33	34.87	90.53
20.34	22.13	23.87	25.57	27.22	28.82	30.38	31.90	33.38	80.21
19.38	21.10	22.77	24.39	25.97	27.51	29.01	30.47	31.89	69.88
18.43	20.07	21.66	23.21	24.73	26.20	27.64	29.04	30.40	59.55
17.48	19.03	20.55	22.04	23.48	24.89	26.27	27.61	28.92	49.22
16.52	18.00	19.45	20.86	22.24	23.58	24.89	26.18	27.43	38.90
12.93	14.12	15.29	16.43	17.55	18.65	19.73	20.79	21.82	.00
27.17	29.44	31.62	33.72	35.75	37.70	39.58	41.40	43.15	100.00
25.74	27.90	29.98	31.99	33.93	35.79	37.60	39.34	41.02	86.75
24.18	26.22	28.19	30.10	31.94	33.71	35.43	37.09	38.69	72.30
22.62	24.55	26.41	28.21	29.95	31.63	33.26	34.84	36.37	57.84
21.06	22.87	24.62	26.32	27.96	29.55	31.10	32.59	34.04	43.39
19.50	21.19	22.83	24.42	25.97	27.47	28.93	30.34	31.72	28.93
16.38	17.83	19.25	20.64	21.99	23.31	24.59	25.84	27.06	.00
31.32	33.81	36.19	38.47	40.65	42.73	44.72	46.62	48.44	100.00
29.27	31.62	33.87	36.02	38.09	40.06	41.96	43.77	45.51	82.60
27.02	29.22	31.33	33.35	35.29	37.16	38.95	40.67	42.32	63.62
24.78	26.82	28.79	30.68	32.50	34.25	35.94	37.56	39.13	44.64
22.54	24.43	26.25	28.01	29.71	31.35	32.93	34.46	35.94	25.66
19.51	21.19	22.82	24.40	25.93	27.42	28.86	30.26	31.62	.00
34.76	37.40	39.91	42.29	44.54	46.69	48.72	50.66	52.50	100.00
32.04	34.51	36.86	39.10	41.23	43.26	45.19	47.03	48.78	78.05
29.07	31.35	33.54	35.62	37.61	39.52	41.33	43.07	44.74	54.11
26.10	28.20	30.21	32.15	34.00	35.77	37.48	39.12	40.69	30.17
22.36	24.23	26.03	27.76	29.44	31.06	32.62	34.13	35.59	.00
37.60	40.34	42.92	45.36	47.65	49.81	51.85	53.78	55.60	100.00
34.19	36.74	39.15	41.43	43.59	45.63	47.57	49.40	51.14	73.06
30.48	32.81	35.03	37.14	39.15	41.07	42.89	44.62	46.28	43.68
24.95	26.97	28.91	30.78	32.56	34.28	35.93	37.52	39.05	.00
39.96	42.75	45.37	47.82	50.12	52.28	54.30	56.19	57.98	100.00
35.86	38.45	40.88	43.17	45.33	47.37	49.29	51.11	52.82	67.59
31.39	33.75	35.98	38.10	40.11	42.02	43.83	45.56	47.20	32.24
27.31	29.46	31.51	33.47	35.35	37.14	38.86	40.50	42.07	.00
41.91	44.77	47.36	49.81	52.09	54.22	56.20	58.06	59.80	100.00
29.46	31.71	33.85	35.89	37.83	39.68	41.44	43.11	44.72	.00
43.53	46.35	48.98	51.40	53.66	55.75	57.69	59.50	61.19	100.00
31.41	33.75	35.96	38.06	40.04	41.93	43.72	45.42	47.04	.00
									MONTHS
39.94	42.52	44.91	47.13	49.19	51.12	52.92	54.60	56.18	191.87
32.16	34.52	36.76	38.87	40.87	42.77	44.57	46.28	47.90	124.87
26.92	29.05	31.09	33.03	34.89	36.67	38.38	40.01	41.58	93.94
23.17	25.09	26.93	28.71	30.42	32.07	33.67	35.20	36.68	75.62
20.34	22.08	23.76	25.39	26.97	28.50	29.98	31.41	32.80	63.40
18.14	19.73	21.27	22.77	24.22	25.64	27.02	28.36	29.66	54.63

9½% MORTGAGE YIELD TABLES

SHOWING DISCOUNT (%) AT VARIOUS YIELDS,
MONTHLY PAYMENT RATES AND DUE DATES

DUE DATE	PAYT RATE	YIELD 10%	11%	12%	13%	14%	15%	16%	17%	18%
1 YR	.79	.47	1.41	2.34	3.27	4.18	5.08	5.97	6.85	7.73
	1.00	.47	1.40	2.32	3.23	4.13	5.02	5.90	6.77	7.64
	1.25	.46	1.38	2.29	3.18	4.07	4.95	5.82	6.68	7.53
	1.50	.46	1.36	2.25	3.14	4.01	4.88	5.74	6.59	7.43
	1.75	.45	1.34	2.22	3.09	3.96	4.81	5.66	6.49	7.32
	2.00	.44	1.32	2.19	3.05	3.90	4.74	5.57	6.40	7.22
	2.25	.44	1.30	2.16	3.00	3.84	4.67	5.49	6.31	7.11
	8.77	.26	.79	1.31	1.83	2.34	2.85	3.36	3.86	4.36
2 YRS	.79	.90	2.68	4.43	6.13	7.81	9.45	11.06	12.64	14.19
	1.00	.88	2.62	4.32	5.99	7.62	9.23	10.80	12.34	13.85
	1.25	.85	2.54	4.19	5.81	7.40	8.95	10.48	11.98	13.45
	1.50	.83	2.46	4.06	5.63	7.17	8.68	10.16	11.61	13.04
	1.75	.80	2.38	3.93	5.45	6.94	8.41	9.84	11.25	12.64
	2.00	.77	2.30	3.80	5.27	6.72	8.13	9.52	10.89	12.23
	2.25	.75	2.22	3.67	5.09	6.49	7.86	9.21	10.53	11.83
	4.59	.50	1.49	2.46	3.42	4.37	5.30	6.23	7.14	8.03
3 YRS	.79	1.29	3.82	6.27	8.66	10.97	13.22	15.41	17.53	19.59
	1.00	1.24	3.67	6.04	8.33	10.57	12.74	14.84	16.89	18.88
	1.25	1.18	3.50	5.76	7.95	10.08	12.15	14.17	16.13	18.03
	1.50	1.13	3.33	5.47	7.56	9.59	11.57	13.49	15.36	17.19
	1.75	1.07	3.16	5.19	7.18	9.11	10.99	12.82	14.60	16.34
	2.00	1.01	2.99	4.91	6.79	8.62	10.40	12.14	13.83	15.49
	2.25	.95	2.81	4.63	6.40	8.13	9.82	11.46	13.07	14.64
	3.20	.73	2.16	3.56	4.93	6.28	7.59	8.89	10.15	11.39
4 YRS	.79	1.64	4.84	7.91	10.87	13.72	16.47	19.11	21.66	24.11
	1.00	1.56	4.59	7.51	10.32	13.04	15.65	18.17	20.60	22.95
	1.25	1.46	4.29	7.03	9.67	12.22	14.67	17.05	19.34	21.55
	1.50	1.36	4.00	6.55	9.01	11.39	13.69	15.92	18.07	20.15
	1.75	1.25	3.70	6.07	8.36	10.57	12.71	14.79	16.80	18.74
	2.00	1.15	3.40	5.58	7.70	9.75	11.74	13.66	15.53	17.34
	2.51	.94	2.80	4.60	6.35	8.06	9.73	11.35	12.93	14.47
5 YRS	.79	1.96	5.75	9.37	12.82	16.12	19.27	22.27	25.15	27.89
	1.00	1.83	5.38	8.76	12.00	15.10	18.06	20.90	23.61	26.21
	1.25	1.68	4.93	8.04	11.02	13.88	16.62	19.25	21.77	24.18
	1.50	1.52	4.48	7.32	10.05	12.66	15.18	17.60	19.92	22.16
	1.75	1.37	4.03	6.60	9.07	11.45	13.74	15.95	18.08	20.13
	2.10	1.15	3.41	5.59	7.70	9.74	11.72	13.64	15.49	17.29
6 YRS	.79	2.25	6.57	10.66	14.53	18.20	21.68	24.97	28.09	31.06
	1.00	2.07	6.05	9.83	13.41	16.81	20.05	23.12	26.03	28.81
	1.25	1.85	5.43	8.83	12.07	15.15	18.09	20.89	23.56	26.11
	1.50	1.64	4.80	7.83	10.72	13.49	16.14	18.67	21.09	23.41
	1.83	1.36	3.99	6.52	8.96	11.31	13.57	15.75	17.85	19.88
7 YRS	.79	2.51	7.30	11.80	16.03	20.01	23.75	27.27	30.58	33.70
	1.00	2.27	6.62	10.72	14.58	18.22	21.66	24.91	27.97	30.87
	1.25	1.99	5.80	9.42	12.84	16.08	19.16	22.07	24.84	27.47
	1.63	1.55	4.55	7.41	10.16	12.79	15.30	17.71	20.02	22.24
8 YRS	.79	2.75	7.96	12.82	17.35	21.59	25.54	29.23	32.69	35.91
	1.00	2.44	7.10	11.46	15.55	19.38	22.97	26.34	29.51	32.48
	1.25	2.08	6.07	9.83	13.38	16.72	19.88	22.87	25.70	28.37
	1.49	1.74	5.08	8.26	11.28	14.16	16.91	19.53	22.02	24.40
9 YRS	.79	2.96	8.55	13.72	18.51	22.96	27.08	30.91	34.46	37.76
	1.38	1.91	5.58	9.05	12.34	15.45	18.41	21.20	23.86	26.38
10 YRS	.79	3.15	9.07	14.52	19.53	24.15	28.41	32.34	35.96	39.31
	1.29	2.08	6.06	9.81	13.34	16.66	19.80	22.75	25.55	28.19
UNTIL PAID	1.00	3.03	8.67	13.82	18.52	22.82	26.76	30.38	33.71	36.78
	1.25	2.18	6.34	10.24	13.91	17.35	20.59	23.63	26.50	29.20
	1.50	1.72	5.04	8.20	11.21	14.07	16.80	19.40	21.88	24.25
	1.75	1.43	4.20	6.85	9.41	11.86	14.22	16.48	18.66	20.76
	2.00	1.22	3.60	5.90	8.12	10.26	12.34	14.34	16.28	18.16
	2.25	1.07	3.15	5.18	7.15	9.05	10.91	12.70	14.45	16.15

MORTGAGE YIELD TABLES 9½%

SHOWING DISCOUNT (%) AT VARIOUS YIELDS,
MONTHLY PAYMENT RATES AND DUE DATES

19%	20%	21%	22%	YIELD 23%	24%	25%	26%	27%	BAL REMAIN
8.59	9.45	10.29	11.13	11.96	12.78	13.59	14.39	15.19	100.00
8.49	9.34	10.18	11.00	11.82	12.63	13.44	14.23	15.02	97.39
8.38	9.21	10.04	10.85	11.66	12.46	13.25	14.04	14.81	94.25
8.26	9.08	9.90	10.70	11.50	12.29	13.07	13.84	14.61	91.12
8.14	8.96	9.76	10.55	11.34	12.12	12.89	13.65	14.41	87.99
8.02	8.82	9.62	10.40	11.18	11.94	12.70	13.46	14.20	84.85
7.91	8.70	9.48	10.25	11.01	11.77	12.52	13.26	14.00	81.72
4.85	5.34	5.83	6.32	6.80	7.27	7.74	8.21	8.68	.00
15.70	17.19	18.65	20.08	21.48	22.85	24.20	25.52	26.82	100.00
15.33	16.79	18.21	19.61	20.98	22.32	23.64	24.93	26.20	94.52
14.89	16.30	17.68	19.04	20.38	21.68	22.97	24.23	25.46	87.94
14.44	15.81	17.16	18.48	19.78	21.05	22.29	23.52	24.72	81.36
13.99	15.32	16.63	17.91	19.17	20.41	21.62	22.81	23.98	74.78
13.55	14.84	16.10	17.35	18.57	19.77	20.95	22.10	23.24	68.20
13.10	14.35	15.58	16.78	17.97	19.13	20.28	21.40	22.50	61.62
8.92	9.79	10.65	11.50	12.33	13.16	13.97	14.78	15.57	.00
21.60	23.54	25.44	27.28	29.06	30.80	32.49	34.13	35.72	100.00
20.82	22.70	24.53	26.31	28.04	29.72	31.36	32.95	34.50	91.36
19.89	21.69	23.45	25.16	26.82	28.43	30.01	31.54	33.03	80.99
18.96	20.68	22.36	24.00	25.59	27.14	28.65	30.12	31.56	70.63
18.03	19.67	21.28	22.84	24.37	25.85	27.30	28.71	30.08	60.26
17.10	18.66	20.20	21.69	23.14	24.56	25.95	27.30	28.61	49.90
16.16	17.66	19.11	20.53	21.92	23.27	24.59	25.88	27.14	39.53
12.61	13.81	14.98	16.12	17.25	18.35	19.43	20.50	21.54	.00
26.48	28.75	30.95	33.06	35.10	37.06	38.96	40.78	42.54	100.00
25.21	27.38	29.49	31.51	33.47	35.35	37.17	38.93	40.62	87.89
23.68	25.74	27.73	29.65	31.51	33.30	35.03	36.71	38.32	73.36
22.15	24.10	25.98	27.79	29.55	31.25	32.89	34.49	36.03	58.83
20.63	22.45	24.22	25.93	27.59	29.20	30.75	32.26	33.73	44.30
19.10	20.81	22.46	24.07	25.63	27.14	28.61	30.04	31.43	29.77
15.98	17.44	18.87	20.26	21.62	22.94	24.23	25.49	26.72	.00
30.52	33.03	35.42	37.72	39.91	42.00	44.01	45.92	47.76	100.00
28.69	31.07	33.35	35.53	37.61	39.61	41.53	43.37	45.13	84.08
26.50	28.72	30.85	32.90	34.86	36.75	38.56	40.29	41.97	64.97
24.30	26.37	28.36	30.27	32.11	33.88	35.58	37.23	38.81	45.87
22.11	24.02	25.86	27.64	29.36	31.01	32.61	34.16	35.65	26.76
19.04	20.73	22.37	23.96	25.50	27.00	28.45	29.85	31.22	.00
33.87	36.53	39.06	41.46	43.73	45.90	47.95	49.90	51.76	100.00
31.44	33.95	36.34	38.60	40.76	42.82	44.77	46.64	48.41	79.89
28.54	30.86	33.07	35.18	37.20	39.12	40.96	42.72	44.41	55.75
25.63	27.76	29.80	31.75	33.63	35.43	37.15	38.81	40.40	31.62
21.83	23.71	25.52	27.27	28.96	30.59	32.16	33.68	35.14	.00
36.64	39.40	42.01	44.47	46.78	48.97	51.03	52.98	54.82	100.00
33.60	36.19	38.63	40.95	43.14	45.21	47.17	49.03	50.80	75.28
29.96	32.33	34.58	36.72	38.76	40.70	42.55	44.30	45.98	45.61
24.36	26.40	28.36	30.23	32.03	33.77	35.43	37.03	38.57	.00
38.93	41.76	44.41	46.89	49.21	51.39	53.44	55.36	57.16	100.00
35.28	37.91	40.39	42.72	44.91	46.98	48.93	50.77	52.51	70.21
30.90	33.29	35.56	37.71	39.75	41.69	43.53	45.27	46.94	34.47
26.67	28.84	30.91	32.89	34.78	36.58	38.32	39.97	41.56	.00
40.83	43.69	46.35	48.83	51.14	53.30	55.31	57.19	58.95	100.00
28.77	31.04	33.21	35.26	37.22	39.09	40.86	42.56	44.18	.00
42.41	45.28	47.93	50.40	52.68	54.80	56.78	58.62	60.33	100.00
30.68	33.04	35.28	37.40	39.41	41.31	43.12	44.84	46.47	.00

									MONTHS
39.62	42.24	44.67	46.92	49.02	50.97	52.79	54.50	56.09	198.92
31.75	34.16	36.43	38.58	40.61	42.53	44.35	46.08	47.72	127.23
26.51	28.67	30.74	32.71	34.59	36.40	38.12	39.78	41.36	95.15
22.78	24.72	26.59	28.38	30.12	31.79	33.40	34.95	36.44	76.37
19.97	21.73	23.43	25.08	26.67	28.21	29.71	31.15	32.56	63.90
17.80	19.40	20.95	22.46	23.93	25.36	26.75	28.10	29.42	54.99

113

MORTGAGE YIELD TABLES

SHOWING DISCOUNT (%) AT VARIOUS YIELDS,
MONTHLY PAYMENT RATES AND DUE DATES

DUE DATE	PAYT RATE	YIELD								
		10%	11%	12%	13%	14%	15%	16%	17%	18%
1 YR	.81	.24	1.18	2.11	3.03	3.94	4.85	5.74	6.62	7.50
	1.00	.23	1.17	2.09	3.00	3.90	4.80	5.68	6.56	7.42
	1.25	.23	1.15	2.06	2.96	3.85	4.73	5.60	6.47	7.32
	1.50	.23	1.13	2.03	2.92	3.80	4.66	5.52	6.37	7.22
	1.75	.22	1.12	2.00	2.88	3.74	4.60	5.45	6.28	7.11
	2.00	.22	1.10	1.97	2.83	3.69	4.53	5.37	6.19	7.01
	2.25	.22	1.08	1.94	2.79	3.63	4.46	5.29	6.10	6.91
	8.78	.13	.66	1.18	1.70	2.21	2.72	3.23	3.73	4.23
2 YRS	.81	.45	2.23	3.98	5.70	7.38	9.02	10.64	12.22	13.77
	1.00	.44	2.19	3.90	5.57	7.22	8.83	10.41	11.96	13.48
	1.25	.43	2.12	3.78	5.41	7.00	8.57	10.10	11.61	13.08
	1.50	.41	2.05	3.66	5.24	6.79	8.31	9.79	11.26	12.69
	1.75	.40	1.99	3.55	5.07	6.57	8.04	9.49	10.90	12.29
	2.00	.39	1.92	3.43	4.91	6.36	7.78	9.18	10.55	11.90
	2.25	.38	1.86	3.31	4.74	6.15	7.52	8.88	10.20	11.51
	4.60	.25	1.24	2.22	3.18	4.13	5.07	5.99	6.90	7.80
3 YRS	.81	.65	3.18	5.65	8.04	10.36	12.62	14.81	16.95	19.02
	1.00	.62	3.07	5.45	7.77	10.02	12.20	14.33	16.39	18.40
	1.25	.59	2.93	5.20	7.41	9.56	11.64	13.67	15.65	17.57
	1.50	.56	2.79	4.95	7.05	9.09	11.09	13.02	14.91	16.74
	1.75	.54	2.64	4.69	6.69	8.63	10.53	12.37	14.17	15.92
	2.00	.51	2.50	4.44	6.33	8.17	9.97	11.72	13.43	15.09
	2.25	.48	2.35	4.18	5.97	7.71	9.41	11.07	12.69	14.26
	3.21	.36	1.80	3.20	4.58	5.93	7.26	8.55	9.82	11.07
4 YRS	.81	.82	4.03	7.12	10.10	12.96	15.72	18.38	20.94	23.40
	1.00	.78	3.84	6.79	9.64	12.38	15.02	17.56	20.02	22.38
	1.25	.73	3.60	6.36	9.02	11.60	14.08	16.47	18.79	21.02
	1.50	.68	3.35	5.92	8.41	10.82	13.14	15.39	17.56	19.65
	1.75	.63	3.10	5.49	7.80	10.04	12.20	14.30	16.33	18.29
	2.00	.58	2.85	5.06	7.19	9.26	11.27	13.21	15.10	16.93
	2.52	.47	2.33	4.14	5.91	7.63	9.30	10.93	12.52	14.07
5 YRS	.81	.98	4.79	8.43	11.90	15.22	18.39	21.42	24.31	27.07
	1.00	.92	4.51	7.94	11.22	14.35	17.35	20.22	22.97	25.59
	1.25	.85	4.14	7.29	10.31	13.20	15.97	18.63	21.18	23.62
	1.50	.77	3.76	6.63	9.39	12.04	14.59	17.04	19.39	21.65
	1.75	.69	3.39	5.98	8.48	10.89	13.21	15.44	17.60	19.67
	2.11	.58	2.84	5.04	7.16	9.21	11.21	13.13	15.00	16.81
6 YRS	.81	1.12	5.47	9.59	13.49	17.19	20.69	24.01	27.16	30.14
	1.00	1.04	5.08	8.91	12.55	16.00	19.28	22.40	25.36	28.17
	1.25	.93	4.56	8.01	11.30	14.43	17.41	20.25	22.96	25.54
	1.50	.83	4.04	7.11	10.04	12.85	15.53	18.10	20.55	22.91
	1.84	.68	3.33	5.88	8.34	10.70	12.98	15.18	17.29	19.33
7 YRS	.81	1.25	6.08	10.62	14.89	18.90	22.67	26.22	29.56	32.71
	1.00	1.15	5.57	9.74	13.67	17.37	20.87	24.17	27.28	30.22
	1.25	1.00	4.89	8.56	12.04	15.34	18.46	21.42	24.23	26.90
	1.65	.78	3.80	6.69	9.45	12.10	14.64	17.07	19.39	21.63
8 YRS	.81	1.37	6.63	11.54	16.11	20.39	24.38	28.11	31.60	34.86
	1.00	1.24	5.98	10.43	14.59	18.50	22.16	25.59	28.81	31.84
	1.25	1.05	5.12	8.95	12.56	15.97	19.19	22.23	25.11	27.82
	1.50	.87	4.24	7.45	10.50	13.41	16.18	18.82	21.33	23.73
9 YRS	.81	1.48	7.12	12.35	17.19	21.68	25.85	29.72	33.31	36.65
	1.39	.96	4.66	8.17	11.49	14.63	17.61	20.44	23.12	25.66
10 YRS	.81	1.58	7.56	13.07	18.14	22.81	27.12	31.09	34.76	38.16
	1.31	1.04	5.07	8.85	12.42	15.78	18.94	21.93	24.76	27.42
UNTIL PAID	1.00	1.56	7.43	12.77	17.63	22.07	26.12	29.84	33.26	36.40
	1.25	1.11	5.38	9.38	13.13	16.65	19.96	23.07	25.99	28.74
	1.50	.87	4.26	7.47	10.54	13.45	16.23	18.87	21.40	23.80
	1.75	.72	3.53	6.23	8.82	11.31	13.70	16.00	18.21	20.33
	2.00	.62	3.03	5.35	7.60	9.77	11.87	13.90	15.87	17.76
	2.25	.54	2.65	4.70	6.68	8.61	10.49	12.30	14.07	15.78

SHOWING DISCOUNT (%) AT VARIOUS YIELDS,
MONTHLY PAYMENT RATES AND DUE DATES

19%	20%	21%	22%	YIELD 23%	24%	25%	26%	27%	BAL REMAIN
8.36	9.22	10.07	10.91	11.74	12.56	13.37	14.18	14.97	100.00
8.28	9.13	9.97	10.80	11.62	12.43	13.24	14.03	14.82	97.65
8.16	9.00	9.83	10.65	11.46	12.26	13.06	13.84	14.62	94.51
8.05	8.88	9.69	10.50	11.30	12.09	12.87	13.65	14.42	91.37
7.94	8.75	9.56	10.35	11.14	11.92	12.69	13.46	14.22	88.23
7.82	8.62	9.42	10.20	10.98	11.75	12.51	13.27	14.02	85.10
7.71	8.50	9.28	10.06	10.82	11.58	12.33	13.08	13.81	81.96
4.73	5.22	5.71	6.19	6.67	7.15	7.62	8.09	8.56	.00
15.29	16.78	18.24	19.68	21.08	22.46	23.81	25.14	26.43	100.00
14.96	16.43	17.86	19.26	20.64	21.99	23.31	24.61	25.89	95.05
14.53	15.95	17.34	18.71	20.05	21.36	22.65	23.92	25.16	88.46
13.66	15.00	16.31	17.60	18.86	20.11	21.32	22.52	23.69	75.27
13.22	14.52	15.79	17.04	18.27	19.48	20.66	21.82	22.96	68.67
12.79	14.04	15.28	16.49	17.68	18.85	20.00	21.13	22.23	62.08
8.69	9.56	10.42	11.27	12.11	12.94	13.76	14.56	15.36	.00
21.03	22.98	24.88	26.73	28.52	30.27	31.96	33.61	35.21	100.00
20.35	22.24	24.09	25.88	27.62	29.31	30.96	32.56	34.12	92.20
19.44	21.26	23.02	24.74	26.42	28.04	29.63	31.17	32.67	81.79
18.53	20.27	21.96	23.61	25.21	26.77	28.29	29.77	31.22	71.38
17.62	19.28	20.90	22.47	24.01	25.50	26.96	28.38	29.76	60.98
16.71	18.29	19.83	21.34	22.80	24.23	25.62	26.98	28.31	50.57
15.80	17.30	18.77	20.20	21.60	22.96	24.29	25.59	26.86	40.17
12.29	13.49	14.67	15.82	16.95	18.05	19.14	20.20	21.25	.00
25.78	28.07	30.28	32.40	34.45	36.42	38.33	40.16	41.93	100.00
24.66	26.86	28.98	31.03	33.00	34.91	36.74	38.52	40.23	89.05
23.17	25.25	27.26	29.20	31.07	32.88	34.63	36.32	37.95	74.44
21.68	23.64	25.54	27.37	29.15	30.86	32.52	34.13	35.68	59.84
20.19	22.03	23.82	25.54	27.22	28.84	30.41	31.93	33.41	45.23
18.70	20.42	22.09	23.71	25.29	26.82	28.30	29.74	31.13	30.63
15.58	17.05	18.48	19.88	21.24	22.57	23.87	25.13	26.37	.00
29.72	32.24	34.65	36.96	39.17	41.28	43.30	45.23	47.08	100.00
28.11	30.51	32.82	35.02	37.13	39.16	41.10	42.95	44.73	85.58
25.96	28.21	30.37	32.44	34.42	36.33	38.16	39.92	41.61	66.34
23.82	25.91	27.92	29.85	31.71	33.50	35.22	36.88	38.48	47.11
21.68	23.61	25.47	27.26	29.00	30.67	32.29	33.85	35.35	27.88
18.57	20.27	21.92	23.52	25.07	26.57	28.03	29.45	30.82	.00
32.97	35.66	38.21	40.63	42.93	45.11	47.18	49.15	51.02	100.00
30.84	33.38	35.80	38.10	40.29	42.37	44.35	46.24	48.04	81.75
28.00	30.35	32.59	34.73	36.77	38.72	40.58	42.37	44.07	57.42
25.16	27.31	29.38	31.36	33.25	35.07	36.82	38.49	40.10	33.09
21.29	23.18	25.01	26.77	28.47	30.11	31.69	33.22	34.70	.00
35.67	38.47	41.10	43.58	45.92	48.12	50.21	52.17	54.03	100.00
33.00	35.63	38.11	40.46	42.68	44.78	46.77	48.66	50.45	77.54
29.43	31.84	34.12	36.30	38.36	40.33	42.20	43.98	45.67	47.59
23.77	25.82	27.79	29.68	31.50	33.25	34.92	36.53	38.08	.00
37.91	40.77	43.44	45.95	48.30	50.50	52.57	54.52	56.34	100.00
34.69	37.36	39.88	42.25	44.48	46.58	48.56	50.43	52.20	72.89
30.39	32.82	35.13	37.31	39.38	41.35	43.21	44.98	46.67	36.75
26.02	28.21	30.30	32.29	34.20	36.03	37.77	39.44	41.04	.00
39.76	42.65	45.34	47.85	50.20	52.38	54.42	56.33	58.11	100.00
28.08	30.37	32.56	34.63	36.61	38.50	40.29	42.00	43.63	.00
41.29	44.20	46.89	49.39	51.71	53.86	55.86	57.73	59.46	100.00
29.95	32.33	34.59	36.73	38.76	40.69	42.52	44.25	45.90	.00
									MONTHS
39.29	41.96	44.44	46.73	48.85	50.83	52.67	54.39	56.00	206.86
31.34	33.79	36.09	38.28	40.34	42.29	44.13	45.88	47.54	129.73
26.10	28.29	30.38	32.38	34.29	36.12	37.86	39.54	41.14	96.41
22.38	24.34	26.23	28.05	29.81	31.50	33.12	34.69	36.20	77.13
19.60	21.38	23.09	24.76	26.37	27.92	29.43	30.90	32.31	64.42
17.45	19.06	20.63	22.16	23.64	25.08	26.49	27.85	29.17	55.37

MORTGAGE YIELD TABLES

SHOWING DISCOUNT (%) AT VARIOUS YIELDS,
MONTHLY PAYMENT RATES AND DUE DATES

DUE DATE	PAYT RATE	YIELD								
		11%	12%	13%	14%	15%	16%	17%	18%	19%
1 YR	.83	.94	1.88	2.80	3.71	4.62	5.51	6.40	7.27	8.14
	1.00	.93	1.86	2.77	3.68	4.57	5.46	6.34	7.21	8.06
	1.25	.92	1.83	2.73	3.63	4.51	5.38	6.25	7.11	7.95
	1.50	.91	1.81	2.70	3.58	4.45	5.31	6.16	7.01	7.84
	1.75	.89	1.78	2.66	3.52	4.38	5.23	6.07	6.91	7.73
	2.00	.88	1.75	2.62	3.47	4.32	5.16	5.99	6.81	7.62
	2.25	.87	1.73	2.58	3.42	4.26	5.08	5.90	6.71	7.51
	8.79	.53	1.05	1.57	2.08	2.60	3.10	3.61	4.11	4.60
2 YRS	.83	1.79	3.54	5.26	6.94	8.59	10.21	11.80	13.35	14.88
	1.00	1.75	3.47	5.16	6.81	8.43	10.02	11.57	13.10	14.60
	1.25	1.70	3.37	5.00	6.61	8.18	9.72	11.23	12.72	14.17
	1.50	1.65	3.26	4.85	6.40	7.93	9.43	10.89	12.33	13.75
	1.75	1.60	3.16	4.70	6.20	7.68	9.13	10.55	11.95	13.32
	2.00	1.54	3.06	4.54	6.00	7.43	8.84	10.22	11.57	12.90
	2.25	1.49	2.95	4.39	5.80	7.18	8.54	9.88	11.19	12.47
	4.61	.99	1.97	2.94	3.89	4.83	5.76	6.67	7.57	8.46
3 YRS	.83	2.55	5.02	7.42	9.75	12.02	14.22	16.36	18.44	20.46
	1.00	2.47	4.87	7.20	9.46	11.66	13.80	15.88	17.90	19.87
	1.25	2.35	4.64	6.87	9.03	11.13	13.18	15.17	17.10	18.98
	1.50	2.24	4.41	6.53	8.59	10.60	12.55	14.45	16.30	18.10
	1.75	2.12	4.19	6.20	8.16	10.07	11.92	13.73	15.49	17.21
	2.00	2.01	3.96	5.87	7.72	9.53	11.30	13.01	14.69	16.32
	2.25	1.89	3.74	5.53	7.29	9.00	10.67	12.30	13.89	15.44
	3.23	1.44	2.85	4.23	5.59	6.92	8.22	9.50	10.75	11.97
4 YRS	.83	3.22	6.33	9.32	12.20	14.97	17.64	20.22	22.70	25.08
	1.00	3.09	6.07	8.94	11.71	14.37	16.94	19.42	21.81	24.11
	1.25	2.89	5.68	8.37	10.97	13.48	15.90	18.23	20.48	22.66
	1.50	2.69	5.30	7.81	10.24	12.58	14.85	17.04	19.16	21.20
	1.75	2.49	4.91	7.24	9.50	11.69	13.80	15.85	17.83	19.75
	2.00	2.30	4.52	6.68	8.76	10.79	12.75	14.66	16.50	18.30
	2.54	1.87	3.69	5.46	7.19	8.87	10.51	12.10	13.66	15.18
5 YRS	.83	3.83	7.49	10.99	14.33	17.51	20.56	23.47	26.25	28.91
	1.00	3.63	7.10	10.42	13.60	16.63	19.54	22.31	24.97	27.52
	1.25	3.33	6.52	9.58	12.51	15.31	18.00	20.58	23.05	25.42
	1.50	3.03	5.94	8.73	11.41	13.99	16.47	18.84	21.13	23.33
	1.75	2.73	5.36	7.89	10.32	12.67	14.93	17.11	19.21	21.23
	2.12	2.28	4.48	6.62	8.69	10.69	12.63	14.51	16.33	18.09
6 YRS	.83	4.38	8.53	12.45	16.18	19.71	23.05	26.22	29.23	32.08
	1.00	4.10	7.99	11.68	15.18	18.51	21.67	24.67	27.52	30.23
	1.25	3.68	7.18	10.52	13.69	16.71	19.59	22.34	24.96	27.45
	1.50	3.26	6.38	9.35	12.20	14.92	17.52	20.01	22.39	24.67
	1.85	2.67	5.24	7.71	10.09	12.39	14.60	16.72	18.77	20.75
7 YRS	.83	4.87	9.44	13.74	17.79	21.59	25.17	28.54	31.72	34.71
	1.00	4.50	8.74	12.73	16.50	20.06	23.41	26.57	29.56	32.38
	1.25	3.95	7.69	11.22	14.57	17.75	20.76	23.62	26.32	28.89
	1.66	3.04	5.96	8.74	11.41	13.97	16.42	18.76	21.01	23.17
8 YRS	.83	5.31	10.25	14.87	19.19	23.22	26.99	30.51	33.80	36.88
	1.00	4.84	9.37	13.62	17.60	21.32	24.82	28.10	31.19	34.08
	1.25	4.15	8.05	11.73	15.21	18.48	21.58	24.50	27.26	29.87
	1.52	3.40	6.64	9.72	12.65	15.44	18.10	20.64	23.06	25.37
9 YRS	.83	5.70	10.98	15.87	20.41	24.62	28.53	32.16	35.54	38.69
	1.41	3.74	7.28	10.63	13.81	16.81	19.67	22.37	24.94	27.38
10 YRS	.83	6.05	11.62	16.74	21.47	25.83	29.85	33.56	37.00	40.18
	1.32	4.06	7.89	11.49	14.89	18.09	21.11	23.96	26.66	29.21
UNTIL PAID	1.00	6.12	11.67	16.71	21.29	25.47	29.30	32.80	36.01	38.97
	1.25	4.38	8.48	12.33	15.93	19.31	22.49	25.47	28.28	30.92
	1.50	3.45	6.73	9.85	12.82	15.65	18.34	20.90	23.34	25.67
	1.75	2.86	5.60	8.23	10.76	13.18	15.51	17.75	19.90	21.97
	2.00	2.44	4.80	7.08	9.28	11.40	13.46	15.44	17.36	19.22
	2.25	2.14	4.21	6.22	8.17	10.06	11.90	13.68	15.41	17.09

MORTGAGE YIELD TABLES   10%

SHOWING DISCOUNT (%) AT VARIOUS YIELDS,
MONTHLY PAYMENT RATES AND DUE DATES

20%	21%	22%	23%	YIELD 24%	25%	26%	27%	28%	BAL REMAIN
9.00	9.84	10.68	11.52	12.34	13.15	13.96	14.75	15.54	100.00
8.91	9.76	10.59	11.41	12.23	13.03	13.83	14.62	15.40	97.91
8.79	9.62	10.44	11.26	12.06	12.86	13.64	14.42	15.20	94.76
8.67	9.49	10.30	11.10	11.89	12.68	13.46	14.23	14.99	91.62
8.55	9.35	10.15	10.94	11.73	12.50	13.27	14.03	14.78	88.48
8.42	9.22	10.01	10.79	11.56	12.32	13.08	13.83	14.57	85.34
8.30	9.09	9.86	10.63	11.39	12.15	12.89	13.63	14.36	82.20
5.09	5.58	6.07	6.55	7.03	7.50	7.97	8.44	8.90	.00
16.37	17.84	19.28	20.68	22.07	23.42	24.75	26.05	27.33	100.00
16.06	17.50	18.91	20.30	21.65	22.99	24.29	25.57	26.83	95.59
15.60	17.00	18.37	19.72	21.04	22.33	23.60	24.85	26.07	98.98
15.13	16.49	17.83	19.13	20.42	21.68	22.91	24.13	25.32	82.37
14.67	15.99	17.28	18.55	19.80	21.03	22.23	23.41	24.56	75.76
14.20	15.48	16.74	17.97	19.18	20.37	21.54	22.69	23.81	69.15
13.74	14.98	16.19	17.39	18.57	19.72	20.85	21.96	23.06	62.53
9.33	10.20	11.05	11.89	12.72	13.54	14.35	15.14	15.93	.00
22.42	24.33	26.18	27.99	29.74	31.44	33.09	34.70	36.26	100.00
21.78	23.64	25.44	27.20	28.90	30.56	32.18	33.74	35.27	93.04
20.81	22.59	24.33	26.01	27.65	29.25	30.80	32.31	33.78	82.59
19.85	21.55	23.21	24.83	26.40	27.93	29.42	30.87	32.29	72.15
18.88	20.51	22.10	23.64	25.15	26.62	28.05	29.44	30.80	61.70
17.92	19.47	20.98	22.46	23.90	25.30	26.67	28.00	29.31	51.25
16.95	18.43	19.87	21.27	22.64	23.98	25.29	26.57	27.82	40.81
13.18	14.35	15.51	16.64	17.75	18.84	19.91	20.96	21.99	.00
27.38	29.60	31.74	33.80	35.79	37.70	39.54	41.32	43.04	100.00
26.33	28.48	30.54	32.53	34.46	36.31	38.10	39.83	41.49	90.21
24.76	26.79	28.74	30.64	32.46	34.23	35.93	37.58	39.17	75.53
23.18	25.10	26.95	28.74	30.47	32.14	33.76	35.33	36.85	60.85
21.61	23.41	25.15	26.84	28.48	30.06	31.60	33.08	34.53	46.17
20.03	21.72	23.35	24.94	26.48	27.98	29.43	30.84	32.21	31.49
16.65	18.09	19.50	20.87	22.21	23.51	24.78	26.02	27.23	.00
31.45	33.88	36.21	38.43	40.55	42.59	44.53	46.39	48.18	100.00
29.95	32.28	34.51	36.65	38.69	40.65	42.53	44.33	46.06	87.09
27.69	29.88	31.97	33.98	35.90	37.76	39.53	41.24	42.88	67.73
25.44	27.47	29.43	31.31	33.11	34.86	36.53	38.15	39.70	48.38
23.18	25.07	26.88	28.63	30.32	31.96	33.53	35.05	36.52	29.02
19.80	21.46	23.07	24.63	26.14	27.61	29.04	30.42	31.76	.00
34.79	37.36	39.80	42.12	44.31	46.40	48.39	50.28	52.07	100.00
32.81	35.26	37.59	39.80	41.91	43.92	45.83	47.66	49.39	83.65
29.83	32.10	34.27	36.34	38.31	40.20	42.00	43.73	45.37	59.12
26.85	28.95	30.95	32.87	34.71	36.48	38.17	39.80	41.36	34.59
22.66	24.50	26.27	27.98	29.63	31.23	32.77	34.25	35.69	.00
37.53	40.18	42.69	45.05	47.28	49.38	51.37	53.25	55.02	100.00
35.05	37.57	39.96	42.21	44.35	46.37	48.28	50.09	51.81	79.84
31.34	33.65	35.86	37.95	39.94	41.83	43.64	45.36	47.00	49.60
25.24	27.23	29.13	30.96	32.72	34.41	36.04	37.60	39.10	.00
39.77	42.48	45.01	47.39	49.62	51.71	53.68	55.53	57.26	100.00
36.80	39.36	41.77	44.03	46.17	48.18	50.08	51.87	53.56	75.64
32.35	34.69	36.90	39.00	41.00	42.89	44.68	46.39	48.01	39.09
27.58	29.69	31.70	33.62	35.47	37.23	38.91	40.53	42.07	.00
41.61	44.34	46.88	49.25	51.46	53.53	55.46	57.27	58.96	100.00
29.70	31.90	34.00	36.00	37.90	39.71	41.44	43.09	44.66	.00
43.12	45.85	48.38	50.73	52.91	54.95	56.84	58.60	60.25	100.00
31.62	33.90	36.07	38.12	40.06	41.91	43.67	45.33	46.92	.00
									MONTHS
41.69	44.21	46.53	48.69	50.70	52.56	54.30	55.92	57.44	215.91
33.41	35.76	37.97	40.07	42.04	43.91	45.69	47.37	48.96	132.38
27.90	30.02	32.05	33.98	35.83	37.60	39.29	40.91	42.46	97.72
23.96	25.88	27.72	29.49	31.20	32.85	34.43	35.96	37.43	77.92
21.02	22.75	24.43	26.06	27.63	29.16	30.63	32.06	33.45	64.95
18.72	20.31	21.85	23.35	24.80	26.22	27.59	28.93	30.23	55.75

10¼%   MORTGAGE YIELD TABLES

SHOWING DISCOUNT (%) AT VARIOUS YIELDS,
MONTHLY PAYMENT RATES AND DUE DATES

DUE DATE	PAYT RATE	YIELD								
		11%	12%	13%	14%	15%	16%	17%	18%	19%
1 YR	.85	.71	1.64	2.57	3.48	4.39	5.28	6.17	7.04	7.91
	1.00	.70	1.63	2.55	3.45	4.35	5.24	6.12	6.99	7.85
	1.25	.69	1.61	2.51	3.40	4.29	5.17	6.03	6.89	7.74
	1.50	.68	1.58	2.47	3.36	4.23	5.09	5.95	6.80	7.63
	1.75	.67	1.56	2.44	3.31	4.17	5.02	5.86	6.70	7.52
	2.00	.66	1.54	2.40	3.26	4.11	4.95	5.78	6.60	7.42
	2.25	.65	1.51	2.37	3.21	4.05	4.88	5.70	6.51	7.31
	8.80	.40	.92	1.44	1.95	2.47	2.97	3.48	3.98	4.48
2 YRS	.85	1.34	3.10	4.82	6.51	8.16	9.79	11.38	12.94	14.47
	1.00	1.32	3.04	4.74	6.40	8.03	9.62	11.19	12.72	14.22
	1.25	1.28	2.95	4.60	6.21	7.79	9.34	10.86	12.35	13.81
	1.50	1.24	2.86	4.46	6.02	7.55	9.06	10.53	11.98	13.40
	1.75	1.20	2.77	4.32	5.83	7.32	8.77	10.20	11.61	12.98
	2.00	1.16	2.68	4.17	5.64	7.08	8.49	9.88	11.24	12.57
	2.25	1.12	2.59	4.03	5.45	6.84	8.21	9.55	10.86	12.16
	4.63	.75	1.73	2.70	3.65	4.59	5.52	6.44	7.34	8.23
3 YRS	.85	1.91	4.39	6.80	9.14	11.42	13.63	15.78	17.86	19.89
	1.00	1.86	4.27	6.62	8.91	11.12	13.28	15.37	17.41	19.39
	1.25	1.77	4.08	6.32	8.50	10.62	12.68	14.68	16.63	18.52
	1.50	1.68	3.88	6.01	8.09	10.11	12.07	13.99	15.85	17.66
	1.75	1.60	3.68	5.71	7.68	9.60	11.47	13.29	15.07	16.80
	2.00	1.51	3.48	5.40	7.27	9.09	10.87	12.60	14.29	15.93
	2.25	1.42	3.28	5.09	6.86	8.59	10.27	11.91	13.51	15.07
	3.24	1.08	2.50	3.89	5.25	6.58	7.89	9.17	10.42	11.65
4 YRS	.85	2.42	5.54	8.54	11.44	14.22	16.91	19.49	21.99	24.39
	1.00	2.33	5.34	8.24	11.03	13.72	16.32	18.82	21.23	23.56
	1.25	2.18	5.00	7.72	10.34	12.87	15.31	17.67	19.94	22.14
	1.50	2.03	4.66	7.20	9.65	12.02	14.31	16.52	18.66	20.72
	1.75	1.88	4.32	6.68	8.96	11.16	13.30	15.37	17.37	19.30
	2.00	1.73	3.98	6.15	8.26	10.31	12.29	14.21	16.08	17.88
	2.55	1.40	3.23	5.01	6.75	8.44	10.08	11.69	13.25	14.77
5 YRS	.85	2.87	6.56	10.07	13.43	16.64	19.70	22.63	25.43	28.11
	1.00	2.74	6.26	9.62	12.83	15.90	18.84	21.65	24.34	26.92
	1.25	2.52	5.75	8.84	11.80	14.64	17.36	19.97	22.47	24.87
	1.50	2.29	5.23	8.06	10.78	13.38	15.89	18.29	20.61	22.83
	1.75	2.06	4.72	7.28	9.75	12.12	14.41	16.61	18.74	20.78
	2.14	1.71	3.93	6.08	8.16	10.17	12.12	14.01	15.84	17.62
6 YRS	.85	3.28	7.46	11.42	15.17	18.72	22.09	25.29	28.32	31.19
	1.00	3.10	7.05	10.79	14.35	17.72	20.92	23.97	26.86	29.61
	1.25	2.78	6.34	9.72	12.94	16.01	18.93	21.71	24.36	26.89
	1.50	2.47	5.63	8.65	11.53	14.29	16.93	19.45	21.87	24.18
	1.87	2.01	4.59	7.08	9.48	11.79	14.01	16.16	18.22	20.21
7 YRS	.85	3.65	8.26	12.60	16.68	20.51	24.12	27.53	30.73	33.75
	1.00	3.41	7.72	11.78	15.62	19.23	22.64	25.85	28.89	31.76
	1.25	2.99	6.79	10.39	13.80	17.03	20.08	22.98	25.73	28.34
	1.67	2.29	5.22	8.03	10.72	13.30	15.77	18.13	20.40	22.57
8 YRS	.85	3.98	8.97	13.63	17.99	22.06	25.86	29.42	32.74	35.86
	1.00	3.67	8.29	12.62	16.67	20.47	24.03	27.38	30.51	33.46
	1.25	3.15	7.13	10.88	14.42	17.75	20.90	23.88	26.69	29.34
	1.53	2.56	5.82	8.93	11.89	14.70	17.39	19.95	22.39	24.72
9 YRS	.85	4.27	9.60	14.55	19.13	23.39	27.34	31.02	34.43	37.61
	1.42	2.81	6.39	9.77	12.97	16.01	18.89	21.62	24.22	26.68
10 YRS	.85	4.54	10.16	15.35	20.13	24.53	28.60	32.37	35.84	39.06
	1.34	3.06	6.92	10.56	13.99	17.23	20.28	23.16	25.89	28.46
UNTIL PAID	1.00	4.74	10.52	15.75	20.49	24.81	28.74	32.33	35.63	38.65
	1.25	3.35	7.56	11.50	15.19	18.65	21.89	24.94	27.80	30.49
	1.50	2.62	5.97	9.15	12.17	15.05	17.79	20.39	22.88	25.24
	1.75	2.17	4.95	7.62	10.19	12.65	15.01	17.28	19.47	21.56
	2.00	1.85	4.24	6.55	8.77	10.93	13.01	15.01	16.96	18.83
	2.25	1.61	3.71	5.74	7.71	9.63	11.48	13.28	15.03	16.73

MORTGAGE YIELD TABLES 10¼%

SHOWING DISCOUNT (%) AT VARIOUS YIELDS,
MONTHLY PAYMENT RATES AND DUE DATES

20%	21%	22%	23%	YIELD 24%	25%	26%	27%	28%	BAL REMAIN
8.77	9.62	10.46	11.29	12.12	12.93	13.74	14.54	15.33	100.00
8.70	9.54	10.38	11.20	12.02	12.83	13.63	14.42	15.21	98.17
8.58	9.41	10.24	11.05	11.86	12.66	13.45	14.23	15.00	95.02
8.46	9.28	10.09	10.90	11.69	12.48	13.26	14.03	14.80	91.88
8.34	9.15	9.95	10.75	11.53	12.31	13.08	13.84	14.59	88.73
8.22	9.02	9.81	10.59	11.37	12.13	12.89	13.64	14.38	85.59
8.10	8.89	9.67	10.44	11.20	11.96	12.70	13.44	14.18	82.44
4.97	5.46	5.94	6.42	6.90	7.38	7.85	8.32	8.78	.00
15.96	17.43	18.87	20.29	21.67	23.03	24.36	25.67	26.95	100.00
15.70	17.15	18.56	19.95	21.32	22.66	23.97	25.25	26.51	96.13
15.24	16.65	18.03	19.38	20.71	22.01	23.29	24.54	25.77	89.51
14.79	16.16	17.50	18.81	20.10	21.37	22.61	23.83	25.03	82.88
14.34	15.66	16.96	18.24	19.49	20.73	21.93	23.12	24.28	76.25
13.88	15.17	16.43	17.67	18.89	20.08	21.25	22.41	23.54	69.62
13.43	14.67	15.90	17.10	18.28	19.44	20.58	21.69	22.79	62.99
9.11	9.97	10.83	11.67	12.50	13.32	14.13	14.93	15.72	.00
21.86	23.78	25.64	27.45	29.21	30.91	32.58	34.19	35.76	100.00
21.31	23.18	25.00	26.77	28.49	30.16	31.78	33.36	34.90	93.88
20.37	22.16	23.91	25.60	27.26	28.86	30.43	31.95	33.43	83.40
19.42	21.14	22.81	24.44	26.02	27.57	29.07	30.53	31.95	72.91
18.48	20.12	21.72	23.27	24.79	26.27	27.71	29.11	30.48	62.43
17.54	19.10	20.62	22.11	23.56	24.97	26.35	27.70	29.01	51.94
16.59	18.08	19.53	20.94	22.33	23.68	24.99	26.28	27.53	41.46
12.86	14.04	15.20	16.34	17.46	18.55	19.62	20.67	21.71	.00
26.70	28.93	31.08	33.15	35.15	37.07	38.93	40.72	42.44	100.00
25.80	27.96	30.05	32.06	34.00	35.87	37.68	39.42	41.10	91.39
24.26	26.31	28.28	30.19	32.04	33.82	35.54	37.20	38.81	76.63
22.72	24.65	26.52	28.33	30.07	31.76	33.40	34.98	36.51	61.88
21.18	22.99	24.75	26.46	28.11	29.71	31.26	32.76	34.21	47.12
19.64	21.34	22.99	24.59	26.14	27.65	29.12	30.54	31.92	32.36
16.26	17.71	19.12	20.49	21.84	23.15	24.42	25.67	26.88	.00
30.67	33.11	35.45	37.69	39.83	41.88	43.84	45.71	47.51	100.00
29.38	31.74	33.99	36.16	38.23	40.21	42.11	43.93	45.67	88.63
27.17	29.38	31.49	33.53	35.47	37.35	39.14	40.87	42.53	69.14
24.96	27.02	28.99	30.90	32.72	34.48	36.18	37.81	39.38	49.66
22.76	24.66	26.49	28.27	29.97	31.62	33.21	34.75	36.23	30.17
19.34	21.01	22.62	24.19	25.72	27.19	28.62	30.01	31.36	.00
33.92	36.51	38.97	41.31	43.52	45.63	47.63	49.54	51.35	100.00
32.24	34.70	37.07	39.31	41.45	43.49	45.42	47.27	49.03	85.58
29.30	31.61	33.80	35.90	37.90	39.81	41.63	43.38	45.05	60.85
26.39	28.51	30.54	32.48	34.34	36.13	37.84	39.49	41.07	36.12
22.13	23.98	25.77	27.49	29.15	30.76	32.31	33.80	35.25	.00
36.59	39.27	41.80	44.18	46.44	48.56	50.57	52.47	54.26	100.00
34.46	37.02	39.44	41.73	43.90	45.95	47.89	49.73	51.48	82.19
30.82	33.17	35.41	37.53	39.55	41.48	43.30	45.05	46.70	51.66
24.66	26.66	28.58	30.43	32.20	33.90	35.54	37.11	38.63	.00
38.78	41.51	44.07	46.48	48.73	50.85	52.84	54.71	56.47	100.00
36.23	38.83	41.28	43.58	45.75	47.79	49.72	51.54	53.26	78.44
31.86	34.23	36.48	38.62	40.64	42.56	44.38	46.11	47.75	41.49
26.95	29.07	31.10	33.04	34.90	36.68	38.38	40.01	41.57	.00
40.57	43.33	45.90	48.30	50.55	52.64	54.59	56.43	58.14	100.00
29.02	31.25	33.37	35.38	37.30	39.13	40.87	42.54	44.13	.00
42.04	44.81	47.37	49.75	51.97	54.03	55.95	57.74	59.41	100.00
30.90	33.21	35.39	37.47	39.43	41.30	43.07	44.76	46.36	.00
									MONTHS
41.42	43.98	46.35	48.54	50.57	52.45	54.21	55.84	57.37	226.36
33.03	35.41	37.67	39.79	41.80	43.69	45.49	47.19	48.80	135.20
27.50	29.65	31.71	33.67	35.54	37.34	39.05	40.69	42.26	99.08
23.58	25.52	27.38	29.18	30.91	32.57	34.17	35.71	37.20	78.73
20.65	22.41	24.11	25.75	27.34	28.85	30.37	31.81	33.21	65.49
18.38	19.98	21.54	23.05	24.52	25.94	27.33	28.68	29.99	56.13

10½% MORTGAGE YIELD TABLES

SHOWING DISCOUNT (%) AT VARIOUS YIELDS,
MONTHLY PAYMENT RATES AND DUE DATES

DUE DATE	PAYT RATE	YIELD 11%	12%	13%	14%	15%	16%	17%	18%	19%
1 YR	.87	.47	1.41	2.33	3.25	4.15	5.05	5.94	6.82	7.69
	1.00	.47	1.40	2.32	3.23	4.13	5.02	5.90	6.77	7.63
	1.25	.46	1.38	2.28	3.18	4.07	4.95	5.82	6.68	7.53
	1.50	.46	1.36	2.25	3.14	4.01	4.88	5.74	6.58	7.42
	1.75	.45	1.34	2.22	3.09	3.95	4.81	5.65	6.49	7.32
	2.00	.44	1.32	2.19	3.05	3.90	4.74	5.57	6.40	7.21
	2.25	.44	1.30	2.16	3.00	3.84	4.67	5.49	6.30	7.11
	8.81	.26	.79	1.31	1.82	2.34	2.85	3.35	3.85	4.35
2 YRS	.87	.89	2.66	4.38	6.07	7.73	9.36	10.96	12.52	14.05
	1.00	.88	2.62	4.32	5.99	7.62	9.23	10.80	12.34	13.85
	1.25	.85	2.54	4.19	5.81	7.40	8.95	10.48	11.98	13.45
	1.50	.83	2.46	4.06	5.63	7.17	8.68	10.17	11.62	13.05
	1.75	.80	2.38	3.93	5.45	6.95	8.41	9.85	11.26	12.64
	2.00	.78	2.30	3.81	5.28	6.72	8.14	9.53	10.90	12.24
	2.25	.75	2.23	3.68	5.10	6.50	7.87	9.22	10.54	11.84
	4.64	.50	1.48	2.45	3.41	4.35	5.28	6.20	7.11	8.00
3 YRS	.87	1.27	3.76	6.18	8.53	10.82	13.04	15.19	17.29	19.32
	1.00	1.24	3.68	6.04	8.34	10.58	12.75	14.86	16.91	18.90
	1.25	1.19	3.51	5.77	7.96	10.09	12.17	14.19	16.15	18.06
	1.50	1.13	3.34	5.49	7.58	9.61	11.59	13.52	15.40	17.22
	1.75	1.07	3.17	5.21	7.20	9.13	11.02	12.85	14.64	16.38
	2.00	1.01	3.00	4.93	6.81	8.65	10.44	12.18	13.88	15.54
	2.25	.95	2.83	4.65	6.43	8.17	9.86	11.51	13.12	14.70
	3.25	.72	2.14	3.54	4.90	6.24	7.55	8.84	10.10	11.33
4 YRS	.87	1.61	4.75	7.77	10.67	13.47	16.17	18.77	21.28	23.69
	1.00	1.56	4.60	7.53	10.35	13.07	15.69	18.22	20.65	23.00
	1.25	1.46	4.31	7.05	9.70	12.26	14.72	17.10	19.40	21.62
	1.50	1.36	4.02	6.58	9.05	11.45	13.76	15.99	18.15	20.23
	1.75	1.26	3.72	6.10	8.41	10.63	12.79	14.88	16.90	18.85
	2.00	1.16	3.43	5.63	7.76	9.82	11.82	13.76	15.64	17.47
	2.56	.94	2.77	4.56	6.31	8.00	9.66	11.27	12.84	14.37
5 YRS	.87	1.92	5.62	9.16	12.53	15.76	18.85	21.80	24.61	27.31
	1.00	1.84	5.40	8.80	12.05	15.16	18.14	20.98	23.70	26.31
	1.25	1.69	4.96	8.09	11.09	13.96	16.72	19.36	21.89	24.32
	1.50	1.54	4.52	7.38	10.13	12.77	15.30	17.73	20.07	22.32
	1.75	1.39	4.08	6.67	9.16	11.57	13.88	16.11	18.26	20.33
	2.15	1.14	3.37	5.53	7.63	9.65	11.61	13.51	15.36	17.14
6 YRS	.87	2.19	6.39	10.38	14.15	17.73	21.13	24.35	27.40	30.30
	1.00	2.08	6.09	9.89	13.50	16.92	20.17	23.26	26.19	28.98
	1.25	1.87	5.48	8.91	12.18	15.29	18.25	21.07	23.76	26.33
	1.50	1.66	4.87	7.93	10.86	13.66	16.33	18.89	21.33	23.67
	1.88	1.34	3.94	6.45	8.87	11.19	13.43	15.59	17.66	19.67
7 YRS	.87	2.43	7.08	11.45	15.56	19.43	23.08	26.51	29.74	32.78
	1.00	2.29	6.68	10.81	14.71	18.38	21.85	25.12	28.20	31.11
	1.25	2.02	5.88	9.54	13.00	16.29	19.39	22.34	25.13	27.78
	1.69	1.53	4.49	7.32	10.03	12.62	15.11	17.49	19.78	21.97
8 YRS	.87	2.65	7.69	12.40	16.79	20.90	24.74	28.33	31.69	34.84
	1.00	2.48	7.19	11.60	15.73	19.60	23.23	26.63	29.83	32.82
	1.25	2.12	6.18	10.01	13.61	17.01	20.21	23.24	26.10	28.80
	1.54	1.71	5.00	8.13	11.12	13.96	16.67	19.25	21.72	24.07
9 YRS	.87	2.85	8.23	13.22	17.86	22.16	26.15	29.87	33.32	36.54
	1.44	1.88	5.49	8.90	12.14	15.21	18.11	20.87	23.49	25.98
10 YRS	.87	3.02	8.71	13.95	18.78	23.24	27.36	31.17	34.69	37.95
	1.35	2.04	5.95	9.63	13.09	16.36	19.45	22.36	25.11	27.72
UNTIL PAID	1.00	3.27	9.30	14.74	19.66	24.12	28.18	31.87	35.24	38.33
	1.25	2.28	6.60	10.64	14.42	17.96	21.28	24.39	27.31	30.06
	1.50	1.77	5.19	8.43	11.51	14.44	17.22	19.87	22.40	24.80
	1.75	1.46	4.29	7.00	9.61	12.11	14.50	16.81	19.02	21.14
	2.00	1.24	3.67	6.00	8.26	10.44	12.54	14.58	16.54	18.44
	2.25	1.08	3.20	5.26	7.25	9.19	11.06	12.89	14.65	16.37

MORTGAGE YIELD TABLES 10½%

SHOWING DISCOUNT (%) AT VARIOUS YIELDS,
MONTHLY PAYMENT RATES AND DUE DATES

| | | | | YIELD | | | | | BAL REMAIN |
20%	21%	22%	23%	24%	25%	26%	27%	28%	
8.55	9.40	10.24	11.07	11.90	12.71	13.52	14.32	15.11	100.00
8.49	9.33	10.17	11.00	11.82	12.63	13.43	14.22	15.01	98.43
8.37	9.21	10.03	10.85	11.66	12.46	13.25	14.03	14.81	95.28
8.25	9.08	9.89	10.70	11.49	12.28	13.06	13.84	14.60	92.13
8.14	8.95	9.75	10.55	11.33	12.11	12.88	13.65	14.40	88.98
8.02	8.82	9.61	10.40	11.17	11.94	12.70	13.45	14.20	85.83
7.90	8.69	9.47	10.25	11.01	11.77	12.52	13.26	13.99	82.68
4.84	5.33	5.82	6.30	6.78	7.26	7.73	8.20	8.66	.00
15.55	17.03	18.47	19.89	21.28	22.64	23.98	25.28	26.57	100.00
15.33	16.79	18.21	19.61	20.98	22.32	23.64	24.93	26.20	96.68
14.89	16.30	17.69	19.05	20.38	21.69	22.97	24.23	25.47	90.03
14.45	15.82	17.17	18.49	19.78	21.06	22.30	23.53	24.73	83.39
14.00	15.34	16.64	17.93	19.19	20.42	21.64	22.83	24.00	76.74
13.56	14.85	16.12	17.37	18.59	19.79	20.97	22.13	23.26	70.10
13.12	14.37	15.60	16.81	17.99	19.16	20.30	21.42	22.53	63.46
8.88	9.75	10.61	11.45	12.28	13.11	13.92	14.72	15.51	.00
21.30	23.22	25.09	26.91	28.67	30.39	32.06	33.68	35.26	100.00
20.84	22.73	24.56	26.34	28.07	29.75	31.39	32.98	34.53	94.74
19.92	21.73	23.48	25.19	26.86	28.47	30.05	31.58	33.07	84.21
19.00	20.73	22.41	24.05	25.64	27.20	28.71	30.18	31.62	73.69
18.08	19.73	21.34	22.90	24.43	25.92	27.37	28.78	30.16	63.16
17.15	18.73	20.26	21.76	23.22	24.64	26.03	27.38	28.70	52.64
16.23	17.73	19.19	20.61	22.01	23.36	24.69	25.98	27.25	42.11
12.54	13.73	14.89	16.04	17.16	18.25	19.33	20.39	21.42	.00
26.02	28.26	30.42	32.50	34.51	36.44	38.31	40.11	41.84	100.00
25.26	27.45	29.55	31.58	33.54	35.43	37.25	39.01	40.71	92.58
23.76	25.82	27.82	29.74	31.61	33.40	35.14	36.82	38.44	77.75
22.25	24.20	26.09	27.91	29.67	31.38	33.03	34.62	36.17	62.92
20.74	22.58	24.35	26.07	27.74	29.35	30.91	32.43	33.90	48.08
19.24	20.95	22.62	24.23	25.80	27.32	28.80	30.23	31.63	33.25
15.86	17.32	18.74	20.12	21.47	22.78	24.06	25.32	26.54	.00
29.88	32.34	34.70	36.95	39.11	41.17	43.14	45.03	46.84	100.00
28.80	31.19	33.47	35.66	37.75	39.76	41.68	43.52	45.28	90.19
26.64	28.87	31.01	33.07	35.04	36.93	38.75	40.49	42.17	70.57
24.48	26.56	28.56	30.48	32.33	34.11	35.82	37.47	39.05	50.96
22.32	24.25	26.10	27.89	29.62	31.28	32.89	34.44	35.94	31.34
18.87	20.55	22.18	23.75	25.29	26.77	28.21	29.61	30.97	.00
33.05	35.66	38.14	40.50	42.73	44.86	46.88	48.80	50.62	100.00
31.62	34.14	36.54	38.81	40.98	43.04	45.00	46.87	48.65	87.54
28.77	31.10	33.32	35.43	37.47	39.41	41.26	43.02	44.71	62.61
25.91	28.06	30.11	32.08	33.97	35.78	37.51	39.17	40.77	37.68
21.60	23.46	25.26	27.00	28.67	30.29	31.85	33.35	34.81	.00
35.65	38.36	40.91	43.32	45.59	47.74	49.77	51.68	53.50	100.00
33.87	36.47	38.92	41.25	43.45	45.53	47.49	49.36	51.13	84.59
30.30	32.68	34.95	37.11	39.16	41.10	42.96	44.72	46.40	53.76
24.07	26.09	28.03	29.89	31.67	33.39	35.04	36.62	38.15	.00
37.78	40.54	43.13	45.56	47.85	49.99	52.00	53.89	55.67	100.00
35.64	38.29	40.77	43.12	45.32	47.40	49.35	51.20	52.94	81.32
31.35	33.77	36.05	38.22	40.27	42.22	44.06	45.82	47.48	43.95
26.31	28.46	30.50	32.46	34.33	36.13	37.84	39.48	41.06	.00
39.53	42.32	44.92	47.35	49.62	51.74	53.73	55.58	57.32	100.00
28.34	30.59	32.73	34.76	36.70	38.55	40.31	41.99	43.59	.00
40.96	43.76	46.36	48.78	51.02	53.12	55.06	56.88	58.58	100.00
30.18	32.51	34.72	36.81	38.80	40.69	42.48	44.18	45.80	.00

									MONTHS
41.16	43.77	46.17	48.39	50.44	52.35	54.12	55.77	57.32	238.69
32.64	35.07	37.36	39.51	41.55	43.47	45.29	47.01	48.64	138.20
27.09	29.28	31.36	33.35	35.25	37.07	38.80	40.46	42.05	100.49
23.19	25.15	27.04	28.86	30.60	32.29	33.91	35.47	36.97	79.56
20.28	22.06	23.77	25.43	27.04	28.60	30.10	31.56	32.97	66.04
18.03	19.65	21.22	22.75	24.23	25.67	27.07	28.43	29.75	56.53

10¾% MORTGAGE YIELD TABLES

SHOWING DISCOUNT (%) AT VARIOUS YIELDS,
MONTHLY PAYMENT RATES AND DUE DATES

DUE DATE	PAYT RATE	YIELD								
		11%	12%	13%	14%	15%	16%	17%	18%	19%
1 YR	.90	.24	1.17	2.10	3.02	3.92	4.82	5.71	6.59	7.46
	1.00	.23	1.17	2.09	3.00	3.90	4.79	5.68	6.55	7.42
	1.25	.23	1.15	2.06	2.96	3.85	4.73	5.60	6.46	7.32
	1.50	.23	1.13	2.03	2.92	3.79	4.66	5.52	6.37	7.21
	1.75	.22	1.12	2.00	2.87	3.74	4.60	5.44	6.28	7.11
	2.00	.22	1.10	1.97	2.83	3.69	4.53	5.36	6.19	7.01
	2.25	.22	1.08	1.94	2.79	3.63	4.46	5.29	6.10	6.91
	8.83	.13	.66	1.18	1.70	2.21	2.72	3.22	3.72	4.22
2 YRS	.90	.45	2.21	3.94	5.64	7.30	8.94	10.53	12.10	13.64
	1.00	.44	2.19	3.90	5.57	7.22	8.83	10.41	11.96	13.48
	1.25	.43	2.12	3.78	5.41	7.00	8.57	10.10	11.61	13.08
	1.50	.42	2.06	3.66	5.24	6.79	8.31	9.80	11.26	12.69
	1.75	.40	1.99	3.55	5.08	6.58	8.05	9.49	10.91	12.30
	2.00	.39	1.93	3.43	4.91	6.37	7.79	9.19	10.56	11.91
	2.25	.38	1.86	3.32	4.75	6.15	7.53	8.89	10.22	11.52
	4.65	.25	1.24	2.21	3.17	4.11	5.05	5.97	6.87	7.77
3 YRS	.90	.64	3.14	5.56	7.92	10.22	12.44	14.61	16.71	18.76
	1.00	.62	3.08	5.46	7.78	10.03	12.21	14.34	16.41	18.41
	1.25	.60	2.93	5.21	7.42	9.57	11.66	13.69	15.67	17.60
	1.50	.57	2.79	4.96	7.06	9.11	11.11	13.05	14.94	16.78
	1.75	.54	2.65	4.71	6.71	8.66	10.56	12.41	14.21	15.96
	2.00	.51	2.51	4.45	6.35	8.20	10.01	11.76	13.47	15.14
	2.25	.48	2.36	4.20	6.00	7.75	9.45	11.12	12.74	14.32
	3.26	.36	1.79	3.19	4.56	5.90	7.21	8.51	9.77	11.01
4 YRS	.90	.81	3.96	6.99	9.91	12.73	15.44	18.05	20.57	22.99
	1.00	.79	3.85	6.81	9.66	12.41	15.05	17.60	20.06	22.43
	1.25	.73	3.61	6.38	9.06	11.64	14.13	16.53	18.85	21.09
	1.50	.68	3.36	5.95	8.45	10.87	13.20	15.46	17.63	19.74
	1.75	.63	3.12	5.52	7.85	10.10	12.28	14.38	16.42	18.39
	2.00	.58	2.87	5.09	7.25	9.33	11.35	13.31	15.21	17.05
	2.57	.47	2.31	4.11	5.86	7.57	9.23	10.85	12.43	13.97
5 YRS	.90	.96	4.68	8.24	11.64	14.89	17.99	20.96	23.79	26.50
	1.00	.93	4.53	7.97	11.27	14.41	17.42	20.30	23.06	25.69
	1.25	.85	4.16	7.33	10.37	13.28	16.06	18.74	21.30	23.75
	1.50	.77	3.79	6.69	9.47	12.14	14.70	17.17	19.53	21.81
	1.75	.70	3.42	6.05	8.57	11.00	13.34	15.60	17.77	19.86
	2.16	.57	2.82	4.99	7.09	9.13	11.10	13.02	14.87	16.66
6 YRS	.90	1.09	5.33	9.34	13.14	16.75	20.17	23.41	26.49	29.41
	1.00	1.05	5.12	8.97	12.63	16.10	19.40	22.53	25.51	28.33
	1.25	.94	4.60	8.09	11.40	14.56	17.56	20.42	23.15	25.75
	1.50	.84	4.09	7.20	10.17	13.01	15.72	18.31	20.79	23.16
	1.89	.67	3.29	5.82	8.25	10.59	12.84	15.01	17.11	19.12
7 YRS	.90	1.22	5.90	10.31	14.45	18.35	22.03	25.49	28.75	31.82
	1.00	1.16	5.62	9.83	13.79	17.52	21.04	24.37	27.50	30.46
	1.25	1.02	4.95	8.67	12.19	15.53	18.69	21.68	24.52	27.21
	1.70	.77	3.75	6.60	9.33	11.95	14.45	16.86	19.16	21.37
8 YRS	.90	1.33	6.41	11.16	15.59	19.74	23.61	27.24	30.63	33.81
	1.00	1.25	6.06	10.55	14.77	18.71	22.41	25.87	29.12	32.17
	1.25	1.07	5.21	9.11	12.78	16.24	19.51	22.59	25.50	28.24
	1.56	.86	4.18	7.34	10.35	13.22	15.95	18.55	21.04	23.41
9 YRS	.90	1.42	6.86	11.90	16.58	20.93	24.96	28.72	32.21	35.46
	1.45	.94	4.59	8.03	11.30	14.40	17.33	20.12	22.76	25.27
10 YRS	.90	1.51	7.26	12.56	17.44	21.95	26.12	29.97	33.53	36.83
	1.36	1.02	4.97	8.69	12.19	15.49	18.61	21.55	24.33	26.96
UNTIL PAID	1.00	1.69	8.02	13.70	18.81	23.43	27.61	31.40	34.86	38.02
	1.25	1.16	5.61	9.76	13.64	17.26	20.66	23.84	26.82	29.62
	1.50	.90	4.38	7.69	10.83	13.81	16.65	19.35	21.91	24.36
	1.75	.74	3.61	6.37	9.02	11.55	13.99	16.32	18.57	20.72
	2.00	.63	3.08	5.45	7.74	9.95	12.08	14.14	16.13	18.05
	2.25	.55	2.69	4.77	6.79	8.74	10.64	12.48	14.26	16.00

SHOWING DISCOUNT (%) AT VARIOUS YIELDS,
MONTHLY PAYMENT RATES AND DUE DATES

| | | | | YIELD | | | | | BAL |
20%	21%	22%	23%	24%	25%	26%	27%	28%	REMAIN
8.32	9.17	10.02	10.85	11.68	12.49	13.30	14.10	14.90	100.00
8.27	9.12	9.96	10.79	11.61	12.42	13.23	14.02	14.81	98.69
8.16	9.00	9.82	10.64	11.45	12.25	13.05	13.83	14.61	95.53
8.05	8.87	9.69	10.50	11.29	12.09	12.87	13.64	14.41	92.38
7.93	8.75	9.55	10.35	11.14	11.92	12.69	13.45	14.21	89.23
7.82	8.62	9.41	10.20	10.98	11.75	12.51	13.26	14.01	86.08
7.71	8.50	9.28	10.05	10.82	11.58	12.33	13.07	13.81	82.92
4.72	5.21	5.69	6.18	6.66	7.13	7.60	8.07	8.54	.00
15.15	16.62	18.07	19.49	20.88	22.25	23.59	24.90	26.19	100.00
14.97	16.43	17.86	19.26	20.64	21.99	23.31	24.61	25.89	97.22
14.53	15.95	17.35	18.71	20.05	21.37	22.66	23.92	25.16	90.56
14.10	15.48	16.83	18.16	19.46	20.74	22.00	23.23	24.44	83.90
13.67	15.01	16.32	17.61	18.88	20.12	21.34	22.54	23.71	77.24
13.24	14.53	15.81	17.06	18.29	19.50	20.68	21.84	22.99	70.58
12.80	14.06	15.30	16.51	17.70	18.87	20.02	21.15	22.26	63.92
8.65	9.52	10.38	11.23	12.07	12.89	13.70	14.51	15.30	.00
20.74	22.67	24.55	26.37	28.14	29.87	31.54	33.17	34.75	100.00
20.37	22.26	24.11	25.90	27.65	29.34	30.99	32.59	34.15	95.60
19.47	21.29	23.06	24.78	26.45	28.08	29.67	31.21	32.71	85.03
18.57	20.31	22.00	23.65	25.26	26.83	28.35	29.83	31.28	74.47
17.67	19.33	20.95	22.53	24.07	25.57	27.03	28.45	29.84	63.90
16.77	18.35	19.90	21.41	22.88	24.31	25.71	27.07	28.40	53.34
15.87	17.38	18.85	20.28	21.68	23.05	24.39	25.69	26.96	42.77
12.22	13.42	14.58	15.73	16.85	17.96	19.04	20.10	21.14	.00
25.33	27.58	29.76	31.85	33.87	35.81	37.69	39.50	41.25	100.00
24.72	26.92	29.05	31.10	33.07	34.98	36.82	38.60	40.31	93.79
23.25	25.33	27.35	29.29	31.17	32.98	34.74	36.43	38.07	78.88
21.78	23.74	25.65	27.49	29.27	30.99	32.65	34.26	35.82	63.96
20.30	22.15	23.95	25.68	27.36	28.99	30.57	32.09	33.58	49.05
18.83	20.57	22.25	23.88	25.46	26.99	28.48	29.93	31.33	34.14
15.47	16.93	18.35	19.74	21.10	22.42	23.71	24.96	26.19	.00
29.09	31.57	33.94	36.21	38.38	40.46	42.45	44.35	46.17	100.00
28.22	30.63	32.94	35.15	37.27	39.30	41.24	43.10	44.89	91.77
26.10	28.36	30.53	32.60	34.60	36.51	38.35	40.11	41.80	72.02
23.99	26.09	28.11	30.06	31.93	33.72	35.45	37.12	38.72	52.28
21.88	23.83	25.70	27.51	29.25	30.94	32.56	34.13	35.64	32.53
18.40	20.09	21.73	23.31	24.85	26.35	27.80	29.20	30.57	.00
32.18	34.81	37.31	39.69	41.94	44.08	46.12	48.06	49.90	100.00
31.02	33.57	36.00	38.30	40.50	42.59	44.58	46.47	48.27	89.53
28.22	30.59	32.84	34.99	37.04	39.00	40.87	42.66	44.37	64.40
25.43	27.60	29.69	31.68	33.59	35.42	37.17	38.85	40.47	39.27
21.07	22.94	24.75	26.50	28.19	29.81	31.38	32.90	34.37	.00
34.71	37.44	40.02	42.45	44.75	46.92	48.96	50.90	52.73	100.00
33.26	35.90	38.39	40.75	42.98	45.09	47.09	48.99	50.78	87.03
29.76	32.19	34.49	36.67	38.75	40.72	42.60	44.39	46.09	55.91
23.48	25.52	27.47	29.34	31.14	32.87	34.53	36.13	37.67	.00
36.79	39.58	42.20	44.65	46.96	49.13	51.16	53.08	54.88	100.00
35.04	37.73	40.26	42.64	44.88	46.99	48.98	50.85	52.62	84.25
30.84	33.29	35.61	37.81	39.90	41.87	43.74	45.52	47.20	46.46
25.67	27.84	29.90	31.88	33.77	35.57	37.30	38.96	40.55	.00
38.49	41.31	43.95	46.41	48.70	50.85	52.86	54.74	56.50	100.00
27.66	29.92	32.08	34.14	36.09	37.96	39.74	41.43	43.05	.00
39.89	42.72	45.36	47.80	50.08	52.20	54.17	56.02	57.74	100.00
29.45	31.81	34.04	36.16	38.16	40.07	41.88	43.60	45.24	.00
									MONTHS
40.91	43.56	46.00	48.25	50.33	52.26	54.05	55.71	57.27	253.61
32.24	34.72	37.04	39.23	41.30	43.25	45.09	46.83	48.48	141.41
26.68	28.90	31.02	33.03	34.96	36.80	38.55	40.23	41.83	101.97
22.79	24.78	26.69	28.53	30.30	32.00	33.64	35.22	36.73	80.42
19.90	21.70	23.44	25.12	26.74	28.31	29.83	31.30	32.73	66.61
17.68	19.31	20.90	22.44	23.94	25.39	26.80	28.17	29.51	56.93

MORTGAGE YIELD TABLES

SHOWING DISCOUNT (%) AT VARIOUS YIELDS,
MONTHLY PAYMENT RATES AND DUE DATES

DUE DATE	PAYT RATE	12%	13%	14%	15%	16%	17%	18%	19%	20%
						YIELD				
1 YR	.92	.94	1.87	2.78	3.69	4.59	5.48	6.36	7.23	8.10
	1.00	.93	1.86	2.77	3.68	4.57	5.46	6.33	7.20	8.06
	1.25	.92	1.83	2.73	3.63	4.52	5.38	6.25	7.10	7.95
	1.50	.91	1.81	2.69	3.57	4.44	5.31	6.16	7.00	7.84
	1.75	.89	1.78	2.66	3.52	4.38	5.23	6.07	6.90	7.73
	2.00	.88	1.75	2.62	3.47	4.32	5.16	5.98	6.80	7.62
	2.25	.87	1.73	2.58	3.42	4.26	5.08	5.90	6.71	7.51
	8.84	.53	1.05	1.57	2.08	2.59	3.10	3.60	4.10	4.59
2 YRS	.92	1.77	3.51	5.21	6.87	8.51	10.11	11.68	13.23	14.74
	1.00	1.75	3.47	5.16	6.81	8.43	10.02	11.57	13.10	14.60
	1.25	1.70	3.37	5.00	6.61	8.18	9.72	11.24	12.72	14.17
	1.50	1.65	3.27	4.85	6.41	7.93	9.43	10.90	12.34	13.75
	1.75	1.60	3.16	4.70	6.21	7.69	9.14	10.56	11.96	13.33
	2.00	1.54	3.06	4.55	6.01	7.44	8.85	10.23	11.58	12.91
	2.25	1.49	2.96	4.39	5.81	7.19	8.55	9.89	11.20	12.49
	4.66	.99	1.96	2.93	3.87	4.81	5.73	6.64	7.54	8.42
3 YRS	.92	2.51	4.95	7.31	9.62	11.85	14.02	16.14	18.19	20.18
	1.00	2.47	4.87	7.20	9.47	11.68	13.82	15.90	17.92	19.89
	1.25	2.36	4.65	6.88	9.04	11.15	13.20	15.19	17.13	19.01
	1.50	2.24	4.42	6.55	8.61	10.62	12.58	14.48	16.33	18.13
	1.75	2.13	4.20	6.22	8.18	10.09	11.96	13.77	15.54	17.26
	2.00	2.01	3.98	5.89	7.75	9.57	11.34	13.06	14.74	16.38
	2.25	1.90	3.75	5.56	7.32	9.04	10.71	12.35	13.94	15.50
	3.27	1.43	2.84	4.21	5.56	6.88	8.17	9.44	10.69	11.91
4 YRS	.92	3.16	6.21	9.15	11.98	14.70	17.33	19.86	22.30	24.65
	1.00	3.10	6.09	8.96	11.74	14.41	16.98	19.47	21.86	24.17
	1.25	2.90	5.70	8.40	11.01	13.52	15.95	18.29	20.55	22.73
	1.50	2.71	5.32	7.84	10.28	12.64	14.92	17.12	19.24	21.30
	1.75	2.51	4.94	7.29	9.56	11.75	13.88	15.94	17.93	19.86
	2.00	2.31	4.55	6.73	8.83	10.87	12.85	14.76	16.62	18.42
	2.58	1.85	3.66	5.42	7.13	8.80	10.43	12.02	13.56	15.07
5 YRS	.92	3.75	7.33	10.74	14.01	17.13	20.12	22.97	25.70	28.31
	1.00	3.65	7.13	10.47	13.65	16.70	19.61	22.40	25.07	27.62
	1.25	3.35	6.56	9.63	12.58	15.40	18.10	20.69	23.18	25.56
	1.50	3.06	5.99	8.80	11.50	14.10	16.59	18.99	21.29	23.50
	1.75	2.76	5.41	7.97	10.43	12.80	15.08	17.28	19.39	21.43
	2.17	2.26	4.44	6.56	8.61	10.59	12.51	14.38	16.18	17.93
6 YRS	.92	4.26	8.30	12.13	15.76	19.21	22.48	25.58	28.52	31.31
	1.00	4.13	8.04	11.75	15.28	18.62	21.80	24.81	27.68	30.40
	1.25	3.71	7.25	10.61	13.81	16.86	19.76	22.53	25.16	27.67
	1.50	3.30	6.46	9.47	12.35	15.10	17.72	20.24	22.64	24.94
	1.90	2.64	5.18	7.63	9.98	12.25	14.44	16.55	18.58	20.54
7 YRS	.92	4.72	9.16	13.34	17.27	20.98	24.47	27.75	30.85	33.77
	1.00	4.54	8.82	12.85	16.64	20.23	23.60	26.79	29.80	32.63
	1.25	4.00	7.79	11.37	14.76	17.97	21.01	23.89	26.62	29.22
	1.71	3.00	5.88	8.63	11.27	13.79	16.21	18.53	20.76	22.89
8 YRS	.92	5.13	9.92	14.39	18.57	22.49	26.15	29.58	32.79	35.79
	1.00	4.90	9.49	13.78	17.80	21.56	25.09	28.40	31.51	34.42
	1.25	4.22	8.19	11.94	15.46	18.79	21.92	24.88	27.67	30.31
	1.57	3.35	6.54	9.57	12.47	15.22	17.85	20.36	22.75	25.03
9 YRS	.92	5.49	10.58	15.31	19.70	23.78	27.57	31.10	34.39	37.45
	1.46	3.68	7.16	10.46	13.58	16.54	19.36	22.02	24.56	26.97
10 YRS	.92	5.81	11.16	16.10	20.66	24.87	28.77	32.37	35.71	38.81
	1.38	3.99	7.74	11.28	14.62	17.77	20.74	23.55	26.21	28.72
UNTIL PAID	1.00	6.66	12.60	17.93	22.72	27.04	30.94	34.49	37.72	40.67
	1.25	4.58	8.84	12.82	16.54	20.01	23.26	26.31	29.16	31.84
	1.50	3.56	6.93	10.13	13.17	16.06	18.81	21.42	23.90	26.26
	1.75	2.92	5.73	8.41	10.99	13.46	15.83	18.10	20.29	22.38
	2.00	2.49	4.89	7.21	9.44	11.60	13.69	15.70	17.64	19.52
	2.25	2.17	4.27	6.31	8.29	10.21	12.07	13.87	15.62	17.32

SHOWING DISCOUNT (%) AT VARIOUS YIELDS,
MONTHLY PAYMENT RATES AND DUE DATES

21%	22%	23%	24%	YIELD 25%	26%	27%	28%	29%	BAL REMAIN
8.95	9.79	10.63	11.46	12.27	13.08	13.89	14.68	15.46	100.00
8.91	9.75	10.58	11.40	12.22	13.03	13.82	14.61	15.40	98.95
8.79	9.62	10.44	11.25	12.05	12.85	13.64	14.42	15.19	95.79
8.66	9.48	10.29	11.09	11.89	12.67	13.45	14.22	14.98	92.64
8.54	9.35	10.15	10.94	11.72	12.50	13.26	14.02	14.77	89.48
8.42	9.22	10.00	10.78	11.55	12.32	13.07	13.82	14.56	86.32
8.30	9.08	9.86	10.63	11.39	12.14	12.89	13.63	14.36	83.17
5.08	5.57	6.05	6.53	7.01	7.48	7.95	8.42	8.88	.00
16.22	17.67	19.09	20.49	21.86	23.20	24.52	25.81	27.08	100.00
16.06	17.50	18.91	20.30	21.65	22.99	24.29	25.57	2C.83	97.77
15.60	17.00	18.37	19.72	21.04	22.34	23.61	24.86	26.08	91.10
15.14	16.50	17.83	19.14	20.43	21.69	22.93	24.14	25.33	84.42
14.68	16.00	17.29	18.57	19.81	21.04	22.24	23.42	24.58	77.74
14.22	15.50	16.75	17.99	19.20	20.39	21.56	22.71	23.83	71.07
13.75	14.99	16.21	17.41	18.59	19.74	20.88	21.99	23.09	64.39
9.30	10.16	11.01	11.85	12.67	13.49	14.29	15.09	15.87	.00
22.12	24.00	25.83	27.61	29.34	31.02	32.66	34.25	35.79	100.00
21.80	23.66	25.47	27.22	28.93	30.57	32.19	33.78	35.30	96.46
20.84	22.63	24.36	26.05	27.69	29.29	30.84	32.35	33.83	85.86
19.89	21.60	23.26	24.88	26.45	27.99	29.48	30.93	32.35	75.25
18.93	20.56	22.15	23.70	25.21	26.68	28.12	29.51	30.87	64.65
17.98	19.53	21.05	22.53	23.97	25.38	26.75	28.09	29.40	54.04
17.02	18.50	19.95	21.36	22.73	24.08	25.39	26.67	27.92	43.44
13.10	14.28	15.43	16.55	17.66	18.74	19.81	20.85	21.88	.00
26.91	29.09	31.20	33.23	35.19	37.07	38.89	40.65	42.34	100.00
26.39	28.54	30.61	32.60	34.53	36.38	38.18	39.91	41.58	95.00
24.84	26.87	28.83	30.73	32.56	34.33	36.04	37.69	39.28	80.01
23.28	25.20	27.06	28.86	30.59	32.27	33.90	35.47	36.99	65.03
21.73	23.53	25.29	26.98	28.62	30.21	31.76	33.25	34.70	50.04
20.17	21.87	23.51	25.11	26.65	28.16	29.62	31.03	32.41	35.05
16.53	17.97	19.36	20.72	22.05	23.35	24.61	25.84	27.05	.00
30.80	33.19	35.47	37.66	39.75	41.75	43.67	45.50	47.26	100.00
30.06	32.40	34.64	36.78	38.83	40.80	42.68	44.48	46.21	93.37
27.84	30.03	32.13	34.15	36.08	37.94	39.72	41.44	43.08	73.49
25.62	27.66	29.63	31.52	33.34	35.08	36.75	38.39	39.95	53.61
23.40	25.30	27.12	28.89	30.59	32.23	33.81	35.34	36.82	33.73
19.63	21.28	22.87	24.42	25.92	27.38	28.80	30.17	31.50	.00
33.96	36.48	38.88	41.15	43.31	45.37	47.32	49.18	50.95	100.00
32.99	35.45	37.79	40.01	42.13	44.15	46.06	47.89	49.63	91.55
30.07	32.35	34.53	36.61	38.59	40.49	42.30	44.03	45.68	66.22
27.14	29.25	31.27	33.20	35.05	36.83	38.53	40.16	41.73	40.88
22.42	24.25	26.00	27.70	29.34	30.92	32.45	33.93	35.35	.00
36.53	39.13	41.58	43.90	46.09	48.16	50.12	51.97	53.72	100.00
35.32	37.85	40.25	42.51	44.65	46.68	48.60	50.42	52.14	89.53
31.67	34.01	36.23	38.33	40.34	42.24	44.05	45.78	47.42	58.10
24.94	26.91	28.80	30.61	32.35	34.03	35.64	37.19	38.68	.00
38.61	41.26	43.74	46.07	48.26	50.32	52.26	54.08	55.80	100.00
37.16	39.74	42.16	44.43	46.58	48.60	50.50	52.29	53.99	87.26
32.80	35.16	37.40	39.51	41.51	43.41	45.21	46.92	48.55	49.05
27.21	29.30	31.29	33.19	35.02	36.76	38.43	40.03	41.57	.00
40.31	42.97	45.46	47.79	49.96	51.99	53.90	55.69	57.36	100.00
29.26	31.44	33.51	35.49	37.37	39.16	40.88	42.51	44.07	.00
41.68	44.35	46.83	49.14	51.28	53.29	55.16	56.90	58.53	100.00
31.10	33.36	35.49	37.52	39.45	41.28	43.02	44.67	46.25	.00
									MONTHS
43.36	45.84	48.12	50.23	52.17	53.98	55.66	57.22	58.68	272.32
34.36	36.73	38.95	41.05	43.03	44.89	46.66	48.33	49.90	144.85
28.52	30.66	32.71	34.66	36.52	38.30	40.00	41.62	43.17	103.50
24.40	26.34	28.20	29.99	31.71	33.37	34.96	36.50	37.98	81.31
21.34	23.10	24.79	26.43	28.02	29.56	31.04	32.48	33.88	67.19
18.97	20.58	22.13	23.64	25.11	26.53	27.92	29.26	30.57	57.34

MORTGAGE YIELD TABLES

SHOWING DISCOUNT (%) AT VARIOUS YIELDS,
MONTHLY PAYMENT RATES AND DUE DATES

DUE DATE	PAYT RATE	YIELD								
		12%	13%	14%	15%	16%	17%	18%	19%	20%
1 YR	.94	.70	1.63	2.55	3.46	4.36	5.25	6.14	7.01	7.87
	1.00	.70	1.63	2.54	3.45	4.35	5.24	6.11	6.98	7.84
	1.25	.69	1.60	2.51	3.40	4.29	5.16	6.03	6.89	7.74
	1.50	.68	1.58	2.47	3.35	4.23	5.09	5.95	6.79	7.63
	1.75	.67	1.56	2.44	3.31	4.17	5.02	5.86	6.70	7.52
	2.00	.66	1.54	2.40	3.26	4.11	4.95	5.78	6.60	7.41
	2.25	.65	1.51	2.37	3.21	4.05	4.87	5.69	6.50	7.31
	8.85	.39	.92	1.44	1.95	2.46	2.97	3.47	3.97	4.47
2 YRS	.94	1.33	3.07	4.77	6.45	8.08	9.69	11.27	12.81	14.33
	1.00	1.32	3.04	4.74	6.40	8.03	9.62	11.19	12.72	14.22
	1.25	1.28	2.95	4.60	6.21	7.79	9.34	10.86	12.35	13.81
	1.50	1.24	2.86	4.46	6.02	7.56	9.06	10.54	11.98	13.40
	1.75	1.20	2.77	4.32	5.83	7.32	8.78	10.21	11.61	12.99
	2.00	1.16	2.68	4.18	5.65	7.09	8.50	9.89	11.25	12.58
	2.25	1.12	2.59	4.04	5.46	6.85	8.22	9.56	10.88	12.17
	4.67	.74	1.72	2.68	3.64	4.57	5.50	6.41	7.31	8.20
3 YRS	.94	1.88	4.33	6.71	9.01	11.26	13.44	15.56	17.62	19.62
	1.00	1.86	4.28	6.63	8.91	11.13	13.29	15.39	17.43	19.41
	1.25	1.77	4.08	6.33	8.51	10.63	12.69	14.70	16.65	18.55
	1.50	1.69	3.89	6.02	8.10	10.13	12.10	14.02	15.88	17.70
	1.75	1.60	3.69	5.72	7.70	9.63	11.50	13.33	15.11	16.84
	2.00	1.52	3.49	5.42	7.30	9.12	10.91	12.64	14.34	15.99
	2.25	1.43	3.30	5.12	6.89	8.62	10.31	11.96	13.56	15.13
	3.29	1.08	2.48	3.86	5.22	6.54	7.84	9.11	10.36	11.59
4 YRS	.94	2.37	5.44	8.39	11.23	13.97	16.61	19.15	21.60	23.96
	1.00	2.34	5.35	8.26	11.06	13.76	16.36	18.86	21.28	23.61
	1.25	2.19	5.02	7.74	10.37	12.91	15.36	17.73	20.01	22.21
	1.50	2.04	4.68	7.23	9.69	12.07	14.37	16.59	18.74	20.81
	1.75	1.89	4.34	6.72	9.01	11.23	13.38	15.45	17.46	19.41
	2.00	1.75	4.01	6.20	8.33	10.39	12.38	14.32	16.19	18.01
	2.60	1.39	3.21	4.97	6.70	8.37	10.01	11.60	13.15	14.67
5 YRS	.94	2.81	6.41	9.85	13.14	16.28	19.28	22.15	24.90	27.52
	1.00	2.75	6.28	9.66	12.88	15.97	18.92	21.74	24.44	27.02
	1.25	2.53	5.78	8.89	11.87	14.73	17.46	20.08	22.60	25.01
	1.50	2.31	5.28	8.13	10.86	13.49	16.01	18.43	20.76	22.99
	1.75	2.08	4.77	7.36	9.85	12.25	14.55	16.78	18.92	20.98
	2.19	1.70	3.89	6.02	8.08	10.08	12.01	13.89	15.70	17.46
6 YRS	.94	3.20	7.26	11.12	14.78	18.25	21.54	24.66	27.63	30.44
	1.00	3.12	7.09	10.86	14.43	17.83	21.05	24.11	27.01	29.77
	1.25	2.81	6.40	9.81	13.05	16.14	19.09	21.89	24.56	27.11
	1.50	2.50	5.70	8.76	11.67	14.46	17.13	19.67	22.11	24.44
	1.92	1.98	4.54	7.00	9.38	11.66	13.86	15.98	18.03	20.00
7 YRS	.94	3.54	8.02	12.23	16.19	19.93	23.45	26.76	29.89	32.84
	1.00	3.44	7.79	11.89	15.75	19.39	22.82	26.06	29.12	32.00
	1.25	3.03	6.88	10.52	13.97	17.23	20.32	23.25	26.03	28.66
	1.73	2.26	5.16	7.93	10.59	13.15	15.57	17.91	20.15	22.30
8 YRS	.94	3.85	8.68	13.19	17.41	21.36	25.06	28.52	31.76	34.80
	1.00	3.72	8.39	12.77	16.86	20.70	24.29	27.66	30.83	33.79
	1.25	3.20	7.25	11.07	14.66	18.04	21.23	24.24	27.09	29.77
	1.58	2.52	5.73	8.80	11.71	14.49	17.14	19.67	22.08	24.39
9 YRS	.94	4.12	9.26	14.03	18.46	22.59	26.42	29.99	33.31	36.41
	1.48	2.76	6.28	9.61	12.76	15.75	18.59	21.29	23.84	26.28
10 YRS	.94	4.36	9.77	14.76	19.37	23.63	27.57	31.22	34.60	37.73
	1.39	3.00	6.79	10.37	13.74	16.92	19.92	22.76	25.45	27.99
UNTIL PAID	1.00	5.20	11.45	17.02	22.00	26.47	30.49	34.13	37.44	40.44
	1.25	3.50	7.89	11.98	15.79	19.35	22.68	25.79	28.70	31.44
	1.50	2.71	6.15	9.42	12.52	15.46	18.25	20.91	23.44	25.84
	1.75	2.22	5.07	7.80	10.41	12.92	15.33	17.63	19.85	21.97
	2.00	1.88	4.32	6.67	8.93	11.12	13.23	15.27	17.24	19.14
	2.25	1.64	3.77	5.83	7.83	9.77	11.65	13.48	15.24	16.96

SHOWING DISCOUNT (%) AT VARIOUS YIELDS,
MONTHLY PAYMENT RATES AND DUE DATES

21%	22%	23%	24%	YIELD 25%	26%	27%	28%	29%	BAL REMAIN
8.73	9.57	10.41	11.24	12.06	12.87	13.67	14.46	15.25	100.00
8.70	9.54	10.37	11.20	12.01	12.82	13.62	14.41	15.20	99.21
8.58	9.41	10.23	11.05	11.85	12.65	13.44	14.22	14.99	96.05
8.46	9.28	10.09	10.89	11.69	12.48	13.25	14.03	14.79	92.89
8.34	9.15	9.95	10.74	11.53	12.30	13.07	13.83	14.58	89.73
8.22	9.02	9.81	10.59	11.36	12.13	12.89	13.64	14.38	86.57
8.10	8.89	9.67	10.44	11.20	11.95	12.70	13.44	14.17	83.41
4.96	5.44	5.93	6.41	6.89	7.36	7.83	8.30	8.76	.00
15.81	17.27	18.70	20.10	21.47	22.82	24.14	25.43	26.70	100.00
15.70	17.15	18.56	19.95	21.32	22.66	23.97	25.25	26.52	98.33
15.25	16.65	18.03	19.39	20.71	22.02	23.29	24.55	25.78	91.63
14.80	16.16	17.50	18.82	20.11	21.38	22.62	23.84	25.04	84.94
14.35	15.67	16.98	18.25	19.51	20.74	21.95	23.13	24.30	78.25
13.89	15.18	16.45	17.69	18.90	20.10	21.27	22.43	23.56	71.55
13.44	14.69	15.92	17.12	18.30	19.46	20.60	21.72	22.82	64.86
9.07	9.94	10.79	11.63	12.46	13.27	14.08	14.87	15.66	.00
21.57	23.46	25.30	27.08	28.82	30.51	32.15	33.75	35.30	100.00
21.33	23.20	25.02	26.79	28.51	30.19	31.81	33.39	34.93	97.34
20.40	22.19	23.94	25.64	27.29	28.90	30.47	31.99	33.47	86.69
19.46	21.18	22.86	24.49	26.07	27.62	29.12	30.59	32.01	76.05
18.53	20.17	21.77	23.33	24.85	26.34	27.78	29.18	30.56	65.40
17.59	19.16	20.69	22.18	23.63	25.05	26.43	27.78	29.10	54.75
16.66	18.15	19.61	21.03	22.41	23.77	25.09	26.38	27.64	44.11
12.79	13.96	15.12	16.25	17.36	18.45	19.52	20.56	21.59	.00
26.24	28.43	30.55	32.59	34.56	36.46	38.29	40.05	41.75	100.00
25.86	28.02	30.11	32.13	34.07	35.95	37.76	39.50	41.19	96.23
24.34	26.39	28.37	30.28	32.13	33.92	35.64	37.31	38.92	81.17
22.82	24.75	26.63	28.44	30.19	31.89	33.53	35.12	36.65	66.10
21.29	23.12	24.89	26.60	28.25	29.86	31.41	32.92	34.38	51.03
19.77	21.48	23.14	24.75	26.31	27.83	29.30	30.73	32.11	35.96
16.14	17.58	18.98	20.35	21.68	22.99	24.26	25.49	26.70	.00
30.03	32.44	34.73	36.93	39.04	41.05	42.98	44.83	46.60	100.00
29.49	31.85	34.12	36.29	38.36	40.35	42.25	44.08	45.82	95.00
27.32	29.53	31.66	33.69	35.65	37.53	39.33	41.06	42.72	74.98
25.14	27.21	29.19	31.10	32.94	34.71	36.41	38.05	39.62	54.97
22.97	24.88	26.73	28.51	30.23	31.89	33.49	35.03	36.52	34.96
19.17	20.82	22.43	23.99	25.50	26.96	28.39	29.77	31.11	.00
33.11	35.65	38.07	40.36	42.54	44.61	46.58	48.45	50.24	100.00
32.40	34.89	37.26	39.52	41.66	43.71	45.65	47.50	49.26	93.61
29.53	31.85	34.06	36.16	38.17	40.09	41.92	43.67	45.35	68.07
26.67	28.80	30.85	32.80	34.68	36.47	38.20	39.85	41.43	42.53
21.90	23.74	25.51	27.21	28.86	30.46	31.99	33.48	34.92	.00
35.62	38.24	40.72	43.06	45.27	47.36	49.33	51.20	52.97	100.00
34.72	37.30	39.73	42.03	44.20	46.26	48.21	50.05	51.80	92.07
31.15	33.52	35.77	37.91	39.94	41.87	43.71	45.45	47.12	60.34
24.36	26.35	28.25	30.08	31.83	33.52	35.15	36.71	38.21	.00
37.65	40.32	42.83	45.19	47.40	49.48	51.44	53.29	55.02	100.00
36.58	39.20	41.66	43.97	46.15	48.20	50.13	51.96	53.67	90.34
32.30	34.70	36.97	39.12	41.15	43.07	44.90	46.63	48.28	51.69
26.59	28.69	30.70	32.62	34.46	36.22	37.90	39.52	41.06	.00
39.30	42.00	44.51	46.87	49.07	51.13	53.06	54.87	56.56	100.00
28.59	30.79	32.88	34.87	36.78	38.59	40.32	41.96	43.54	.00
40.64	43.34	45.85	48.19	50.37	52.40	54.29	56.06	57.72	100.00
30.39	32.67	34.83	36.88	38.82	40.67	42.43	44.10	45.69	.00

21%	22%	23%	24%	25%	26%	27%	28%	29%	MONTHS
43.19	45.70	48.01	50.14	52.10	53.93	55.62	57.19	58.65	297.13
34.00	36.41	38.67	40.80	42.80	44.70	46.48	48.17	49.77	148.56
28.12	30.30	32.38	34.36	36.24	38.04	39.76	41.41	42.98	105.11
24.02	25.98	27.86	29.67	31.42	33.09	34.71	36.26	37.75	82.22
20.97	22.75	24.47	26.12	27.73	29.28	30.78	32.24	33.64	67.79
18.63	20.25	21.82	23.34	24.82	26.26	27.66	29.02	30.34	57.76

11½% MORTGAGE YIELD TABLES

SHOWING DISCOUNT (%) AT VARIOUS YIELDS,
MONTHLY PAYMENT RATES AND DUE DATES

DUE DATE	PAYT RATE	12%	13%	14%	15%	16%	17%	18%	19%	20%
1 YR	.96	.47	1.40	2.32	3.23	4.13	5.03	5.91	6.78	7.65
	1.25	.46	1.38	2.28	3.18	4.07	4.94	5.81	6.67	7.52
	1.50	.45	1.36	2.25	3.13	4.01	4.88	5.73	6.58	7.42
	1.75	.45	1.34	2.22	3.09	3.95	4.81	5.65	6.49	7.32
	2.00	.44	1.32	2.19	3.05	3.90	4.74	5.57	6.39	7.21
	2.25	.44	1.30	2.15	3.00	3.84	4.67	5.49	6.30	7.11
	2.50	.43	1.28	2.12	2.96	3.78	4.60	5.41	6.21	7.00
	8.86	.26	.79	1.31	1.82	2.33	2.84	3.34	3.84	4.34
2 YRS	.96	.89	2.63	4.34	6.02	7.66	9.27	10.85	12.40	13.92
	1.25	.85	2.54	4.19	5.81	7.40	8.96	10.48	11.98	13.45
	1.50	.83	2.46	4.06	5.63	7.18	8.69	10.17	11.63	13.05
	1.75	.80	2.38	3.94	5.46	6.95	8.42	9.86	11.27	12.65
	2.00	.78	2.31	3.81	5.28	6.73	8.15	9.54	10.91	12.25
	2.25	.75	2.23	3.68	5.11	6.51	7.88	9.23	10.55	11.85
	2.50	.72	2.15	3.55	4.93	6.28	7.61	8.92	10.20	11.46
	4.68	.50	1.48	2.44	3.40	4.34	5.26	6.18	7.08	7.97
3 YRS	.96	1.25	3.71	6.10	8.41	10.67	12.86	14.98	17.05	19.06
	1.25	1.19	3.51	5.77	7.97	10.11	12.19	14.21	16.18	18.09
	1.50	1.13	3.34	5.50	7.59	9.63	11.62	13.55	15.43	17.26
	1.75	1.07	3.18	5.22	7.22	9.16	11.05	12.89	14.68	16.42
	2.00	1.02	3.01	4.95	6.84	8.68	10.47	12.22	13.93	15.59
	2.25	.96	2.84	4.67	6.46	8.20	9.90	11.56	13.18	14.76
	2.50	.90	2.67	4.40	6.08	7.73	9.33	10.90	12.43	13.92
	3.30	.72	2.13	3.52	4.87	6.20	7.51	8.79	10.04	11.27
4 YRS	.96	1.58	4.66	7.62	10.48	13.23	15.88	18.44	20.90	23.28
	1.25	1.47	4.32	7.08	9.73	12.30	14.77	17.16	19.46	21.68
	1.50	1.37	4.03	6.61	9.09	11.50	13.82	16.06	18.23	20.32
	1.75	1.27	3.74	6.14	8.46	10.70	12.86	14.96	16.99	18.96
	2.00	1.17	3.46	5.67	7.82	9.89	11.91	13.86	15.76	17.59
	2.25	1.07	3.17	5.20	7.18	9.09	10.96	12.76	14.52	16.23
	2.61	.93	2.75	4.53	6.26	7.94	9.59	11.19	12.75	14.27
5 YRS	.96	1.87	5.49	8.95	12.26	15.42	18.44	21.33	24.09	26.74
	1.25	1.70	4.99	8.14	11.15	14.04	16.81	19.47	22.01	24.45
	1.50	1.55	4.55	7.44	10.21	12.86	15.42	17.87	20.22	22.48
	1.75	1.40	4.12	6.74	9.26	11.68	14.02	16.27	18.43	20.52
	2.00	1.25	3.69	6.04	8.31	10.50	12.62	14.67	16.64	18.55
	2.20	1.13	3.34	5.48	7.55	9.56	11.51	13.39	15.22	16.99
6 YRS	.96	2.13	6.23	10.11	13.79	17.29	20.60	23.75	26.74	29.57
	1.25	1.89	5.53	8.99	12.28	15.42	18.40	21.25	23.95	26.53
	1.50	1.68	4.93	8.03	10.99	13.82	16.52	19.10	21.57	23.93
	1.75	1.47	4.33	7.07	9.69	12.21	14.63	16.96	19.19	21.33
	1.93	1.32	3.90	6.38	8.77	11.07	13.28	15.42	17.48	19.46
7 YRS	.96	2.36	6.87	11.12	15.11	18.88	22.43	25.77	28.92	31.90
	1.25	2.04	5.96	9.66	13.17	16.48	19.62	22.60	25.42	28.09
	1.50	1.77	5.18	8.41	11.49	14.43	17.22	19.88	22.41	24.82
	1.74	1.51	4.43	7.22	9.90	12.46	14.92	17.28	19.54	21.70
8 YRS	.96	2.56	7.44	11.99	16.25	20.24	23.97	27.46	30.74	33.81
	1.25	2.16	6.29	10.18	13.84	17.28	20.53	23.60	26.49	29.21
	1.50	1.82	5.31	8.62	11.77	14.75	17.59	20.28	22.84	25.28
	1.60	1.68	4.93	8.01	10.96	13.76	16.43	18.98	21.41	23.74
9 YRS	.96	2.74	7.93	12.75	17.23	21.40	25.27	28.88	32.24	35.37
	1.49	1.85	5.40	8.76	11.94	14.96	17.82	20.54	23.13	25.58
10 YRS	.96	2.90	8.37	13.41	18.08	22.39	26.37	30.06	33.48	36.65
	1.41	2.00	5.84	9.45	12.85	16.07	19.10	21.97	24.68	27.25
UNTIL PAID	1.25	2.39	6.91	11.11	15.02	18.67	22.08	25.26	28.24	31.02
	1.50	1.83	5.35	8.68	11.84	14.84	17.69	20.39	22.96	25.40
	1.75	1.50	4.39	7.17	9.82	12.37	14.81	17.15	19.40	21.56
	2.00	1.27	3.74	6.12	8.41	10.63	12.76	14.83	16.82	18.74
	2.25	1.10	3.26	5.34	7.37	9.33	11.23	13.07	14.86	16.60
	2.50	.98	2.89	4.75	6.56	8.32	10.03	11.70	13.32	14.90

MORTGAGE YIELD TABLES 11½%

SHOWING DISCOUNT (%) AT VARIOUS YIELDS, MONTHLY PAYMENT RATES AND DUE DATES

21%	22%	23%	24%	YIELD 25%	26%	27%	28%	29%	BAL REMAIN
8.50	9.35	10.19	11.02	11.84	12.65	13.45	14.25	15.03	100.00
8.37	9.20	10.03	10.84	11.65	12.45	13.24	14.02	14.80	96.31
8.25	9.07	9.89	10.69	11.49	12.28	13.06	13.83	14.60	93.15
8.13	8.95	9.75	10.54	11.33	12.11	12.88	13.64	14.39	89.98
8.02	8.82	9.61	10.39	11.17	11.94	12.70	13.45	14.21	86.82
7.90	8.69	9.47	10.24	11.01	11.76	12.51	13.26	13.99	83.66
7.79	8.56	9.33	10.09	10.85	11.59	12.33	13.06	13.79	80.49
4.83	5.32	5.81	6.29	6.76	7.24	7.71	8.18	8.64	.00
15.41	16.87	18.30	19.70	21.08	22.43	23.75	25.05	26.32	100.00
14.89	16.31	17.69	19.05	20.39	21.69	22.98	24.24	25.47	92.17
14.45	15.83	17.17	18.50	19.79	21.07	22.32	23.54	24.74	85.46
14.01	15.35	16.65	17.94	19.20	20.44	21.65	22.84	24.01	78.75
13.57	14.87	16.14	17.38	18.61	19.81	20.99	22.15	23.28	72.04
13.13	14.39	15.62	16.83	18.01	19.18	20.32	21.45	22.55	65.33
12.69	13.91	15.10	16.27	17.42	18.55	19.66	20.75	21.82	58.62
8.85	9.71	10.56	11.41	12.24	13.06	13.87	14.66	15.45	.00
21.01	22.91	24.76	26.55	28.29	29.99	31.64	33.24	34.80	100.00
19.95	21.76	23.52	25.23	26.89	28.51	30.09	31.63	33.12	87.53
19.04	20.77	22.45	24.10	25.69	27.25	28.76	30.24	31.68	76.84
18.12	19.78	21.39	22.96	24.49	25.98	27.44	28.85	30.23	66.16
17.21	18.79	20.33	21.83	23.29	24.72	26.11	27.47	28.79	55.47
16.30	17.80	19.27	20.70	22.09	23.46	24.79	26.08	27.35	44.78
15.38	16.81	18.20	19.56	20.89	22.19	23.46	24.70	25.91	34.10
12.47	13.65	14.81	15.95	17.06	18.15	19.23	20.28	21.31	.00
25.57	27.77	29.90	31.95	33.93	35.84	37.68	39.45	41.16	100.00
23.83	25.90	27.90	29.84	31.70	33.50	35.24	36.92	38.55	82.33
22.34	24.30	26.19	28.02	29.79	31.50	33.16	34.76	36.31	67.18
20.86	22.70	24.48	26.21	27.88	29.50	31.07	32.59	34.06	52.04
19.37	21.10	22.77	24.39	25.97	27.50	28.98	30.42	31.82	36.89
17.88	19.49	21.06	22.58	24.06	25.50	26.90	28.26	29.58	21.74
15.75	17.19	18.60	19.98	21.32	22.62	23.90	25.14	26.36	.00
29.26	31.68	33.99	36.21	38.33	40.36	42.30	44.16	45.94	100.00
26.78	29.02	31.17	33.23	35.21	37.11	38.93	40.68	42.36	76.50
24.66	26.74	28.75	30.68	32.54	34.33	36.05	37.70	39.30	56.35
22.53	24.47	26.33	28.13	29.87	31.55	33.16	34.72	36.23	36.20
20.40	22.19	23.91	25.58	27.20	28.76	30.28	31.74	33.16	16.06
18.71	20.37	21.99	23.55	25.07	26.55	27.98	29.37	30.71	.00
32.27	34.82	37.26	39.57	41.76	43.85	45.84	47.73	49.53	100.00
28.99	31.34	33.57	35.71	37.74	39.69	41.54	43.32	45.01	69.96
26.19	28.35	30.42	32.40	34.30	36.12	37.86	39.53	41.13	44.20
23.39	25.36	27.26	29.09	30.85	32.55	34.18	35.74	37.26	18.45
21.38	23.22	25.00	26.72	28.38	29.99	31.54	33.03	34.48	.00
34.70	37.35	39.85	42.21	44.45	46.56	48.55	50.44	52.23	100.00
30.62	33.03	35.31	37.48	39.54	41.49	43.35	45.12	46.81	62.62
27.12	29.32	31.42	33.42	35.33	37.15	38.90	40.57	42.17	30.58
23.78	25.78	27.70	29.54	31.31	33.01	34.63	36.22	37.74	.00
36.68	39.38	41.92	44.30	46.54	48.65	50.63	52.49	54.25	100.00
31.79	34.23	36.53	38.71	40.77	42.73	44.58	46.34	48.01	54.40
27.60	29.81	31.91	33.92	35.83	37.66	39.40	41.06	42.65	15.31
25.96	28.08	30.10	32.04	33.89	35.67	37.37	39.00	40.56	.00
38.29	41.02	43.57	45.95	48.18	50.26	52.22	54.05	55.77	100.00
27.91	30.13	32.25	34.26	36.18	38.01	39.75	41.42	43.01	.00
39.60	42.33	44.88	47.25	49.45	51.51	53.43	55.23	56.91	100.00
29.68	31.98	34.16	36.23	38.20	40.07	41.84	43.53	45.14	.00
									MONTHS
33.63	36.08	38.38	40.55	42.58	44.50	46.31	48.02	49.63	152.58
27.73	29.94	32.04	34.05	35.96	37.79	39.53	41.19	42.78	106.79
23.63	25.61	27.52	29.36	31.12	32.81	34.45	36.01	37.52	83.17
20.60	22.40	24.13	25.81	27.43	29.00	30.52	31.98	33.40	68.40
18.28	19.91	21.50	23.04	24.54	25.99	27.40	28.77	30.10	58.19
16.44	17.94	19.39	20.82	22.20	23.55	24.86	26.14	27.39	50.69

SHOWING DISCOUNT (%) AT VARIOUS YIELDS,
MONTHLY PAYMENT RATES AND DUE DATES

DUE DATE	PAYT RATE	YIELD								
		12%	13%	14%	15%	16%	17%	18%	19%	20%
1 YR	.98	.23	1.17	2.09	3.00	3.90	4.80	5.68	6.56	7.42
	1.25	.23	1.15	2.06	2.96	3.85	4.73	5.60	6.46	7.31
	1.50	.23	1.13	2.03	2.91	3.79	4.66	5.52	6.37	7.21
	1.75	.22	1.12	2.00	2.87	3.74	4.59	5.44	6.28	7.11
	2.00	.22	1.10	1.97	2.83	3.68	4.53	5.36	6.19	7.01
	2.25	.22	1.08	1.94	2.79	3.63	4.46	5.28	6.10	6.91
	2.50	.21	1.07	1.91	2.75	3.58	4.40	5.21	6.01	6.80
	8.87	.13	.66	1.18	1.69	2.20	2.71	3.22	3.72	4.21
2 YRS	.98	.44	2.19	3.91	5.59	7.23	8.85	10.43	11.99	13.51
	1.25	.43	2.12	3.78	5.41	7.00	8.57	10.11	11.61	13.09
	1.50	.42	2.06	3.67	5.25	6.79	8.31	9.80	11.27	12.70
	1.75	.40	1.99	3.55	5.08	6.58	8.06	9.50	10.92	12.31
	2.00	.39	1.93	3.44	4.92	6.37	7.80	9.20	10.57	11.92
	2.25	.38	1.86	3.32	4.75	6.16	7.54	8.90	10.23	11.54
	2.50	.36	1.80	3.21	4.59	5.95	7.28	8.60	9.88	11.15
	4.70	.25	1.23	2.20	3.16	4.10	5.03	5.94	6.85	7.74
3 YRS	.98	.63	3.09	5.49	7.81	10.07	12.27	14.41	16.48	18.50
	1.25	.60	2.94	5.22	7.43	9.58	11.68	13.72	15.70	17.62
	1.50	.57	2.80	5.08	7.08	9.13	11.13	13.08	14.97	16.81
	1.75	.54	2.66	4.72	6.73	8.68	10.59	12.44	14.24	16.00
	2.00	.51	2.52	4.47	6.37	8.23	10.04	11.80	13.52	15.19
	2.25	.48	2.37	4.22	6.02	7.78	9.49	11.16	12.79	14.38
	2.50	.45	2.23	3.97	5.67	7.33	8.94	10.52	12.07	13.57
	3.31	.36	1.78	3.17	4.53	5.87	7.17	8.46	9.71	10.95
4 YRS	.98	.79	3.88	6.86	9.73	12.50	15.16	17.73	20.21	22.59
	1.25	.74	3.62	6.40	9.09	11.67	14.17	16.58	18.91	21.15
	1.50	.69	3.38	5.98	8.49	10.92	13.26	15.52	17.71	19.82
	1.75	.64	3.14	5.56	7.89	10.16	12.35	14.46	16.51	18.50
	2.00	.59	2.90	5.13	7.30	9.40	11.43	13.40	15.31	17.17
	2.25	.54	2.66	4.71	6.70	8.64	10.52	12.34	14.12	15.84
	2.62	.47	2.30	4.08	5.82	7.51	9.16	10.77	12.34	13.86
5 YRS	.98	.94	4.58	8.06	11.38	14.56	17.60	20.51	23.29	25.95
	1.25	.86	4.19	7.37	10.43	13.35	16.15	18.84	21.41	23.86
	1.50	.78	3.82	6.74	9.54	12.23	14.81	17.29	19.68	21.96
	1.75	.71	3.46	6.11	8.66	11.11	13.48	15.75	17.94	20.05
	2.00	.63	3.10	5.48	7.78	9.99	12.14	14.21	16.20	18.14
	2.21	.57	2.79	4.94	7.03	9.05	11.00	12.90	14.73	16.52
6 YRS	.98	1.07	5.19	9.10	12.81	16.33	19.67	22.84	25.84	28.70
	1.25	.95	4.65	8.16	11.50	14.68	17.71	20.59	23.34	25.95
	1.50	.85	4.14	7.29	10.29	13.16	15.90	18.52	21.02	23.41
	1.75	.74	3.64	6.42	9.08	11.64	14.09	16.44	18.70	20.87
	1.94	.66	3.26	5.75	8.16	10.47	12.70	14.85	16.92	18.92
7 YRS	.98	1.18	5.73	10.01	14.04	17.83	21.41	24.78	27.96	30.96
	1.25	1.03	5.02	8.78	12.34	15.72	18.91	21.93	24.79	27.51
	1.50	.89	4.36	7.65	10.78	13.76	16.60	19.30	21.87	24.32
	1.75	.76	3.70	6.51	9.21	11.80	14.27	16.65	18.92	21.11
8 YRS	.98	1.28	6.20	10.79	15.09	19.11	22.88	26.41	29.71	32.81
	1.25	1.09	5.31	9.27	13.00	16.51	19.81	22.93	25.87	28.65
	1.50	.92	4.48	7.86	11.06	14.10	16.98	19.72	22.33	24.80
	1.61	.84	4.11	7.23	10.20	13.02	15.72	18.29	20.74	23.09
9 YRS	.98	1.37	6.61	11.48	16.00	20.21	24.12	27.77	31.16	34.33
	1.50	.93	4.51	7.90	11.11	14.16	17.05	19.80	22.40	24.88
10 YRS	.98	1.45	6.98	12.08	16.79	21.14	25.17	28.91	32.37	35.57
	1.42	1.00	4.88	8.53	11.97	15.21	18.28	21.18	23.92	26.51
UNTIL PAID	1.25	1.22	5.88	10.21	14.23	17.97	21.46	24.72	27.76	30.60
	1.50	.93	4.52	7.93	11.15	14.21	17.11	19.86	22.48	24.96
	1.75	.76	3.70	6.52	9.22	11.81	14.29	16.67	18.95	21.13
	2.00	.64	3.14	5.56	7.88	10.13	12.29	14.38	16.40	18.35
	2.25	.56	2.73	4.85	6.89	8.88	10.80	12.66	14.47	16.23
	2.50	.49	2.42	4.30	6.13	7.91	9.64	11.32	12.96	14.55

SHOWING DISCOUNT (%) AT VARIOUS YIELDS,
MONTHLY PAYMENT RATES AND DUE DATES

21%	22%	23%	24%	YIELD 25%	26%	27%	28%	29%	BAL REMAIN
8.28	9.13	9.97	10.80	11.62	12.43	13.24	14.03	14.82	100.00
8.16	8.99	9.82	10.64	11.45	12.25	13.04	13.83	14.60	96.57
8.04	8.87	9.68	10.49	11.29	12.08	12.86	13.64	14.40	93.40
7.93	8.74	9.55	10.34	11.13	11.91	12.68	13.45	14.21	90.24
7.82	8.62	9.41	10.20	10.97	11.74	12.51	13.26	14.01	87.07
7.70	8.49	9.28	10.05	10.82	11.58	12.33	13.07	13.81	83.90
7.59	8.37	9.14	9.90	10.66	11.41	12.15	12.88	13.61	80.73
4.71	5.20	5.68	6.16	6.64	7.12	7.59	8.06	8.52	.00
15.00	16.46	17.90	19.31	20.69	22.04	23.37	24.67	25.95	100.00
14.54	15.96	17.35	18.72	20.06	21.37	22.66	23.93	25.17	92.71
14.11	15.49	16.84	18.17	19.47	20.75	22.01	23.24	24.45	85.99
13.68	15.02	16.33	17.62	18.89	20.13	21.35	22.55	23.73	79.26
13.25	14.55	15.82	17.08	18.31	19.51	20.70	21.86	23.01	72.53
12.82	14.08	15.32	16.53	17.72	18.90	20.05	21.18	22.29	65.81
12.39	13.61	14.81	15.98	17.14	18.28	19.39	20.49	21.57	59.08
8.62	9.49	10.34	11.19	12.02	12.84	13.65	14.45	15.24	.00
20.46	22.37	24.22	26.02	27.77	29.47	31.13	32.74	34.30	100.00
19.50	21.32	23.09	24.81	26.49	28.12	29.71	31.26	32.76	88.38
18.60	20.35	22.05	23.70	25.31	26.88	28.40	29.89	31.34	77.65
17.71	19.38	21.01	22.59	24.13	25.63	27.10	28.52	29.91	66.92
16.82	18.41	19.96	21.47	22.95	24.39	25.79	27.15	28.49	56.19
15.93	17.44	18.92	20.36	21.77	23.14	24.48	25.79	27.06	45.47
15.04	16.48	17.88	19.25	20.59	21.89	23.17	24.42	25.64	34.74
12.16	13.34	14.50	15.64	16.76	17.86	18.93	19.99	21.03	.00
24.89	27.11	29.25	31.31	33.30	35.22	37.07	38.85	40.58	100.00
23.32	25.41	27.43	29.38	31.26	33.08	34.84	36.54	38.17	83.51
21.87	23.84	25.75	27.60	29.38	31.11	32.78	34.39	35.96	68.28
20.41	22.27	24.07	25.81	27.50	29.14	30.72	32.25	33.74	53.05
18.96	20.70	22.39	24.03	25.62	27.16	28.66	30.11	31.52	37.83
17.51	19.14	20.71	22.25	23.74	25.19	26.60	27.97	29.30	22.60
15.35	16.81	18.22	19.60	20.95	22.26	23.54	24.79	26.01	.00
28.49	30.93	33.26	35.49	37.62	39.66	41.62	43.49	45.29	100.00
26.24	28.51	30.68	32.77	34.77	36.69	38.53	40.30	42.00	78.03
24.16	26.27	28.31	30.26	32.14	33.94	35.68	37.35	38.96	57.75
22.08	24.04	25.93	27.75	29.50	31.20	32.83	34.41	35.93	37.47
20.00	21.81	23.55	25.24	26.87	28.45	29.98	31.46	32.89	17.18
18.24	19.92	21.54	23.11	24.64	26.13	27.56	28.96	30.32	.00
31.42	34.00	36.45	38.78	40.99	43.10	45.10	47.01	48.82	100.00
28.94	30.82	33.09	35.25	37.31	39.28	41.16	42.95	44.67	71.87
25.70	27.89	29.99	31.99	33.91	35.75	37.52	39.21	40.83	45.91
22.96	24.96	26.88	28.73	30.51	32.23	33.87	35.46	36.99	19.94
20.85	22.71	24.50	26.23	27.90	29.52	31.08	32.58	34.04	.00
33.79	36.46	38.99	41.37	43.62	45.75	47.77	49.67	51.48	100.00
30.08	32.52	34.84	37.04	39.12	41.11	42.99	44.79	46.50	64.95
26.65	28.88	31.01	33.03	34.97	36.82	38.59	40.28	41.90	32.60
23.20	25.21	27.15	29.00	30.79	32.50	34.15	35.73	37.26	.00
35.72	38.45	41.01	43.42	45.68	47.81	49.81	51.70	53.47	100.00
31.27	33.74	36.08	38.30	40.39	42.37	44.25	46.03	47.73	57.17
27.16	29.40	31.54	33.57	35.51	37.36	39.12	40.81	42.42	17.64
25.32	27.46	29.51	31.46	33.33	35.12	36.83	38.48	40.05	.00
37.28	40.04	42.62	45.03	47.28	49.39	51.37	53.23	54.97	100.00
27.24	29.48	31.61	33.64	35.58	37.43	39.19	40.87	42.47	.00
38.55	41.32	43.90	46.30	48.54	50.62	52.57	54.39	56.09	100.00
28.96	31.29	33.49	35.58	37.57	39.45	41.25	42.95	44.58	.00
									MONTHS
33.26	35.76	38.10	40.29	42.36	44.30	46.13	47.86	49.49	156.96
27.32	29.57	31.70	33.74	35.68	37.53	39.29	40.97	42.58	108.56
23.23	25.24	27.18	29.03	30.82	32.53	34.18	35.77	37.30	84.14
20.23	22.04	23.80	25.49	27.13	28.72	30.25	31.73	33.16	69.02
17.93	19.58	21.18	22.73	24.24	25.71	27.13	28.51	29.86	58.63
16.11	17.62	19.09	20.52	21.92	23.28	24.60	25.89	27.15	51.01

MORTGAGE YIELD TABLES

SHOWING DISCOUNT (%) AT VARIOUS YIELDS, MONTHLY PAYMENT RATES AND DUE DATES

DUE DATE	PAYT RATE	YIELD 13%	14%	15%	16%	17%	18%	19%	20%	21%
1 YR	1.00	.93	1.86	2.77	3.67	4.57	5.45	6.33	7.20	8.05
	1.25	.92	1.83	2.73	3.62	4.51	5.38	6.24	7.10	7.94
	1.50	.91	1.80	2.69	3.57	4.44	5.30	6.16	7.00	7.83
	1.75	.89	1.78	2.65	3.52	4.38	5.23	6.07	6.90	7.72
	2.00	.88	1.75	2.62	3.47	4.32	5.15	5.98	6.80	7.61
	2.25	.87	1.73	2.58	3.42	4.25	5.08	5.90	6.70	7.50
	2.50	.86	1.70	2.54	3.37	4.19	5.00	5.81	6.61	7.39
	8.88	.52	1.05	1.56	2.07	2.58	3.09	3.59	4.09	4.58
2 YRS	1.00	1.75	3.47	5.16	6.81	8.43	10.02	11.57	13.10	14.60
	1.25	1.70	3.37	5.00	6.61	8.18	9.72	11.24	12.72	14.18
	1.50	1.65	3.27	4.85	6.41	7.94	9.43	10.90	12.34	13.76
	1.75	1.60	3.16	4.70	6.21	7.69	9.14	10.57	11.97	13.34
	2.00	1.55	3.06	4.55	6.01	7.45	8.85	10.24	11.59	12.92
	2.25	1.49	2.96	4.40	5.81	7.20	8.56	9.90	11.21	12.50
	2.50	1.44	2.86	4.25	5.61	6.96	8.27	9.57	10.84	12.09
	4.71	.99	1.96	2.91	3.86	4.79	5.71	6.62	7.51	8.39
3 YRS	1.00	2.47	4.88	7.21	9.48	11.69	13.83	15.91	17.94	19.91
	1.25	2.36	4.65	6.89	9.06	11.16	13.22	15.21	17.15	19.04
	1.50	2.25	4.43	6.56	8.63	10.64	12.60	14.51	16.36	18.17
	1.75	2.13	4.21	6.23	8.20	10.12	11.99	13.81	15.58	17.30
	2.00	2.02	3.99	5.91	7.78	9.60	11.37	13.10	14.79	16.43
	2.25	1.91	3.77	5.58	7.35	9.08	10.76	12.40	14.00	15.56
	2.50	1.79	3.55	5.26	6.93	8.55	10.15	11.70	13.21	14.69
	3.32	1.42	2.82	4.19	5.53	6.84	8.13	9.39	10.63	11.84
4 YRS	1.00	3.11	6.10	8.98	11.76	14.44	17.02	19.51	21.91	24.22
	1.25	2.91	5.72	8.43	11.05	13.57	16.00	18.35	20.62	22.80
	1.50	2.72	5.34	7.88	10.33	12.69	14.98	17.19	19.32	21.39
	1.75	2.52	4.97	7.33	9.61	11.82	13.96	16.03	18.03	19.97
	2.00	2.33	4.59	6.78	8.90	10.95	12.94	14.87	16.74	18.55
	2.25	2.14	4.21	6.22	8.18	10.08	11.92	13.71	15.44	17.13
	2.63	1.84	3.63	5.38	7.08	8.74	10.35	11.93	13.46	14.96
5 YRS	1.00	3.66	7.16	10.51	13.71	16.77	19.69	22.49	25.16	27.72
	1.25	3.37	6.60	9.69	12.65	15.49	18.20	20.81	23.30	25.69
	1.50	3.08	6.03	8.87	11.59	14.20	16.71	19.12	21.44	23.66
	1.75	2.79	5.47	8.05	10.53	12.92	15.23	17.44	19.57	21.63
	2.00	2.50	4.91	7.23	9.48	11.64	13.74	15.76	17.71	19.60
	2.22	2.24	4.40	6.50	8.53	10.49	12.40	14.25	16.04	17.78
6 YRS	1.00	4.15	8.09	11.82	15.37	18.73	21.92	24.95	27.83	30.57
	1.25	3.75	7.31	10.70	13.93	17.00	19.92	22.71	25.36	27.88
	1.50	3.34	6.54	9.58	12.49	15.27	17.92	20.46	22.88	25.20
	1.75	2.94	5.76	8.46	11.05	13.54	15.92	18.21	20.41	22.52
	1.96	2.61	5.12	7.54	9.87	12.12	14.28	16.37	18.38	20.32
7 YRS	1.00	4.58	8.89	12.96	16.78	20.39	23.79	27.00	30.02	32.88
	1.25	4.05	7.88	11.51	14.93	18.18	21.25	24.16	26.91	29.53
	1.50	3.52	6.87	10.06	13.09	15.97	18.71	21.32	23.80	26.17
	1.77	2.96	5.80	8.52	11.12	13.62	16.01	18.30	20.51	22.62
8 YRS	1.00	4.96	9.59	13.93	17.99	21.79	25.35	28.69	31.82	34.75
	1.25	4.29	8.33	12.13	15.71	19.08	22.25	25.24	28.06	30.73
	1.50	3.63	7.07	10.33	13.43	16.36	19.15	21.80	24.31	26.70
	1.63	3.30	6.44	9.43	12.28	15.00	17.60	20.07	22.43	24.69
9 YRS	1.00	5.29	10.20	14.77	19.02	22.97	26.66	30.09	33.29	36.28
	1.52	3.61	7.04	10.28	13.36	16.28	19.05	21.68	24.18	26.56
10 YRS	1.00	5.58	10.73	15.50	19.90	23.97	27.75	31.25	34.50	37.51
	1.43	3.91	7.60	11.07	14.35	17.45	20.38	23.14	25.76	28.24
UNTIL PAID	1.25	4.81	9.27	13.41	17.25	20.83	24.16	27.27	30.18	32.89
	1.50	3.68	7.15	10.45	13.56	16.52	19.32	21.98	24.51	26.91
	1.75	3.00	5.87	8.61	11.24	13.76	16.17	18.48	20.70	22.83
	2.00	2.54	4.99	7.34	9.62	11.81	13.93	15.97	17.94	19.84
	2.25	2.21	4.34	6.41	8.42	10.36	12.25	14.08	15.85	17.57
	2.50	1.95	3.85	5.70	7.49	9.24	10.94	12.59	14.20	15.77

SHOWING DISCOUNT (%) AT VARIOUS YIELDS,
MONTHLY PAYMENT RATES AND DUE DATES

| | | | | YIELD | | | | | BAL REMAIN |
22%	23%	24%	25%	26%	27%	28%	29%	30%	
8.90	9.74	10.58	11.40	12.21	13.02	13.82	14.61	15.39	100.00
8.78	9.61	10.43	11.24	12.05	12.84	13.63	14.41	15.18	96.83
8.66	9.48	10.29	11.09	11.88	12.67	13.44	14.21	14.97	93.66
8.54	9.35	10.14	10.93	11.72	12.49	13.26	14.02	14.77	90.49
8.42	9.21	10.00	10.78	11.55	12.31	13.07	13.82	14.56	87.32
8.30	9.08	9.86	10.62	11.39	12.14	12.88	13.62	14.35	84.15
8.17	8.95	9.71	10.47	11.22	11.96	12.70	13.42	14.15	80.98
5.07	5.56	6.04	6.52	6.99	7.47	7.93	8.40	8.86	.00
16.06	17.50	18.91	20.30	21.66	22.99	24.29	25.57	26.83	100.00
15.60	17.00	18.38	19.72	21.05	22.34	23.61	24.86	26.08	93.26
15.15	16.51	17.84	19.15	20.44	21.70	22.94	24.15	25.34	86.51
14.69	16.01	17.31	18.58	19.83	21.05	22.26	23.44	24.60	79.77
14.23	15.51	16.77	18.01	19.22	20.41	21.58	22.73	23.86	73.03
13.77	15.01	16.23	17.43	18.61	19.77	20.90	22.02	23.11	66.28
13.31	14.51	15.70	16.86	18.00	19.12	20.22	21.31	22.37	59.54
9.26	10.12	10.97	11.80	12.62	13.44	14.24	15.03	15.81	.00
21.82	23.68	25.49	27.25	28.96	30.62	32.23	33.81	35.33	100.00
20.87	22.66	24.40	26.09	27.73	29.33	30.88	32.40	33.87	89.23
19.93	21.64	23.30	24.92	26.50	28.04	29.54	30.99	32.41	78.46
18.98	20.62	22.21	23.76	25.28	26.75	28.19	29.58	30.95	67.69
18.03	19.60	21.12	22.60	24.05	25.46	26.84	28.18	29.49	56.92
17.09	18.57	20.02	21.44	22.82	24.17	25.49	26.77	28.02	46.15
16.14	17.55	18.93	20.28	21.59	22.88	24.14	25.36	26.56	35.38
13.03	14.20	15.34	16.46	17.56	18.64	19.70	20.74	21.76	.00
26.45	28.60	30.67	32.67	34.60	36.46	38.26	39.99	41.66	100.00
24.91	26.95	28.92	30.82	32.66	34.43	36.14	37.80	39.39	84.69
23.38	25.31	27.17	28.97	30.71	32.40	34.03	35.60	37.13	69.39
21.84	23.66	25.42	27.12	28.77	30.37	31.91	33.41	34.87	54.08
20.31	22.01	23.66	25.27	26.82	28.33	29.80	31.22	32.60	38.78
18.77	20.36	21.91	23.42	24.88	26.30	27.68	29.03	30.34	23.47
16.42	17.84	19.23	20.58	21.90	23.19	24.44	25.67	26.86	.00
30.17	32.52	34.76	36.91	38.97	40.94	42.82	44.63	46.36	100.00
27.99	30.18	32.29	34.32	36.26	38.12	39.91	41.63	43.28	79.58
25.80	27.85	29.83	31.72	33.55	35.31	37.00	38.62	40.19	59.17
23.61	25.52	27.36	29.13	30.84	32.49	34.08	35.62	37.10	38.75
21.42	23.19	24.89	26.54	28.14	29.68	31.17	32.62	34.02	18.33
19.46	21.09	22.68	24.21	25.70	27.15	28.56	29.92	31.25	.00
33.17	35.64	37.98	40.22	42.34	44.36	46.29	48.12	49.86	100.00
30.29	32.59	34.78	36.87	38.86	40.76	42.58	44.32	45.97	73.82
27.42	29.54	31.57	33.52	35.38	37.17	38.88	40.52	42.09	47.65
24.55	26.50	28.37	30.17	31.90	33.57	35.17	36.72	38.20	21.47
22.19	24.00	25.74	27.42	29.05	30.62	32.13	33.60	35.02	.00
35.57	38.12	40.53	42.80	44.95	46.99	48.91	50.73	52.46	100.00
32.00	34.35	36.58	38.70	40.72	42.63	44.45	46.18	47.82	67.33
28.43	30.59	32.64	34.61	36.48	38.27	39.98	41.62	43.18	34.66
24.64	26.59	28.46	30.26	31.99	33.65	35.24	36.78	38.26	.00
37.51	40.10	42.53	44.82	46.97	48.99	50.90	52.70	54.39	100.00
33.25	35.62	37.80	40.00	42.01	43.92	45.72	47.44	49.06	60.02
28.98	31.15	33.21	35.18	37.05	38.84	40.55	42.18	43.73	20.04
26.85	28.91	30.88	32.76	34.57	36.30	37.95	39.54	41.06	.00
39.07	41.67	44.11	46.39	48.53	50.53	52.41	54.17	55.83	100.00
28.82	30.97	33.02	34.98	36.84	38.62	40.31	41.93	43.48	.00
40.32	42.93	45.36	47.62	49.73	51.71	53.55	55.28	56.90	100.00
30.59	32.82	34.93	36.93	38.84	40.65	42.37	44.01	45.58	.00
									MONTHS
35.43	37.81	40.04	42.14	44.11	45.96	47.71	49.36	50.92	161.75
29.19	31.36	33.42	35.39	37.26	39.05	40.75	42.38	43.93	110.41
24.87	26.83	28.71	30.51	32.25	33.92	35.52	37.06	38.55	85.15
21.68	23.46	25.17	26.83	28.43	29.98	31.48	32.92	34.32	69.66
19.24	20.85	22.42	23.95	25.43	26.86	28.26	29.61	30.93	59.07
17.30	18.78	20.23	21.64	23.01	24.34	25.65	26.91	28.15	51.34

● FHA LOAN QUALIFICATION ●

To qualify for a government-insured loan the borrower must have:

> A satisfactory credit record.
> The cash needed at closing of the mortgage.
> A steady income sufficient to make the monthly mortgage payments without difficulty.

FHA sets no age limits nor does it say you must have a certain income to buy a home at a certain price.

Let's take a look at some of the FHA considerations.

First, FHA is concerned with the Total Monthly Housing Expenses. This monthly figure includes:

1. The monthly principal and interest loan payment.
2. Hazard (fire) insurance.
3. Property taxes.
4. Maintenance estimates.
5. Estimated utilities.

Now the total figure of Total Monthly Housing Expenses should not exceed 35% of the borrower's net income. Net income is less federal income taxes only.

At this point several factors must be kept in mind if the borrower's income doesn't qualify.

1. Total indebtedness is a prime factor in any marginal situation.
2. Future income prospects. Will borrower's income increase?

A judgment decision.

The tables on pages 135-167 are designed to help qualify FHA buyers. For example:

Mr. and Mrs. Renter wish to purchase a home with an FHA appraised value of $40,000. From the Loan-to-Value Table on p. 139, we find the maximum regular Sec. 203(b) loan is $37,250. From pgs. 154 & 162, we find that a $37,250 loan at 8.5% for 30 years calls for monthly payments of $301.91. The property taxes are $1,200 per year, and from Tables on page 137, we find this equals $100 per month. The three-year fire insurance premium is $450, and from the Tables on page 137, we find this equals $12.50 per month. The monthly total of payments, taxes and insurance is $413.41.

Mr. Renter earns $480 per week, and from the Tables on page 136, this equals $2,080 per month. Mr. Renter clearly has enough income to qualify for the loan, providing he meets the other requirements.

MONTHLY PAYMENT TO INCOME RATIO

Monthly Income Required

Monthly Payment *P.I.T.I.	3 to 1	3½ to 1	4 to 1	4½ to 1	5 to 1
200	600	700	800	900	1000
205	615	718	820	923	1025
210	630	735	840	945	1050
215	645	753	860	968	1075
220	660	770	880	990	1100
225	675	788	900	1013	1125
230	690	805	920	1035	1150
235	705	823	940	1058	1175
240	720	840	960	1080	1200
245	735	858	980	1103	1225
250	750	875	1000	1125	1250
255	765	893	1020	1148	1275
260	780	910	1040	1170	1300
265	795	928	1060	1193	1325
270	810	945	1080	1215	1350
275	825	963	1100	1238	1375
280	840	980	1120	1260	1400
285	855	998	1140	1283	1425
290	870	1015	1160	1305	1450
295	885	1033	1180	1328	1475
300	900	1050	1200	1350	1500
305	915	1068	1220	1373	1525
310	930	1085	1240	1395	1550
315	945	1103	1260	1418	1575
320	960	1120	1280	1440	1600
325	975	1138	1300	1463	1625
330	990	1155	1320	1485	1650
335	1005	1173	1340	1508	1675
340	1020	1190	1360	1530	1700
345	1035	1208	1380	1553	1725
350	1050	1225	1400	1575	1750
355	1065	1243	1420	1598	1775
360	1080	1260	1440	1620	1800
365	1095	1278	1460	1643	1825
370	1110	1295	1480	1665	1850
375	1125	1313	1500	1688	1875
380	1140	1330	1520	1710	1900
385	1155	1348	1540	1733	1925
390	1170	1365	1560	1755	1950
395	1185	1383	1580	1778	1975
400	1200	1400	1600	1800	2000
405	1215	1418	1620	1823	2025
410	1230	1435	1640	1845	2050
415	1245	1453	1660	1868	2075
420	1260	1470	1680	1890	2100
425	1275	1488	1700	1913	2125
430	1290	1505	1720	1935	2150
435	1305	1523	1740	1958	2175
440	1320	1540	1760	1980	2200
445	1335	1558	1780	2003	2225
450	1350	1575	1800	2025	2250
455	1365	1593	1820	2048	2275
460	1380	1610	1840	2070	2300
465	1395	1628	1860	2093	2325
470	1410	1645	1880	2115	2350
475	1425	1663	1900	2138	2375
480	1440	1680	1920	2160	2400
485	1455	1698	1940	2183	2425
490	1470	1715	1960	2205	2450
495	1485	1733	1980	2228	2475

Monthly Income Required

Monthly Payment *P.I.T.I.	3 to 1	3½ to 1	4 to 1	4½ to 1	5 to 1
500	1500	1750	2000	2250	2500
505	1515	1768	2020	2273	2525
510	1530	1785	2040	2295	2550
515	1545	1803	2060	2318	2575
520	1560	1820	2080	2340	2600
525	1575	1838	2100	2363	2625
530	1590	1855	2120	2385	2650
535	1605	1873	2140	2408	2675
540	1620	1890	2160	2430	2700
545	1635	1908	2180	2453	2725
550	1650	1925	2200	2475	2750
555	1665	1943	2220	2498	2775
560	1680	1960	2240	2520	2800
565	1695	1978	2260	2543	2825
570	1710	1995	2280	2565	2850
575	1725	2013	2300	2588	2875
580	1740	2030	2320	2610	2900
585	1755	2048	2340	2633	2925
590	1770	2065	2360	2655	2950
595	1785	2083	2380	2678	2975
600	1800	2100	2400	2700	3000
605	1815	2118	2420	2723	3025
610	1830	2135	2440	2745	3050
615	1845	2153	2460	2768	3075
620	1860	2170	2480	2790	3100
625	1875	2188	2500	2813	3125
630	1890	2205	2520	2835	3150
635	1905	2223	2540	2858	3175
640	1920	2240	2560	2880	3200
645	1935	2258	2580	2903	3225
650	1950	2275	2600	2925	3250
655	1965	2293	2620	2948	3275
660	1980	2310	2640	2970	3300
665	1995	2328	2660	2993	3325
670	2010	2345	2680	3015	3350
675	2025	2363	2700	3038	3375
680	2040	2380	2720	3060	3400
685	2055	2398	2740	3083	3425
690	2070	2415	2760	3105	3450
695	2085	2433	2780	3128	3475
700	2100	2450	2800	3150	3500
705	2115	2468	2820	3173	3525
710	2130	2485	2840	3195	3550
715	2145	2503	2860	3218	3575
720	2160	2520	2880	3240	3600
725	2175	2538	2900	3263	3625
730	2190	2555	2920	3285	3650
735	2205	2573	2940	3308	3675
740	2220	2590	2960	3330	3700
745	2235	2608	2980	3353	3725
750	2250	2625	3000	3375	3750
755	2265	2643	3020	3398	3775
760	2280	2660	3040	3420	3800
765	2295	2678	3060	3443	3825
770	2310	2695	3080	3465	3850
775	2325	2713	3100	3488	3875
780	2340	2730	3120	3510	3900
785	2355	2748	3140	3533	3925
790	2370	2765	3160	3555	3950
795	2385	2783	3180	3578	3975

*Principal Interest Taxes Insurance

INCOME CONVERSION TABLES

YEAR	MONTH	WEEK	HOUR	YEAR	MONTH	WEEK	HOUR
8320.00	693.33	160	4.00	20800.00	1733.33	400	10.00
8528.00	710.67	164	4.10	21008.00	1750.67	404	10.10
8736.00	728.00	168	4.20	21216.00	1768.00	408	10.20
8944.00	745.33	172	4.30	21424.00	1785.33	412	10.30
9152.00	762.67	176	4.40	21632.00	1802.67	416	10.40
9360.00	780.00	180	4.50	21840.00	1820.00	420	10.50
9568.00	797.33	184	4.60	22048.00	1837.33	424	10.60
9776.00	814.67	188	4.70	22256.00	1854.67	428	10.70
9984.00	832.00	192	4.80	22464.00	1872.00	432	10.80
10192.00	849.33	196	4.90	22672.00	1889.33	436	10.90
10400.00	866.67	200	5.00	22880.00	1906.67	440	11.00
10608.00	884.00	204	5.10	23088.00	1924.00	444	11.10
10816.00	901.33	208	5.20	23296.00	1941.33	448	11.20
11024.00	918.67	212	5.30	23504.00	1958.67	452	11.30
11232.00	936.00	216	5.40	23712.00	1976.00	456	11.40
11440.00	953.33	220	5.50	23920.00	1993.33	460	11.50
11648.00	970.67	224	5.60	24128.00	2010.67	464	11.60
11856.00	988.00	228	5.70	24336.00	2028.00	468	11.70
12064.00	1005.33	232	5.80	24544.00	2045.33	472	11.80
12272.00	1022.67	236	5.90	24752.00	2062.67	476	11.90
12480.00	1040.00	240	6.00	24960.00	2080.00	480	12.00
12688.00	1057.33	244	6.10	25168.00	2097.33	484	12.10
12896.00	1074.67	248	6.20	25376.00	2114.67	488	12.20
13104.00	1092.00	252	6.30	25584.00	2132.00	492	12.30
13312.00	1109.33	256	6.40	25792.00	2149.33	496	12.40
13520.00	1126.67	260	6.50	26000.00	2166.67	500	12.50
13728.00	1144.00	264	6.60	26208.00	2184.00	504	12.60
13936.00	1161.33	268	6.70	26416.00	2201.33	508	12.70
14144.00	1178.67	272	6.80	26624.00	2218.67	512	12.80
14352.00	1196.00	276	6.90	26832.00	2236.00	516	12.90
14560.00	1213.33	280	7.00	27040.00	2253.33	520	13.00
14768.00	1230.67	284	7.10	27248.00	2270.67	524	13.10
14976.00	1248.00	288	7.20	27456.00	2288.00	528	13.20
15184.00	1265.33	292	7.30	27664.00	2305.33	532	13.30
15392.00	1282.67	296	7.40	27872.00	2322.67	536	13.40
15600.00	1300.00	300	7.50	28080.00	2340.00	540	13.50
15808.00	1317.33	304	7.60	28288.00	2357.33	544	13.60
16016.00	1334.67	308	7.70	28496.00	2374.67	548	13.70
16224.00	1352.00	312	7.80	28704.00	2392.00	552	13.80
16432.00	1369.33	316	7.90	28912.00	2409.33	556	13.90
16640.00	1386.67	320	8.00	29120.00	2426.67	560	14.00
16848.00	1404.00	324	8.10	29328.00	2444.00	564	14.10
17056.00	1421.33	328	8.20	29536.00	2461.33	568	14.20
17264.00	1438.67	332	8.30	29744.00	2478.67	572	14.30
17472.00	1456.00	336	8.40	29952.00	2496.00	576	14.40
17680.00	1473.33	340	8.50	30160.00	2513.33	580	14.50
17888.00	1490.67	344	8.60	30368.00	2530.67	584	14.60
18096.00	1508.00	348	8.70	30576.00	2548.00	588	14.70
18304.00	1525.33	352	8.80	30784.00	2565.33	592	14.80
18512.00	1542.67	356	8.90	30992.00	2582.67	596	14.90
18720.00	1560.00	360	9.00	31200.00	2600.00	600	15.00
18928.00	1577.33	364	9.10	31408.00	2617.33	604	15.10
19136.00	1594.67	368	9.20	31616.00	2634.67	608	15.20
19344.00	1612.00	372	9.30	31824.00	2652.00	612	15.30
19552.00	1629.33	376	9.40	32032.00	2669.33	616	15.40
19760.00	1646.67	380	9.50	32240.00	2686.67	620	15.50
19968.00	1664.00	384	9.60	32448.00	2704.00	624	15.60
20176.00	1681.33	388	9.70	32656.00	2721.33	628	15.70
20384.00	1698.67	392	9.80	32864.00	2738.67	632	15.80
20592.00	1716.00	396	9.90	33072.00	2756.00	636	15.90

MONTHLY TAX AND
INSURANCE CONVERTER

Tax or Insurance Premium	1/12TH	1/36TH	Tax or Insurance Premium	1/12TH	1/36TH	Tax or Insurance Premium	1/12TH	1/36TH
150	12.50	4.17	750	62.50	20.83	1350	112.50	37.50
160	13.33	4.44	760	63.33	21.11	1360	113.33	37.78
170	14.17	4.72	770	64.17	21.39	1370	114.17	38.06
180	15.00	5.00	780	65.00	21.67	1380	115.00	38.33
190	15.83	5.28	790	65.83	21.94	1390	115.83	38.61
200	16.67	5.56	800	66.67	22.22	1400	116.67	38.89
210	17.50	5.83	810	67.50	22.50	1410	117.50	39.17
220	18.33	6.11	820	68.33	22.78	1420	118.33	39.44
230	19.17	6.39	830	69.17	23.06	1430	119.17	39.72
240	20.00	6.67	840	70.00	23.33	1440	120.00	40.00
250	20.83	6.94	850	70.83	23.61	1450	120.83	40.28
260	21.67	7.22	860	71.67	23.89	1460	121.67	40.56
270	22.50	7.50	870	72.50	24.17	1470	122.50	40.83
280	23.33	7.78	880	73.33	24.44	1480	123.33	41.11
290	24.17	8.06	890	74.17	24.72	1490	124.17	41.39
300	25.00	8.33	900	75.00	25.00	1500	125.00	41.67
310	25.83	8.61	910	75.83	25.28	1510	125.83	41.94
320	26.67	8.89	920	76.67	25.56	1520	126.67	42.22
330	27.50	9.17	930	77.50	25.83	1530	127.50	42.50
340	28.33	9.44	940	78.33	26.11	1540	128.33	42.78
350	29.17	9.72	950	79.17	26.39	1550	129.17	43.06
360	30.00	10.00	960	80.00	26.67	1560	130.00	43.33
370	30.83	10.28	970	80.83	26.94	1570	130.83	43.61
380	31.67	10.56	980	81.67	27.22	1580	131.67	43.89
390	32.50	10.83	990	82.50	27.50	1590	132.50	44.17
400	33.33	11.11	1000	83.33	27.78	1600	133.33	44.44
410	34.17	11.39	1010	84.17	28.06	1610	134.17	44.72
420	35.00	11.67	1020	85.00	28.33	1620	135.00	45.00
430	35.83	11.94	1030	85.83	28.61	1630	135.83	45.28
440	36.67	12.22	1040	86.67	28.89	1640	136.67	45.56
450	37.50	12.50	1050	87.50	29.17	1650	137.50	45.83
460	38.33	12.78	1060	88.33	29.44	1660	138.33	46.11
470	39.17	13.06	1070	89.17	29.72	1670	139.17	46.39
480	40.00	13.33	1080	90.00	30.00	1680	140.00	46.67
490	40.83	13.61	1090	90.83	30.28	1690	140.83	46.94
500	41.67	13.89	1100	91.67	30.56	1700	141.67	47.22
510	42.50	14.17	1110	92.50	30.83	1710	142.50	47.50
520	43.33	14.44	1120	93.33	31.11	1720	143.33	47.78
530	44.17	14.72	1130	94.17	31.39	1730	144.17	48.06
540	45.00	15.00	1140	95.00	31.67	1740	145.00	48.33
550	45.83	15.28	1150	95.83	31.94	1750	145.83	48.61
560	46.67	15.56	1160	96.67	32.22	1760	146.67	48.89
570	47.50	15.83	1170	97.50	32.50	1770	147.50	49.17
580	48.33	16.11	1180	98.33	32.78	1780	148.33	49.44
590	49.17	16.39	1190	99.17	33.06	1790	149.17	49.72
600	50.00	16.67	1200	100.00	33.33	1800	150.00	50.00
610	50.83	16.94	1210	100.83	33.61	1810	150.83	50.28
620	51.67	17.22	1220	101.67	33.89	1820	151.67	50.56
630	52.50	17.50	1230	102.50	34.17	1830	152.50	50.83
640	53.33	17.78	1240	103.33	34.44	1840	153.33	51.11
650	54.17	18.06	1250	104.17	34.72	1850	154.17	51.39
660	55.00	18.33	1260	105.00	35.00	1860	155.00	51.67
670	55.83	18.61	1270	105.83	35.28	1870	155.83	51.94
680	56.67	18.89	1280	106.67	35.56	1880	156.67	52.22
690	57.50	19.17	1290	107.50	35.83	1890	157.50	52.50
700	58.33	19.44	1300	108.33	36.11	1900	158.33	52.78
710	59.17	19.72	1310	109.17	36.39	1910	159.17	53.06
720	60.00	20.00	1320	110.00	36.67	1920	160.00	53.33
730	60.83	20.28	1330	110.83	36.94	1930	160.83	53.61
740	61.67	20.56	1340	111.67	37.22	1940	161.67	53.89

LOAN TO VALUE RATIOS FOR FHA LOANS

APPROVED NEW CONSTRUCTION—APPROVED EXISTING CONSTRUCTION, LESS THAN
ONE YEAR OLD—EXISTING CONSTRUCTION OVER ONE YEAR OLD

	MAXIMUM LOANS			MAXIMUM LOANS			MAXIMUM LOANS	
Appraised Value	REGULAR 203-B	VETERAN 203-B	Appraised Value	REGULAR 203-B	VETERAN 203-B	Appraised Value	REGULAR 203-B	VETERAN 203-B
15100	14647	14900	21100	20467	20900	27100	26140	26690
15200	14744	15000	21200	20564	21000	27200	26230	26780
15300	14841	15100	21300	20661	21100	27300	26320	26870
15400	14938	15200	21400	20758	21200	27400	26410	26960
15500	15035	15300	21500	20855	21300	27500	26500	27050
15600	15132	15400	21600	20952	21400	27600	26590	27140
15700	15229	15500	21700	21049	21500	27700	26680	27230
15800	15326	15600	21800	21146	21600	27800	26770	27320
15900	15423	15700	21900	21243	21700	27900	26860	27410
16000	15520	15800	22000	21340	21800	28000	26950	27500
16100	15617	15900	22100	21437	21900	28100	27040	27590
16200	15714	16000	22200	21534	22000	28200	27130	27680
16300	15811	16100	22300	21631	22100	28300	27220	27770
16400	15908	16200	22400	21728	22200	28400	27310	27860
16500	16005	16300	22500	21825	22300	28500	27400	27950
16600	16102	16400	22600	21922	22400	28600	27490	28040
16700	16199	16500	22700	22019	22500	28700	27580	28130
16800	16296	16600	22800	22116	22600	28800	27670	28220
16900	16393	16700	22900	22213	22700	28900	27760	28310
17000	16490	16800	23000	22310	22800	29000	27850	28400
17100	16587	16900	23100	22407	22900	29100	27940	28490
17200	16684	17000	23200	22504	23000	29200	28030	28580
17300	16781	17100	23300	22601	23100	29300	28120	28670
17400	16878	17200	23400	22698	23200	29400	28210	28760
17500	16975	17300	23500	22795	23300	29500	28300	28850
17600	17072	17400	23600	22892	23400	29600	28390	28940
17700	17169	17500	23700	22989	23500	29700	28480	29030
17800	17266	17600	23800	23086	23600	29800	28570	29120
17900	17363	17700	23900	23183	23700	29900	28660	29210
18000	17460	17800	24000	23280	23800	30000	28750	29300
18100	17557	17900	24100	23377	23900	30100	28840	29390
18200	17654	18000	24200	23474	24000	30200	28930	29480
18300	17751	18100	24300	23571	24100	30300	29020	29570
18400	17848	18200	24400	23668	24200	30400	29110	29660
18500	17945	18300	24500	23765	24300	30500	29200	29750
18600	18042	18400	24600	23862	24400	30600	29290	29840
18700	18139	18500	24700	23959	24500	30700	29380	29930
18800	18236	18600	24800	24056	24600	30800	29470	30020
18900	18333	18700	24900	24153	24700	30900	29560	30110
19000	18430	18800	25000	24250	24800	31000	29650	30200
19100	18527	18900	25100	24340	24890	31100	29740	30290
19200	18624	19000	25200	24430	24980	31200	29830	30380
19300	18721	19100	25300	24520	25070	31300	29920	30470
19400	18818	19200	25400	24610	25160	31400	30010	30560
19500	18915	19300	25500	24700	25250	31500	30100	30650
19600	19012	19400	25600	24790	25340	31600	30190	30740
19700	19109	19500	25700	24880	25430	31700	30280	30830
19800	19206	19600	25800	24970	25520	31800	30370	30920
19900	19303	19700	25900	25060	25610	31900	30460	31010
20000	19400	19800	26000	25150	25700	32000	30550	31100
20100	19497	19900	26100	25240	25790	32100	30640	31190
20200	19594	20000	26200	25330	25880	32200	30730	31280
20300	19691	20100	26300	25420	25970	32300	30820	31370
20400	19788	20200	26400	25510	26060	32400	30910	31460
20500	19885	20300	26500	25600	26150	32500	31000	31550
20600	19982	20400	26600	25690	26240	32600	31090	31640
20700	20079	20500	26700	25780	26330	32700	31180	31730
20800	20176	20600	26800	25870	26420	32800	31270	31820
20900	20273	20700	26900	25960	26510	32900	31360	31910
21000	20370	20800	27000	26050	26600	33000	31450	32000

LOAN TO VALUE RATIOS FOR FHA LOANS

APPROVED NEW CONSTRUCTION—APPROVED EXISTING CONSTRUCTION, LESS THAN
ONE YEAR OLD—EXISTING CONSTRUCTION OVER ONE YEAR OLD

	MAXIMUM LOANS			MAXIMUM LOANS			MAXIMUM LOANS	
Appraised Value	REGULAR 203-B	VETERAN 203-B	Appraised Value	REGULAR 203-B	VETERAN 203-B	Appraised Value	REGULAR 203-B	VETERAN 203-B
33100	31540	32090	39100	36530	37285	50200	45410	46720
33200	31630	32180	39200	36610	37370	50400	45570	46890
33300	31720	32270	39300	36690	37455	50600	45730	47060
33400	31810	32360	39400	36770	37540	50800	45890	47230
33500	31900	32450	39500	36850	37625	51000	46050	47400
33600	31990	32540	39600	36930	37710	51200	46210	47570
33700	32080	32630	39700	37010	37795	51400	46370	47740
33800	32170	32720	39800	37090	37880	51600	46530	47910
33900	32260	32810	39900	37170	37965	51800	46690	48080
34000	32350	32900	40000	37250	38050	52000	46850	48250
34100	32440	32990	40200	37410	38220	52200	47010	48420
34200	32530	33080	40400	37570	38390	52400	47170	48590
34300	32620	33170	40600	37730	38560	52600	47330	48760
34400	32710	33260	40800	37890	38730	52800	47490	48930
34500	32800	33350	41000	38050	38900	53000	47650	49100
34600	32890	33440	41200	38210	39070	53200	47810	49270
34700	32980	33530	41400	38370	39240	53400	47970	49440
34800	33070	33620	41600	38530	39410	53600	48130	49610
34900	33160	33710	41800	38690	39580	53800	48290	49780
35000	33250	33800	42000	38850	39750	54000	48450	49950
35100	33330	33885	42200	39010	39920	54200	48610	50120
35200	33410	33970	42400	39170	40090	54400	48770	50290
35300	33490	34055	42600	39330	40260	54600	48930	50460
35400	33570	34140	42800	39490	40430	54800	49090	50630
35500	33650	34225	43000	39650	40600	55000	49250	50800
35600	33730	34310	43200	39810	40770	55200	49410	50970
35700	33810	34395	43400	39970	40940	55400	49570	51140
35800	33890	34480	43600	40130	41110	55600	49730	51310
35900	33970	34565	43800	40290	41280	55800	49890	51480
36000	34050	34650	44000	40450	41450	56000	50050	51650
36100	34130	34735	44200	40610	41620	56200	50210	51820
36200	34210	34820	44400	40770	41790	56400	50370	51990
36300	34290	34905	44600	40930	41960	56600	50530	52160
36400	34370	34990	44800	41090	42130	56800	50690	52330
36500	34450	35075	45000	41250	42300	57000	50850	52500
36600	34530	35160	45200	41410	42470	57200	51010	52670
36700	34610	35245	45400	41570	42640	57400	51170	52840
36800	34690	35330	45600	41730	42810	57600	51330	53010
36900	34770	35415	45800	41890	42980	57800	51490	53180
37000	34850	35500	46000	42050	43150	58000	51650	53350
37100	34930	35585	46200	42210	43320	58200	51810	53520
37200	35010	35670	46400	42370	43490	58400	51970	53690
37300	35090	35755	46600	42530	43660	58600	52130	53860
37400	35170	35840	46800	42690	43830	58800	52290	54030
37500	35250	35925	47000	42850	44000	59000	52450	54200
37600	35330	36010	47200	43010	44170	59200	52610	54370
37700	35410	36095	47400	43170	44340	59400	52770	54540
37800	35490	36180	47600	43330	44510	59600	52930	54710
37900	35570	36265	47800	43490	44680	59800	53090	54880
38000	35650	36350	48000	43650	44850	60000	53250	55050
38100	35730	36435	48200	43810	45020	60200	53410	55220
38200	35810	36520	48400	43970	45190	60400	53570	55390
38300	35890	36605	48600	44130	45360	60600	53730	55560
38400	35970	36690	48800	44290	45530	60800	53890	55730
38500	36050	36775	49000	44450	45700	61000	54050	55900
38600	36130	36860	49200	44610	45870	61200	54210	56070
38700	36210	36945	49400	44770	46040	61400	54370	56240
38800	36290	37030	49600	44930	46210	61600	54530	56410
38900	36370	37115	49800	45090	46380	61800	54690	56580
39000	36450	37200	50000	45250	46550	62000	54850	56750

MONTHLY PAYMENTS FOR 25-YR. FHA LOANS

INCLUDING FIRST YEAR ½% MORTGAGE INSURANCE PREMIUMS

AMOUNT	INTEREST							
	7.00%	7.25%	7.50%	7.75%	8.00%	8.25%	8.50%	8.75%
50	.37	.38	.39	.40	.41	.41	.42	.43
100	.75	.76	.78	.80	.81	.83	.85	.86
250	1.87	1.91	1.95	1.99	2.03	2.07	2.12	2.16
500	3.75	3.83	3.91	3.99	4.07	4.16	4.24	4.33
10000	74.84	76.44	78.04	79.74	81.34	83.04	84.74	86.44
10100	75.59	77.20	78.82	80.54	82.15	83.87	85.60	87.31
10200	76.33	77.97	79.60	81.33	82.96	84.71	86.44	88.18
10300	77.08	78.73	80.38	82.14	83.79	85.54	87.29	89.04
10400	77.83	79.49	81.17	82.93	84.60	86.37	88.13	89.90
10500	78.58	80.27	81.95	83.73	85.41	87.20	88.98	90.77
10600	79.33	81.03	82.72	84.53	86.22	88.02	89.83	91.63
10700	80.08	81.79	83.50	85.32	87.03	88.85	90.67	92.49
10800	80.83	82.55	84.28	86.12	87.85	89.68	91.53	93.36
10900	81.57	83.32	85.06	86.91	88.66	90.52	92.37	94.23
11000	82.32	84.08	85.84	87.71	89.48	91.35	93.22	95.09
11100	83.07	84.84	86.63	88.52	90.29	92.18	94.07	95.95
11200	83.81	85.62	87.41	89.31	91.10	93.01	94.91	96.82
11300	84.57	86.38	88.19	90.11	91.92	93.84	95.76	97.68
11400	85.32	87.14	88.97	90.90	92.73	94.67	96.60	98.54
11500	86.07	87.91	89.75	91.70	93.54	95.50	97.46	99.42
11600	86.81	88.67	90.52	92.49	94.35	96.33	98.31	100.28
11700	87.56	89.43	91.30	93.29	95.17	97.16	99.15	101.14
11800	88.31	90.19	92.09	94.10	95.99	97.99	100.00	102.00
11900	89.05	90.97	92.87	94.89	96.80	98.82	100.84	102.87
12000	89.81	91.73	93.65	95.69	97.61	99.65	101.69	103.73
12100	90.56	92.49	94.43	96.49	98.42	100.48	102.54	104.60
12200	91.30	93.26	95.21	97.28	99.23	101.31	103.39	105.47
12300	92.05	94.02	95.99	98.08	100.05	102.15	104.24	106.33
12400	92.80	94.78	96.77	98.87	100.87	102.98	105.08	107.19
12500	93.55	95.55	97.55	99.68	101.68	103.81	105.93	108.06
12600	94.29	96.31	98.33	100.48	102.49	104.63	106.78	108.92
12700	95.04	97.08	99.11	101.27	103.30	105.46	107.62	109.78
12800	95.80	97.84	99.89	102.07	104.12	106.29	108.47	110.65
12900	96.54	98.61	100.67	102.86	104.93	107.12	109.32	111.52
13000	97.29	99.37	101.45	103.66	105.74	107.96	110.17	112.38
13100	98.04	100.13	102.23	104.46	106.56	108.79	111.02	113.24
13200	98.78	100.90	103.01	105.26	107.37	109.62	111.86	114.11
13300	99.53	101.66	103.80	106.06	108.19	110.45	112.71	114.97
13400	100.28	102.43	104.58	106.85	109.00	111.28	113.55	115.83
13500	101.04	103.20	105.36	107.65	109.81	112.11	114.40	116.71
13600	101.78	103.96	106.13	108.45	110.62	112.93	115.26	117.57
13700	102.53	104.72	106.91	109.24	111.43	113.77	116.10	118.43
13800	103.28	105.48	107.69	110.04	112.26	114.60	116.95	119.29
13900	104.02	106.25	108.47	110.84	113.07	115.43	117.79	120.16
14000	104.77	107.01	109.26	111.64	113.88	116.26	118.64	121.02
14100	105.52	107.78	110.04	112.44	114.69	117.09	119.49	121.88
14200	106.27	108.55	110.82	113.23	115.50	117.92	120.33	122.76
14300	107.02	109.31	111.60	114.03	116.32	118.75	121.19	123.62
14400	107.77	110.07	112.38	114.82	117.13	119.59	122.03	124.48
14500	108.52	110.84	113.16	115.62	117.95	120.42	122.88	125.35
14600	109.26	111.60	113.93	116.43	118.76	121.24	123.73	126.21
14700	110.01	112.36	114.72	117.22	119.57	122.07	124.57	127.07
14800	110.76	113.13	115.50	118.02	120.39	122.90	125.42	127.93
14900	111.51	113.90	116.28	118.81	121.20	123.73	126.26	128.81
15000	112.26	114.66	117.06	119.61	122.01	124.56	127.12	129.67
15100	113.01	115.42	117.84	120.41	122.82	125.40	127.97	130.53
15200	113.75	116.19	118.62	121.20	123.64	126.23	128.81	131.40
15300	114.50	116.95	119.40	122.01	124.46	127.06	129.66	132.26
15400	115.25	117.71	120.19	122.80	125.27	127.89	130.50	133.12
15500	116.00	118.49	120.97	123.60	126.08	128.72	131.35	133.99

MONTHLY PAYMENTS FOR 25-YR. FHA LOANS

INCLUDING FIRST YEAR ½% MORTGAGE INSURANCE PREMIUMS

AMOUNT	INTEREST							
	9.00%	9.25%	9.50%	9.75%	10.00%	10.25%	10.50%	10.75%
50	.44	.45	.46	.47	.47	.48	.49	.50
100	.88	.90	.91	.93	.95	.97	.99	1.00
250	2.20	2.24	2.29	2.33	2.37	2.42	2.46	2.51
500	4.41	4.50	4.58	4.67	4.76	4.85	4.94	5.03
10000	88.15	89.85	91.55	93.35	95.05	96.85	98.65	100.45
10100	89.03	90.75	92.46	94.28	96.00	97.82	99.64	101.45
10200	89.91	91.64	93.38	95.21	96.95	98.78	100.62	102.46
10300	90.79	92.54	94.29	96.15	97.90	99.75	101.61	103.47
10400	91.67	93.44	95.21	97.08	98.85	100.73	102.60	104.47
10500	92.55	94.34	96.12	98.02	99.81	101.70	103.59	105.48
10600	93.43	95.24	97.04	98.95	100.75	102.66	104.57	106.48
10700	94.32	96.14	97.96	99.88	101.70	103.63	105.56	107.48
10800	95.20	97.04	98.87	100.82	102.65	104.60	106.54	108.48
10900	96.08	97.93	99.79	101.75	103.60	105.56	107.53	109.49
11000	96.96	98.83	100.70	102.68	104.55	106.53	108.52	110.50
11100	97.84	99.73	101.61	103.61	105.51	107.51	109.51	111.50
11200	98.72	100.62	102.53	104.55	106.46	108.47	110.49	112.51
11300	99.60	101.53	103.45	105.49	107.41	109.44	111.48	113.51
11400	100.49	102.43	104.37	106.42	108.36	110.41	112.46	114.51
11500	101.37	103.33	105.28	107.35	109.31	111.38	113.45	115.52
11600	102.25	104.22	106.19	108.28	110.25	112.34	114.43	116.52
11700	103.13	105.12	107.11	109.21	111.20	113.31	115.43	117.53
11800	104.01	106.02	108.02	110.15	112.16	114.29	116.41	118.53
11900	104.89	106.91	108.95	111.09	113.11	115.25	117.40	119.54
12000	105.77	107.82	109.86	112.02	114.06	116.22	118.38	120.54
12100	106.66	108.72	110.77	112.95	115.01	117.19	119.37	121.54
12200	107.54	109.61	111.69	113.88	115.96	118.15	120.35	122.55
12300	108.42	110.51	112.60	114.82	116.91	119.12	121.34	123.56
12400	109.30	111.41	113.52	115.75	117.86	120.10	122.33	124.56
12500	110.18	112.31	114.43	116.68	118.82	121.07	123.32	125.57
12600	111.06	113.20	115.35	117.62	119.76	122.03	124.30	126.57
12700	111.94	114.11	116.27	118.55	120.71	123.00	125.29	127.57
12800	112.83	115.01	117.18	119.49	121.66	123.97	126.27	128.57
12900	113.71	115.90	118.10	120.42	122.61	124.93	127.26	129.58
13000	114.59	116.80	119.01	121.35	123.56	125.90	128.25	130.59
13100	115.47	117.70	119.92	122.28	124.51	126.88	129.24	131.59
13200	116.35	118.59	120.84	123.22	125.47	127.84	130.22	132.60
13300	117.23	119.49	121.76	124.16	126.42	128.81	131.21	133.60
13400	118.11	120.40	122.68	125.09	127.37	129.78	132.19	134.60
13500	119.00	121.30	123.59	126.02	128.32	130.75	133.18	135.61
13600	119.88	122.19	124.50	126.95	129.26	131.71	134.17	136.62
13700	120.76	123.09	125.42	127.88	130.21	132.68	135.16	137.62
13800	121.64	123.99	126.33	128.82	131.17	133.66	136.14	138.62
13900	122.52	124.88	127.25	129.76	132.12	134.62	137.13	139.63
14000	123.40	125.78	128.17	130.69	133.07	135.59	138.11	140.63
14100	124.29	126.69	129.08	131.62	134.02	136.56	139.10	141.63
14200	125.17	127.58	130.00	132.55	134.97	137.52	140.08	142.64
14300	126.05	128.48	130.91	133.49	135.92	138.49	141.07	143.65
14400	126.93	129.38	131.83	134.42	136.87	139.47	142.06	144.65
14500	127.81	130.28	132.74	135.35	137.83	140.44	143.05	145.66
14600	128.69	131.17	133.66	136.29	138.77	141.40	144.03	146.66
14700	129.57	132.08	134.58	137.22	139.72	142.37	145.02	147.66
14800	130.46	132.98	135.49	138.16	140.67	143.34	146.00	148.66
14900	131.34	133.87	136.41	139.09	141.62	144.30	146.99	149.67
15000	132.22	134.77	137.32	140.02	142.57	145.27	147.98	150.68
15100	133.10	135.67	138.23	140.95	143.52	146.25	148.97	151.68
15200	133.98	136.56	139.15	141.88	144.48	147.21	149.95	152.69
15300	134.86	137.46	140.07	142.83	145.43	148.18	150.94	153.69
15400	135.74	138.37	140.99	143.76	146.38	149.15	151.92	154.69
15500	136.63	139.27	141.90	144.69	147.33	150.12	152.91	155.70

MONTHLY PAYMENTS FOR 25-YR. FHA LOANS

INCLUDING FIRST YEAR ½% MORTGAGE INSURANCE PREMIUMS

AMOUNT	INTEREST							
	7.00%	7.25%	7.50%	7.75%	8.00%	8.25%	8.50%	8.75%
15600	116.74	119.25	121.74	124.40	126.89	129.54	132.20	134.86
15700	117.50	120.01	122.52	125.19	127.70	130.37	133.05	135.72
15800	118.25	120.77	123.30	125.99	128.52	131.21	133.90	136.58
15900	118.99	121.54	124.08	126.78	129.34	132.04	134.74	137.45
16000	119.74	122.30	124.86	127.59	130.15	132.87	135.59	138.31
16100	120.49	123.06	125.65	128.39	130.96	133.70	136.44	139.17
16200	121.23	123.83	126.43	129.18	131.77	134.53	137.28	140.04
16300	121.98	124.60	127.21	129.98	132.59	135.36	138.13	140.91
16400	122.74	125.36	127.99	130.77	133.40	136.19	138.98	141.77
16500	123.49	126.13	128.77	131.57	134.21	137.03	139.83	142.64
16600	124.23	126.89	129.54	132.37	135.03	137.85	140.68	143.50
16700	124.98	127.65	130.32	133.17	135.84	138.68	141.52	144.36
16800	125.73	128.41	131.11	133.97	136.66	139.51	142.37	145.22
16900	126.47	129.18	131.89	134.76	137.47	140.34	143.21	146.09
17000	127.22	129.95	132.67	135.56	138.28	141.17	144.06	146.96
17100	127.98	130.71	133.45	136.36	139.09	142.00	144.92	147.82
17200	128.72	131.48	134.23	137.15	139.90	142.84	145.76	148.69
17300	129.47	132.24	135.01	137.95	140.73	143.67	146.61	149.55
17400	130.22	133.00	135.79	138.75	141.54	144.50	147.45	150.41
17500	130.97	133.77	136.57	139.55	142.35	145.33	148.30	151.28
17600	131.71	134.53	137.35	140.35	143.16	146.15	149.15	152.14
17700	132.46	135.30	138.13	141.14	143.97	146.98	149.99	153.01
17800	133.22	136.06	138.91	141.94	144.79	147.81	150.85	153.87
17900	133.96	136.83	139.69	142.73	145.60	148.65	151.69	154.74
18000	134.71	137.59	140.47	143.53	146.42	149.48	152.54	155.60
18100	135.46	138.35	141.25	144.33	147.23	150.31	153.39	156.46
18200	136.20	139.12	142.03	145.13	148.04	151.14	154.23	157.33
18300	136.95	139.88	142.82	145.93	148.86	151.97	155.08	158.19
18400	137.70	140.65	143.60	146.72	149.67	152.80	155.92	159.06
18500	138.45	141.42	144.38	147.52	150.48	153.63	156.78	159.93
18600	139.20	142.18	145.15	148.32	151.29	154.46	157.63	160.79
18700	139.95	142.94	145.93	149.11	152.11	155.29	158.47	161.65
18800	140.70	143.70	146.71	149.91	152.93	156.12	159.32	162.51
18900	141.44	144.47	147.49	150.71	153.74	156.95	160.16	163.38
19000	142.19	145.23	148.28	151.51	154.55	157.78	161.01	164.24
19100	142.94	146.00	149.06	152.31	155.36	158.61	161.86	165.11
19200	143.68	146.77	149.84	153.10	156.17	159.44	162.71	165.98
19300	144.44	147.53	150.62	153.90	156.99	160.28	163.56	166.84
19400	145.19	148.29	151.40	154.69	157.81	161.11	164.40	167.70
19500	145.94	149.06	152.18	155.49	158.62	161.94	165.25	168.57
19600	146.68	149.82	152.95	156.30	159.43	162.76	166.10	169.43
19700	147.43	150.58	153.74	157.09	160.24	163.59	166.94	170.29
19800	148.18	151.34	154.52	157.89	161.06	164.42	167.79	171.16
19900	148.92	152.12	155.30	158.68	161.87	165.25	168.64	172.03
20000	149.68	152.88	156.08	159.48	162.68	166.09	169.49	172.89
20100	150.43	153.64	156.86	160.28	163.50	166.92	170.34	173.75
20200	151.17	154.41	157.64	161.07	164.31	167.75	171.18	174.62
20300	151.92	155.17	158.42	161.88	165.13	168.58	172.03	175.48
20400	152.67	155.93	159.21	162.67	165.94	169.41	172.87	176.35
20500	153.42	156.70	159.99	163.47	166.75	170.24	173.72	177.22
20600	154.16	157.47	160.76	164.27	167.56	171.06	174.56	178.08
20700	154.92	158.23	161.54	165.06	168.37	171.90	175.42	178.94
20800	155.67	158.99	162.32	165.86	169.20	172.73	176.27	179.80
20900	156.41	159.76	163.10	166.65	170.01	173.56	177.11	180.67
21000	157.16	160.52	163.88	167.46	170.82	174.39	177.96	181.53
21100	157.91	161.28	164.67	168.26	171.63	175.22	178.81	182.40
21200	158.65	162.05	165.45	169.05	172.44	176.05	179.65	183.27
21300	159.40	162.82	166.23	169.85	173.26	176.88	180.51	184.13
21400	160.15	163.58	167.01	170.64	174.07	177.72	181.35	184.99
21500	160.91	164.35	167.79	171.44	174.89	178.55	182.20	185.86

142

MONTHLY PAYMENTS FOR 25-YR. FHA LOANS

INCLUDING FIRST YEAR ½% MORTGAGE INSURANCE PREMIUMS

AMOUNT	INTEREST							
	9.00%	9.25%	9.50%	9.75%	10.00%	10.25%	10.50%	10.75%
15600	137.51	140.16	142.81	145.62	148.27	151.08	153.89	156.71
15700	138.39	141.06	143.73	146.55	149.22	152.05	154.89	157.71
15800	139.27	141.96	144.64	147.49	150.18	153.03	155.87	158.71
15900	140.15	142.85	145.56	148.43	151.13	153.99	156.86	159.72
16000	141.03	143.75	146.48	149.36	152.08	154.96	157.84	160.72
16100	141.91	144.66	147.39	150.29	153.03	155.93	158.83	161.72
16200	142.80	145.55	148.31	151.22	153.98	156.89	159.81	162.73
16300	143.68	146.45	149.22	152.16	154.93	157.86	160.80	163.74
16400	144.56	147.35	150.14	153.09	155.88	158.84	161.79	164.74
16500	145.44	148.25	151.05	154.02	156.84	159.81	162.78	165.75
16600	146.32	149.14	151.96	154.96	157.78	160.77	163.76	166.75
16700	147.20	150.04	152.89	155.89	158.73	161.74	164.75	167.75
16800	148.08	150.95	153.80	156.83	159.68	162.71	165.73	168.76
16900	148.97	151.84	154.72	157.76	160.63	163.67	166.72	169.76
17000	149.85	152.74	155.63	158.69	161.58	164.64	167.71	170.77
17100	150.73	153.64	156.54	159.62	162.53	165.62	168.70	171.77
17200	151.61	154.53	157.46	160.55	163.48	166.58	169.68	172.78
17300	152.49	155.43	158.37	161.50	164.44	167.55	170.67	173.78
17400	153.37	156.33	159.30	162.43	165.39	168.52	171.65	174.78
17500	154.25	157.24	160.21	163.36	166.34	169.49	172.64	175.79
17600	155.14	158.13	161.12	164.29	167.28	170.45	173.62	176.80
17700	156.02	159.03	162.04	165.22	168.23	171.42	174.62	177.80
17800	156.90	159.93	162.95	166.16	169.18	172.40	175.60	178.80
17900	157.78	160.82	163.87	167.09	170.14	173.36	176.59	179.81
18000	158.66	161.72	164.79	168.03	171.09	174.33	177.57	180.81
18100	159.54	162.62	165.70	168.96	172.04	175.30	178.56	181.81
18200	160.42	163.52	166.62	169.89	172.99	176.26	179.54	182.82
18300	161.31	164.42	167.53	170.83	173.94	177.23	180.53	183.83
18400	162.19	165.32	168.45	171.76	174.89	178.21	181.52	184.83
18500	163.07	166.22	169.36	172.69	175.85	179.18	182.51	185.84
18600	163.95	167.11	170.27	173.63	176.79	180.14	183.49	186.84
18700	164.83	168.01	171.20	174.56	177.74	181.11	184.48	187.84
18800	165.71	168.92	172.11	175.50	178.69	182.08	185.46	188.84
18900	166.60	169.81	173.03	176.43	179.64	183.04	186.45	189.86
19000	167.48	170.71	173.94	177.36	180.59	184.01	187.44	190.86
19100	168.36	171.61	174.85	178.29	181.54	184.99	188.43	191.86
19200	169.24	172.50	175.77	179.22	182.50	185.95	189.41	192.87
19300	170.12	173.40	176.68	180.17	183.45	186.92	190.40	193.87
19400	171.00	174.30	177.61	181.10	184.40	187.89	191.38	194.87
19500	171.88	175.21	178.52	182.03	185.35	188.86	192.37	195.88
19600	172.77	176.10	179.43	182.96	186.29	189.82	193.35	196.89
19700	173.65	177.00	180.35	183.89	187.24	190.79	194.35	197.89
19800	174.53	177.90	181.26	184.83	188.19	191.77	195.33	198.89
19900	175.41	178.79	182.18	185.76	189.15	192.73	196.32	199.90
20000	176.29	179.69	183.09	186.70	190.10	193.70	197.30	200.90
20100	177.17	180.59	184.01	187.63	191.05	194.67	198.29	201.90
20200	178.05	181.49	184.93	188.56	192.00	195.63	199.27	202.91
20300	178.94	182.39	185.84	189.50	192.95	196.60	200.26	203.92
20400	179.82	183.29	186.76	190.43	193.90	197.57	201.25	204.92
20500	180.70	184.19	187.67	191.36	194.86	198.55	202.24	205.93
20600	181.58	185.08	188.58	192.29	195.80	199.51	203.22	206.93
20700	182.46	185.98	189.50	193.23	196.75	200.48	204.21	207.93
20800	183.34	186.88	190.42	194.17	197.70	201.45	205.19	208.93
20900	184.22	187.78	191.34	195.10	198.65	202.41	206.18	209.95
21000	185.11	188.68	192.25	196.03	199.60	203.38	207.17	210.95
21100	185.99	189.58	193.16	196.96	200.55	204.36	208.16	211.95
21200	186.87	190.47	194.08	197.89	201.51	205.32	209.14	212.96
21300	187.75	191.37	194.99	198.84	202.46	206.29	210.13	213.96
21400	188.63	192.27	195.92	199.77	203.41	207.26	211.11	214.96
21500	189.51	193.17	196.83	200.70	204.36	208.23	212.10	215.97

MONTHLY PAYMENTS FOR 25-YR. FHA LOANS

INCLUDING FIRST YEAR ½% MORTGAGE INSURANCE PREMIUMS

AMOUNT	INTEREST							
	7.00%	7.25%	7.50%	7.75%	8.00%	8.25%	8.50%	8.75%
21600	161.65	165.11	168.56	172.24	175.70	179.37	183.05	186.72
21700	162.40	165.87	169.34	173.04	176.51	180.20	183.89	187.58
21800	163.15	166.63	170.13	173.84	177.33	181.03	184.74	188.45
21900	163.89	167.40	170.91	174.63	178.14	181.86	185.58	189.32
22000	164.64	168.17	171.69	175.43	178.95	182.69	186.44	190.18
22100	165.39	168.93	172.47	176.23	179.76	183.53	187.29	191.04
22200	166.14	169.70	173.25	177.02	180.58	184.36	188.13	191.91
22300	166.89	170.46	174.03	177.82	181.40	185.19	188.98	192.77
22400	167.64	171.22	174.81	178.62	182.21	186.02	189.82	193.63
22500	168.39	171.99	175.59	179.42	183.02	186.85	190.67	194.51
22600	169.13	172.75	176.37	180.22	183.83	187.67	191.52	195.37
22700	169.88	173.52	177.15	181.01	184.64	188.50	192.37	196.23
22800	170.63	174.28	177.93	181.81	185.46	189.34	193.22	197.09
22900	171.38	175.05	178.71	182.60	186.28	190.17	194.06	197.96
23000	172.13	175.81	179.49	183.40	187.09	191.00	194.91	198.82
23100	172.88	176.57	180.27	184.21	187.90	191.83	195.76	199.68
23200	173.62	177.34	181.05	185.00	188.71	192.66	196.60	200.56
23300	174.37	178.10	181.84	185.80	189.53	193.49	197.45	201.42
23400	175.12	178.86	182.62	186.59	190.34	194.32	198.30	202.28
23500	175.87	179.64	183.40	187.39	191.15	195.16	199.15	203.15
23600	176.62	180.40	184.17	188.19	191.97	195.98	200.00	204.01
23700	177.37	181.16	184.95	188.98	192.78	196.81	200.84	204.87
23800	178.12	181.92	185.73	189.79	193.60	197.64	201.69	205.73
23900	178.86	182.69	186.51	190.58	194.41	198.47	202.53	206.61
24000	179.61	183.45	187.30	191.38	195.22	199.30	203.38	207.47
24100	180.36	184.21	188.08	192.18	196.03	200.13	204.24	208.33
24200	181.10	184.99	188.86	192.97	196.84	200.97	205.08	209.20
24300	181.85	185.75	189.64	193.77	197.67	201.80	205.93	210.06
24400	182.61	186.51	190.42	194.56	198.48	202.63	206.77	210.92
24500	183.36	187.28	191.20	195.37	199.29	203.46	207.62	211.79
24600	184.10	188.04	191.97	196.17	200.10	204.28	208.47	212.66
24700	184.85	188.80	192.76	196.96	200.91	205.11	209.32	213.52
24800	185.60	189.56	193.54	197.76	201.73	205.94	210.17	214.38
24900	186.34	190.34	194.32	198.55	202.54	206.78	211.01	215.25
25000	187.09	191.10	195.10	199.35	203.35	207.61	211.86	216.11
25100	187.85	191.86	195.88	200.15	204.17	208.44	212.71	216.97
25200	188.59	192.63	196.66	200.94	204.98	209.27	213.55	217.84
25300	189.34	193.39	197.44	201.75	205.80	210.10	214.40	218.71
25400	190.09	194.15	198.23	202.54	206.61	210.93	215.25	219.57
25500	190.84	194.92	199.01	203.34	207.42	211.76	216.10	220.44
25600	191.58	195.69	199.78	204.14	208.23	212.59	216.95	221.30
25700	192.33	196.45	200.56	204.93	209.04	213.42	217.79	222.16
25800	193.09	197.21	201.34	205.73	209.87	214.25	218.64	223.02
25900	193.83	197.98	202.12	206.52	210.68	215.08	219.48	223.89
26000	194.58	198.74	202.90	207.33	211.49	215.91	220.33	224.76
26100	195.33	199.50	203.69	208.13	212.30	216.74	221.19	225.62
26200	196.07	200.27	204.47	208.92	213.11	217.57	222.03	226.49
26300	196.82	201.04	205.25	209.72	213.93	218.41	222.88	227.35
26400	197.57	201.80	206.03	210.51	214.74	219.24	223.72	228.21
26500	198.33	202.57	206.81	211.31	215.56	220.07	224.57	229.08
26600	199.07	203.33	207.58	212.11	216.37	220.89	225.42	229.94
26700	199.82	204.09	208.36	212.91	217.18	221.72	226.26	230.81
26800	200.57	204.85	209.15	213.71	218.00	222.55	227.12	231.67
26900	201.31	205.62	209.93	214.50	218.81	223.38	227.96	232.54
27000	202.06	206.38	210.71	215.30	219.62	224.22	228.81	233.40
27100	202.81	207.15	211.49	216.10	220.43	225.05	229.66	234.26
27200	203.55	207.92	212.27	216.89	221.25	225.88	230.50	235.13
27300	204.31	208.68	213.05	217.69	222.07	226.71	231.35	235.99
27400	205.06	209.44	213.83	218.49	222.88	227.54	232.19	236.86
27500	205.81	210.21	214.61	219.29	223.69	228.37	233.05	237.73

MONTHLY PAYMENTS FOR 25-YR. FHA LOANS

INCLUDING FIRST YEAR ½% MORTGAGE INSURANCE PREMIUMS

AMOUNT	INTEREST							
	9.00%	9.25%	9.50%	9.75%	10.00%	10.25%	10.50%	10.75%
21600	190.39	194.07	197.74	201.63	205.30	209.19	213.08	216.98
21700	191.28	194.97	198.66	202.56	206.25	210.16	214.08	217.98
21800	192.16	195.87	199.57	203.50	207.20	211.14	215.06	218.98
21900	193.04	196.76	200.49	204.43	208.16	212.10	216.05	219.99
22000	193.92	197.66	201.40	205.37	209.11	213.07	217.03	220.99
22100	194.80	198.56	202.32	206.30	210.06	214.04	218.02	221.99
22200	195.68	199.46	203.24	207.23	211.01	215.00	219.00	223.00
22300	196.56	200.36	204.15	208.17	211.96	215.97	219.99	224.01
22400	197.45	201.26	205.07	209.10	212.91	216.94	220.98	225.01
22500	198.33	202.16	205.98	210.03	213.86	217.92	221.97	226.02
22600	199.21	203.05	206.89	210.96	214.81	218.88	222.95	227.02
22700	200.09	203.95	207.81	211.90	215.76	219.85	223.94	228.02
22800	200.97	204.85	208.73	212.84	216.71	220.82	224.92	229.02
22900	201.85	205.75	209.65	213.77	217.66	221.78	225.91	230.04
23000	202.73	206.65	210.56	214.70	218.61	222.75	226.90	231.04
23100	203.62	207.55	211.47	215.63	219.56	223.73	227.89	232.04
23200	204.50	208.44	212.39	216.56	220.52	224.69	228.87	233.05
23300	205.38	209.34	213.30	217.50	221.47	225.66	229.86	234.05
23400	206.26	210.24	214.22	218.44	222.42	226.63	230.84	235.05
23500	207.14	211.14	215.14	219.37	223.37	227.60	231.83	236.06
23600	208.02	212.04	216.05	220.30	224.31	228.56	232.81	237.07
23700	208.90	212.94	216.97	221.23	225.26	229.53	233.81	238.07
23800	209.79	213.84	217.88	222.17	226.21	230.51	234.79	239.07
23900	210.67	214.73	218.80	223.10	227.17	231.47	235.78	240.08
24000	211.55	215.63	219.71	224.04	228.12	232.44	236.76	241.08
24100	212.43	216.53	220.62	224.97	229.07	233.41	237.75	242.08
24200	213.31	217.42	221.55	225.90	230.02	234.37	238.73	243.09
24300	214.19	218.33	222.46	226.84	230.97	235.34	239.72	244.10
24400	215.08	219.23	223.38	227.77	231.92	236.31	240.71	245.10
24500	215.96	220.13	224.29	228.70	232.87	237.29	241.70	246.11
24600	216.84	221.02	225.20	229.63	233.82	238.25	242.68	247.11
24700	217.72	221.92	226.12	230.57	234.77	239.22	243.67	248.11
24800	218.60	222.82	227.04	231.51	235.72	240.19	244.65	249.11
24900	219.48	223.71	227.96	232.44	236.67	241.15	245.64	250.13
25000	220.36	224.62	228.87	233.37	237.62	242.12	246.63	251.13
25100	221.25	225.52	229.78	234.30	238.57	243.10	247.62	252.13
25200	222.13	226.41	230.70	235.23	239.53	244.06	248.60	253.14
25300	223.01	227.31	231.61	236.17	240.48	245.03	249.59	254.14
25400	223.89	228.21	232.53	237.11	241.43	246.00	250.57	255.15
25500	224.77	229.11	233.45	238.04	242.38	246.97	251.56	256.15
25600	225.65	230.00	234.36	238.97	243.32	247.93	252.54	257.16
25700	226.53	230.91	235.28	239.90	244.27	248.90	253.54	258.16
25800	227.42	231.81	236.19	240.84	245.22	249.88	254.52	259.16
25900	228.30	232.70	237.11	241.77	246.18	250.84	255.51	260.17
26000	229.18	233.60	238.02	242.70	247.13	251.81	256.49	261.17
26100	230.06	234.50	238.93	243.64	248.08	252.78	257.48	262.17
26200	230.94	235.39	239.86	244.57	249.03	253.74	258.46	263.19
26300	231.82	236.30	240.77	245.51	249.98	254.71	259.45	264.19
26400	232.70	237.20	241.69	246.44	250.93	255.68	260.44	265.19
26500	233.59	238.10	242.60	247.37	251.88	256.66	261.43	266.20
26600	234.47	238.99	243.51	248.30	252.83	257.62	262.41	267.20
26700	235.35	239.89	244.43	249.24	253.78	258.59	263.40	268.20
26800	236.23	240.79	245.34	250.18	254.73	259.56	264.38	269.20
26900	237.11	241.68	246.27	251.11	255.68	260.52	265.37	270.22
27000	237.99	242.59	247.18	252.04	256.63	261.49	266.36	271.22
27100	238.87	243.49	248.09	252.97	257.58	262.47	267.35	272.22
27200	239.76	244.38	249.01	253.90	258.53	263.43	268.33	273.23
27300	240.64	245.28	249.92	254.84	259.49	264.40	269.32	274.23
27400	241.52	246.18	250.84	255.78	260.44	265.37	270.30	275.23
27500	242.40	247.08	251.76	256.71	261.39	266.34	271.29	276.24

MONTHLY PAYMENTS FOR 25-YR. FHA LOANS

INCLUDING FIRST YEAR ½% MORTGAGE INSURANCE PREMIUMS

AMOUNT	INTEREST							
	7.00%	7.25%	7.50%	7.75%	8.00%	8.25%	8.50%	8.75%
27600	206.55	210.97	215.39	220.09	224.50	229.19	233.90	238.59
27700	207.30	211.73	216.17	220.88	225.31	230.03	234.74	239.45
27800	208.05	212.50	216.95	221.68	226.13	230.86	235.59	240.31
27900	208.79	213.27	217.73	222.47	226.95	231.69	236.43	241.18
28000	209.55	214.03	218.51	223.27	227.76	232.52	237.28	242.04
28100	210.30	214.79	219.29	224.08	228.57	233.35	238.13	242.91
28200	211.04	215.56	220.07	224.87	229.38	234.18	238.98	243.78
28300	211.79	216.32	220.86	225.67	230.20	235.01	239.83	244.64
28400	212.54	217.08	221.64	226.46	231.01	235.85	240.67	245.50
28500	213.29	217.86	222.42	227.26	231.82	236.68	241.52	246.37
28600	214.03	218.62	223.19	228.06	232.64	237.50	242.37	247.23
28700	214.79	219.38	223.97	228.85	233.45	238.33	243.21	248.10
28800	215.54	220.14	224.75	229.66	234.27	239.16	244.06	248.96
28900	216.28	220.91	225.53	230.45	235.08	239.99	244.91	249.83
29000	217.03	221.67	226.32	231.25	235.89	240.82	245.76	250.69
29100	217.78	222.43	227.10	232.05	236.70	241.66	246.61	251.55
29200	218.52	223.21	227.88	232.84	237.51	242.49	247.45	252.42
29300	219.27	223.97	228.66	233.64	238.34	243.32	248.30	253.28
29400	220.03	224.73	229.44	234.43	239.15	244.15	249.14	254.15
29500	220.78	225.50	230.22	235.24	239.96	244.98	249.99	255.02
29600	221.52	226.26	230.99	236.04	240.77	245.80	250.85	255.88
29700	222.27	227.02	231.78	236.83	241.58	246.63	251.69	256.74
29800	223.02	227.78	232.56	237.63	242.40	247.47	252.54	257.60
29900	223.76	228.56	233.34	238.42	243.21	248.30	253.38	258.47
30000	224.51	229.32	234.12	239.22	244.03	249.13	254.23	259.33
30100	225.26	230.08	234.90	240.02	244.84	249.96	255.08	260.20
30200	226.01	230.85	235.68	240.82	245.65	250.79	255.92	261.07
30300	226.76	231.61	236.46	241.62	246.47	251.62	256.78	261.93
30400	227.51	232.37	237.25	242.41	247.28	252.45	257.62	262.79
30500	228.26	233.14	238.03	243.21	248.09	253.29	258.47	263.66
30600	229.00	233.90	238.80	244.01	248.90	254.11	259.32	264.52
30700	229.75	234.67	239.58	244.80	249.72	254.94	260.16	265.38
30800	230.50	235.43	240.36	245.60	250.54	255.77	261.01	266.25
30900	231.25	236.20	241.14	246.40	251.35	256.60	261.85	267.12
31000	232.00	236.96	241.92	247.20	252.16	257.43	262.71	267.98
31100	232.75	237.72	242.71	248.00	252.97	258.26	263.56	268.84
31200	233.49	238.49	243.49	248.79	253.78	259.10	264.40	269.71
31300	234.24	239.25	244.27	249.59	254.60	259.93	265.25	270.57
31400	234.99	240.02	245.05	250.38	255.42	260.76	266.09	271.43
31500	235.74	240.79	245.83	251.18	256.23	261.59	266.94	272.31
31600	236.49	241.55	246.60	251.99	257.04	262.41	267.79	273.17
31700	237.24	242.31	247.38	252.78	257.85	263.24	268.64	274.03
31800	237.99	243.07	248.17	253.58	258.67	264.07	269.49	274.89
31900	238.73	243.84	248.95	254.37	259.48	264.91	270.33	275.76
32000	239.48	244.60	249.73	255.17	260.29	265.74	271.18	276.62
32100	240.23	245.37	250.51	255.97	261.11	266.57	272.03	277.48
32200	240.97	246.14	251.29	256.76	261.92	267.40	272.87	278.36
32300	241.72	246.90	252.07	257.57	262.74	268.23	273.72	279.22
32400	242.48	247.66	252.85	258.36	263.55	269.06	274.57	280.09
32500	243.23	248.43	253.63	259.16	264.36	269.89	275.42	280.95
32600	243.97	249.19	254.41	259.96	265.17	270.72	276.27	281.81
32700	244.72	249.95	255.19	260.75	265.98	271.55	277.11	282.67
32800	245.47	250.72	255.97	261.55	266.81	272.38	277.96	283.53
32900	246.21	251.49	256.75	262.34	267.62	273.21	278.80	284.41
33000	246.96	252.25	257.53	263.14	268.43	274.04	279.65	285.27
33100	247.72	253.01	258.31	263.95	269.24	274.87	280.51	286.13
33200	248.46	253.78	259.09	264.74	270.05	275.70	281.35	287.00
33300	249.21	254.54	259.88	265.54	270.87	276.54	282.20	287.86
33400	249.96	255.30	260.66	266.33	271.68	277.37	283.04	288.72
33500	250.71	256.08	261.44	267.13	272.50	278.20	283.89	289.59

MONTHLY PAYMENTS FOR 25-YR. FHA LOANS

INCLUDING FIRST YEAR ½% MORTGAGE INSURANCE PREMIUMS

AMOUNT	INTEREST							
	9.00%	9.25%	9.50%	9.75%	10.00%	10.25%	10.50%	10.75%
27600	243.28	247.97	252.67	257.64	262.33	267.30	272.27	277.25
27700	244.16	248.88	253.59	258.57	263.28	268.27	273.27	278.25
27800	245.04	249.78	254.50	259.51	264.23	269.25	274.25	279.25
27900	245.93	250.67	255.42	260.44	265.19	270.21	275.24	280.26
28000	246.81	251.57	256.33	261.37	266.14	271.18	276.22	281.26
28100	247.69	252.47	257.24	262.31	267.09	272.15	277.21	282.26
28200	248.57	253.36	258.17	263.24	268.04	273.11	278.19	283.28
28300	249.45	254.26	259.08	264.18	268.99	274.08	279.18	284.28
28400	250.33	255.17	260.00	265.11	269.94	275.05	280.17	285.28
28500	251.21	256.07	260.91	266.04	270.89	276.03	281.16	286.29
28600	252.10	256.96	261.82	266.97	271.84	276.99	282.14	287.29
28700	252.98	257.86	262.74	267.90	272.79	277.96	283.13	288.29
28800	253.86	258.76	263.65	268.85	273.74	278.93	284.11	289.29
28900	254.74	259.65	264.58	269.78	274.69	279.89	285.10	290.31
29000	255.62	260.55	265.49	270.71	275.64	280.86	286.09	291.31
29100	256.50	261.46	266.40	271.64	276.59	281.84	287.08	292.31
29200	257.38	262.35	267.32	272.57	277.54	282.80	288.06	293.32
29300	258.27	263.25	268.23	273.51	278.50	283.77	289.05	294.32
29400	259.15	264.15	269.15	274.44	279.45	284.74	290.03	295.32
29500	260.03	265.05	270.06	275.38	280.40	285.71	291.02	296.33
29600	260.91	265.94	270.98	276.31	281.34	286.67	292.00	297.34
29700	261.79	266.84	271.90	277.24	282.29	287.64	293.00	298.34
29800	262.67	267.75	272.81	278.18	283.24	288.62	293.98	299.34
29900	263.56	268.64	273.73	279.11	284.20	289.58	294.97	300.35
30000	264.44	269.54	274.64	280.04	285.15	290.55	295.95	301.35
30100	265.32	270.44	275.55	280.98	286.10	291.52	296.94	302.35
30200	266.20	271.33	276.47	281.91	287.05	292.48	297.92	303.37
30300	267.08	272.23	277.39	282.85	288.00	293.45	298.91	304.37
30400	267.96	273.14	278.31	283.78	288.95	294.42	299.90	305.37
30500	268.84	274.04	279.22	284.71	289.90	295.40	300.89	306.38
30600	269.73	274.93	280.13	285.64	290.85	296.36	301.87	307.38
30700	270.61	275.83	281.05	286.57	291.80	297.33	302.86	308.38
30800	271.49	276.73	281.96	287.52	292.75	298.30	303.84	309.38
30900	272.37	277.62	282.89	288.45	293.70	299.26	304.83	310.40
31000	273.25	278.52	283.80	289.38	294.65	300.23	305.82	311.40
31100	274.13	279.43	284.71	290.31	295.60	301.20	306.81	312.40
31200	275.01	280.32	285.63	291.24	296.55	302.17	307.79	313.41
31300	275.90	281.22	286.54	292.18	297.51	303.14	308.78	314.41
31400	276.78	282.12	287.46	293.11	298.46	304.11	309.76	315.41
31500	277.66	283.02	288.37	294.05	299.41	305.08	310.75	316.43
31600	278.54	283.91	289.29	294.98	300.35	306.04	311.73	317.43
31700	279.42	284.81	290.21	295.91	301.30	307.01	312.73	318.43
31800	280.30	285.72	291.12	296.85	302.25	307.99	313.71	319.43
31900	281.18	286.61	292.04	297.78	303.20	308.95	314.70	320.44
32000	282.07	287.51	292.95	298.71	304.16	309.92	315.68	321.44
32100	282.95	288.41	293.86	299.64	305.11	310.89	316.67	322.44
32200	283.83	289.30	294.78	300.58	306.06	311.85	317.65	323.46
32300	284.71	290.20	295.70	301.52	307.01	312.82	318.64	324.46
32400	285.59	291.10	296.62	302.45	307.96	313.79	319.63	325.46
32500	286.47	292.01	297.53	303.38	308.91	314.77	320.62	326.47
32600	287.35	292.90	298.44	304.31	309.86	315.73	321.60	327.47
32700	288.24	293.80	299.36	305.24	310.81	316.70	322.59	328.47
32800	289.12	294.70	300.27	306.19	311.76	317.67	323.57	329.47
32900	290.00	295.59	301.19	307.12	312.71	318.63	324.56	330.49
33000	290.88	296.49	302.11	308.05	313.66	319.60	325.55	331.49
33100	291.76	297.39	303.02	308.98	314.61	320.57	326.54	332.49
33200	292.64	298.29	303.94	309.91	315.56	321.54	327.52	333.50
33300	293.52	299.19	304.85	310.85	316.52	322.51	328.51	334.50
33400	294.41	300.09	305.77	311.78	317.47	323.48	329.49	335.50
33500	295.29	300.99	306.68	312.72	318.42	324.45	330.48	336.52

147

MONTHLY PAYMENTS FOR 25-YR. FHA LOANS

INCLUDING FIRST YEAR ½% MORTGAGE INSURANCE PREMIUMS

AMOUNT	INTEREST							
	7.00%	7.25%	7.50%	7.75%	8.00%	8.25%	8.50%	8.75%
33600	251.45	256.84	262.21	267.93	273.31	279.02	284.74	290.46
33700	252.20	257.60	262.99	268.72	274.12	279.85	285.58	291.32
33800	252.96	258.36	263.77	269.53	274.94	280.68	286.44	292.18
33900	253.70	259.13	264.55	270.32	275.75	281.51	287.28	293.05
34000	254.45	259.89	265.34	271.12	276.56	282.35	288.13	293.91
34100	255.20	260.65	266.12	271.92	277.37	283.18	288.98	294.77
34200	255.94	261.42	266.90	272.71	278.19	284.01	289.82	295.64
34300	256.69	262.19	267.68	273.51	279.01	284.84	290.67	296.51
34400	257.44	262.95	268.46	274.30	279.82	285.67	291.51	297.37
34500	258.20	263.72	269.24	275.11	280.63	286.50	292.37	298.24
34600	258.94	264.48	270.01	275.91	281.44	287.32	293.22	299.10
34700	259.69	265.24	270.80	276.70	282.25	288.16	294.06	299.96
34800	260.44	266.00	271.58	277.50	283.07	288.99	294.91	300.82
34900	261.18	266.77	272.36	278.29	283.89	289.82	295.75	301.69
35000	261.93	267.54	273.14	279.09	284.70	290.65	296.60	302.56
35100	262.68	268.30	273.92	279.89	285.51	291.48	297.45	303.42
35200	263.42	269.07	274.70	280.69	286.32	292.31	298.30	304.29
35300	264.18	269.83	275.48	281.49	287.14	293.14	299.15	305.15
35400	264.93	270.59	276.27	282.28	287.95	293.98	299.99	306.01
35500	265.68	271.36	277.05	283.08	288.76	294.81	300.84	306.88
35600	266.42	272.12	277.82	283.88	289.58	295.63	301.69	307.74
35700	267.17	272.89	278.60	284.67	290.39	296.46	302.53	308.61
35800	267.92	273.65	279.38	285.47	291.21	297.29	303.38	309.47
35900	268.66	274.42	280.16	286.27	292.02	298.12	304.23	310.34
36000	269.42	275.18	280.94	287.07	292.83	298.95	305.08	311.20
36100	270.17	275.94	281.73	287.87	293.64	299.79	305.93	312.06
36200	270.91	276.71	282.51	288.66	294.45	300.62	306.77	312.93
36300	271.66	277.47	283.29	289.46	295.28	301.45	307.62	313.80
36400	272.41	278.24	284.07	290.25	296.09	302.28	308.46	314.66
36500	273.16	279.01	284.85	291.05	296.90	303.11	309.31	315.53
36600	273.90	279.77	285.62	291.86	297.71	303.93	310.17	316.39
36700	274.66	280.53	286.40	292.65	298.52	304.76	311.01	317.25
36800	275.41	281.29	287.19	293.45	299.34	305.60	311.86	318.11
36900	276.15	282.06	287.97	294.24	300.15	306.43	312.70	318.98
37000	276.90	282.82	288.75	295.04	300.97	307.26	313.55	319.85
37100	277.65	283.59	289.53	295.84	301.78	308.09	314.40	320.71
37200	278.39	284.36	290.31	296.63	302.59	308.92	315.24	321.58
37300	279.14	285.12	291.09	297.44	303.41	309.75	316.10	322.44
37400	279.90	285.88	291.87	298.23	304.22	310.58	316.94	323.30
37500	280.65	286.65	292.65	299.03	305.03	311.42	317.79	324.17
37600	281.39	287.41	293.43	299.83	305.84	312.24	318.64	325.03
37700	282.14	288.17	294.21	300.62	306.66	313.07	319.48	325.90
37800	282.89	288.93	294.99	301.42	307.48	313.90	320.33	326.76
37900	283.63	289.71	295.77	302.22	308.29	314.73	321.17	327.63
38000	284.38	290.47	296.55	303.02	309.10	315.56	322.03	328.49
38100	285.13	291.23	297.33	303.82	309.91	316.39	322.88	329.35
38200	285.88	292.00	298.11	304.61	310.72	317.23	323.72	330.22
38300	286.63	292.76	298.90	305.41	311.54	318.06	324.57	331.08
38400	287.38	293.52	299.68	306.20	312.36	318.89	325.41	331.95
38500	288.13	294.29	300.46	307.00	313.17	319.72	326.26	332.82
38600	288.87	295.06	301.23	307.80	313.98	320.54	327.11	333.68
38700	289.62	295.82	302.01	308.60	314.79	321.37	327.96	334.54
38800	290.37	296.58	302.79	309.40	315.61	322.20	328.81	335.40
38900	291.12	297.35	303.57	310.19	316.42	323.04	329.65	336.27
39000	291.87	298.11	304.36	310.99	317.23	323.87	330.50	337.13
39100	292.62	298.87	305.14	311.79	318.05	324.70	331.35	338.00
39200	293.36	299.64	305.92	312.58	318.86	325.53	332.19	338.86
39300	294.11	300.41	306.70	313.38	319.68	326.36	333.04	339.73
39400	294.86	301.17	307.48	314.18	320.49	327.19	333.89	340.59
39500	295.61	301.94	308.26	314.98	321.30	328.02	334.74	341.46

MONTHLY PAYMENTS FOR 25-YR. FHA LOANS

INCLUDING FIRST YEAR ½% MORTGAGE INSURANCE PREMIUMS

AMOUNT	INTEREST							
	9.00%	9.25%	9.50%	9.75%	10.00%	10.25%	10.50%	10.75%
33600	296.17	301.88	307.59	313.65	319.36	325.41	331.46	337.52
33700	297.05	302.78	308.52	314.58	320.31	326.38	332.46	338.52
33800	297.93	303.68	309.43	315.52	321.26	327.36	333.44	339.52
33900	298.81	304.58	310.35	316.45	322.21	328.32	334.43	340.53
34000	299.69	305.48	311.26	317.38	323.17	329.29	335.41	341.53
34100	300.58	306.38	312.17	318.31	324.12	330.26	336.40	342.53
34200	301.46	307.27	313.09	319.25	325.07	331.22	337.38	343.55
34300	302.34	308.17	314.01	320.19	326.02	332.19	338.37	344.55
34400	303.22	309.07	314.93	321.12	326.97	333.16	339.36	345.55
34500	304.10	309.98	315.84	322.05	327.92	334.14	340.35	346.56
34600	304.98	310.87	316.75	322.98	328.86	335.10	341.33	347.56
34700	305.86	311.77	317.67	323.91	329.82	336.07	342.32	348.56
34800	306.75	312.67	318.58	324.85	330.77	337.04	343.30	349.56
34900	307.63	313.56	319.50	325.79	331.72	338.00	344.29	350.58
35000	308.51	314.46	320.42	326.72	332.67	338.97	345.28	351.58
35100	309.39	315.36	321.33	327.65	333.62	339.94	346.27	352.58
35200	310.27	316.26	322.25	328.58	334.57	340.91	347.25	353.59
35300	311.15	317.16	323.16	329.52	335.53	341.88	348.24	354.59
35400	312.04	318.06	324.08	330.45	336.48	342.85	349.22	355.59
35500	312.92	318.96	324.99	331.39	337.43	343.82	350.21	356.61
35600	313.80	319.85	325.90	332.32	338.37	344.78	351.19	357.61
35700	314.68	320.75	326.83	333.25	339.32	345.75	352.19	358.61
35800	315.56	321.65	327.74	334.19	340.27	346.73	353.17	359.61
35900	316.44	322.55	328.66	335.12	341.22	347.69	354.16	360.62
36000	317.32	323.45	329.57	336.05	342.18	348.66	355.14	361.62
36100	318.21	324.35	330.48	336.98	343.13	349.63	356.13	362.62
36200	319.09	325.24	331.40	337.92	344.08	350.59	357.11	363.64
36300	319.97	326.14	332.31	338.86	345.03	351.56	358.11	364.64
36400	320.85	327.04	333.24	339.79	345.98	352.53	359.09	365.64
36500	321.73	327.94	334.15	340.72	346.93	353.51	360.08	366.65
36600	322.61	328.84	335.06	341.65	347.87	354.47	361.06	367.65
36700	323.49	329.74	335.98	342.58	348.83	355.44	362.05	368.65
36800	324.38	330.64	336.89	343.52	349.78	356.41	363.03	369.65
36900	325.26	331.53	337.81	344.46	350.73	357.37	364.02	370.67
37000	326.14	332.43	338.72	345.39	351.68	358.34	365.01	371.67
37100	327.02	333.33	339.64	346.32	352.63	359.31	366.00	372.67
37200	327.90	334.22	340.56	347.25	353.58	360.28	366.98	373.68
37300	328.78	335.13	341.47	348.19	354.54	361.25	367.97	374.68
37400	329.66	336.03	342.39	349.12	355.49	362.22	368.95	375.68
37500	330.55	336.93	343.30	350.05	356.44	363.19	369.94	376.70
37600	331.43	337.82	344.21	350.99	357.38	364.15	370.92	377.70
37700	332.31	338.72	345.14	351.92	358.33	365.12	371.92	378.70
37800	333.19	339.62	346.05	352.86	359.28	366.10	372.90	379.70
37900	334.07	340.51	346.97	353.79	360.23	367.06	373.89	380.71
38000	334.95	341.42	347.88	354.72	361.19	368.03	374.87	381.71
38100	335.83	342.32	348.79	355.65	362.14	369.00	375.86	382.71
38200	336.72	343.21	349.71	356.59	363.09	369.96	376.84	383.73
38300	337.60	344.11	350.62	357.53	364.04	370.93	377.84	384.73
38400	338.48	345.01	351.55	358.46	364.99	371.90	378.82	385.73
38500	339.36	345.91	352.46	359.39	365.94	372.88	379.81	386.74
38600	340.24	346.81	353.37	360.32	366.88	373.84	380.79	387.74
38700	341.12	347.71	354.29	361.25	367.84	374.81	381.78	388.74
38800	342.00	348.61	355.20	362.19	368.79	375.78	382.76	389.75
38900	342.89	349.50	356.12	363.13	369.74	376.74	383.75	390.76
39000	343.77	350.40	357.03	364.06	370.69	377.71	384.74	391.76
39100	344.65	351.30	357.95	364.99	371.64	378.68	385.73	392.76
39200	345.53	352.19	358.87	365.92	372.59	379.65	386.71	393.77
39300	346.41	353.10	359.78	366.86	373.54	380.62	387.70	394.77
39400	347.29	354.00	360.70	367.79	374.50	381.59	388.68	395.77
39500	348.17	354.90	361.61	368.72	375.45	382.56	389.67	396.79

MONTHLY PAYMENTS FOR 25-YR. FHA LOANS

INCLUDING FIRST YEAR ½% MORTGAGE INSURANCE PREMIUMS

AMOUNT	INTEREST							
	7.00%	7.25%	7.50%	7.75%	8.00%	8.25%	8.50%	8.75%
39600	296.36	302.70	309.03	315.78	322.11	328.85	335.59	342.32
39700	297.11	303.46	309.82	316.57	322.92	329.68	336.43	343.18
39800	297.86	304.22	310.60	317.37	323.75	330.51	337.28	344.05
39900	298.60	304.99	311.38	318.16	324.56	331.34	338.12	344.92
40000	299.35	305.76	312.16	318.96	325.37	332.17	338.97	345.78
40100	300.10	306.52	312.94	319.76	326.18	333.00	339.83	346.64
40200	300.84	307.29	313.72	320.56	326.99	333.83	340.67	347.51
40300	301.60	308.05	314.50	321.36	327.81	334.67	341.52	348.37
40400	302.35	308.81	315.29	322.15	328.62	335.50	342.36	349.23
40500	303.10	309.58	316.07	322.95	329.44	336.33	343.21	350.11
40600	303.84	310.34	316.84	323.75	330.25	337.15	344.06	350.97
40700	304.59	311.11	317.62	324.54	331.06	337.98	344.91	351.83
40800	305.34	311.87	318.40	325.34	331.88	338.81	345.76	352.69
40900	306.08	312.64	319.18	326.14	332.69	339.64	346.60	353.56
41000	306.83	313.40	319.96	326.94	333.50	340.48	347.45	354.42
41100	307.59	314.16	320.75	327.74	334.31	341.31	348.30	355.28
41200	308.33	314.93	321.53	328.53	335.12	342.14	349.14	356.16
41300	309.08	315.69	322.31	329.33	335.95	342.97	349.99	357.02
41400	309.83	316.45	323.09	330.12	336.76	343.80	350.84	357.88
41500	310.58	317.23	323.87	330.92	337.57	344.63	351.69	358.75
41600	311.32	317.99	324.64	331.73	338.38	345.45	352.54	359.61
41700	312.07	318.75	325.42	332.52	339.19	346.29	353.38	360.47
41800	312.83	319.51	326.21	333.32	340.01	347.12	354.23	361.33
41900	313.57	320.28	326.99	334.11	340.82	347.95	355.07	362.21
42000	314.32	321.04	327.77	334.91	341.64	348.78	355.92	363.07
42100	315.07	321.81	328.55	335.71	342.45	349.61	356.78	363.93
42200	315.81	322.58	329.33	336.50	343.26	350.44	357.62	364.80
42300	316.56	323.34	330.11	337.31	344.08	351.27	358.47	365.66
42400	317.31	324.10	330.89	338.10	344.89	352.11	359.31	366.52
42500	318.07	324.87	331.67	338.90	345.70	352.94	360.16	367.39
42600	318.81	325.63	332.45	339.70	346.51	353.76	361.01	368.26
42700	319.56	326.39	333.23	340.49	347.33	354.59	361.85	369.12
42800	320.31	327.15	334.01	341.29	348.15	355.43	362.71	369.98
42900	321.05	327.93	334.79	342.08	348.96	356.25	363.55	370.85
43000	321.80	328.69	335.57	342.89	349.77	357.08	364.40	371.71
43200	323.30	330.22	337.13	344.48	351.39	358.75	366.09	373.44
43400	324.80	331.74	338.70	346.07	353.03	360.41	367.78	375.17
43600	326.29	333.28	340.25	347.67	354.65	362.06	369.49	376.90
43800	327.79	334.80	341.81	349.27	356.28	363.73	371.18	378.62
44000	329.29	336.33	343.38	350.86	357.90	365.39	372.87	380.36
44200	330.78	337.86	344.94	352.45	359.53	367.05	374.57	382.09
44400	332.28	339.39	346.50	354.05	361.16	368.71	376.26	383.81
44600	333.77	340.92	348.05	355.65	362.78	370.37	377.96	385.55
44800	335.28	342.44	349.62	357.24	364.42	372.03	379.65	387.27
45000	336.77	343.97	351.18	358.83	366.04	373.69	381.35	389.00
45200	338.26	345.51	352.74	360.43	367.66	375.36	383.04	390.73
45400	339.77	347.03	354.31	362.02	369.29	377.02	384.73	392.46
45600	341.26	348.56	355.86	363.62	370.92	378.67	386.44	394.19
45800	342.76	350.09	357.42	365.22	372.55	380.33	388.13	395.91
46000	344.25	351.62	358.98	366.81	374.17	382.00	389.82	397.65
46200	345.75	353.15	360.55	368.40	375.80	383.66	391.51	399.38
46400	347.25	354.67	362.11	369.99	377.43	385.32	393.21	401.10
46600	348.74	356.21	363.66	371.60	379.05	386.98	394.91	402.83
46800	350.24	357.73	365.23	373.19	380.68	388.64	396.60	404.56
47000	351.74	359.26	366.79	374.78	382.31	390.30	398.30	406.29
47200	353.23	360.80	368.35	376.37	383.93	391.96	399.99	408.02
47400	354.73	362.32	369.91	377.97	385.56	393.63	401.68	409.75
47600	356.23	363.85	371.47	379.57	387.19	395.28	403.38	411.48
47800	357.73	365.37	373.03	381.16	388.82	396.94	405.08	413.20
48000	359.22	366.91	374.59	382.76	390.44	398.61	406.77	414.93

MONTHLY PAYMENTS FOR 25-YR. FHA LOANS

INCLUDING FIRST YEAR ½% MORTGAGE INSURANCE PREMIUMS

AMOUNT	9.00%	9.25%	9.50%	9.75%	10.00%	10.25%	10.50%	10.75%
39600	349.06	355.79	362.52	369.66	376.39	383.52	390.65	397.79
39700	349.94	356.69	363.44	370.59	377.34	384.49	391.65	398.79
39800	350.82	357.59	364.36	371.53	378.29	385.46	392.63	399.79
39900	351.70	358.48	365.28	372.46	379.24	386.43	393.62	400.80
40000	352.58	359.39	366.19	373.39	380.20	387.40	394.60	401.80
40100	353.46	360.29	367.11	374.32	381.15	388.37	395.59	402.80
40200	354.34	361.18	368.02	375.25	382.10	389.33	396.57	403.82
40300	355.23	362.08	368.93	376.20	383.05	390.30	397.57	404.82
40400	356.11	362.98	369.86	377.13	384.00	391.27	398.55	405.82
40500	356.99	363.88	370.77	378.06	384.95	392.25	399.54	406.83
40600	357.87	364.77	371.68	378.99	385.89	393.21	400.52	407.83
40700	358.75	365.68	372.60	379.92	386.85	394.18	401.51	408.83
40800	359.63	366.58	373.51	380.86	387.80	395.15	402.49	409.84
40900	360.52	367.47	374.43	381.80	388.75	396.11	403.48	410.85
41000	361.40	368.37	375.34	382.73	389.70	397.08	404.47	411.85
41100	362.28	369.27	376.26	383.66	390.65	398.05	405.46	412.85
41200	363.16	370.16	377.18	384.59	391.60	399.02	406.44	413.86
41300	364.04	371.06	378.09	385.53	392.55	399.99	407.43	414.86
41400	364.92	371.97	379.01	386.46	393.51	400.96	408.41	415.86
41500	365.80	372.87	379.92	387.39	394.46	401.93	409.40	416.88
41600	366.69	373.76	380.83	388.33	395.40	402.89	410.38	417.88
41700	367.57	374.66	381.75	389.26	396.35	403.86	411.38	418.88
41800	368.45	375.56	382.67	390.20	397.30	404.83	412.36	419.88
41900	369.33	376.45	383.59	391.13	398.25	405.80	413.35	420.89
42000	370.21	377.35	384.50	392.06	399.21	406.77	414.33	421.89
42100	371.09	378.26	385.41	392.99	400.16	407.74	415.32	422.89
42200	371.97	379.15	386.33	393.92	401.11	408.70	416.30	423.91
42300	372.86	380.05	387.24	394.87	402.06	409.67	417.30	424.91
42400	373.74	380.95	388.16	395.80	403.01	410.64	418.28	425.91
42500	374.62	381.85	389.08	396.73	403.96	411.62	419.27	426.92
42600	375.50	382.74	389.99	397.66	404.90	412.58	420.25	427.92
42700	376.38	383.65	390.91	398.59	405.86	413.55	421.24	428.92
42800	377.26	384.55	391.82	399.53	406.81	414.52	422.22	429.93
42900	378.14	385.44	392.74	400.46	407.76	415.48	423.21	430.94
43000	379.03	386.34	393.65	401.40	408.71	416.45	424.20	431.94
43200	380.79	388.13	395.49	403.26	410.61	418.39	426.17	433.95
43400	382.55	389.94	397.32	405.13	412.52	420.33	428.14	435.95
43600	384.31	391.73	399.14	407.00	414.41	422.26	430.11	437.97
43800	386.08	393.53	400.98	408.87	416.31	424.20	432.09	439.97
44000	387.84	395.32	402.81	410.73	418.21	426.14	434.06	441.98
44200	389.60	397.12	404.64	412.59	420.12	428.07	436.03	444.00
44400	391.37	398.92	406.47	414.47	422.02	430.01	438.01	446.00
44600	393.13	400.71	408.30	416.33	423.91	431.95	439.98	448.01
44800	394.89	402.52	410.13	418.20	425.82	433.89	441.95	450.02
45000	396.65	404.31	411.96	420.07	427.72	435.82	443.93	452.03
45200	398.42	406.10	413.80	421.93	429.62	437.76	445.90	454.04
45400	400.18	407.90	415.63	423.80	431.53	439.70	447.87	456.04
45600	401.94	409.70	417.45	425.66	433.42	441.63	449.84	458.06
45800	403.71	411.50	419.28	427.54	435.32	443.57	451.82	460.06
46000	405.47	413.29	421.12	429.40	437.22	445.51	453.79	462.07
46200	407.23	415.09	422.95	431.26	439.13	447.44	455.76	464.09
46400	409.00	416.89	424.78	433.14	441.03	449.38	457.74	466.09
46600	410.76	418.68	426.61	435.00	442.92	451.32	459.71	468.10
46800	412.52	420.49	428.44	436.87	444.83	453.26	461.68	470.11
47000	414.28	422.28	430.27	438.74	446.73	455.19	463.66	472.12
47200	416.05	424.07	432.11	440.60	448.63	457.13	465.63	474.13
47400	417.81	425.87	433.94	442.47	450.54	459.07	467.60	476.13
47600	419.57	427.67	435.76	444.33	452.43	461.00	469.57	478.15
47800	421.34	429.47	437.59	446.21	454.33	462.94	471.55	480.15
48000	423.10	431.26	439.43	448.07	456.23	464.88	473.52	482.16

MONTHLY PAYMENTS FOR 25-YR. FHA LOANS

INCLUDING FIRST YEAR ½% MORTGAGE INSURANCE PREMIUMS

AMOUNT	INTEREST							
	7.00%	7.25%	7.50%	7.75%	8.00%	8.25%	8.50%	8.75%
48200	360.71	368.44	376.15	384.35	392.06	400.27	408.46	416.67
48400	362.22	369.96	377.72	385.94	393.70	401.93	410.16	418.39
48600	363.71	371.49	379.27	387.54	395.32	403.58	411.86	420.12
48800	365.21	373.02	380.83	389.14	396.95	405.25	413.55	421.85
49000	366.71	374.55	382.40	390.73	398.58	406.91	415.24	423.58
49200	368.20	376.08	383.96	392.32	400.20	408.57	416.94	425.31
49400	369.70	377.61	385.52	393.92	401.83	410.24	418.63	427.03
49600	371.19	379.14	387.07	395.52	403.45	411.89	420.33	428.77
49800	372.70	380.66	388.64	397.11	405.09	413.55	422.03	430.49
50000	374.19	382.19	390.20	398.70	406.71	415.21	423.72	432.22
50200	375.68	383.73	391.76	400.30	408.33	416.88	425.41	433.96
50400	377.18	385.25	393.33	401.89	409.97	418.54	427.10	435.68
50600	378.68	386.78	394.88	403.49	411.59	420.19	428.81	437.41
50800	380.18	388.31	396.44	405.09	413.22	421.86	430.50	439.13
51000	381.67	389.84	398.00	406.68	414.84	423.52	432.19	440.87
51200	383.17	391.37	399.57	408.27	416.47	425.18	433.89	442.60
51400	384.67	392.89	401.13	409.86	418.10	426.84	435.58	444.32
51600	386.16	394.43	402.68	411.47	419.72	428.50	437.28	446.06
51800	387.66	395.95	404.25	413.06	421.36	430.16	438.97	447.78
52000	389.16	397.48	405.81	414.65	422.98	431.82	440.67	449.51
52200	390.65	399.01	407.37	416.25	424.60	433.49	442.36	451.24
52400	392.15	400.54	408.93	417.84	426.23	435.15	444.05	452.97
52600	393.64	402.07	410.49	419.44	427.86	436.80	445.76	454.70
52800	395.15	403.59	412.05	421.03	429.49	438.46	447.45	456.42
53000	396.64	405.13	413.61	422.63	431.11	440.13	449.14	458.16
53200	398.13	406.66	415.17	424.22	432.74	441.79	450.83	459.89
53400	399.64	408.18	416.74	425.81	434.37	443.45	452.53	461.61
53600	401.13	409.71	418.29	427.42	435.99	445.11	454.23	463.35
53800	402.63	411.24	419.85	429.01	437.62	446.77	455.92	465.07
54000	404.12	412.77	421.42	430.60	439.25	448.43	457.62	466.80
54200	405.62	414.30	422.98	432.19	440.87	450.09	459.31	468.53
54400	407.12	415.83	424.54	433.79	442.50	451.76	461.00	470.26
54600	408.61	417.36	426.09	435.39	444.13	453.41	462.70	471.99
54800	410.11	418.88	427.66	436.98	445.76	455.07	464.40	473.71
55000	411.61	420.41	429.22	438.57	447.38	456.74	466.09	475.45
55200	413.10	421.95	430.78	440.17	449.00	458.40	467.78	477.18
55400	414.60	423.47	432.35	441.76	450.64	460.06	469.48	478.90
55600	416.10	425.00	433.90	443.36	452.26	461.71	471.18	480.63
55800	417.60	426.52	435.46	444.96	453.89	463.38	472.87	482.36
56000	419.09	428.06	437.02	446.55	455.52	465.04	474.56	484.09
56200	420.58	429.59	438.59	448.14	457.14	466.70	476.26	485.82
56400	422.09	431.11	440.15	449.73	458.77	468.37	477.95	487.55
56600	423.58	432.65	441.70	451.34	460.39	470.02	479.65	489.28
56800	425.08	434.17	443.27	452.93	462.03	471.68	481.35	491.00
57000	426.58	435.70	444.83	454.52	463.65	473.34	483.04	492.73
57200	428.07	437.23	446.39	456.12	465.27	475.01	484.73	494.47
57400	429.57	438.76	447.95	457.71	466.90	476.67	486.43	496.19
57600	431.06	440.29	449.51	459.31	468.53	478.32	488.13	497.92
57800	432.57	441.81	451.07	460.90	470.16	479.99	489.82	499.65
58000	434.06	443.35	452.63	462.50	471.78	481.65	491.51	501.38
58200	435.55	444.88	454.19	464.09	473.41	483.31	493.21	503.11
58400	437.05	446.40	455.76	465.68	475.04	484.97	494.90	504.83
58600	438.55	447.93	457.31	467.29	476.66	486.63	496.60	506.57
58800	440.05	449.46	458.87	468.88	478.29	488.29	498.30	508.29
59000	441.54	450.99	460.44	470.47	479.92	489.95	499.99	510.02
59200	443.04	452.52	462.00	472.06	481.54	491.62	501.68	511.76
59400	444.54	454.04	463.56	473.66	483.17	493.28	503.37	513.48
59600	446.03	455.58	465.11	475.26	484.80	494.93	505.08	515.21
59800	447.53	457.10	466.68	476.85	486.43	496.59	506.77	516.93
60000	449.03	458.63	468.24	478.45	488.05	498.26	508.46	518.67

MONTHLY PAYMENTS FOR 25-YR. FHA LOANS

INCLUDING FIRST YEAR ½% MORTGAGE INSURANCE PREMIUMS

AMOUNT	INTEREST							
	9.00%	9.25%	9.50%	9.75%	10.00%	10.25%	10.50%	10.75%
48200	424.86	433.06	441.26	449.93	458.14	466.81	475.49	484.18
48400	426.62	434.86	443.09	451.81	460.04	468.75	477.47	486.18
48600	428.39	436.65	444.92	453.67	461.93	470.69	479.44	488.19
48800	430.15	438.45	446.75	455.54	463.84	472.63	481.41	490.20
49000	431.91	440.25	448.58	457.40	465.74	474.56	483.39	492.21
49200	433.68	442.04	450.41	459.27	467.64	476.50	485.36	494.22
49400	435.44	443.84	452.25	461.14	469.55	478.44	487.33	496.22
49600	437.20	445.64	454.07	463.00	471.44	480.37	489.30	498.24
49800	438.96	447.44	455.90	464.88	473.34	482.31	491.28	500.24
50000	440.73	449.23	457.74	466.74	475.24	484.25	493.25	502.25
50200	442.49	451.02	459.57	468.60	477.15	486.18	495.22	504.27
50400	444.25	452.83	461.40	470.48	479.05	488.12	497.20	506.27
50600	446.02	454.62	463.23	472.34	480.94	490.06	499.17	508.28
50800	447.78	456.42	465.06	474.21	482.85	492.00	501.14	510.29
51000	449.54	458.22	466.89	476.07	484.75	493.93	503.12	512.30
51200	451.31	460.01	468.72	477.94	486.65	495.87	505.09	514.31
51400	453.07	461.81	470.56	479.81	488.56	497.81	507.06	516.32
51600	454.83	463.61	472.38	481.67	490.45	499.74	509.03	518.33
51800	456.59	465.41	474.21	483.55	492.35	501.68	511.01	520.33
52000	458.36	467.20	476.05	485.41	494.25	503.62	512.98	522.34
52200	460.12	468.99	477.88	487.27	496.16	505.55	514.95	524.36
52400	461.88	470.80	479.71	489.15	498.06	507.49	516.93	526.36
52600	463.65	472.59	481.53	491.01	499.95	509.43	518.90	528.37
52800	465.41	474.39	483.37	492.88	501.86	511.37	520.87	530.38
53000	467.17	476.19	485.20	494.74	503.76	513.30	522.85	532.39
53200	468.93	477.98	487.03	496.61	505.66	515.24	524.82	534.40
53400	470.70	479.78	488.87	498.48	507.56	517.18	526.79	536.41
53600	472.46	481.57	490.69	500.34	509.46	519.11	528.76	538.42
53800	474.22	483.38	492.52	502.22	511.36	521.05	530.74	540.42
54000	475.99	485.17	494.36	504.08	513.26	522.99	532.71	542.43
54200	477.75	486.96	496.19	505.94	515.17	524.92	534.68	544.45
54400	479.51	488.77	498.02	507.81	517.07	526.86	536.66	546.45
54600	481.27	490.56	499.84	509.68	518.96	528.80	538.63	548.46
54800	483.04	492.36	501.68	511.55	520.87	530.74	540.60	550.47
55000	484.80	494.16	503.51	513.41	522.77	532.67	542.58	552.48
55200	486.56	495.95	505.34	515.28	524.67	534.61	544.55	554.49
55400	488.33	497.75	507.18	517.15	526.57	536.55	546.52	556.50
55600	490.09	499.54	509.00	519.01	528.47	538.48	548.49	558.51
55800	491.85	501.35	510.83	520.89	530.37	540.42	550.47	560.51
56000	493.61	503.14	512.66	522.75	532.27	542.36	552.44	562.52
56200	495.38	504.93	514.50	524.61	534.18	544.29	554.41	564.54
56400	497.14	506.74	516.33	526.48	536.08	546.23	556.39	566.54
56600	498.90	508.53	518.15	528.35	537.97	548.17	558.36	568.55
56800	500.67	510.33	519.99	530.22	539.88	550.11	560.33	570.56
57000	502.43	512.12	521.82	532.08	541.78	552.04	562.31	572.57
57200	504.19	513.92	523.65	533.95	543.68	553.98	564.28	574.58
57400	505.95	515.72	525.49	535.82	545.58	555.92	566.25	576.59
57600	507.72	517.51	527.31	537.68	547.48	557.85	568.22	578.60
57800	509.48	519.32	529.14	539.56	549.38	559.79	570.20	580.60
58000	511.24	521.11	530.97	541.42	551.28	561.73	572.17	582.61
58200	513.01	522.90	532.81	543.28	553.19	563.66	574.14	584.63
58400	514.77	524.70	534.64	545.15	555.09	565.60	576.12	586.63
58600	516.53	526.50	536.46	547.02	556.98	567.54	578.09	588.64
58800	518.30	528.30	538.30	548.89	558.89	569.48	580.06	590.65
59000	520.06	530.09	540.13	550.75	560.79	571.41	582.04	592.66
59200	521.82	531.89	541.96	552.62	562.69	573.34	584.01	594.67
59400	523.58	533.69	543.79	554.49	564.59	575.29	585.98	596.68
59600	525.35	535.48	545.62	556.35	566.49	577.22	587.95	598.69
59800	527.11	537.29	547.45	558.23	568.39	579.16	589.93	600.69
60000	528.87	539.08	549.28	560.09	570.29	581.10	591.90	602.70

MONTHLY PAYMENTS FOR 30-YR. FHA LOANS

INCLUDING FIRST YEAR ½% MORTGAGE INSURANCE PREMIUMS

AMOUNT	INTEREST							
	7.00%	7.25%	7.50%	7.75%	8.00%	8.25%	8.50%	8.75%
50	.35	.36	.37	.38	.39	.40	.40	.41
100	.71	.72	.74	.76	.77	.79	.81	.83
250	1.77	1.81	1.85	1.89	1.94	1.98	2.02	2.07
500	3.54	3.63	3.71	3.80	3.88	3.97	4.06	4.15
10000	70.75	72.45	74.15	75.85	77.55	79.35	81.05	82.85
10100	71.46	73.17	74.89	76.61	78.32	80.14	81.86	83.68
10200	72.16	73.90	75.63	77.36	79.10	80.93	82.68	84.51
10300	72.87	74.62	76.37	78.12	79.88	81.74	83.49	85.34
10400	73.57	75.34	77.12	78.89	80.66	82.53	84.30	86.17
10500	74.28	76.08	77.86	79.65	81.43	83.32	85.11	87.00
10600	75.00	76.80	78.60	80.40	82.20	84.11	85.91	87.82
10700	75.70	77.52	79.34	81.16	82.98	84.90	86.72	88.65
10800	76.41	78.24	80.08	81.92	83.75	85.70	87.53	89.49
10900	77.11	78.97	80.82	82.67	84.53	86.50	88.35	90.31
11000	77.82	79.69	81.56	83.44	85.31	87.29	89.16	91.14
11100	78.53	80.41	82.31	84.20	86.08	88.08	89.97	91.97
11200	79.24	81.15	83.05	84.95	86.86	88.87	90.78	92.79
11300	79.95	81.87	83.79	85.71	87.63	89.67	91.59	93.62
11400	80.65	82.59	84.53	86.47	88.41	90.46	92.40	94.45
11500	81.36	83.32	85.27	87.23	89.18	91.25	93.22	95.29
11600	82.07	84.04	86.01	87.98	89.96	92.05	94.02	96.11
11700	82.77	84.76	86.75	88.75	90.74	92.84	94.83	96.94
11800	83.48	85.48	87.50	89.51	91.51	93.64	95.64	97.77
11900	84.19	86.22	88.24	90.26	92.29	94.43	96.45	98.59
12000	84.90	86.94	88.98	91.02	93.06	95.22	97.26	99.42
12100	85.61	87.66	89.72	91.78	93.83	96.01	98.07	100.26
12200	86.31	88.39	90.46	92.53	94.61	96.80	88.89	101.08
12300	87.02	89.11	91.20	93.29	95.39	97.61	99.70	101.91
12400	87.72	89.83	91.94	94.06	96.17	98.40	100.51	102.74
12500	88.43	90.57	92.69	94.82	96.94	99.19	101.32	103.57
12600	89.15	91.29	93.43	95.57	97.71	99.98	102.12	104.39
12700	89.85	92.01	94.17	96.33	98.49	100.77	102.93	105.22
12800	90.56	92.73	94.91	97.09	99.26	101.57	103.75	106.06
12900	91.26	93.46	95.65	97.84	100.04	102.37	104.56	106.88
13000	91.97	94.18	96.39	98.61	100.82	103.16	105.37	107.71
13100	92.68	94.90	97.14	99.37	101.59	103.95	106.18	108.54
13200	93.38	95.64	97.88	100.12	102.37	104.74	106.99	109.36
13300	94.10	96.36	98.62	100.88	103.14	105.54	107.80	110.19
13400	94.80	97.08	99.36	101.64	103.92	106.33	108.61	111.03
13500	95.51	97.81	100.10	102.40	104.69	107.12	109.43	111.86
13600	96.22	98.53	100.84	103.15	105.47	107.92	110.23	112.68
13700	96.92	99.25	101.58	103.92	106.25	108.71	111.04	113.51
13800	97.63	99.97	102.33	104.68	107.02	109.51	111.85	114.34
13900	98.33	100.71	103.07	105.43	107.80	110.30	112.66	115.16
14000	99.05	101.43	103.81	106.19	108.57	111.09	113.47	115.99
14100	99.76	102.15	104.55	106.95	109.34	111.88	114.28	116.83
14200	100.46	102.88	105.29	107.70	110.12	112.68	115.10	117.65
14300	101.17	103.60	106.03	108.46	110.90	113.48	115.91	118.48
14400	101.87	104.32	106.77	109.23	111.68	114.27	116.72	119.31
14500	102.58	105.05	107.52	109.99	112.45	115.06	117.53	120.14
14600	103.30	105.78	108.26	110.74	113.22	115.85	118.33	120.96
14700	104.00	106.50	109.00	111.50	114.00	116.64	119.14	121.80
14800	104.71	107.22	109.74	112.26	114.77	117.44	119.96	122.63
14900	105.41	107.95	110.48	113.01	115.55	118.24	120.77	123.45
15000	106.12	108.67	111.22	113.78	116.33	119.03	121.58	124.28
15100	106.83	109.39	111.97	114.54	117.10	119.82	122.39	125.11
15200	107.53	110.13	112.71	115.29	117.88	120.61	123.20	125.93
15300	108.25	110.85	113.45	116.05	118.65	121.41	124.01	126.76
15400	108.95	111.57	114.19	116.81	119.43	122.20	124.82	127.60
15500	109.66	112.30	114.93	117.57	120.20	122.99	125.64	128.43

MONTHLY PAYMENTS FOR 30-YR. FHA LOANS

INCLUDING FIRST YEAR ½% MORTGAGE INSURANCE PREMIUMS

AMOUNT	INTEREST							
	9.00%	9.25%	9.50%	9.75%	10.00%	10.25%	10.50%	10.75%
50	.42	.43	.44	.45	.46	.47	.48	.49
100	.85	.86	.88	.90	.92	.94	.96	.97
250	2.11	2.16	2.20	2.25	2.30	2.34	2.39	2.44
500	4.24	4.33	4.42	4.51	4.60	4.70	4.79	4.88
10000	84.65	86.45	88.26	90.16	91.96	93.86	95.66	97.56
10100	85.51	87.32	89.14	91.06	92.88	94.80	96.62	98.53
10200	86.35	88.19	90.02	91.96	93.80	95.73	97.57	99.51
10300	87.20	89.05	90.90	92.86	94.71	96.67	98.53	100.48
10400	88.04	89.91	91.78	93.76	95.63	97.61	99.48	101.46
10500	88.89	90.78	92.67	94.66	96.55	98.55	100.45	102.44
10600	89.73	91.64	93.55	95.56	97.48	99.49	101.40	103.41
10700	90.58	92.51	94.44	96.47	98.40	100.43	102.36	104.39
10800	91.43	93.37	95.32	97.37	99.31	101.37	103.31	105.36
10900	92.28	94.24	96.20	98.27	100.23	102.30	104.27	106.34
11000	93.12	95.10	97.08	99.17	101.15	103.24	105.22	107.31
11100	93.97	95.96	97.96	100.07	102.07	104.18	106.18	108.29
11200	94.81	96.83	98.84	100.97	102.99	105.12	107.14	109.27
11300	95.66	97.69	99.73	101.88	103.91	106.06	108.10	110.24
11400	96.51	98.56	100.61	102.78	104.83	107.00	109.05	111.22
11500	97.36	99.43	101.50	103.68	105.75	107.94	110.01	112.19
11600	98.20	100.29	102.38	104.58	106.67	108.87	110.96	113.16
11700	99.05	101.15	103.26	105.48	107.59	109.81	111.92	114.14
11800	99.89	102.01	104.14	106.38	108.50	110.75	112.88	115.12
11900	100.74	102.88	105.02	107.29	109.43	111.69	113.84	116.10
12000	101.58	103.75	105.91	108.19	110.35	112.63	114.79	117.07
12100	102.44	104.61	106.79	109.09	111.27	113.57	115.75	118.04
12200	103.28	105.48	107.67	109.99	112.19	114.50	116.70	119.02
12300	104.13	106.34	108.55	110.89	113.10	115.44	117.66	119.99
12400	104.97	107.20	109.43	111.79	114.02	116.38	118.61	120.98
12500	105.82	108.07	110.32	112.69	114.95	117.33	119.58	121.95
12600	106.66	108.93	111.21	113.60	115.87	118.26	120.53	122.92
12700	107.52	109.80	112.09	114.50	116.79	119.20	121.49	123.90
12800	108.36	110.66	112.97	115.40	117.70	120.14	122.44	124.87
12900	109.21	111.53	113.85	116.30	118.62	121.07	123.40	125.85
13000	110.05	112.39	114.73	117.20	119.54	122.01	124.35	126.82
13100	110.90	113.25	115.61	118.10	120.46	122.96	125.32	127.80
13200	111.74	114.12	116.49	119.01	121.39	123.89	126.27	128.78
13300	112.59	114.99	117.38	119.91	122.30	124.83	127.23	129.75
13400	113.44	115.85	118.26	120.81	123.22	125.77	128.18	130.73
13500	114.29	116.72	119.15	121.71	124.14	126.71	129.14	131.70
13600	115.13	117.58	120.03	122.61	125.06	127.64	130.09	132.67
13700	115.98	118.44	120.91	123.51	125.98	128.58	131.06	133.66
13800	116.82	119.30	121.79	124.41	126.90	129.53	132.01	134.63
13900	117.67	120.17	122.68	125.32	127.82	130.46	132.97	135.61
14000	118.52	121.04	123.56	126.22	128.74	131.40	133.92	136.58
14100	119.37	121.90	124.44	127.12	129.66	132.34	134.88	137.55
14200	120.21	122.77	125.32	128.02	130.58	133.27	135.83	138.53
14300	121.06	123.63	126.20	128.92	131.49	134.21	136.79	139.51
14400	121.90	124.49	127.08	129.82	132.41	135.16	137.75	140.49
14500	122.75	125.36	127.97	130.73	133.34	136.10	138.71	141.46
14600	123.59	126.23	128.86	131.63	134.26	137.03	139.66	142.43
14700	124.45	127.09	129.74	132.53	135.18	137.97	140.62	143.41
14800	125.29	127.95	130.62	133.43	136.09	138.91	141.57	144.38
14900	126.14	128.82	131.50	134.33	137.01	139.84	142.53	145.36
15000	126.98	129.68	132.38	135.23	137.93	140.78	143.49	146.34
15100	127.83	130.54	133.26	136.13	138.86	141.73	144.45	147.31
15200	128.67	131.41	134.15	137.04	139.78	142.66	145.40	148.29
15300	129.53	132.28	135.03	137.94	140.69	143.60	146.36	149.26
15400	130.37	133.14	135.91	138.84	141.61	144.54	147.31	150.24
15500	131.22	134.01	136.80	139.74	142.53	145.48	148.27	151.21

MONTHLY PAYMENTS FOR 30-YR. FHA LOANS

INCLUDING FIRST YEAR ½% MORTGAGE INSURANCE PREMIUMS

AMOUNT	INTEREST							
	7.00%	7.25%	7.50%	7.75%	8.00%	8.25%	8.50%	8.75%
15600	110.37	113.02	115.67	118.32	120.98	123.79	126.44	129.25
15700	111.07	113.74	116.41	119.09	121.76	124.58	127.25	130.08
15800	111.78	114.46	117.16	119.85	122.53	125.38	128.06	130.91
15900	112.48	115.20	117.90	120.60	123.31	126.17	128.87	131.73
16000	113.20	115.92	118.64	121.36	124.08	126.96	129.68	132.56
16100	113.91	116.64	119.38	122.12	124.85	127.75	130.50	133.40
16200	114.61	117.37	120.12	122.87	125.63	128.55	131.31	134.22
16300	115.32	118.09	120.86	123.63	126.41	129.35	132.12	135.05
16400	116.02	118.81	121.60	124.40	127.19	130.14	132.93	135.88
16500	116.73	119.54	122.35	125.16	127.96	130.93	133.74	136.71
16600	117.44	120.27	123.09	125.91	128.73	131.72	134.54	137.53
16700	118.15	120.99	123.83	126.67	129.51	132.51	135.35	138.37
16800	118.86	121.71	124.57	127.43	130.28	133.31	136.17	139.20
16900	119.56	122.44	125.31	128.18	131.06	134.11	136.98	140.02
17000	120.27	123.16	126.05	128.95	131.84	134.90	137.79	140.85
17100	120.98	123.88	126.79	129.71	132.61	135.69	138.60	141.68
17200	121.68	124.61	127.54	130.46	133.39	136.48	139.41	142.50
17300	122.39	125.34	128.28	131.22	134.16	137.28	140.22	143.33
17400	123.10	126.06	129.02	131.98	134.94	138.07	141.04	144.17
17500	123.81	126.79	129.76	132.74	135.71	138.87	141.85	145.00
17600	124.52	127.51	130.50	133.49	136.49	139.66	142.65	145.82
17700	125.22	128.23	131.24	134.26	137.27	140.45	143.46	146.65
17800	125.93	128.95	131.99	135.02	138.04	141.25	144.27	147.48
17900	126.63	129.69	132.73	135.77	138.82	142.04	145.08	148.30
18000	127.35	130.41	133.47	136.53	139.59	142.83	145.89	149.14
18100	128.06	131.13	134.21	137.29	140.36	143.62	146.71	149.97
18200	128.76	131.86	134.95	138.04	141.14	144.42	147.52	150.79
18300	129.47	132.58	135.69	138.80	141.92	145.22	148.33	151.62
18400	130.17	133.30	136.43	139.57	142.70	146.01	149.14	152.45
18500	130.88	134.03	137.18	140.33	143.47	146.80	149.95	153.28
18600	131.59	134.76	137.92	141.08	144.24	147.59	150.75	154.10
18700	132.30	135.48	138.66	141.84	145.02	148.38	151.57	154.94
18800	133.01	136.20	139.40	142.60	145.79	149.18	152.38	155.77
18900	133.71	136.93	140.14	143.35	146.58	149.98	153.19	156.59
19000	134.42	137.65	140.88	144.12	147.35	150.77	154.00	157.42
19100	135.13	138.37	141.62	144.88	148.12	151.56	154.81	158.25
19200	135.83	139.10	142.37	145.63	148.90	152.35	155.62	159.07
19300	136.54	139.83	143.11	146.39	149.67	153.15	156.43	159.91
19400	137.25	140.55	143.85	147.15	150.45	153.94	157.25	160.74
19500	137.96	141.28	144.59	147.91	151.22	154.74	158.06	161.57
19600	138.67	142.00	145.33	148.66	152.00	155.53	158.86	162.39
19700	139.37	142.72	146.07	149.43	152.78	156.32	159.67	163.22
19800	140.08	143.44	146.82	150.19	153.55	157.12	160.48	164.05
19900	140.78	144.17	147.56	150.94	154.33	157.91	161.29	164.87
20000	141.49	144.90	148.30	151.70	155.10	158.70	162.10	165.71
20100	142.21	145.62	149.04	152.46	155.87	159.49	162.92	166.54
20200	142.91	146.35	149.78	153.21	156.65	160.29	163.73	167.36
20300	143.62	147.07	150.52	153.97	157.43	161.09	164.54	168.19
20400	144.32	147.79	151.26	154.74	158.21	161.88	165.35	169.02
20500	145.03	148.52	152.01	155.50	158.98	162.67	166.16	169.85
20600	145.74	149.25	152.75	156.25	159.75	163.46	166.96	170.68
20700	146.45	149.97	153.49	157.01	160.53	164.25	167.78	171.51
20800	147.16	150.69	154.23	157.77	161.30	165.06	168.59	172.34
20900	147.86	151.42	154.97	158.52	162.09	165.85	169.40	173.16
21000	148.57	152.14	155.71	159.29	162.86	166.64	170.21	173.99
21100	149.28	152.86	156.45	160.05	163.63	167.43	171.02	174.82
21200	149.98	153.59	157.20	160.80	164.41	168.22	171.83	175.64
21300	150.69	154.32	157.94	161.56	165.18	169.02	172.64	176.48
21400	151.40	155.04	158.68	162.32	165.96	169.81	173.46	177.31
21500	152.11	155.77	159.42	163.08	166.73	170.61	174.27	178.14

MONTHLY PAYMENTS FOR 30-YR. FHA LOANS

INCLUDING FIRST YEAR ½% MORTGAGE INSURANCE PREMIUMS

AMOUNT	INTEREST							
	9.00%	9.25%	9.50%	9.75%	10.00%	10.25%	10.50%	10.75%
15600	132.06	134.87	137.68	140.64	143.45	146.41	149.23	152.19
15700	132.91	135.73	138.56	141.54	144.38	147.36	150.19	153.17
15800	133.75	136.59	139.44	142.45	145.29	148.30	151.14	154.14
15900	134.60	137.47	140.33	143.35	146.21	149.23	152.10	155.12
16000	135.45	138.33	141.21	144.25	147.13	150.17	153.05	156.09
16100	136.30	139.19	142.09	145.15	148.05	151.11	154.01	157.06
16200	137.14	140.06	142.97	146.05	148.97	152.04	154.96	158.05
16300	137.99	140.92	143.85	146.95	149.88	152.99	155.93	159.02
16400	138.83	141.78	144.73	147.85	150.81	153.93	156.88	160.00
16500	139.68	142.65	145.63	148.76	151.73	154.87	157.84	160.97
16600	140.53	143.52	146.51	149.66	152.65	155.80	158.79	161.94
16700	141.38	144.38	147.39	150.56	153.57	156.74	159.75	162.92
16800	142.22	145.24	148.27	151.46	154.48	157.68	160.70	163.89
16900	143.07	146.11	149.15	152.36	155.40	158.61	161.67	164.88
17000	143.91	146.97	150.03	153.26	156.33	159.56	162.62	165.85
17100	144.76	147.83	150.92	154.17	157.25	160.50	163.58	166.82
17200	145.60	148.71	151.80	155.07	158.17	161.43	164.53	167.80
17300	146.46	149.57	152.68	155.97	159.08	162.37	165.49	168.77
17400	147.30	150.43	153.56	156.87	160.00	163.31	166.44	169.75
17500	148.15	151.30	154.45	157.77	160.92	164.25	167.41	170.73
17600	148.99	152.16	155.33	158.67	161.84	165.19	168.36	171.70
17700	149.84	153.02	156.21	159.58	162.77	166.13	169.32	172.68
17800	150.68	153.88	157.10	160.48	163.68	167.07	170.27	173.65
17900	151.54	154.76	157.98	161.38	164.60	168.00	171.23	174.63
18000	152.38	155.62	158.86	162.28	165.52	168.94	172.18	175.60
18100	153.23	156.48	159.74	163.18	166.44	169.88	173.14	176.58
18200	154.07	157.35	160.62	164.08	167.36	170.81	174.10	177.56
18300	154.92	158.21	161.50	164.98	168.28	171.76	175.06	178.53
18400	155.76	159.07	162.39	165.89	169.20	172.70	176.01	179.51
18500	156.61	159.95	163.28	166.79	170.12	173.64	176.97	180.48
18600	157.46	160.81	164.16	167.69	171.04	174.57	177.92	181.45
18700	158.31	161.67	165.04	168.59	171.96	175.51	178.88	182.43
18800	159.15	162.53	165.92	169.49	172.87	176.45	179.84	183.41
18900	160.00	163.40	166.80	170.39	173.80	177.39	180.80	184.39
19000	160.84	164.26	167.68	171.30	174.72	178.33	181.75	185.36
19100	161.69	165.12	168.57	172.20	175.64	179.27	182.71	186.33
19200	162.54	166.00	169.45	173.10	176.56	180.20	183.66	187.31
19300	163.39	166.86	170.33	174.00	177.47	181.14	184.62	188.28
19400	164.23	167.72	171.21	174.90	178.39	182.08	185.58	189.27
19500	165.08	168.59	172.10	175.80	179.31	183.03	186.54	190.24
19600	165.92	169.45	172.98	176.70	180.24	183.96	187.49	191.21
19700	166.77	170.31	173.87	177.61	181.16	184.90	188.45	192.19
19800	167.61	171.18	174.75	178.51	182.07	185.84	189.40	193.16
19900	168.47	172.05	175.63	179.41	182.99	186.77	190.36	194.14
20000	169.31	172.91	176.51	180.31	183.91	187.71	191.31	195.12
20100	170.16	173.77	177.39	181.21	184.83	188.65	192.28	196.09
20200	171.00	174.64	178.27	182.11	185.76	189.59	193.23	197.07
20300	171.85	175.50	179.15	183.02	186.67	190.53	194.19	198.04
20400	172.69	176.36	180.04	183.92	187.59	191.47	195.14	199.02
20500	173.55	177.24	180.93	184.82	188.51	192.41	196.10	199.99
20600	174.39	178.10	181.81	185.72	189.43	193.34	197.05	200.96
20700	175.24	178.96	182.69	186.62	190.35	194.28	198.02	201.95
20800	176.08	179.82	183.57	187.52	191.26	195.23	198.97	202.92
20900	176.93	180.69	184.45	188.42	192.19	196.16	199.93	203.90
21000	177.77	181.55	185.34	189.33	193.11	197.10	200.88	204.87
21100	178.62	182.42	186.22	190.23	194.03	198.04	201.84	205.84
21200	179.47	183.29	187.10	191.13	194.95	198.97	202.79	206.82
21300	180.32	184.15	187.98	192.03	195.86	199.91	203.75	207.80
21400	181.16	185.01	188.86	192.93	196.78	200.86	204.71	208.78
21500	182.01	185.88	189.75	193.83	197.71	201.80	205.67	209.75

MONTHLY PAYMENTS FOR 30-YR. FHA LOANS

INCLUDING FIRST YEAR ½% MORTGAGE INSURANCE PREMIUMS

AMOUNT	INTEREST							
	7.00%	7.25%	7.50%	7.75%	8.00%	8.25%	8.50%	8.75%
21600	152.82	156.49	160.16	163.83	167.51	171.40	175.07	178.96
21700	153.52	157.21	160.90	164.60	168.29	172.19	175.88	179.79
21800	154.23	157.93	161.65	165.36	169.06	172.99	176.69	180.62
21900	154.93	158.66	162.39	166.11	169.84	173.78	177.50	181.45
22000	155.64	159.39	163.13	166.87	170.61	174.57	178.32	182.28
22100	156.36	160.11	163.87	167.63	171.38	175.36	179.13	183.11
22200	157.06	160.84	164.61	168.38	172.16	176.16	179.94	183.93
22300	157.77	161.56	165.35	169.14	172.94	176.96	180.75	184.76
22400	158.47	162.28	166.09	169.91	173.72	177.75	181.56	185.59
22500	159.18	163.01	166.84	170.67	174.49	178.54	182.37	186.42
22600	159.89	163.74	167.58	171.42	175.26	179.33	183.17	187.25
22700	160.59	164.46	168.32	172.18	176.04	180.12	183.99	188.08
22800	161.31	165.18	169.06	172.94	176.81	180.93	184.80	188.91
22900	162.01	165.91	169.80	173.69	177.60	181.72	185.61	189.73
23000	162.72	166.63	170.54	174.46	178.37	182.51	186.42	190.56
23100	163.43	167.35	171.28	175.22	179.14	183.30	187.23	191.39
23200	164.13	168.08	172.03	175.97	179.92	184.09	188.04	192.22
23300	164.84	168.81	172.77	176.73	180.69	184.89	188.86	193.05
23400	165.54	169.53	173.51	177.49	181.47	185.68	189.67	193.88
23500	166.26	170.26	174.25	178.25	182.24	186.48	190.48	194.71
23600	166.97	170.98	174.99	179.00	183.02	187.27	191.28	195.53
23700	167.67	171.70	175.73	179.77	183.80	188.06	192.09	196.36
23800	168.38	172.42	176.47	180.53	184.57	188.86	192.90	197.19
23900	169.08	173.15	177.22	181.28	185.35	189.65	193.71	198.02
24000	169.79	173.88	177.96	182.04	186.12	190.44	194.53	198.85
24100	170.51	174.60	178.70	182.80	186.89	191.24	195.34	199.68
24200	171.21	175.33	179.44	183.55	187.68	192.03	196.15	200.50
24300	171.92	176.05	180.18	184.31	188.45	192.83	196.96	201.33
24400	172.62	176.77	180.92	185.08	189.23	193.62	197.77	202.16
24500	173.33	177.50	181.67	185.84	190.00	194.41	198.58	203.00
24600	174.04	178.22	182.41	186.59	190.77	195.20	199.38	203.82
24700	174.74	178.95	183.15	187.35	191.55	195.99	200.20	204.65
24800	175.46	179.67	183.89	188.11	192.32	196.80	201.01	205.48
24900	176.16	180.40	184.63	188.86	193.11	197.59	201.82	206.30
25000	176.87	181.12	185.37	189.63	193.88	198.38	202.63	207.13
25100	177.58	181.84	186.11	190.39	194.65	199.17	203.44	207.96
25200	178.28	182.57	186.86	191.14	195.43	199.96	204.25	208.79
25300	178.99	183.30	187.60	191.90	196.20	200.76	205.07	209.62
25400	179.69	184.02	188.34	192.66	196.98	201.55	205.88	210.45
25500	180.41	184.75	189.08	193.42	197.75	202.35	206.69	211.28
25600	181.12	185.47	189.82	194.17	198.53	203.14	207.49	212.10
25700	181.82	186.19	190.56	194.94	199.31	203.93	208.30	212.93
25800	182.53	186.91	191.30	195.70	200.08	204.73	209.11	213.76
25900	183.23	187.64	192.05	196.45	200.86	205.52	209.92	214.59
26000	183.94	188.37	192.79	197.21	201.63	206.31	210.74	215.42
26100	184.65	189.09	193.53	197.97	202.40	207.11	211.55	216.25
26200	185.36	189.82	194.27	198.72	203.19	207.90	212.36	217.07
26300	186.07	190.54	195.01	199.48	203.96	208.70	213.17	217.90
26400	186.77	191.26	195.75	200.25	204.74	209.49	213.98	218.73
26500	187.48	191.99	196.50	201.01	205.51	210.28	214.79	219.57
26600	188.19	192.71	197.24	201.76	206.28	211.07	215.60	220.39
26700	188.89	193.44	197.98	202.52	207.06	211.86	216.41	221.22
26800	189.60	194.16	198.72	203.28	207.83	212.67	217.22	222.05
26900	190.31	194.89	199.46	204.03	208.62	213.46	218.03	222.87
27000	191.02	195.61	200.20	204.80	209.39	214.25	218.84	223.70
27100	191.73	196.33	200.94	205.56	210.16	215.04	219.65	224.53
27200	192.43	197.06	201.69	206.31	210.94	215.83	220.46	225.36
27300	193.14	197.78	202.43	207.07	211.71	216.63	221.28	226.19
27400	193.84	198.51	203.17	207.83	212.49	217.43	222.09	227.02
27500	194.56	199.24	203.91	208.59	213.26	218.22	222.90	227.85

MONTHLY PAYMENTS FOR 30-YR. FHA LOANS

INCLUDING FIRST YEAR ½% MORTGAGE INSURANCE PREMIUMS

AMOUNT	INTEREST							
	9.00%	9.25%	9.50%	9.75%	10.00%	10.25%	10.50%	10.75%
21600	182.85	186.74	190.63	194.74	198.63	202.73	206.62	210.72
21700	183.70	187.61	191.52	195.64	199.55	203.67	207.58	211.70
21800	184.55	188.47	192.40	196.54	200.46	204.61	208.53	212.67
21900	185.40	189.34	193.28	197.44	201.38	205.54	209.49	213.66
22000	186.24	190.20	194.16	198.34	202.30	206.48	210.45	214.63
22100	187.09	191.06	195.04	199.24	203.23	207.43	211.41	215.60
22200	187.93	191.93	195.92	200.15	204.15	208.36	212.36	216.58
22300	188.78	192.79	196.81	201.05	205.06	209.30	213.32	217.55
22400	189.62	193.66	197.69	201.95	205.98	210.24	214.27	218.53
22500	190.48	194.53	198.58	202.85	206.90	211.18	215.23	219.51
22600	191.32	195.39	199.46	203.75	207.82	212.11	216.19	220.48
22700	192.17	196.25	200.34	204.65	208.74	213.06	217.15	221.46
22800	193.01	197.11	201.22	205.55	209.66	214.00	218.10	222.43
22900	193.86	197.98	202.11	206.46	210.58	214.93	219.06	223.41
23000	194.70	198.85	202.99	207.36	211.50	215.87	220.01	224.38
23100	195.56	199.71	203.87	208.26	212.42	216.81	220.97	225.35
23200	196.40	200.58	204.75	209.16	213.34	217.74	221.92	226.34
23300	197.25	201.44	205.63	210.06	214.25	218.68	222.89	227.31
23400	198.09	202.30	206.51	210.96	215.18	219.63	223.84	228.29
23500	198.94	203.17	207.40	211.87	216.10	220.57	224.80	229.26
23600	199.78	204.03	208.29	212.77	217.02	221.50	225.75	230.23
23700	200.63	204.90	209.17	213.67	217.94	222.44	226.71	231.21
23800	201.48	205.76	210.05	214.57	218.85	223.38	227.66	232.19
23900	202.33	206.63	210.93	215.47	219.77	224.31	228.63	233.17
24000	203.17	207.49	211.81	216.37	220.69	225.26	229.58	234.14
24100	204.02	208.35	212.69	217.27	221.62	226.20	230.54	235.11
24200	204.86	209.22	213.58	218.18	222.54	227.13	231.49	236.09
24300	205.71	210.09	214.46	219.08	223.45	228.07	232.45	237.06
24400	206.56	210.95	215.34	219.98	224.37	229.01	233.40	238.04
24500	207.41	211.82	216.23	220.88	225.29	229.95	234.37	239.02
24600	208.25	212.68	217.11	221.78	226.21	230.89	235.32	239.99
24700	209.10	213.54	217.99	222.68	227.14	231.83	236.28	240.97
24800	209.94	214.40	218.87	223.59	228.05	232.77	237.23	241.94
24900	210.79	215.27	219.76	224.49	228.97	233.70	238.19	242.92
25000	211.63	216.14	220.64	225.39	229.89	234.64	239.14	243.89
25100	212.49	217.00	221.52	226.29	230.81	235.58	240.10	244.87
25200	213.33	217.87	222.40	227.19	231.73	236.51	241.06	245.85
25300	214.18	218.73	223.28	228.09	232.65	237.46	242.02	246.82
25400	215.02	219.59	224.16	228.99	233.57	238.40	242.97	247.80
25500	215.87	220.46	225.04	229.90	234.49	239.34	243.93	248.77
25600	216.71	221.33	225.94	230.80	235.41	240.27	244.88	249.74
25700	217.57	222.19	226.82	231.70	236.33	241.21	245.84	250.73
25800	218.41	223.05	227.70	232.60	237.24	242.15	246.80	251.70
25900	219.26	223.92	228.58	233.50	238.16	243.09	247.76	252.68
26000	220.10	224.78	229.46	234.40	239.09	244.03	248.71	253.65
26100	220.95	225.64	230.34	235.31	240.01	244.97	249.67	254.62
26200	221.79	226.51	231.23	236.21	240.93	245.90	250.62	255.60
26300	222.64	227.38	232.11	237.11	241.84	246.84	251.58	256.57
26400	223.49	228.24	232.99	238.01	242.76	247.78	252.54	257.56
26500	224.34	229.11	233.88	238.91	243.68	248.72	253.50	258.53
26600	225.18	229.97	234.76	239.81	244.61	249.66	254.45	259.50
26700	226.03	230.83	235.64	240.72	245.53	250.60	255.41	260.48
26800	226.87	231.69	236.53	241.62	246.44	251.54	256.36	261.45
26900	227.72	232.57	237.41	242.52	247.36	252.47	257.32	262.43
27000	228.57	233.43	238.29	243.42	248.28	253.41	258.27	263.41
27100	229.42	234.29	239.17	244.32	249.20	254.35	259.24	264.38
27200	230.26	235.16	240.05	245.22	250.12	255.29	260.19	265.36
27300	231.11	236.02	240.93	246.12	251.04	256.23	261.15	266.33
27400	231.95	236.88	241.81	247.03	251.96	257.17	262.10	267.31
27500	232.80	237.75	242.71	247.93	252.88	258.11	263.06	268.28

MONTHLY PAYMENTS FOR 30-YR. FHA LOANS

INCLUDING FIRST YEAR ½% MORTGAGE INSURANCE PREMIUMS

AMOUNT	7.00%	7.25%	7.50%	7.75%	8.00%	8.25%	8.50%	8.75%
27600	195.27	199.96	204.65	209.34	214.04	219.01	223.70	228.67
27700	195.97	200.68	205.39	210.11	214.82	219.80	224.51	229.50
27800	196.68	201.40	206.13	210.87	215.59	220.60	225.32	230.34
27900	197.38	202.13	206.88	211.62	216.37	221.39	226.14	231.16
28000	198.09	202.86	207.62	212.38	217.14	222.18	226.95	231.99
28100	198.80	203.58	208.36	213.14	217.91	222.98	227.76	232.82
28200	199.51	204.31	209.10	213.89	218.70	223.77	228.57	233.64
28300	200.22	205.03	209.84	214.65	219.47	224.57	229.38	234.47
28400	200.92	205.75	210.58	215.42	220.25	225.36	230.19	235.30
28500	201.63	206.48	211.32	216.18	221.02	226.15	231.00	236.14
28600	202.34	207.20	212.07	216.93	221.79	226.94	231.81	236.96
28700	203.04	207.93	212.81	217.69	222.57	227.73	232.62	237.79
28800	203.75	208.65	213.55	218.45	223.34	228.54	233.43	238.62
28900	204.46	209.38	214.29	219.20	224.13	229.33	234.24	239.44
29000	205.17	210.10	215.03	219.97	224.90	230.12	235.05	240.27
29100	205.88	210.82	215.77	220.73	225.67	230.91	235.86	241.11
29200	206.58	211.55	216.52	221.48	226.45	231.70	236.68	241.93
29300	207.29	212.27	217.26	222.24	227.22	232.50	237.49	242.76
29400	207.99	213.00	218.00	223.00	228.00	233.30	238.30	243.59
29500	208.70	213.73	218.74	223.76	228.78	234.09	239.11	244.42
29600	209.42	214.45	219.48	224.51	229.55	234.88	239.91	245.24
29700	210.12	215.17	220.22	225.28	230.33	235.67	240.72	246.07
29800	210.83	215.89	220.96	226.04	231.10	236.47	241.53	246.91
29900	211.53	216.62	221.71	226.79	231.88	237.26	242.35	247.73
30000	212.24	217.34	222.45	227.55	232.65	238.05	243.16	248.56
30100	212.95	218.07	223.19	228.31	233.42	238.85	243.97	249.39
30200	213.65	218.80	223.93	229.06	234.21	239.64	244.78	250.21
30300	214.37	219.52	224.67	229.82	234.98	240.44	245.59	251.04
30400	215.07	220.24	225.41	230.59	235.76	241.23	246.40	251.88
30500	215.78	220.97	226.15	231.35	236.53	242.02	247.21	252.71
30600	216.49	221.69	226.90	232.10	237.30	242.81	248.02	253.53
30700	217.19	222.42	227.64	232.86	238.08	243.61	248.83	254.36
30800	217.90	223.14	228.38	233.62	238.85	244.41	249.64	255.19
30900	218.61	223.87	229.12	234.37	239.64	245.20	250.45	256.01
31000	219.32	224.59	229.86	235.14	240.41	245.99	251.26	256.84
31100	220.03	225.31	230.60	235.90	241.18	246.78	252.07	257.68
31200	220.73	226.04	231.35	236.65	241.96	247.57	252.89	258.50
31300	221.44	226.76	232.09	237.41	242.73	248.37	253.70	259.33
31400	222.14	227.49	232.83	238.17	243.51	249.17	254.51	260.16
31500	222.85	228.22	233.57	238.93	244.29	249.96	255.32	260.99
31600	223.57	228.94	234.31	239.68	245.06	250.75	256.12	261.81
31700	224.27	229.66	235.05	240.45	245.84	251.54	256.93	262.65
31800	224.98	230.38	235.79	241.21	246.61	252.34	257.74	263.48
31900	225.68	231.11	236.54	241.96	247.39	253.13	258.56	264.30
32000	226.39	231.83	237.28	242.72	248.16	253.92	259.37	265.13
32100	227.10	232.56	238.02	243.48	248.93	254.72	260.18	265.96
32200	227.80	233.29	238.76	244.23	249.72	255.51	260.99	266.78
32300	228.52	234.01	239.50	244.99	250.49	256.31	261.80	267.61
32400	229.22	234.73	240.24	245.76	251.27	257.10	262.61	268.45
32500	229.93	235.46	240.98	246.52	252.04	257.89	263.43	269.28
32600	230.64	236.18	241.73	247.27	252.81	258.68	264.23	270.10
32700	231.34	236.90	242.47	248.03	253.59	259.48	265.04	270.93
32800	232.05	237.63	243.21	248.79	254.36	260.28	265.85	271.76
32900	232.75	238.36	243.95	249.54	255.15	261.07	266.66	272.58
33000	233.47	239.08	244.69	250.31	255.92	261.86	267.47	273.42
33100	234.18	239.80	245.43	251.07	256.69	262.65	268.28	274.25
33200	234.88	240.53	246.18	251.82	257.47	263.44	269.10	275.07
33300	235.59	241.25	246.92	252.58	258.24	264.24	269.91	275.90
33400	236.29	241.98	247.66	253.34	259.02	265.04	270.72	276.73
33500	237.00	242.71	248.40	254.10	259.80	265.83	271.53	277.56

MONTHLY PAYMENTS FOR 30-YR. FHA LOANS

INCLUDING FIRST YEAR ½% MORTGAGE INSURANCE PREMIUMS

AMOUNT	INTEREST							
	9.00%	9.25%	9.50%	9.75%	10.00%	10.25%	10.50%	10.75%
27600	233.64	238.62	243.59	248.83	253.84	258.40	264.01	269.26
27700	234.50	239.48	244.47	249.73	254.72	259.98	264.98	270.24
27800	235.34	240.34	245.35	250.63	255.63	260.93	265.93	271.21
27900	236.19	241.21	246.23	251.53	256.56	261.86	266.89	272.19
28000	237.03	242.07	247.11	252.44	257.48	262.80	267.84	273.16
28100	237.88	242.93	248.00	253.34	258.40	263.74	268.80	274.13
28200	238.72	243.81	248.88	254.24	259.32	264.67	269.75	275.11
28300	239.58	244.67	249.76	255.14	260.23	265.61	270.71	276.09
28400	240.42	245.53	250.64	256.04	261.15	266.55	271.67	277.07
28500	241.27	246.40	251.53	256.94	262.08	267.50	272.63	278.04
28600	242.11	247.26	252.41	257.84	263.00	268.43	273.58	279.01
28700	242.96	248.12	253.30	258.75	263.92	269.37	274.54	279.99
28800	243.80	248.98	254.18	259.65	264.83	270.31	275.49	280.96
28900	244.65	249.86	255.06	260.55	265.75	271.24	276.45	281.95
29000	245.50	250.72	255.94	261.45	266.67	272.18	277.41	282.92
29100	246.35	251.58	256.82	262.35	267.59	273.13	278.37	283.89
29200	247.19	252.45	257.70	263.25	268.52	274.06	279.32	284.87
29300	248.04	253.31	258.58	264.16	269.43	275.00	280.28	285.84
29400	248.88	254.17	259.47	265.06	270.35	275.94	281.23	286.82
29500	249.73	255.05	260.36	255.96	271.27	276.88	282.19	287.80
29600	250.58	255.91	261.24	266.86	272.19	277.81	283.15	288.77
29700	251.43	256.77	262.12	267.76	273.11	278.75	284.11	289.75
29800	252.27	257.63	263.00	268.66	274.03	279.70	285.06	290.72
29900	253.12	258.50	263.88	269.56	274.95	280.63	286.02	291.70
30000	253.96	259.36	264.77	270.47	275.87	281.57	286.97	292.67
30100	254.81	260.22	265.65	271.37	276.79	282.51	287.93	293.64
30200	255.65	261.10	266.53	272.27	277.71	283.44	288.88	294.63
30300	256.51	261.96	267.41	273.17	278.62	284.38	289.85	295.60
30400	257.35	262.82	268.29	274.07	279.54	285.33	290.80	296.58
30500	258.20	263.69	269.18	274.97	280.47	286.27	291.76	297.55
30600	259.04	264.55	270.06	275.88	281.39	287.20	292.71	298.52
30700	259.89	265.41	270.95	276.78	282.31	288.14	293.67	299.50
30800	260.73	266.28	271.83	277.68	283.23	289.08	294.62	300.48
30900	261.59	267.15	272.71	278.58	284.14	290.01	295.59	301.46
31000	262.43	268.01	273.59	279.48	285.06	290.96	296.54	302.43
31100	263.28	268.87	274.47	280.38	285.99	291.90	297.50	303.40
31200	264.12	269.74	275.35	281.29	286.91	292.83	298.45	304.38
31300	264.97	270.60	276.24	282.19	287.82	293.77	299.41	305.35
31400	265.81	271.46	277.12	283.09	288.74	294.71	300.36	306.34
31500	266.66	272.34	278.01	283.99	289.66	295.65	301.33	307.31
31600	267.51	273.20	278.89	284.89	290.58	296.58	302.28	308.28
31700	268.36	274.06	279.77	285.79	291.50	297.53	303.24	309.26
31800	269.20	274.92	280.65	286.69	292.42	298.47	304.19	310.23
31900	270.05	275.79	281.53	287.60	293.34	299.40	305.15	311.21
32000	270.89	276.65	282.42	288.50	294.26	300.34	306.10	312.18
32100	271.74	277.52	283.30	289.40	295.18	301.28	307.06	313.16
32200	272.59	278.39	284.18	290.30	296.10	302.21	308.02	314.14
32300	273.44	279.25	285.06	291.20	297.01	303.16	308.98	315.11
32400	274.28	280.11	285.94	292.10	297.94	304.10	309.93	316.09
32500	275.13	280.98	286.83	293.01	298.86	305.04	310.89	317.06
32600	275.97	281.84	287.72	293.91	299.78	305.97	311.84	318.03
32700	276.82	282.70	288.60	294.81	300.70	306.91	312.80	319.02
32800	277.66	283.57	289.48	295.71	301.61	307.85	313.76	319.99
32900	278.52	284.44	290.36	296.61	302.53	308.79	314.72	320.97
33000	279.36	285.30	291.24	297.51	303.46	309.73	315.67	321.94
33100	280.21	286.16	292.12	298.41	304.38	310.67	316.63	322.91
33200	281.07	287.03	293.00	299.32	305.30	311.60	317.58	323.89
33300	281.90	287.89	293.89	300.22	306.21	312.54	318.54	324.86
33400	282.74	288.76	294.77	301.12	307.13	313.48	319.50	325.85
33500	283.60	289.63	295.66	302.02	308.05	314.42	320.46	326.82

MONTHLY PAYMENTS FOR 30-YR. FHA LOANS

INCLUDING FIRST YEAR ½% MORTGAGE INSURANCE PREMIUMS

AMOUNT	INTEREST							
	7.00%	7.25%	7.50%	7.75%	8.00%	8.25%	8.50%	8.75%
33600	237.72	243.43	249.14	254.85	260.57	266.62	272.33	278.38
33700	238.42	244.15	249.88	255.62	261.35	267.41	273.14	279.22
33800	239.13	244.87	250.62	256.38	262.12	268.21	273.96	280.05
33900	239.83	245.60	251.37	257.13	262.90	269.00	274.77	280.87
34000	240.54	246.32	252.11	257.89	263.67	269.80	275.58	281.70
34100	241.25	247.05	252.85	258.65	264.44	270.59	276.39	282.53
34200	241.95	247.78	253.59	259.40	265.23	271.38	277.20	283.35
34300	242.67	248.50	254.33	260.16	266.00	272.18	278.01	284.19
34400	243.37	249.22	255.07	260.93	266.78	272.97	278.82	285.02
34500	244.08	249.95	255.81	261.69	267.55	273.76	279.64	285.85
34600	244.79	250.67	256.56	262.44	268.32	274.55	280.44	286.67
34700	245.49	251.39	257.30	263.20	269.10	275.35	281.25	287.50
34800	246.20	252.12	258.04	263.96	269.88	276.15	282.06	288.33
34900	246.90	252.85	258.78	264.71	270.66	276.94	282.87	289.15
35000	247.62	253.57	259.52	265.48	271.43	277.73	283.68	289.99
35100	248.33	254.29	260.26	266.24	272.20	278.52	284.50	290.82
35200	249.03	255.02	261.00	266.99	272.98	279.31	285.31	291.64
35300	249.74	255.74	261.75	267.75	273.75	280.11	286.12	292.47
35400	250.44	256.46	262.49	268.51	274.53	280.91	286.93	293.30
35500	251.15	257.20	263.23	269.27	275.31	281.70	287.74	294.13
35600	251.86	257.92	263.97	270.02	276.08	282.49	288.54	294.95
35700	252.57	258.64	264.71	270.79	276.86	283.28	289.35	295.79
35800	253.28	259.36	265.45	271.55	277.63	284.08	290.17	296.62
35900	253.98	260.09	266.20	272.30	278.41	284.87	290.98	297.44
36000	254.69	260.81	266.94	273.06	279.18	285.67	291.79	298.27
36100	255.40	261.54	267.68	273.82	279.95	286.46	292.60	299.10
36200	256.10	262.27	268.42	274.57	280.74	287.25	293.41	299.92
36300	256.81	262.99	269.16	275.33	281.51	288.05	294.22	300.76
36400	257.52	263.71	269.90	276.10	282.29	288.84	295.03	301.59
36500	258.23	264.44	270.64	276.86	283.06	289.63	295.85	302.42
36600	258.94	265.16	271.39	277.61	283.83	290.42	296.65	303.24
36700	259.64	265.88	272.13	278.37	284.61	291.22	297.46	304.07
36800	260.35	266.61	272.87	279.13	285.39	292.02	298.27	304.90
36900	261.05	267.34	273.61	279.88	286.17	292.81	299.08	305.72
37000	261.77	268.06	274.35	280.65	286.94	293.60	299.89	306.56
37100	262.48	268.78	275.09	281.41	287.71	294.39	300.71	307.39
37200	263.18	269.51	275.83	282.16	288.49	295.18	301.52	308.21
37300	263.89	270.23	276.58	282.92	289.26	295.99	302.33	309.04
37400	264.59	270.95	277.32	283.68	290.04	296.78	303.14	309.87
37500	265.30	271.69	278.06	284.44	290.82	297.57	303.95	310.70
37600	266.01	272.41	278.80	285.19	291.59	298.36	304.75	311.53
37700	266.72	273.13	279.54	285.96	292.37	299.15	305.56	312.36
37800	267.43	273.85	280.28	286.72	293.14	299.95	306.38	313.19
37900	268.13	274.58	281.03	287.47	293.92	300.74	307.19	314.01
38000	268.84	275.30	281.77	288.23	294.69	301.54	308.00	314.84
38100	269.55	276.02	282.51	288.99	295.46	302.33	308.81	315.67
38200	270.25	276.76	283.25	289.74	296.25	303.12	309.62	316.49
38300	270.96	277.48	283.99	290.50	297.02	303.92	310.43	317.33
38400	271.67	278.20	284.73	291.27	297.80	304.71	311.25	318.16
38500	272.38	278.93	285.47	292.03	298.57	305.50	312.06	318.99
38600	273.09	279.65	286.22	292.78	299.34	306.29	312.86	319.81
38700	273.79	280.37	286.96	293.54	300.12	307.09	313.67	320.64
38800	274.50	281.10	287.70	294.30	300.90	307.89	314.48	321.47
38900	275.20	281.83	288.44	295.05	301.68	308.68	315.29	322.30
39000	275.91	282.55	289.18	295.82	302.45	309.47	316.10	323.13
39100	276.63	283.27	289.92	296.58	303.22	310.26	316.92	323.96
39200	277.33	284.00	290.66	297.33	304.00	311.05	317.73	324.78
39300	278.04	284.72	291.41	298.09	304.77	311.86	318.54	325.61
39400	278.74	285.44	292.15	298.85	305.55	312.65	319.35	326.44
39500	279.45	286.18	292.89	299.61	306.33	313.44	320.16	327.27

MONTHLY PAYMENTS FOR 30-YR. FHA LOANS

INCLUDING FIRST YEAR ½% MORTGAGE INSURANCE PREMIUMS

AMOUNT	INTEREST							
	9.00%	9.25%	9.50%	9.75%	10.00%	10.25%	10.50%	10.75%
33600	284.44	290.49	296.54	302.92	308.97	315.36	321.41	327.79
33700	285.29	291.35	297.42	303.82	309.90	316.30	322.37	328.77
33800	286.13	292.21	298.30	304.73	310.81	317.24	323.32	329.74
33900	286.98	293.08	299.19	305.63	311.73	318.17	324.28	330.72
34000	287.82	293.94	300.07	306.53	312.65	319.11	325.23	331.70
34100	288.67	294.81	300.95	307.43	313.57	320.05	326.20	332.67
34200	289.52	295.68	301.83	308.33	314.49	320.99	327.15	333.65
34300	290.37	296.54	302.71	309.23	315.41	321.93	328.11	334.62
34400	291.21	297.40	303.59	310.13	316.33	322.87	329.06	335.60
34500	292.06	298.27	304.48	311.04	317.25	323.81	330.02	336.57
34600	292.90	299.13	305.37	311.94	318.17	324.74	330.97	337.55
34700	293.75	300.00	306.25	312.84	319.09	325.68	331.94	338.53
34800	294.60	300.86	307.13	313.74	320.00	326.62	332.89	339.50
34900	295.45	301.73	308.01	314.64	320.92	327.56	333.85	340.48
35000	296.29	302.59	308.89	315.54	321.85	328.50	334.80	341.45
35100	297.14	303.45	309.77	316.45	322.77	329.44	335.76	342.42
35200	297.98	304.32	310.66	317.35	323.69	330.37	336.71	343.40
35300	298.83	305.19	311.54	318.25	324.60	331.31	337.68	344.38
35400	299.67	306.05	312.42	319.15	325.52	332.25	338.63	345.36
35500	300.53	306.92	313.31	320.05	326.44	333.20	339.59	346.33
35600	301.37	307.78	314.19	320.95	327.37	334.13	340.54	347.30
35700	302.22	308.64	315.07	321.86	328.29	335.07	341.50	348.28
35800	303.06	309.50	315.96	322.76	329.20	336.01	342.45	349.25
35900	303.91	310.37	316.84	323.66	330.12	336.94	343.41	350.24
36000	304.75	311.24	317.72	324.56	331.04	337.88	344.37	351.21
36100	305.60	312.10	318.60	325.46	331.96	338.83	345.33	352.18
36200	306.45	312.97	319.48	326.36	332.89	339.76	346.28	353.16
36300	307.30	313.83	320.36	327.26	333.80	340.70	347.24	354.13
36400	308.14	314.69	321.24	328.17	334.72	341.64	348.19	355.11
36500	308.99	315.56	322.14	329.07	335.64	342.58	349.15	356.09
36600	309.83	316.43	323.02	329.97	336.56	343.51	350.11	357.06
36700	310.68	317.29	323.90	330.87	337.48	344.45	351.07	358.04
36800	311.53	318.15	324.78	331.77	338.39	345.39	352.02	359.01
36900	312.38	319.02	325.66	332.67	339.32	346.33	352.98	359.99
37000	313.22	319.88	326.54	333.58	340.24	347.27	353.93	360.96
37100	314.07	320.74	327.43	334.48	341.16	348.21	354.89	361.93
37200	314.91	321.61	328.31	335.38	342.08	349.14	355.84	362.92
37300	315.76	322.48	329.19	336.28	342.99	350.08	356.81	363.89
37400	316.60	323.34	330.07	337.18	343.91	351.03	357.76	364.87
37500	317.46	324.21	330.96	338.08	344.83	351.97	358.72	365.84
37600	318.30	325.07	331.84	338.98	345.76	352.90	359.67	366.81
37700	319.15	325.93	332.72	339.89	346.68	353.84	360.63	367.79
37800	319.99	326.79	333.61	340.79	347.59	354.78	361.58	368.77
37900	320.84	327.67	334.49	341.69	348.51	355.71	362.55	369.75
38000	321.68	328.53	335.37	342.59	349.43	356.65	363.50	370.72
38100	322.53	329.39	336.25	343.49	350.35	357.60	364.46	371.69
38200	323.38	330.26	337.13	344.39	351.28	358.53	365.41	372.67
38300	324.23	331.12	338.01	345.30	352.19	359.47	366.37	373.64
38400	325.07	331.98	338.90	346.20	353.11	360.41	367.32	374.63
38500	325.92	332.85	339.79	347.10	354.03	361.35	368.29	375.60
38600	326.76	333.72	340.67	348.00	354.95	362.28	369.24	376.57
38700	327.61	334.58	341.55	348.90	355.87	363.23	370.20	377.55
38800	328.46	335.44	342.43	349.80	356.79	364.17	371.15	378.52
38900	329.31	336.31	343.31	350.70	357.71	365.10	372.11	379.50
39000	330.15	337.17	344.19	351.61	358.63	366.04	373.06	380.47
39100	331.00	338.03	345.08	352.51	359.55	366.98	374.02	381.45
39200	331.84	338.91	345.96	353.41	360.47	367.91	374.98	382.43
39300	332.69	339.77	346.84	354.31	361.38	368.86	375.94	383.40
39400	333.54	340.63	347.72	355.21	362.31	369.80	376.89	384.38
39500	334.39	341.50	348.61	356.11	363.23	370.74	377.85	385.35

MONTHLY PAYMENTS FOR 30-YR. FHA LOANS

INCLUDING FIRST YEAR ½% MORTGAGE INSURANCE PREMIUMS

AMOUNT	7.00%	7.25%	7.50%	7.75%	8.00%	8.25%	8.50%	8.75%
39600	280.16	286.90	293.63	300.36	307.10	314.23	320.96	328.10
39700	280.86	287.62	294.37	301.13	307.88	315.02	321.78	328.93
39800	281.58	288.34	295.11	301.89	308.65	315.82	322.59	329.76
39900	282.28	289.07	295.85	302.64	309.43	316.61	323.40	330.58
40000	282.99	289.79	296.60	303.40	310.20	317.41	324.21	331.41
40100	283.70	290.51	297.34	304.16	310.98	318.20	325.02	332.24
40200	284.40	291.25	298.08	304.91	311.76	318.99	325.83	333.07
40300	285.11	291.97	298.82	305.67	312.53	319.79	326.64	333.90
40400	285.82	292.69	299.56	306.44	313.31	320.58	327.46	334.73
40500	286.53	293.42	300.30	307.20	314.08	321.37	328.27	335.56
40600	287.24	294.14	301.05	307.95	314.85	322.17	329.07	336.38
40700	287.94	294.86	301.79	308.71	315.63	322.96	329.88	337.21
40800	288.65	295.58	302.53	309.47	316.41	323.76	330.69	338.04
40900	289.35	296.32	303.27	310.22	317.19	324.55	331.50	338.87
41000	290.06	297.04	304.01	310.99	317.96	325.34	332.31	339.70
41100	290.78	297.76	304.75	311.75	318.73	326.13	333.13	340.53
41200	291.48	298.49	305.49	312.50	319.51	326.92	333.94	341.35
41300	292.19	299.21	306.24	313.26	320.28	327.73	334.75	342.18
41400	292.89	299.93	306.98	314.02	321.06	328.52	335.56	343.01
41500	293.60	300.67	307.72	314.78	321.84	329.31	336.37	343.85
41600	294.31	301.39	308.46	315.53	322.61	330.10	337.17	344.67
41700	295.01	302.11	309.20	316.30	323.39	330.89	337.99	345.50
41800	295.73	302.83	309.94	317.06	324.16	331.69	338.80	346.33
41900	296.43	303.56	310.68	317.81	324.94	332.48	339.61	347.15
42000	297.14	304.28	311.43	318.57	325.71	333.28	340.42	347.98
42100	297.85	305.00	312.17	319.33	326.49	334.07	341.23	348.81
42200	298.55	305.74	312.91	320.08	327.27	334.86	342.04	349.64
42300	299.26	306.46	313.65	320.84	328.04	335.66	342.85	350.47
42400	299.96	307.18	314.39	321.61	328.82	336.45	343.67	351.30
42500	300.68	307.91	315.13	322.37	329.59	337.24	344.48	352.13
42600	301.39	308.63	315.88	323.12	330.36	338.04	345.28	352.95
42700	302.09	309.35	316.62	323.88	331.14	338.83	346.09	353.78
42800	302.80	310.07	317.36	324.64	331.92	339.63	346.90	354.62
42900	303.50	310.81	318.10	325.39	332.70	340.42	347.71	355.44
43000	304.21	311.53	318.84	326.16	333.47	341.21	348.53	356.27
43200	305.63	312.98	320.32	327.67	335.02	342.79	350.15	357.92
43400	307.04	314.42	321.81	329.19	336.57	344.39	351.77	359.58
43600	308.46	315.88	323.29	330.70	338.12	345.97	353.38	361.24
43800	309.88	317.32	324.77	332.23	339.67	347.56	355.01	362.90
44000	311.29	318.77	326.26	333.74	341.22	349.15	356.63	364.55
44200	312.70	320.23	327.74	335.25	342.78	350.73	358.25	366.21
44400	314.11	321.67	329.22	336.78	344.33	352.32	359.88	367.87
44600	315.54	323.12	330.71	338.29	345.87	353.91	361.49	369.52
44800	316.95	324.56	332.19	339.81	347.43	355.50	363.11	371.19
45000	318.36	326.02	333.67	341.33	348.98	357.08	364.74	372.84
45200	319.78	327.47	335.15	342.84	350.53	358.66	366.36	374.49
45400	321.19	328.91	336.64	344.36	352.09	360.26	367.98	376.16
45600	322.61	330.37	338.12	345.87	353.63	361.84	369.60	377.81
45800	324.02	331.81	339.60	347.40	355.18	363.43	371.22	379.47
46000	325.44	333.26	341.09	348.91	356.73	365.02	372.84	381.12
46200	326.85	334.71	342.57	350.42	358.29	366.60	374.46	382.78
46400	328.26	336.16	344.05	351.95	359.84	368.19	376.09	384.44
46600	329.69	337.61	345.53	353.46	361.38	369.78	377.70	386.09
46800	331.10	339.05	347.02	354.98	362.94	371.37	379.32	387.76
47000	332.51	340.51	348.50	356.50	364.49	372.95	380.95	389.41
47200	333.93	341.96	349.98	358.01	366.04	374.54	382.57	391.06
47400	335.34	343.40	351.47	359.53	367.60	376.13	384.19	392.73
47600	336.76	344.86	352.95	361.04	369.14	377.71	385.81	394.38
47800	338.17	346.30	354.43	362.57	370.69	379.30	387.43	396.04
48000	339.59	347.75	355.92	364.08	372.24	380.89	389.05	397.69

MONTHLY PAYMENTS FOR 30-YR. FHA LOANS

INCLUDING FIRST YEAR ½% MORTGAGE INSURANCE PREMIUMS

AMOUNT	9.00%	9.25%	9.50%	9.75%	10.00%	10.25%	10.50%	10.75%
39600	335.23	342.36	349.49	357.02	364.15	371.67	378.80	386.32
39700	336.08	343.22	350.38	357.92	365.07	372.61	379.76	387.31
39800	336.92	344.08	351.26	358.82	365.98	373.55	380.72	388.28
39900	337.77	344.96	352.14	359.72	366.90	374.48	381.68	389.26
40000	338.61	345.82	353.02	360.62	367.82	375.43	382.63	390.23
40100	339.47	346.68	353.90	361.52	368.75	376.37	383.59	391.21
40200	340.31	347.55	354.78	362.43	369.67	377.30	384.54	392.18
40300	341.16	348.41	355.66	363.33	370.58	378.24	385.50	393.16
40400	342.00	349.27	356.55	364.23	371.50	379.18	386.46	394.14
40500	342.85	350.15	357.44	365.13	372.42	380.12	387.42	395.11
40600	343.69	351.01	358.32	366.03	373.34	381.06	388.37	396.08
40700	344.55	351.87	359.20	366.93	374.27	382.00	389.33	397.06
40800	345.39	352.73	360.08	367.83	375.18	382.94	390.28	398.03
40900	346.24	353.60	360.96	368.74	376.10	383.87	391.24	399.01
41000	347.08	354.46	361.85	369.64	377.02	384.81	392.19	399.99
41100	347.93	355.32	362.73	370.54	377.94	385.75	393.16	400.96
41200	348.77	356.20	363.61	371.44	378.86	386.69	394.11	401.94
41300	349.62	357.06	364.49	372.34	379.77	387.63	395.07	402.91
41400	350.47	357.92	365.37	373.24	380.70	388.57	396.02	403.89
41500	351.32	358.79	366.26	374.15	381.62	389.51	396.98	404.86
41600	352.16	359.65	367.15	375.05	382.54	390.44	397.93	405.84
41700	353.01	360.51	368.03	375.95	383.46	391.38	398.90	406.82
41800	353.85	361.38	368.91	376.85	384.37	392.32	399.85	407.79
41900	354.70	362.25	369.79	377.75	385.29	393.26	400.81	408.77
42000	355.55	363.11	370.67	378.65	386.22	394.20	401.76	409.74
42100	356.40	363.97	371.55	379.55	387.14	395.14	402.72	410.71
42200	357.24	364.84	372.43	380.46	388.06	396.07	403.67	411.70
42300	358.09	365.70	373.32	381.36	388.97	397.01	404.64	412.67
42400	358.93	366.56	374.20	382.26	389.89	397.95	405.59	413.65
42500	359.78	367.44	375.09	383.16	390.81	398.90	406.55	414.62
42600	360.62	368.30	375.97	384.06	391.74	399.83	407.50	415.59
42700	361.48	369.16	376.85	384.96	392.66	400.77	408.46	416.57
42800	362.32	370.02	377.73	385.87	393.57	401.71	409.41	417.54
42900	363.17	370.89	378.62	386.77	394.49	402.64	410.37	418.53
43000	364.01	371.75	379.50	387.67	395.41	403.58	411.33	419.50
43200	365.70	373.49	381.26	389.47	397.25	405.46	413.24	421.45
43400	367.40	375.21	383.02	391.27	399.09	407.34	415.15	423.40
43600	369.09	376.94	384.80	393.08	400.93	409.21	417.07	425.35
43800	370.78	378.67	386.56	394.88	402.76	411.10	418.98	427.30
44000	372.48	380.40	388.32	396.68	404.61	412.97	420.89	429.25
44200	374.17	382.13	390.09	398.49	406.45	414.84	422.80	431.21
44400	375.86	383.86	391.85	400.29	408.28	416.73	424.72	433.16
44600	377.56	385.59	393.62	402.09	410.13	418.60	426.63	435.10
44800	379.25	387.31	395.38	403.90	411.96	420.48	428.54	437.06
45000	380.94	389.04	397.15	405.70	413.80	422.35	430.46	439.01
45200	382.63	390.78	398.91	407.50	415.65	424.23	432.37	440.96
45400	384.33	392.50	400.67	409.31	417.48	426.11	434.28	442.92
45600	386.02	394.23	402.45	411.11	419.32	427.98	436.20	444.86
45800	387.71	395.96	404.21	412.91	421.16	429.87	438.11	446.81
46000	389.41	397.69	405.97	414.72	423.00	431.74	440.02	448.77
46200	391.10	399.42	407.74	416.52	424.84	433.61	441.94	450.72
46400	392.79	401.15	409.50	418.32	426.67	435.50	443.85	452.67
46600	394.49	402.88	411.27	420.12	428.52	437.37	445.76	454.61
46800	396.18	404.60	413.04	421.93	430.35	439.25	447.68	456.57
47000	397.87	406.34	414.80	423.73	432.19	441.13	449.59	458.52
47200	399.57	408.07	416.56	425.53	434.04	443.00	451.50	460.47
47400	401.26	409.79	418.32	427.34	435.87	444.88	453.42	462.43
47600	402.95	411.52	420.10	429.14	437.71	446.76	455.33	464.37
47800	404.64	413.25	421.86	430.94	439.55	448.64	457.24	466.32
48000	406.34	414.98	423.62	432.75	441.39	450.51	459.15	468.28

MONTHLY PAYMENTS FOR 30-YR. FHA LOANS

INCLUDING FIRST YEAR ½% MORTGAGE INSURANCE PREMIUMS

AMOUNT	INTEREST							
	7.00%	7.25%	7.50%	7.75%	8.00%	8.25%	8.50%	8.75%
48200	341.00	349.20	357.40	365.59	373.80	382.47	390.67	399.35
48400	342.41	350.65	358.88	367.12	375.35	384.06	392.30	401.01
48600	343.84	352.10	360.36	368.63	376.89	385.65	393.91	402.66
48800	345.25	353.54	361.85	370.15	378.45	387.24	395.53	404.33
49000	346.66	355.00	363.33	371.67	380.00	388.82	397.16	405.98
49200	348.07	356.45	364.81	373.18	381.55	390.41	398.78	407.63
49400	349.49	357.89	366.30	374.70	383.11	392.00	400.40	409.30
49600	350.91	359.35	367.78	376.21	384.65	393.58	402.02	410.95
49800	352.32	360.79	369.26	377.74	386.20	395.17	403.64	412.61
50000	353.74	362.24	370.75	379.25	387.75	396.76	405.26	414.27
50200	355.15	363.69	372.25	380.76	389.31	398.34	406.89	415.92
50400	356.56	365.14	373.71	382.29	390.86	399.93	408.51	417.58
50600	357.99	366.59	375.19	383.80	392.40	401.52	410.12	419.23
50800	359.40	368.03	376.68	385.32	393.96	403.11	411.74	420.90
51000	360.81	369.49	378.16	386.84	395.51	404.69	413.37	422.55
51200	362.22	370.94	379.64	388.35	397.06	406.28	414.99	424.20
51400	363.64	372.38	381.13	389.87	398.62	407.87	416.61	425.87
51600	365.06	373.83	382.61	391.38	400.16	409.45	418.23	427.52
51800	366.47	375.28	384.09	392.91	401.71	411.04	419.85	429.18
52000	367.89	376.73	385.58	394.42	403.26	412.63	421.47	430.84
52200	369.30	378.18	387.06	395.93	404.82	414.21	423.10	432.49
52400	370.71	379.63	388.54	397.46	406.37	415.80	424.72	434.15
52600	372.14	381.08	390.02	398.97	407.91	417.39	426.33	435.81
52800	373.55	382.52	391.51	400.49	409.47	418.98	427.95	437.47
53000	374.96	383.98	392.99	402.01	411.02	420.56	429.58	439.12
53200	376.37	385.43	394.47	403.52	412.57	422.15	431.20	440.77
53400	377.79	386.87	395.96	405.04	414.13	423.74	432.82	442.44
53600	379.21	388.32	397.44	406.55	415.67	425.32	434.44	444.09
53800	380.62	389.77	398.92	408.08	417.22	426.92	436.06	445.75
54000	382.04	391.22	400.41	409.59	418.77	428.50	437.68	447.41
54200	383.45	392.67	401.89	411.10	420.33	430.08	439.31	449.06
54400	384.86	394.12	403.37	412.63	421.88	431.67	440.93	450.72
54600	386.28	395.57	404.85	414.14	423.42	433.26	442.54	452.38
54800	387.70	397.01	406.34	415.66	424.98	434.85	444.17	454.04
55000	389.11	398.47	407.82	417.18	426.53	436.43	445.79	455.69
55200	390.52	399.92	409.30	418.69	428.08	438.02	447.41	457.35
55400	391.94	401.36	410.79	420.21	429.64	439.61	449.03	459.01
55600	393.36	402.81	412.27	421.72	431.18	441.19	450.65	460.66
55800	394.77	404.26	413.75	423.25	432.73	442.79	452.27	462.32
56000	396.19	405.71	415.24	424.76	434.28	444.37	453.89	463.98
56200	397.60	407.16	416.72	426.27	435.84	445.95	455.52	465.63
56400	399.01	408.61	418.20	427.80	437.39	447.54	457.14	467.29
56600	400.43	410.06	419.68	429.31	438.93	449.13	458.75	468.95
56800	401.85	411.50	421.17	430.83	440.49	450.72	460.38	470.61
57000	403.26	412.95	422.65	432.35	442.04	452.30	462.00	472.26
57200	404.67	414.41	424.13	433.86	443.59	453.89	463.62	473.92
57400	406.09	415.85	425.62	435.38	445.15	455.48	465.24	475.58
57600	407.51	417.30	427.10	436.89	446.69	457.06	466.86	477.23
57800	408.92	418.75	428.58	438.42	448.24	458.66	468.48	478.89
58000	410.33	420.20	430.06	439.93	449.80	460.24	470.10	480.55
58200	411.75	421.65	431.55	441.44	451.35	461.82	471.73	482.20
58400	413.16	423.10	433.03	442.97	452.90	463.41	473.35	483.86
58600	414.58	424.55	434.51	444.48	454.44	465.00	474.96	485.52
58800	416.00	425.99	436.00	446.00	456.00	466.59	476.59	487.18
59000	417.41	427.44	437.48	447.52	457.55	468.17	478.21	488.83
59200	418.82	428.90	438.96	449.03	459.10	469.76	479.83	490.49
59400	420.24	430.34	440.45	450.55	460.66	471.35	481.46	492.15
59600	421.66	431.79	441.93	452.06	462.20	472.93	483.07	493.80
59800	423.07	433.24	443.41	453.59	463.75	474.53	484.69	495.47
60000	424.48	434.69	444.89	455.10	465.31	476.11	486.31	497.12

MONTHLY PAYMENTS FOR 30-YR. FHA LOANS

INCLUDING FIRST YEAR ½% MORTGAGE INSURANCE PREMIUMS

AMOUNT	INTEREST							
	9.00%	9.25%	9.50%	9.75%	10.00%	10.25%	10.50%	10.75%
48200	408.03	416.71	425.39	434.55	443.23	452.38	461.07	470.23
48400	409.72	418.44	427.15	436.35	445.07	454.27	462.98	472.18
48600	411.42	420.17	428.92	438.16	446.91	456.14	464.90	474.13
48800	413.11	421.89	430.69	439.96	448.74	458.02	466.81	476.08
49000	414.80	423.63	432.45	441.76	450.59	459.90	468.72	478.03
49200	416.50	425.36	434.21	443.56	452.43	461.77	470.63	479.99
49400	418.19	427.08	435.98	445.37	454.26	463.65	472.55	481.94
49600	419.88	428.82	437.75	447.17	456.10	465.53	474.46	483.88
49800	421.58	430.54	439.51	448.97	457.94	467.41	476.37	485.84
50000	423.27	432.27	441.28	450.78	459.78	469.28	478.29	487.79
50200	424.96	434.01	443.04	452.58	461.62	471.16	480.20	489.74
50400	426.65	435.73	444.80	454.38	463.46	473.04	482.11	491.69
50600	428.35	437.46	446.57	456.19	465.30	474.91	484.03	493.64
50800	430.04	439.18	448.34	457.99	467.13	476.80	485.94	495.59
51000	431.73	440.92	450.10	459.79	468.98	478.67	487.85	497.54
51200	433.43	442.65	451.86	461.60	470.82	480.54	489.77	499.50
51400	435.12	444.37	453.63	463.40	472.65	482.42	491.68	501.45
51600	436.81	446.11	455.40	465.20	474.50	484.30	493.59	503.39
51800	438.51	447.83	457.16	467.01	476.33	486.18	495.50	505.35
52000	440.20	449.56	458.93	468.81	478.17	488.05	497.42	507.30
52200	441.89	451.30	460.69	470.61	480.02	489.93	499.33	509.25
52400	443.59	453.02	462.45	472.41	481.85	491.81	501.24	511.21
52600	445.28	454.75	464.23	474.22	483.69	493.68	503.16	513.15
52800	446.97	456.48	465.99	476.02	485.52	495.57	505.07	515.10
53000	448.66	458.21	467.75	477.82	487.37	497.44	506.98	517.06
53200	450.36	459.94	469.51	479.63	489.21	499.31	508.90	519.01
53400	452.05	461.66	471.28	481.43	491.04	501.20	510.81	520.96
53600	453.74	463.40	473.05	483.23	492.89	503.07	512.72	522.91
53800	455.44	465.12	474.81	485.04	494.72	504.95	514.64	524.86
54000	457.13	466.85	476.58	486.84	496.56	506.83	516.55	526.81
54200	458.82	468.59	478.34	488.64	498.41	508.70	518.46	528.76
54400	460.52	470.31	480.10	490.45	500.24	510.58	520.38	530.72
54600	462.21	472.04	481.88	492.25	502.08	512.45	522.29	532.66
54800	463.90	473.77	483.64	494.05	503.92	514.34	524.20	534.61
55000	465.60	475.50	485.40	495.86	505.76	516.21	526.11	536.57
55200	467.29	477.23	487.17	497.66	507.60	518.08	528.03	538.52
55400	468.98	478.96	488.93	499.46	509.44	519.97	529.94	540.47
55600	470.67	480.69	490.70	501.26	511.28	521.84	531.85	542.42
55800	472.37	482.41	492.47	503.07	513.11	523.72	533.77	544.37
56000	474.06	484.14	494.23	504.87	514.95	525.60	535.68	546.32
56200	475.75	485.88	495.99	506.67	516.80	527.47	537.59	548.28
56400	477.45	487.60	497.75	508.48	518.63	529.35	539.51	550.23
56600	479.14	489.33	499.53	510.28	520.47	531.23	541.42	552.17
56800	480.83	491.06	501.29	512.08	522.31	533.11	543.33	554.13
57000	482.53	492.79	503.05	513.89	524.15	534.98	545.25	556.08
57200	484.22	494.52	504.82	515.69	525.99	536.86	547.16	558.03
57400	485.91	496.25	506.58	517.49	527.83	538.74	549.07	559.98
57600	487.61	497.98	508.35	519.30	529.67	540.61	550.99	561.93
57800	489.30	499.70	510.12	521.10	531.50	542.49	552.90	563.88
58000	490.99	501.44	511.88	522.90	533.35	544.37	554.81	565.83
58200	492.68	503.17	513.64	524.70	535.19	546.24	556.73	567.79
58400	494.38	504.89	515.41	526.51	537.02	548.12	558.64	569.74
58600	496.07	506.62	517.18	528.31	538.86	550.00	560.55	571.68
58800	497.76	508.35	518.94	530.11	540.70	551.88	562.46	573.64
59000	499.46	510.08	520.70	531.92	542.54	553.75	564.38	575.59
59200	501.15	511.81	522.47	533.72	544.38	555.63	566.29	577.54
59400	502.84	513.54	524.23	535.52	546.21	557.50	568.20	579.50
59600	504.54	515.27	526.00	537.33	548.06	559.38	570.12	581.44
59800	506.23	516.99	527.77	539.13	549.89	561.27	572.03	583.39
60000	507.92	518.73	529.53	540.93	551.74	563.14	573.94	585.35

PRORATIONS FROM JAN. 1st TO PRORATION DATE

DATE	JAN Days Past	% of 360	FEB Days Past	% of 360	MAR Days Past	% of 360	APR Days Past	% of 360	MAY Days Past	% of 360	JUN Days Past	% of 360	DATE
1	1	.28	31	8.61	61	16.94	91	25.28	121	33.61	151	41.94	1
2	2	.56	32	8.89	62	17.22	92	25.56	122	33.89	152	42.22	2
3	3	.83	33	9.17	63	17.50	93	25.83	123	34.17	153	42.50	3
4	4	1.11	34	9.44	64	17.78	94	26.11	124	34.44	154	42.78	4
5	5	1.39	35	9.72	65	18.06	95	26.39	125	34.72	155	43.06	5
6	6	1.67	36	10.00	66	18.33	96	26.67	126	35.00	156	43.33	6
7	7	1.94	37	10.28	67	18.61	97	26.94	127	35.28	157	43.61	7
8	8	2.22	38	10.56	68	18.89	98	27.22	128	35.56	158	43.89	8
9	9	2.50	39	10.83	69	19.17	99	27.50	129	35.83	159	44.17	9
10	10	2.78	40	11.11	70	19.44	100	27.78	130	36.11	160	44.44	10
11	11	3.06	41	11.39	71	19.72	101	28.06	131	36.39	161	44.72	11
12	12	3.33	42	11.67	72	20.00	102	28.33	132	36.67	162	45.00	12
13	13	3.61	43	11.94	73	20.28	103	28.61	133	36.94	163	45.28	13
14	14	3.89	44	12.22	74	20.56	104	28.89	134	37.22	164	45.56	14
15	15	4.17	45	12.50	75	20.83	105	29.17	135	37.50	165	45.83	15
16	16	4.44	46	12.78	76	21.11	106	29.44	136	37.78	166	46.11	16
17	17	4.72	47	13.06	77	21.39	107	29.72	137	38.06	167	46.39	17
18	18	5.00	48	13.33	78	21.67	108	30.00	138	38.33	168	46.67	18
19	19	5.28	49	13.61	79	21.94	109	30.28	139	38.61	169	46.94	19
20	20	5.56	50	13.89	80	22.22	110	30.56	140	38.89	170	47.22	20
21	21	5.83	51	14.17	81	22.50	111	30.83	141	39.17	171	47.50	21
22	22	6.11	52	14.44	82	22.78	112	31.11	142	39.44	172	47.78	22
23	23	6.39	53	14.72	83	23.06	113	31.39	143	39.72	173	48.06	23
24	24	6.67	54	15.00	84	23.33	114	31.67	144	40.00	174	48.33	24
25	25	6.94	55	15.28	85	23.61	115	31.94	145	40.28	175	48.61	25
26	26	7.22	56	15.56	86	23.89	116	32.22	146	40.56	176	48.89	26
27	27	7.50	57	15.83	87	24.17	117	32.50	147	40.83	177	49.17	27
28	28	7.78	58	16.11	88	24.44	118	32.78	148	41.11	178	49.44	28
29	29	8.06	59	16.39	89	24.72	119	33.06	149	41.39	179	49.72	29
30	30	8.33	60	16.67	90	25.00	120	33.33	150	41.67	180	50.00	30

PRORATIONS FROM PRORATION DATE TO DEC. 31st

DATE	JAN Days to Come	% of 360	FEB Days to Come	% of 360	MAR Days to Come	% of 360	APR Days to Come	% of 360	MAY Days to Come	% of 360	JUN Days to Come	% of 360	DATE
1	360	100.00	330	91.67	300	83.33	270	75.00	240	66.67	210	58.33	1
2	359	99.72	329	91.39	299	83.06	269	74.72	239	66.39	209	58.06	2
3	358	99.44	328	91.11	298	82.78	268	74.44	238	66.11	208	57.78	3
4	357	99.17	327	90.83	297	82.50	267	74.17	237	65.83	207	57.50	4
5	356	98.89	326	90.56	296	82.22	266	73.89	236	65.56	206	57.22	5
6	355	98.61	325	90.28	295	81.94	265	73.61	235	65.28	205	56.94	6
7	354	98.33	324	90.00	294	81.67	264	73.33	234	65.00	204	56.67	7
8	353	98.06	323	89.72	293	81.39	263	73.06	233	64.72	203	56.39	8
9	352	97.78	322	89.44	292	81.11	262	72.78	232	64.44	202	56.11	9
10	351	97.50	321	89.17	291	80.83	261	72.50	231	64.17	201	55.83	10
11	350	97.22	320	88.89	290	80.56	260	72.22	230	63.89	200	55.56	11
12	349	96.94	319	88.61	289	80.28	259	71.94	229	63.61	199	55.28	12
13	348	96.67	318	88.33	288	80.00	258	71.67	228	63.33	198	55.00	13
14	347	96.39	317	88.06	287	79.72	257	71.39	227	63.06	197	54.72	14
15	346	96.11	316	87.78	286	79.44	256	71.11	226	62.78	196	54.44	15
16	345	95.83	315	87.50	285	79.17	255	70.83	225	62.50	195	54.17	16
17	344	95.56	314	87.22	284	78.89	254	70.56	224	62.22	194	53.89	17
18	343	95.28	313	86.94	283	78.61	253	70.28	223	61.94	193	53.61	18
19	342	95.00	312	86.67	282	78.33	252	70.00	222	61.67	192	53.33	19
20	341	94.72	311	86.39	281	78.06	251	69.72	221	61.39	191	53.06	20
21	340	94.44	310	86.11	280	77.78	250	69.44	220	61.11	190	52.78	21
22	339	94.17	309	85.83	279	77.50	249	69.17	219	60.83	189	52.50	22
23	338	93.89	308	85.56	278	77.22	248	68.89	218	60.56	188	52.22	23
24	337	93.61	307	85.28	277	76.94	247	68.61	217	60.28	187	51.94	24
25	336	93.33	306	85.00	276	76.67	246	68.33	216	60.00	186	51.67	25
26	335	93.06	305	84.72	275	76.39	245	68.06	215	59.72	185	51.39	26
27	334	92.78	304	84.44	274	76.11	244	67.78	214	59.44	184	51.11	27
28	333	92.50	303	84.17	273	75.83	243	67.50	213	59.17	183	50.83	28
29	332	92.22	302	83.89	272	75.56	242	67.22	212	58.89	182	50.56	29
30	331	91.94	301	83.61	271	75.28	241	66.94	211	58.61	181	50.28	30

PRORATIONS FROM JAN. 1st TO PRORATION DATE

DATE	JUL Days Past	JUL % of 360	AUG Days Past	AUG % of 360	SEP Days Past	SEP % of 360	OCT Days Past	OCT % of 360	NOV Days Past	NOV % of 360	DEC Days Past	DEC % of 360	DATE
1	181	50.28	211	58.61	241	66.94	271	75.28	301	83.61	331	91.94	1
2	182	50.56	212	58.89	242	67.22	272	75.56	302	83.89	332	92.22	2
3	183	50.83	213	59.17	243	67.50	273	75.83	303	84.17	333	92.50	3
4	184	51.11	214	59.44	244	67.78	274	76.11	304	84.44	334	92.78	4
5	185	51.39	215	59.72	245	68.06	275	76.39	305	84.72	335	93.06	5
6	186	51.67	216	60.00	246	68.33	276	76.67	306	85.00	336	93.33	6
7	187	51.94	217	60.28	247	68.61	277	76.94	307	85.28	337	93.61	7
8	188	52.22	218	60.56	248	68.89	278	77.22	308	85.56	338	93.89	8
9	189	52.50	219	60.83	249	69.17	279	77.50	309	85.83	339	94.17	9
10	190	52.78	220	61.11	250	69.44	280	77.78	310	86.11	340	94.44	10
11	191	53.06	221	61.39	251	69.72	281	78.06	311	86.39	341	94.72	11
12	192	53.33	222	61.67	252	70.00	282	78.33	312	86.67	342	95.00	12
13	193	53.61	223	61.94	253	70.28	283	78.61	313	86.94	343	95.28	13
14	194	53.89	224	62.22	254	70.56	284	78.89	314	87.22	344	95.56	14
15	195	54.17	225	62.50	255	70.83	285	79.17	315	87.50	345	95.83	15
16	196	54.44	226	62.78	256	71.11	286	79.44	316	87.78	346	96.11	16
17	197	54.72	227	63.06	257	71.39	287	79.72	317	88.06	347	96.39	17
18	198	55.00	228	63.33	258	71.67	288	80.00	318	88.33	348	96.67	18
19	199	55.28	229	63.61	259	71.94	289	80.28	319	88.61	349	96.94	19
20	200	55.56	230	63.89	260	72.22	290	80.56	320	88.89	350	97.22	20
21	201	55.83	231	64.17	261	72.50	291	80.83	321	89.17	351	97.50	21
22	202	56.11	232	64.44	262	72.78	292	81.11	322	89.44	352	97.78	22
23	203	56.39	233	64.72	263	73.06	293	81.39	323	89.72	353	98.06	23
24	204	56.67	234	65.00	264	73.33	294	81.67	324	90.00	354	98.33	24
25	205	56.94	235	65.28	265	73.61	295	81.94	325	90.28	355	98.61	25
26	206	57.22	236	65.56	266	73.89	296	82.22	326	90.56	356	98.89	26
27	207	57.50	237	65.83	267	74.17	297	82.50	327	90.83	357	99.17	27
28	208	57.78	238	66.11	268	74.44	298	82.78	328	91.11	358	99.44	28
29	209	58.06	239	66.39	269	74.72	299	83.06	329	91.39	359	99.72	29
30	210	58.33	240	66.67	270	75.00	300	83.33	330	91.67	360	100.00	30

PRORATIONS FROM PRORATION DATE TO DEC. 31st

DATE	JUL Days to Come	JUL % of 360	AUG Days to Come	AUG % of 360	SEP Days to Come	SEP % of 360	OCT Days to Come	OCT % of 360	NOV Days to Come	NOV % of 360	DEC Days to Come	DEC % of 360	DATE
1	180	50.00	150	41.67	120	33.33	90	25.00	60	16.67	30	8.33	1
2	179	49.72	149	41.39	119	33.06	89	24.72	59	16.39	29	8.06	2
3	178	49.44	148	41.11	118	32.78	88	24.44	58	16.11	28	7.78	3
4	177	49.17	147	40.83	117	32.50	87	24.17	57	15.83	27	7.50	4
5	176	48.89	146	40.56	116	32.22	86	23.89	56	15.56	26	7.22	5
6	175	48.61	145	40.28	115	31.94	85	23.61	55	15.28	25	6.94	6
7	174	48.33	144	40.00	114	31.67	84	23.33	54	15.00	24	6.67	7
8	173	48.06	143	39.72	113	31.39	83	23.06	53	14.72	23	6.39	8
9	172	47.78	142	39.44	112	31.11	82	22.78	52	14.44	22	6.11	9
10	171	47.50	141	39.17	111	30.83	81	22.50	51	14.17	21	5.83	10
11	170	47.22	140	38.89	110	30.56	80	22.22	50	13.89	20	5.56	11
12	169	46.94	139	38.61	109	30.28	79	21.94	49	13.61	19	5.28	12
13	168	46.67	138	38.33	108	30.00	78	21.67	48	13.33	18	5.00	13
14	167	46.39	137	38.06	107	29.72	77	21.39	47	13.06	17	4.72	14
15	166	46.11	136	37.78	106	29.44	76	21.11	46	12.78	16	4.44	15
16	165	45.83	135	37.50	105	29.17	75	20.83	45	12.50	15	4.17	16
17	164	45.56	134	37.22	104	28.89	74	20.56	44	12.22	14	3.89	17
18	163	45.28	133	36.94	103	28.61	73	20.28	43	11.94	13	3.61	18
19	162	45.00	132	36.67	102	28.33	72	20.00	42	11.67	12	3.33	19
20	161	44.72	131	36.39	101	28.06	71	19.72	41	11.39	11	3.06	20
21	160	44.44	130	36.11	100	27.78	70	19.44	40	11.11	10	2.78	21
22	159	44.17	129	35.83	99	27.50	69	19.17	39	10.83	9	2.50	22
23	158	43.89	128	35.56	98	27.22	68	18.89	38	10.56	8	2.22	23
24	157	43.61	127	35.28	97	26.94	67	18.61	37	10.28	7	1.94	24
25	156	43.33	126	35.00	96	26.67	66	18.33	36	10.00	6	1.67	25
26	155	43.06	125	34.72	95	26.39	65	18.06	35	9.72	5	1.39	26
27	154	42.78	124	34.44	94	26.11	64	17.78	34	9.44	4	1.11	27
28	153	42.50	123	34.17	93	25.83	63	17.50	33	9.17	3	.83	28
29	152	42.22	122	33.89	92	25.56	62	17.22	32	8.89	2	.56	29
30	151	41.94	121	33.61	91	25.28	61	16.94	31	8.61	1	.28	30

PRORATIONS FROM JAN. 1st TO PRORATION DATE

DATE	JAN Days Past	JAN % of 365	FEB Days Past	FEB % of 365	MAR Days Past	MAR % of 365	APR Days Past	APR % of 365	MAY Days Past	MAY % of 365	JUN Days Past	JUN % of 365	DATE
1	1	.27	32	8.77	60	16.44	91	24.93	121	33.15	152	41.64	1
2	2	.55	33	9.04	61	16.71	92	25.21	122	33.42	153	41.92	2
3	3	.82	34	9.32	62	16.99	93	25.48	123	33.70	154	42.19	3
4	4	1.10	35	9.59	63	17.26	94	25.75	124	33.97	155	42.47	4
5	5	1.37	36	9.86	64	17.53	95	26.03	125	34.25	156	42.74	5
6	6	1.64	37	10.14	65	17.81	96	26.30	126	34.52	157	43.01	6
7	7	1.92	38	10.41	66	18.08	97	26.58	127	34.79	158	43.29	7
8	8	2.19	39	10.68	67	18.36	98	26.85	128	35.07	159	43.56	8
9	9	2.47	40	10.96	68	18.63	99	27.12	129	35.34	160	43.84	9
10	10	2.74	41	11.23	69	18.90	100	27.40	130	35.62	161	44.11	10
11	11	3.01	42	11.51	70	19.18	101	27.67	131	35.89	162	44.38	11
12	12	3.29	43	11.78	71	19.45	102	27.95	132	36.16	163	44.66	12
13	13	3.56	44	12.05	72	19.73	103	28.22	133	36.44	164	44.93	13
14	14	3.84	45	12.33	73	20.00	104	28.49	134	36.71	165	45.21	14
15	15	4.11	46	12.60	74	20.27	105	28.77	135	36.99	166	45.48	15
16	16	4.38	47	12.88	75	20.55	106	29.04	136	37.26	167	45.75	16
17	17	4.66	48	13.15	76	20.82	107	29.32	137	37.53	168	46.03	17
18	18	4.93	49	13.42	77	21.10	108	29.59	138	37.81	169	46.30	18
19	19	5.21	50	13.70	78	21.37	109	29.86	139	38.08	170	46.58	19
20	20	5.48	51	13.97	79	21.64	110	30.14	140	38.36	171	46.85	20
21	21	5.75	52	14.25	80	21.92	111	30.41	141	38.63	172	47.12	21
22	22	6.03	53	14.52	81	22.19	112	30.68	142	38.90	173	47.40	22
23	23	6.30	54	14.79	82	22.47	113	30.96	143	39.18	174	47.67	23
24	24	6.58	55	15.07	83	22.74	114	31.23	144	39.45	175	47.95	24
25	25	6.85	56	15.34	84	23.01	115	31.51	145	39.73	176	48.22	25
26	26	7.12	57	15.62	85	23.29	116	31.78	146	40.00	177	48.49	26
27	27	7.40	58	15.89	86	23.56	117	32.05	147	40.27	178	48.77	27
28	28	7.67	59	16.16	87	23.84	118	32.33	148	40.55	179	49.04	28
29	29	7.95			88	24.11	119	32.60	149	40.82	180	49.32	29
30	30	8.22			89	24.38	120	32.88	150	41.10	181	49.59	30
31	31	8.49			90	24.66			151	41.37			31

PRORATIONS FROM PRORATION DATE TO DEC. 31st

DATE	JAN Days to Come	JAN % of 365	FEB Days to Come	FEB % of 365	MAR Days to Come	MAR % of 365	APR Days to Come	APR % of 365	MAY Days to Come	MAY % of 365	JUN Days to Come	JUN % of 365	DATE
1	365	100.00	334	91.51	306	83.84	275	75.34	245	67.12	214	58.63	1
2	364	99.73	333	91.23	305	83.56	274	75.07	244	66.85	213	58.36	2
3	363	99.45	332	90.96	304	83.29	273	74.79	243	66.58	212	58.08	3
4	362	99.18	331	90.68	303	83.01	272	74.52	242	66.30	211	57.81	4
5	361	98.90	330	90.41	302	82.74	271	74.25	241	66.03	210	57.53	5
6	360	98.63	329	90.14	301	82.47	270	73.97	240	65.75	209	57.26	6
7	359	98.36	328	89.86	300	82.19	269	73.70	239	65.48	208	56.99	7
8	358	98.08	327	89.59	299	81.92	268	73.42	238	65.21	207	56.71	8
9	357	97.81	326	89.32	298	81.64	267	73.15	237	64.93	206	56.44	9
10	356	97.53	325	89.04	297	81.37	266	72.88	236	64.66	205	56.16	10
11	355	97.26	324	88.77	296	81.10	265	72.60	235	64.38	204	55.89	11
12	354	96.99	323	88.49	295	80.82	264	72.33	234	64.11	203	55.62	12
13	353	96.71	322	88.22	294	80.55	263	72.05	233	63.84	202	55.34	13
14	352	96.44	321	87.95	293	80.27	262	71.78	232	63.56	201	55.07	14
15	351	96.16	320	87.67	292	80.00	261	71.51	231	63.29	200	54.79	15
16	350	95.89	319	87.40	291	79.73	260	71.23	230	63.01	199	54.52	16
17	349	95.62	318	87.12	290	79.45	259	70.96	229	62.74	198	54.25	17
18	348	95.34	317	86.85	289	79.18	258	70.68	228	62.47	197	53.97	18
19	347	95.07	316	86.58	288	78.90	257	70.41	227	62.19	196	53.70	19
20	346	94.79	315	86.30	287	78.63	256	70.14	226	61.92	195	53.42	20
21	345	94.52	314	86.03	286	78.36	255	69.86	225	61.64	194	53.15	21
22	344	94.25	313	85.75	285	78.08	254	69.59	224	61.37	193	52.88	22
23	343	93.97	312	85.48	284	77.81	253	69.32	223	61.10	192	52.60	23
24	342	93.70	311	85.21	283	77.53	252	69.04	222	60.82	191	52.33	24
25	341	93.42	310	84.93	282	77.26	251	68.77	221	60.55	190	52.05	25
26	340	93.15	309	84.66	281	76.99	250	68.49	220	60.27	189	51.78	26
27	339	92.88	308	84.38	280	76.71	249	68.22	219	60.00	188	51.51	27
28	338	92.60	307	84.11	279	76.44	248	67.95	218	59.73	187	51.23	28
29	337	92.33			278	76.16	247	67.67	217	59.45	186	50.96	29
30	336	92.05			277	75.89	246	67.40	216	59.18	185	50.68	30
31	335	91.78			276	75.62			215	58.90	184		31

PRORATIONS FROM JAN. 1st TO PRORATION DATE

DATE	JUL Days Past	JUL % of 365	AUG Days Past	AUG % of 365	SEP Days Past	SEP % of 365	OCT Days Past	OCT % of 365	NOV Days Past	NOV % of 365	DEC Days Past	DEC % of 365	DATE
1	182	49.86	213	58.36	244	66.85	274	75.07	305	83.56	335	91.78	1
2	183	50.14	214	58.63	245	67.12	275	75.34	306	83.84	336	92.05	2
3	184	50.41	215	58.90	246	67.40	276	75.62	307	84.11	337	92.33	3
4	185	50.68	216	59.18	247	67.67	277	75.89	308	84.38	338	92.60	4
5	186	50.96	217	59.45	248	67.95	278	76.16	309	84.66	339	92.88	5
6	187	51.23	218	59.73	249	68.22	279	76.44	310	84.93	340	93.15	6
7	188	51.51	219	60.00	250	68.49	280	76.71	311	85.21	341	93.42	7
8	189	51.78	220	60.27	251	68.77	281	76.99	312	85.48	342	93.70	8
9	190	52.05	221	60.55	252	69.04	282	77.26	313	85.75	343	93.97	9
10	191	52.33	222	60.82	253	69.32	283	77.53	314	86.03	344	94.25	10
11	192	52.60	223	61.10	254	69.59	284	77.81	315	86.30	345	94.52	11
12	193	52.88	224	61.37	255	69.86	285	78.08	316	86.58	346	94.79	12
13	194	53.15	225	61.64	256	70.14	286	78.36	317	86.85	347	95.07	13
14	195	53.42	226	61.92	257	70.41	287	78.63	318	87.12	348	95.34	14
15	196	53.70	227	62.19	258	70.68	288	78.90	319	87.40	349	95.62	15
16	197	53.97	228	62.47	259	70.96	289	79.18	320	87.67	350	95.89	16
17	198	54.25	229	62.74	260	71.23	290	79.45	321	87.95	351	96.16	17
18	199	54.52	230	63.01	261	71.51	291	79.73	322	88.22	352	96.44	18
19	200	54.79	231	63.29	262	71.78	292	80.00	323	88.49	353	96.71	19
20	201	55.07	232	63.56	263	72.05	293	80.27	324	88.77	354	96.99	20
21	202	55.34	233	63.84	264	72.33	294	80.55	325	89.04	355	97.26	21
22	203	55.62	234	64.11	265	72.60	295	80.82	326	89.32	356	97.53	22
23	204	55.89	235	64.38	266	72.88	296	81.10	327	89.59	357	97.81	23
24	205	56.16	236	64.66	267	73.15	297	81.37	328	89.86	358	98.08	24
25	206	56.44	237	64.93	268	73.42	298	81.64	329	90.14	359	98.36	25
26	207	56.71	238	65.21	269	73.70	299	81.92	330	90.41	360	98.63	26
27	208	56.99	239	65.48	270	73.97	300	82.19	331	90.68	361	98.90	27
28	209	57.26	240	65.75	271	74.25	301	82.47	332	90.96	362	99.18	28
29	210	57.53	241	66.03	272	74.52	302	82.74	333	91.23	363	99.45	29
30	211	57.81	242	66.30	273	74.79	303	83.01	334	91.51	364	99.73	30
31	212	58.08	243	66.58			304	83.29			365	100.00	31

PRORATIONS FROM PRORATION DATE TO DEC. 31st

DATE	JUL Days to Come	JUL % 365	AUG Days to Come	AUG % 365	SEP Days to Come	SEP % 365	OCT Days to Come	OCT % 365	NOV Days to Come	NOV % 365	DEC Days to Come	DEC % 365	DATE
1	184	50.41	153	41.92	122	33.42	92	25.21	61	16.71	31	8.49	1
2	183	50.14	152	41.64	121	33.15	91	24.93	60	16.44	30	8.22	2
3	182	49.86	151	41.37	120	32.88	90	24.66	59	16.16	29	7.95	3
4	181	49.59	150	41.10	119	32.60	89	24.38	58	15.89	28	7.67	4
5	180	49.32	149	40.82	118	32.33	88	24.11	57	15.62	27	7.40	5
6	179	49.04	148	40.55	117	32.05	87	23.84	56	15.34	26	7.12	6
7	178	48.77	147	40.27	116	31.78	86	23.56	55	15.07	25	6.85	7
8	177	48.49	146	40.00	115	31.51	85	23.29	54	14.79	24	6.58	8
9	176	48.22	145	39.73	114	31.23	84	23.01	53	14.52	23	6.30	9
10	175	47.95	144	39.45	113	30.96	83	22.74	52	14.25	22	6.03	10
11	174	47.67	143	39.18	112	30.68	82	22.47	51	13.97	21	5.75	11
12	173	47.40	142	38.90	111	30.41	81	22.19	50	13.70	20	5.48	12
13	172	47.12	141	38.63	110	30.14	80	21.92	49	13.42	19	5.21	13
14	171	46.85	140	38.36	109	29.86	79	21.64	48	13.15	18	4.93	14
15	170	46.58	139	38.08	108	29.59	78	21.37	47	12.88	17	4.66	15
16	169	46.30	138	37.81	107	29.32	77	21.10	46	12.60	16	4.38	16
17	168	46.03	137	37.53	106	29.04	76	20.82	45	12.33	15	4.11	17
18	167	45.75	136	37.26	105	28.77	75	20.55	44	12.05	14	3.84	18
19	166	45.48	135	36.99	104	28.49	74	20.27	43	11.78	13	3.56	19
20	165	45.21	134	36.71	103	28.22	73	20.00	42	11.51	12	3.29	20
21	164	44.93	133	36.44	102	27.95	72	19.73	41	11.23	11	3.01	21
22	163	44.66	132	36.16	101	27.67	71	19.45	40	10.96	10	2.74	22
23	162	44.38	131	35.89	100	27.40	70	19.18	39	10.68	9	2.47	23
24	161	44.11	130	35.62	99	27.12	69	18.90	38	10.41	8	2.19	24
25	160	43.84	129	35.34	98	26.85	68	18.63	37	10.14	7	1.92	25
26	159	43.56	128	35.07	97	26.58	67	18.36	36	9.86	6	1.64	26
27	158	43.29	127	34.79	96	26.30	66	18.08	35	9.59	5	1.37	27
28	157	43.01	126	34.52	95	26.03	65	17.81	34	9.32	4	1.10	28
29	156	42.74	125	34.25	94	25.75	64	17.53	33	9.04	3	.82	29
30	155	42.47	124	33.97	93	25.48	63	17.26	32	8.77	2	.55	30
31	154	42.19	123	33.70			62	16.99			1	.27	31

EQUITY BUILD-UP

15 YEAR TERM

IN PERCENT OF ORIGINAL LOAN AMOUNT
FOR FIRST 10 YEARS

15 YEAR TERM

YEAR	ANN. %	CUM. %	ANN. %	CUM. %	ANN. %	CUM. %	ANN. %	CUM. %	ANN. %	CUM. %	YEAR
	6.00%		6.25%		6.50%		6.75%		7.00%		
1	4.2	4.2	4.2	4.2	4.1	4.1	4.0	4.0	3.9	3.9	1
2	4.5	8.7	4.4	8.6	4.3	8.4	4.3	8.3	4.2	8.1	2
3	4.8	13.5	4.7	13.3	4.6	13.1	4.6	12.8	4.5	12.6	3
4	5.1	18.6	5.0	18.3	4.9	18.0	4.9	17.7	4.8	17.4	4
5	5.4	24.0	5.3	23.6	5.3	23.3	5.2	22.9	5.2	22.6	5
6	5.7	29.7	5.7	29.3	5.6	28.9	5.6	28.5	5.5	28.1	6
7	6.1	35.8	6.0	35.4	6.0	34.9	6.0	34.5	5.9	34.1	7
8	6.4	42.2	6.4	41.8	6.4	41.3	6.4	40.9	6.4	40.4	8
9	6.8	49.1	6.8	48.6	6.8	48.2	6.8	47.7	6.8	47.3	9
10	7.3	56.4	7.3	55.9	7.3	55.5	7.3	55.0	7.3	54.6	10
	7.25%		7.50%		7.75%		8.00%		8.25%		
1	3.8	3.8	3.8	3.8	3.7	3.7	3.6	3.6	3.5	3.5	1
2	4.1	7.9	4.0	7.8	4.0	7.6	3.9	7.5	3.8	7.3	2
3	4.4	12.4	4.4	12.2	4.3	11.9	4.2	11.7	4.2	11.5	3
4	4.8	17.1	4.7	16.8	4.6	16.6	4.6	16.3	4.5	16.0	4
5	5.1	22.2	5.1	21.9	5.0	21.6	4.9	21.2	4.9	20.9	5
6	5.5	27.7	5.5	27.4	5.4	27.0	5.4	26.6	5.3	26.2	6
7	5.9	33.7	5.9	33.2	5.8	32.8	5.8	32.4	5.8	32.0	7
8	6.4	40.0	6.3	39.6	6.3	39.1	6.3	38.7	6.3	38.3	8
9	6.8	46.8	6.8	46.4	6.8	45.9	6.8	45.5	6.8	45.1	9
10	7.3	54.2	7.4	53.7	7.4	53.3	7.4	52.9	7.4	52.4	10
	8.50%		8.75%		9.00%		9.25%		9.50%		
1	3.4	3.4	3.4	3.4	3.3	3.3	3.2	3.2	3.2	3.2	1
2	3.8	7.2	3.7	7.1	3.6	6.9	3.5	6.8	3.5	6.6	2
3	4.1	11.3	4.0	11.1	4.0	10.9	3.9	10.7	3.8	10.5	3
4	4.4	15.7	4.4	15.5	4.3	15.2	4.3	14.9	4.2	14.7	4
5	4.8	20.6	4.8	20.3	4.7	19.9	4.7	19.6	4.6	19.3	5
6	5.3	25.8	5.2	25.5	5.2	25.1	5.1	24.7	5.1	24.4	6
7	5.7	31.6	5.7	31.2	5.7	30.8	5.6	30.4	5.6	30.0	7
8	6.2	37.8	6.2	37.4	6.2	37.0	6.2	36.5	6.1	36.1	8
9	6.8	44.6	6.8	44.2	6.8	43.7	6.8	43.3	6.7	42.9	9
10	7.4	52.0	7.4	51.6	7.4	51.1	7.4	50.7	7.4	50.3	10
	9.75%		10.00%		10.25%		10.50%		10.75%		
1	3.1	3.1	3.0	3.0	3.0	3.0	2.9	2.9	2.8	2.8	1
2	3.4	6.5	3.3	6.4	3.3	6.3	3.2	6.1	3.2	6.0	2
3	3.8	10.3	3.7	10.1	3.6	9.9	3.6	9.7	3.5	9.5	3
4	4.1	14.4	4.1	14.2	4.0	13.9	4.0	13.7	3.9	13.4	4
5	4.6	19.0	4.5	18.7	4.5	18.4	4.4	18.1	4.4	17.8	5
6	5.0	24.0	5.0	23.7	4.9	23.3	4.9	23.0	4.8	22.6	6
7	5.5	29.6	5.5	29.2	5.5	28.8	5.4	28.4	5.4	28.0	7
8	6.1	35.7	6.1	35.3	6.1	34.9	6.0	34.4	6.0	34.0	8
9	6.7	42.4	6.7	42.0	6.7	41.6	6.7	41.1	6.7	40.7	9
10	7.4	49.9	7.4	49.4	7.4	49.0	7.4	48.6	7.4	48.1	10
	11.00%		11.25%		11.50%		11.75%		12.00%		
1	2.8	2.8	2.7	2.7	2.7	2.7	2.6	2.6	2.5	2.5	1
2	3.1	5.9	3.0	5.8	3.0	5.6	2.9	5.5	2.9	5.4	2
3	3.5	9.3	3.4	9.1	3.3	9.0	3.3	8.8	3.2	8.6	3
4	3.9	13.2	3.8	12.9	3.7	12.7	3.7	12.5	3.6	12.3	4
5	4.3	17.5	4.2	17.2	4.2	16.9	4.1	16.6	4.1	16.3	5
6	4.8	22.3	4.8	22.0	4.7	21.6	4.7	21.3	4.6	21.0	6
7	5.3	27.6	5.3	27.3	5.3	26.9	5.2	26.5	5.2	26.2	7
8	6.0	33.6	5.9	33.2	5.9	32.8	5.9	32.4	5.9	32.0	8
9	6.7	40.3	6.7	39.9	6.6	39.4	6.6	39.0	6.6	38.6	9
10	7.4	47.7	7.4	47.3	7.4	46.9	7.4	46.5	7.4	46.0	10

20 YEAR TERM — IN PERCENT OF ORIGINAL LOAN AMOUNT FOR FIRST 10 YEARS — **20 YEAR TERM**

YEAR	6.00% ANN. %	6.00% CUM. %	6.25% ANN. %	6.25% CUM. %	6.50% ANN. %	6.50% CUM. %	6.75% ANN. %	6.75% CUM. %	7.00% ANN. %	7.00% CUM. %	YEAR
1	2.7	2.7	2.6	2.6	2.5	2.5	2.4	2.4	2.4	2.4	1
2	2.8	5.5	2.8	5.5	2.7	5.2	2.6	5.1	2.6	4.9	2
3	3.0	8.5	2.9	8.3	2.9	8.1	2.8	7.9	2.7	7.7	3
4	3.2	11.7	3.1	11.4	3.1	11.1	3.0	10.9	2.9	10.6	4
5	3.4	15.1	3.3	14.8	3.3	14.4	3.2	14.1	3.1	13.7	5
6	3.6	18.7	3.5	18.3	3.5	17.9	3.4	17.5	3.4	17.1	6
7	3.8	22.5	3.8	22.1	3.7	21.6	3.7	21.2	3.6	20.7	7
8	4.1	26.6	4.0	26.1	4.0	25.6	3.9	25.1	3.9	24.6	8
9	4.3	30.9	4.3	30.4	4.2	29.8	4.2	29.3	4.2	28.8	9
10	4.6	35.5	4.5	34.9	4.5	34.3	4.5	33.8	4.5	33.2	10

YEAR	7.25% ANN. %	7.25% CUM. %	7.50% ANN. %	7.50% CUM. %	7.75% ANN. %	7.75% CUM. %	8.00% ANN. %	8.00% CUM. %	8.25% ANN. %	8.25% CUM. %	YEAR
1	2.3	2.3	2.2	2.2	2.2	2.2	2.1	2.1	2.1	2.1	1
2	2.5	4.8	2.4	4.7	2.4	4.5	2.3	4.4	2.2	4.3	2
3	2.7	7.5	2.6	7.3	2.5	7.1	2.5	6.9	2.4	6.7	3
4	2.9	10.3	2.8	10.1	2.7	9.8	2.7	9.6	2.6	9.3	4
5	3.1	13.4	3.0	13.1	3.0	12.8	2.9	12.5	2.8	12.2	5
6	3.3	16.7	3.3	16.4	3.2	16.0	3.1	15.6	3.1	15.3	6
7	3.6	20.3	3.5	19.9	3.5	19.4	3.4	19.0	3.4	18.6	7
8	3.8	24.1	3.8	23.7	3.7	23.2	3.7	22.7	3.6	22.3	8
9	4.1	28.2	4.1	27.7	4.0	27.2	4.0	26.7	4.0	26.2	9
10	4.4	32.7	4.4	32.1	4.4	31.6	4.3	31.1	4.3	30.5	10

YEAR	8.50% ANN. %	8.50% CUM. %	8.75% ANN. %	8.75% CUM. %	9.00% ANN. %	9.00% CUM. %	9.25% ANN. %	9.25% CUM. %	9.50% ANN. %	9.50% CUM. %	YEAR
1	2.0	2.0	1.9	1.9	1.9	1.9	1.8	1.8	1.8	1.8	1
2	2.2	4.2	2.1	4.0	2.0	3.9	2.0	3.8	1.9	3.7	2
3	2.4	6.5	2.3	6.3	2.2	6.2	2.2	6.0	2.1	5.8	3
4	2.6	9.1	2.5	8.8	2.5	8.6	2.4	8.4	2.3	8.2	4
5	2.8	11.9	2.7	11.6	2.7	11.3	2.6	11.0	2.6	10.7	5
6	3.0	14.9	3.0	14.6	2.9	14.2	2.9	13.9	2.8	13.6	6
7	3.3	18.2	3.3	17.8	3.2	17.4	3.2	17.0	3.1	16.7	7
8	3.6	21.8	3.6	21.4	3.5	20.9	3.5	20.5	3.4	20.1	8
9	3.9	25.7	3.9	25.3	3.8	24.8	3.8	24.3	3.8	23.8	9
10	4.3	30.0	4.2	29.5	4.2	29.0	4.2	28.5	4.1	28.0	10

YEAR	9.75% ANN. %	9.75% CUM. %	10.00% ANN. %	10.00% CUM. %	10.25% ANN. %	10.25% CUM. %	10.50% ANN. %	10.50% CUM. %	10.75% ANN. %	10.75% CUM. %	YEAR
1	1.7	1.7	1.7	1.7	1.6	1.6	1.6	1.6	1.5	1.5	1
2	1.9	3.6	1.8	3.5	1.8	3.4	1.7	3.3	1.7	3.2	2
3	2.1	5.7	2.0	5.5	2.0	5.3	1.9	5.2	1.9	5.0	3
4	2.3	7.9	2.2	7.7	2.2	7.5	2.1	7.3	2.1	7.1	4
5	2.5	10.5	2.5	10.2	2.4	9.9	2.4	9.7	2.3	9.4	5
6	2.8	13.2	2.7	12.9	2.7	12.6	2.6	12.3	2.6	12.0	6
7	3.1	16.3	3.0	15.9	3.0	15.6	2.9	15.2	2.9	14.9	7
8	3.4	19.7	3.3	19.3	3.3	18.8	3.2	18.4	3.2	18.0	8
9	3.7	23.4	3.7	22.9	3.6	22.5	3.6	22.0	3.5	21.6	9
10	4.1	27.5	4.1	27.0	4.0	26.5	4.0	26.0	3.9	25.5	10

YEAR	11.00% ANN. %	11.00% CUM. %	11.25% ANN. %	11.25% CUM. %	11.50% ANN. %	11.50% CUM. %	11.75% ANN. %	11.75% CUM. %	12.00% ANN. %	12.00% CUM. %	YEAR
1	1.5	1.5	1.4	1.4	1.4	1.4	1.3	1.3	1.3	1.3	1
2	1.6	3.1	1.6	3.0	1.5	2.9	1.5	2.8	1.4	2.7	2
3	1.8	4.9	1.8	4.8	1.7	4.6	1.7	4.5	1.6	4.4	3
4	2.0	6.9	2.0	6.7	1.9	6.5	1.9	6.4	1.8	6.2	4
5	2.3	9.2	2.2	8.9	2.2	8.7	2.1	8.5	2.1	8.3	5
6	2.5	11.7	2.5	11.4	2.4	11.1	2.4	10.9	2.3	10.6	6
7	2.8	14.5	2.8	14.2	2.7	13.9	2.7	13.5	2.6	13.2	7
8	3.1	17.7	3.1	17.3	3.0	16.9	3.0	16.5	3.0	16.2	8
9	3.5	21.2	3.5	20.7	3.4	20.3	3.4	19.9	3.3	19.5	9
10	3.9	25.1	3.9	24.6	3.8	24.1	3.8	23.7	3.8	23.3	10

EQUITY BUILD-UP

YEAR	6.00% ANN. %	6.00% CUM. %	6.25% ANN. %	6.25% CUM. %	6.50% ANN. %	6.50% CUM. %	6.75% ANN. %	6.75% CUM. %	7.00% ANN. %	7.00% CUM. %	YEAR
1	1.8	1.8	1.7	1.7	1.7	1.7	1.6	1.6	1.5	1.5	1
2	1.9	3.7	1.8	3.5	1.8	3.4	1.7	3.3	1.6	3.2	2
3	2.0	5.7	1.9	5.5	1.9	5.3	1.8	5.1	1.8	4.9	3
4	2.1	7.8	2.1	7.5	2.0	7.3	1.9	7.1	1.9	6.8	4
5	2.3	10.1	2.2	9.7	2.1	9.4	2.1	9.1	2.0	8.8	5
6	2.4	12.5	2.3	12.1	2.3	11.7	2.2	11.4	2.2	11.0	6
7	2.5	15.0	2.5	14.6	2.4	14.2	2.4	13.7	2.3	13.3	7
8	2.7	17.7	2.7	17.2	2.6	16.8	2.5	16.3	2.5	15.8	8
9	2.9	20.6	2.8	20.1	2.8	19.5	2.7	19.0	2.7	18.5	9
10	3.1	23.6	3.0	23.1	3.0	22.5	2.9	21.9	2.9	21.4	10

YEAR	7.25% ANN. %	7.25% CUM. %	7.50% ANN. %	7.50% CUM. %	7.75% ANN. %	7.75% CUM. %	8.00% ANN. %	8.00% CUM. %	8.25% ANN. %	8.25% CUM. %	YEAR
1	1.5	1.5	1.4	1.4	1.4	1.4	1.3	1.3	1.3	1.3	1
2	1.6	3.1	1.5	2.9	1.5	2.8	1.4	2.7	1.4	2.6	2
3	1.7	4.8	1.6	4.6	1.6	4.4	1.5	4.3	1.5	4.1	3
4	1.8	6.6	1.8	6.4	1.7	6.1	1.7	5.9	1.6	5.7	4
5	2.0	8.5	1.9	8.3	1.9	8.0	1.8	7.7	1.7	7.5	5
6	2.1	10.7	2.1	10.3	2.0	10.0	2.0	9.7	1.9	9.4	6
7	2.3	12.9	2.2	12.5	2.2	12.2	2.1	11.8	2.1	11.4	7
8	2.4	15.4	2.4	14.9	2.3	14.5	2.3	14.1	2.2	13.7	8
9	2.6	18.0	2.6	17.5	2.5	17.0	2.5	16.6	2.4	16.1	9
10	2.8	20.8	2.8	20.3	2.7	19.8	2.7	19.2	2.6	18.7	10

YEAR	8.50% ANN. %	8.50% CUM. %	8.75% ANN. %	8.75% CUM. %	9.00% ANN. %	9.00% CUM. %	9.25% ANN. %	9.25% CUM. %	9.50% ANN. %	9.50% CUM. %	YEAR
1	1.2	1.2	1.2	1.2	1.1	1.1	1.1	1.1	1.0	1.0	1
2	1.3	2.5	1.3	2.4	1.2	2.3	1.2	2.2	1.1	2.2	2
3	1.4	4.0	1.4	3.8	1.3	3.7	1.3	3.5	1.2	3.4	3
4	1.6	5.5	1.5	5.3	1.5	5.1	1.4	4.9	1.4	4.8	4
5	1.7	7.2	1.6	7.0	1.6	6.7	1.5	6.5	1.5	6.3	5
6	1.8	9.1	1.8	8.8	1.7	8.5	1.7	8.2	1.7	7.9	6
7	2.0	11.1	2.0	10.7	1.9	10.4	1.9	10.1	1.8	9.7	7
8	2.2	13.3	2.1	12.9	2.1	12.5	2.0	12.1	2.0	11.7	8
9	2.4	15.6	2.3	15.2	2.3	14.8	2.2	14.3	2.2	13.9	9
10	2.6	18.2	2.5	17.7	2.5	17.3	2.5	16.8	2.4	16.3	10

YEAR	9.75% ANN. %	9.75% CUM. %	10.00% ANN. %	10.00% CUM. %	10.25% ANN. %	10.25% CUM. %	10.50% ANN. %	10.50% CUM. %	10.75% ANN. %	10.75% CUM. %	YEAR
1	1.0	1.0	.9	.9	.9	.9	.9	.9	.8	.8	1
2	1.1	2.1	1.0	2.0	1.0	1.9	1.0	1.8	.9	1.8	2
3	1.2	3.3	1.2	3.1	1.1	3.0	1.1	2.9	1.0	2.8	3
4	1.3	4.6	1.3	4.4	1.2	4.3	1.2	4.1	1.2	4.0	4
5	1.5	6.0	1.4	5.8	1.4	5.6	1.3	5.4	1.3	5.2	5
6	1.6	7.7	1.6	7.4	1.5	7.1	1.5	6.9	1.4	6.7	6
7	1.8	9.4	1.7	9.1	1.7	8.8	1.6	8.5	1.6	8.2	7
8	1.9	11.4	1.9	11.0	1.9	10.7	1.8	10.3	1.8	10.0	8
9	2.1	13.5	2.1	13.1	2.1	12.7	2.0	12.4	2.0	12.0	9
10	2.4	15.9	2.3	15.4	2.3	15.0	2.2	14.6	2.2	14.2	10

YEAR	11.00% ANN. %	11.00% CUM. %	11.25% ANN. %	11.25% CUM. %	11.50% ANN. %	11.50% CUM. %	11.75% ANN. %	11.75% CUM. %	12.00% ANN. %	12.00% CUM. %	YEAR
1	.8	.8	.8	.8	.7	.7	.7	.7	.7	.7	1
2	.9	1.7	.9	1.6	.8	1.6	.8	1.5	.8	1.4	2
3	1.0	2.7	1.0	2.6	.9	2.5	.9	2.4	.9	2.3	3
4	1.1	3.8	1.1	3.7	1.0	3.5	1.0	3.4	1.0	3.3	4
5	1.2	5.0	1.2	4.9	1.2	4.7	1.1	4.5	1.1	4.3	5
6	1.4	6.4	1.3	6.2	1.3	6.0	1.3	5.8	1.2	5.6	6
7	1.5	8.0	1.5	7.7	1.5	7.5	1.4	7.2	1.4	7.0	7
8	1.7	9.7	1.7	9.4	1.6	9.1	1.6	8.8	1.6	8.5	8
9	1.9	11.6	1.9	11.3	1.8	10.9	1.8	10.6	1.8	10.3	9
10	2.1	13.8	2.1	13.4	2.1	13.0	2.0	12.6	2.0	12.2	10

EQUITY BUILD-UP

30 YEAR TERM

IN PERCENT OF ORIGINAL LOAN AMOUNT FOR FIRST 10 YEARS

YEAR	6.00% ANN.%	CUM.%	6.25% ANN.%	CUM.%	6.50% ANN.%	CUM.%	6.75% ANN.%	CUM.%	7.00% ANN.%	CUM.%	YEAR
1	1.2	1.2	1.2	1.2	1.1	1.1	1.1	1.1	1.0	1.0	1
2	1.3	2.5	1.2	2.4	1.2	2.3	1.1	2.2	1.1	2.1	2
3	1.4	3.9	1.3	3.7	1.3	3.6	1.2	3.4	1.2	3.3	3
4	1.5	5.4	1.4	5.2	1.4	4.9	1.3	4.7	1.3	4.5	4
5	1.6	6.9	1.5	6.7	1.4	6.4	1.4	6.1	1.3	5.9	5
6	1.7	8.6	1.6	8.3	1.5	7.9	1.5	7.6	1.4	7.3	6
7	1.8	10.4	1.7	10.0	1.6	9.6	1.6	9.2	1.5	8.9	7
8	1.9	12.2	1.8	11.8	1.8	11.3	1.7	10.9	1.7	10.5	8
9	2.0	14.2	1.9	13.7	1.9	13.2	1.8	12.7	1.8	12.3	9
10	2.1	16.3	2.1	15.8	2.0	15.2	2.0	14.7	1.9	14.2	10

YEAR	7.25% ANN.%	CUM.%	7.50% ANN.%	CUM.%	7.75% ANN.%	CUM.%	8.00% ANN.%	CUM.%	8.25% ANN.%	CUM.%	YEAR
1	1.0	1.0	.9	.9	.9	.9	.8	.8	.8	.8	1
2	1.0	2.0	1.0	1.9	.9	1.8	.9	1.7	.9	1.7	2
3	1.1	3.1	1.1	3.0	1.0	2.9	1.0	2.7	.9	2.6	3
4	1.2	4.3	1.2	4.1	1.1	4.0	1.1	3.8	1.0	3.6	4
5	1.3	5.6	1.2	5.4	1.2	5.2	1.1	4.9	1.1	4.7	5
6	1.4	7.0	1.3	6.7	1.3	6.4	1.2	6.2	1.2	5.9	6
7	1.5	8.5	1.4	8.2	1.4	7.8	1.3	7.5	1.3	7.2	7
8	1.6	10.1	1.6	9.7	1.5	9.3	1.5	9.0	1.4	8.6	8
9	1.7	11.8	1.7	11.4	1.6	11.0	1.6	10.6	1.5	10.2	9
10	1.9	13.7	1.8	13.2	1.8	12.7	1.7	12.3	1.7	11.8	10

YEAR	8.50% ANN.%	CUM.%	8.75% ANN.%	CUM.%	9.00% ANN.%	CUM.%	9.25% ANN.%	CUM.%	9.50% ANN.%	CUM.%	YEAR
1	.8	.8	.7	.7	.7	.7	.7	.7	.6	.6	1
2	.8	1.6	.8	1.5	.7	1.4	.7	1.4	.7	1.3	2
3	.9	2.5	.9	2.4	.8	2.2	.8	2.1	.8	2.0	3
4	1.0	3.4	1.0	3.3	.9	3.1	.9	3.0	.9	2.9	4
5	1.1	4.5	1.0	4.3	1.0	4.1	.9	3.9	.9	3.8	5
6	1.2	5.7	1.1	5.4	1.1	5.2	1.0	5.0	1.0	4.7	6
7	1.3	6.9	1.2	6.6	1.2	6.4	1.1	6.1	1.1	5.8	7
8	1.4	8.3	1.3	8.0	1.3	7.6	1.2	7.3	1.2	7.0	8
9	1.5	9.8	1.4	9.4	1.4	9.0	1.4	8.7	1.3	8.3	9
10	1.6	11.4	1.6	11.0	1.5	10.6	1.5	10.2	1.4	9.8	10

YEAR	9.75% ANN.%	CUM.%	10.00% ANN.%	CUM.%	10.25% ANN.%	CUM.%	10.50% ANN.%	CUM.%	10.75% ANN.%	CUM.%	YEAR
1	.6	.6	.6	.6	.5	.5	.5	.5	.5	.5	1
2	.6	1.2	.6	1.2	.6	1.1	.6	1.1	.5	1.0	2
3	.7	1.9	.7	1.8	.6	1.8	.6	1.7	.6	1.6	3
4	.8	2.7	.7	2.6	.7	2.5	.7	2.4	.7	2.2	4
5	.9	3.6	.8	3.4	.8	3.3	.8	3.1	.7	3.0	5
6	1.0	4.5	.9	4.3	.9	4.1	.9	4.0	.8	3.8	6
7	1.0	5.6	1.0	5.4	1.0	5.1	.9	4.9	.9	4.7	7
8	1.2	6.7	1.1	6.5	1.1	6.2	1.0	5.9	1.0	5.7	8
9	1.3	8.0	1.2	7.7	1.2	7.4	1.2	7.1	1.1	6.8	9
10	1.4	9.4	1.4	9.1	1.3	8.7	1.3	8.4	1.2	8.1	10

YEAR	11.00% ANN.%	CUM.%	11.25% ANN.%	CUM.%	11.50% ANN.%	CUM.%	11.75% ANN.%	CUM.%	12.00% ANN.%	CUM.%	YEAR
1	.5	.5	.4	.4	.4	.4	.4	.4	.4	.4	1
2	.5	1.0	.5	.9	.5	.9	.4	.8	.4	.8	2
3	.6	1.5	.5	1.4	.5	1.4	.5	1.3	.5	1.2	3
4	.6	2.1	.6	2.0	.6	1.9	.5	1.8	.5	1.8	4
5	.7	2.8	.7	2.7	.6	2.6	.6	2.5	.6	2.3	5
6	.8	3.6	.7	3.4	.7	3.3	.7	3.1	.7	3.0	6
7	.9	4.5	.8	4.3	.8	4.1	.8	3.9	.7	3.7	7
8	1.0	5.5	.9	5.2	.9	5.0	.9	4.8	.8	4.6	8
9	1.1	6.5	1.0	6.3	1.0	6.0	1.0	5.8	.9	5.5	9
10	1.2	7.7	1.2	7.4	1.1	7.1	1.1	6.9	1.1	6.6	10

EQUITY BUILD-UP

IN PERCENT OF ORIGINAL LOAN AMOUNT FOR FIRST 10 YEARS

YEAR	6.00% ANN. %	CUM. %	6.25% ANN. %	CUM. %	6.50% ANN. %	CUM. %	6.75% ANN. %	CUM. %	7.00% ANN. %	CUM. %	YEAR
1	.9	.9	.8	.8	.8	.8	.7	.7	.7	.7	1
2	.9	1.8	.9	1.7	.8	1.6	.8	1.5	.7	1.4	2
3	1.0	2.8	.9	2.6	.9	2.5	.8	2.3	.8	2.2	3
4	1.0	3.8	1.0	3.6	.9	3.4	.9	3.2	.8	3.1	4
5	1.1	4.9	1.0	4.7	1.0	4.4	1.0	4.2	.9	4.0	5
6	1.2	6.1	1.1	5.8	1.1	5.5	1.0	5.2	1.0	5.0	6
7	1.2	7.3	1.2	7.0	1.1	6.6	1.1	6.3	1.0	6.0	7
8	1.3	8.6	1.3	8.2	1.2	7.8	1.2	7.5	1.1	7.1	8
9	1.4	10.0	1.3	9.6	1.3	9.1	1.2	8.7	1.2	8.3	9
10	1.5	11.5	1.4	11.0	1.4	10.5	1.3	10.1	1.3	9.6	10

YEAR	7.25% ANN. %	CUM. %	7.50% ANN. %	CUM. %	7.75% ANN. %	CUM. %	8.00% ANN. %	CUM. %	8.25% ANN. %	CUM. %	YEAR
1	.6	.6	.6	.6	.6	.6	.5	.5	.5	.5	1
2	.7	1.3	.7	1.3	.6	1.2	.6	1.1	.6	1.1	2
3	.7	2.1	.7	2.0	.7	1.9	.6	1.8	.6	1.7	3
4	.8	2.9	.8	2.7	.7	2.6	.7	2.5	.7	2.3	4
5	.9	3.8	.8	3.6	.8	3.4	.7	3.2	.7	3.0	5
6	.9	4.7	.9	4.5	.8	4.2	.8	4.0	.8	3.8	6
7	1.0	5.7	1.0	5.4	.9	5.1	.9	4.9	.8	4.6	7
8	1.1	6.8	1.0	6.5	1.0	6.1	.9	5.8	.9	5.5	8
9	1.2	7.9	1.1	7.6	1.1	7.2	1.0	6.9	1.0	6.5	9
10	1.2	9.2	1.2	8.8	1.2	8.4	1.1	8.0	1.1	7.6	10

YEAR	8.50% ANN. %	CUM. %	8.75% ANN. %	CUM. %	9.00% ANN. %	CUM. %	9.25% ANN. %	CUM. %	9.50% ANN. %	CUM. %	YEAR
1	.5	.5	.5	.5	.4	.4	.4	.4	.4	.4	1
2	.5	1.0	.5	.9	.5	.9	.4	.8	.4	.8	2
3	.6	1.6	.5	1.5	.5	1.4	.5	1.3	.5	1.2	3
4	.6	2.2	.6	2.1	.6	2.0	.5	1.8	.5	1.7	4
5	.7	2.9	.6	2.7	.6	2.6	.6	2.4	.5	2.3	5
6	.7	3.6	.7	3.4	.7	3.2	.6	3.1	.6	2.9	6
7	.8	4.4	.8	4.2	.7	4.0	.7	3.8	.7	3.6	7
8	.9	5.3	.8	5.0	.8	4.8	.8	4.5	.7	4.3	8
9	.9	6.2	.9	5.9	.9	5.6	.8	5.3	.8	5.1	9
10	1.0	7.2	1.0	6.9	1.0	6.6	.9	6.3	.9	6.0	10

YEAR	9.75% ANN. %	CUM. %	10.00% ANN. %	CUM. %	10.25% ANN. %	CUM. %	10.50% ANN. %	CUM. %	10.75% ANN. %	CUM. %	YEAR
1	.4	.4	.3	.3	.3	.3	.3	.3	.3	.3	1
2	.4	.7	.4	.7	.3	.7	.3	.6	.3	.6	2
3	.4	1.2	.4	1.1	.4	1.0	.4	1.0	.3	.9	3
4	.5	1.6	.4	1.5	.4	1.5	.4	1.4	.4	1.3	4
5	.5	2.2	.5	2.0	.5	1.9	.4	1.8	.4	1.7	5
6	.6	2.7	.5	2.6	.5	2.4	.5	2.3	.5	2.2	6
7	.6	3.4	.6	3.2	.6	3.0	.5	2.9	.5	2.7	7
8	.7	4.1	.7	3.9	.6	3.6	.6	3.5	.6	3.3	8
9	.8	4.8	.7	4.6	.7	4.4	.7	4.1	.6	3.9	9
10	.8	5.7	.8	5.4	.8	5.1	.7	4.9	.7	4.6	10

YEAR	11.00% ANN. %	CUM. %	11.25% ANN. %	CUM. %	11.50% ANN. %	CUM. %	11.75% ANN. %	CUM. %	12.00% ANN. %	CUM. %	YEAR
1	.3	.3	.2	.2	.2	.2	.2	.2	.2	.2	1
2	.3	.5	.3	.5	.3	.5	.2	.4	.2	.4	2
3	.3	.9	.3	.8	.3	.8	.3	.7	.3	.7	3
4	.4	1.2	.3	1.1	.3	1.1	.3	1.0	.3	1.0	4
5	.4	1.6	.4	1.5	.4	1.4	.3	1.3	.3	1.3	5
6	.4	2.1	.4	1.9	.4	1.8	.4	1.7	.4	1.6	6
7	.5	2.6	.5	2.4	.4	2.3	.4	2.2	.4	2.0	7
8	.6	3.1	.5	2.9	.5	2.8	.5	2.6	.5	2.5	8
9	.6	3.7	.6	3.5	.6	3.3	.5	3.2	.5	3.0	9
10	.7	4.4	.7	4.2	.6	4.0	.6	3.8	.6	3.6	10

EQUITY BUILD-UP

40 YEAR TERM — IN PERCENT OF ORIGINAL LOAN AMOUNT FOR FIRST 10 YEARS — 40 YEAR TERM

YEAR	6.00% ANN. %	CUM. %	6.25% ANN. %	CUM. %	6.50% ANN. %	CUM. %	6.75% ANN. %	CUM. %	7.00% ANN. %	CUM. %	YEAR
1	.6	.6	.6	.6	.5	.5	.5	.5	.5	.5	1
2	.7	1.3	.6	1.2	.6	1.1	.5	1.0	.5	1.0	2
3	.7	2.0	.7	1.9	.6	1.7	.6	1.6	.5	1.5	3
4	.7	2.7	.7	2.6	.7	2.4	.6	2.2	.6	2.1	4
5	.8	3.5	.7	3.3	.7	3.1	.7	2.9	.6	2.7	5
6	.8	4.3	.8	4.1	.7	3.8	.7	3.6	.7	3.4	6
7	.9	5.2	.8	4.9	.8	4.6	.8	4.4	.7	4.1	7
8	.9	6.2	.9	5.8	.9	5.5	.8	5.2	.8	4.9	8
9	1.0	7.2	1.0	6.8	.9	6.4	.9	6.0	.8	5.7	9
10	1.1	8.2	1.0	7.8	1.0	7.4	.9	7.0	.9	6.6	10

YEAR	7.25% ANN. %	CUM. %	7.50% ANN. %	CUM. %	7.75% ANN. %	CUM. %	8.00% ANN. %	CUM. %	8.25% ANN. %	CUM. %	YEAR
1	.4	.4	.4	.4	.4	.4	.4	.4	.3	.3	1
2	.5	.9	.4	.9	.4	.8	.4	.7	.4	.7	2
3	.5	1.4	.5	1.3	.4	1.2	.4	1.2	.4	1.1	3
4	.5	2.0	.5	1.8	.5	1.7	.5	1.6	.4	1.5	4
5	.6	2.6	.6	2.4	.5	2.2	.5	2.1	.5	2.0	5
6	.6	3.2	.6	3.0	.6	2.8	.5	2.6	.5	2.5	6
7	.7	3.9	.6	3.6	.6	3.4	.6	3.2	.5	3.0	7
8	.7	4.6	.7	4.3	.7	4.1	.6	3.8	.6	3.6	8
9	.8	5.4	.7	5.1	.7	4.8	.7	4.5	.6	4.2	9
10	.8	6.2	.8	5.9	.8	5.6	.7	5.2	.7	4.9	10

YEAR	8.50% ANN. %	CUM. %	8.75% ANN. %	CUM. %	9.00% ANN. %	CUM. %	9.25% ANN. %	CUM. %	9.50% ANN. %	CUM. %	YEAR
1	.3	.3	.3	.3	.3	.3	.2	.2	.2	.2	1
2	.3	.6	.3	.6	.3	.6	.3	.5	.3	.5	2
3	.4	1.0	.3	.9	.3	.9	.3	.8	.3	.8	3
4	.4	1.4	.4	1.3	.4	1.2	.3	1.1	.3	1.1	4
5	.4	1.8	.4	1.7	.4	1.6	.4	1.5	.3	1.4	5
6	.5	2.3	.4	2.2	.4	2.0	.4	1.9	.4	1.8	6
7	.5	2.8	.5	2.7	.5	2.5	.4	2.3	.4	2.2	7
8	.6	3.4	.5	3.2	.5	3.0	.5	2.8	.4	2.6	8
9	.6	4.0	.6	3.8	.5	3.5	.5	3.3	.5	3.1	9
10	.7	4.7	.6	4.4	.6	4.1	.6	3.9	.5	3.7	10

YEAR	9.75% ANN. %	CUM. %	10.00% ANN. %	CUM. %	10.25% ANN. %	CUM. %	10.50% ANN. %	CUM. %	10.75% ANN. %	CUM. %	YEAR
1	.2	.2	.2	.2	.2	.2	.2	.2	.2	.2	1
2	.2	.5	.2	.4	.2	.4	.2	.4	.2	.3	2
3	.3	.7	.2	.7	.2	.6	.2	.6	.2	.5	3
4	.3	1.0	.3	.9	.3	.9	.2	.8	.2	.7	4
5	.3	1.3	.3	1.2	.3	1.1	.3	1.1	.2	1.0	5
6	.3	1.7	.3	1.6	.3	1.4	.3	1.4	.3	1.3	6
7	.4	2.0	.4	1.9	.3	1.8	.3	1.7	.3	1.6	7
8	.4	2.5	.4	2.3	.4	2.2	.4	2.0	.3	1.9	8
9	.5	2.9	.4	2.8	.4	2.6	.4	2.4	.4	2.3	9
10	.5	3.4	.5	3.2	.5	3.0	.4	2.9	.4	2.7	10

YEAR	11.00% ANN. %	CUM. %	11.25% ANN. %	CUM. %	11.50% ANN. %	CUM. %	11.75% ANN. %	CUM. %	12.00% ANN. %	CUM. %	YEAR
1	.1	.1	.1	.1	.1	.1	.1	.1	.1	.1	1
2	.2	.3	.2	.3	.1	.3	.1	.2	.1	.2	2
3	.2	.5	.2	.5	.2	.4	.1	.4	.1	.4	3
4	.2	.7	.2	.6	.2	.6	.2	.6	.2	.5	4
5	.2	.9	.2	.9	.2	.8	.2	.8	.2	.7	5
6	.3	1.2	.2	1.1	.2	1.0	.2	1.0	.2	.9	6
7	.3	1.5	.3	1.4	.3	1.3	.2	1.2	.2	1.1	7
8	.3	1.8	.3	1.7	.3	1.6	.3	1.5	.2	1.4	8
9	.4	2.1	.3	2.0	.3	1.9	.3	1.8	.3	1.6	9
10	.4	2.5	.4	2.4	.4	2.2	.3	2.1	.3	2.0	10

DEPRECIATION

	STRAIGHT LINE		125% S/L		150% S/L		200% S/L		SUM YEARS DIGITS		
YEAR	ANN. %	CUM. %	ANN. %	CUM. %	ANN. %	CUM. %	ANN. %	CUM. %	ANN. %	CUM. %	YEAR
					5 YEAR USEFUL LIFE						
1	20.0	20.0	25.0	25.0	30.0	30.0	40.0	40.0	33.3	33.3	1
2	20.0	40.0	18.8	43.8	21.0	51.0	24.0	64.0	26.7	60.0	2
3	20.0	60.0	14.1	57.8	14.7	65.7	14.4	78.4	20.0	80.0	3
4	20.0	80.0	10.5	68.4	10.3	76.0	8.6	87.0	13.3	93.3	4
5	20.0	100.0	7.9	76.3	7.2	83.2	5.2	92.2	6.7	100.0	5
					10 YEAR USEFUL LIFE						
1	10.0	10.0	12.5	12.5	15.0	15.0	20.0	20.0	18.2	18.2	1
2	10.0	20.0	10.9	23.4	12.8	27.7	16.0	36.0	16.4	34.5	2
3	10.0	30.0	9.6	33.0	10.8	38.6	12.8	48.8	14.5	49.1	3
4	10.0	40.0	8.4	41.4	9.2	47.8	10.2	59.0	12.7	61.8	4
5	10.0	50.0	7.3	48.7	7.8	55.6	8.2	67.2	10.9	72.7	5
6	10.0	60.0	6.4	55.1	6.7	62.3	6.6	73.8	9.1	81.8	6
7	10.0	70.0	5.6	60.7	5.7	67.9	5.2	79.0	7.3	89.1	7
8	10.0	80.0	4.9	65.6	4.8	72.8	4.2	83.2	5.5	94.5	8
9	10.0	90.0	4.3	69.9	4.1	76.8	3.4	86.6	3.6	98.2	9
10	10.0	100.0	3.8	73.7	3.5	80.3	2.7	89.3	1.8	100.0	10
					15 YEAR USEFUL LIFE						
1	6.7	6.7	8.3	8.3	10.0	10.0	13.3	13.3	12.5	12.5	1
2	6.7	13.3	7.6	16.0	9.0	19.0	11.6	24.9	11.7	24.2	2
3	6.7	20.0	7.0	23.0	8.1	27.1	10.0	34.9	10.8	35.0	3
4	6.7	26.7	6.4	29.4	7.3	34.4	8.7	43.6	10.0	45.0	4
5	6.7	33.3	5.9	35.3	6.6	41.0	7.5	51.1	9.2	54.2	5
6	6.7	40.0	5.4	40.7	5.9	46.9	6.5	57.6	8.3	62.5	6
7	6.7	46.7	4.9	45.6	5.3	52.2	5.7	63.3	7.5	70.0	7
8	6.7	53.3	4.5	50.1	4.8	57.0	4.9	68.2	6.7	76.7	8
9	6.7	60.0	4.2	54.3	4.3	61.3	4.2	72.4	5.8	82.5	9
10	6.7	66.7	3.8	58.1	3.9	65.1	3.7	76.1	5.0	87.5	10
					20 YEAR USEFUL LIFE						
1	5.0	5.0	6.3	6.3	7.5	7.5	10.0	10.0	9.5	9.5	1
2	5.0	10.0	5.9	12.1	6.9	14.4	9.0	19.0	9.0	18.6	2
3	5.0	15.0	5.5	17.6	6.4	20.9	8.1	27.1	8.6	27.1	3
4	5.0	20.0	5.1	22.8	5.9	26.8	7.3	34.4	8.1	35.2	4
5	5.0	25.0	4.8	27.6	5.5	32.3	6.6	41.0	7.6	42.9	5
6	5.0	30.0	4.5	32.1	5.1	37.4	5.9	46.9	7.1	50.0	6
7	5.0	35.0	4.2	36.3	4.7	42.1	5.3	52.2	6.7	56.7	7
8	5.0	40.0	4.0	40.3	4.3	46.4	4.8	57.0	6.2	62.9	8
9	5.0	45.0	3.7	44.1	4.0	50.4	4.3	61.3	5.7	68.6	9
10	5.0	50.0	3.5	47.6	3.7	54.1	3.9	65.1	5.2	73.8	10
					25 YEAR USEFUL LIFE						
1	4.0	4.0	5.0	5.0	6.0	6.0	8.0	8.0	7.7	7.7	1
2	4.0	8.0	4.7	9.7	5.6	11.6	7.4	15.4	7.4	15.1	2
3	4.0	12.0	4.5	14.3	5.3	16.9	6.8	22.1	7.1	22.2	3
4	4.0	16.0	4.3	18.5	5.0	21.9	6.2	28.4	6.8	28.9	4
5	4.0	20.0	4.1	22.6	4.7	26.6	5.7	34.1	6.5	35.4	5
6	4.0	24.0	3.9	26.5	4.4	31.0	5.3	39.4	6.2	41.5	6
7	4.0	28.0	3.7	30.2	4.1	35.2	4.9	44.2	5.8	47.4	7
8	4.0	32.0	3.5	33.7	3.9	39.0	4.5	48.7	5.5	52.9	8
9	4.0	36.0	3.3	37.0	3.7	42.7	4.1	52.8	5.2	58.2	9
10	4.0	40.0	3.2	40.1	3.4	46.1	3.8	56.6	4.9	63.1	10

DEPRECIATION

<table>
<tr><th colspan="12">M E T H O D</th></tr>
<tr><th rowspan="2">YEAR</th><th colspan="2">STRAIGHT LINE</th><th colspan="2">125% S/L</th><th colspan="2">150% S/L</th><th colspan="2">200% S/L</th><th colspan="2">SUM YEARS DIGITS</th><th rowspan="2">YEAR</th></tr>
<tr><th>ANN. %</th><th>CUM. %</th><th>ANN. %</th><th>CUM. %</th><th>ANN. %</th><th>CUM. %</th><th>ANN. %</th><th>CUM. %</th><th>ANN. %</th><th>CUM. %</th></tr>

<tr><td colspan="12" align="center">30 YEAR USEFUL LIFE</td></tr>
<tr><td>1</td><td>3.3</td><td>3.3</td><td>4.2</td><td>4.2</td><td>5.0</td><td>5.0</td><td>6.7</td><td>6.7</td><td>6.5</td><td>6.5</td><td>1</td></tr>
<tr><td>2</td><td>3.3</td><td>6.7</td><td>4.0</td><td>8.2</td><td>4.7</td><td>9.7</td><td>6.2</td><td>12.9</td><td>6.2</td><td>12.7</td><td>2</td></tr>
<tr><td>3</td><td>3.3</td><td>10.0</td><td>3.8</td><td>12.0</td><td>4.5</td><td>14.3</td><td>5.8</td><td>18.7</td><td>6.0</td><td>18.7</td><td>3</td></tr>
<tr><td>4</td><td>3.3</td><td>13.3</td><td>3.7</td><td>15.7</td><td>4.3</td><td>18.5</td><td>5.4</td><td>24.1</td><td>5.8</td><td>24.5</td><td>4</td></tr>
<tr><td>5</td><td>3.3</td><td>16.7</td><td>3.5</td><td>19.2</td><td>4.1</td><td>22.6</td><td>5.1</td><td>29.2</td><td>5.6</td><td>30.1</td><td>5</td></tr>
<tr><td>6</td><td>3.3</td><td>20.0</td><td>3.4</td><td>22.5</td><td>3.9</td><td>26.5</td><td>4.7</td><td>33.9</td><td>5.4</td><td>35.5</td><td>6</td></tr>
<tr><td>7</td><td>3.3</td><td>23.3</td><td>3.2</td><td>25.8</td><td>3.7</td><td>30.2</td><td>4.4</td><td>38.3</td><td>5.2</td><td>40.6</td><td>7</td></tr>
<tr><td>8</td><td>3.3</td><td>26.7</td><td>3.1</td><td>28.9</td><td>3.5</td><td>33.7</td><td>4.1</td><td>42.4</td><td>4.9</td><td>45.6</td><td>8</td></tr>
<tr><td>9</td><td>3.3</td><td>30.0</td><td>3.0</td><td>31.8</td><td>3.3</td><td>37.0</td><td>3.8</td><td>46.3</td><td>4.7</td><td>50.3</td><td>9</td></tr>
<tr><td>10</td><td>3.3</td><td>33.3</td><td>2.8</td><td>34.7</td><td>3.2</td><td>40.1</td><td>3.6</td><td>49.8</td><td>4.5</td><td>54.8</td><td>10</td></tr>

<tr><td colspan="12" align="center">33 1/3 YEAR USEFUL LIFE</td></tr>
<tr><td>1</td><td>3.0</td><td>3.0</td><td>3.8</td><td>3.7</td><td>4.5</td><td>4.5</td><td>6.0</td><td>6.0</td><td>5.8</td><td>5.8</td><td>1</td></tr>
<tr><td>2</td><td>3.0</td><td>6.0</td><td>3.6</td><td>7.4</td><td>4.3</td><td>8.8</td><td>5.6</td><td>11.6</td><td>5.7</td><td>11.5</td><td>2</td></tr>
<tr><td>3</td><td>3.0</td><td>9.0</td><td>3.5</td><td>10.8</td><td>4.1</td><td>12.9</td><td>5.3</td><td>16.9</td><td>5.5</td><td>17.0</td><td>3</td></tr>
<tr><td>4</td><td>3.0</td><td>12.0</td><td>3.3</td><td>14.2</td><td>3.9</td><td>16.8</td><td>5.0</td><td>21.9</td><td>5.3</td><td>22.3</td><td>4</td></tr>
<tr><td>5</td><td>3.0</td><td>15.0</td><td>3.2</td><td>17.4</td><td>3.7</td><td>20.6</td><td>4.7</td><td>26.6</td><td>5.1</td><td>27.4</td><td>5</td></tr>
<tr><td>6</td><td>3.0</td><td>18.0</td><td>3.1</td><td>20.5</td><td>3.6</td><td>24.1</td><td>4.4</td><td>31.0</td><td>5.0</td><td>32.3</td><td>6</td></tr>
<tr><td>7</td><td>3.0</td><td>21.0</td><td>3.0</td><td>23.5</td><td>3.4</td><td>27.6</td><td>4.1</td><td>35.2</td><td>4.8</td><td>37.1</td><td>7</td></tr>
<tr><td>8</td><td>3.0</td><td>24.0</td><td>2.9</td><td>26.3</td><td>3.3</td><td>30.8</td><td>3.9</td><td>39.0</td><td>4.6</td><td>41.7</td><td>8</td></tr>
<tr><td>9</td><td>3.0</td><td>27.0</td><td>2.8</td><td>29.1</td><td>3.1</td><td>33.9</td><td>3.7</td><td>42.7</td><td>4.4</td><td>46.1</td><td>9</td></tr>
<tr><td>10</td><td>3.0</td><td>30.0</td><td>2.7</td><td>31.8</td><td>3.0</td><td>36.9</td><td>3.4</td><td>46.1</td><td>4.3</td><td>50.4</td><td>10</td></tr>

<tr><td colspan="12" align="center">35 YEAR USEFUL LIFE</td></tr>
<tr><td>1</td><td>2.9</td><td>2.9</td><td>3.6</td><td>3.6</td><td>4.3</td><td>4.3</td><td>5.7</td><td>5.7</td><td>5.6</td><td>5.6</td><td>1</td></tr>
<tr><td>2</td><td>2.9</td><td>5.7</td><td>3.4</td><td>7.0</td><td>4.1</td><td>8.4</td><td>5.4</td><td>11.1</td><td>5.4</td><td>11.0</td><td>2</td></tr>
<tr><td>3</td><td>2.9</td><td>8.6</td><td>3.3</td><td>10.3</td><td>3.9</td><td>12.3</td><td>5.1</td><td>16.2</td><td>5.2</td><td>16.2</td><td>3</td></tr>
<tr><td>4</td><td>2.9</td><td>11.4</td><td>3.2</td><td>13.5</td><td>3.8</td><td>16.1</td><td>4.8</td><td>21.0</td><td>5.1</td><td>21.3</td><td>4</td></tr>
<tr><td>5</td><td>2.9</td><td>14.3</td><td>3.1</td><td>16.6</td><td>3.6</td><td>19.7</td><td>4.5</td><td>25.5</td><td>4.9</td><td>26.2</td><td>5</td></tr>
<tr><td>6</td><td>2.9</td><td>17.1</td><td>3.0</td><td>19.6</td><td>3.4</td><td>23.1</td><td>4.3</td><td>29.7</td><td>4.8</td><td>31.0</td><td>6</td></tr>
<tr><td>7</td><td>2.9</td><td>20.0</td><td>2.9</td><td>22.5</td><td>3.3</td><td>26.4</td><td>4.0</td><td>33.8</td><td>4.6</td><td>35.6</td><td>7</td></tr>
<tr><td>8</td><td>2.9</td><td>22.9</td><td>2.8</td><td>25.2</td><td>3.2</td><td>29.6</td><td>3.8</td><td>37.5</td><td>4.4</td><td>40.0</td><td>8</td></tr>
<tr><td>9</td><td>2.9</td><td>25.7</td><td>2.7</td><td>27.9</td><td>3.0</td><td>32.6</td><td>3.6</td><td>41.1</td><td>4.3</td><td>44.3</td><td>9</td></tr>
<tr><td>10</td><td>2.9</td><td>28.6</td><td>2.6</td><td>30.5</td><td>2.9</td><td>35.5</td><td>3.4</td><td>44.5</td><td>4.1</td><td>48.4</td><td>10</td></tr>

<tr><td colspan="12" align="center">40 YEAR USEFUL LIFE</td></tr>
<tr><td>1</td><td>2.5</td><td>2.5</td><td>3.1</td><td>3.1</td><td>3.8</td><td>3.7</td><td>5.0</td><td>5.0</td><td>4.9</td><td>4.9</td><td>1</td></tr>
<tr><td>2</td><td>2.5</td><td>5.0</td><td>3.0</td><td>6.2</td><td>3.6</td><td>7.4</td><td>4.7</td><td>9.7</td><td>4.8</td><td>9.6</td><td>2</td></tr>
<tr><td>3</td><td>2.5</td><td>7.5</td><td>2.9</td><td>9.1</td><td>3.5</td><td>10.8</td><td>4.5</td><td>14.3</td><td>4.6</td><td>14.3</td><td>3</td></tr>
<tr><td>4</td><td>2.5</td><td>10.0</td><td>2.8</td><td>11.9</td><td>3.3</td><td>14.2</td><td>4.3</td><td>18.5</td><td>4.5</td><td>18.8</td><td>4</td></tr>
<tr><td>5</td><td>2.5</td><td>12.5</td><td>2.8</td><td>14.7</td><td>3.2</td><td>17.4</td><td>4.1</td><td>22.6</td><td>4.4</td><td>23.2</td><td>5</td></tr>
<tr><td>6</td><td>2.5</td><td>15.0</td><td>2.7</td><td>17.3</td><td>3.1</td><td>20.5</td><td>3.9</td><td>26.5</td><td>4.3</td><td>27.4</td><td>6</td></tr>
<tr><td>7</td><td>2.5</td><td>17.5</td><td>2.6</td><td>19.9</td><td>3.0</td><td>23.5</td><td>3.7</td><td>30.2</td><td>4.1</td><td>31.6</td><td>7</td></tr>
<tr><td>8</td><td>2.5</td><td>20.0</td><td>2.5</td><td>22.4</td><td>2.9</td><td>26.3</td><td>3.5</td><td>33.7</td><td>4.0</td><td>35.6</td><td>8</td></tr>
<tr><td>9</td><td>2.5</td><td>22.5</td><td>2.4</td><td>24.9</td><td>2.8</td><td>29.1</td><td>3.3</td><td>37.0</td><td>3.9</td><td>39.5</td><td>9</td></tr>
<tr><td>10</td><td>2.5</td><td>25.0</td><td>2.3</td><td>27.2</td><td>2.7</td><td>31.8</td><td>3.2</td><td>40.1</td><td>3.8</td><td>43.3</td><td>10</td></tr>

<tr><td colspan="12" align="center">50 YEAR USEFUL LIFE</td></tr>
<tr><td>1</td><td>2.0</td><td>2.0</td><td>2.5</td><td>2.5</td><td>3.0</td><td>3.0</td><td>4.0</td><td>4.0</td><td>3.9</td><td>3.9</td><td>1</td></tr>
<tr><td>2</td><td>2.0</td><td>4.0</td><td>2.4</td><td>4.9</td><td>2.9</td><td>5.9</td><td>3.8</td><td>7.8</td><td>3.8</td><td>7.8</td><td>2</td></tr>
<tr><td>3</td><td>2.0</td><td>6.0</td><td>2.4</td><td>7.3</td><td>2.8</td><td>8.7</td><td>3.7</td><td>11.5</td><td>3.8</td><td>11.5</td><td>3</td></tr>
<tr><td>4</td><td>2.0</td><td>8.0</td><td>2.3</td><td>9.6</td><td>2.7</td><td>11.5</td><td>3.5</td><td>15.1</td><td>3.7</td><td>15.2</td><td>4</td></tr>
<tr><td>5</td><td>2.0</td><td>10.0</td><td>2.3</td><td>11.9</td><td>2.7</td><td>14.1</td><td>3.4</td><td>18.5</td><td>3.6</td><td>18.8</td><td>5</td></tr>
<tr><td>6</td><td>2.0</td><td>12.0</td><td>2.2</td><td>14.1</td><td>2.6</td><td>16.7</td><td>3.3</td><td>21.7</td><td>3.5</td><td>22.4</td><td>6</td></tr>
<tr><td>7</td><td>2.0</td><td>14.0</td><td>2.1</td><td>16.2</td><td>2.5</td><td>19.2</td><td>3.1</td><td>24.9</td><td>3.5</td><td>25.8</td><td>7</td></tr>
<tr><td>8</td><td>2.0</td><td>16.0</td><td>2.1</td><td>18.3</td><td>2.4</td><td>21.6</td><td>3.0</td><td>27.9</td><td>3.4</td><td>29.2</td><td>8</td></tr>
<tr><td>9</td><td>2.0</td><td>18.0</td><td>2.0</td><td>20.4</td><td>2.4</td><td>24.0</td><td>2.9</td><td>30.7</td><td>3.3</td><td>32.5</td><td>9</td></tr>
<tr><td>10</td><td>2.0</td><td>20.0</td><td>2.0</td><td>22.4</td><td>2.3</td><td>26.3</td><td>2.8</td><td>33.5</td><td>3.2</td><td>35.7</td><td>10</td></tr>
</table>

DOCUMENTARY STAMPS

Although the Federal Revenue Stamp Law was repealed effective January 1, 1968, the table is still useful for finding sales prices by looking up the amount of Revenue Stamps on deeds.

OVER	NOT EXCEEDING	REVENUE STAMPS	OVER	NOT EXCEEDING	REVENUE STAMPS
100	500	.55	25000	25500	28.05
500	1000	1.10	25500	26000	28.60
1000	1500	1.65	26000	26500	29.15
1500	2000	2.20	26500	27000	29.70
2000	2500	2.75	27000	27500	30.25
2500	3000	3.30	27500	28000	30.80
3000	3500	3.85	28000	28500	31.35
3500	4000	4.40	28500	29000	31.90
4000	4500	4.95	29000	29500	32.45
4500	5000	5.50	29500	30000	33.00
5000	5500	6.05	30000	30500	33.55
5500	6000	6.60	30500	31000	34.10
6000	6500	7.15	31000	31500	34.65
6500	7000	7.70	31500	32000	35.20
7000	7500	8.25	32000	32500	35.75
7500	8000	8.80	32500	33000	36.30
8000	8500	9.35	33000	33500	36.85
8500	9000	9.90	33500	34000	37.40
9000	9500	10.45	34000	34500	37.95
9500	10000	11.00	34500	35000	38.50
10000	10500	11.55	35000	35500	39.05
10500	11000	12.10	35500	36000	39.60
11000	11500	12.65	36000	36500	40.15
11500	12000	13.20	36500	37000	40.70
12000	12500	13.75	37000	37500	41.25
12500	13000	14.30	37500	38000	41.80
13000	13500	14.85	38000	38500	42.35
13500	14000	15.40	38500	39000	42.90
14000	14500	15.95	39000	39500	43.45
14500	15000	16.50	39500	40000	44.00
15000	15500	17.05	40000	40500	44.55
15500	16000	17.60	40500	41000	45.10
16000	16500	18.15	41000	41500	45.65
16500	17000	18.70	41500	42000	46.20
17000	17500	19.25	42000	42500	46.75
17500	18000	19.80	42500	43000	47.30
18000	18500	20.35	43000	43500	47.85
18500	19000	20.90	43500	44000	48.40
19000	19500	21.45	44000	44500	48.95
19500	20000	22.00	44500	45000	49.50
20000	20500	22.55	45000	45500	50.05
20500	21000	23.10	45500	46000	50.60
21000	21500	23.65	46000	46500	51.15
21500	22000	24.20	46500	47000	51.70
22000	22500	24.75	47000	47500	52.25
22500	23000	25.30	47500	48000	52.80
23000	23500	25.85	48000	48500	53.35
23500	24000	26.40	48500	49000	53.90
24000	24500	26.95	49000	49500	54.45
24500	25000	27.50	49500	50000	55.00

DOCUMENTARY STAMPS

Although the Federal Revenue Stamp Law was repealed effective January 1, 1968, the table is still useful for finding sales prices by looking up the amount of Revenue Stamps on deeds.

OVER	NOT EXCEEDING	REVENUE STAMPS	OVER	NOT EXCEEDING	REVENUE STAMPS
50000	50500	55.55	75000	75500	83.05
50500	51000	56.10	75500	76000	83.60
51000	51500	56.65	76000	76500	84.15
51500	52000	57.20	76500	77000	84.70
52000	52500	57.75	77000	77500	85.25
52500	53000	58.30	77500	78000	85.80
53000	53500	58.85	78000	78500	86.35
53500	54000	59.40	78500	79000	86.90
54000	54500	59.95	79000	79500	87.45
54500	55000	60.50	79500	80000	88.00
55000	55500	61.05	80000	80500	88.55
55500	56000	61.60	80500	81000	89.10
56000	56500	62.15	81000	81500	89.65
56500	57000	62.70	81500	82000	90.20
57000	57500	63.25	82000	82500	90.75
57500	58000	63.80	82500	83000	91.30
58000	58500	64.35	83000	83500	91.85
58500	59000	64.90	83500	84000	92.40
59000	59500	65.45	84000	84500	92.95
59500	60000	66.00	84500	85000	93.50
60000	60500	66.55	85000	85500	94.05
60500	61000	67.10	85500	86000	94.60
61000	61500	67.65	86000	86500	95.15
61500	62000	68.20	86500	87000	95.70
62000	62500	68.75	87000	87500	96.25
62500	63000	69.30	87500	88000	96.80
63000	63500	69.85	88000	88500	97.35
63500	64000	70.40	88500	89000	97.90
64000	64500	70.95	89000	89500	98.45
64500	65000	71.50	89500	90000	99.00
65000	65500	72.05	90000	90500	99.55
65500	66000	72.60	90500	91000	100.10
66000	66500	73.15	91000	91500	100.65
66500	67000	73.70	91500	92000	101.20
67000	67500	74.25	92000	92500	101.75
67500	68000	74.80	92500	93000	102.30
68000	68500	75.35	93000	93500	102.85
68500	69000	75.90	93500	94000	103.40
69000	69500	76.45	94000	94500	103.95
69500	70000	77.00	94500	95000	104.50
70000	70500	77.55	95000	95500	105.05
70500	71000	78.10	95500	96000	105.60
71000	71500	78.65	96000	96500	106.15
71500	72000	79.20	96500	97000	106.70
72000	72500	79.75	97000	97500	107.25
72500	73000	80.30	97500	98000	107.80
73000	73500	80.85	98000	98500	108.35
73500	74000	81.40	98500	99000	108.90
74000	74500	81.95	99000	99500	109.45
74500	75000	82.50	99500	100000	110.00

— INSTRUCTIONS — DEFINITIONS —
— HOW TO USE THE TABLES —

• CONSTANT ANNUAL PERCENT (CAP) •

(pages 48 & 49)

This table is designed to find the Annual Debt Service (ADS) on a loan with a fully amortizing (FA) loan payment. You will need to know the interest rate, the term of the loan, and the loan amount.

Example: $100,000 loan, a 30-year term, and a 8.5% interest rate.

Turn to page 48 and locate the point of intersection of the 8.5% interest rate column and the 30-year row. The figure located at this intersection is 9.23% (CAP). 9.23% (CAP) multiplied by $100,000 is $9,230 (ADS). The annual debt service of $9,230 is the same as the monthly payment times 12.

Alternate Uses:

Problem 2: To find the original loan amount when you know the term, interest rate, and monthly payment (FA).

Example: A 20-year term, a 10% interest rate, and a $482.52 monthly payment (FA).

Turn to page 49 and locate the constant annual percent of 11.58 at the intersection of the 20-year row and the 10% interest-rate column.
Divide the annual debt service (12 X 482.52) by 11.58% (or .1158) to find the original loan amount of $50,000.

Problem 3: To find the unknown interest rate on a loan when you know the loan amount, the annual debt service (ADS), and the term of the loan.

Example: A $25,000 loan, a monthly payment (FA) of $216.96, and a term of 20 years.

Divide the annual debt service (216.96 X 12) by $25,000 (loan amount) to find the constant annual percent of 10.41.

Turn to page 48 or 49 and locate the 20-year term row. Follow that row across in each section until you locate the 10.41* figure in the 8.5% interest rate column on page 48. This indicates that the desired interest rate for the above example is 8.5%.

Problem 4: To find the remaining term of a loan when you know the loan balance, interest rate, and annual debt service (ADS).

Example: A $30,000 balance, a 10% interest, and a monthly payment of $300.

Divide the annual debt service ($300 X 12) by $30,000 to get the constant annual percent (CAP) of 12.00. Turn to page 49 and find the 10% interest rate column. Follow that column down until you find the 12.00* figure in the 18-year row. The remaining term for this example is 18 years.

* You may need to interpolate at this point.

• LOAN PROGRESS CHARTS •

(pages 60 thru 81)

The purpose of these tables is to show the balance remaining in principal on a loan at a given point during the term of the loan. The user can see the progress of a loan from the end of the 1st year to 1 year prior to maturity.

You will need to know the interest rate, the original term in years, the current age of the loan and the original loan amount.

Example: A 15-year original term loan, $25,500 original loan amount and a 10% interest rate. What is the principal balance remaining at the end of 10 years (current age)?

Turn to page 73 and locate the point of intersection of the 15-year original term column and the 10-year row. The figure located at this intersection is 506($). This $506 represents the amount of principal still owed for every $1000.00 of original loan amount. Divide $25,500 by 1000 to find the number of $1,000.00 units. The answer of 25.5 is multiplied by $506 to arrive at $12,900.00 which is the principal balance still owed on the example loan.

•MORTGAGE YIELD TABLES•

(pages 86 thru 133)

These tables are designed to tell the user the percent (%) of discount required on a loan (note) to achieve a desired yield. You will need the interest rate, the term, the desired yield and the monthly payback rate.

Example: A 4-year $100,000 loan, at 8.5% interest rate, with a 1.5% payment rate ($1500 per month), and the desired yield is 15%.

Turn to page 104 and locate the point of intersection of the 15% yield column and the 1.5% payment rate row in the 4-year section. The figure at that intersection is 15.84%. This means the loan must be discounted 15.84% to yield 15%. Therefore, the $100,000 loan is discounted $15,840, and the purchase price is $84,160.00.

Alternate Usage — Problem 2:
Given the percent of discount on a loan, what is the yield? You will need to do some interpolation on this technique.

Example: A 5-year loan, 10% interest rate, 1.00% payback rate and a 20% discount.

Turn to the 10% page (p. 116) and locate the 1.00% payback row in the 5-year section. Follow that row across until you arrive at a percent (%) close to 20%. In this case, 19.54 (closest to 20%) is located in the 16% column. Therefore, the yield is only slightly higher than 16% because in the next highest column of 17% the percent of discount is 22.31 (%).

Please note the unique layout features of the tables. Within each due date (term of loan) section, the first payment rate row is always interest only, and the last payment rate row is always fully amortizing. The last column on the right-facing pages shows the remaining balance on the loan (% of original loan balance) at the due date. The last section of each two-page group is the "until paid" section. In this section, the last column is the number of months until the loan is paid.

184

•PRORATIONS OF TAXES, RENTS AND REBATES OF OTHER ANNUAL FIGURES•

(pages 168 thru 171)

These charts utilize the actual 365-day calendar (pages 170-171) and the 360-day financial calendar (pages 168-169). The purpose of these charts is to determine the exact number of days from January 1st to any given date. The chart will also indicate the percentage that period in time is of 100%. (100% represents the total 365 days in the year or the 360 days).

Example: An annual property tax bill of $1075.00 and escrow closes on June 21, 1976. What percent (%) of the total bill is chargeable to the present owner if an actual day calendar is used?

Turn to page 170. Locate the point of intersection of the number 21 in the first column on the left side of the page and the June column. The figure at that point of intersection is 172, and the figure located to the right of it is 47.12. This means that 47.12% of the $1075.00 property tax bill is chargeable to the present owner. Since we are using the actual calendar, this also means that there are 172 days between January 1st and June 21st. No allowance is made for leap year.

•EQUITY BUILD-UP TABLES•

(pages 172 thru 177)

These tables allow the user to determine how much equity (amortization of principal) he will gain each year as he makes his loan payments. He can also determine the cumulative equity build-up for the holding period of the loan.

Example: A $30,000 loan at 8% for 30 years has been paid for 10 years. What is the equity build-up in the 10th year and what is the cumulative equity build-up for the 10-year holding period?

Turn to page 175 and locate the 10th-year row in the 8% interest rate columns. The annual equity build-up is 1.7%. Therefore, $30,000 X 0.017 equals $510 equity build-up for the 10th year. The cumulative equity build-up is 12.3%. Therefore, $30,000 X 0.123 equals $3690.00 cumulative equity build-up for the first 10 years of the loan.

• REMAINING BALANCE TABLES •

(pages 82 thru 85)

These tables offer a slightly different version of the Loan Progress Charts. They cover loans with 10-year terms or less and monthly payments represented by monthly payback rates. These payback rates start at interest only and are incremented gradually to the fully amortizing rate.

Example: A loan with a 5-year due date, 8.5% interest rate, an original loan of $95,000.00 and a 1% monthly payback rate ($950.00 per month).

Turn to page 83 and locate the point of intersection of the 1% payback rate column and the 5-year due date in the 8.5% section. The figure at that intersection is 783($). This represents the amount still owed in principal for every $1000.00 of original loan amount. Divide the $95,000.00 by 1000 to find the number of $1000.00 units. The answer of 95 is multiplied by 783 to arrive at the $74,400.00 principal balance still owed on the loan.

Note that this balance remaining is after the 60th monthly payment is made. If you need to know the 60th *balloon payment* on this 5-year loan, just add the balance remaining to the 60th regular monthly payment. In the above example the balloon payment is equal to $950.00, plus $74,400.00 or $75,-350.00.

• DEFINITIONS •

Amortized Loan — a loan that will be completely paid off during its term.

Remaining Balance — amount of principal left unpaid on a loan at the end of a given term (due date).

Balloon Payment — is the remaining balance, plus one monthly payment.

Discount ($) — current loan balance less purchase price.

Payback Rate (%) — monthly payment divided by present amount of loan.

Payment Rate (%) — exact same meaning as payback rate.

Purchase Price ($) — current loan balance less discount.

Constant Annual Percent (%) — is the monthly payment times 12 (or the annual debt service), divided by the loan amount.

Yield — the annualized percentage return on invested dollars, considering the interest to be received over the term of the note, and the amount of discount.

Term — the exact length (number of months or years) of the loan, until the loan is fully amortized or until the unpaid balance is due and payable.

Due Date — the exact same meaning as the term of the loan.

Until Paid (UTP) — the term of the loan will run until the principal reduction portion of the monthly payment pays off the entire loan amount.

Daily Proration — the exact number of days between January 1 and any other day in the year (except leap year). This number is also represented as a percent of the total year in our tables. Daily proration can be calculated for either a 365-day year or a 360-day year.

Equity Buildup — the principal portion of the loan that is paid off each period by the payment.

Interpolation — estimation of the correct answer to a problem that lies between two known answers.

Straight Line Depreciation — equal annual depreciation amounts over the useful lifetime of the property.

Declining Balance Depreciation — annual depreciation is based on a fixed percentage of the current undepreciated value of the property.

Sum of the Years Digits (SYD) Depreciation — annual depreciation is based on a declining percentage of the original undepreciated value of the property.

Useful Lifetime — the number of years chosen as the life of the property for purposes of calculating depreciation.

GROSS AND NET SELLING PRICES

GROSS	96% of GROSS (4% Comm.)	95% of GROSS (5% Comm.)	94% of GROSS (6% Comm.)	93% of GROSS (7% Comm.)
10000	9600	9500	9400	9300
10500	10080	9975	9870	9765
11000	10560	10450	10340	10230
11500	11040	10925	10810	10695
12000	11520	11400	11280	11160
12500	12000	11875	11750	11625
13000	12480	12350	12220	12090
13500	12960	12825	12690	12555
14000	13440	13300	13160	13020
14500	13920	13775	13630	13485
15000	14400	14250	14100	13950
15500	14880	14725	14570	14415
16000	15360	15200	15040	14880
16500	15840	15675	15510	15345
17000	16320	16150	15980	15810
17500	16800	16625	16450	16275
18000	17280	17100	16920	16740
18500	17760	17575	17390	17205
19000	18240	18050	17860	17670
19500	18720	18525	18330	18135
20000	19200	19000	18800	18600
20500	19680	19475	19270	19065
21000	20160	19950	19740	19530
21500	20640	20425	20210	19995
22000	21120	20900	20680	20460
22500	21600	21375	21150	20925
23000	22080	21850	21620	21390
23500	22560	22325	22090	21855
24000	23040	22800	22560	22320
24500	23520	23275	23030	22785
25000	24000	23750	23500	23250
25500	24480	24225	23970	23715
26000	24960	24700	24440	24180
26500	25440	25175	24910	24645
27000	25920	25650	25380	25110
27500	26400	26125	25850	25575
28000	26880	26600	26320	26040
28500	27360	27075	26790	26505
29000	27840	27550	27260	26970
29500	28320	28025	27730	27435
30000	28800	28500	28200	27900
30500	29280	28975	28670	28365
31000	29760	29450	29140	28830
31500	30240	29925	29610	29295
32000	30720	30400	30080	29760
32500	31200	30875	30550	30225
33000	31680	31350	31020	30690
33500	32160	31825	31490	31155
34000	32640	32300	31960	31620
34500	33120	32775	32430	32085
35000	33600	33250	32900	32550
35500	34080	33725	33370	33015
36000	34560	34200	33840	33480
36500	35040	34675	34310	33945
37000	35520	35150	34780	34410
37500	36000	35625	35250	34875
38000	36480	36100	35720	35340
38500	36960	36575	36190	35805
39000	37440	37050	36660	36270
39500	37920	37525	37130	36735

GROSS	96% of GROSS (4% Comm.)	95% of GROSS (5% Comm.)	94% of GROSS (6% Comm.)	93% of GROSS (7% Comm.)
40000	38400	38000	37600	37200
41000	39360	38950	38540	38130
42000	40320	39900	39480	39060
43000	41280	40850	40420	39990
44000	42240	41800	41360	40920
45000	43200	42750	42300	41850
46000	44160	43700	43240	42780
47000	45120	44650	44180	43710
48000	46080	45600	45120	44640
49000	47040	46550	46060	45570
50000	48000	47500	47000	46500
51000	48960	48450	47940	47430
52000	49920	49400	48880	48360
53000	50880	50350	49820	49290
54000	51840	51300	50760	50220
55000	52800	52250	51700	51150
56000	53760	53200	52640	52080
57000	54720	54150	53580	53010
58000	55680	55100	54520	53940
59000	56640	56050	55460	54870
60000	57600	57000	56400	55800
61000	58560	57950	57340	56730
62000	59520	58900	58280	57660
63000	60480	59850	59220	58590
64000	61440	60800	60160	59520
65000	62400	61750	61100	60450
66000	63360	62700	62040	61380
67000	64320	63650	62980	62310
68000	65280	64600	63920	63240
69000	66240	65550	64860	64170
70000	67200	66500	65800	65100
71000	68160	67450	66740	66030
72000	69120	68400	67680	66960
73000	70080	69350	68620	67890
74000	71040	70300	69560	68820
75000	72000	71250	70500	69750
76000	72960	72200	71440	70680
77000	73920	73150	72380	71610
78000	74880	74100	73320	72540
79000	75840	75050	74260	73470
80000	76800	76000	75200	74400
81000	77760	76950	76140	75330
82000	78720	77900	77080	76260
83000	79680	78850	78020	77190
84000	80640	79800	78960	78120
85000	81600	80750	79900	79050
86000	82560	81700	80840	79980
87000	83520	82650	81780	80910
88000	84480	83600	82720	81840
89000	85440	84550	83660	82770
90000	86400	85500	84600	83700
91000	87360	86450	85540	84630
92000	88320	87400	86480	85560
93000	89280	88350	87420	86490
94000	90240	89300	88360	87420
95000	91200	90250	89300	88350
96000	92160	91200	90240	89280
97000	93120	92150	91180	90210
98000	94080	93100	92120	91140
99000	95040	94050	93060	92070

• CHECKLIST •

BUYER'S CLOSING COSTS:

Fees

- Escrow
- Legal
- Loan
- Appraisal
- Notary
- Recording
- Pest Control
- Title & Fire Insurance

- Credit Report
- Security Deposit
- Impound Account
- Trust Fund
- Prorated Taxes, Interest and Rents
- Accounting Charges

SELLER'S CLOSING COSTS:

- Sales Commissions
- Fees
    Escrow
    Legal
    Pest Control
    Recording
    Reconveyance
    Notary
    Trust Fund
- Title Insurance

- Prepayment Penalty
- Revenue Stamps, State and Local
- Transfer Taxes
- Property Taxes
- Security Deposit
- Prorated Rents, Taxes, and Interest
- Impound Account
- Points on Gov't Insured Loans

BROKER'S ESCROW CHECK LIST:

- Check all commission allocations
- Buyer Credit Report, loan commitment, and loan application
- Pest Control Inspection, other required inspections
- Check to eliminate any possible contingencies
- Possible deposit increase
- Occupancy permit
- Fire insurance
- Closing instructions (buyer sign)
- Notify sale to M.L.S. (if applicable)
- Title report ambiguities (final and preliminary)
- Lender-Payoff demands, statement of condition and assumption papers
- Seller's instructions signed
- Check for possible seller 2nd trust deed, or other loans
- Seller's forwarding address and phone

RESIDENTIAL SALES:

- Collect personal data on owner • When can owner move?
- Title – all interested parties • Degree of urgency for selling
- Inspect property • Date purchased and last time listed

Legal location, nearest cross streets, access to freeways, schools, churches, shopping, public transportation and recreation. Is the view good?

SITE CONSIDERATION:

Lot size, location, zoning and legal description.

- Amenities — underground utilities, pool, fences (type), patio and landscaping • Levels or stories — How many?
- Age, style and design (basement)
- Quality of construction
- Garage — How many cars?
- Exterior and roof condition
- Wiring, plumbing, sewer, heating, air-conditioning, insulation, weather stripping, floors, screens and intercom system

INTERIOR:

Floor plan, square feet, number of bedrooms and baths, living room (size), if dining room (size), family room, laundry room, carpeting, draperies, unusual items and overall condition.

- Kitchen — List all appliances (type and size)

FINANCING:

- Current loan balance, monthly payment (P & I), interest rate, loan number, original loan amount, term and lender.
- Prepayment penalty
- Due dates and balloon payment
- Is loan transferable? What is fee?
- Is there a 2nd trust deed? Can it be discounted?
- FHA or GI points — will seller pay?
- Possible seller financing. Get commitment!
- Installment sales • Get new loan commitment

PRICE:

Asking price. Check comparables.

•INCOME-PRODUCING PROPERTY•

Date all information.
Property location, name, and type.
Highest and best use??

- Personal data on owner — Name, address, phone, occupation, and business phone, and TAX BRACKET
- Is owner manager? Who is? Personal data on manager
- Vested title. Check all interests • Is owner a dealer?
- Depreciation — Method, deduction and useful life
- Owner's attorney, accountant, and bookkeeper
- Acquisition date and personal property costs
- Last time listed and what price • Inspect property
- Selling reason and urgency • Investment objectives
- Type of transaction: Sale, sale-lease back, exchange, installment sale

Location Related Conditions:

- Nearness to business, public transportation, freeways, shopping, service facilities (banks, restaurants, etc.), schools, churches, recreation, parking and traffic patterns in the area

Site Related Conditions:

- Size — Dimensions
- Zoning, codes, legal description
- Zoning future • Loading and potential moving problems
- All details on parking conditions, paving?
- Amenities — pools, patios, and landscaping
- Easements and deed restrictions • Expansion possibilities

Considerations for Improvements:

- Age and design of building • Sewer and toilet facilities
- Number of stories and units or offices • Pest control
- Lighting intensity and floor load level • Type of construction
- Heating, plumbing, air-conditioning, electrical, sprinklers, ventilation, burglar and fire control, waterheating, soundproofing, insulation, roof, and general condition of interior and exterior • Garbage and laundry facilities
- Basements, storage, and elevators • Expansion possibilities
- Dimensions of all rooms and offices

• Expenses to Consider:

- Hazard and liability insurance
- Workmen's compensation insurance
- Property and Income taxes
- Garbage, sewer, elevator and pool service
- Landscaping care
- Legal, accounting, and management fees
- Advertising
- Reserves
- Social Security
- Utilities
- Salaries

• Financing (existing and new)

- Current loan balance, interest rate and monthly payment for each loan
- Details on current lender with loan numbers
- Prepayment penalties
- Due dates and balloon payments
- Is loan transferable? What is fee?
- Original loan date and amount
- Is there a second involved? Can it be discounted?
- New loan commitment.
  Amount, rate, term, monthly payment, loan fee, and lender.
- Seller financing — establish terms
- Consider installment sale

• Price:

- Suggested or asking
- Check cap rate and gross multiplier
- Comparables

• General Considerations:

- Title report (preliminary)
- Survey report and area map with photographs
- Plot plan
- Recent inspection reports
- Certified operating statement (5 years)
- Copies of leases, rental agreements, and management contracts
- Inventory of personal property
- Statistical reports on economic and population growth